Lecture Notes of the Institute for Computer Sciences, Social Informatics and Telecommunications Engineering 500

The LNICST series publishes ICST's conferences, symposia and workshops.

LNICST reports state-of-the-art results in areas related to the scope of the Institute. The type of material published includes

- Proceedings (published in time for the respective event)
- Other edited monographs (such as project reports or invited volumes)

LNICST topics span the following areas:

- General Computer Science
- E-Economy
- E-Medicine
- Knowledge Management
- Multimedia
- Operations, Management and Policy
- Social Informatics
- Systems

Feifei Gao · Jun Wu · Yun Li · Honghao Gao
Editors

Communications and Networking

17th EAI International Conference, Chinacom 2022
Virtual Event, November 19–20, 2022
Proceedings

 Springer

Editors
Feifei Gao
Tsinghua University
Beijing, China

Yun Li
Chongqing University
Chongqing, China

Jun Wu
Fudan University
Shanghai, China

Honghao Gao
Shanghai University
Shanghai, China

ISSN 1867-8211   ISSN 1867-822X (electronic)
Lecture Notes of the Institute for Computer Sciences, Social Informatics
and Telecommunications Engineering
ISBN 978-3-031-34789-4   ISBN 978-3-031-34790-0 (eBook)
https://doi.org/10.1007/978-3-031-34790-0

This Springer imprint is published by the registered company Springer Nature Switzerland AG
The registered company address is: Gewerbestrasse 11, 6330 Cham, Switzerland

Preface

We are delighted to introduce the proceedings of the 17th European Alliance for Innovation (EAI) International Conference on Communications and Networking in China (Chinacom 2022). This conference brought together researchers, developers and practitioners around the world who are interested in communications and networking from the viewpoint of Signal Processing, Communication Optimization, Scheduling, Artificial Intelligence and so on.

The technical program of Chinacom 2022 consisted of 31 papers in oral presentation sessions at the main conference tracks. The conference sessions were: Session 1 - Signal Processing and Communication Optimization; Session 2 - Scheduling and Transmission Optimization; Session 3 - Network Communication Performance Enhancement; Session 4 - Deep Learning Applications and Optimization; Session 5 - Deep Learning and Network Performance Optimization; Session 6 - Edge Computing and Artificial Intelligence Applications. Apart from high-quality technical paper presentations, the technical program also featured three keynote speeches. The first keynote speech was delivered by Guangyi Liu from China Mobile. The second keynote speech was delivered by Yuantao Gu from Tsinghua University. The third keynote speech was delivered by Junhui Zhao from Southeast University.

Coordination with the steering chair, Imrich Chlamtac, was essential for the success of the conference. We sincerely appreciate his constant support and guidance. It was also a great pleasure to work with such an excellent organizing committee team for their hard work in organizing and supporting the conference. In particular, the Technical Program Committee, led by our TPC Co-Chairs Yueshen Xu, Caijun Zhong and Lisheng Fan, completed the peer-review process of technical papers and made a high-quality technical program. We are also grateful to Conference Manager Mikita Yelnitski for her support and all the authors who submitted their papers to the Chinacom 2022 conference.

We strongly believe that the Chinacom conference provides a good forum for all researchers, developers and practitioners to discuss all science and technology aspects that are relevant to collaborative computing. We also expect that the future Chinacom conferences will be as successful and stimulating, as indicated by the contributions presented in this volume.

November 2022

Feifei Gao
Jun Wu
Yun Li
Honghao Gao

Organization

Steering Committee

Chair

Imrich Chlamtac   University of Trento, Italy

Members

Changjun Jiang (Vice President)   Tongji University, China
Qianbin Chen (Vice President)   Chongqing University of Posts and
                                      Telecommunications, China
Honghao Gao   Shanghai University, China

Organizing Committee

General Chair

Feifei Gao   Tsinghua University, China

General Co-chairs

Jun Wu   Fudan University, China
Yun Li   Chongqing University of Posts and
                                      Telecommunications, China
Honghao Gao   Shanghai University, China

TPC Chairs and Co-chairs

Yueshen Xu   Xidian University, China
Caijun Zhong   Zhejiang University, China
Lisheng Fan   Guangzhou University, China

Web Chair

Honghao Gao   Shanghai University, China

Publicity and Social Media Chairs

Rui Li   Xidian University, China
Yucong Duan   Hainan University, China

Workshops Chair

Yuyu Yin   Hangzhou Dianzi University, China

Sponsorship and Exhibits Chair

Honghao Gao   Shanghai University, China

Publications Chair

Youhuizi Li   Hangzhou Dianzi University, China

Local Chair

Yushen Xu   Xidian University, China

Technical Program Committee

Honghao Gao	Shanghai University, China
Mingqi Li	Shanghai Advanced Research Institute, Chinese Academy of Sciences, China
Sherali Zeadally	University of Kentucky, USA
Chongbin Xu	Fudan University, China
An Liu	Zhejiang University, China
Tien-Wen Sung	Fujian University of Technology, China
Taiping Cui	Chongqing University of Posts and Telecommunications, China
Ding Xu	Nanjing University of Posts and Telecommunications, China
Hui Zhao	Chongqing University of Posts and Telecommunications, China

Contents

Network Communication Performance Enhancement

Deep Learning Applications and Optimization

Signal Processing and Communication Optimization

A Routing Strategy for GEO/LEO Satellite Network Based on Dynamic Delay Prediction and Link Control

Xixi Zheng[1,2,3], Jing Liu[1], Junrong Li[2], Dong Lv[4], Junle Liao[4], Xiang Chen[2,3]([✉]), and Terngyin Hsu[5]

[1] College of Electronics and Information Engineering, Shenzhen University, Shenzhen, China
[2] School of Electronics and Information Technology, Sun Yat-sen University, Guangzhou, China
chenxiang@mail.sysu.edu.cn
[3] Research Institute of Tsinghua University in Shenzhen (RITS), Shenzhen, China
[4] IPLOOK Technologies Co., Ltd., Guangzhou, China
[5] Department of Computer Science, National Chiao Tung University, Hsinchu, Taiwan

Abstract. As an important part of modern communication, the satellite communication is attracting more and more attention. In recent years, the low earth orbit (LEO) satellite constellations are being developed vigorously. To achieve better performance and flexibility, many researchers have proposed to combine the LEO and geostationary earth orbit (GEO) satellites to construct a double-layer network. However, this double-layer structure brings significant challenges to the design of routing strategy. In this paper, we propose a routing strategy for GEO/LEO satellite network based on dynamic delay prediction and link control. In particular, we craft a link cost function that comprehensively considers the link load, queuing delay, processing delay and transmission delay. The cost function can provide more accurate estimation of the link delay compared with the existing methods roughly using hop counts. Based on it, the proposed double-layer strategy can not only optimize the end-to-end delay but also achieve better traffic balance. Simulations on STK and OPNET verify that the proposed approach can greatly improve the performance of packet loss rate, end-to-end delay and throughput.

Keywords: GEO/LEO double-layer satellite network · Routing strategy · Clustering mechanism · Layered transmission

1 Introduction

LEO satellite mobile communication systems are of great significance in national development and improving people's life. Due to the feature of low orbital altitude, the relative movement of LEO satellites on different planes is relatively fast, which might cause poor communication effect when the LEO satellites carry heavy traffic [1]. In addition, the distribution of users is usually uneven due to terrain, climate and economy, which can result in significant load imbalance between different satellites [2]. In this case, the satellite networks will be prone to link congestion if only single layer routing within LEO

© ICST Institute for Computer Sciences, Social Informatics and Telecommunications Engineering 2023
Published by Springer Nature Switzerland AG 2023. All Rights Reserved
F. Gao et al. (Eds.): ChinaCom 2022, LNICST 500, pp. 3–17, 2023.
https://doi.org/10.1007/978-3-031-34790-0_1

constellations is considered [3]. Moreover, the LEO single layer routing is usually with high latency and unstable robustness, which prompts more and more systems to adopt multi-layer satellite routing that involves medium earth orbit (MEO) or GEO satellites.

Compared with single-layer satellite networks, multi-layer satellite networks have many advantages, such as good invulnerability, high spectrum utilization, flexible networking and large capacity, which are more potential for the development of satellite networks in the future. However, the multi-layer satellite networks contain numerous nodes and links, which makes the network topology change more frequently and the routing design more challenging. In the literature of multi-layer satellite routing, most strategies adopt the idea of hierarchical grouping to reduce complexity. Among the representative studies, Akyildiz et al. [4] proposes the idea of layering and grouping concurrently for LEO/MEO/GEO three-layer satellite networks. According to the coverage of high-layer satellites, low-layer satellites are divided into several groups, and the high-layer satellites as group managers collect topological information within the group and recalculate routing table when a group switch occurs. This algorithm provides a good management strategy for multi-layer satellite networks. Nonetheless, it fails to take into account the link load and thus is unable to deal with traffic burst well.

In order to balance traffic effectively and improve network congestion response capability, many other strategies have been proposed for multi-layer satellite networks in recent years. For example, the authors in [5] adopt a double-layer satellite routing strategy based on hop number limit and cluster management. Two LEO satellites on the same orbital plane are designated as cluster headers to collect network link information, and then the information is collected to GEO satellites. A certain hop number threshold and queuing delay threshold are used to judge whether the GEO-assisted routing is needed. In [6], a method based on hop limit and link control is proposed, which is based on clustering and grouping of double-layer satellite management mode. LEO satellites are grouped according to the coverage relationship between the upper and lower layers, and the nearest GEO satellite is a group manager in the mode. The strategy reduces the number of inter-satellite links between layers and the complexity of connection relations, and improves the efficiency of network management. Besides, the link load factor is taken into consideration in this work.

Furthermore, in addition to the optimization of the double-layer satellite management strategy, many scholars have made some innovations in routing mode and link weight. In [7], a new double-layer satellite routing strategy calculation is proposed, which sets different routing patterns according to the different coverage relationship between the source address and destination address. This strategy takes the GEO satellites as cluster headers as the cluster header, and makes different processing patterns according to the different number of GEO satellites covering LEO satellites, so as to ensure that there is a manager for each LEO satellite throughout. Besides, the inter-cluster and intra-cluster routes are distinguished by whether the cluster headers of the source and destination LEO are the same. The delivery of the routing table is not period but triggered by the variation of link conditions, which is more efficient. In [8], the authors propose a new link weight calculation method for double-layer routing, which takes not only the propagation and queuing delays but also the residual bandwidth into consideration to improve the response speed to link congestion.

At present, most of the existing double-layer satellite routing algorithms use the number of hops as a crucial metric to determine routes. However, the propagation delay between satellites often changes greatly with their relative motion, and the queuing delay also changes with the alteration of traffic. Consequently, in double-layer routing, it is not reasonable enough to regard the hop counts as the equivalent of delay. In this context, this paper proposes a new double-layer routing strategy. We craft a novel cost function based on dynamic delay estimation and queue load. Using this function as a metric, we further propose a clustered link control method to optimize the routing efficiency and traffic balance.

The rest of the article is organized as follows. Section 2 briefly introduces the architecture of the double-layer satellite network. Section 3 introduces the routing strategy based on dynamic delay estimation and cluster management. Section 4 presents and analyzes the simulation results based on the OPNET simulation platform. Finally, Sect. 5 concludes this paper.

2 GEO/LEO Satellite Network Architecture

2.1 Double-Layer Satellite Network Model

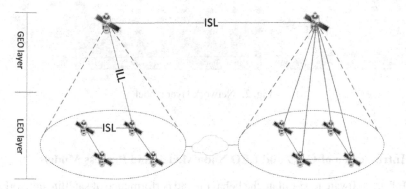

Fig. 1. GEO/LEO double layer satellite network architecture

Compared with single-layer network, multi-layer network can exploit the advantages of different layers, which are the wide coverage of the high-layer satellites and the low transmission delay of the low-layer ones. There are two kinds of links in double-layer satellite networks, namely inter-satellite link (ISL) and inter-layer link (ILL). We consider a Architecture for LEO/GEO satellite networks, and its network structure is shown in Fig. 1.

The LEO satellite constellation in this paper adopts the inclined orbit design, and 216 LEO satellites are built based on OPNET, as shown in Fig. 2. The LEO satellites are evenly distributed on 12 orbital planes, with 18 satellites on each orbital plane. The altitude of the orbit of LEO satellites is 1,150 km. Each satellite has 4 links, which are fixed inter-satellite links (ISL) and used to communicate with its adjacent satellites in four directions.

Considering the coverage characteristics of GEO satellites, this paper uses three GEO satellites to realize the coverage of all LEO satellites. This is because three GEO satellites can cover most of the Earth's surface except the polar region, they can meet the requirements of routing strategy. The altitude of the orbit of GEO satellites is 36,000 km. The longitudes of the three GEO satellites are −80°, 40° and 160° respectively. Regardless of the process of service interaction between satellites and users, all services are generated randomly by the LEO satellites.

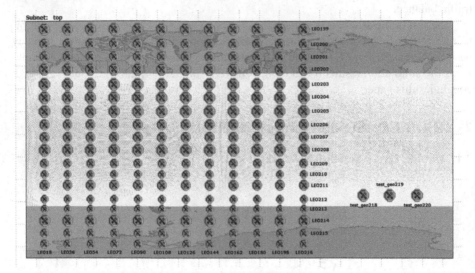

Fig. 2. Network layer model

2.2   Introduction of GEO and LEO Node Models and Process Models

OPNET is a software to simulate the behavior and performance of satellite networks. We use OPNET as a tool to design and verify our strategy in this work. The OPNET satellite node domain is mainly used to simulate the communication function of satellite nodes to realize the resume and data forwarding of the inter-satellite routing table. As shown in Fig. 3, each GEO node consists of the following modules: two sets of inter-satellite link models for communication with other GEO satellites, a set of inter-layer link modules for communication with the LEO satellites, a central processing module named net and a packet destruction module named sink.

Each LEO satellite node consists of the following models: four sets of inter-satellite link models for LEO layer communication, a set of inter-satellite link models for communication with the GEO satellites, a central processing model named net, a packet sending model named app_gen and a packet destroying model named sink, as shown in Fig. 4. The packet generating model is used to simulate traffic from the users while the destroying model is to simulate that the packets have been delivered to the users. Queue is a special component in OPNET, which can be used to buffer packets. In this work, each link is equipped with a queue. When the queue if full, the packet will be automatically discarded. Eight statistical lines are used to feedback the queue length and queue delay of the four inter-satellite links to the central processing model.

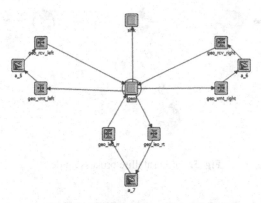

Fig. 3. GEO satellite node model

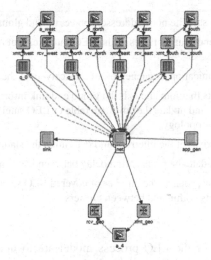

Fig. 4. LEO satellite node model

Process models are the lowest layer of three-layer modeling architecture in OPNET for realizing the jump of code and protocol and thus controlling the action of each node. The GEO process model is a key module to realize centralized routing strategy. In addition to the basic functions of receiving and forwarding data packets, the GEO process model also has several other functions, which include updating the global network topology information. Figure 5 shows the GEO satellite process model, and Table 1 shows the functions of the various states of the GEO process model.

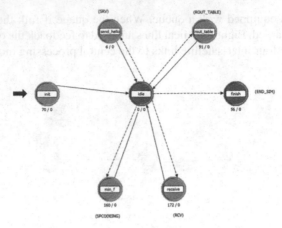

Fig. 5. GEO satellite process model

Table 1. Functions of states in the GEO satellite process model

state	function
init	Initialize GEO satellite node addresses, object id, and global network topology, etc.
rout_table	Periodically send routing tables to the LEO satellites that are registered within the cluster
min_f	Set the communication frequency of all transceivers of the GEO nodes
receive	Receive packets that join and exit the group and link information packets from LEO satellites, and update the coverage table of LEO satellites in the group and the global network topology
idle	Wait for the arrival of the interrupt and determine the status of the next hop
time	Periodically update the propagation delay between LEO satellites
finish	Collect statistics, such as the number of covered LEO satellites and the number of received packets within and between clusters

The main functions of the LEO process model are to update the GEO satellite currently accessed, record the information of adjacent satellites through hello packets, upload the information to the GEO satellite, and update the local routing information with the routing tables received from the GEO manager. Figure 6 shows the process model of the central processing module of the LEO satellite node models, and Table 2 shows the functions of the various states of the LEO process model.

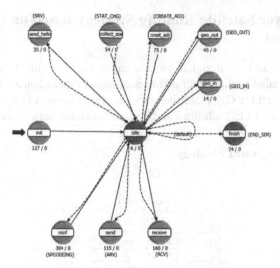

Fig. 6. LEO satellite process model

Table 2. Functions of states in LEO satellite process model

state	function
init	Initialize satellite node addresses, object id and the number of orbital planes and other parameters
send_hello	Sends hello packets to obtain information about the neighboring nodes
creat_adj	Send the link information of this node to the GEO manager
minf	Set the communication frequency of all transceivers of the LEO satellite nodes
send	Forward the data packets generated by the app_gen module according to the routing table
receive	Receive data packets from other satellites, hello packets, and routing tables from the GEO manager
geo_out	Update the GEO manager number and send packages to exit the group of the old GEO manager
geo_in	Send packages to join the group of the new GEO manager
collect_stat	Collect queue delay and queue occupancy length
finish	Calculate throughput, packet loss rate, and average end-to-end delay

3 Double-Layer Satellite Routing Strategy Based on Cluster Management

In order to reduce the cost of signal packets and collect the global network topology information more quickly, this paper adopts a strategy of hierarchical cluster to manage the double-layer satellites. GEO satellites serve as cluster headers to dynamically collect the link information of LEO satellites and update the global network topology.

3.1 Cluster Management Strategy

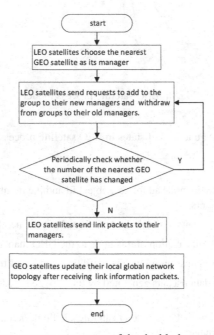

Fig. 7. Cluster management strategy of the double-layer satellite network

In practice, each GEO satellite cannot establish inter-satellite links with all the LEO satellites. Therefore, in this work, the LEO satellites are divided into three groups according to the GEO satellite that they are accessing. Each LEO satellite is only linked to its nearest GEO satellite and all the LEO satellites linked to the same GEO satellite form a group. Figure 7 is the specific flow chart of the clustering management strategy in this paper. More details of the cluster management strategy are as below:

- LEO satellites periodically check whether it is necessary to make handover between the GEO satellites through the "shortest distance" criterion. If necessary, the LEO satellite need to send packets to inform the old GEO manager of exiting and the new one of joining.
- GEO satellites will update the local registration table of LEO satellites after receiving packages of exiting or joining the group from LEO satellites.

- After confirming the unique manager number, LEO satellites send link information packets to the corresponding GEO manager.
- GEO satellites update the local network topology table of LEO layer and deliver routing tables to the LEO satellites after receiving link information packets from the LEO satellites and forwarding link information packets to their neighboring GEO satellites. The link information packet contains information of queuing delay, link cost between the satellite and its neighbors, and the addresses of the satellite and its neighbors.

3.2 Link Cost Design

Delay is an important metric for routing design, which usually consists of the propagation delay related to inter-satellite distance and queuing delay related to the traffic load. However, the existing works either consider the minimization of delay but fail to balance the traffic [5], or only consider part of the factors that infect the total delay [8]. Therefore, in this work, we propose a comprehensive link cost function that takes queuing delay, processing delay, propagation delay and queue load into consideration. This method can not only keep the end-to-end delay relatively low but also balance the network load and improve the response speed to local congestion. The proposed cost function is determined by queue occupancy ratio and delay, which is given by

$$W_0 = \alpha \cdot \frac{Q(i,j)}{Q_{max}} + \beta \cdot \frac{D_p(i,j) + D_q(i,j) + D_d(i,j)}{D_{min}} \tag{1}$$

Here, $Q(i,j)$ is the queue occupation length of the link between the LEO satellite i and j, and Q_{max} is the total length of the queue. D_{min} denotes the minimal total delay, which is the sum of the propagation delay and queuing delay, of all the LEO satellite links. $D_p(i,j)$ means the propagation delay between the LEO satellite nodes i and j link. $D_q(i,j)$ denotes the queuing delay of the link between the LEO satellite nodes i and j, $D_d(i,j)$ means the processing delay of the link between the LEO satellite nodes i and j, which refers to the time from receiving the packet to sending the packet.

In link cost function (1), α and β represent the importance of delay and queue load in the link cost evaluation model. In the routing strategy presented in this paper, the delay and the queue load have almost the same importance, but in order to improve the response speed to the queue load, α and β are set to 0.6, 0.4 relatively.

3.3 Design of the Double-Layer Satellite Routing Strategy

The double-layer satellite routing strategy in this paper is designed based on Dijkstra algorithm, which solves the problem of the shortest path of single source on non-negatively weighted directed graph. The weight of Dijkstra algorithm adopts the link cost defined by (1). Combing the cluster management described in Sect. 3.1 and the link cost function proposed in Sect. 3.2, we design a GEO/LEO double-layer satellite routing strategy as shown in Fig. 8.

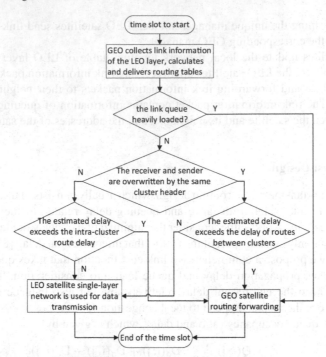

Fig. 8. Double-layer routing strategy

To leverage the low-latency advantage of the LEO satellites, the packets are preferentially routed in the LEO layer. And they are diverted to the GEO satellites only when:

Case 1: The current path is congested. When the queue load of the LEO satellites reaches a certain load threshold, the packets arriving after will be routed via the GEO satellites to reduce packet loss.

Case 2: The source and the destination nodes are covered by the same GEO manager, and the delay of "intra-cluster routing" is lower than the predicted delay of the LEO layer.

Case 3: The source and the destination nodes are covered by different GEO managers, but the delay of "inter-cluster routing" is lower than the predicted delay of the LEO layer.

Among them, intra-cluster routing refers to the forwarding of data packets via only one GEO satellite, while inter-cluster routing refers to the forwarding of data packets via two GEO satellites. The case 2 and 3 usually occur when the LEO constellation is bearing massive amount of traffic.

4 Verification of Simulation Results

4.1 Simulation Environment Setting

In order to evaluate the communication performance of the double-layer satellite network under the actual high-speed motion condition, this paper build a simulation environment of double-layer satellite network based on OPNET and STK. The orbit files generated by STK can be used to approximate real trajectory of satellites. By exporting the orbit files into OPNET, the double-layer satellite constellation scene can be rapidly built. The link parameters of the double-layer satellite network are shown in Table 3. The size of data packets is set to a constant value of 128b, and the size of the other signal packets is specified as 0.25b.

Table 3. Link parameters

Link type	sending rate/(Mbit · s^{-1})	queue length/kb
LEO inter-satellite link	1.5	12.5
GEO inter-satellite link	64	125
The link between the layers	64	12.5

We compare the performance of our strategy with the one based on hop limit proposed by [5] in several aspects, including packet loss rate, throughput and delay. For convenience, in the following, we will refer to the hop-limit method as the traditional strategy. In order to simulate network congestion at different levels, the rate of package generation for 18 satellites were randomly assigned in the LEO network layer. The packet transmission rate is constant. The packet sending time is 5 s, and the total simulation time is 30 s.

4.2 Average End-to-End Delay

Figure 9 shows the end-to-end delay comparison of the two routing strategies with different data traffic. Among them, the hop threshold of the traditional strategy is set to 10 according to the scale of LEO satellites. For our algorithm when the queue occupancy ratio is greater than 0.75, it is perceived as severe congestion. Apparently, with the increase of packet generation rate, the average delay of both strategies increases. However, the proposed method can reduce the delay by 10–50 ms compared with the traditional one. This is because the link load is added into the link cost calculation. Therefore, the GEO satellites can bypass those LEO satellites with high link load. The link cost function is helpful to balance the link load of the LEO layer and reduce the queuing delay and eventually reduces the total end-to-end delay.

In addition, when the link load of LEO layer is high, the routing strategy proposed in this paper can compare the total delay of LEO satellite transmission with the total delay of GEO transmission for data packets, then choose a route mode with lower delay, which also reduces the end-to-end delay of packet transmission to a certain extent.

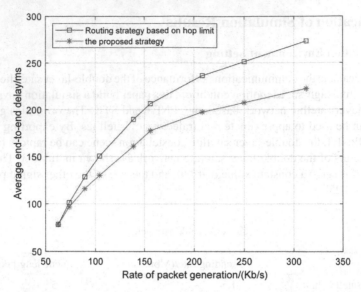

Fig. 9. The average end-to-end latency varies with different traffic

4.3 Throughput

Figure 10 shows the throughput comparison of the two routing strategies with different traffic. When the rate of packet generation is less than 600 Kb/s, the two strategies have close performance in throughput. This is because both strategies take into account the shunting of data packets of the double-layer satellite network. When the rate of packet generation is more than 600 Kb/s, the advantages of the proposed routing strategy are more obvious. At this time, the LEO satellites have achieve their maximal capacities to deal with packet routing and a large number of packets need to be transmitted via GEO satellites. Therefore, the different criteria of the strategies on whether to transmit packets via GEO satellites bring different results. The traditional method uses the number of hops to determine data shunting. However, when the traffic is heavy and unevenly distributed, the number of hops cannot reveal the delay accurately since the queuing delays of different nodes are various but is not taken into consideration. This limits the throughput of the traditional method when the rate of packet generation is relatively high.

However, instead of quantifying the delay by hop number, the routing strategy proposed in this paper uses the historical LEO transmission delay to dynamically estimate the current transmission delay. Moreover, the link load limit is added into the routing strategy. When the link load exceeds the set threshold, the packets are sent directly through GEO satellites, which further reduces the loss of packets and improves the throughput. When the rate of packet generation is about 1100Kb/s, the proposed strategy can improve the throughput of the system by about 16.18% compared with the traditional method.

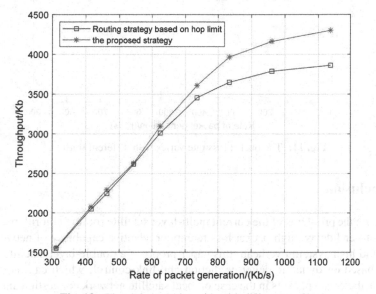

Fig. 10. Throughput varies with with different traffic

4.4 Packet Loss Rate

Figure 11 shows the packet loss rate comparison of the two routing strategies with different traffic. Apparently, the proposed routing strategy can effectively reduce the packet loss rate in the case of congestion. When the rate of packet generation is about 800 Kb/s, it is about 7.5% lower than the traditional routing strategy based on hop limit. There are two reasons for this. First, the routing strategy based on hop limit does not set the threshold of link load. When the link load of LEO satellites exceeds the queue length and does not meet the conditions of GEO transmission, this strategy will cause the loss of data packets to some extent. Secondly, the link cost function of routing strategy based on hop limit only considers the hop number. The hop number can not fully indicate the load of the link, so the response to local network congestion is relatively slow, resulting in a poor ability to balance traffic. However, the link cost function proposed in this paper takes the link load into account. When calculating the routing table, it can avoid the path with higher link load, so it can balance the traffic of LEO layer better and reduce packet loss.

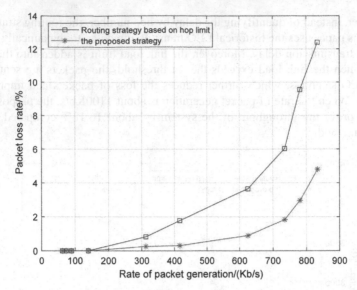

Fig. 11. The packet loss rate varies with different traffic

5 Conclusion

Considering the problems of the current multi-layer satellite routing algorithms, such as high end-to-end delay, high packet loss rate, poor adaptive capability of network congestion and high system overhead, this paper proposes a double-layer satellite routing strategy based on dynamic delay prediction and link control, which can more effectively distribute data packets in the case of local satellite network congestion and reduce the flow pressure in the LEO satellite layer. In addition, in order to improve the self-adaptability of the double-layer satellite routing strategy to network congestion, a new link cost function is proposed, which comprehensively considers the link load and delay in different aspects. Compared with the traditional routing strategy based on hop limit, the proposed approach can reduce the end-to-end delay by 10–50 ms with different volume of traffic, efficiently reduce the packet loss rate by around 7.5% and increase the system throughput by about 16.18% when the traffic is relatively heavy.

Acknowledgment. This research is supported in part by the State's Key Project of Research and Development Plan under Grants (2019YFE0196400), and in part by the Shenzhen Natural Science Foundation under Grant JCYJ20200109143016563.

References

1. Feng, X.: Research on QoS routing protocol in multi-layer satellite network. Master thesis. Harbin Institute of Technology (2016)
2. Wang, J., Guo, Y., Sun, L., Zhou, J., Han, C.: Load balancing algorithm for multi-traffic in double layered satellite network. Syst. Eng. Electron. **38**(9), 2156–2161 (2016)

3. Wang, J., Ji, B., Sun, L., Zhou, J., Han, C.: Multi-path and multi-service routing strategy for LEO/GEO satellite networks. J. Nanjing Univ. Posts Telecommun. (Nat. Sci. Edn.) **37**(6), 36–43 (2017)
4. Akyildiz, I.F., Ekici, E., Bender, M.D.: MLSR: a novel routing algorithm for multilayered satellite IP networks. IEEE/ACM Trans. Netw. **10**(3), 411–424 (2002)
5. Zhang, T., Li, Y., Zhao, S.: Optimization design of routing algorithm based on GEO/LEO double-layer satellite network. Comput. Eng. **46**(7), 198–205 (2020)
6. Chen, J.: Research on multi-layered satellite network routing strategy. Master thesis. Harbin Institute of Technology (2015)
7. Pan, Y.: Research of routing techniques in satellite networks. Master thesis. Beijing University of Posts and Telecommunications (2017)
8. Research on multi-service routing algorithm for satellite networks. Master thesis. Dalian University (2016)

The APC Algorithm of Solving Large-Scale Linear Systems: A Generalized Analysis

Jiyan Zhang, Yue Xue, Yuan Qi$^{(\boxtimes)}$, and Jiale Wang

Beijing University of Posts and Telecommunications, Beijing, China
{zhangjiyan,runfordream,qiyuan,wangjiale}@bupt.edu.cn

Abstract. A new algorithm called accelerated projection-based consensus (APC) has recently emerged as a promising approach to solve large-scale systems of linear equations in a distributed fashion. The algorithm uses a federated computational architecture, and attracts increasing research interest; however, it's performance analysis is still incomplete, e.g., the error performance under noisy condition has not yet been investigated. In this paper, we focus on providing a generalized analysis by the use of the linear system theory, such that the error performance of the APC algorithm for solving linear systems in presence of additive noise can be clarified. We specifically provide a closed-form expression of the error of solution attained by the APC algorithm. Numerical results demonstrate the error performance of the APC algorithm, validating the presented analysis.

Keywords: Large-scale systems · linear equations · distributed algorithms · performance analysis

1 Introduction

Solving large-scale systems of linear equations is a fundamental problem in various signal processing, control theory, and machine learning applications [1–5]. Recently, *Azizan-Ruhi*, *Avestimehrm*, and *Hassibi* developed the APC algorithm for distributed solution of large-scale systems of linear equations [1]. APC offers significant speed-up relative to other distributed methods such as the well-known alternating direction method of multipliers (ADMM) method [1], making the algorithm appealing for many applications [1,5,6]. The APC algorithm was used by the probabilistic load flow calculation of power systems for the privacy-preserving purpose [6]. Inspired by the APC algorithm, our previous work designed a distributed channel estimation algorithm for mmWave massive MIMO communication systems [5].

This work is sponsored in part by the National Natural Science Foundation of China (grant no. 61971058, 61801048, 61631004, 62071063) and Beijing Natural Science Foundation (grant no. L202014, L192002).

F. Gao et al. (Eds.): ChinaCom 2022, LNICST 500, pp. 18–32, 2023.
https://doi.org/10.1007/978-3-031-34790-0_2

One distinguishing attribute of the APC algorithm is that it's computational architecture is a *federated* architecture (also known as the *server-worker* distributed architecture [7,8]). A federated architecture comprises of one server (master) and multiple agents (workers) [7–12]. Research attention has increasingly focused on the development of novel algorithms to distributed computation [2,7–13], including those with the federated architecture [7–12]; thus, the APC algorithm also attracts increasing research interest [3,7–13]. There are a number of references on the topics related to the APC algorithm, e.g., distributed algorithms for systems of linear equations [2], for state estimation [3], for gradient-descent method [7,9], for linear transforms [10,11], for coded matrix multiplication [12], and for phase retrieval [13].

However, the seminal work on the APC algorithm [1] only considers a model setting wherein the system is free from noise, while noise is an unavoidable factor in real systems. It is still unconfirmed whether the APC algorithm can effectively solve linear systems with the existence of noise; in other words, researchers still lack a clear understanding of the robustness of the algorithm under the noisy condition. Therefore, this study aims at deriving the analytical results by considering the additive noise. Specifically, we generalize the analysis of the APC algorithm by utilizing the linear system theory (see Theorem 1), such that the error performance of the algorithm for solving linear systems is clarified in presence of noise (see Theorem 3). Note that the study in this paper derives analytical results which can be reduced to those in [1], by letting the elements of noise vector be zeros; in this sense, the analysis conducted in this paper is the generalized one. Moreover, we provide closed-form expressions to two important parameters of the APC algorithm (see Remark 1).

Notations : Let $\mathbb{C}$ be the complex field. We write $\| \cdot \|_2$ for the ℓ_2 norm of a vector. For a matrix $\mathbf{A}$, $\lambda_{min}(\mathbf{A})$ and $\lambda_{max}(\mathbf{A})$ are the smallest and largest eigenvalues, respectively, and $\rho(\mathbf{A})$ is the spectral radius of $\mathbf{A}$, i.e., the largest absolute value of its eigenvalues. When $\mathbf{A}$ has full column rank, we let $\mathbf{A}^\dagger = \left(\mathbf{A}^H \mathbf{A}\right)^{-1} \mathbf{A}^H$ be the Moore-Penrose pseudoinverse of $\mathbf{A}$. If span($\mathbf{A}$) is the span of columns in $\mathbf{A}$, then $\mathbf{P}_{\mathbf{A}}^{\perp} = \mathbf{I} - \mathbf{A}\mathbf{A}^\dagger$ is the projection onto the orthogonal complement of span($\mathbf{A}$). For a block diagonal matrix $\mathbf{A} = \text{diag}(\mathbf{A}_{11}, \cdots, \mathbf{A}_{kk})$, one can write $\mathbf{A} = \mathbf{A}_{11} \bigoplus \mathbf{A}_{22} \bigoplus \cdots \bigoplus \mathbf{A}_{kk}$ that is the direct sum of the matrices $\mathbf{A}_{11}, \cdots, \mathbf{A}_{kk}$ [14]. Let $\mathbf{I}_N \in \mathbb{C}^{N \times N}$ be the identity matrix and $\mathbf{0}_N \in \mathbb{C}^N$ ($\mathbf{O}_N \in \mathbb{C}^{N \times N}$) be the all-zero vector (matrix).

2   Model

Consider the problem of solving a large-scale system of linear equations

$$\mathbf{A}\mathbf{x} = \mathbf{y}, \tag{1}$$

where $\mathbf{A} \in \mathbb{C}^{M \times s}$ has full column rank, $\mathbf{x} \in \mathbb{C}^s$, and

$$\mathbf{y} = \mathbf{A}\mathbf{x}^* + \tilde{\mathbf{w}} \in \mathbb{C}^M. \tag{2}$$

As usual, $\mathbf{A}$ and $\mathbf{y}$ are known matrix and vector, respectively. While $\tilde{\mathbf{w}} = [\tilde{w}_1, \cdots, \tilde{w}_M]^T$ is an unknown noise vector (not necessarily Gaussian noise) in this paper.

We can apply the APC algorithm (presented in Algorithm 1) to find the solution to (1), which will obtain an estimate of $\mathbf{x}^*$. The formal description of APC [1] is provided as Algorithm 1. The implementation of the APC algorithm requires M distributed agents and one server. Every agent computes a solution to its own private equation, while all these agents can run in a parallel fashion. The server calculates the average of these M solutions and regards it as the global solution.

The APC algorithm runs for T iterations. Initially, the algorithm executes the following computations: $\mathbf{x}_\ell(0) = \mathbf{A}_\ell^H \left(\mathbf{A}_\ell \mathbf{A}_\ell^H \right)^{-1} y_\ell$ in every agent, and $\overline{\mathbf{x}}(0) = \frac{1}{M} \sum_{\ell=1}^{M} \mathbf{x}_\ell(0)$ in the server. After that, the computations are performed iteratively; that is, for $t = 0, \cdots, T-1$, the APC algorithm goes through the following steps: $\mathbf{x}_\ell(t+1) = \mathbf{x}_\ell(t) + \gamma \mathbf{P}_\ell^\perp \left(\overline{\mathbf{x}}(t) - \mathbf{x}_\ell(t) \right)$ and $\overline{\mathbf{x}}(t+1) = \frac{\eta}{M} \sum_{\ell=1}^{M} \mathbf{x}_\ell(t+1) + (1-\eta)\overline{\mathbf{x}}(t)$, with the agents and server, respectively.

Algorithm 1: The APC Algorithm for Finding the Solution $\tilde{\mathbf{x}}$ to $\mathbf{A}\mathbf{x} = \mathbf{y}$

Input: $\mathbf{y} = [y_1, \cdots, y_M]^T \in \mathbb{C}^M$, $\mathbf{A} \in \mathbb{C}^{M \times s}$, and T.
Output: $\tilde{\mathbf{z}} \in \mathbb{C}^s$.
1 Let $\mathbf{A}_\ell \in \mathbb{C}^{1 \times s}$ denote the ℓ-th row of $\mathbf{A}$;
2 $t = 0$;
  /* Computations in every agent: */
3 **for** $\ell = 1 : M$ **do**
4      $\mathbf{P}_\ell^\perp = \mathbf{I}_s - \mathbf{A}_\ell^H \left(\mathbf{A}_\ell \mathbf{A}_\ell^H \right)^{-1} \mathbf{A}_\ell$;
5      $\mathbf{z}_\ell(0) = \mathbf{A}_\ell^H \left(\mathbf{A}_\ell \mathbf{A}_\ell^H \right)^{-1} y_\ell$;   // Initializing each $\mathbf{z}_\ell(0)$
6 **end**
  /* Computations in the server: */
7 $\overline{\mathbf{z}}(0) = \frac{1}{M} \sum_{\ell=1}^{M} \mathbf{z}_\ell(0)$;
8 **while** $t \leq T - 1$ **do**
    /* Computations in every agent: */
9   **for** $\ell = 1 : M$ **do**
10         $\mathbf{z}_\ell(t+1) = \mathbf{z}_\ell(t) + \gamma \mathbf{P}_\ell^\perp \left(\overline{\mathbf{z}}(t) - \mathbf{z}_\ell(t) \right)$;
11   **end**
    /* Computations in the server: */
12      $\overline{\mathbf{z}}(t+1) = \frac{\eta}{M} \sum_{\ell=1}^{M} \mathbf{z}_\ell(t+1) + (1-\eta)\overline{\mathbf{z}}(t)$;
13      $t = t + 1$;
14 **end**
15 $\tilde{\mathbf{z}} = \overline{\mathbf{z}}(t+1)$;

To clarify how to set the parameters γ and η, we define

$$\mathbf{X} = \frac{1}{M} \sum_{\ell=1}^{M} \mathbf{A}_\ell^H \left(\mathbf{A}_\ell \mathbf{A}_\ell^H \right)^{-1} \mathbf{A}_\ell, \tag{3}$$

and denote the eigenvalues of $\mathbf{X}$ by θ_i, $1 \leq i \leq s$, where

$$\theta_s \leq \cdots \leq \theta_1 \tag{4}$$

with $\theta_s = \theta_{min} = \lambda_{min}(\mathbf{X}) \geq 0$ and $\theta_1 = \theta_{max} = \lambda_{max}(\mathbf{X}) \leq 1$ [1]. It is known from [14, Theorem 2.5.6] that $\theta_1, \cdots, \theta_s$ are real-valued.

Remark 1: The parameters γ and η in the APC algorithm are set as follows:

$$\gamma = \frac{2\left(\sqrt{\theta_{max}}\sqrt{\theta_{min}} + 1\right) - 2\sqrt{(1 - \theta_{max})(1 - \theta_{min})}}{\left(\sqrt{\theta_{max}} + \sqrt{\theta_{min}}\right)^2}, \tag{5}$$

$$\eta = \frac{2\left(\sqrt{\theta_{max}}\sqrt{\theta_{min}} + 1\right) + 2\sqrt{(1 - \theta_{max})(1 - \theta_{min})}}{\left(\sqrt{\theta_{max}} + \sqrt{\theta_{min}}\right)^2}, \tag{6}$$

which satisfy [1]

$$\theta_{max}\eta\gamma = \left(1 + \sqrt{(\gamma - 1)(\eta - 1)}\right)^2, \tag{7}$$

$$\theta_{min}\eta\gamma = \left(1 - \sqrt{(\gamma - 1)(\eta - 1)}\right)^2. \tag{8}$$

Note here that the seminal work [1] of the APC algorithm provided an indirect way of finding the optimal γ and η, which requires to solve an optimizing problem and might only achieve near-optimal values in practical use. While in this paper we present closed-form expressions of the optimal γ and η, i.e., (5) and (6), respectively, so as to simplify the parameter setting as well as the forthcoming performance analysis.

Moreover, we define

$$\alpha = \frac{\sqrt{\kappa(\mathbf{X})} - 1}{\sqrt{\kappa(\mathbf{X})} + 1}, \tag{9}$$

where $\kappa(\mathbf{X}) = \frac{\theta_{max}}{\theta_{min}} \geq 1$ that is the condition number of $\mathbf{X}$ [1].

3   Analysis

In this section, we conduct a performance analysis of the APC algorithm, in terms of the error of solution (Definition 1). We are now going to present the main results whose proofs are given in Appendix.

Lemma 1. *Consider Algorithm 1, and assume that $\mathbf{A}_\ell$ is the ℓ-th row of $\mathbf{A}$ (see Line 1). Then, the projection matrix onto the nullspace of $\mathbf{A}_\ell^H$ can be expressed as*

$$\mathbf{P}_\ell^\perp = \mathbf{I}_s - \mathbf{A}_\ell^H\left(\mathbf{A}_\ell\mathbf{A}_\ell^H\right)^{-1}\mathbf{A}_\ell, \tag{10}$$

which is calculated and used in Algorithm 1 (see Line 4 and Line 10, respectively). Moreover, $\mathbf{A}_\ell\mathbf{P}_\ell^\perp = \mathbf{0}_L^T$ and $\left(\mathbf{P}_\ell^\perp\right)^2 = \mathbf{P}_\ell^\perp$.

Definition 1. *Let*

$$e_\ell(t) = x_\ell(t) - x^*, \tag{11}$$

$$\bar{e}(t) = \bar{x}(t) - x^* = \frac{1}{M} \sum_{\ell=1}^{M} e_\ell(t). \tag{12}$$

The key recursions in the APC algorithm, i.e., Line 10 and Line 12 of Algorithm 1, can be reformulated as

$$e_\ell(t+1) = e_\ell(t) + \gamma P_\ell^\perp \left(\bar{e}(t) - e_\ell(t) \right), \tag{13}$$

$$\bar{e}(t+1) = \frac{\eta}{M} \sum_{\ell=1}^{M} e_\ell(t+1) + (1-\eta)\bar{e}(t). \tag{14}$$

It follows from (2) that $y_\ell = \mathbf{A}_\ell x^* + \hat{w}_\ell$, while every $\mathbf{x}_\ell(t)$ computed in Line 5 or Line 10 of Algorithm 1 should be a solution of $y_\ell = \mathbf{A}_\ell x$, i.e.,

$$y_\ell = \mathbf{A}_\ell \mathbf{x}_\ell(t). \tag{15}$$

This can be verified using the fact that, as long as $\mathbf{A}_\ell \mathbf{x}_\ell(0) = y_\ell$, $\mathbf{A}_\ell \mathbf{x}_\ell(t+1) = \mathbf{A}_\ell \mathbf{x}_\ell(t) + \gamma \mathbf{A}_\ell \mathbf{P}_\ell^\perp (\bar{\mathbf{x}}(t) - \mathbf{x}_\ell(t)) = \mathbf{A}_\ell \mathbf{x}_\ell(t) = y_\ell$ holds true for all $t \geq 0$, according to Lemma 1. Therefore,

$$\mathbf{P}_\ell^\perp e_\ell(t) = e_\ell(t) - \mathbf{A}_\ell^H \left(\mathbf{A}_\ell \mathbf{A}_\ell^H \right)^{-1} (\mathbf{A}_\ell \mathbf{x}_\ell(t) - \mathbf{A}_\ell x^*)$$

$$= e_\ell(t) - \mathbf{A}_\ell^H \left(\mathbf{A}_\ell \mathbf{A}_\ell^H \right)^{-1} \tilde{w}_\ell, \tag{16}$$

which allows us to rewrite (13) as

$$e_\ell(t+1) = (1-\gamma)e_\ell(t) + \gamma \mathbf{P}_\ell^\perp \bar{e}(t) + \gamma \mathbf{A}_\ell^H \left(\mathbf{A}_\ell \mathbf{A}_\ell^H \right)^{-1} \tilde{w}_\ell. \tag{17}$$

From (14) and (17), we can develop a state-space equation to describe the key recursions of the APC algorithm as follows:

$$\mathbf{d}(t+1) = \mathbf{G}\mathbf{d}(t) + \tilde{\mathbf{w}}_d, \tag{18}$$

where

$$\mathbf{d}(t) = \begin{bmatrix} e_1(t) \\ \vdots \\ e_M(t) \\ \bar{e}(t) \end{bmatrix}, \quad \tilde{\mathbf{w}}_d = \gamma \begin{bmatrix} \mathbf{A}_1^H \left(\mathbf{A}_1 \mathbf{A}_1^H \right)^{-1} \tilde{w}_1 \\ \vdots \\ \mathbf{A}_M^H \left(\mathbf{A}_M \mathbf{A}_M^H \right)^{-1} \tilde{w}_M \\ \mathbf{0}_s \end{bmatrix}, \tag{19}$$

$$\mathbf{G} = \begin{bmatrix} (1-\gamma)\mathbf{I}_{Ms} & \gamma \begin{bmatrix} \mathbf{P}_1^\perp \\ \vdots \\ \mathbf{P}_M^\perp \end{bmatrix} \\ \frac{\eta(1-\gamma)}{M} \begin{bmatrix} \mathbf{I}_s \cdots \mathbf{I}_s \end{bmatrix} & \mathbf{B} \end{bmatrix}, \tag{20}$$

with $\mathbf{B} = \frac{\eta\gamma}{M} \sum_{\ell=1}^{M} \mathbf{P}_\ell^\perp + (1-\eta)\mathbf{I}_s = -\eta\gamma\mathbf{X} + (1-\eta+\eta\gamma)\mathbf{I}_s$.

Lemma 2. G *have* $(M + 1)s$ *eigenvalues, among which there are* $(M - 1)s$ *eigenvalues that are equal to* $1 - \gamma$, *and* $2s$ *eigenvalues* $\xi_{1,\pm}, \cdots, \xi_{s,\pm}$, *where* $\xi_{i,\pm}$ $(i = 1, \cdots, s)$ *are the solutions of the quadratic equation*

$$\xi^2 + (\eta\gamma(1 + \theta_i) + \gamma + \eta + 2)\xi + (\gamma + 1)(\eta + 1) = 0, \tag{21}$$

such that

$$\xi_{i,\pm} = \frac{\theta_{max} + \theta_{min} - 2\theta_i}{\left(\sqrt{\theta_{max}} + \sqrt{\theta_{min}}\right)^2} \pm \frac{2\sqrt{(\theta_i - \theta_{max})(\theta_i - \theta_{min})}}{\left(\sqrt{\theta_{max}} + \sqrt{\theta_{min}}\right)^2}. \tag{22}$$

If $\theta_{min} < \theta_i < \theta_{max}$, *then* $(\theta_i - \theta_{max})(\theta_i - \theta_{min}) < 0$ *and thus* $\xi_{i,\pm}$ *are complex-valued.*

Lemma 3. *For* G, *the spectral radius* $\rho(G) = \alpha < 1$, *so that* $\lim_{t \to \infty} G^t = 0_{(M+1)s}$, *where* α *is defined in* (9), *and* t *is a positive integer. Besides, the Neumann series* $\sum_{l=0}^{\infty} G^l$ *converges, i.e.,* $\sum_{l=0}^{\infty} G^l = (I - G)^{-1}$.

Because the system (18) is in the form of a discrete-time state-space equation, its closed-form solution can be directly obtained by applying the linear system theory [15].

Theorem 1. *The solution to the system* (18) *can be written as*

$$d(t) = G^t d(0) + \left(\sum_{l=0}^{t-1} G^l\right) \tilde{w}_d, \tag{23}$$

where $G^t d(0)$ *and* $\left(\sum_{l=0}^{t-1} G^l\right) \tilde{w}_d$ *are the zero-input and zero-state responses, respectively* [15, (4.20)].

Use Lemma 3 to show that

$$\sum_{l=0}^{t-1} G^l = \sum_{l=0}^{\infty} G^l - G^t \left(\sum_{l=0}^{\infty} G^l\right) = (I - G^t)(I - G)^{-1}. \tag{24}$$

Substituting this result into (23) produces

$$d(t) = G^t d(0) + (I - G^t)(I - G)^{-1} \tilde{w}_d, \tag{25}$$

which suggests that

$$d(\infty) := \lim_{t \to \infty} d(t) = (I - G)^{-1} \tilde{w}_d. \tag{26}$$

Observe that the behavior of $d(t)$ relies heavily on G and G^t, so we will apply the Jordan canonical form theorem to the coming analysis.

Theorem 2. *There exists a nonsingular matrix* $\boldsymbol{S} \in \mathbb{C}^{(M+1)s \times (M+1)s}$, *and there are positive integers* $q, n_1, \cdots, n_q$ *with* $n_1 + \cdots + n_q = (M+1)s$, *and scalars* $\xi_1, \cdots, \xi_q \in \{1 - \gamma, \xi_{1,\pm}, \xi_{2,\pm}, \cdots, \xi_{s,\pm}\}$ *such that*

$$G = S^{-1} J S, \tag{27}$$

where $\boldsymbol{J} = \boldsymbol{J}_{n_1}(\xi_1) \bigoplus \cdots \bigoplus \boldsymbol{J}_{n_q}(\xi_q)$ *is a Jordan matrix, and* $\boldsymbol{J}_{n_l}(\xi_l), l = 1, \cdots, q$, *are Jordan blocks*[1]. *(Jordan Canonical Form [14, Theorem 3.1.11])*

This theorem has an important consequence. Precisely, we have the following corollary.

Corollary 1. *Let* $\boldsymbol{G}$ *be given. Then* $\boldsymbol{G}^t = \boldsymbol{S}^{-1} \boldsymbol{J}^t \boldsymbol{S}$.

Next, we investigate the properties of $\boldsymbol{J}^t$ by establishing two lemmas (i.e., Lemmas 4 and 6 given below) that identify the features of Jordan blocks with different eigenvalues of $\boldsymbol{G}$.

Lemma 4. *The number of Jordan blocks of* $\boldsymbol{G}$ *corresponding to eigenvalue* $1 - \gamma$ *is* $(M-1)s$, *such that every Jordan block is 1-by-1. (Jordan Blocks with Eigenvalue* $1 - \gamma$ *of* $\boldsymbol{G}$)

The next result aims to provide insights into Jordan blocks with eigenvalues $\xi_{i,\pm}, i = 1, \cdots, s$. Before stating this result, we will first give an explicit formula for the eigenvectors associated with these eigenvalues.

Lemma 5. *Let* $\boldsymbol{\Lambda} = diag(\theta_1, \cdots, \theta_s)$, *where* $\theta_1, \cdots, \theta_s$ *are the eigenvalues of* $\boldsymbol{X}$, *see (3) and (4). Then*

(a) $\boldsymbol{X}$ *has* s *orthonormal eigenvectors, denoted by* $\boldsymbol{v}_1, \cdots, \boldsymbol{v}_s$, *where* $\boldsymbol{v}_i$ *is the eigenvector associated with eigenvalue* θ_i *of* $\boldsymbol{X}$, $i = 1, \cdots, s$.
(b) *Every scalar* $\xi \in \{\xi_{1,\pm}, \cdots, \xi_{s,\pm}\}$ *(such that* ξ *is a solution to (21)) and*

$$\boldsymbol{v}_G(\xi) = \begin{bmatrix} -\frac{\gamma}{1-\gamma-\xi} \boldsymbol{P}_1^\perp \boldsymbol{v}_i \\ -\frac{\gamma}{1-\gamma-\xi} \boldsymbol{P}_2^\perp \boldsymbol{v}_i \\ \vdots \\ \boldsymbol{v}_i \end{bmatrix}, \tag{28}$$

form an eigenvalue-eigenvector pair for $\boldsymbol{G}$.

Lemma 6. *The number of Jordan blocks of* $\boldsymbol{G}$ *corresponding to every eigenvalue* $\xi \in \{\xi_{1,\pm}, \cdots, \xi_{s,\pm}\}$ *is at most 2, where each Jordan block is either 1-by-1 or 2-by-2. (Jordan Blocks with Eigenvalues* $\xi_{i,\pm}, i = 1, \cdots, s$, *of* $\boldsymbol{G}$)

The preceding results (including Lemmas 4 and 6) motivate the property of $\boldsymbol{J}^t$, as shown by the following lemma.

---

[1] The Jordan block $\boldsymbol{J}_{n_l}(\xi_l)$ is an n_l-by-n_l upper triangular matrix in which ξ_l appears n_l times on the main diagonal; if $n_l > 1$, there are $n_l - 1$ elements 1 in the super-diagonal; all other elements are 0 [14].

Lemma 7. *For the Jordan matrix $\boldsymbol{J}$ in (27), we have*

$$\boldsymbol{J}^t = \boldsymbol{J}^t_{n_1}(\xi_1) \bigoplus \cdots \bigoplus \boldsymbol{J}^t_{n_q}(\xi_q), \tag{29}$$

where

$$\boldsymbol{J}^t_n(\xi) = \begin{bmatrix} \xi^t & \binom{t}{1}\xi^{t-1} & \cdots & \binom{t}{n-1}\xi^{t-n+1} \\ 0 & \xi^t & \cdots & \binom{t}{n-2}\xi^{t-n+2} \\ \vdots & \vdots & \ddots & \vdots \\ 0 & 0 & \cdots & \xi^t \end{bmatrix}, \tag{30}$$

and $n_l \in \{1,2\}$ for all $l = 1, \cdots, q$.

After obtaining Corollary 1 and Lemma 7, the mechanism governing the convergence of $\boldsymbol{G}^t$ (in (25)) to zero is better understood. Now we are in a position to give a formulation that characterizes the behavior of $\boldsymbol{d}(t)$.

Theorem 3. *Consider the solution $\boldsymbol{d}(t)$ of the state-space equation (18). We have*

$$\boldsymbol{d}(t) = \boldsymbol{d}(\infty) + \boldsymbol{G}^t \left(\boldsymbol{d}(0) - \left(\boldsymbol{I}_{(M+1)s} - \boldsymbol{G} \right)^{-1} \tilde{\boldsymbol{w}}_d \right), \tag{31}$$

since $\boldsymbol{d}(\infty) = \left(\boldsymbol{I}_{(M+1)s} - \boldsymbol{G} \right)^{-1} \tilde{\boldsymbol{w}}_d$, such that

$$\boldsymbol{d}(t) = \left(\boldsymbol{I}_{(M+1)s} - \boldsymbol{G} \right)^{-1} \tilde{\boldsymbol{w}}_d + \left(\boldsymbol{I}_{(M+1)s} - \boldsymbol{G} \right)^{-1} \boldsymbol{\epsilon}, \tag{32}$$

where

$$\boldsymbol{\epsilon} = \boldsymbol{G}^t \left(\left(\boldsymbol{I}_{(M+1)s} - \boldsymbol{G} \right) \boldsymbol{d}(0) - \tilde{\boldsymbol{w}}_d \right). \tag{33}$$

Moreover, $\|\boldsymbol{\epsilon}\|_2 = O\left(\alpha^t\right)$.

Theorem 4. *Consider the problem of solving a large-scale system (1) of linear equations, we have*

$$\bar{\boldsymbol{x}}(t) - \boldsymbol{x}^* = \frac{1}{(1+\eta)M} \boldsymbol{X}^{-1} \boldsymbol{A}^H \boldsymbol{\Xi} \tilde{\boldsymbol{w}} + \frac{1}{\gamma(1+\eta)} \boldsymbol{X}^{-1} \bar{\boldsymbol{\epsilon}}, \tag{34}$$

where

$$\bar{\boldsymbol{\epsilon}} = \left[\frac{1}{M} \boldsymbol{I}_s \; \frac{1}{M} \boldsymbol{I}_s \; \cdots \; \boldsymbol{I}_s \right] \boldsymbol{\epsilon}. \tag{35}$$

Moreover, $\|\bar{\boldsymbol{\epsilon}}\|_2 = O\left(\alpha^t\right)$.

Theorem 3 characterizes the error of solution attained by the APC algorithm when the system (1) is faced with unknown noise $\tilde{\boldsymbol{w}}$ as in (2). It is easy to see that Theorem 3 is a generalization of Theorem 1 derived in [1], because by letting $\tilde{\boldsymbol{w}}$ be the all-zero vector in Theorem 3, our obtained result can be reduced to Theorem 1 of [1].

4   Numerical Results

In this section, we carry out a serise of simulations to evaluate the performance of the APC algorithm in the complex white gaussian noise scenarios with the aim to verify the main result (Theorem 3). The noise vector $\tilde{\mathbf{w}}$ has independent identically distributed elements satisfying $\tilde{w}_i \sim CN(0, P_n)$. By letting the iteration number T vary, we focus on the mean square error (MSE) performance which defined as:

$$\text{MSE} = \mathbb{E}\left\{\|\mathbf{x}^* - \tilde{\mathbf{x}}\|_2^2\right\}. \tag{36}$$

We mainly consider the influence of three factors: the algorithm parameter M, the condition number of matrix $\mathbf{X}$ (i.e., $\kappa(\mathbf{X})$), and the noise power P_n.

Figure 1 shows the MSE performance of the APC algorithm with different size of matrix $\mathbf{A}$. We set $\kappa(\mathbf{X}) = 1.6$ (i.e., $\alpha = 0.23$), and the noise power $P_n = 1.0\text{e}{-}4$. When $M = \{8, 32, 128\}$, the simulation results are shown in Fig. 1. We can find that lines are similar to the exponential decay curve. No matter what M is equal to, the algorithm can quickly converge after $T = 4$. When $T \geq 5$, $\|\bar{\epsilon}\|_2 = O\left(0.23^T\right)$ in (34) is small enough ($\|\bar{\epsilon}\|_2 \leq 10^{-3}$) to be neglected.

Figure 2 is plotted with $M = 32$ and $P_n = 1.0\text{e}{-}4$. It shows the influence of $\kappa(\mathbf{X})$ on the MSE performance. By comparing the curves, we can observe that if we keep M and P_n the same, the converged value of the MSE varies only slightly. But there are differences in convergence speed. When the condition number is larger, the convergence speed is lower. Specifically, when $\kappa(\mathbf{X}) = 1.56$, the algorithm converges after 3 iterations; but when $\kappa(\mathbf{X})$ increases to 6.0, while the algorithm needs 9 iterations to achieve the convergence. Combined with (9), we can analyze that the closer $\kappa(\mathbf{X})$ is to 1, the closer α is to 0, and the faster $\|\bar{\epsilon}\|_2$ decreases which influences the MSE performance according to (32) and (36). The theoretical analysis is in accordance with the simulation results.

Figure 3 illustrates the effect of the noise power P_n on the MSE performance for the APC algorithm. Let P_n gradually increase from $1.0\text{e}{-}5$ to $1.0\text{e}{-}3$. It can be seen that the increase of P_n does not have evident influence on the convergence speed of the algorithm, but the final MSE performance (after the algorithm converges) will getting worse. We also plot ADMM method in Fig. 3 as the comparison algorithm. The figure clearly presents that, ADMM needs 30 times iterations to decrease the MSE to 0.74 with $P_n = 1.0\text{e}{-}5$, but APC gets convergence by 5 times iterations under higher noise level ($P_n = 1.0\text{e}{-}3$). Comparing with ADMM, APC can achieve better MSE performance with faster convergence in the scene with higher noise level.

In summary, as the value of T increases, $\frac{1}{\gamma(1+\eta)}\mathbf{X}^{-1}\bar{\epsilon}$ in (34) tends to 0, the error of APC algorithm will only be effected by $\frac{1}{(1+\eta)M}\mathbf{X}^{-1}\mathbf{A}^H\mathbf{\Xi}\tilde{\mathbf{w}}$ in (34). In other words, the error is determined by the noise level after enough iterations. This fits with Theorem 3.

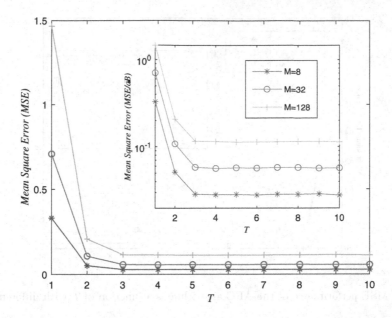

Fig. 1. MSE performance of the APC algorithm as a function of T with different M.

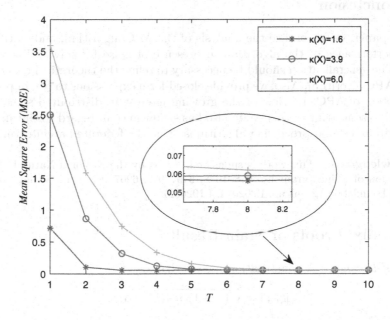

Fig. 2. MSE performance of the APC algorithm as a function of T with different $\kappa\left(\mathbf{X}\right)$.

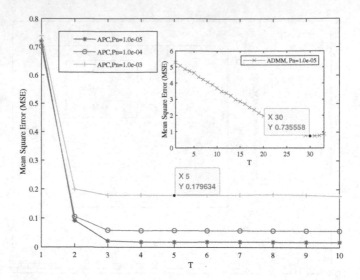

Fig. 3. MSE performance of the APC algorithm as a function of T with different P_n.

5   Conclusion

In this paper, we generalize the analysis of the APC algorithm, and clarify the error performance of the algorithm in presence of noise for solving linear systems. The generalization should be necessary to refine the theoretical framework of the APC algorithm. Also, we provide closed-form expressions to two important parameters of APC. In view of the growing interest in distributed signal processing, to some degree, this study also has significance in regard to the analysis of distributed signal processing algorithms using the federated architecture.

Acknowledgment. This work is sponsored in part by the National Natural Science Foundation of China (grant no. 61801048, 61971058, 62071063) and Beijing Natural Science Foundation (grant no. L202014, L192002).

Appendix: Proofs of Main Results

Proof of Lemma 3: A computation reveals that

$$|\xi_{i,\pm}| = \sqrt{(\gamma - 1)(\eta - 1)} = \alpha, \tag{37}$$

for all $i = 1, \cdots, s$. Then, it's a simple consequence of Lemma A.2 that $\rho(\mathbf{G}) = \alpha < 1$ [1], i.e., the largest magnitude eigenvalue of $\mathbf{G}$ is less than 1. This implies that $\lim_{t \to \infty} \mathbf{G}^t = \mathbf{O}_{(M+1)s}$ and $\sum_{l=0}^{\infty} \mathbf{G}^l = (\mathbf{I} - \mathbf{G})^{-1}$ [16]. ∎

Proof of Lemma 4: All we need to do is to show that the geometric multiplicity of eigenvalue $1 - \gamma$ is $(M-1)s$ [14, 16]. We begin by noting that

$$\mathbf{G} - (1-\gamma)\mathbf{I} = \begin{bmatrix} \mathbf{O}_{Ms} & \gamma \begin{bmatrix} \mathbf{P}_1^\perp \\ \vdots \\ \mathbf{P}_M^\perp \end{bmatrix} \\ \frac{\eta(1-\gamma)}{M} \begin{bmatrix} \mathbf{I}_s & \cdots & \mathbf{I}_s \end{bmatrix} \mathbf{B} - (1-\gamma)\mathbf{I}_s \end{bmatrix}.$$

Applying elementary row and column operations [14], we can transform $\mathbf{G} - (1-\gamma)\mathbf{I}$ into a simple form

$$\mathbf{G}_T = \begin{bmatrix} \mathbf{O}_{Ms} & \gamma \begin{bmatrix} \mathbf{P}_1^\perp \\ \vdots \\ \mathbf{P}_M^\perp \end{bmatrix} \\ \frac{\eta(1-\gamma)}{M} \begin{bmatrix} \mathbf{O}_s & \cdots & \mathbf{O}_s & \mathbf{I}_s \end{bmatrix} & \mathbf{O}_s \end{bmatrix}.$$

Since elementary operations do not change the rank of a matrix [14], it follows that

$$\operatorname{rank}(\mathbf{G} - (1-\gamma)\mathbf{I}) = \operatorname{rank}(\mathbf{G}_T) \leq 2\,s. \tag{38}$$

The geometric multiplicity of eigenvalue $1 - \gamma$ of $\mathbf{G}$ is equal to $(M+1)s - \operatorname{rank}(\mathbf{G} - (1-\gamma)\mathbf{I})$ that is not less than $(M-1)s$ according to (38). Furthermore, the geometric multiplicity should not be larger than algebraic multiplicity, i.e., $(M-1)s$, for $1 - \gamma$, and thus can only be $(M-1)s$ [14, Theorem 1.4.10]. This implies that the number of Jordan blocks of $\mathbf{G}$ corresponding to $1-\gamma$, is $(M-1)s$ [14]. Finally, because the geometric and algebraic multiplicities of $1-\gamma$ are equal, every Jordan block corresponding to $1 - \gamma$ is 1-by-1 [14]. ∎

Proof of Lemma 5: First note that $\mathbf{X}$ is Hermitian and $\mathbf{X}$ is unitarily diagonalizable [14, Theorem 2.5.6]. Then, applying [14, Theorem 2.5.3] yields the assertion (a).

To prove the assertion (b), let us verify whether $\mathbf{v}_G(\xi)$ satisfies the eigenvalue-eigenvector equation $(\mathbf{G} - \xi\mathbf{I})\mathbf{v}_G(\xi) = \mathbf{0}_{(M+1)s}$, where

$$\mathbf{G} - \xi\mathbf{I}_{(M+1)s} = \begin{bmatrix} (1-\gamma-\xi)\mathbf{I}_{Ms} & \gamma \begin{bmatrix} \mathbf{P}_1^\perp \\ \vdots \\ \mathbf{P}_M^\perp \end{bmatrix} \\ \frac{\eta(1-\gamma)}{M} \begin{bmatrix} \mathbf{I}_s & \cdots & \mathbf{I}_s \end{bmatrix} & \mathbf{B} - \xi\mathbf{I}_s \end{bmatrix}.$$

On the one hand, it is easy to check that

$$\begin{bmatrix} (1-\gamma-\xi)\mathbf{I}_{ML} & \gamma \begin{bmatrix} \mathbf{P}_1^\perp \\ \vdots \\ \mathbf{P}_M^\perp \end{bmatrix} \end{bmatrix} \mathbf{v}_G(\xi) = \mathbf{0}_{Ms}. \tag{39}$$

On the other hand, since $\mathbf{X}\mathbf{v}_i = \theta_i\mathbf{v}_i$ and $\frac{\sum_{\ell=1}^M \mathbf{P}_\ell^\perp}{M} = \mathbf{I}_s - \mathbf{X}$, we have $\frac{\sum_{\ell=1}^M \mathbf{P}_\ell^\perp}{M}\mathbf{v}_i = (1 - \theta_i)\mathbf{v}_i$ and $(\mathbf{B} - \xi\mathbf{I}_s)\mathbf{v}_i = (-\eta\gamma\theta_i + 1 - \eta + \eta\gamma - \xi)\mathbf{v}_i$. As (21) ensures that $-\frac{\eta\gamma(1-\gamma)}{1-\gamma-\xi}(1 - \theta) - \eta\gamma\theta + 1 - \eta + \eta\gamma - \xi = 0$ if $\xi \neq 1 - \gamma$, it yields

$$\left[\frac{\eta(1-\gamma)}{M}\begin{bmatrix}\mathbf{I}_s & \cdots & \mathbf{I}_s\end{bmatrix}\mathbf{B} - \xi\mathbf{I}_s\right]\mathbf{v}_G(\xi)$$

$$= \left[-\frac{\eta\gamma(1-\gamma)}{(1-\gamma-\xi)}\frac{\sum_{\ell=1}^M \mathbf{P}_\ell^\perp}{M} + (\mathbf{B} - \xi\mathbf{I}_s)\right]\mathbf{v}_i = \mathbf{0}_s. \tag{40}$$

Finally, (39) and (40) together imply that $(\mathbf{G} - \xi\mathbf{I})\mathbf{v}_G(\xi) = \mathbf{0}_{(M+1)s}$ which completes the proof of the assertion (b). ∎

Proof of Lemma 6: It follows from (22) that $\xi_{1,+} = \xi_{1,-}$ and $\xi_{s,+} = \xi_{s,-}$ since $\theta_s = \theta_{min}$ and $\theta_1 = \theta_{max}$, while $\xi_{i,+} \neq \xi_{i,-}$ if $\theta_{min} < \theta_i < \theta_{max}$. One of the consequences of Lemma 5 is that the number of linearly dependent eigenvectors associated with every eigenvalue $\xi \in \{\xi_{1,\pm}, \cdots, \xi_{s,\pm}\}$ is not larger than 2. Therefore, the geometric multiplicity of ξ is 1, and the Jordan block of $\mathbf{G}$ with eigenvalue ξ is 2-by-2, when $\xi = \xi_{1,+} = \xi_{1,-}$ or $\xi = \xi_{s,+} = \xi_{s,-}$. If $\xi = \xi_{i,+}$ or $\xi = \xi_{i,-}$ with $\xi_{i,+} \neq \xi_{i,-}$, then the geometric multiplicity of ξ is 2 such that the Jordan block with eigenvalue ξ is 1-by-1. ∎

Proof of Lemma 7: It can easily be verified by using the property of direct sum together with [16, (7.10.7)]. ∎

Proof of Theorem 2: Combining (25) and (26) yields (31), and then multiplying on both sides of (31) by $\mathbf{I}_{(M+1)s} - \mathbf{G}$ produces (33). By the Rayleigh quotient theorem [16] and Corollary 1, we obtain

$$\|\boldsymbol{\epsilon}\|_2 \leq \|\mathbf{J}^t\|_2 \|(\mathbf{I}_{(M+1)s} - \mathbf{G})\mathbf{d}(0) - \tilde{\mathbf{w}}_d\|_2, \tag{41}$$

where $\|\mathbf{J}^t\|_2 = O(\alpha^t)$ [15].

The remaining part of the proof is to derive an upper bound on $\|(\mathbf{I}_{(M+1)s} - \mathbf{G})\mathbf{d}(0) - \tilde{\mathbf{w}}_d\|_2$. First, it is clear that

$$\mathbf{d}(0) = \begin{bmatrix} -\mathbf{P}_1^\perp\mathbf{x}^* + \mathbf{A}_1^H\left(\mathbf{A}_1\mathbf{A}_1^H\right)^{-1}\tilde{w}_1 \\ \vdots \\ -\mathbf{P}_M^\perp\mathbf{x}^* + \mathbf{A}_M^H\left(\mathbf{A}_M\mathbf{A}_M^H\right)^{-1}\tilde{w}_M \\ -\frac{1}{M}\sum_{\ell=1}^M \mathbf{P}_\ell^\perp\mathbf{x}^* + \frac{1}{M}\sum_{\ell=1}^M \mathbf{A}_\ell^H\left(\mathbf{A}_\ell\mathbf{A}_\ell^H\right)^{-1}\tilde{w}_\ell \end{bmatrix}, \tag{42}$$

according to the initialization of the APC algorithm as in Line 5 of Algorithm 1 together with (19), and thus

$$\left(\mathbf{I}_{(M+1)s} - \mathbf{G}\right)\mathbf{d}(0) - \tilde{\mathbf{w}}_d = \begin{bmatrix} -\gamma\mathbf{P}_1^\perp\left(\mathbf{x}^* + \bar{\mathbf{e}}(0)\right) \\ \vdots \\ -\gamma\mathbf{P}_M^\perp\left(\mathbf{x}^* + \bar{\mathbf{e}}(0)\right) \\ -\eta\gamma\mathbf{X}\bar{\mathbf{e}}(0) \end{bmatrix}.$$

This yields

$$\left\|\left(\mathbf{I}_{(M+1)s} - \mathbf{G}\right)\mathbf{d}(0) - \tilde{\mathbf{w}}_d\right\|_2^2 \leq 2\gamma^2 M \left(1 - \theta_{min}\right)\|\mathbf{x}^*\|_2^2$$
$$+ \left(2\gamma^2 M \left(1 - \theta_{min}\right) + \eta^2\gamma^2\theta_{max}^2\right)\|\bar{\mathbf{e}}(0)\|_2^2.$$

Then, since $\|\bar{\mathbf{e}}(0)\|_2^2 \leq \frac{\sum_{\ell=1}^{M}\|\mathbf{e}_\ell(0)\|_2^2}{M}$, it follows from Lemma 1 and (42) that

$$\|\bar{\mathbf{e}}(0)\|_2^2 \leq \frac{M\left(\mathbf{x}^*\right)^H\left(\mathbf{I} - \mathbf{X}\right)\mathbf{x}^* + \sum_{\ell=1}^{M}\left(\mathbf{A}_\ell\mathbf{A}_\ell^H\right)^{-2}\tilde{w}_\ell}{M}$$

$$\leq (1 - \theta_{min})\|\mathbf{x}^*\|_2^2 + \frac{\sum_{\ell=1}^{M}\left(\mathbf{A}_\ell\mathbf{A}_\ell^H\right)^{-2}\tilde{w}_\ell}{M},$$

and

$$\left\|\left(\mathbf{I}_{(M+1)s} - \mathbf{G}\right)\mathbf{d}(0) - \tilde{\mathbf{w}}_d\right\|_2 \leq \left(2\gamma^2 M \left(1 - \theta_{min}\right) + \eta^2\gamma^2\theta_{max}^2\right)$$

$$\times \left((2 - \theta_{min})\|\mathbf{x}^*\|_2^2 + \frac{\sum_{\ell=1}^{M}\left(\mathbf{A}_\ell\mathbf{A}_\ell^H\right)^{-2}\tilde{w}_\ell}{M}\right).$$

Substituting this inequality into (41) gives $\|\epsilon\|_2 = O\left(\alpha^t\right)$.   ∎

Proof of Theorem 3: Observe that

$$\left[\tfrac{1}{M}\mathbf{I}_s \; \tfrac{1}{M}\mathbf{I}_s \; \cdots \; \mathbf{I}_s\right]\mathbf{d}(t) = 2\bar{\mathbf{e}}(t),$$
$$\left[\tfrac{1}{M}\mathbf{I}_s \; \tfrac{1}{M}\mathbf{I}_s \; \cdots \; \mathbf{I}_s\right]\mathbf{G}\mathbf{d}(t) = (2\mathbf{I}_s - \gamma(1+\eta)\mathbf{X})\,\bar{\mathbf{e}}(t).$$

A calculation also shows that $\left[\tfrac{1}{M}\mathbf{I}_s \; \tfrac{1}{M}\mathbf{I}_s \; \cdots \; \mathbf{I}_s\right]\tilde{\mathbf{w}}_d = \tfrac{\gamma}{M}\mathbf{A}^H\mathbf{\Xi}\tilde{\mathbf{w}}$. Combining these results, we get

$$\gamma(1+\eta)\mathbf{X}\bar{\mathbf{e}}(t) = \frac{\gamma}{M}\mathbf{A}^H\mathbf{\Xi}\tilde{\mathbf{w}} + \left[\tfrac{1}{M}\mathbf{I}_s \; \tfrac{1}{M}\mathbf{I}_s \; \cdots \; \mathbf{I}_s\right]\epsilon,$$

which can be rewritten as (34). From Theorem 1, it follows that $\|\epsilon\|_2 = O\left(\alpha^t\right)$. Finally, based on the definition in (12), Theorem 3 can be verified.   ∎

References

1. Azizan-Ruhi, N., Lahouti, F., Avestimehrm, A., Hassibi, B.: Distributed solution of large-scale linear systems via accelerated projection based consensus. IEEE Trans. Sig. Process. **67**(14), 3806–3817 (2019)
2. Alaviani, S., Elia, N.: A distributed algorithm for solving linear algebraic equations over random networks. IEEE Trans. Autom. Control **66**(5), 2399–2406 (2021)
3. Zivojevic, D., et al.: Distributed weighted least-squares and Gaussian belief propagation: an integrated approach. In: Proceedings of 2021 IEEE International Conference on Communications, Control, and Computing Technologies for Smart Grids (SmartGridComm), pp. 432–437 (2021)

4. Wang, X., Mou, S., Sun, D.: Improvement of a distributed algorithm for solving linear equations. IEEE Trans. Ind. Electron. **64**(4), 3113–3117 (2017)
5. Zuo, C., Deng, H., Zhang, J., Qi, Y.: Distributed channel estimation algorithm for mmWave massive MIMO communication systems. In: Proceedings of 2021 IEEE 94th Vehicular Technology Conference (VTC2021-Fall), pp. 1–6 (2021)
6. Jia, M., Wang, Y., Shen, C., Hug, G.: Privacy-preserving distributed probabilistic load flow. IEEE Trans. Power Syst. **36**(2), 1616–1627 (2021)
7. Chakrabarti, K., Gupta, N., Chopra, N.: Iterative pre-conditioning to expedite the gradient-descent method. In: Proceedings of 2020 American Control Conference (ACC), pp. 3977–3982 (2020)
8. Li, T., Sahu, A.K., Talwalkar, A., Smith, V.: Federated learning: challenges, methods, and future directions. IEEE Sig. Process. Mag. **37**(3), 50–60 (2020)
9. Chakrabarti, K., Gupta, N., Chopra, N.: Robustness of iteratively pre-conditioned gradient-descent method: the case of distributed linear regression problem. In: Proceedings of 2021 American Control Conference (ACC), pp. 2248–2253 (2021)
10. Dutta, S., Cadambe, V., Grover, P.: Short-Dot: computing large linear transforms distributedly using coded short dot product. In: Proceedings of the 30th International Conference on Neural Information Processing Systems (NIPS), pp. 2092–2100 (2016)
11. Dutta, S., Cadambe, V., Grover, P.: Short-Dot: computing large linear transforms distributedly using coded short dot products. IEEE Trans. Inf. Theory **65**(10), 6171–6193 (2019)
12. Dutta, S., et al.: On the optimal recovery threshold of coded matrix multiplication. IEEE Trans. Inf. Theory **66**(1), 278–301 (2020)
13. Zhao, Z., Lu, S., Hong, M., Palomar, D.: Distributed optimization for generalized phase retrieval over networks. In: Proceedings of 2018 52nd Asilomar Conference on Signals, Systems and Computers, pp. 48–52 (2018)
14. Horn, R., Johnson, C.: Matrix Analysis. Cambridge University Press, 2nd ed., Cambridge, USA (2013)
15. Chen, C.: Linear System Theory and Design. Oxford University Press, 3rd ed., Oxford, USA (1999)
16. Meyer, C.: Matrix Analysis and Applied Linear Algebra. Cambridge University Press, Cambridge (2000)

A Low-Cost Semihosting Approach to Debug DSP Application

Tao Huang[1], Haoqi Ren[1], Zhifeng Zhang[1], Bin Tan[2], and Jun Wu[3(✉)]

[1] Department of Computer Science, Tongji University, Shanghai, China
{2030798,renhaoqi,zhangzf}@tongji.edu.cn
[2] School of Electronic and Information Engineering, Jinggangshan University, Ji'an, China
tanbin@jgsu.edu.cn
[3] School of Computer Science, Fudan University, Shanghai, China
wujun@fudan.edu.cn

Abstract. Applications of digital signal processor (DSP) involve large amounts of data processing. In order to be able to improve the speed of DSP application development, it is necessary to be able to implement debugging functions that can support File I/O at a small cost of modification. This paper proposes a complete set of implementation methods of the semihosting debugging function on a DSP without an operating system, including hardware support and software algorithms. On hardware, this article adds only one self-trapping instruction to support semihosting debugging. In software, this article is based on the GDB File I/O extension protocol to design and implement the debugging agent software and C language library underlying file operations. And after optimizing library files and application source code, the I/O speed of the architecture can meet users' debugging needs. This solution can realize the semihosting debugging function for DSP chip at a low cost and has good performance. Therefore, provides more powerful debugging functions for DSP application development. In assembly level debugging, observing the execution of each assembly instruction can also verify the instruction execution of the chip itself. The addition of file operation can greatly validate the chip with larger data.

Keywords: DSP · Semihosting · GDB · Embedded debugging

1 Introduction

Nowadays, digital signal processing technology can be seen everywhere in people's daily lives, and digital signal processing algorithms often involve the real-time processing of large-scale data. So, in many devices, a separate DSP is always been used to complete the data-processing tasks, creating a huge market and application demand for DSP. In recent years, the development and application of deep learning have put forward higher demands on large-scale parallel computing [1]. Compared to general-purpose processors, DSP can process larger amounts of data simultaneously, but its control instructions are much simpler in order to reduce power consumption and silicon area. Therefore, how to quickly debug and verify it at various stages has become a difficult problem.

© ICST Institute for Computer Sciences, Social Informatics and Telecommunications Engineering 2023
Published by Springer Nature Switzerland AG 2023. All Rights Reserved
F. Gao et al. (Eds.): ChinaCom 2022, LNICST 500, pp. 33–43, 2023.
https://doi.org/10.1007/978-3-031-34790-0_3

The development and production of a chip often goes through multiple stages. As the number of transistors integrated on a single chip and the complexity of the on-chip system and microprocessor design continues to grow and increase, FPGA prototype verification before tape-out became an indispensable part of each design team [2]. Using FPGA and the debugging system as prototype can improve the verification speed [3, 4], but the digital signal processing application is characterized by the processing of a large amount of data, how to complete the verification of large-scale data during debugging is a challenge.

In general, large-scale data is often validated using file comparisons. In the field of debugging, you can simply divide the debugging method into two types, local debugging and embedded debugging [5, 6]. Local debugging is the most common. In this mode, the debugged program runs together with the debugger software on a PC, and the debugger debugs the program through the debugging interface provided by the operating system. The input and output of the program is managed by the operating system, and the result file can be easily obtained. Under embedded debugging [7], the debugger runs on the host PC and the program being debugged runs on the target machine. In the field of embedded debugging, in order to input and output files, the semihosting mechanism is required. Semihosting mode [8] refers to the delivery of input/output requests from application code to the host which running the debugger, using the host's file I/O system for input/output functionality. As for DSP, its control instructions are generally relatively simple, so usually it is difficult to run a fully functional and powerful operating system, let alone a file system. To debug it for file I/O, the only choice is the semihosting approach.

This article primarily describes the design of a semihosting debugging approach that requires only minimum hardware support and the associated hardware and software design and implementation. Hardware, the scheme implements a self-trapping instruction for the DSP to support semihosting debugging and connects to the host based on the JTAG interface. On the software, we base on the open-source debugger GDB to complete debugging agent software and corresponding C language libraries.

This article is organized as follows: The second part describes the relevant work in the field of debugging. The third part describes in detail the semihosting design we proposed. The fourth part is application optimization and validation. The fifth part is a summary of this article.

2   Related Work

Embedded debugging systems are divided into three categories: hardware debugging, software debugging and simulator debugging [9]. Software debugging requires the corresponding system and software support on the embedded hardware, and simulator debugging is a complete simulation of the embedded hardware on the host. The most widely used is hardware debugging, which can achieve completely realistic and reliable debugging effects, and does not require hardware support for the operating system.

There are two kinds of hardware debugging: in-circuit emulator (ICE) and on-chip debugger [10–13]. In-circuit emulator is a set of computer systems specifically designed to simulate the target CPU or MCU [14, 15]. The system generally contains an emulator motherboard, the processor embedded in the motherboard has exactly the same function as the processor to be debugged, and in order to achieve the purpose of debugging, its hardware has been specially modified. Using ICE to debug is essentially a hardware debugging method that been implemented by using the corresponding ICE to replace the processor [16–18].

ICE has not been used on a large scale due to its excessive cost and poor scalability. On the contrary, the on-chip debugger has been widely used due to its low hardware overhead and cost. On-chip debugging is to add a hardware circuit module specifically for debugging, which is called the on-chip debugger, inside the processor at the beginning of the processor hardware design [19–21]. In embedded debugging field, most users only use some basic debugging functions, such as breakpoints, single steps, register access, memory access, and so on. Therefore, on-chip debugging has become the first choice for most users.

The classic semihosting mechanism in the field of debugging is proposed by ARM [22], who implements or simulates the half-master mechanism in both hardware debugging and simulator debugging. However, the semihosting mechanism in ARM hardware debugging requires more hardware support. It must use an emulator that supports the semihosting mechanism for debugging [23], which has higher requirements for hardware versions and cumbersome development process.

Based on the above related considerations, this paper adopts the on-chip debugging method in order to implement the semihosting function on DSP quickly and at low cost. And in order to reduce the dependence on the emulator, this article will use software to provide appropriate support for the semihosting mechanism as much as possible.

3   Semihosting Approach

SWIFT processor is a high-performance DSP chip developed by Tongji University, which uses VLIW (Very Long Instruction Word) [24] technology and self-developed instruction set, and has high parallelistic vector computing capability. Consider power consumption and silicon area, the SWIFT instruction set omits a large number of control instructions. In order to be able to more easily and quickly verify and debug applications on the SWIFT processor, we need to support semihosting debugging with minimal changes.

3.1   GDB-Based Semihosting Architecture

The SWIFT DSP has a debugging system consists of a debug module, a JTAG tap on hardware and a debug agent (proxy), GDB on the software, as shown in Fig. 1.

GDB (The GNU Project Debugger) is a powerful open-source debugger. The structure of the GDB target side is relatively separate from other parts, which reduces the difficulty and effort of porting and adapting the new hardware architecture. GDB has thus become the first choice for many new chips. GDB is controlled by IDE in the debug system, execute what the user wants. Not only is GDB capable of debugging programs on the host, its simple RSP protocol also provides the basis for remote debugging. GDB using RSP protocol to send command and data to the debug proxy and get the result from it.

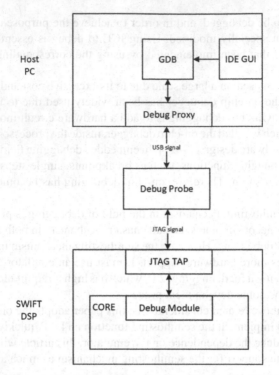

Fig. 1. The embedded debugging system Architecture for SWIFT DSP.

The debug proxy gets the GDB command and drive the Debug Probe to connect with the target machine, which is SWIFT DSP. Debug Probe in this system is simply a convertor translate USB signals to JTAG signals. JTAG TAP and Debug module control the core and using JTAG interface to communicate with the host.

The RSP protocol GDB used has an extension protocol, File-I/O Remote Protocol Extension, which can implement remote File I/O function. The File I/O Remote Protocol extension allows remote target to complete various system calls over GDB using the host's file system and console I/O. The target's system call is converted to a remote protocol packet to GDB, which then performs the desired action on the PC host system and returns the response packet to the remote target. This can simulate file system operations on targets without file system.

Based on File-I/O Remote Protocol Extension, this debug system can achieve semihosting operations with several modifications.

One semihosting operation based on GDB is performed as the procedure below:

1. Processor requires file manipulation.
2. Processor stalls and sends a request to debug module.
3. The request is sent to GDB via debug probe.
4. GDB performs the file operation.

5. GDB get the result and feed back to processor.

In traditional semihosting architectures, a debug probe is required to support semi-hosting mode. When the processor makes a request outward through the debug module, the probe will interact with the hardware to obtain the necessary information after receiving the request. This process is transparent to the user, which limits the user's hardware choice and prevents the user from making corresponding changes and optimizations on the software. In order to avoid hardware limitations, this paper's approach only uses the probe made of ordinary USB-JTAG communication chip. And the software does the necessary job.

3.2 Hardware Support

As the semihosting procedure shown in Sect. 3.1, DSP has to have the ability to stall autonomously and send the request to JTAG interface. To help DSP implement semi-hosting function with minimal changes, we added a instruction TRAP for SWIFT DSP. The way TRAP instruction works is shown in Fig. 2.

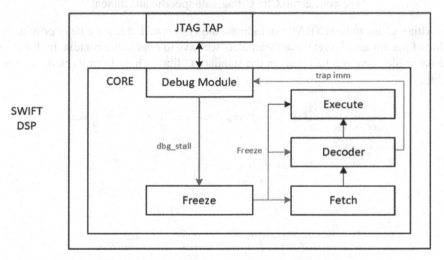

Fig. 2. How TRAP works in SWIFT DSP.

The immediate value followed by the TRAP instruction indicates which system call was made. The decoder of DSP decodes the TRAP instruction into a signal trap with an immediate value. Signal trap is passed into the debug module, causes the signal "dbg_stall", which generates several freeze signals to stall the core. The freeze signals are connected to the pipeline of SWIFT DSP. In order to stop in the right position, we only freeze the fetch module and the decoder of the processor to let the former instructions execute normally.

At the same time, the immediate value is also passed into the debug module, which is placed in the first half of the DRR (debug reason register). DRR was originally used to indicate what has happened that caused SWIFT DSP to stop. But the number of events only used the lower 14 bits. We use the high 18 bits of DRR for the immediate value of instruction "TRAP". The debug proxy learns the status of the core by polling for the registers of the core.

3.3 Software Support

The debug proxy controls the interaction between the debug probe and GDB. The debug proxy knows that DSP has been paused and gets the immediate value of TRAP by the value of the debug reason register. But the system call requires various parameters, taking read as an example, (1) is the open function supported by GDB. (2) is the packet content GDB need and (3) is what GDB feed back to proxy after performed the system call.

$$\text{int open(const char} * \text{pathname, int flags);} \tag{1}$$

$$\text{'Fopen,pathptr/len,flags,mode'} \tag{2}$$

$$\text{'Fretcode,errno,Ctrl-C flag;call-specific attachment'} \tag{3}$$

Although instruction TRAP can indicate the system call, it is not able to provide the value of parameters. To get these parameters we have to refer to the context. In that case, the basic file operating functions in the standard C library have been written as shown in Fig. 3.

```
int myopen(const char *pathname, int length, int flags,
int *errorno)
{
    int a;
    __builtin_dsp_trap(1);
    return a;
}

int open(const char *pathname, int flags)
{
    int length = strlen(pathname) + 1;
    return myopen(pathname, length, flags, &errno);
}
```

Fig. 3. The "open" and "myopen" function in C standard library

We design the parameter format of the function "myopen" according to the parameter information required by the RSP protocol of GDB and the format of the reply. In the function "open" of the standard library, the parameter value required by protocol is first calculated, and then the important function "myopen" is called.

```
myopen:                                              # @myopen
    addi  GR30, GR30, -256
    load32  GR2, GR30, 67
    load32  GR3, GR30, 66
    store32 GR4, GR30, 63
    store32 GR5, GR30, 62
    store32 GR3, GR30, 61
    store32 GR2, GR30, 60
    trap  1
    load32  GR2, GR30, 59
    addi  GR30, GR30, 256
    ret GR31
    nop
    nop

open:                                                # @open
    ...
    call  strlen
    ...
    call  __errno
    nop
    nop
    store32 GR2, GR30, 3
    ...
    store32 GR18, GR30, 2
    call  myopen
    nop
    nop
    ...
    ret GR31
    nop
    nop
```

Fig. 4. The assembly code of "open" and "myopen" function

The assembly code generated by compiling these functions by compiler is shown in Fig. 4. The GR30 is the stack register for SWIFT. After entering the function "my-open", the processor first modifies the value of the stack register and therefore enters the corresponding function stack area. Then compiler want the parameters are stored in a contiguous chunk of memory. So, it starts to collect them from memory or registers.

Finally, the parameters are stored in the memory address of GR30+63/62/61/60. Therefore, proxy only needs to read the value of GR30 to get the address where all parameters are stored in memory. When the processor encounters a trap instruction to stop, the proxy drives debug probe to read the memory to get the value of the parameter. Then proxy gets all the information it needed and combined the data in RSP protocol format and sent it to GDB.

GDB performs the corresponding operation on the host and returned the result to proxy. The proxy needs to give feedback to the processor by writing the returned data to memory. According to the assembly of the function "myopen", the address value of the global variable "errno" is stored at address of "GR30+60". When the proxy encounter a GDB execution failure, the reason for the failure can be stored to the corresponding address. After executing the TRAP instruction, the processor loads the data at "GR30+59" into GR2 and returns it to the upper function as the end. Therefore, the return value "fd" or failure code "−1" after GDB executing the function "open" can be placed at address of "GR30+59". In this way, the SWIFT processor finishes executing the function "open". Similarly, we can implement the common file I/O functions supported by GDB, such as close, read, write, etc.

This method relies on how the compiler compiles functions such as "myopen", and more specifically on the size of the function stack. However, functions such as "myread" and "mywrite" are used in the standard library, and the standard library is provided to the users in the form of a static library, and the assembly in the static library is fixed and will not be modified by the user. The compiler does not frequently modify the size of the function stack. Also, the position of these parameters could be listed in the configure file of the toolchain. It allows us to modify the stack without recompile the proxy.

4   Validation and Optimization

To validate the semihosting system, we use a development board containing two Xilinx VU440 FPGA chips to build the prototype verification system. The structural diagram of the development board is shown in the Fig. 5. SWIFT DSP has ultra-long vector parallel processing capability that cannot be implemented on a single VU440 chip, so we use time-division multiplexing to logically split it and implement it on two FPGAs. Due to the board level delay, the consequent main frequency can only be around 20 MHz. And the JTAG clock must lower than the main frequency of DSP. We use the FT2232HL development board as the debug probe, the structure diagram is shown in the Fig. 6. The board uses the FT2232H chip, which supports a USB2.0 high-speed interface that converts USB signals to a variety of serial signals, including JTAG. The manufacturer FTDI also provides the basic driver library file for the chip. Facilitates the writing of debugging proxy.

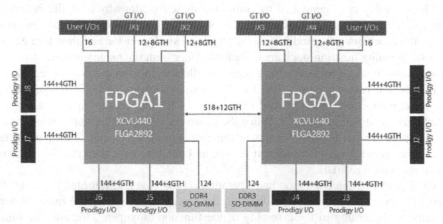

Fig. 5. The architecture of FPGA development board

Fig. 6. The appearance of the FT2232HL development board

We tested this prototype verification system with a commonly used digital signal processing program that includes FTT algorithm. Without optimization, the running time is unbearable, taking 14 min to complete according to Table 1. This is because the bottleneck of program speed is file operation.

Table 1. The running time of a digital signal processing program in 20 MHz FPGA

Before optimization	After optimization
14 min 20 s	9 s

In SWIFT's C language library, the underlying layer of commonly used input and output functions is implemented with read and write functions, such as printf, fread, fwrite, etc. In DSP applications, programmers are used to call input and output functions frequently, and the amount of data for I/O is very large, as the amount of data in a single I/O operation is very small. Each time SWIFT executes an I/O operation, it has to go through the transmission and conversion process from the processor's debug module to the debug probe, proxy, and GDB. Its rate is much lower than that of local I/O. Too many I/O operations can greatly slow down the speed of the SWIFT processor, and caused the result of 14 min in Table 1.

To improve its speed, we optimize it in our program. In the C language standard library, the FILE struct is used to flag a file, and we add a data member "char buf[MAXBUF]" to the FILE struct to cache data read in from the remote host. When there is no data in the buffer, calling the input function will directly read the MAXBUF size data from the remote host. And when there is data in the buffer, the program reads the data from the buffer and returns.

The optimization of the output function follows a similar principle, reducing the number of I/O and increasing the amount of data for a single IO. For example, the implementation of the function "printf" can first call "sprinf" to store data in contiguous memory and then output it to the remote host.

As seen in Table 1, after optimization, the running time is reduced to 9 s. The file operation is no longer the bottleneck as the main frequency is only 20 MHz in FPGA. The running speed after optimization can meet users' debugging need.

5 Conclusion

In this article, we proposed a complete and simple semihosting debugging approach based on the SWIFT DSP. The solution does not rely on too much hardware, only requires the processor to support self-trapping instructions, and can use the most versatile USB to JTAG serial port chip as a debug probe, reducing the cost of developing and using. On the software side, we used libraries and proxy to read the relevant parameters of I/O functions and write back the results, which is convenient for modification and debugging. Libraries and applications can be I/O optimized to get close to the speed of traditional semihosting methods.

We used FPGA to build a prototype system, FT2232HL board to connect FPGA and PC host. After code optimization, the running speed of program met most user's need in debugging. Given the speed of the DSP clock and JTAG clock, it could be called a satisfactory performance.

The approach is based on an open-source debugger, which greatly reduces the development workload of the semihosting function and can quickly provide the available semihosting function to various processors. Providing more powerful functions for application debugging can accelerate the speed of application development and adaptation, and provide great help for a new DSP chip to seize the market.

Acknowledgment. The authors thank the editors and the anonymous reviewers for their invaluable comments to help to improve the quality of this paper. This work was supported by the Key-Area Research and Development Program of Guangdong Province under Grant 2018B010115002, National Natural Science Foundation of China under Grants 61831018 and U21A20452, the Outstanding youth project of Natural Science Foundation of Jiangxi Province 20212ACB212001, and the S&T plan projects of Jiangxi Province Education Department GJJ201003.

References

1. Kuschnero, V.M., Schaedler, M., Bluemm, C., et al.: Advances in deep learning for digital signal processing in coherent optical modems. In: Optical Fiber Communication Conference (2020)
2. Austin, T., Larson, E., et al.: SimpleScalar: an infrastructure for computer system modeling. Computer **35**, 59–67 (2002)
3. Nadal, J., Baghdadi, A.: Parallel and flexible 5G LDPC decoder architecture targeting FPGA. IEEE Trans. Very Large Scale Integr. (VLSI) Syst. **29**(6), 1141–1151 (2021). https://doi.org/10.1109/TVLSI.2021.3072866
4. Weng, O., Khodamoradi, A., Kastner, R.: Hardware-efficient residual networks for FPGAs (2021)
5. Berger, A.S.: An overview of the tools for embedded design and debug (2020)
6. Berger, A.S.: Best practices for debugging embedded software (2020)

7. Hossain, F., Iry, J., Kulkarni, N., et al.: Method and system for remote debug protocol proxying for production debugging; selective session and user routing for debugging in multi-tenant cloud computing infrastructure. US (2014)
8. Prado, B., Dantas, D., Bispo, K., et al.: A virtual prototype semihosting approach for early simulation of cyber-physical systems. In: 2018 IEEE Symposium on Computers and Communications (ISCC). IEEE (2018)
9. Chance, G., Ghobrial, A., Mcareavey, K., et al.: On determinism of game engines used for simulation-based autonomous vehicle verification (2021)
10. Lee, H., Hyunggoy, Oh., Kang, S.: On-chip error detection reusing built-in self-repair for silicon debug. IEEE Access 9, 56443–56456 (2021). https://doi.org/10.1109/ACCESS.2021.3071517
11. Mitra, S., Barrett, C., Lin, D., et al.: Post-silicon validation and debug using symbolic quick error detection (2018)
12. Cao, Y., Hao, Z., Palombo, H., et al.: A post-silicon trace analysis approach for system-on-chip protocol debug. In: 2017 IEEE 35th International Conference on Computer Design (ICCD). IEEE (2017)
13. Merten, M., Huhn, S., Drechsler, R.: A codeword-based compactor for on-chip generated debug data using two-stage artificial neural networks. In: 2021 IEEE International Symposium on Defect and Fault Tolerance in VLSI and Nanotechnology Systems (DFT), pp. 1–6. IEEE (2021)
14. Petrović, P.B.: A new electronically controlled floating/grounded meminductor emulator based on single MO-VDTA. Analog Integr. Circuits Signal Process. 110, 185–195 (2021)
15. Minati, L., Mancinelli, M., Frasca, M., et al.: An analog electronic emulator of non-linear dynamics in optical microring resonators. Chaos Solitons Fractals 153, 111410 (2021)
16. Kumar, V., Dubey, S.K., Islam, A.: A Current-Mode Memristor Emulator Circuit (2020)
17. Barboni, L.: A passive circuit-emulator for a current-controlled memristor (2020)
18. Zhu, M., Wang, C., Deng, Q., et al.: Locally active memristor with three coexisting pinched hysteresis loops and its emulator circuit. Int. J. Bifurcation Chaos (2020)
19. Berger, A., Barr, M., et al.: On-chip debug. Embed. Syst. Program. (2003)
20. Berger, A.S.: On-chip debugging resources (2020)
21. Backer, J., Hely, D., Karri, R.: Secure design-for-debug for systems-on-chip. In: Test Conference. IEEE (2015)
22. Yiu, J.: Input and output software examples - ScienceDirect. The Definitive Guide to ARM® CORTEX®-M3 and CORTEX®-M4 Processors (Third Edition), pp. 583–604 (2014)
23. Yiu, J.: Getting Started with the ARM RealView Development Suite. Elsevier Inc. (2011)
24. Uzan, D., Kahn, R., Weiss, S.: Perceptron based filtering of futile prefetches in embedded VLIW DSPs. J. Syst. Architect. 110(3), 101826 (2020)

Reinforcement Learning Based Preamble Resource Allocation Scheme for Access Control in Machine-to-Machine Communication

Hongyu Liu[1(✉)], Bei Liu[1,2], Hui Gao[3], Xibin Xu[4], and Xin Su[4]

[1] School of Communication and Information Engineering,
Chongqing University of Posts and Telecommunications,
Chongqing, China
S200131182@stu.cqupt.edu.cn

[2] Beijing National Research Center for Information Science and Technology,
Tsinghua University, Beijing, China
liubei@mail.tsinghua.edu.cn

[3] Beijing University of Posts and Telecommunications, Beijing, China
huigao@bupt.edu.cn

[4] Department of Electronic Engineering Tsinghua University, Beijing, China
{xuxb,suxin}@tsinghua.edu.cn

Abstract. With the rapid development of Internet of Things (IoT) technology, the number of large numbers of Machine Type Communication (MTC) devices involved in M2M has increased dramatically. When large scale MTC devices access the base station at the same time in a short period of time, this can cause traffic overload and lead to a sharp drop in the success rate of access of MTC devices. 3GPP has proposed the access class barring (ACB) scheme to defer access requests from certain activated MTC devices to avoid congestion at the base station (BS). In this paper, we propose a dynamic ACB scheme for grouping MTC devices and a resource allocation scheme for preamble. First, MTC devices are classified into two categories according to their characteristics: delay-sensitive and energy-constrained. The two categories use separate preamble resources, and a temporary ACB factor is calculated for each time slot based on the current preamble resources and the number of devices. The preamble resources are reallocated based on this temporary ACB factor using reinforcement learning methods, and then the ACB factor is dynamically adjusted according to the new preamble resources. Simulation results show that the solution improves the access success rate of M2M devices, reducing the total service time of delay-sensitive devices by 40% compared to the traditional solution, while reducing the access collision rate of energy-constrained devices by 30%.

Keywords: Machine-to-machine communications · Random Access Control · Q-learning

Supported by the National Key R&D Program of China under Grant 2020YFB1806702.

1   Introduction

The widespread adoption of the IoT [1] in various fields such as industry, agriculture, healthcare and transportation has stimulated an explosive growth in the number of IoT devices. With the growth of the IoT devices, M2M communication is expected to become one of the main drivers of cellular networks [2,3] M2M communication, also known as MTC, refers to communication between machine devices without human intervention. Many devices can be triggered almost simultaneously and attempt to access a base station via a random access channel (RACH), which can cause a surge in M2M traffic. M2M communication, as the key part of IoT development, is essential for efficient data transfer from machines and devices to the network for various IoT applications such as smart metering, healthcare, smart appliances, surveillance, security and logistics tracking. Studies from 3GPP and the literature have shown that the physical random access channel (PRACH) of a cell can be severely overloaded when tens of thousands of MTDs wake up and attempt to access the cell in a highly synchronised manner. However, traditional access control methods may not be able to handle overload in the radio access network (RAN) and core network (CN), which can lead to severe congestion and delays. The problem becomes worse if a faulty device keeps trying to access the network, resulting in a large proportion of machine communication devices not being able to gain access before the maximum number of allowed attempts is exceeded. The ACB scheme is easy to implement and is very effective for congestion control, therefore it is defined as a viable scheme by the Radio Resource Control specification. In the first step of the RACH process, the base station broadcasts an ACB factor p to all UEs before the start of each time slot via system messages, with p taking values from 0 to 1. In the same time slot, each UE generates a random number between 0 and 1 and compares it with the value of p before attempting to access the PRACH channel. If the random number is less than the broadcast ACB factor p, the UE device will continue to access the base station. Otherwise, the UE device is denied access at this time slot and the process is repeated at the next time slot or after being blocked for a certain amount of time. In this way, the ACB reduces the number of access requests per time slot.

The size of the ACB factor is fixed in traditional ACB schemes, which can significantly improve access success rates in large-scale burst access scenarios, but at the cost of a dramatic increase in access latency. We consider a large-scale IoT scenario such as the smart city in Fig. 1, where devices are divided into delay-sensitive devices and energy-constrained devices. For example, self-driving cars need to communicate with nearby vehicles with low latency, while fixed devices in the surrounding environment, such as surveillance cameras, have low data rates and infrequent transmissions. The size of the signalling packets used in the wireless network to synchronise sensor devices to the base station or to resolve contention between sensor devices can be much larger than the size of the user data packets used for sensor transmissions. Therefore, for the sensor class of devices, where energy constraints are a key feature, access collisions should be avoided as much as possible. When these two types of devices coexist, the traditional ACB scheme with a fixed ACB factor is clearly not suitable for this scenario, and the traditional ACB scheme does not take good care of the access characteristics of both types of devices.

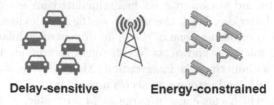

Delay-sensitive   **Energy-constrained**

Fig. 1. A massive IoT network

To solve the above problems, this paper proposes an access control strategy and a dynamic preamble grouping scheme based on reinforcement learning that is applicable to the coexistence scenario of two types of devices. The main contributions of this paper are summarized as follows.

1. We divide MTCD into two groups according to realistic scenarios, while dynamically assigning the preamble resources to the two types of devices, which complete the random access process through the ACB mechanism.
2. We propose a method for preamble resource allocation through reinforcement learning. A temporary ACB factor is calculated in each time slot based on the current resources, and the preamble resources are reallocated based on this temporary ACB factor to enable both types of devices to use the preamble resources efficiently.
3. Based on the derived values of ACB factors for delay-sensitive devices in related work, the ACB factors for energy-constrained devices are derived and the optimal ACB factors are calculated based on the number of activated devices and the size of the leading resources.
4. Simulation results show that the scheme results in lower collision rates for energy-constrained devices, reduced congestion conflicts, and significantly lower total service times for delay-sensitive devices.

The rest of this paper is organized as follows Sect. 2 provides an initial introduction to the work related to random access control and the random access process. In Sect. 3, we detail the design of our proposed scheme. In Sect. 4, the performance of our proposed scheme is evaluated by comparing it with a typical conventional scheme. Section 5 contains concluding remarks.

2   Related Work

To improve the latency performance of traditional ACB schemes while maintaining their access success rate, various works have proposed dynamic adjustment of the ACB factor over time. The article [4] uses the QOE of device delay mapping as the objective function for reinforcement learning. Due to the different device characteristics, different delay mapping functions can better differentiate devices and achieve priority access to low latency devices. The article [5] proposes a dual-Q learning-based ACB mechanism to determine the ACB parameters, which is able to dynamically adapt to different traffic conditions when M2M and H2H communications coexist, with three different configurations allowing a trade-off between the probability of successful access and the average access latency. The article [6] proposes a dynamic ACB approach where the value of the ACB factor changes adaptively within each time slot depending on the service load. In order to find the optimal ACB factor the article proposes a method to estimate the number of devices based on the information obtained by the base station. The article [7] proposes the use of a reinforcement learning method called dueling deep Q networks to dynamically adjust the ban factor and average ban time. Computer simulations show that for a given access delay and energy consumption tolerance, our design can achieve significantly higher energy satisfaction while maintaining comparable delay satisfaction compared to schemes that focus only on restriction factor adjustment. The article [8] presents a new deep reinforcement learning algorithm that is first used to dynamically adjust the ACB factor in a uniform priority network. The algorithm is then further enhanced to adapt to different MTCDs with different quality of service (Qos) requirements. article [9] combines ACB and extended access limits (EAB) to increase access latency while reducing the conflict probability, resulting in higher energy efficiency. With respect to the allocation of leading resources, the article [10] determines the optimal value of the ACB factor to reduce traffic overload in the ideal case where the eNodeB knows the number of backlogged MTC devices. To make better use of the random access resources shared between human users and MTC devices in LTE networks, methods are proposed to dynamically allocate the preamble resources for MTC devices. Most dynamic ACB solutions focus only on tuning the ACB factor, and the derivation of the ACB factor is based on reducing the latency as well as the total service time of the system, with no consideration given to energy-constrained devices.

3   System Model

3.1   Random Access Process

In current cellular networks, UEs need to perform random access processes to achieve uplink synchronisation with the base station and to obtain radio channel access resources. The two types of random access are competition-based and non-competition-based. This paper focuses on the contention-based random access process. This process consists of four steps.

1. Preamble (MSG1): In the first step, all UEs that pass the ACB test randomly select a preamble and transmit it on the physical random access channel.
2. RAR (MSG2): In the second step, the base station confirms that all the preamble have been successfully received using the Random Access Request Response (RAR), which contains the identification of the detected preamble and the uplink permission for the Step 3 message MSG3.

3. Connection request (MSG3): In step 3, the UE sends the MSG3 of its ID in the PUSCH after receiving its corresponding RAR within the random access response window size time. When two UEs have selected the same preamble in step 1, both UEs will be granted the same block of time-frequency resources for uplink transmission of MSG3, when a conflict occurs.
4. Contention resolution (MSG4): In step 4, the base station broadcasts the contention solution containing the IDs of the UEs that have successfully decoded MSG3 without any response to the conflicting MSG3s and declares access failure in the contention solution for those UEs that have selected the conflicting preamble.

3.2   System Traffic Model

We assume that 54 preamble are available and that there are a total of N MTC devices in a cell. As these devices are not synchronised, they will not be active at the same time, but will be active for a short T_A period. We refer to this time as the activation time. Each device is activated with probability $f(t)$ over a time horizon of length T_A. The popular choice for modelling service volume bursts proposed in 3GPP is the beta distribution with the following expression for $f(t), B(\alpha, \beta)$ as a function of β, where $\alpha = 3, \beta = 4$.

$$f(t) = \frac{t^{\alpha-1}(T_A - t)^{\beta-1}}{T_A^{\alpha+\beta-1} B(\alpha, \beta)}, 0 \leq t \leq T_A \tag{1}$$

In this system model, time is divided into consecutive time slots, each represented by an integer $i = 1, 2 \cdots \cdots$. Thus T_A can be divided into I_A time slots, with I_A denoting the number of $RACH$ in the T_A time range, where the duration of the ith time slot is from the t_{i-1} moment to t_i. It is assumed that the activation of the MTC device is completed at the beginning of the time slot. Denote the number of newly activated devices in time slot i by λ_i, where $i = 1, 2 \cdots \cdots I_A$. The λ_i depends specifically on the distribution of the activated traffic $f(t)$ and the total number of devices N, with the expression

$$\lambda_i = N \int_{t_{i-1}}^{t_i} f(t)dt, i = 1, 2 \cdots \cdots I_A \tag{2}$$

4   Proposed Preamble Allocation and Access Control Scheme

The number of MTC devices that need to be accessed in each time slot plays a crucial role in the design of the ACB scheme. The number of MTC devices that need to be accessed in each time slot is unknown to both base stations and terminals because of the inconsistent activation times of MTC devices. A number of methods have been proposed by a large number of research institutions to estimate the number of devices in a time slot, and the estimated number of devices in [4] is very close to the actual number of devices. In this paper, the number of MTC devices to be accessed in each time slot is known by default and the ACB scheme for two types of devices is proposed.

4.1 Dynamic Adjustment of ACB Factor

In the scenario we set up, assuming $M = 54$ preamble are available and a total of N MTC devices are active at time T_A, we classify these N devices into two categories: delay-sensitive (DSD) and energy-constrained (ECD). Our ACB scheme is different for different types of devices, and the number of these two types of devices is N_D and N_E. So we have

$$N_D + N_E = N \tag{3}$$

Correspondingly, the number of preamble owned by the two types of devices are M_D and M_E respectively.

$$M_D + M_E = M \tag{4}$$

ACB Factor for Delay-Sensitive Devices. Delay-sensitive devices need to be connected to the network as soon as possible, so the total service time needs to be reduced. The total service time is defined as the number of time slots consumed between the activation of the device and the successful transmission of the preamble. Given the number of access devices $N_i = n$ at each time slot, the ideal ACB factor for the minimum total service time according to article [10] is

$$p_D = min(1, \frac{M_D}{n_D}) \tag{5}$$

ACB Factor for Energy-Constrained Devices. What needs to be considered for this class of devices is the energy consumed during the whole random access process because of the energy constraint. When multiple devices select the same preamble, the base station detects a preamble collision, and the device that selected the preamble fails this access and needs to initiate random access again after waiting for an avoidance interval. When the probability of preamble collision is high, the device needs to initiate random access several times, which will consume a lot of energy because of the uplink transmission. Therefore, for energy-constrained devices, our solution focuses on reducing their collision probability.

In time slot i, it is assumed that n MTC devices randomly select one of the preamble sequences with equal probability. The total number of preamble is M and the probability of selecting preamble m is $1/M$. Let $P_m = 0, P_m = 1, P_m > 1$ denote the three cases of unselected preamble, successful transmission and collision occurring instead.

The probability that the preamble m is not selected is

$$P(P_m = 0) = (1 - \frac{1}{M})^n \tag{6}$$

The probability of successful transmission of the preamble m is

$$P(P_m = 1) = C_n^1 \times \frac{1}{M} \times (1 - \frac{1}{M})^{n-1} \tag{7}$$

The probability of a collision of the preamble m is

$$P(P_m > 1) = 1 - P(P_m = 0) - P(P_m = 1) = 1 - (1 - \frac{1}{M})^n - \frac{n}{M} \times (1 - \frac{1}{M})^{n-1} \quad (8)$$

Let C_i be the number of conflicting preamble in time slot i and p be the ACB factor for that time slot. Since the collision and non-collision events for each preamble are independent and identically distributed binomial distributions, the expectation of the number of conflicting preamble can be found as

$$E(C_i) = \sum_{m=1}^{M} P(P_m > 1) = M \times \left[1 - (1 - \frac{1}{M})^{np} - \frac{np}{M} \times (1 - \frac{1}{M})^{np-1} \right] \quad (9)$$

$$\approx M - (M + np)e^{-\frac{np}{M}}$$

Similarly let S_i be the number of preamble successfully transmitted in time slot i as

$$E(S_i) = \sum_{m=1}^{M} P(P_m = 1) = np \times (1 - \frac{1}{M})^{np-1} \approx np \times e^{-\frac{np}{M}} \quad (10)$$

The ACB factor for delay-sensitive devices is derived by maximising the access success preamble per time slot, and the number of collisions needs to be considered for energy-constrained devices, so calculating the ACB factor for energy-efficient devices requires a combination of the above two equations to consider.

$$E(X_i) = E(S_i) - E(C_i) = (M + 2np) \cdot e^{-\frac{np}{M}} - M \quad (11)$$

Derive for p

$$\frac{d}{dp}E(X_i) = (n - \frac{2n^2 p}{M}) \cdot e^{-\frac{np}{M}} \quad (12)$$

Letting the equation be 0, we obtain $p = \frac{M}{2n}$. So the ACB factor for the energy-constrained device is set to $\frac{M}{2n}$.

4.2   Reinforcement Learning Based Preamble Resource Allocation

The number of preamble per time slot is finite, and the ultimate goal of both device types is to successfully access the network; both access strategies cater for more devices to access while ensuring their access characteristics. We consider the use of reinforcement learning to solve the problem of preamble allocation, as it enables the use of computer simulations to generate reasonable solutions without the need to build complex theoretical models that allow devices to use the least amount of leading resources while maintaining the minimum service time. the ACB factor maximises the use of the limited number of preamble for access control to minimise the total service time for the delay-sensitive class of devices and the energy-constrained devices access characteristics. Therefore, the allocation of preamble is an efficient use of resources, reducing the number of preamble when the number of device activations is low and increasing the number of preamble when the number of device activations is high, focusing on the access of latency-sensitive devices in the process.

Let S denote a finite set of possible environment states and let A denote a finite set of admissible actions to be taken. At RA slot t, BS perceives the current state $s_t = s \in S$ of the environment and take an action $a_t = a \in A$ based on both the perceived state and its past experience. The action a_t changes the environment state from s_t to $s_{t+1} = s' \in S$. When that happens, the system receives the reward r_t. The goal of the system is to find an optimal strategy The goal of the system is to find an optimal strategy.

$$\pi^*(s) = \underset{a \in A}{\mathrm{argmax}}(Q^*(s, a)) \tag{13}$$

$Q^*(s, a)$ is the optimal Q value, which is defined as

$$Q_t(s, a) = Q_t(s, a) + \alpha(r_t(s, a) + \gamma_t \max_{a_{t+1} \in A} Q_t(s_{t+1}, a_{t+1}) - Q_t(s, a)) \tag{14}$$

$\alpha(0 \leq \alpha \leq 1)$ is the learning rate and $\gamma(0 \leq \gamma \leq 1)$ is the discount rate. When the learning rate is 0, the Q value is never updated. When the learning rate is set to higher, learning will be rapid and the discount factor will be weighted more heavily on the current reward than the reward.

In this paper, we build a QL algorithm to allocate preamble resource to increase the number of successful accesses to delay sensitive devices in each time slot. The state space consists of the ACB factor of the current time slot. The size of the ACB factor is related to the number of preamble and the number of devices to be accessed. The ACB factor calculated from the state of the current pool of preamble and the number of devices in the current time slot is used as the state, and the action is selected to update the pool of preamble, and the recalculated ACB factor is the ACB factor of the current time slot. The size of the ACB factor as a state is discrete into intervals $(0, 0.01), (0.01, 0.1), (0.1, 0.3), (0.3, 0.5), (0.5, 0.7), (0.7, 1)$, when P is large, indicating that the number of devices is small or the number of preamble is assigned high at this time, so that the number of preamble can be reduced to another class of devices. The action space is represented by A. The number of preamble for delay-sensitive device is incremented or decremented to adjust the allocation of preamble resources for each time slot, and these actions are decremented or incremented by $\delta_i(\delta_i \in \{-10, -7, -5, -3, -1, 0, +1, +3, 5, +7, +10\})$ or kept at their current values. To balance the use of learning and exploration, the QL algorithm uses the $\epsilon - greey$ method. When an action needs to be selected, the BS primarily selects the action a with the largest $Q(s, a)$ in state s. The BS randomly selects the action a with probability ϵ from the allowed actions in state s.

The reward function focuses on the number of successful accesses to delay-sensitive devices, reducing the restriction on delay-sensitive devices by assigning them more leading resources in the presence of network congestion, and the relative energy-limited because of the reduction in leading resources, the ACB will be more restrictive. The number of successful delay-sensitive devices and the number of successful energy-constrained devices are weighted and summed, and then divided by the total number of preamble M-normalised

$$r_t(s,a) = \frac{\omega N_L^t + (1 - \omega)N_E^t}{M} \tag{15}$$

N_L^t is the number of delay-sensitive devices successfully accessed, N_E^t is the number of energy-constrained devices successfully accessed, and ω is the smoothing factor.

Algorithm 1: RL-based preamble resource allocation algorithm

Input: The number of current time slot devices and the number of preamble are used to obtain a temporary ACB factor according to (5)(12)

Output: The number of increments and decrements in the preamble of delay-sensitive devices

1 Initialise the number of preamble available to the device;
2 **for** *episode = 0, 1, 2, ... * **do**
3   **while** *Number of devices connected n < Total number of devices N* **do**
4   Calculation of a temporary ACB factor based on the number of devices that currently need to be accessed and the number of preamble;
5   Select an action $a^n = i$, $i \in A$ based on the greedy policy, where i represents the number of increments and decrements in the preamble;
6   Calculate the ACB factor for this time slot according to (5)(12);
7       $n+ =$ Number of successfully accessed devices;
8   **end**
9 **end**

---

5   Performance Evaluation

In this section, we validate the effectiveness of the proposed scheme in terms of both the collision rate of energy-constrained devices and the total service time of both types of devices.

5.1   Comparison of Collision Rates for ECD

The collision rate refers to the ratio of the number of devices with failed access at time slot t to the number of devices initiating access. Figure 2 shows the ACB

Table 1. RACH Configuration

Parameter	Setting
Preamble number M	54
Total number of M2M devices N	30000
DSD number	10000
ECD number	20000
Backoff indicator	20 ms

factor for DSDs is set with the goal of the shortest total service time and lowest latency, and does not take into account the collision rate. When an ECD uses a dedicated ACB factor, the collision rate is reduced compared to sharing the same ACB factor with a low-latency device. The reduced collision rate means that the ECD initiates accesses less often, saving the energy required to initiate accesses.

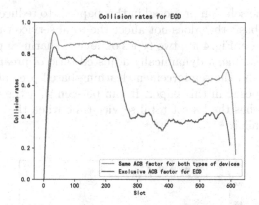

Fig. 2. Collision rate per time slot for ECD

5.2 The Impact of Preamble Resource Allocation on the Probability of Access Success

When DSD and ECD coexist, the percentage of preamble allocated affects access performance. In scenarios where the proportion of DSDs is $10\%, 20\%$ and 30% respectively, Fig. 3 shows that when the proportion of DSDs is 10%, the number of successfully accessed devices first increases and then decreases as the number of preamble allocated to DSDs increases. The analysis leads to the conclusion that the optimal allocation of the preamble is different for different proportions of DSDs. In a practical scenario, after estimating the actual number of DSDs and ECDs, the optimal allocation of preamble can be chosen to obtain the optimal probability of successful access.

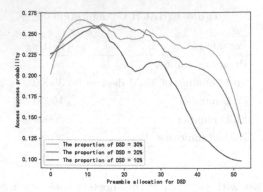

Fig. 3. Different preamble allocation affects the access success probability

5.3   The Impact of the Number of Preamble Resources on the Total Service Time

The objective of the solution proposed in this paper is to reduce the total service time of DSD on a basis that does not affect the total service time of all devices. The schemes shown in Fig. 4 are two types of devices sharing a pool of preamble, a fixed ratio of preamble, a dynamically adjusted ratio of preamble as proposed in the paper [11], and the reinforcement learning-based preamble resource allocation scheme proposed in this paper. It can be seen that the proposed scheme DSD in this paper has the lowest total service time when the total service time of all devices is similar.

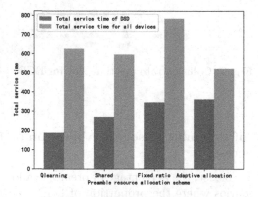

Fig. 4. The impact of the preamble resource allocation scheme on total service time

6   Conclusion

In this paper, we focus on the coexistence of large-scale DSD and ECD in cellular communication systems, and propose an access control strategy and a dynamic preamble grouping scheme based on reinforcement learning for the coexistence of the two types of devices, taking full account of the QoS requirements of DSDs, and dividing the preamble into two groups. In this paper, we use the current ACB factor for each time slot to allocate the preamble resources by reinforcement learning, and the ACB factor is dynamically updated according to the number of preamble and the number of devices. The paper verifies the feasibility and effectiveness of the scheme using Python simulations. The collision rate of energy-limited devices is reduced by 30%, while dynamically adjusting the number of preamble has a significant effect on reducing the total service time of DSD devices by 40% compared to the conventional scheme.

References

1. Nguyen, D.C., Ding, M., Pathirana, P.N., Seneviratne, A., Li, J., Niyato, D., Dobre, O., Poor, H.V.: 6g internet of things: A comprehensive survey. IEEE Internet Things J. **9**(1), 359–383 (2022). https://doi.org/10.1109/JIOT.2021.3103320
2. Wu, H., Zhu, C., La, R.J., Liu, X., Zhang, Y.: Fasa: Accelerated s-aloha using access history for event-driven m2m communications. IEEE/ACM Trans. Netw. **21**(6), 1904–1917 (2013). https://doi.org/10.1109/TNET.2013.2241076
3. Laya, A., Alonso, L., Alonso-Zarate, J.: Is the random access channel of lte and lte-a suitable for m2m communications? a survey of alternatives. IEEE Commun. Surv. Tutor. **16**(1), 4–16 (2014). https://doi.org/10.1109/SURV.2013.111313.00244
4. Zhang, D., Liu, J., Zhou, W.: Acb scheme based on reinforcement learning in m2m communication. In: GLOBECOM 2020–2020 IEEE Global Communications Conference, pp. 1–6 (2020). https://doi.org/10.1109/GLOBECOM42002.2020.9322144
5. Pacheco-Paramo, D., Tello-Oquendo, L.: Adjustable access control mechanism in cellular mtc networks: A double q-learning approach. In: 2019 IEEE Fourth Ecuador Technical Chapters Meeting (ETCM), pp. 1–6 (2019). https://doi.org/10.1109/ETCM48019.2019.9014871
6. Haider Shah, S.W., Riaz, A.T., Iqbal, K.: Congestion control through dynamic access class barring for bursty mtc traffic in future cellular networks. In: 2018 International Conference on Frontiers of Information Technology (FIT), pp. 176 181 (2018). https://doi.org/10.1109/FIT.2018.00038
7. Bui, A.T.H., Pham, A.T.: Deep reinforcement learning-based access class barring for energy-efficient mmtc random access in lte networks. IEEE Access **8**, 227657–227666 (2020). https://doi.org/10.1109/ACCESS.2020.3045811
8. Chen, Z., Smith, D.B.: Heterogeneous machine-type communications in cellular networks: Random access optimization by deep reinforcement learning. In: 2018 IEEE International Conference on Communications (ICC), pp. 1–6 (2018). https://doi.org/10.1109/ICC.2018.8422775
9. Toor, W.T., Jin, H.: Combined access barring for energy and delay constrained machine type communications. In: 2018 International Conference on Information and Communication Technology Convergence (ICTC), pp. 130–132 (2018). https://doi.org/10.1109/ICTC.2018.8539640

10. Duan, S., Shah-Mansouri, V., Wang, Z., Wong, V.W.S.: D-acb: Adaptive congestion control algorithm for bursty m2m traffic in lte networks. IEEE Trans. Veh. Technol. **65**(12), 9847–9861 (2016). https://doi.org/10.1109/TVT.2016.2527601
11. Zhao, X., Wang, C., Wang, W.: Dynamic preamble grouping and access control scheme in machine-to-machine communication. In: 2019 11th International Conference on Wireless Communications and Signal Processing (WCSP), pp. 1–6 (2019). https://doi.org/10.1109/WCSP.2019.8928049

Adaptive Orthogonal Basis Scheme for OTFS

Yinhua Jia[1](✉)(iD), Sen Wang[2], Jing Jin[2], and Hang Long[1]

[1] Wireless Signal Processing and Network Lab Key Laboratory of Universal Wireless Communications, Ministry of Education Beijing University of Posts and Telecommunications, Beijing 100876, China
jiayinhua@163.com

[2] China Mobile Research Institute, Beijing, China

Abstract. Orthogonal time frequency space (OTFS) modulation can provide significant error performance than orthogonal frequency division multiplexing (OFDM) modulation in the high-speed scenario. However, the fractional Doppler effects cause Doppler diffusion. In this paper, we analyze the Doppler diffusion from both the formula and geometric levels. In order to alleviate Doppler diffusion, we propose an adaptive orthogonal basis scheme by using the Doppler shifts feedback of the receiver. Our scheme alter the matrix of the inverse symplectic finite Fourier transform (ISFFT) by the feedback. This scheme makes it possible to estimate the channel more accurately. In the simulation results, we show that the bit error rate (BER) and block error rate (BLER) performance of our proposed scheme is not affected compared with OTFS. In addition, our scheme can work even if the Doppler domain dimension is limited and the Doppler shifts feedback of the receiver is inaccurate.

Keywords: OTFS · delay-Doppler channel · fractional Doppler effect

1 Introduction

The sixth-generation (6G) era is expected to ultra-reliable wireless communication in the high-speed scenario such as high-speed railway, vehicle to everything (V2X) and low-earth-orbit satellites (LEOS) communications [3,14,15]. While the orthogonal frequency division multiplexing (OFDM) modulation deployed in the fifth-generation (5G) mobile systems can achieve high spectral efficiency, it is not robust to time-varying channels with Doppler shifts [1,2,4,5,16]. In order to realize robust transmission, a new two-dimensional (2D) modulation scheme as orthogonal time-frequency space (OTFS) was proposed [1].

In OTFS, the information symbols are multiplexed in the delay-Doppler domain rather than the time-frequency domain as the OFDM [5]. The delay-Doppler domain symbols are transformed into the time-frequency domain via the inverse symplectic finite Fourier transform (ISFFT). Relying on this 2D orthogonal transform, the OTFS modulation represents the time-varying multipath channel into the delay-Doppler domain, making all transmitted symbols

F. Gao et al. (Eds.): ChinaCom 2022, LNICST 500, pp. 57–68, 2023.
https://doi.org/10.1007/978-3-031-34790-0_5

experience the quasi-stationary channel [1–5]. Furthermore, the delay-Doppler domain channel presents sparse characters since the delay and the Doppler shift of the channel are limited for a wide-band system [6–9]. In addition, the channel representation demonstrates attractive properties such as separability, compactness, and stability which have the potential to be exploited for OTFS system design [3, 14, 15].

The sparse character of the channel provides the possibility to estimate the delay and Doppler shift [2]. However, interference cancellation is still necessary. In the OTFS system, Raviteja *et al.* simplify the OTFS input-output relation characterizing the interference [7]. In the case of an ideal waveform, there is no inter-carrier interference (ICI) and inter-symbol interference (ISI) occurs. while inter-Doppler interference (IDI) is still present due to unavoidable fractional Doppler effects.

In this paper, we analyze the unavoidable fractional Doppler effects in the case of an ideal waveform. Further, we show the Doppler diffusion caused by fractional Doppler effects and analyze the diffusion both on the formula and geometric level. Specially, we propose an adaptive orthogonal basis scheme to alleviate this diffusion. Finally, our results show that with coding and ideal channel estimation, the bit error rate (BER) and block error rate (BLER) performances of adaptive orthogonal basis are not affected compared with OTFS. Our scheme can work even when the Doppler domain dimension is limited and the Doppler shifts feedback from the receiver is inaccurate.

The rest of the paper is organized as follows. Section 2 reviews the diagram of the OTFS system. Next, we analyze the fractional Doppler effects in Sect. 3 and propose an adaptive orthogonal basis scheme in Sect. 4. Numerical results are presented in Sect. 5 to verify the performance of our proposed scheme and our conclusions are finally shown in Sect. 6.

Notations: Boldface capital letters stand for matrices and lower-case letters stand for column vectors. The transpose, conjugate, conjugate transpose, and inverse of a matrix are denoted by $(\cdot)^T$, $(\cdot)^*$, $(\cdot)^H$, $(\cdot)^{-1}$, respectively. $\|\mathbf{s}\|$ is the ℓ_2-norm of the vector $\mathbf{s}$. $\delta(\cdot)$ denotes the Dirac delta function. $[\cdot]_N$ is the modulo operator of divider N. $\mathbf{0}$, $\mathbf{I}_L$ and $\mathbf{F}_L$ represent zero matrix, identity matrix with the order L and L−order normalized discrete Fourier transform (DFT) matrix, respectively. The operator $\text{diag}\{\mathbf{x}\}$ creates a diagonal matrix with the elements of vector $\mathbf{x}$.

2   System Model

We consider an OTFS system with M subcarriers with the sub-carrier bandwidth of Δf and N symbols with the length of T. The total bandwidth and total duration of OTFS system are $B = M\Delta f$ and $T_f = NT$. Moreover, the OTFS system is critically sampled $T\Delta f = 1$.

In this section, we introduce the diagram of the OTFS system. Figure 1 shows the transceiver diagram of the OTFS system [6]. The modulator first maps the delay-Doppler information symbols $x[k, l]$ to the time-frequency symbols $X[n, m]$ by using the ISFFT. Next, the Heisenberg transform is applied

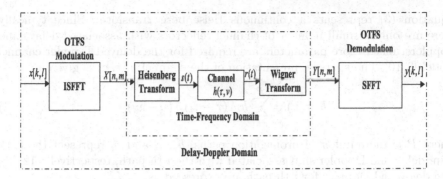

Fig. 1. The transceiver of the OTFS.

to $X[n, m]$ to generate the time domain signal $s(t)$ for transmission over the channel. At the receiver, the received time-domain signal is mapped to the time-frequency domain through the Wigner transform (the inverse of the Heisenberg Transform), and then to the delay-Doppler domain using SFFT for symbol demodulation.

In the following subsection, we will give the matrix expression of the above process from the transmitter, channel and receiver.

2.1 Transmitter

First, using the ISFFT to map the delay-Doppler information symbols to the time-frequency domain. It can be expressed as

$$\mathbf{X} = \mathbf{F}_M \mathbf{X_{DD}} \mathbf{F}_N^H \tag{1}$$

where $\mathbf{X_{DD}} \in \mathbb{C}^{M \times N}$ represents the matrix form of the delay-Doppler domain symbols $x[k, l]$ and $\mathbf{X} \in \mathbb{C}^{M \times N}$ is the time-frequency domain symbol matrix.

Next, the transmitted symbols are mapped into the time domain by ultilizing the Heisenberg transform, which can be expressed as

$$\mathbf{S} = \mathbf{F}_M^H \mathbf{X} = \mathbf{X_{DD}} \mathbf{F}_N^H \tag{2}$$

where $\mathbf{S} \in \mathbb{C}^{M \times N}$ is the time domain symbol matrix.

2.2 Channel

The signal $s(t)$ is transmitted over a time-varying channel with channel response $h(\tau, v)$, which characterizes the channel to an impulse with delay τ and Doppler v [1]. The received signal is given by

$$r(t) = \iint h(\tau, v) s(t - \tau) e^{j2\pi v(t - \tau)} \tag{3}$$

Equation (3) represents a continuous Heisenberg transform. Since typically there are only a small number of channel reflectors with associated delays and Dopplers, much more parameters are required for the delayed Doppler channel model [8,10]. The sparse representation of the channel $h(\tau, v)$ is given as

$$h(\tau, v) = \sum_{i=1}^{P} h_i \delta(\tau - \tau_i) \delta(v - v_i) \tag{4}$$

where P is the number of propagation paths, h_i, τ_i and v_i represent the path gain, delay and Doppler shift associated with the i-th path, respectively [12,13]. The delay and Doppler for i-th path are expressed as

$$\tau_i = \frac{l_{\tau_i}}{M\Delta f}, v_i = \frac{k_{v_i} + \kappa_{v_i}}{NT} \tag{5}$$

where l_{τ_i}, k_{τ_i} are integers and real $-1/2 < \kappa_{v_i} \leq 1/2$. l_{τ_i}, k_{τ_i} represent the delay tap and Doppler tap corresponding to the delay τ_i and Doppler frequency v_i, respectively. And κ_{v_i} represent the fractional Doppler shift from the nearest Doppler tap k_{τ_i} [12,13].

To obtain discrete time domain representation, $s(t)$ and $r(t)$ are sampled at the interval of T/M [18], expressed by vector $\mathbf{s}$ and $\mathbf{r}$. In addition, the relation of $\mathbf{s}$ and $\mathbf{S}$ shown as

$$\mathbf{s} = vec(\mathbf{S}) \tag{6}$$

2.3 Receiver

After removal of CP at the receiver, received signal can be written as [18]

$$\mathbf{r} = \mathbf{Hs} + \mathbf{n} \tag{7}$$

where $\mathbf{n}$ is white Gaussion noise vector with elemental variance $\sigma_{\mathbf{n}}^2$ and $\mathbf{H}$ is the equivalent time domain channel matrix and can be represented by (4)

$$\mathbf{H} = \sum_{i=1}^{P} h_i \mathbf{\Pi}^{l_{\tau_i}} \mathbf{\Delta}^{k_{v_i} + \kappa_{v_i}} \tag{8}$$

where $\mathbf{\Pi}$ is a forward cyclic shift permutation matrix,

$$\mathbf{\Pi} = [e_2, e_3, \ldots, e_{MN}, e_1] \tag{9}$$

where e_i is the i-th column of the identity matrix $\mathbf{I}_{MN}$. $\mathbf{\Delta}$ is a diagonal matrix expressed as

$$\mathbf{\Delta} = \text{diag}\{1, e^{\frac{j2\pi}{MN}}, \ldots, e^{\frac{j2\pi(MN-1)}{MN}}\} \tag{10}$$

We reshape $\mathbf{r}$ to received time domain symbol matrix $\mathbf{R} \in \mathbb{C}^{M \times N}$ and the matrix $\mathbf{R}$ is transformed to the delay-Doppler domain through the Wigner transform (the inverse of the Heisenberg Transform) and the SFFT respectively. It can be expressed as

$$\mathbf{r} = vec(\mathbf{R}) \tag{11}$$

$$\mathbf{Y} = \mathbf{F}_M \mathbf{R} \tag{12}$$

$$\mathbf{Y_{DD}} = \mathbf{F}_M^H \mathbf{Y} \mathbf{F}_N = \mathbf{R} \mathbf{F}_N \tag{13}$$

where $\mathbf{Y} \in \mathbb{C}^{M \times N}$ and $\mathbf{Y_{DD}} \in \mathbb{C}^{M \times N}$ are the time-frequency domain and the delay-Doppler domain received symbol matrix.

3 Fractional Doppler Effects Analysis

In Sect. 2.2, we introduce the i-th path delay and Doppler τ_i and v_i. Since the resolution of the sampling time $1/M\Delta f$ is sufficient to approximate the path delays to the nearest sampling points in typical wide-band systems [7], we do not need to consider the fractional delay effects. However, we cannot ignore the fractional Doppler effects.

In order to analyze the fractional Doppler effects independently, we analyze the case of ideal waveforms and consider the simple channel estimation scheme [11,12]. In this scheme, we set the delay-Doppler domain symbol matrix $\mathbf{X_{DD}}_{sch}$ as

$$\mathbf{X_{DD}}_{sch}(m, n) = \begin{cases} 1, (m, n) = (0, n_k) \\ 0, others \end{cases} \tag{14}$$

$$m \in [0, 1, \ldots, M-1], n, n_k \in [0, 1, \ldots, N-1]$$

We recall (1) that the ISFFT process is combined by the matrix $\mathbf{F}_M$ and $\mathbf{F}_N^H$. The elements of $\mathbf{F}_N$ can be expressed as

$$\mathbf{F}_N(m, n) = \frac{1}{\sqrt{N}} e^{-j2\pi \frac{mn}{M}} \quad m, n \in [0, 1, \ldots, M-1] \tag{15}$$

According to (2), $\mathbf{X_{DD}}_{sch}$ is transformed to the time domain. Then transmitting through the ideal channel with $\sigma_{\mathbf{n}}^2 = 0$, (7) can be written as

$$\mathbf{r}_{sch} = \mathbf{H}\mathbf{s}_{sch} \tag{16}$$

Finally, we reshape $\mathbf{r}_{sch}$ to $\mathbf{R}_{sch}$ and obtain $\mathbf{Y_{DD}}_{sch}$ by (12) and (13),

$$\mathbf{Y_{DD}}_{sch} = \mathbf{R}_{sch} \mathbf{F}_N \tag{17}$$

where $\mathbf{Y_{DD}}_{sch}$ contains all paths channel response in the delay-Doppler domain. Focus on the i-th path channel response, it can be expressed from (10) and (15)

$$\sum_{k=0}^{N-1} e^{j2\pi(\frac{(k v_i + \kappa v_i)(1+kM)}{MN})} e^{j2\pi(\frac{(n_k - 1 - m)k}{N})} \tag{18}$$

$$= e^{j2\pi \frac{k v_i + \kappa v_i}{MN}} \sum_{k=0}^{N-1} e^{j2\pi \frac{(f_d' + n_k - 1 - m)}{N}} \tag{19}$$

where $m \in [0, N-1]$ and $k_{v_i} + \kappa_{v_i}$ represents the i-th path Doppler. Futhermore, we can derive (19) as

$$\sum_{k=0}^{N-1} e^{j2\pi\frac{(k_{v_i}+\kappa_{v_i}+n_k-1-m)}{N}} = \begin{cases} N, k_{v_i} + \kappa_{v_i} + n_k - 1 - m = 0 \\ 0, k_{v_i} + \kappa_{v_i} + n_k - 1 - m \neq 0 \end{cases} \tag{20}$$

When κ_{v_i} is zero, since n_k is an integer, we have $m = k_{v_i} + \kappa_{v_i} + n_k - 1$ is also an integer. That means only one impulse in the Doppler domain according to (20). But when κ_{v_i} is not zero , m is a decimal. That means the one impulse will diffuse to the whole Doppler domain. We refer to this diffusion as the fractional Doppler effect. In practice, the diffusion is not serious when the fractional Doppler is close to 0, which is shown in the left part of Fig. 2. Conversely, the diffusion is serious when the fractional Doppler is close to 0.5, which is shown in the right part of Fig. 2.

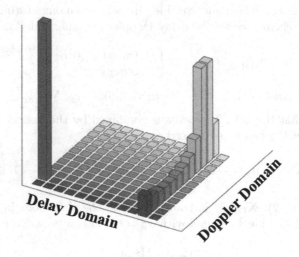

Fig. 2. Schematic diagram: $\kappa_{v_i} = 0$ and $\kappa_{v_i} = 0.5$.

Next, we try to make a geometric analysis of the Doppler diffusion. $\mathbf{F}_N$ can be regarded as a matrix composed of N orthogonal column vectors, which can be considered as channel vectors generated by N consecutive integer Doppler values. The channel estimation process can be looked upon as N vectors to represent the estimated channel vector. When the channel vector and N column vectors are not orthogonal, they cannot be represented by the matrix $\mathbf{F}_N$, so the results are serious diffusion in the Doppler domain.

4 Adaptive Orthogonal Basis Scheme

In Sect. 3, we analyze the fractional Doppler effects and serious diffusion in the Doppler domain. To alleviate this diffusion, we propose an adaptive orthogonal basis scheme based on OTFS. In the previous section, we know the Doppler shifts of the time-varying channel are changing. If receiver feedback the Doppler shift value at a certain time and we can calculate the channel vector from it. Based on this channel vector, we use adaptive our scheme to alleviate the Doppler diffusion. In particular, even if the Doppler is changing or inaccurate, our proposed scheme can work normally within an error range.

Next, we will introduce the implementation of our scheme. Our scheme aims to alter the DFT matrix $\mathbf{F}_N$: Replace the corresponding column vector of the $\mathbf{F}_N$ with the calculated channel vector to form an orthogonal basis transformation matrix. After applying the adaptive orthogonal basis, the effect of alleviating diffusion is changed from Fig. 2 to Fig. 3.

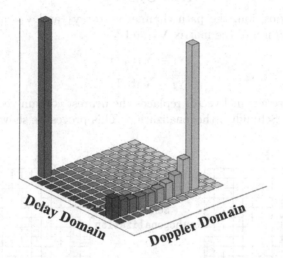

Fig. 3. Schematic diagram of adaptive orthogonal basis.

Taking the two-path channel as an example, we introduce the specific method in this scheme. We set $f_{Doppler1}$ and $f_{Doppler2}$ to represent two path Doppler shift values. According to (8) and (10), channel matrices of the two paths are expressed as

$$
\mathbf{H}_1 = \begin{bmatrix}
\delta^0 & \delta^M & \dots & \delta^{(N-1)M} \\
\delta^1 & \delta^{M+1} & \dots & \delta^{(N-1)M} \\
\vdots & \vdots & \ddots & \vdots \\
\delta^{M-2} & \delta^{2M-2} & \dots & \delta^{NM-2} \\
\delta^{M-1} & \delta^{2M-1} & \dots & \delta^{NM-1},
\end{bmatrix} \tag{21}
$$

$$\mathbf{H}_2 = \begin{bmatrix} \xi^0 & \xi^M & \cdots & \xi^{(N-1)M} \\ \xi^1 & \xi^{M+1} & \cdots & \xi^{(N-1)M} \\ \vdots & \vdots & \ddots & \vdots \\ \xi^{M-2} & \xi^{2M-2} & \cdots & \xi^{NM-2} \\ \xi^{M-1} & \xi^{2M-1} & \cdots & \xi^{NM-1}, \end{bmatrix} \tag{22}$$

where $\delta = e^{\frac{j2\pi f_{Doppler1}}{MN}}$ and $\xi = e^{\frac{j2\pi f_{Doppler2}}{MN}}$. Then, we perform the singular value decomposition (SVD) of channel matrices. It can be expressed as

$$\mathbf{H}_1 = \mathbf{U}_1 \mathbf{\Sigma}_1 \mathbf{V}_1^T \tag{23}$$

$$\mathbf{H}_2 = \mathbf{U}_2 \mathbf{\Sigma}_2 \mathbf{V}_2^T \tag{24}$$

After decomposition, the path channel vector $\mathbf{v}_1$ and $\mathbf{v}_2$ can be obtained from the first column of the matrix $\mathbf{V}_1$ and $\mathbf{V}_2$

$$\mathbf{v}_1 = \mathbf{V}_1(:,1) \tag{25}$$

$$\mathbf{v}_2 = \mathbf{V}_2(:,1) \tag{26}$$

Finally, we use channel vector replaces the nearest column vector in $\mathbf{F}_N$ and obtain $\mathbf{Q}_N$ after Schmidt orthogonalization. This process is shown in Fig. 4.

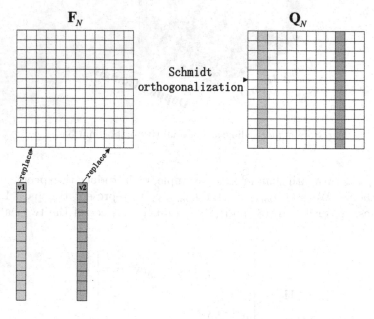

Fig. 4. Schematic diagram of adaptive orthogonal basis.

Compared with OTFS, the advantages of adaptive orthogonal basis scheme are improving the accuracy of channel estimation and reducing the cost of guard symbols by alleviating Doppler diffusion.

5   Simulation Results

In this section, we present the simulation results with coding and ideal channel estimation to compare the BER and BLER performance of our proposed scheme and OTFS. In addition, we show the performance of different symbols number N for the OTFS systems. Furthermore, the performance of different Doppler shifts feedback from the receiver is also shown.

The simulation setup is illustrated in Table 1. For channel model, we use two-path channel model, and the path delay, path Doppler and path power are $[0, 50/9]\,\mu s$, $[1.25, -3.125]$kHz and $[0, 0]$dB, respectively.

Table 1. Simulation Parameters

Parameter	Value
Carrier frequency	4 GHz
Number of subcarriers(M)	120
Number of symbols(N)	12
Subcarrier spacing(Δf)	15 kHz
CP length	$25/9\,\mu s$
Modulation	4-QAM

In Fig. 5, we compare the BER of different symbols number N in the Doppler domain. We use the channel estimation in [17] and compare the case of $N = 12$, $N = 24$ and $N = 48$. We can see that the performance is better as N increases. Obviously, the larger the N, the smaller the fractional Doppler effect [7]. In order to better verify the performance of our scheme, we limit the number of symbols to $N = 12$.

In Fig. 6, we compare the BER and BLER performance of the OTFS and our proposed adaptive orthogonal basis scheme. For fairness, we choose the ideal channel estimation with coding. It can be obtained that the adaptive orthogonal basis scheme has the advantage of alleviating Doppler diffusion without affecting performance. This advantage will further bring benefits, such as reducing pilot symbols expenses and obtaining channel estimation gains.

In practice, the Doppler shift feedback from the receiver is inaccurate, we further evaluate the performance of our scheme in the presence of Doppler error. We consider two Doppler error cases: ± 0.3 kHz and ± 1 kHz. In Fig. 7, we show the BER and BLER performance of our scheme with different Doppler error cases. We can see that the BER loss of two error cases at -2 dB are 0.1 dB and 0.2 dB respectively, the BLER loss are smaller. It can be obtained that our proposed scheme can work even when the number of symbols is limited and the Doppler shifts feedback from the receiver is inaccurate.

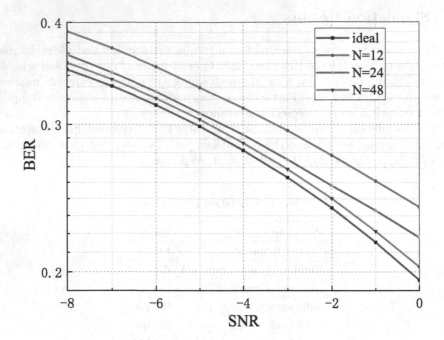

Fig. 5. The BER of different symbols number N in OTFS.

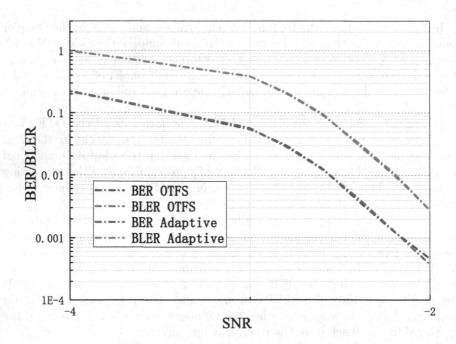

Fig. 6. The BER and BLER performance of the OTFS and our proposed scheme.

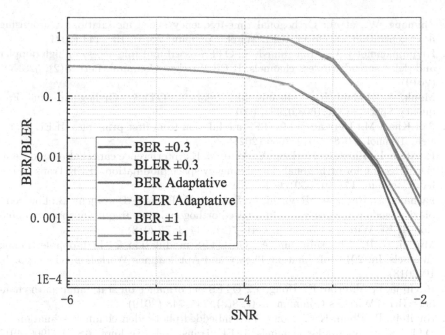

Fig. 7. The performance of our scheme with different Doppler error cases.

6   Conclusion

In this paper, we have analyzed the unavoidable fractional Doppler effects in the case of ideal waveform and show the cause of diffusion from both formula and geometric levels. In particular, we proposed an adaptive orthogonal basis scheme to alleviate the Doppler diffusion. In our scheme, we modified the matrix of the inverse symplectic finite Fourier transform by using the Doppler shifts feedback of the receiver. In the simulation results, we show that the BER and BLER performance of our proposed scheme are not affected compared with OTFS when coding and ideal channel estimation. And our scheme can work even when the number of symbols N is limited and the Doppler shifts feedback from the receiver is inaccurate.

ACKNOWLEDGEMENTS. This work is supported by National Natural Science Foundation of China (No. 61931005) and Beijing University of Posts and Telecommunications-China Mobile Research Institute Joint Innovation Center.

References

1. Hadani, R, et al.: Orthogonal Time Frequency Space Modulation. In: 2017 IEEE Wireless Communications and Networking Conference (WCNC), pp. 1–6(2016)
2. Hadani, R., et al.: Orthogonal Time Frequency Space (OTFS) modulation for millimeter-wave communications systems. In: 2017 IEEE MTT-S International Microwave Symposium (IMS), pp. 681–683(2017)

3. Zhiqiang, W., et al.: Orthogonal time-frequency space modulation: a promising next-generation waveform. IEEE Wirel. Commun. **28**(3), 136–144 (2021)
4. Khammammetti, V., Mohammed, S.: OTFS-based multiple-access in high doppler and delay spread wireless channels. IEEE Wireless Commun. Lett. **8**(2), 528–531 (2019)
5. Monk, A., Hadani, R., Tsatsanis, M., Rakib, S.: OTFS - Orthogonal Time Frequency Space. arXiv:1608.02993. (2016)
6. Saif Khan, M.: Derivation of OTFS modulation from first principles. IEEE Trans. Veh. Technol. **70**(8), 7619–7636 (2021)
7. Raviteja, P., Phan, K.T., Hong, Y., Viterbo, E.: Interference cancellation and iterative detection for orthogonal time frequency space modulation. IEEE Trans. Wireless Commun. **17**(10), 6501–6515 (2018)
8. Farhang, A., RezazadehReyhani, A., Doyle, L.E., Farhang-Boroujeny, B.: Low complexity modem structure for ofdm-based orthogonal time frequency space modulation. IEEE Wireless Commun. Lett. **7**(3), 344–347 (2018)
9. Murali, K. R., Chockalingam, A.: On OTFS modulation for high-doppler fading channels. In: 2018 Information Theory and Applications Workshop (ITA), pp. 1–10(2018)
10. Raviteja, P., Viterbo, E., Hong, Y.: OTFS performance on static multipath channels. IEEE Wireless Commun. Lett. **8**(3), 745–748 (2019)
11. Raviteja, P., Phan, K.T., Hong, Y.: Embedded pilot-aided channel estimation for OTFS in delay-doppler channels. IEEE Trans. Veh. Technol. **68**(5), 4906–4917 (2019)
12. Raviteja, P., Phan, K.T., Hong, Y., Viterbo, E.: Embedded delay-doppler channel estimation for orthogonal time frequency space modulation. In: 2018 IEEE 88th Vehicular Technology Conference (VTC-Fall), pp. 1–5 (2018)
13. Wenqian, S., Linglong, D., Jianping, A., Pingzhi, F., Robert, W.H.: Channel estimation for orthogonal time frequency space (OTFS) massive MIMO. IEEE Trans. Signal Process. **67**(16), 4204–4217 (2019)
14. 6G Vision and Candidate Technologies White Paper (2021). http://www.caict.ac.cn/english/news/202106/P020210608349616163475.pdf
15. Yiqing, Z., et al.: Service-aware 6G: an intelligent and open network based on the convergence of communication, computing and caching. Digital Commun. Netw. **6**(3), 253–260 (2020)
16. Yiqing, Z., Jiangzhou, W., Sawahashi, M.: Downlink transmission of broadband OFCDM Systems-part II: effect of Doppler shift. IEEE Trans. Commun. **54**(6), 1097–1108 (2006)
17. Yixiao, L. and Sen, W. and Jing, J. and Wei, X. and Hang, L.: Doppler Shift Estimation Based Channel Estimation for Orthogonal Time Frequency Space System. In: 2021 IEEE 94th Vehicular Technology Conference (VTC2021-Fall), pp. 1–6(2021)
18. Raviteja, P., Hong, Y., Viterbo, E., Biglieri, E.: Practical pulse-shaping waveforms for reduced-cyclic-prefix OTFS. IEEE Trans. Veh. Technol. **68**(1), 957–961 (2019)

Scheduling and Transmission Optimization

Random Access Preamble Sequence Design in High-Speed Scenario

Ziyuan Qiu[1]([✉]), Sen Wang[2], Qixing Wang[2], Wenxi He[3], and Hang Long[1]

[1] Wireless Signal Processing and Network Lab, Key Laboratory of Universal Wireless Communication, Ministry of Education, Beijing University of Posts and Telecommunications, Beijing, China
qiuziyuan@bupt.edu.cn
[2] China Mobile Research Institute, Beijing, China
[3] Purple Mountain Laboratories, Nanjing, China

Abstract. Random access preamble sequences are sent from the user equipment (UE) to gNodeB though Physical Random Access Channel to access to the network. In high-speed scenarios, the performance of random access based on Zadoff-Chu sequences degrades due to the Doppler frequency offset which breaks the sub-carrier orthogonality. In this paper, a random access preamble sequence with linear change in phase is proposed based on the analysis of the influence of frequency offset on the correlation results of random access preamble sequence. The method of decreasing the peak-to-average power ratio of time domain sequence and the random access preamble sequence design compatible with orthogonal time-frequency space technology are proposed. The false detection rate and the timing error distribution are evaluated. The simulation results show that the proposed designs of random access preamble sequence are insensitive to frequency offset, and the detection performance and timing performance are almost unaffected by frequency offset.

Keywords: Random access · Doppler shift · OTFS

1 Introduction

The random access procedure is very important in realizing user equipment (UE) access to the network and uplink timing synchronization, in which UE sends a random access preamble to gNodeB (gNB) through Physical Random Access Channel (PRACH), and the gNB determines whether any UE accesses to the network and which UE accesses to the network by detecting the random access preamble sequence in the received signal based on peak energy and position of sequence correlation [1]. In 5G new radio (NR) system, random access preambles are generated based on the Zadoff-Chu (ZC) sequences. The good correlation of the ZC sequence avoids the problems of access conflict and inter-user interference when multiple UEs access [2, 3].

The Doppler frequency offset caused by the rapid movement of the UE will destroy the good correlation of the ZC sequence, thus affecting the random access performance.

© ICST Institute for Computer Sciences, Social Informatics and Telecommunications Engineering 2023
Published by Springer Nature Switzerland AG 2023. All Rights Reserved
F. Gao et al. (Eds.): ChinaCom 2022, LNICST 500, pp. 71–83, 2023.
https://doi.org/10.1007/978-3-031-34790-0_6

For the problem of random access in high-speed scenarios, Refs. [4] and [5] analyzed that the frequency offset would lead to the leakage of the peak energy of sequence correlation, resulting in multiple pseudo-peaks. Refs. [6] and [7] proposed a multi-window combined detection method at the receiver to overcome the problem of leakage of the peak energy, but its detection performance in high-speed scenarios will still deteriorate. Refs. [8] and [9] proposed frequency offset estimation methods based on PRACH, and then detect the random access preamble after frequency offset compensation, but it can only estimate the frequency offset in a certain range, and it is only suitable for a single frequency offset scenario.

According to the influence of frequency offset on peak energy and position of correlation, this paper designs an anti-frequency offset random access preamble sequence. On this basis, a method to solve the problem of large Peak-to-Average Power Ratio (PAPR) of time domain sequence is given. Considering the compatibility with multi-carrier modulation technology in 6G, this paper also proposes the design of anti-frequency offset random access sequences based on Orthogonal Time and Frequency Space (OTFS). The sequences proposed in this paper can meet the demand for the number of available sequences in the cell, and the demand for random access preamble detection and timing performance with the traditional single window detection method.

The rest of this paper is organized as follows. Section 2 describes the system model. Section 3 analyzes the influence of frequency offset on peak position and energy of correlation result. Section 4 puts forward an anti-frequency offset random access preamble sequence design and a method to decrease the PAPR, and Sect. 5 gives the design of random access preamble sequence based on OTFS. Section 6 presents the simulation results followed by the conclusion in Sect. 7.

Notations: $|\cdot|$ denotes the absolute value, $\langle \cdot \rangle$ represents rounding up, and $(\cdot)^*$ denotes the conjugate.

2 System Model

The 5G standard specifies [10] that the random access preamble sequences are generated from ZC sequences and different preambles are obtained by cyclic shift to meet the requirements of cell reuse. The rules for generating random access preamble sequences defined in 3GPP 38.211 protocol [10] can be denoted as

$$
\begin{aligned}
x_u(n) &= e^{-j\frac{\pi u n(n+1)}{L_{RA}}}, n = 0, 1, ..., L_{RA} - 1 \\
x_{u,v}(n) &= x_u[(n + C_v) \bmod L_{RA}]
\end{aligned}
\tag{1}
$$

where u is the physical root sequence number, L_{RA} refers to the length of ZC sequence, C_v is the cyclic shift, mod refers to Modulo operation. $x_{u,v}(n)$ is the random access preamble sequence generated by cyclic-shifting the root sequence $x_u(n)$.

Figure 1 shows the procedure of PRACH transmitter and receiver in the 5G system. $Y(m)$ is the frequency domain expression of $x_{u,v}(n)$. The time domain sequence $x_t(p)$ is obtained by $Y(m)$ with sub-carrier mapping and Inverse Fast Fourier Transform (IFFT), and then adds Cyclic Prefix (CP) to get random access transmission signal.

The gNB removes CP of received random access signal and then obtains the time domain sequence $x_r(p)$ denoted as

$$x_r(p) = Hx_t(p)e^{j\frac{2\pi \Delta f}{N_{FFT}\Delta f_{RA}}p} + q(p) \quad p = 0, 1, \cdots, N_{FFT}-1 \tag{2}$$

where H is the Line of Sight (LOS) channel gain, Δf denotes the Doppler frequency offset, N_{FFT} refers to the size of Fast Fourier Transform (FFT), Δf_{RA} is sub-carrier interval, and $q(p)$ refers to the noise [11]. Then $x_r(p)$ is transformed into the frequency domain sequence $Y_r(m)$ by FFT and sub-carrier de-mapping. The root sequence $Y_{root}(m)$ is the frequency domain expression of $x_u(n)$. Using the method of frequency domain correlation detection, $Y_r(m)$ and $Y_{root}(m)$ are conjugated multiplied to get $Y_c(m)$, and then the time domain correlation result is obtained through Inverse Discrete Fourier Transform (IDFT). Next, receiver implements preamble detection and timing estimation according to the energy and position of the peak of the time domain correlation result.

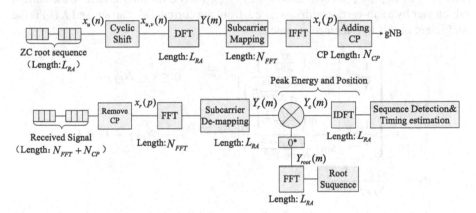

Fig. 1. System Model

3   Influence of Frequency Offset on Correlation Receiver

In high-speed scenarios, the frequency offset leads to the leakage of the peak energy of the correlation result of ZC sequence, which will reduce the detection performance and timing accuracy.

Reference [12] analyzes the influence of frequency offset on the correlation result of general sequence in the frequency domain. Without considering the noise, the result of the frequency domain correlation result at the receiver is simplified as

$$Y_c(m) \approx |K(0)|Y_{c,pre}(m) + Y_{c,interf}(m) \quad m = 0, 1, \ldots, L_{RA}-1 \tag{3}$$

where L_{RA} is the sequence length. Set

$$Y_{c,pre}(m) = HY(m)Y_{root}(m)^*$$

$$Y_{c,interf}(m) = \sum_{k=1}^{L_{RA}-1} Y_{c,interf,k}(m) - \sum_{k=-(L_{RA}-1)}^{-1} Y_{c,interf,k}(m)$$

$$Y_{c,interf,k}(m) = H|K(k)|Y_{1,k}(m)Y_{root}(m)^* \qquad (4)$$

$$Y_{1,k}(m) = \begin{cases} Y(m+k), \max(0,-k) \leq m \leq \min(L_{RA}-1, L_{RA}-1-k) \\ 0, \text{else} \end{cases}$$

$$k = -(L_{RA}-1), -(L_{RA}-2), \cdots, -1, 1, 2, \cdots, L_{RA}-1$$

where H is the LOS channel gain, $Y_{c,pre}(m)$ refers to the frequency domain correlation result without frequency offset, while $Y_c(m)$ has an additional interference $Y_{c,interf}(m)$ consisting of $Y_{c,interf,k}(m)$ compared to it. $Y_{c,interf,k}(m)$ is the interference to the current sub-carrier by a sub-carrier with distance k from the current sub-carrier, and $K(k)$ is the coefficient of this interference, denotes as

$$K(k) = \begin{cases} \dfrac{1}{N}e^{j\theta_0} \left| \dfrac{\sin\left(\frac{\Delta f}{\Delta f^{RA}}\pi\right)}{\sin\left(\frac{\Delta f+k\Delta f^{RA}}{N_{FFT}\Delta f^{RA}}\pi\right)} \right| e^{j(\frac{-k}{N_{FFT}})\pi}, 0 \leq k \leq N_{FFT}-1 \\[20pt] \dfrac{1}{N}e^{j\theta_0} \left| \dfrac{\sin\left(\frac{\Delta f}{\Delta f^{RA}}\pi\right)}{\sin\left(\frac{\Delta f+k\Delta f^{RA}}{N_{FFT}\Delta f^{RA}}\pi\right)} \right| e^{j(\frac{-k}{N_{seq}}+1)\pi}, -(N_{FFT}-1) \leq k < 0 \end{cases} \qquad (5)$$

$$\theta_0 = \frac{(N_{FFT}-1)\Delta f\pi}{N_{FFT}\Delta f^{RA}}$$

where N_{FFT} is the FFT size. The absolute value of $K(k)$ decreases to close to 0 as the absolute value of k increases.

The time domain correlation result can be denoted as

$$x_c(p) \approx |K(0)|x_{c,pre}(p) + x_{c,interf}(p)\, p = 0, 1, \ldots, L_{RA}-1 \qquad (6)$$

where $x_c(p)$, $x_{c,pre}(p)$ and $x_{c,interf}(p)$ are the time domain expressions corresponding to the terms in Eq. (3), and

$$x_{c,interf}(p) = \sum_{k=1}^{L_{RA}-1} x_{c,interf,k}(p) - \sum_{k=-(L_{RA}-1)}^{-1} x_{c,interf,k}(p) \qquad (7)$$

$x_{c,interf,k}(p)$ is the time domain expression of $Y_{c,interf,k}(m)$. Set p_c, $p_{c,pre}$, $p_{c,interf}$ and $p_{c,interf,k}$ to be the peak positions of $x_c(p)$, $x_{c,pre}(p)$, $x_{c,interf}(p)$ and $x_{c,interf,k}(p)$ respectively. According to (6) and (7), when $p_{c,interf,k} = p_{c,pre}$, the frequency offset has no effect on the peak position of the correlation result, but the peak energy is slightly affected; when $p_{c,interf,k} \neq p_{c,pre}$, the peak energy and position of the correlation result are greatly affected by the frequency offset.

Applying the ZC sequence to the above analysis, results in an offset $kd_u\langle N_{FFT}/L_{RA}\rangle$ in $p_{c,interf,k}$ compared to $p_{c,pre}$ [12]. du is defined as

$$d_u = \begin{cases} q, \ 0 \leq q < L_{RA}/2 \\ L_{RA} - q, \ else \end{cases} \quad (8)$$

$$(uq) \bmod L_{RA} = 1$$

Figure 2 shows the peak position relationships between $x_{c,pre}(p)$ and $x_{c,interf,k}(p)$ with different values of d_u. When $d_u = 1$, both the peak energy and position of ZC sequence have affected by frequency offset. When $d_u \neq 1$, the offset of the peak position of the interference leads to multiple pseudo-peaks instead of only one main peak in the correlation result. In addition, as the frequency offset increases, the energy of the main peak decreases and the energy of the pseudo-peak increases. When the frequency offset is equal to the sub-carrier interval, the energy will be concentrated on the pseudo-peak, and the energy of the main peak is too weak to be detected, so the detection and timing performance of the random access seriously decreases.

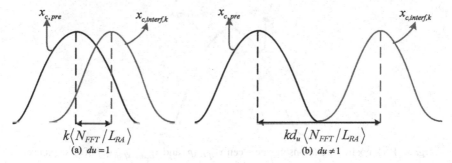

Fig. 2. Peak position relationship between $x_{c,pre}(p)$ and $x_{c,interf,k}(p)$ of ZC sequence

4   The Design of Random Access Preamble Sequence

4.1   Anti-frequency Offset Random Access Preamble Sequence

Based on the analysis of the influence of frequency offset on the correlation result in Sect. 3, a sequence with a constant module value of 1 and linear change in phase are proposed as the random access preamble sequence in frequency domain, which is defined as

$$X(m) = e^{jm\left(\theta_h + \frac{2\pi C_v}{L_{RA}}\right)} \quad m = 0, 1, \cdots, L_{RA} - 1 \quad (9)$$

where C_v is cyclic shift, and θ_h refers to phase slope, that is, the phase difference between two points in the sequence when the cyclic shift is 0, $\theta_h \in [0, 2\pi)$.

The module value of the frequency domain sequence is constant, and the corresponding time domain sequence has good autocorrelation characteristic. Applying $X(m)$ to

Eq. (4), the result of time domain correlation calculation without frequency offset can be denoted as

$$x_{c,pre}(p) = \sum_{L_{RA}} e^{jm\left(\frac{2\pi(C_v+p)}{L_{RA}}\right)} \quad p = 1, 2, \ldots, L_{RA} - 1 \tag{10}$$

and the kth interference can be denoted as

$$x_{c,interf,k}(p) = H|K(k)| \sum_{L_{RA}} e^{jk\theta_h} \cdot e^{jm\left(\frac{2\pi(C_v+p)}{L_{RA}}\right)} \quad p = 1, 2, \ldots, L_{RA} - 1 \tag{11}$$

where $\max(0, -k) \leq m \leq \min(L_{RA} - 1, L_{RA} - 1 - k)$. It is easy to get that the peak position of the kth interference and the correlation without frequency offset are the same from (10) and (11), that is $p_{c,interf,k} = p_{c,pre}$. Figure 3 shows the peak position relationships between $x_{c,pre}(p)$ and $x_{c,interf,k}(p)$ of X sequence. According to Sect. 3, $X(m)$ avoid influence of frequency offset on peak position of correlation result effectively.

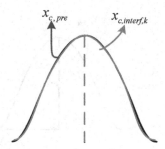

Fig. 3. Peak position relationships between $x_{c,pre}(p)$ and $x_{c,interf,k}(p)$ of X sequence

According to (7), the interference of the correlation result at receiver is essentially the sum of all kth Interference. In fact, it is not enough to achieve $p_{c,interf,k} = p_{c,pre}$. It is necessary to further determine whether $p_{c,interf} = p_{c,pre}$ is satisfied. According to (7) and (11), the interference of the correlation result at receiver can be denoted as

$$x_{c,interf}(p) = H \sum_{m=0}^{L_{RA}-1} e^{j\left(\frac{2\pi m(C_v+p)}{L_{RA}}\right)} \cdot \left[\sum_{k=1}^{L_{RA}-m-1} |K(k)|e^{jk\theta_h} - \sum_{k=-m}^{-1} |K(k)|e^{jk\theta_h} \right] \tag{12}$$

From Eq. (12), it can be found that after summing all the kth interferences the peak position may change due to θ_h and the characteristic of $K(k)$. Let

$$G(m) = \sum_{k=1}^{L_{RA}-m-1} |K(k)|e^{jk\theta_h} - \sum_{k=-m}^{-1} |K(k)|e^{jk\theta_h} \tag{13}$$

When the absolute value and phase of $G(m)$ are constant, $p_{c,interf} = p_{c,pre}$. According to Eq. (5), $|K(k)|$ takes its maximum value at $k = 0$, the larger $|k|$, the smaller $|K(k)|$, and $|K(k)| = |K(k - L_{RA})|, k = 1, 2, \ldots, L_{RA} - 1$. On this basis, the absolute value and phase of $G(m)$ are constant when $\theta_h = \pi$. As $|\theta_h - \pi|$ increases, the absolute value and phase of $G(m)$ will vary more significantly with m, and vary greatest with m when $\theta_h = 0$. Consider θ_h as close to π as possible, but not close to 0.

4.2 Anti-frequency Offset Random Access Preamble Sequence with Low PAPR

The time domain expression of $X(m)$ can be denoted as

$$x(p) = \frac{1}{\sqrt{L_{RA}}} \frac{\sin\left(\frac{L_{RA}}{2}\right)}{\sin\left(\frac{\theta_h}{2} + \frac{(p+C_v)\pi}{L_{RA}}\right)} e^{j\left[\frac{(L_{RA}-1)\theta_h}{2} + \frac{(p+C_v)\pi}{L_{RA}}\right]} p = 0, 1, \ldots, L_{RA} - 1 \quad (14)$$

It can be obtained that the time domain sequence has a significant peak at $\left(\left|\theta_h L_{RA}/2\pi\right|\right) - C_v$ with a high PAPR. A high PAPR in the time domain sequence increases the demands on the linear power amplifiers of transmitter and receiver and reduces transmission efficiency. The linear change in phase of the $X(m)$ makes it resistant to frequency offset, but also introduces the problem of large PAPR of the time domain sequence. Consider reducing the PAPR of the time domain sequence by appropriately reducing the linear characteristics of the sequence, while meeting the requirement of random access performance.

According to analysis in Sect. 3 $|K(k)|$ close to 0 when $|k|$ is large. It can be ignored whether $Y_{c,interf,k}(m)$ with large $|k|$ is affected by frequency offset, which is the frequency domain correlation result of sequence with cyclic shift k and root sequence. On the other hand, the sequence only needs to keep a linear change in phase over a certain length.

Thus, a spliced sequence of multiple X sequences is proposed. In order to achieve a balance between the anti-frequency offset and low PAPR characteristics, the length of each subsequence is set to be equal and the phase slope difference between adjacent subsequences is equal, with the phase slope distributed around π. The spliced sequence is defined as

$$Xa(m) = \begin{cases} e^{jm(\pi - b'\Delta\theta + \Delta\theta + \frac{2\pi C_v}{L_{RA}})}, & m = 0, 1, \cdots, L_b - 1 \\ \cdots \\ e^{jm(\pi - \Delta\theta + \frac{2\pi C_v}{L_{RA}})}, & m = (b' - 2)L_b, (b' - 2)L_b+1, \cdots, (b' - 1)L_b - 1 \\ e^{jm(\pi + \frac{2\pi C_v}{L_{RA}})}, & m = (b' - 1)L_b, (b' - 1)L_b+1, \cdots, b'L_b - 1 \\ \cdots \\ e^{jm(\pi + b\Delta\theta - b'\Delta\theta + \frac{2\pi C_v}{L_{RA}})}, & m = (b-1)L_b, (b-1)L_b+1, \cdots, L_{RA} - 1 \end{cases}$$

$$(15)$$

where b is the number of subsequence, $b' = \langle b/2 \rangle$, $L_b = \langle L_{RA}/b \rangle$ refers to the length of subsequence, $\Delta\theta$ is the difference of phase slope between adjacent subsequences, C_v denotes the cyclic shift. The stronger the linearity of the sequence, the better characteristic of anti-frequency offset and the higher PAPR of the time domain sequence. Increasing the number of subsequences or increasing the phase slope difference of adjacent sub-sequences weakens the sequence linearity, which will deteriorate the anti-frequency offset characteristic. Therefore, the number of subsequences and the phase slope differ-ence need to be set according to different scenarios to control the phase linearity of the sequences.

5   The Design of Random Access Preamble Sequence Based on OTFS

The OTFS technology proposed for 6G enables highly reliable, high-speed data trans-mission in doubly-selective fading channel, which modulates data directly in the Delay-Doppler (DD) domain and extends over the time-frequency domain [13]. Consider designing a random access preamble sequence in the DD domain. Discrete signals in DD domain can be transformed into the time-frequency domain though an M-point FFT and an N-point IFFT on the columns and rows of a $M \times N$ DD domain signal matrix, respectively. Thus, define the random access preamble sequences in the DD domain as

$$\text{Xo}[k, l] = \begin{cases} 1 & k = a, l = 0 \\ 0 & else \end{cases} \begin{cases} k = 0, 1, \ldots, M - 1 \\ l = 0, 1, \ldots, N - 1 \end{cases} \tag{16}$$

After IFFT, the signal of time-frequency domain can be denoted as

$$x[m, n] = \frac{1}{\sqrt{NM}} \sum_{l=0}^{N-1} \sum_{k=0}^{M-1} \text{Xo}[k, l] e^{j2\pi(\frac{nl}{N} - \frac{mk}{M})} = \frac{1}{\sqrt{NM}} e^{-j\frac{2\pi am}{M}} \begin{cases} m = 0, 1, \ldots, M - 1 \\ n = 0, 1, \ldots, N - 1 \end{cases} \tag{17}$$

It is obtained that the signal is linear change in phase in the frequency domain and can be regarded as an X sequence with $\theta_h + 2\pi C_v/M = -2\pi a/M$ in Sect. 4.1. The value of a is determined by the phase slope θ_h and the cyclic shift C_v.

Several 1s are placed at different locations in the delay domain as random access preamble sequences of different UEs for different UEs in the DD domain, and then the time-frequency domain signals are obtained though Inverse Symplectic Finite Fourier Transform (ISFFT). The sequences of different users are orthogonal in the time domain, which leads to multiple separated peaks in the time domain correlation results. Different UEs are identified based on the peak locations. The maximum number of UEs for random access that can be carried in an OTFS frame is determined by the length of the delay domain and the timing error tolerance of channel.

In addition, it can be found that the time-frequency domain signal includes N OFDM symbols based on Eq. (17). The receiver performs correlation on the N OFDM symbols respectively. The detection performance can be improved by combining the N correlation results in high-speed scenario.

6   Simulation Results and Analysis

In this section, the detection performance and timing performance of the proposed anti-frequency offset random access preamble sequence are simulated and evaluated in high-speed scenarios and compared with the performance of PRACH format 0 defined in

3GPP 38.211 protocol [10]. The simulations are carried out on Additive White Gaussian Noise (AWGN) channel and Tapped Delay Line-D (TDL-D) channel respectively and the antenna configuration and channel model are based on the 3GPP 38.104 protocol [14]. In the case of restricted type A for ZC sequence, the receiver in simulation adopts multiple-windows combined detection algorithm [6, 7], while in all other cases the conventional receiver with single-window detection algorithm is adopted [15]. For OTFS-based random access preamble sequence, only the correlation result of the first OFDM symbol received is used for detection and timing. Table 1 and Table 2 show the system simulation parameters and sequence design parameters respectively.

Table 1. System simulation parameters

Parameters	Values
Carrier Frequency	2.6 GHz
Bandwidth	40 MHz
Sub-carrier Interval	1.25 kHz
Antenna Configuration	1Tx, 2Rx
Delay Spread	TDL-D: 300 ns
Time Error Tolerance	AWGN: 1.04 μs TDL-D:2.55 μs

Table 2. Sequence Design parameters

Parameters	Values
PRACH format 0 (ZC sequence)	Unrestricted (0Hz), restricted type A (625 Hz\1340 Hz): $u = 40, C_v = 0$
Anti-frequency offset sequence (X sequence)	$C_v = 0, \theta_h = \pi / 2$
Low PAPR sequence (Xa sequence)	$M = 1024, d = 10, \Delta 0 = \pi / 20, C_v = 0$
OTFS-based sequence (Xo sequence)	$N = 12, M = 1024, a = 257, C_v = 0$

6.1 Detection Performance

This section evaluates the detection performance of different random access preamble sequence based on 3GPP 38.104 protocol [14], which specifies that the PRACH detection performance must meet the false alarm probability of no more than 0.1% and the false detection rate of less than 1%. While satisfying the false alarm probability, the signal-to-noise ratio (SNR) at the false detection rate of 1% is taken as the metric of detection performance.

From Fig. 4 and Fig. 5, the detection performance of X sequence on AWGN and TDL-D is almost unaffected by frequency offset, while the performance of Xa and Xo sequence is slightly degraded with increasing frequency offset. The performance degradation of Xa and Xo sequence at 1340 Hz is less than 0.5 dB compared to no frequency offset.

In addition, the sequence proposed in this paper has a significant performance gain over the ZC sequence. When the frequency offset is 1340 Hz, the performance gain of X, Xa and Xo sequence are 0.91 dB, 0.76 dB and 1.82 dB respectively compared to the ZC sequence on AWGN, and the performance gain are 1.28 dB, 1.02 dB and 2.35 dB on TDL-D. And the performance gain of 625 Hz will larger than that frequency offset of 1340 Hz. The reason is that when frequency offset is 625 Hz, i.e., half the sub-carrier interval, the energy of peak spreads more, the pseudo-peak in the correlation result is the almost same energy as the main peak, while at a frequency offset close to the sub-carrier interval (1340 Hz), the correlation results still only have a distinct peak, which leads to better detection performance at frequency offset of 1340 Hz than 625 Hz.

The Xo sequence has the same phase slope as the X sequence, and its sequence length is 1024, which is larger than the sequence length of the X sequence, resulting in its detection performance is slightly better than that of the X sequence. Combining the correlation of all OFDM symbols in receiver, the performance gain is approximately 8 dB compared to receiver using only the correlation of the first OFDM symbol.

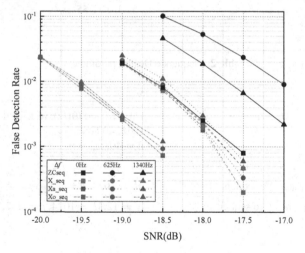

Fig. 4. Detection performance on AWGN

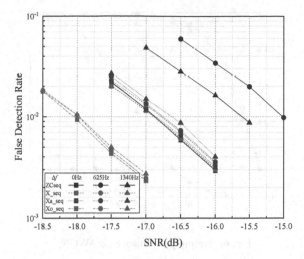

Fig. 5. Detection Performance on TDL-D

The PAPRs of the X and Xa sequences are evaluated in the simulations and are 187.8 and 6.2 respectively. Thus, the Xa sequence is achieving a large decrease in PAPR at the expense of slight anti-frequency offset characteristic.

6.2 Timing Performance

This section evaluates the timing performance of different random access preamble sequences based on the timing error distribution, the specific method is with the limitation of timing error tolerance, timing based on the peak position of the correlation results, the difference with the ideal peak position as the timing error, $\Delta t = 1/\Delta f_{RA} \cdot N_{IFFT}$ as the unit of timing error, statistics to obtain the timing error Cumulative Distribution Function (CDF).

Figure 6 and Fig. 7 show the timing error distributions of the ZC, X and Xa sequences for SNR of -18 dB on AWGN and -16 dB on TDL-D, respectively. It can be found that the timing errors of the sequences on both channels are controlled within 13 Δt. With the influence of frequency offset, the timing performance of the ZC sequence based on the multiple-window combined detection algorithm slightly decreases, the timing error distribution of the X sequence is the same as when there is no frequency offset. The timing performance of the Xa sequence decreases due to frequency offset, and the larger the frequency offset, the larger the timing error. The reason is that the linear characteristic of the Xa sequence is weakened compared to the X sequence, and its anti-frequency offset characteristic is consequently weakened, resulting in a larger peak position offset. However, the timing error of Xa sequence is still controlled within 13 Δt, which is less than 16 Δt, the timing accuracy of PRACH in 5G NR system [16] and satisfies the requirement of PRACH timing performance.

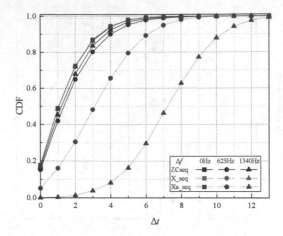

Fig. 6. Timing performance on AWGN

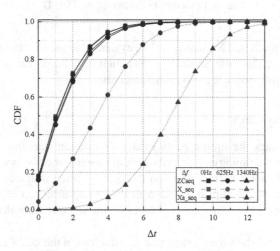

Fig. 7. Timing performance on TDL-D

7 Conclusion

This paper proposes a design of anti-frequency offset random access preamble sequence for high-speed scenarios, replacing the random access preamble sequence generated from the ZC sequence, avoiding the problem of frequency offset destroying the good correlation of the ZC sequence, which causes random access performance degradation. This paper also provides a method to reduce the time-domain PAPR of this sequence, as well as a sequence design method based on OTFS. According to the simulation results on AWGN and TDL-D channels, it is concluded that the proposed sequence is insensitive to frequency offset and can improve the detection performance and timing performance of random access in high-speed scenarios.

Acknowledgement. This work is supported by National Natural Science Foundation of China (No. 61931005) and Beijing University of Posts and Telecommunications-China Mobile Research Institute Joint Innovation Center.

References

1. Sanguinetti, L., Morelli, M., Marchetti, L.: A random access algorithm for LTE systems. Trans. Emerging Telecommun. Technol. **24**(1), 49–58 (2012)
2. Kim, J., Munir, D., Hasan, S., et al.: Enhancement of LTE RACH through extended random access process. Electron. Lett. **50**(19), 1399–1400 (2014)
3. Leyva-Mayorga, I., Tello-Oquendo, L., Pla, V., et al.: On the accurate performance evaluation of the LTE-A random access procedure and the access class barring scheme. IEEE Trans. Wireless Commun. **16**(12), 7785–7799 (2017)
4. Hua, M., Wang, M., Yang, W., et al.: Analysis of the frequency offset effect on random access signals. IEEE Trans. Commun. **61**(11), 4728–4740 (2013)
5. Thota, J., Aijaz, A.: On performance evaluation of random access enhancements for 5G uRLLC. In: 2019 IEEE Wireless Communications and Networking Conference (WCNC), pp. 1–7 (IEEE)
6. Huang, C., Ma, W., Luo, L.: Detection of random access preamble sequences in ultra high speed mobile environment. Syst. Eng. Electron. Technol. **40**(09), 2100–2105 (2018)
7. Min, T., Wen, W., Xu, Z.: High-speed mobile receiver algorithm in LTE system. Mobile Commun. **42**(6), 73–79 (2018)
8. Cao. A., Xiao, P., Tafazolli, R.: Frequency offset estimation based on PRACH preambles in LTE. In: 2014 11th International Symposium on Wireless Communications Systems, Barcelona, Spain, pp. 22–26 (2014)
9. Jun, W., Bao, G., Liu, S., et al.: Frequency offset estimation based on peak power ratio in LTE system. J. China Univers. Posts Telecommun. **2013**(6), 49–54 (2013)
10. 3GPP TS 38.211 V16.3.0. NR; Physical Channels and Modulation (2020)
11. Zhang, Y., Zhang, Z., Hu, X.: An improved preamble detection method for LTE PRACH based on Doppler frequency offset correction. In: Liu, X., Cheng, D., Jinfeng, L. (eds.) ChinaCom 2018. LNICST, vol. 262, pp. 573-582. Doi. Springer, Cham (2019). https://doi.org/10.1007/978-3-030-06161-6_56
12. He, W., Du, Y., Long, H.: Analysis of frequency offset effect on prach in 5g nr systems. In: 2019 14th International Conference on Communications and Networking in China (ChinaCom), Shanghai, China, pp. 679–692 (2019)
13. Long, H., Wang, S., Xu, L., et al.: OTFS technology research and prospect. Telecommun. Sci. **37**(09), 57–63 (2021)
14. 3GPP TS 38.104 V16.3.0. NR; Base Station (BS) Radio Transmission and Reception (2020)
15. Chen, Y., Wen, X., Zheng, W.: Random access algorithm of LTE TDD system based on frequency domain detection. In: 2009 Fifth International Conference on Semantics, Knowledge and Grid, pp. 346–350 (2009)
16. 3GPP TS 38.213 V16.3.0. NR; Physical layer procedures for control (2020)

Privacy-Aware Task Allocation with Service Differentiation for Mobile Edge Computing: Multi-armed Bandits Approach

Hangfan Li[1,2], Lin Shi[1], Xiaoxiong Zhong[1,2,3(✉)], Yun Ji[2], and Sheng Zhang[2]

[1] Guilin University of Electronic Technology, Guilin 541004, China
[2] Graduate School at Shenzhen, Tsinghua University, Shenzhen 518055, China
[3] Peng Cheng Laboratory, Shenzhen 518000, People's Republic of China
xixzhong@gmail.com

Abstract. With the development of fifth generation (5G) technology, mobile edge computing (MEC) is becoming an essential architecture which is envisioned as a cloud extension version. MEC system can push the resources from cloud side to edge side, aiming to solve many computation intensive problems. The task offloading policy is vital and has an important influence on MEC system. Meanwhile, privacy leakage may occur during the task offloading period which may degrade MEC system performance. The attention on these issues is lack according to existing works. Inspired by this, we present a privacy-preserving aware Multi-Armed Bandits based task allocation algorithm, Privacy Upper Confidence Bound (pUCB), to find a balance between the privacy preserving and the efficiency of task processing. In addition, we take regret analysis of the proposed algorithm. The extensive simulation results show that pUCB scheme can achieve a higher optimal rate, a lower lock rate and less total time cost comparing with traditional Multi-arm bandits (MAB) based algorithm.

Keywords: Mobile Edge Computing (MEC) · Privacy Preserving · Multi-armed Bandits (MAB)

1 Introduction

With the development of the 5G, communication among individuals is becoming more frequency all over the world. Cloud computing has been unable to meet the requirements of task computing or transmission under certain circumstances. MEC [1] has been presented to address these issues, which can bring storage and computation resources closer to edge devices. Computation task will

H. Li and L. Shi—Co-first authors. This work was supported by The Major Key Project of PCL (Grant No. PCL2021A02), National Natural Science Foundation of China (Grant Nos. 61802221) and the Guangdong Talent Project 2021TQ06X117.

be offloaded to edge device, which can reduce delay. Due to the limited computing resources of edge devices, the servers are unable to provide unlimited computational offload services for all tasks among edge devices. Therefore, designing an effective task offloading mechanism and maximizing system performance are challenging issues.

Multi-armed bandits (MAB) framework is wildly used in decision making area which provide a solution of the above issues. In [1], coexisting users are becoming research targets and decentralized task offloading strategies DEBO is proposed to achieve a close-to-optimal performance in MEC system. In [2] and [3], online learning policies based on adversary MAB framework are proposed to deal with peer and flows competition. In [4], MAB based SAGE algorithm is proposed to offer a better performance under different quality of service requirements (QoS). In [5], virtual machines or servers in abundance are used to execute edge computing tasks and Multi-Agent MAB based CB-UCB and DB-UCB are proposed to minimize task computing delay. In [6], an MAB based algorithm is proposed to deal with the uncertainty of MEC system considering energy-efficient and delay-sensitive for a dynamic environment MEC system.

Wang et al. [7] and Gong et al. [8] proposed a novel location-privacy aware service migration scheme and privacy aware online task assignment for MEC. They jointly consider migration cost, user-perceived delay, and the risk of location privacy leakage for making service migration decisions, which is formulated as an MDP process. However, they did not consider differentiated service for MEC. How could we design an efficient resource optimization mechanism for differentiated service MEC when considering privacy preserving, and how could we guarantee the optimal task offloading strategy perform better?

To answer these questions, we present a privacy-preserving aware MAB based algorithm for differentiated service MEC, privacy UCB, which can reach a balance between protecting privacy and task processing efficiency. The contributions of this article are shown as follows:

- We propose an MAB based algorithm for differentiated service (difference type of task like video.mp4 or document.txt) MEC, whose goal are maximizing the resource usage in MEC system and considering privacy preserving at the same time. In proposed scheme, we characterize the delay in task processing of different task types from three computation models: local computation, edge computation and cloud computation. To the best of our knowledge, this scheme is the first work combining MAB algorithms and privacy protecting in differentiated service.
- For privacy preserving in task allocation, we define accumulated privacy quantity (APQ) to quantitative privacy, which aims to reduce the risk of personal privacy leakage. And then, we formulate the optimization problem based on traditional algorithms in differentiated service MEC system. In addition, we take regret analysis of the Privacy Upper Confidence Bound.
- We conduct extensive experiments to evaluate the performance of the proposed scheme. In the simulation results, the proposed algorithm can achieve

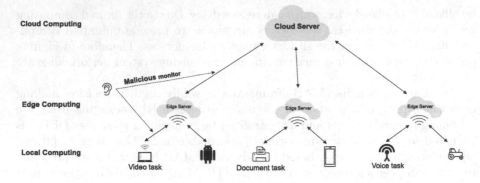

Fig. 1. Traditional MEC System Model

a higher optimal rate, a lower lock rate and total time cost comparing with existing traditional MAB based algorithms.

2 System Model and Problem Formulation

In this section, we firstly introduce our multi-servers computing system based on MEC system. Then we define the delay model for a single task processed by the system. Finally, we propose pUCB for differentiated service in MEC.

2.1 System Model and Useful Notions

In this paper, we consider an MEC system, in where the servers are divided into two categories: N edge servers and one cloud servers indexed by $\{S_1, S_2, \ldots, S_N\}$ where S_1 represents the cloud server and the remaining elements represents the edge servers. We hold a plenty of local devices (LDs) could be denoted by $\{u_1, u_2, \ldots, u_I\}$ and a finite round horizon $\{1, 2, \ldots, t, \ldots, T\}$. The system contains three parts: local devices, edge servers (ES) and one cloud server (CS), which are shown in Fig. 1. Firstly, to simulate reality, LD will generate tasks with random type (task type will be defined later) and size. A task is a command for transmission or handle different types of files or projects. Tasks will be offloaded to a selected server by some strategies where the task can only be computed on edge side, cloud side or local side. Delay-sensitive computing tasks have high requirement on response time, but task size is usually small. Therefore, we assume that a task can be processed before LD moving to another cell MEC system.

2.2 Task Generation

Before considering the privacy quantity, we formulate the overall delay for a task execution process based on the proposed model. For each u_i task will be generated in each round. Task in each round can be defined as a tuple:

$$h_{i,t}^\theta = \left(\mu_{i,t}^\theta, r_{i,t}^\theta, \tau_{i,t}^\theta\right) \tag{1}$$

where $\mu_{i,t}^\theta$ represents the size of task, $r_{i,t}^\theta$ represents the size of result (usually the returned result size is much smaller than the task size) and $\tau_{i,t}^\theta$ represents the time deadline of current task. θ is the type of the task and, for simplicity, in our system, $\theta \in \{$ document, voice, video $\}$.

Once a task has been generated, it should be processed and get feedback. According to the MEC model, we assume that each local device will choose a method to handle the task independently. In this section, we introduce three kinds of computing patterns that can be selected by the local device: local computing pattern, edge computing pattern and cloud computing pattern.

Local Compute Pattern (LCP). Under LCP, the task will be processed by local CPU and get the feedback. So, the delay $d_{i,t,local}^\theta$ can be defined as follow:

$$d_{i,t,local}^\theta = \frac{\mu_{i,t}^\theta}{v_{local}} \tag{2}$$

where v_{local} represents the maximum computing speed of the current LD. For example, $d_{1,2,local}^{voice}$ represents the delay of the task that generated by the first LD in this network in round 2 processing under LCP pattern and the type of task is voice.

Edge Computing Pattern (ECP). Under ECP the tasks will be offloaded to edge servers and the overall process contains three steps: task upload, task execution and result feedback. Task upload delay $d_{i\to n,t}^\theta$ and transmission rate $rate_{i\to n}$ can be written as:

$$d_{i\to n,t}^\theta = \frac{\mu_{i,t}^\theta}{rate_{i\to n}}, n \neq 1 \tag{3}$$

$$rate_{i\to n} = W \log_2 (1 + SNR_{i\to n}), n \neq 1 \tag{4}$$

where $SNR_{i\to n}$ represents signal to noise ratio and W represents the channel bandwidth. After receiving tasks, edge server starts the task execution process. Task execution delay can be written as:

$$d_{i,n,t}^\theta = \frac{\mu_{i,t}^\theta}{v_n} \tag{5}$$

where v_n represents the stander capacity of edge server n (bit/sec). Comparing to the cloud server, the capacity of edge server is not strong as cloud server. So the actual capacity of edge server might fluctuate around v_n.

In the end, edge server needs to transmit the result back to the user. So, the download delay from edge server to the local device $d_{n\to i,t}^\theta$ and the transmission rate $rate_{n\to i}$ can be written as:

$$d_{n\to i,t}^\theta = \frac{r_{i,t}^\theta}{rate_{n\to i}}, n \neq 1 \tag{6}$$

So, the task delay under ECP can be defined as follows:

$$d_{ECP}^{\theta} = d_{i \to n,t}^{\theta} + d_{i,n,t}^{\theta} + d_{n \to i,t}^{\theta} \tag{7}$$

Cloud Computing Pattern (CCP). Under CCP, the task will be offload to CS and the overall process contain three steps as same as the ECP: task upload, task execution and result feedback.

The task uploading delay can be written as:

$$d_{i \to 1,t}^{\theta} = \frac{\mu_{i,t}^{\theta}}{rate_{i \to 1}} \tag{8}$$

Due to the long distance between LDs and cloud servers, the signal to noise $SNR_{i \to 1}$ might fluctuate up and down according to the instant network environment.

We assume that the CS is the first server among the server group. After receiving tasks, CS starts the task execution process. Task execution delay can be written as:

$$d_{i,1,t}^{\theta} = \frac{\mu_{i,t}^{\theta}}{rate_{i,1}} \tag{9}$$

where v_1 represents the capacity of the cloud server.

After finishing the tasks, CS needs to give out feedback. So, the download delay can be written as:

$$d_{1 \to i,t}^{\theta} = \frac{\mu_{i,t}^{\theta}}{rate_{1 \to i}} \tag{10}$$

So, the task delay under CCP, can be defined as follows:

$$d_{CCP}^{\theta} = d_{i \to 1,t}^{\theta} + d_{i,1,t}^{\theta} + d_{1 \to i,t}^{\theta} \tag{11}$$

Pattern Selection Vector. A task can only be processed by one computing pattern. So, the pattern selection vector π_t can be written as:

$$\pi_t \in \{\pi_{local}, \pi_{edge}, \pi_{cloud}\} \tag{12}$$

where $\pi_{local} = \begin{bmatrix} 1 & 0 & 0 \end{bmatrix}$ represents LCP, $\pi_{edge} = \begin{bmatrix} 0 & 1 & 0 \end{bmatrix}$ represents ECP and $\pi_{cloud} = \begin{bmatrix} 0 & 0 & 1 \end{bmatrix}$ represents CCP. In addition, the task delay vector can be written as:

$$D_{i,t}^{\theta} = \begin{bmatrix} d_{LCP}^{\theta} & d_{ECP}^{\theta} & d_{CCP}^{\theta} \end{bmatrix} \tag{13}$$

therefore, the total delay for a task can be written as:

$$\pi_t \begin{bmatrix} D_{i,t}^{\theta} \end{bmatrix}^{\mathrm{T}} \tag{14}$$

where $[\cdot]^{\mathrm{T}}$ represents the vector transpose.

Quantity of Privacy and Problem Formulation. The protection of privacy is an essential problem in today's digital society, and it is also an important index to measure the quality of algorithms and the overall system. In our system, due to the limited computing resources, it is impossible to deploy the high security encryption algorithm on both user side and server side. Therefore, it is necessary to control the frequency of task uploading to the ES and CS. The risk of privacy leakage is closely bound up with the times of task uploading.

In general, malicious monitors can obtain user (users are LDs in this paper) information from their unloading habits and task unloading probability through illegal ways. Because of the homogeneity of the edge local area network, if the malicious monitor finds a security hole within the system, it is convenient to duplicate the illegal behavior to the whole edge network. Through the combination of these two means, it can be more accurate to identify whether the target user is in the current network, the crime cost is low, and the profit is large.

Therefore, only if we quantify the privacy, we can protect user information. The privacy quantity $q_{i,t}^{\theta}$ can be written as:

$$q_{i,t}^{\theta} = \ln \frac{p_{i,t}^{\theta}}{\bar{p}_{\theta}} \tag{15}$$

where $p_{i,t}^{\theta}$ represents the probability of LD i uploading the task in round t and $\bar{p}_{\theta}$ is the average probability to upload the θ task within MEC system.

If $q_{i,t}^{\theta} > 0$, it means that the task processing method selected by the user has strong personal habit characteristics which is easy to disclose personal privacy. Otherwise, if $q_{i,t}^{\theta} < 0$, it means that current task processing method is universality which helps to reduce the accumulated privacy quantity and reduce the risk of personal privacy leakage. Then the Accumulated Privacy Quantity (APQ) of current LD can be written as:

$$Q_i = \sum_{t=1}^{T} \left(1 - \pi_t \pi_{local}^{\mathrm{T}}\right) q_{i,t}^{\theta} \tag{16}$$

As a result, the final problem for a single LD can be defined as follows:

$$\mathbf{P1} : \text{minimize} \sum_{i=1}^{I} \sum_{t=1}^{T} \pi_t \left[D_{i,t}^{\theta}\right]^{\mathrm{T}}, \forall \theta \tag{17}$$

$$\text{s.t.} \pi_t \in \{\pi_{local}, \pi_{edge}, \pi_{cloud}\} \tag{17a}$$

$$Q_i < Q_{target} \tag{17b}$$

$$D_{i,t}^{\theta} < \tau_{i,t}^{\theta} \tag{17c}$$

$$n \in [1, N] \tag{17d}$$

$$t \in [1, T] \tag{17e}$$

Constraint 1 implies that the task offload approach is limited in three patterns: LCP, ECP, CCP. Based on realistic considerations, constraint 2 and 3 are

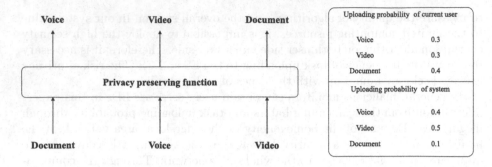

Fig. 2. Traditional MEC System Model

protections on privacy and delay respectively. Constraint 4 and 5 implies that the number of edge server and round horizon are finite. Focused on a normal LD, we need to minimize its total time cost and APQ. Self-locking will occur once the task overtimes to complete and the APQ surpasses its target.

3   Algorithm and Regret Analysis

It is evident that the optimization problem P1 mentioned in section two is easy to solve if we know the key information e.g., server capability, upload-download link state and system resource utilization. However, all this information is not available in advance, and it is infeasible to achieve the optimization in P1 if we result from uncertainty of backhaul information.

We exploit an MAB framework to find a solution to deal with such incomplete priori information situation, which is shown in Algorithm 1. In the MEC system, each user generates different kinds of tasks anytime and anywhere. After each task uploading decisions, the algorithm observe the reward (the shorter time took, the bigger reward got). The size and type of tasks cannot be determined, but the server for processing tasks can be selected, called Action. The collection of actions is called the Action Pool. Hence, the MEC system can learn the distribution from empirical information and determine action selection. We denote $A = \{a_1, \ldots, a_E, a_l, a_c\}$ as the action pool where $a_1 \sim a_E$ represents ECP, a_l represents the LCP and a_c represents the CCP. Inputting such an action pool, we can get the fastest task processing action. Different from classic UCB1 algorithm, in lines 6~8, it is designed to solve privacy protection problem. According to the definition of quantity of privacy, malicious monitor could only get the regular pattern (often upload some specific type of tasks) of task offloading but not the actual information. Therefore, we can use privacy preserving function to add a misleading task type to protect the regular pattern. As shown in Fig. 2, privacy preserving function could be defined followed confidentiality principle which means the function could totally follow random rule. In our paper, we set the privacy preserving function as follow: set the most common type (the smallest type uploading probability difference between users and the system) as

---

Algorithm 1. Privacy-UCB algorithm

Input:

An Action pool with K actions;

1: Try each action $a_m \in A$ in action pool at first;
2: for $l = K + 1 : T$ do
3:    Estimate the optimistic bound from previous training;
4:    $a_m = \overline{a_m} + \sqrt{\frac{2\ln t}{\omega_m}}$;
     $\overline{a_m}$ denote the average delay;
     ω_m denote the number of times of action m has been chosen;
5:    Try action $a_m = \min a_m$, for all $a_m \in A$
6:    if $Q_{i,t} \geq \varepsilon Q_{target}$ then
7:       According to the privacy preserving function, add a different type of task as
         enclosure to mislead the malicious monitors;
8:    end if
9:    if $D_{i,t}^\theta < \tau_{i,t}^\theta$ then
10:       Update $\overline{a_m} = \overline{a_m} + \frac{\left(D_{i,t}^\theta - \overline{a_m}\right)}{\omega_m + 1}$;
11:       Update $\omega_m = \omega_m + 1$;
12:       Update $Q_i = Q_i + Q_t$
13:    end if
14: end for

---

the misleading enclosure for the most exposed type (the biggest type uploading probability difference between users and the system) of tasks where the probabilities are known. Others are totally random.

Then, we discuss the complexity of the Algorithm 1. Firstly, to initialize the action pool, we need to take an K times iteration, therefore, the complexity of initial part is O(K). For the exploration part, the complexity is related to the action number K which is also O(K). The complexity of main loop, including privacy protection and delay calculation program, is O(N-K). So, the whole complexity of Algorithm 1 is O(N).

Useful Notation and Regret Analysis. Denote $\mathbb{E}[\cdot]$ as expectation and $\mathbb{P}\{\cdot\}$ as probability. Denote K as the number of actions. The time cost of each action obey different distributions and according to the MEC system, we denote $\mathbb{P}_1, \ldots, \mathbb{P}_K$ as the choosing probability for each actions. Denote $G_i(n)$ as the number of times action i has been choose by LD during its first n tasks and μ^* as the shortest time cost under best strategy. Then the regret comparing to the best strategy could defined as:

$$\mu^* n - \mu_j \sum_{j=1}^{K} \mathbb{E}[G_i(n)] \tag{18}$$

Denote $d_{t,s} = \sqrt{2\ln t/s}$ as the confidence radius distance and $\Delta_i = |\mu_i - \mu^*|$ as the regret of a single round.

Theorem 1. *The average choosing number of $G_i(n)$ of the proposed scheme is limited by an upper bound, which is expressed:*

$$G_i(n) \leq \frac{8 \ln n}{\Delta_i^2} + 1 + \frac{\pi^2}{3} \tag{19}$$

where n represents the number of tasks.

Proof. We first introduce **Chernoff-Hoeffding Inequality.** [9] Let $\mathbb{X}_1, \ldots, \mathbb{X}_n$ be the random variables with common range $[0, 1]$, $\mathbb{E}[\mathbb{X}_t | \mathbb{X}_1, \ldots, \mathbb{X}_{t-1}] = \mu$ and $S_n = \mathbb{X}_1 + \ldots + \mathbb{X}_n$. Then for all $a > 0$:

$$\mathbb{P}\{S_n \geq n\mu + a\} \leq e^{-2a^2/n} \tag{20}$$

$$\mathbb{P}\{S_n \leq n\mu - a\} \leq e^{-2a^2/n} \tag{21}$$

Precisely, for each $t \geq 1$ we bound the indicator function of $I_t = i$ as follows. Let ϕ be an arbitrary positive integer.

$$G_i(n) = 1 + \sum_{t=K+1}^{n} \{T_t = i\}$$

$$\leq \phi + \sum_{t=K+1}^{n} \{T_t = i, T_i(t-1) \geq \phi\}$$

$$\leq \phi + \sum_{t=K+1}^{n} \{\overline{\mathbb{X}}_{T^*(t-1)}^* - d_{t-1} \leq \overline{\mathbb{X}}_{i,T_i(t-1)} + d_{t-1}, T_i(t-1) \geq \phi\} \tag{22}$$

$$\leq \phi + \sum_{t=K+1}^{n} \{\min_{0<r<t} \overline{\mathbb{X}}_r^* + d_{t-1,r} \leq \max_{\phi<s<t} \overline{\mathbb{X}}_{i,s} + d_{t-1,s}\}$$

$$\leq \phi + \sum_{t=1}^{\infty} \sum_{r=1}^{t-1} \sum_{s=\phi}^{t-1} \{\overline{\mathbb{X}}_r^* + d_{t,r} \leq \overline{\mathbb{X}}_{i,s} + d_{t,s}\}$$

Then, at least one of the following must hold:

$$\overline{\mathbb{X}}_r^* \leq \mu^* - d_{t,r}$$
$$\overline{\mathbb{X}}_{i,s} \geq \mu_i + d_{t,s} \tag{23}$$
$$\mu^* < \mu_i + 2d_{t,s}$$

Then according to the Chernoff-Hoeffding Inequality:

$$\mathbb{P}\{\overline{\mathbb{X}}_r^* \leq \mu^* - d_{t,r}\} \leq e^{-4\ln t} = t^{-4} \tag{24}$$

$$\mathbb{P}\{\overline{\mathbb{X}}_r^* \geq \mu^* + d_{t,s}\} \leq e^{-4\ln t} = t^{-4} \tag{25}$$

For $\phi = (8 \ln n)/\Delta_i^*$, $\mu^* < \mu_i + 2d_{t,s}$ is false. Therefore, we have

$$r > (8 \ln n) \tag{26}$$

$$G_i(n) \leq \frac{8 \ln n}{\Delta_i^2} + 1 + \frac{\pi^2}{3} \tag{27}$$

which concludes the proof.

4   Performance Evaluation

In this part, we evaluate the performance of the proposed scheme. The parameters are set as shown in Table 1 and Table 2.

Table 1. Simulation parameters setting for different traffic types.

Type	Offloading probability	Q_i
Voice	0.342	+0.2
Voice	0.342	+0.3
Voice	0.342	−0.05

Table 2. Simulation parameters setting.

Parameter	Value
Local device CPU frequency	2 GHz
Clock cycles required to process a one-bit task	50 clock cycles
Channel bandwidth	1 MHz
SNR between local device and edge server $SNR_{i \to n}$	$2^{20} - 1$
SNR between local device and cloud server $SNR_{i \to 1}$	$2^{20} - 1$
Task size	1MB ∼ 100 MB
Number of edge server	11
Task processing capacity of edge server	10 MB ∼ 30MB
Eps-Greedy algorithm	0.4

Optimal rate is the ratio of optimal choosing tasks to overall tasks.

Locking rate is the ratio of device locking number to total number of LD which is set to 100 in our experiments.

The task number is 300, task size is 30MB, the device capacity = 2.0GHz, the epsilon is 0.4, the temperature of SoftMax algorithm is 0.1 and the number of devices is 100. We suppose that there is no privacy concerning limited (QTarget is big enough to ensure device-locking will never happen) if privacy bound is not a variable.

From Fig. 3 (1), the performance of Epsilon-greedy algorithm converges at around 50 tasks which is the fastest one. However, the optimal rate is bad compared with others. SoftMax algorithm converges at around 75 tasks and the optimal rate is better than the previous one. pUCB algorithm and UCB1 algorithm almost have the same performance. Although they converge slowly around

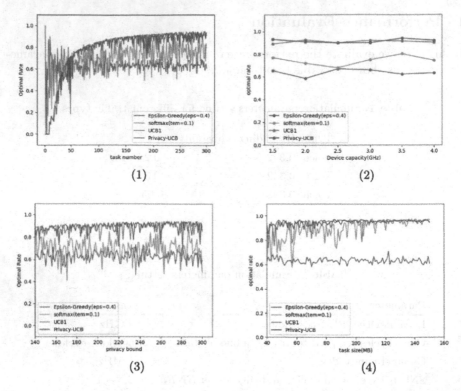

Fig. 3. Optimal rate vs different variables. (1) with task number; (2) with device capacity; (3) with privacy bound; (4) with task size.

100 tasks, but the optimal rate is the best. From Fig. 3 (2), the device capacity has little effect to the optimal rate. In this test, we take the average number of 10 repeated experiments as final report for each CPU frequency. No matter how strong or sick of the CPU performance, local capacity is far less than the server capacity. Therefore, choosing local computing will be a low priority action. The situation of privacy bound and task size is similar with device capacity. From Fig. 3 (3) and Fig. 3 (4), we can confirm the low correlation between optimal rate and these two variables because task size and privacy bound will not influence the capacity of arms directly.

In Fig. 4, it is the most appropriate one to show the difference between pUCB and other traditional MAB algorithms. As we can see, with the increasing of task number, the privacy preserving function plays its due rule. The device lock rate increases rapidly for all algorithms expect pUCB. Combining with the previous test, the desired effect is achieved by using pUCB. The followings are two supplementary trials of the previous one which come to the same conclusion. In Fig. 4 (2) and Fig. 4 (2), device lock rate of pUCB remains zero as the privacy bound increasing and of other three algorithms decline gradually from 100 per-

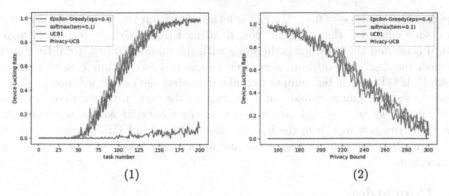

Fig. 4. Device locking rate vs different variables. (1) with task number; (2) with privacy bound.

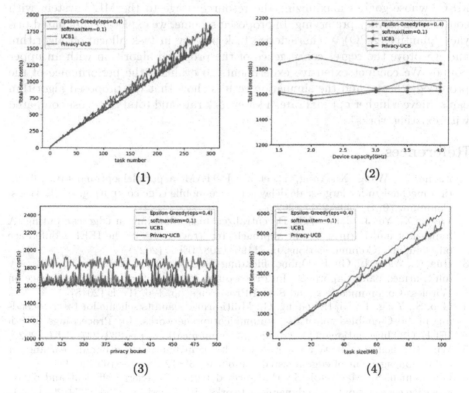

Fig. 5. Total time cost vs different variables. (1) with task number (2) with device capacity; (3) with privacy bound; (4) with task size.

cent to zero. This means, in most cases, pUCB algorithm is a better strategy to acclimatize device to the MEC system.

In Fig. 5 (1), it is a direct confirmation of the previous hypothesis. The time difference required for completion of 300 tasks is 250 s between pUCB and

Epsilon-Greedy (eps = 0.4). We can get the data from the test "total time cost vs device capacity" that the time cost of using Epsilon-Greedy (eps=0.4) algorithm is around 1900 s which is the same with the number in test "total time cost vs task number". In addition, according to the test "total time cost vs privacy bound", if QTarget is big enough to make sure that the device will not lock, the time cost still remains stable and according to the test "total time cost vs task size", it is easy to draw the conclusion that the time cost will grow linearly as the task size growing. From the last four test, we verify pUCB algorithm can get a balance between privacy preserving and algorithm performance in time saving dimension.

5   Conclusion

In this paper, we propose an MAB based algorithm for differentiated service MEC, whose goal is maximizing the resource usage to the MEC system with considering privacy preserving. In proposed scheme, we exploit accumulated privacy quantity (APQ) to characterize task privacy in task allocation algorithm and we prove the regret convergence of the proposed algorithm with an upper bound. We conduct extensive experiments to evaluate the performance of the proposed scheme, and the simulation results show that the proposed algorithm can achieve a higher optimal rate, a lower lock rate and total time cost compared with existing works.

References

1. Zhone, X., Wang, X., Yang, T., et al.: POTAM: a parallel optimal task allocation mechanism for large-scale delay sensitive mobile edge computing. IEEE Trans. Commun. **70**(4), 2499–2517 (2022)
2. Wang, X., Ye, J., John, C.S.: Decentralized task offloading in edge computing: A multi-user multi-armed bandit approach. In: Proceedings of the IEEE Conference on Computer Communications, pp. 1199–1208. IEEE (2022)
3. Hua, C., Wang, L., Gu, P.: Online offloading in dense wireless networks: an adversary multi-armed bandit approach. In: Proceedings of 10th International Conference on Wireless Communications and Signal Processing, pp. 1–6. IEEE (2018)
4. Gao, S., Yang, T., Ni, H., Zhang, G.: Multi-armed bandits scheme for tasks offloading in MEC-enabled maritime communication networks. In: Proceedings of 9th IEEE/CIC International Conference on Communications, pp. 232–237. IEEE (2020)
5. Wu, B., Chen, T., Ni, W., Wang, X.: Multi-agent multi-armed bandit learning for online management of edge-assisted computing **69**(12), 8188–8199 (2021)
6. Ghoorchian, S., Maghsudi, S.: Multi-armed bandit for energy-efficient and delay-sensitive edge computing in dynamic networks with uncertainty **7**(1), 279–293 (2021)
7. Wang, W., Ge, S., Zhou, X.: Location-privacy-aware service migration in mobile edge computing. In: Proceedings of 2020 IEEE Wireless Communications and Networking Conference, pp. 1–6. IEEE (2020)
8. Gone, W., Zhang, B., Li, C.: Privacy-aware online task assignment framework for mobile crowdsensing. In: Proceedings of 2019 IEEE International Conference on Communications, pp. 1–6. IEEE (2019)
9. Auer, P., Cesa-Bianchi, N., Fischer, P.: Finite-time analysis of the multiarmed bandit problem. Mach. Learn. **47**(2), 235–256 (2002)

FTDCN: Full Two-Dimensional Convolution Network for Speech Enhancement in Time-Frequency Domain

Maoqing Liu[1(✉)], Hongqing Liu[1], Yi Zhou[1], and Lu Gan[2]

[1] School of Communication and Information Engineering, Chongqing University of Posts and Telecommunications, Chongqing, China
s200131275@stu.cqupt.edu.cn
[2] College of Engineering, Design and Physical Science, Brunel University, London UB8 3PH, UK

Abstract. The dual-path structure achieves superior performance in monaural speech enhancement (SE), demonstrating the importance of modeling the long-range spectral patterns of a single frame. In this paper, two novel causal temporal convolutional network (TCN) modules, inter-frame complex-valued two-dimensional TCN (Inter-CTTCN) and intra-frame complex-valued two-dimensional TCN (Intra-CTTCN), are proposed to capture the long-range spectral dependence within a single frame and the long-term dependence between frames, respectively. These two lightweight TCN components, which are composed entirely of two-dimensional convolutions, maintain a high dimension feature representation that facilitates the distinction between speech and noise. We join the Inter-CTTCN and Intra-CTTCN with a gated complex-valued convolutional encoder and decoder structure to design a full two-dimensional convolutional network (FTDCN) for SE in the time-frequency (T-F) domain. Using noisy speech as input, the proposed model was experimentally evaluated on the datasets of Interspeech 2020 Deep Noise Suppression Challenge (DNS Challenge 2020). The NB-PESQ of our proposed model exceeds the DNS Challenge 2020 first-placed model by 0.19 and our model requires only 0.8 M parameters.

Keywords: Speech enhancement · Dual-path · End-to-End

1 Introduction

Speech enhancement (SE) can substantially improve speech quality in applications such as hearing aids, pickup devices, and audio-video conferencing systems, enhancing users' experiences. With the developments of deep learning techniques in recent years, the performances of deep learning SE methods surpass those of traditional methods.

The temporal dependency of speech is what deep learning methods mainly model. In that case, long short-term memory (LSTM) [1,2] and temporal convolutional network (TCN) [3,4] are successively proposed to extract long-term

© ICST Institute for Computer Sciences, Social Informatics and Telecommunications Engineering 2023
Published by Springer Nature Switzerland AG 2023. All Rights Reserved
F. Gao et al. (Eds.): ChinaCom 2022, LNICST 500, pp. 97–108, 2023.
https://doi.org/10.1007/978-3-031-34790-0_8

temporal relationships of speech. Compared to LSTM, TCN has the advantage of a flexible receptive field and can be parallelized to improve the model running speed computationally. The TCN was first proposed for sequence modeling, proving that it is superior to LSTM. The speech separation model Conv-TasNet [5] used the TCN structure as a backbone and achieved excellent results. Subsequently, TCNN [6] applied TCN with a convolutional encoder-decoder (CED) structure for the time domain SE task and demonstrated the effectiveness of TCN. For long-range spectral patterns, the recent performance of PHASEN [7], DPCRN [8], and DCCRN+ [9] also demonstrates the importance of TCN structure.

In light of this, we design two causal TCN modules, Intra-CTTCN and Inter-CTTCN, to model the long-range spectral dependence within a single frame and the long-term dependence between frames, respectively. Compared with the original TCN structure, our proposed TCN module makes several optimisations. The two modules consist entirely of two-dimensional convolutions to maintain the advantage of high-dimensional features over low-dimensional ones and reduce the model's size. Adding complex-valued operations make the number of parameters reduced by half. The dilation factor is set to a power of 3 to avoid overlapping operations, thus allowing a larger receptive field of the exact computation. Maintain an appropriate Spectral resolution, as it affects the modelling of the intra-frame harmonic relations. The intra-frame module has frame group convolution kernels in each convolution layer used to model the harmonic relations of a single frame separately.

Finally, a gated complex-valued CED structure that joins Intra-CTTCN and Inter-CTTCN is developed to obtain a full two-dimensional convolution network termed FTDCN. Since the Spectral resolution is large enough, using LayerNorm to normalize each frame in the whole model can achieve better results while maintaining causality. The experiments show that FTDCN achieves better objective metrics than the top model in DNS Challenge 2020, and with a smaller model size.

2   System Overview

In this section, we will show details of the proposed architecture. Figure 1 depicts the general structure of FTDCN, which consists of STFT, encoder, dual-path complex-valued TCN module, decoder, and iSTFT. The output shapes along the channel and frequency axis are 32 and 128 for encoder1 and encoder2, respectively, and 64 and 64 for the other encoders. The output shape of the decoder is symmetrical to the encoder.

2.1   Dual-Path Complex-Valued TCN Module

Inspired by DPCRN [8] and TCNN [6], we propose a dual-path complex-valued TCN module (DPCTM), a causal lightweight module in the T-F domain. It consists of an intra-frame module and an inter-frame module for modeling the

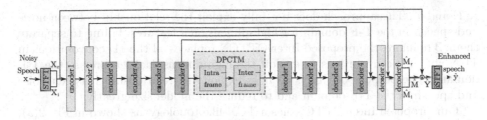

Fig. 1. FTDCN network.

long-range spectral dependence within a single frame and the long-term dependence between frames, respectively. The backbone of the inter-frame module is composed of multiple Inter-CTTCN modules. There is a pointwise convolution (1×1-Conv) at the front and back of the Inter-CTTCNs to perform a fully connected operation on the input channel axes. The intra-frame module is similar to the inter-frame module, but it consists of three parts: 1×1-Conv, Intra-CTTCN modules, and 1×1-Conv, where the number of groups of 1×1-Conv is set to T, which is used to equalize the scale of each frame.

2.2 Inter-frame Complex-Valued Two-Dimensional TCN Module (Inter-CTTCN)

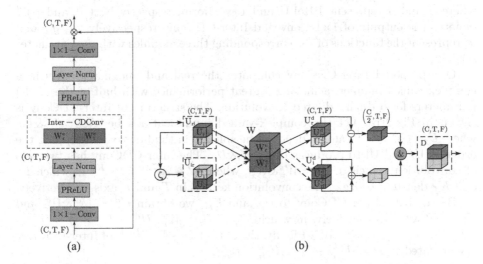

Fig. 2. (a)Proposed Inter-CTTCN. (b)Proposed Inter-CDConv, ζ denotes swapping the order of the two parts on the C axis

We propose Inter-CTTCN for extracting long-term inter-frame dependencies of high-level features. Traditionally, to extract long-term context dependencies with modules like TCN, the encoder output is usually flattened to two dimensions, C

$\times F$ and T. This approach does not fully exploit the relationship between noise and speech in the T-F domain for high-dimensional features, failing to separate them. Therefore, the proposed Inter-CTTCN replaces all the 1D convolutions in TCN with 2D convolutions to exploit the high-dimensional features in the T-F domain. The purpose of this is to fully exploit the relationship between noise and speech in the T-F domain and to reduce the model size greatly.

Our proposed Inter-CTTCN has a TCN-like topology, as shown in Fig. 2(a), where 1×1-Conv is a 2D convolutional layer with a convolutional kernel size of one in both T and F axes. The 1×1-Conv, PReLU, and LayerNorm are used to increase the nonlinearity of the network and act first on the module input $U \in \mathbb{R}^{C\times T\times F}$. In the middle, the inter-frame complex-valued dilated convolution (Inter-CDConv) extends the receptive field of the model to extract the high-level signal's long-term frame-to-frame dependence. The Inter-CDConv is also followed by PReLU and LayerNorm. After that, a layer of 1×1-Conv is employed, which is a fully connected operation on the channel axis of the signal. Finally, the residual path is used to add the module input to the output of the final layer. In a nutshell, the output U_e of the Inter-CTTCN is calculated by

$$\tilde{U}^1 = g_1(U; \psi_1), \tag{1}$$

$$\tilde{U}^{cd} = g_{cd}(\beta(\delta(\tilde{U}^1; \psi_c d))), \tag{2}$$

$$\tilde{U}_e = g_2(\beta(\delta(\tilde{U}^{cd}; \psi_2))) + U, \tag{3}$$

where δ and β represent PReLU and LayerNorm, respectively, $(\tilde{\cdot})^1$ and $(\tilde{\cdot})^{cd}$ denotes the outputs of 1×1-Conv and Inter-CDConv, respectively, g_1, g_{cd} and g_2 represent the functions of the corresponding three modules with the parameter set $\psi_{(\cdot)}$,

Our proposed Inter-CDConv computes the real and imaginary parts in a complex-valued manner, achieving a great performance with half of the model parameters for ordinary dilated convolution. The structure of Inter-CDConv is shown in Fig. 2(b). Let the complex-valued input features be $U_{ri} = U_r \& U_i$, where $U_{ri} \in \mathbb{R}^{C\times T\times F}$, and & denotes the splicing in the first axis. Swapping the order of Ur and Ui to produces $U_{ir} = U_i \& U_r$. The Inter-CDConv has two sets of convolution kernels of $W = W_r^e \& W_i^e$, where $W \in \mathbb{R}^{C\times C\times K_t\times K_f}$ in which K_t and K_f denote the size of the convolution kernels in T and F axis, respectively.

By applying Inter-CDConv to U_{ri} and U_{ri}, we obtain $U_r^d = U_{rr}^d \& U_{ir}^d$ and $U_i^d = U_{ir}^d \& U_{ri}^d$, respectively, in which $U_{rr}^d = U_r \times W_r^e$, $U_{ii}^d = U_i \times W_i^e$, $U_{ir}^d = U_i^d \times W_r^e$ and $U_{ri}^d = U_r^d \times W_i^e$. Finally, the output $D \in \mathbb{R}^{C\times T\times F}$ of Inter-CDConv is calculated as $D = (U_{rr}^d - U_{ir}^d) \& (U_{ir}^d - U_{ri}^d)$.

2.3   Intra-frame Complex-Valued Two-Dimensional TCN Module (Intra-CTTCN)

Recent studies [7–9] have demonstrated the importance of capturing the long-range dependence of spectrograms within a single frame. The reason is that the fundamental frequencies of speech and its harmonics are strongly correlated and

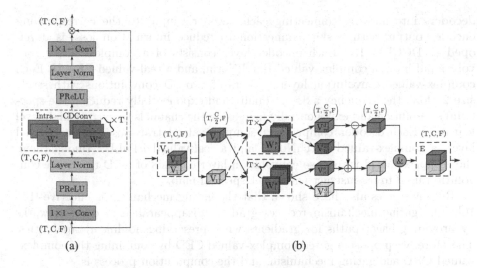

Fig. 3. (a)Proposed Intra-CTTCN. (b)Proposed Intra-CDConv

often distributed in the long-range spectrum within a given frame. Therefore, we propose Intra-CTTCN to capture long-range spectrogram dependencies within a single frame.

The topology of Intra-CTTCN is similar to Inter-CTTCN, shown in Fig. 3(a). The input $V \in \mathbb{R}^{T \times C \times F}$ is fed into the first layer of the module 1×1-Conv, which has T sets of independent convolution kernels of size 1 in both C and F axes, which equalizes the size of each frame in the time scale. The 1×1-Conv is followed by PReLU and LayerNorm, where LayerNorm is normalized to the $[C, F]$ dimension of each frame during training and evaluation. The intermediate Intra-CDConv is shown in Fig. 3(b), which consists of T groups of convolution kernels to perform convolution operations on the spectral map of each frame separately to extract the spectral map long-range dependence. Each group has two convolution kernels for real and imaginary parts, similar to the complex-valued operation equation, the computation process of Intra-CDConv is

$$V_{rr}^d = V_r \times W_r^a, \quad V_{ii}^d = V_i \times W_i^a,$$
$$V_{ri}^d = V_r \times W_i^a, \quad V_{ir}^d = V_i \times W_r^a, \tag{4}$$

$$E = (V_{rr}^d - V_{ii}^d) \& (V_{ri}^d + V_{ir}^d). \tag{5}$$

The Intra-CDConv is followed by PReLU, LayerNorm, and 1×1 conv, and the residual path is also added.

2.4   Gated Complex-Valued Convolutional Encoder and Decoder

The convolutional encoder and decoder (CED) structure has been widely adopted in many applications [10–12]. A complex-valued CED architecture consists of six complex-valued encoder layers and corresponding complex-valued decoders into mirrors, connecting each decoder's input to the corresponding encoder output with a skip connection to reduce information loss, is developed in DCCRN [13]. Each encoder layer consists of a complex-valued convolutional layer, a complex-valued BatchNorm, and a real-valued PPeLU. Each complex-valued convolution layer consists of two 2D convolutions with stride size 2 along the frequency axis, gradually and exponentially reducing the spectrum's resolution and exponentially increasing the channels to extract high-level features. Each decoder comprises a complex-valued transposed convolutional layer, a complex-valued BatchNorm, and a real-valued PPeLU. Among them, the complex-valued transpose convolution layer consists of a 2D transpose convolution used to reconstruct the target spectral map.

Recent studies also have shown that the gating mechanism is effective [14–16]. The gating mechanism reduces gradient disappearance in deep networks by providing linear paths for gradients while preserving nonlinear capabilities. Therefore, we propose a gated complex-valued CED by combining the complex-valued CED and gating mechanism, and the computation process is

$$
\begin{aligned}
\tilde{U}^{rr} &= g_r(I_r; \psi_r), \quad \tilde{U}^{ii} = g_i(I_i; \psi_i), \\
\tilde{U}^{ri} &= g_i(I_r; \psi_i), \quad \tilde{U}^{ir} = g_r(I_i; \psi_r),
\end{aligned} \tag{6}
$$

$$
\tilde{U}^{cc} = (\tilde{U}^{rr} - \tilde{U}^{ii}) \& (\tilde{U}^{ri} + \tilde{U}^{ir}), \tag{7}
$$

$$
\tilde{U}^{G} = \tilde{U}^{cc_2} + g_t(\tilde{U}^{cc_2}; \psi_t), \tag{8}
$$

$$
\tilde{U}_o = \beta(\delta(\tilde{U}^{G})), \tag{9}
$$

where $(\cdot)^{rr}$, $(\cdot)^{ii}$, $(\cdot)^{ri}$, $(\cdot)^{ir}$ represents real part input through real part convolution kernel, imaginary part input through imaginary part convolution kernel, real part input through imaginary part convolution kernel, and imaginary part input through real part convolution kernel, respecitively, $(\cdot)^{cc_1}$ and $(\cdot)^{cc_2}$ represent the output of two complex-valued convolutions that do not share weights, g_r, g_i and g_t represent the functions of the corresponding three modules with the parameter set $\psi_{(.)}$.

2.5   The Final Proposed Framework

DPCTM. We place a 1×1-Conv at the head and tail of the Inter-frame module and stack eight Inter-CTTCNs in the middle. In the Inter-CTTCN, the Inter-CDConv has T sets of convolutional kernels, and the size of each convolutional kernel in the time and frequency axes is set to [3,3]. The dilation factor d on the time axis is set to [1,3,9,27,1,3,9,27], and the dilatation factor on the frequency axis is kept as 1. To maintain the causal constraint, we complement the signal with $(3 - 1) \times d$ zeros at the top of the time axis before Inter-CDConv. The normalized shape of LayerNorm is set to F to maintain the causal constraint.

Similarly, we place a 1×1-Conv at the head and tail of the Intra-frame module, with six Intra-CTTCNs stacking in between. In Intra-CTTCN, Intra-CDConv has only one set of conv kernels, each of size [3,3] conducting convolution on the channel and frequency axes of the signal. Since there is no causal constraint in the channel and frequency axes, the expansion factors of both axes are set to [1,3,9,1,3,9] and the signal is complemented by $\frac{(3-1)\times d}{2}$ zeros in front and behind each of the two axes before Intra-CDConv. To obtain a better normalization performance, we normalize the C and F axes of the signal together, so we set the normalized shape to $[C,F]$, which is still under the causal constraint.

Gated Complex-Valued Convolutional Encoder and Decoder. Within each encoder block, the size of the convolution kernel on the time and frequency axes is set to (2,5). The stride for the cross-correlation of the first and third encoder is set to (1,2) and the others are set to (1,1). This is because we empirically found that the resolution of the input spectrum of DPCTM would reduce the SE effect if it is too small, but it would also increase the computation cost if it is too high. Considering all these factors, we change the frequency in the encoder to a quarter of the original one. Similarly, we set the number of channels in the final output of encoder to 64, compared to the 256 channels of DCCRN, since we want a smaller model size. As with Inter-CTTCN, we set the normalized shape of the LayerNorm after Gated Complex-Valued Convolutional to F to maintain the causal constraint. Note that we are looking forward to one frame in each encoder-decoder pair, which results in a 37.5ms look ahead.

Detailed Parameter Settings. The detailed parameter settings of our proposed model are shown in Table 1. We split the real and imaginary parts of the STFT output into two channels and delete the first point, fill a zero in front of iSTFT and merge the real and imaginary parts of the input. The size of the input and output in the frequency domain is *channels × frames × frequency*, except for Intra-CTTCN, which is *frames × channels × frequency*. For encoder and decoder, the parameters represent *kernel size alone height × kernel size alone width, (stride along height, stride along width), input channels, output channels*. For Intra-CTTCN, the parameters represent *groups of input, kernel size alone height × kernel size alone width, (stride along height, stride along width), channels*. Inter-CTTCN has one less paramete groups of input than Intra-CTTCN.

2.6 Loss Function

We use complex ratio mask (CRM) [17] as the learning target of FDTCN. This network is trained to estimate the mask $\hat{M} = \hat{M}_R + j\hat{M}_I$, where $\hat{M} \in \mathbb{C}^{C\times T\times F}$. Combining $\hat{M}$ with the input $X = X_R + jX_I$, where $X \in \mathbb{C}^{C\times T\times F}$, yields the output $\hat{Y}$, given by

$$\hat{Y} = \hat{M} \times X = (\hat{M}_R + j\hat{M}_I)(X_R + jX_I), \tag{10}$$

Considering the loss functions in the frequency and time domains can better utilize information from both domains, so we propose the following the joint loss function, given by

$$\hat{Y}_{mag} = \|\hat{Y}_r + \hat{Y}_i\|_F, \tag{11}$$

Table 1. Detailed parameter settings of the proposed FTDCN. The meaning of the values represented is described in the text.

layer name	input size	hyperparameters	output size
STFT	1×16000	-	514×T
encoder1	2×T×256	2×5,(1,2),2,32	32×T×128
encoder2	32×T×128	2×5, (1,1), 32, 32	32×T×128
encoder3	32×T×128	2×5, (1,2), 32, 64	64×T×64
encoder4	64×T×64	2×5,(1,1),64,64	64×T×64
encoder5	64×T×64	2×5,(1,1),64,64	64×T×64
encoder6	64×T×64	2×5,(1,1),64,64	64×T×64
reshape	64×T×64	-	T×64×64
Intra-CTTCN	T×64×64	$T,1\times1,(1,1),T$ $\left.\begin{pmatrix}T,1\times1,(1,1),T\\T,3\times3,(1,1),T\\T,3\times3,(1,1),T\\T,1\times1,(1,1),T\\T,1\times1,(1,1),T\\T,3\times3,(3,3),T\\T,3\times3,(3,3),T\\T,1\times1,(1,1),T\\T,1\times1,(1,1),T\\T,3\times3,(9,9),T\\T,3\times3,(9,9),T\\T,1\times1,(1,1),T\end{pmatrix}\right.\times2$ $T,1\times1,(1,1),T$	T×64×64
reshape	T,64,64	-	64 ×T×64
Inter-CTTCN	64×T×64	$1\times1,(1,1),64$ $\left.\begin{pmatrix}1\times1,(1,1),64\\3\times3,(1,1),64\\1\times1,(1,1),64\\1\times1,(1,1),64\\3\times3,(3,1),64\\1\times1,(1,1),64\\1\times1,(1,1),64\\3\times3,(9,1),64\\1\times1,(1,1),64\\1\times1,(1,1),64\\3\times3,(27,1),64\\1\times1,(1,1),64\end{pmatrix}\right.\times2$ $1\times1,(1,1),64$	T×64×64
decoder1	128×T×64	2×5,(1,1),64	64×T×64
decoder2	128×T×64	2×5,(1,1),64	64×T×64
decoder3	128×T×64	2×5,(1,1),64	64×T×64
decoder4	128×T×64	2×5,(1,2),64	32×T×128
decoder5	64×T×64	2×5,(1,1),64	32×T×128
decoder6	64×T×64	2×5,(1,2),64	2×T×256
iSTFT	514×T	-	1×16000

$$Y_{mag} = \|Y_r + Y_i\|_F, \tag{12}$$

$$L_F = 10log_{10}(\|\hat{Y}_r - Y_r\|_F^2 + \|\hat{Y}_i - Y_i\|_F^2 + \|\hat{Y}_{mag} - Y_{mag}\|_F^2), \tag{13}$$

$$L_T = 10log_{10}\frac{\|\frac{\langle\hat{y},y\rangle\hat{y}}{\|Y\|_F^2}\|_F^2}{\|\hat{y} - y\|_F^2}, \tag{14}$$

$$L = L_T + L_F, \tag{15}$$

where $\langle\cdot,\cdot\rangle$ is the inner product of two matrices, and $\|\cdot\|_F$ denotes Frobenius norm.

3   Experimental Setup

3.1   Dataset

In this paper, we use the DNS Challenge 2020 dataset [18] to evaluate FTDCN with the sampling rate at 16 kHz. The clean speech consists of 500 h of speech from 2150 speakers, and noise contains 150 types of noise for 180 h. We made two training dataset to verify the effectiveness of the model, with and without reverberations. For 500 h of the training set with reverberation, the clean speech was first convoluted with random room impulse responses mixed with a reverberation time of 0.3 to 0.6 s and then synthesized randomly with the noise of signal-to-noise ratio (SNR) of –5 to 20 dB. For the training set of 500 h without reverberation, we synthesize clean speech and noise with SNRs in the range of –5 to 20 dB randomly. We use the test set provided by DNS Challenge 2020 containing 150 voices of ten seconds in length to compare with other methods.

3.2   Training Setup

We set the window length to 25 ms, the frameshift to 6.25 ms, and a 512-point FFT. We set the initial learning rate to 0.001 and the weight decay to 0.00001. When we observe that the decreasing trend of the loss curve tends to level off, we usually set it to half of the previous one, and finally, we trained 51 epochs with a learning rate of 0.000025.

3.3   Ablation Studies

Two baseline models are trained for the purposes of ablation studies. First, we trained a model, called FTDCN-E, which differs from FTDCN only in that it removes the intra-frame module from FTDCN. Second, we trained a model that doubles C and halves F of the DPCTM input, calling it FTDCN-D, where the (*stride along height,stride along width*) and *channels* of the six encoders of FTDCN-D are set to (*(1,2), (1,1), (1,2), (1,1), (1,2), (1,1)), (1,2), (1,1)*), (*32,32,64,64,128,128*), and Decoder and DPCTM are changed correspondingly.

4   Results

In Table 2, we compare FTDCN with DNS Challenge 2020 top-ranked methods and baselines together, where NSNet [19] is the DNS Challenge 2020's official baseline network, DTLN [20] and DCCRN [13] are for the real-time track, and Conv-TasNet [5] is for the non-real-time track. Under the condition of the same test set, we directly use the objective scores provided by these authors, where "-"

Table 2. NB-PESQ, WB-PESQ, STOI, SI-SDR on DNS Challenge 2020 test set.

Method	Para.(M)	no Reverb				Reverb			
		NB-PESQ	WB-PESQ	STOI	SI-SDR	NB-PESQ	WB-PESQ	STOI	SI-SDR
Noisy	–	2.45	1.58	91.52	9.07	2.75	1.82	86.62	9.03
NSNet	5.1	2.87	2.15	90.47	15.61	3.08	2.37	90.43	14.72
DTLN	1.0	3.04	–	94.76	16.34	2.70	–	84.68	10.53
Conv-TasNet	5.08	–	2.73	–	–	–	2.75	–	–
DCCRN	3.7	3.27	–	–	–	3.08	–	–	–
TRU-Net	**0.38**	3.36	2.86	96.32	17.55	3.35	2.74	91.29	14.87
FTDCN-E	0.69	3.34	2.81	96.52	18.53	3.29	2.57	90.58	14.57
FTDCN-D	1.43	3.36	2.80	96.41	18.65	3.31	2.62	90.37	14.40
FTDCN	0.82	**3.46**	**2.96**	**96.91**	**19.23**	**3.40**	**2.79**	**91.70**	**15.51**

means this score is not provided, "Para" indicates the parameters of the model, "no Reverb" and "Reverb" represent the test set without and with reverberations, respectively.

The following conclusions can be drawn from Table 2:

1) Comparing FTDCN with FTDCN-E, it shows that the proposed intra-frame module greatly enhances the SE capability with only a slightly increased model size. It illustrates the importance of capturing the long-range spectral dependence and the effectiveness of the intra-frame module.
2) Comparing FTDCN with FTDCN-D, it illustrates the importance of proper frequency resolution, showing that minor F may attenuate the model's ability to model long-range dependencies of speech.
3) Comparing FTDCN with the top-ranked models from DNS Challenge 2020, it demonstrates the excellent noise reduction capability is obtained by our proposed FTDCN, even with a small model size. FTDCN-D also illustrates the importance of maintaining the high dimensionality of the features compared to other methods.

5   Conclusion

In this work, we propose an end-to-end semi-causal lightweight speech enhancement method. To model the intra- and inter-frame dependencies of the speech, we propose two lightweight modules, termed Intra-CTTCN and Inter-CTTCN, by using only convolutions. To utilize the Intra-CTTCN and Inter-CTTCN, we develop a gated complex CED structure to model the real and imaginary parts of the input. The results show that the performance of the proposed model is superior to the top-ranked model in DNS Challenge 2020, even with smaller model size. Future research will explore the possibility of deploying our model to edge devices.

References

1. Tan, K., Wang, D.L.: A convolutional recurrent neural network for real-time speech enhancement. Interspeech **2018**, 3229–3233 (2018)
2. Luo, Y., Mesgarani, N.: Tasnet: time-domain audio separation network for real-time, single-channel speech separation. In: 2018 IEEE International Conference on Acoustics, Speech and Signal Processing (ICASSP), pp. 696–700. IEEE (2018)
3. Bai, S., Kolter, J.Z., Koltun, V.: An empirical evaluation of generic convolutional and recurrent networks for sequence modeling. arXiv preprint arXiv:1803.01271 (2018)
4. Kishore, V., Tiwari, N., Paramasivam, P.: Improved speech enhancement using tcn with multiple encoder-decoder layers. In: Interspeech, pp. 4531–4535 (2020)
5. Luo, Y., Mesgarani, N.: Conv-tasnet: Surpassing ideal time-frequency magnitude masking for speech separation. IEEE/ACM Trans. Audio Speech Lang. Proc. **27**(8), 1256–1266 (2019)
6. Pandey. A., Wang, D.: Tcnn: Temporal convolutional neural network for real-time speech enhancement in the time domain. In: ICASSP 2019–2019 IEEE International Conference on Acoustics, Speech and Signal Processing (ICASSP), pp. 6875–6879. IEEE (2019)
7. Yin, D., Luo, C., Xiong, Z., Zeng, W.: Phasen: A phase-and-harmonics-aware speech enhancement network. In: Proceedings of the AAAI Conference on Artificial Intelligence, vol. 34, pp. 9458–9465 (2020)
8. Le, X., Chen, H., Chen, K., Lu, J.: Dpcrn: Dual-path convolution recurrent network for single channel speech enhancement. arXiv preprint arXiv:2107.05429 (2021)
9. Lv, S., Hu, Y., Zhang, S., Xie, L.: Dccrn+: Channel-wise subband dccrn with snr estimation for speech enhancement. arXiv preprint arXiv:2106.08672 (2021)
10. Ronneberger, O., Fischer, P., Brox, T.: U-net: Convolutional networks for biomedical image segmentation. arXiv preprint arXiv:1505.04597 (2015)
11. Zhao, S., Nguyen, T.H., Ma, B.: Monaural speech enhancement with complex convolutional block attention module and joint time frequency losses. In: ICASSP 2021–2021 IEEE International Conference on Acoustics, Speech and Signal Processing (ICASSP), pp. 6648–6652. IEEE (2021)
12. Choi, H.-S., Kim, J.-H., Huh, J., Kim, A., Ha, J.-W., Lee, K.: Phase-aware speech enhancement with deep complex u-net. In: International Conference on Learning Representations (2018)
13. Hu, Y., et al.: Dccrn: Deep complex convolution recurrent network for phase-aware speech enhancement. arXiv preprint arXiv:2008.00264 (2020)
14. Van Oord, A., Kalchbrenner, N., Kavukcuoglu, K.: Pixel recurrent neural networks. In: International Conference on Machine Learning, pp. 1747–1756. PMLR (2016)
15. Dauphin, Y.N., Fan, A., Auli, M., Grangier, D.: Language modeling with gated convolutional networks. In: International Conference on Machine Learning, pp. 933–941. PMLR (2017)
16. Van den Oord, A., Kalchbrenner, N., Espeholt, L., Vinyals, O., Graves, A., et al.: Conditional image generation with pixelcnn decoders. In: Advances in Neural Information Processing Systems 29 (2016)
17. Williamson, D.S., Wang, Y., Wang, D.: Complex ratio masking for monaural speech separation. IEEE/ACM Trans. Audio Speech Lang. Proc. **24**(3), 483–492 (2015)
18. Reddy, C.K.A., et al.: The interspeech 2020 deep noise suppression challenge: Datasets, subjective speech quality and testing framework. arXiv preprint arXiv:2001.08662 (2020)

19. Xia, Y., Braun, S., Reddy, C.K.A., Dubey, H., Cutler, R., Tashev, I.: Weighted speech distortion losses for neural-network-based real-time speech enhancement. In: ICASSP 2020-2020 IEEE International Conference on Acoustics, Speech and Signal Processing (ICASSP), pp. 871–875. IEEE (2020)
20. Westhausen, N.L., Meyer, B.T.: Dual-signal transformation lstm network for real-time noise suppression. arXiv preprint arXiv:2005.07551 (2020)

Robust Hybrid Beamforming
for Multi-user Millimeter Wave Systems
with Sub-connected Structure

Zhen Luo$^{(\boxtimes)}$, Lang Luo, Xin Zhang, and Hongqing Liu

School of Communication and Information Engineering, Chongqing University of
Posts and Telecommunications, Chongqing 404100, China
luozhen@cqupt.edu.cn, {s210131170,s190131221}@stu.cqupt.edu.cn

Abstract. In this paper, we investigate a millimeter wave multi-user
system to further improve the spectral efficiency. Millimeter wave channels with correlated estimation errors and sub-connected structures are
considered to develop a two-stage hybrid beamforming scheme. In the
first stage, the analog parts of beamformers are designed to maximize
RF-to-RF channel gains. In the second stage, the digital parts of the
beamformers are optimized by utilizing the equivalence between the maximization of mutual information and the minimization of weighted minimum mean square error. The numerical results show that the proposed
scheme has superior performance over other existing designs.

Keywords: millimeter wave · hybrid beamforming · multi-user ·
estimation errors · sub-connected

1   Introduction

With the increasing congestion of sub-6GHz, millimeter wave (mmWave) band
receives wide research interests as the unexploited band for the fifth-generation
mobile communication. The severe path loss caused by short wavelength is the
main obstacle to the utilization of mmWave [1]. Fortunately, short wavelength
also enables small devices to package a large number of antennas. Thus, the
current enabling technology is to develop beamforming schemes which steers
the transmitting/receiving beams in a certain direction to combat the path loss.
However, for conventional multiple-input multiple-output (MIMO) systems with
fully digital beamforming, each transmitting or receiving antenna need to assign
one radio frequency (RF) chain. Applying such structure to mmWave systems
with large antenna arrays results in extremely high power consumption and hardware complexity [2], which is unaffordable in practice. So hybrid beamforming,
which consists of analog part with only phase shifters and digital part with small
number of RF chains, is widely adopted in mmWave beamforming designs due
to the balance of cost, complexity, and system performance.

© ICST Institute for Computer Sciences, Social Informatics and Telecommunications Engineering 2023
Published by Springer Nature Switzerland AG 2023. All Rights Reserved
F. Gao et al. (Eds.): ChinaCom 2022, LNICST 500, pp. 109–121, 2023.
https://doi.org/10.1007/978-3-031-34790-0_9

The hybrid beamforming schemes for multi-user (MU) systems have been studied in literature. In [3], the fully digital beamformer of each user is designed to minimize the total mean square error (MSE) first. Then, the OMP-based algorithm is applied to decompose the fully digital processors into hybrid ones. However, the computational complexity of decomposing a matrix with large antenna arrays is extremely high. To reduce the computational complexity, the two-stage design scheme, which designs analog and digital beamformers successively, is adopted in [4–8]. In [4], the analog beamformers are determined firstly, and the digital beamformers are designed to minimize the sum-MSE. In [5], a joint design method is proposed to avoid the loss of information at each stage. In [6], the analog and digital beamformers are updated iteratively to minimize MSE. In [7], a piecewise successive iterative approximation algorithm is utilized to design analog beamformers, and digital beamformers are designed by piecewise successive approximation to avoid the loss of information. The aforementioned works all adopt fully-connected structures in which each RF chain is connected to all antennas. However, such a structure leads to severe insertion losses and degrades the energy efficiency [9]. Thus, sub-connected structure is adopted in [8]. The analog beamformers are designed to maximize RF-to-RF channel gains, and the digital beamformers are obtained by applying zero-forcing (ZF) strategy to eliminate the inter-user interference.

It is noted that the above works are all based on perfect channel state information (CSI) assumptions. However, CSI imperfectness must be considered in implementations. The estimation errors of angles are considered in [10,11]. In [12], a robust hybrid beamforming scheme is proposed for MU full-duplex systems based on uncorrelated estimation errors. Correlated estimation errors are investigated in [13] for point-to-point mmWave systems, in which the compressed sensing based algorithm applicable for mmWave channels is considered to derive the estimated channel model. To the best of our knowledge, the hybrid beamforming design for MU systems based on correlated estimation errors is still an open problem.

We develop a robust hybrid beamforming scheme with sub-connected structures for MU systems in this paper. Unlike the study in [8], which assumes single data steam users, a more general situation where each user is equipped with multiple RF chains to support multiple data streams is investigated in this paper. The analog parts of beamformers are designed to maximize the gains of RF-to-RF channels. The optimization of digital beamformers is solved iteratively by utilizing the equivalence between the maximization of mutual information and the minimization of weighted minimum mean square error (WMMSE). The main contributions are summarized as follows: 1) A robust hybrid beamforming scheme is proposed for MU mmWave systems based on correlated estimation errors. 2) To improve energy efficiency, the sub-connected structure is adopted in this paper. To the best of our knowledge, this is the first robust design for such system configurations. Performance gains of the proposed design are highlighted by numerical simulations in terms of sum rates and energy efficiencies.

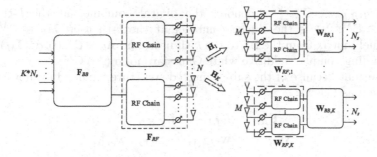

Fig. 1. System model.

Notation: Bold lower case and upper case letters denote vectors and matrices, respectively. $(\cdot)^T$, $(\cdot)^H$, $\text{tr}(\cdot)$, $E(\cdot)$ stand for the matrix transpose, Hermitian transpose, trace and expectation, respectively. $\|\cdot\|_F$ denotes the Frobenius norm. $\mathbf{x}^{(i)}$ is the i-th entry of vector $\mathbf{x}$. $\mathbf{X}(m:n,i)$ denotes the sub-matrix composed of corresponding rows and column of $\mathbf{X}$. $\mathbf{I}_K$ denotes the $K \times K$ identity matrix. $\mathbb{C}^{N \times M}$ is the set of all $N \times M$ complex matrices. $\mathbf{X} \sim \mathcal{CN}(\mathbf{P},\mathbf{K})$ means that $\mathbf{X}$ is a complex Gaussian random matrix with mean $\mathbf{P}$ and covariance matrix $\mathbf{K}$.

2   System and Channel Model

The downlink of the MU mmWave system with sub-connected structure is illustrated in Fig. 1, where a base station (BS) with N antennas serves K users with M antennas on each user. Hybrid structures are employed at the BS and users. The BS is equipped with KN_{rf} RF chains to support KN_s data streams, and each user is equipped with N_{rf} RF chains to support N_s data streams. The number of RF chains is subject to the constraint $N_s \leq N_{rf} \leq \min\{\frac{N}{K}, M\}$. The signal transmitted at the BS can be expressed as

$$\mathbf{x} = \mathbf{F}_{RF}\mathbf{F}_{BB}\mathbf{s}, \tag{1}$$

where $\mathbf{F}_{RF} \in \mathbb{C}^{N \times KN_{rf}}$ denotes the analog precoder at the BS; $\mathbf{F}_{BB} = [\mathbf{F}_{BB,1},\cdots,\mathbf{F}_{BB,K}]$ with $\mathbf{F}_{BB,k} \in \mathbb{C}^{KN_{rf} \times N_s}$, $k \in \{1,2,\cdots,K\}$ denoting the digital precoder at the BS associated with the k-th user; $\mathbf{s} = [\mathbf{s}_1^T,\cdots,\mathbf{s}_K^T]^T \in \mathbb{C}^{KN_s \times 1}$ is the transmitted signal, with $\mathbf{s}_k \in \mathbb{C}^{N_s \times 1}$ is the signal intended for the k-th user, which satisfies $E(\mathbf{s}\mathbf{s}^H) = I_{KN_s}$. The power constraint at the BS is $\sum_{j=1}^{K} \text{tr}\left(\mathbf{F}_{RF}\mathbf{F}_{BB,j}\mathbf{F}_{BB,j}^H\mathbf{F}_{RF}^H\right) = 1$. The combined signal at the k-th user $\mathbf{y}_k$ can be expressed as

$$\mathbf{y}_k = \mathbf{W}_{BB,k}^H\mathbf{W}_{RF,k}^H\mathbf{H}_k\mathbf{F}_{RF}\mathbf{F}_{BB,k}\mathbf{s}_k + \mathbf{W}_{BB,k}^H\mathbf{W}_{RF,k}^H\mathbf{H}_k$$

$$\cdot \mathbf{F}_{RF}\sum_{h=1,h\neq k}^{K}\mathbf{F}_{BB,h}\mathbf{s}_h + \mathbf{W}_{BB,k}^H\mathbf{W}_{RF,k}^H\mathbf{n}_k, \tag{2}$$

where $\mathbf{W}_{BB,k} \in \mathbb{C}^{N_{rf} \times N_s}$ denotes the digital combiner at the k-th user; $\mathbf{W}_{RF,k} \in \mathbb{C}^{M \times N_{rf}}$ is the analog combiner at the k-th user; $\mathbf{H}_k \in \mathbb{C}^{M \times N}$ is the channel matrix from the BS to the k-th user, and $\mathbf{n}_k \sim \mathcal{CN}(\mathbf{0}, \sigma_{\mathbf{n}_k}^2 \mathbf{I}_M)$ is the corresponding complex additive white Gaussian noise (AWGN).

Notice that because of the sub-connected structure, analog beamformers are constrained as follows:

$$\mathbf{F}_{RF} = [\mathbf{f}_{rf,1}, \cdots, \mathbf{f}_{rf,KN_{rf}}], \tag{3}$$

$$\mathbf{W}_{RF,k} = [\mathbf{w}_{rf,k,1}, \cdots, \mathbf{w}_{rf,k,N_{rf}}], \tag{4}$$

where $\mathbf{f}_{rf,p} \in \mathbb{C}^{N \times 1}, p \in \{1, \cdots, KN_{rf}\}$ with non-zero elements in $[(p-1)M_s+1]$-th to pM_s-th element, $\mathbf{w}_{rf,k,q} \in \mathbb{C}^{M \times 1}, q \in \{1, \cdots, N_{rf}\}$ with non-zero elements in $[(q-1)M_d+1]$-th to qM_d-th element. $M_s = \frac{N}{KN_{rf}}$ and $M_d = \frac{M}{N_{rf}}$ are the number of antennas connected to each RF chain at the BS and the k-th user, respectively. In this paper, we assume that M_d of each user is the same for simplicity. As the analog beamformers are implemented by phase shifters, none-zero elements in analog beamforming matrices satisfy that $|\mathbf{f}_{rf,p}^{(c)}| = \sqrt{\frac{1}{M_s}}, |\mathbf{w}_{rf,q}^{(d)}| = \sqrt{\frac{1}{M_d}}$, for $\forall c, d$.

The mmWave channel with a uniform linear array can be formulated as follows

$$\mathbf{H} = \sqrt{\frac{NM}{N_p}} \sum_{m=1}^{N_p} \alpha_m \mathbf{a}_r(\theta_m) \mathbf{a}_t(\phi_m)^H, \tag{5}$$

where N_p is the number of scattering paths; α_m denotes the complex gain of the m-th scattering path; $\mathbf{a}_r$ and $\mathbf{a}_t$ denote the receive and transmit array response vectors with the angle of arrival (AoA) θ_m and the angle of departure (AoD) ϕ_m, respectively. The channel can be rewritten compactly as follows

$$\mathbf{H} = \mathbf{A}_r \mathbf{D} \mathbf{A}_t^H, \tag{6}$$

where $\mathbf{A}_r = [\mathbf{a}_r(\theta_1), \cdots, \mathbf{a}_r(\theta_{N_p})]$ and $\mathbf{A}_t = [\mathbf{a}_t(\phi_1), \cdots, \mathbf{a}_t(\phi_{N_p})]$ are the receive and transmit array response vector sets, respectively. $\mathbf{D}$ is a diagonal matrix, with the m-th diagonal element being $\sqrt{\frac{NM}{N_p}} \alpha_m$. The relationship between the actual channel and the estimated channel can be expressed as [13]

$$\bar{\mathbf{H}} = \mathbf{H} + \mathbf{N}\mathbf{\Phi}, \tag{7}$$

where $\mathbf{\Phi}$ is the estimation processing matrix. $\mathbf{N} \sim \mathcal{CN}(\mathbf{0}, \sigma_e^2 \mathbf{I})$ denotes the AWGN during the training period. The channel model in (7) applies to all the channels in the system, we drop the subscripts here for ease of notation. For more details about the correlated channel model, please refer to [13].

Notice that, the estimation algorithms applicable for mmWave channels will result in correlated errors, as described in (7). So the existing robust designs based on uncorrelated channel model in [12] are not applicable now. In the Sect. 4, the numerical results will show the loss of performance due to the mismatch of the channel model.

3   Robust Hybrid Beamforming Designs

In this section, a two-stage scheme is developed to design hybrid beamformers. In the first stage, the analog beamformers are designed to maximize estimated RF-to-RF channel gains. In the second stage, the digital beamformers are optimized by utilizing the equivalence between the maximization of mutual information and the minimization of WMMSE.

3.1   Analog Beamforming Designs

The RF-to-RF estimated channel at the k-th user can be expressed as

$$\hat{\mathbf{H}}_k = \mathbf{W}_{RF,k}^H \bar{\mathbf{H}}_k \mathbf{F}_{RF}. \tag{8}$$

The gain of the i-th eigenmode in the k-th RF-to-RF estimated channel can be express as

$$\left| \mathbf{w}_{rf,k,i}^H \bar{\mathbf{u}}_{k,i} \bar{\mathbf{v}}_{k,i}^H \mathbf{f}_{rf,(k-1)N_{rf}+i} \right|, \tag{9}$$

where $i \in \{1, \cdots, N_{rf}\}$; $\mathbf{u}_{k,i}$ and $\mathbf{v}_{k,i}$ are the i-th columns in left and right singular matrices i.e., $\bar{\mathbf{U}}_k$ and $\bar{\mathbf{V}}_k$, of $\bar{\mathbf{H}}_k$, with ordered singular value decomposition $\bar{\mathbf{H}}_k = \bar{\mathbf{U}}_k \bar{\mathbf{\Lambda}}_k \bar{\mathbf{V}}_k^H$. The analog beamformers are design as follows

$$\mathbf{w}_{rf,k,i}[(i-1)M_d + 1 : iM_d] =$$
$$\sqrt{\frac{1}{M_d}} \cdot \text{phase}\left\{ \bar{\mathbf{U}}_k[(i-1)M_d + 1 : iM_d, i] \right\}, \tag{10}$$

$$\mathbf{f}_{rf,(k-1)N_{rf}+i}[((k-1)N_{rf} + i - 1)M_s + 1 :$$
$$((k-1)N_{rf} + i)M_s] =$$
$$\sqrt{\frac{1}{M_s}} \cdot \text{phase}\left\{ \bar{\mathbf{V}}_k[(i-1)M_s + 1 : iM_s, i] \right\},$$
$$k \in \{1, \cdots, K\}. \tag{11}$$

Proof. $\mathbf{w}_{rf,k,i}$ and $\mathbf{f}_{rf,(k-1)N_{rf}+i}$ can be expressed as

$$\mathbf{w}_{rf,k,i} = \sqrt{\frac{1}{M_d}} [\mathbf{0}_{1 \times (i-1)M_d}, e^{j\theta_1^{(k,i)}}, \cdots, e^{j\theta_{M_d}^{(k,i)}},$$
$$\mathbf{0}_{1 \times M - iM_d}]^T,$$

$$\mathbf{f}_{rf,(k-1)N_{rf}+i} = \sqrt{\frac{1}{M_s}} [\mathbf{0}_{1 \times (k-1)N_{rf}+i-1)M_s}, e^{j\phi_1^{(k,i)}},$$
$$\cdots, e^{j\phi_{M_s}^{(k,i)}}, \mathbf{0}_{1 \times N-((k-1)N_{rf}+i)M_s}]^T. \tag{12}$$

The polar forms of $\bar{\mathbf{u}}_{k,i}$ and $\bar{\mathbf{v}}_{k,i}$ are $\bar{\mathbf{u}}_{k,i} = [\gamma_1 e^{j\alpha_1^{(k,i)}}, \cdots, \gamma_M e^{j\alpha_M^{(k,i)}}]^T$, $\bar{\mathbf{v}}_{k,i} = [\rho_1 e^{j\beta_1^{(k,i)}}, \cdots, \rho_N e^{j\beta_N^{(k,i)}}]^T$. Then, the gain of the i-th eigenmode in the k-th RF-to-RF estimated channel can be expressed as

$$\left| \mathbf{w}_{rf,k,i}^H \bar{\mathbf{u}}_{k,i} \bar{\mathbf{v}}_{k,i}^H \mathbf{f}_{rf,(k-1)N_{rf}+i} \right| =$$

$$\left| \sqrt{\frac{1}{M_d}} \sum_{f=(i-1)M_d+1}^{iM_d} \gamma_f e^{(\theta_f^{(k,i)} - \alpha_f^{(k,i)})} \right|$$

$$\cdot \left| \sqrt{\frac{1}{M_s}} \sum_{g=((k-1)N_{rf}+i-1)M_s+1}^{((k-1)N_{rf}+i)M_s} \rho_g e^{(\beta_g^{(k,i)} - \phi_g^{(k,i)})} \right|. \tag{13}$$

According to the Cauchy-Schwartz inequality, we have

$$\left| \sqrt{\frac{1}{M_d}} \sum_{f=(i-1)M_d+1}^{iM_d} \gamma_f e^{(\theta_f^{(k,i)} - \alpha_f^{(k,i)})} \right|^2$$

$$\leq \frac{1}{M_d} \sum_{f=(i-1)M_d+1}^{iM_d} |\gamma_f|^2 \sum_{f=(i-1)M_d+1}^{iM_d} \left| e^{(\theta_f^{(k,i)} - \alpha_f^{(k,i)})} \right|^2$$

$$= \frac{1}{M_d} \sum_{f=(i-1)M_d+1}^{iM_d} |\gamma_f|^2. \tag{14}$$

The equality holds when $\theta_f^{(k,i)} = \alpha_f^{(k,i)}$, $\forall f$. Similarly, $|\bar{\mathbf{v}}_{k,i}^H \mathbf{f}_{rf,(k-1)N_{rf}+i}|$ has the maximum when $\beta_g^{(k,i)} = \phi_g^{(k,i)}$, $\forall g$. So we have the conclusion in (10) and (11).

3.2   Digital Beamforming Designs

After determining the analog beamformers, the problem is reduced to optimization of low-dimensional digital beamformers. After fixing the analog beamformers, the k-th effective channel can be constructed as

$$\tilde{\mathbf{H}} = \hat{\mathbf{H}}_k + \mathbf{\Sigma}_k \mathbf{N}_k \mathbf{\Psi}_k \tag{15}$$

where $\mathbf{\Sigma}_k = \mathbf{W}_{RF,k}^H$; $\mathbf{\Psi}_k = \mathbf{\Phi}_k \mathbf{F}_{RF}$. Substituting (15) into (2), the k-th combined signal can be rewritten as

$$\mathbf{y}_k = \mathbf{W}_{BB,k}^H \tilde{\mathbf{H}}_k \mathbf{F}_{BB,k} \mathbf{s}_k + \mathbf{W}_{BB,k}^H \tilde{\mathbf{H}}_k \sum_{h=1,h\neq k}^{K} \mathbf{F}_{BB,h} \mathbf{s}_h$$
$$+ \mathbf{W}_{BB,k}^H \tilde{\mathbf{n}}_k, \tag{16}$$

where $\tilde{\mathbf{n}}_k = \mathbf{W}_{RF,k}^H \mathbf{n}_k$. To simplify the design, the minimum mean square error (MMSE) receiver is adopted, which is given by

$$\mathbf{W}_{BB,k} = \left[\hat{\mathbf{H}}_k \left(\sum_{j=1}^{K} \mathbf{F}_{BB,j} \mathbf{F}_{BB,j}^H \right) \hat{\mathbf{H}}_k^H + \mathbf{Q}_k \right]^{-1} \\ \cdot \hat{\mathbf{H}}_k \mathbf{F}_{BB,k}, \qquad (17)$$

where $\mathbf{Q}_k = \sum_{j=1}^{K} \sigma_e^2 \mathrm{tr} \left(\mathbf{\Psi}_k \mathbf{F}_{BB,j} \mathbf{F}_{BB,j}^H \mathbf{\Psi}_k^H \right) \mathbf{\Sigma}_k \mathbf{\Sigma}_k^H + \mathbf{R}_{\tilde{n}_k}$ is obtained by utilizing Lemma 3 in [14]; $\mathbf{R}_{\tilde{n}_k} = E \left(\tilde{\mathbf{n}}_k \tilde{\mathbf{n}}_k^H \right) = \sigma_{\mathbf{n}_k}^2 \mathbf{W}_{RF,k}^H \mathbf{W}_{RF,k}$.

Then, the digital precoder at the BS is designed to maximize the lower bound of average mutual information, which is given by [15]

$$I_{lb} \left(\mathbf{s}_k, \tilde{\mathbf{y}}_k \right) = -\log \det \mathbf{M}_k, \qquad (18)$$

where $\tilde{\mathbf{y}}_k$ denotes the received signal before combining at the k-th user; $\mathbf{M}_k$ is the MMSE matrix of the k-th user, which can be formulated as

$$\mathbf{M}_k = \mathbf{W}_{BB,k}^H \left[\hat{\mathbf{H}}_k \sum_{j=1}^{K} \left(\mathbf{F}_{BB,j} \mathbf{F}_{BB,j}^H \right) \hat{\mathbf{H}}_k^H + \mathbf{Q}_k \right] \mathbf{W}_{BB,k} \\ - \mathbf{W}_{BB,k}^H \hat{\mathbf{H}}_k \mathbf{F}_{BB,k} - \mathbf{F}_{BB,k}^H \hat{\mathbf{H}}_k^H \mathbf{W}_{BB,k} + \mathbf{I}_{N_s}. \qquad (19)$$

The optimization problem can be formulated as

$$\max_{\{\mathbf{F}_{BB,j}\}} \sum_{j=1}^{K} I_{lb} \left(\mathbf{s}_j, \tilde{\mathbf{y}}_j \right) \qquad (20)$$

$$\text{s.t.} \sum_{j=1}^{K} \mathrm{tr} \left(\mathbf{F}_{RF} \mathbf{F}_{BB,j} \mathbf{F}_{BB,j}^H \mathbf{F}_{RF}^H \right) = 1.$$

It is still difficult to directly solve the above problem. Therefore, the equivalence between the maximization of mutual information and the minimization of WMMSE is utilized in this paper. The minimization problem of WMMSE is formulated as follows

$$\min_{\{\mathbf{F}_{BB,j}, \mathbf{V}_j\}} \sum_{j=1}^{K} \mathrm{tr} \left(\mathbf{V}_j \mathbf{M}_j \right) \qquad (21)$$

$$\text{s.t.} \sum_{j=1}^{K} \mathrm{tr} \left(\mathbf{F}_{RF} \mathbf{F}_{BB,j} \mathbf{F}_{BB,j}^H \mathbf{F}_{RF}^H \right) = 1,$$

where $\mathbf{V}_j$ is a constant weight matrix. Notice that, by setting

$$\mathbf{V}_j = \mathbf{M}_j^{-1}, \qquad (22)$$

the Karush-Kuhn-Tucker (KKT) conditions of problems (20) and (21) can be satisfied simultaneously.

Proof. Taking the derivative of $-\sum_{j=1}^{K} I_{lb}\left(\mathbf{s}_j, \tilde{\mathbf{y}}_j\right)$ w.r.t $\mathbf{F}_{BB,k}$, we have

$$\frac{\partial\left(-\sum_{j=1}^{K} I_{lb}\left(\mathbf{s}_j, \tilde{\mathbf{y}}_j\right)\right)}{\partial \mathbf{F}_{BB,k}} = -\frac{\partial \sum_{j=1}^{K} \operatorname{tr}\left(\mathbf{M}_j \partial \mathbf{M}_j^{-1}\right)}{\partial \mathbf{F}_{BB,k}}, \tag{23}$$

where $\partial \log \det \mathbf{X} = \operatorname{tr}\left(\mathbf{X}^{-1} \partial \mathbf{X}\right)$ is utilized. Similarly, by taking the derivative of $\sum_{j=1}^{K} \operatorname{tr}\left(\mathbf{V}_j \mathbf{M}_j\right)$ w.r.t $\mathbf{F}_{BB,k}$, we have

$$\frac{\partial\left(\sum_{j=1}^{K} \operatorname{tr}\left(\mathbf{V}_j \mathbf{M}_j\right)\right)}{\partial \mathbf{F}_{BB,k}} = \frac{\sum_{j=1}^{K} \operatorname{tr}\left(\partial\left(\left(\mathbf{M}_j^{-1}\right)^{-1}\right) \mathbf{V}_j\right)}{\partial \mathbf{F}_{BB,k}}$$

$$\overset{(a)}{=} -\frac{\sum_{j=1}^{K} \operatorname{tr}\left(\mathbf{M}_j \partial\left(\mathbf{M}_j^{-1}\right) \mathbf{M}_j \mathbf{V}_j\right)}{\partial \mathbf{F}_{BB,k}}, \tag{24}$$

where $\partial \mathbf{X}^{-1} = -\mathbf{X}^{-1} \partial(\mathbf{X}) \mathbf{X}^{-1}$ is utilized in (a). When $\mathbf{V}_j = \mathbf{M}_j^{-1}$, The equivalence of (23) and (24) can be obtained. Considering that the constraints in (20) and (21) are identical, we conclude that the KKT conditions of the two optimization problems can be satisfied simultaneously.

We propose an alternating algorithm to solve the WMMSE problem. By fixing $\mathbf{F}_{BB,h}$, $h \neq k$, the corresponding Lagrange function of solve $\mathbf{F}_{BB,k}$ can be written as follows

$$L_{\mathbf{F}_{BB,k}} = \sum_{j=1}^{K} \operatorname{tr}\left(\mathbf{V}_j \mathbf{M}_j\right) +$$

$$\lambda\left[\sum_{i=1}^{K} \operatorname{tr}\left(\mathbf{F}_{RF} \mathbf{F}_{BB,j} \mathbf{F}_{BB,j}^{H} \mathbf{F}_{RF}^{H}\right) - 1\right], \tag{25}$$

where λ is the Lagrange multiplier. By setting the partial derivative of $L_{\mathbf{F}_{BB,k}}$ to zero. $\mathbf{F}_{BB,k}$ can be solved as

$$\mathbf{F}_{BB,k} = \left\{\sum_{j=1}^{K}\left[\hat{\mathbf{H}}_j^{H} \mathbf{W}_{BB,j} \mathbf{V}_j \mathbf{W}_{BB,j}^{H} \hat{\mathbf{H}}_j + \sigma_e^2 \operatorname{tr}\left(\mathbf{V}_j\right.\right.\right.$$

$$\left.\left.\cdot \mathbf{W}_{BB,j}^{H} \Sigma_j \Sigma_j^{H} \mathbf{W}_{BB,j}\right) \boldsymbol{\Psi}_j^{H} \boldsymbol{\Psi}_j\right] + \lambda \mathbf{F}_{RF}^{H} \mathbf{F}_{RF}\right\}^{-1}$$

$$\cdot \hat{\mathbf{H}}_k^{H} \mathbf{W}_{BB,k} \mathbf{V}_k. \tag{26}$$

Notice that, the optimum λ must be positive and the power constraint is a decreasing function of λ for $\lambda > 0$. Therefore, one-dimensional search techniques can be utilized to λ. We adopt the bisection method by setting the minimum Lagrange multiplier as $\lambda_{min} = 0$ and the maximum Lagrange multiplier as a pre-defined value λ_{max}. By substituting λ into (26), $\mathbf{F}_{BB,k}$ can be obtained. The steps of the proposed robust beamforming scheme for multi-user systems are summarized in Algorithm 1.

Algorithm 1. Proposed robust hybrid beamforming design

Require: Construct $\mathbf{F}_{BB}$ randomly; set λ_{min}, λ_{max}, and the termination criteria ϵ_1 and ϵ_2;

1: Calculate analog precoders $\mathbf{F}_{RF,k}$ for all k according to (3);
2: Calculate analog combiners $\mathbf{W}_{RF,k}^{H}$ for all k according to (4);
3: **repeat**
4:     Update digital combiners $\mathbf{W}_{BB,k}$ for all k according to (17);
5:     Update MMSE matrix $\mathbf{M}_k$ for all k according to (19);
6:     Update weighted matrix $\mathbf{V}_k = \mathbf{M}_k^{-1}$ for all k;
7:     **while** $\lambda_{max} - \lambda_{min} > \epsilon_1$ **do**
8:         setting $\lambda = \frac{\lambda_{max}+\lambda_{min}}{2}$;
9:         calculate $\mathbf{F}_{BB,k}$ for all k according to (26);
10:         **if** $\sum_{j=1}^{K} \text{tr}\left(\mathbf{F}_{RF}\mathbf{F}_{BB,j}\mathbf{F}_{BB,j}^{H}\mathbf{F}_{RF}^{H}\right) < 1$ **then**
11:             $\lambda_{max} = \lambda$;
12:         **else**
13:             $\lambda_{min} = \lambda$;
14:         **end if**
15:     **end while**
16: **until** The change of $\sum_{j=1}^{K} \text{tr}\left(\mathbf{V}_j\mathbf{M}_j\right)$ is below ϵ_2.

Since the constant weighted matrix $\mathbf{V}_k$ is updated with each iteration, it does not ensure that the objective function decreases monotonously. We are unable to directly demonstrate the convergence of the proposed algorithm. Fortunately, its convergence can be proved by proving the convergence of an equivalent optimization problem as follows

$$\min_{\{\mathbf{F}_{BB,j},\mathbf{V}_j\}} \sum_{j=1}^{K} [\text{tr}\left(\mathbf{V}_j\mathbf{M}_j\right) - \log\det\mathbf{V}_j] \tag{27}$$

$$\text{s.t.} \sum_{j=1}^{K} \text{tr}\left(\mathbf{F}_{RF}\mathbf{F}_{BB,j}\mathbf{F}_{BB,j}^{H}\mathbf{F}_{RF}^{H}\right) = 1.$$

When $\mathbf{F}_{BB,j}$ and $\mathbf{V}_j$ are fixed, optimizing (27) w.r.t $\mathbf{W}_{BB,j}$ gives the same result as step 5 in Algorithm 1. Similarly, by fixed other variables, optimizing (27) w.r.t $\mathbf{V}_j$ and $\mathbf{F}_{BB,j}$ gives the same results as steps 6 and 9 in Algorithm 1, respectively. Thus, the objective function in (27) decreases monotonically. A similar procedure was adopted in [16] to prove the monotonous convergence of equivalent problems, in which traditional fully digital transceivers are optimized iteratively under perfect CSI assumptions. According to [16], the objective function in (27) has a lower bound, so the convergence of Algorithm 1 to a local minimum can be guaranteed.

4   Simulation Results

In this section, the sum rate and energy efficiency of the proposed beamforming scheme are evaluated for different configurations. The number of users is

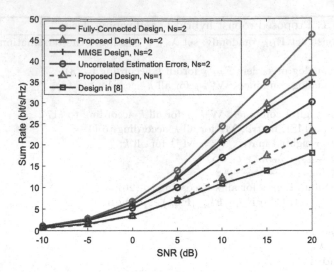

Fig. 2. Sum rate comparison at different SNR.

$K = 4$. The propagation paths for different channels are all set as $N_p = 4$. The elements of mmWave channels, i.e., complex gains of propagation paths, and AWGN matrices obey complex Gaussian distribution. The AoAs and AoDs follow Laplacian distribution with uniformly distributed mean angles over $[-\frac{\pi}{2}, \frac{\pi}{2}]$. The angular spread is restricted to $10°$. The variances of estimation errors for different channels are assumed to be identical for simplicity. The signal-to-noise ratio (SNR) is defined as $10\lg\frac{1}{\sigma_n^2}$. The stopping criteria in Algorithm 1 are set as $\epsilon_1 = 10^{-8}$, $\epsilon_2 = 10^{-4}$. λ_{min} and λ_{max} are set to 0 and 50, respectively. All simulations are averaged over 1000 channel realizations.

Figure 2 shows the sum rate comparison between the proposed design and other existing designs. The fully-connected structure design is obtained by replacing sub-connected structures in the proposed design with fully-connected structures. The MMSE design minimize MSE by replacing the weighted matrix with an identity matrix. The design based on uncorrelated estimation errors is obtained by forcing the covariance matrices to be identity matrices in the proposed design. The antenna configurations are set as $N = 64$, $M = 8$, $\sigma_e^2 = 0.5$, $N_s = N_{rf}$. As we can see, the proposed design is only inferior to the fully-connected design. The proposed design outperforms the MMSE design by 5.28% at SNR = 15 dB. The performance gap caused by model mismatch is quite large. The proposed design outperforms the design based on uncorrelated estimation errors by 25.6% at SNR = 10 dB. Besides, the performance of the non-robust joint design with sub-connected structures in [8], which only applies to single data stream users is also illustrated in the figure. We can see the performance improvement is significant as the number of data streams increases. When the number of data streams reduced to one, the proposed design still outperforms the design in [8] by 27.6% .

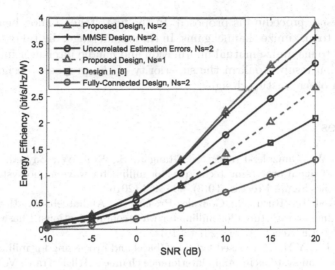

Fig. 3. Energy efficiency at different SNR.

Figure 3 shows the energy efficiency comparison of the designs in Fig. 2. The power consumption at the BS side can be expressed as [2]

$$P_{fully} = N(KN_{rf} + 1)P_{PA} + NKN_{rf}P_{PS} + P_{BB} + KN_{rf}$$
$$\cdot (P_{RFC} + P_{DAC}),$$
$$P_{sub} = NP_{PA} + NP_{PS} + P_{BB} + KN_{rf}(P_{RFC} + P_{DAC}),$$

where P_{PA} denotes the power of power phase amplifiers; P_{PS} denotes the power of phase shifters. P_{BB} denotes the power of baseband processing; P_{RFC} denotes the power of RF chains; P_{DAC} denotes the power of digital-to-analog converts. The power consumption at the user side can be obtained by corresponding substitutions. The value of each component follows [2]. As we can see, although the fully-connected design provides higher sum rate, its energy efficiency is the worst. The sub-connected designs provide better energy efficiency due to the reduced number of phase shifters. The proposed design outperforms the fully-connected design by 226% at SNR = 15 dB. Besides, the proposed design has the best energy efficiency and outperforms the MMSE design and the design based on uncorrelated estimation errors by 5.3% and 25.7% respectively at SNR = 15 dB. Furthermore, with the increase of the number of data streams, the system has higher energy efficiency. Even if the number of data streams is reduced to one, the proposed design outperforms the design in [8] by 24.4% at SNR = 15 dB.

5   Conclusion

Correlated estimation errors and sub-connected structures are considered to design a robust beamforming scheme for MU mmWave systems in this paper. A two-stage design procedure is proposed. In the first stage, analog beamformers are designed to maximize channel gains. In the second stage, digital beamformers are designed to maximize mutual information and handle inter-user interference. The simulation results confirm the superiority of the proposed design in comparison with other existing designs.

References

1. Heath, R.W., Gonzalez-Prelcic, N., Rangan, S., Roh, W., Sayeed, A.M.: An overview of signal processing techniques for millimeter wave mimo systems. IEEE J. Sel. Topics Signal Process. **10**(3), 436–453 (2016)
2. Mendez-Rial, R., Rusu, C., Gonzalez-Prelcic, N., Alkhateeb, A., Heath, R.W.: Hybrid mimo architectures for millimeter wave communications: Phase shifters or switches? IEEE Access **4**, 247–267 (2016)
3. Kim, M., Lee, Y.H.: Mse-based hybrid rf/baseband processing for millimeter-wave communication systems in mimo interference channels. IEEE Trans. Veh. Technol. **64**(6), 2714–2720 (2015)
4. Nguyen, D.H.N., Le, L.B., Le-Ngoc, T., Heath, R.W.: Hybrid mmse precoding and combining designs for mmwave multiuser systems. IEEE Access **5**, 19167–19181 (2017)
5. Wu, X., Liu, D., Yin, F.: Hybrid beamforming for multi-user massive mimo systems. IEEE Trans. Commun. **66**(9), 3879–3891 (2018)
6. Ha, V.N., Nguyen, D.H.N., Frigon, J.F.: System energy-efficient hybrid beamforming for mmwave multi-user systems. IEEE Trans. Green Commun. Netw. **4**(4), 1010–1023 (2020)
7. Zhang, Y., Du, J., Chen, Y., Li, X., Rabie, K.M., Kharel, R.: Near-optimal design for hybrid beamforming in mmwave massive multi-user mimo systems. IEEE Access **8**, 129153–129168 (2020)
8. Li, A., Masouros, C.: Hybrid analog-digital millimeter-wave mu-mimo transmission with virtual path selection. IEEE Commun. Lett. **21**(2), 438–441 (2017)
9. Garcia-Rodriguez, A., Venkateswaran, V., Rulikowski, P., Masouros, C.: Hybrid analog-digital precoding revisited under realistic rf modeling. IEEE Wireless Commun. Lett. **5**(5), 528–531 (2016)
10. Zhao, L., Ng, D.W.K., Yuan, J.: Multi-user precoding and channel estimation for hybrid millimeter wave systems. IEEE J. Sel. Areas Commun. **35**(7), 1576–1590 (2017)
11. Jiang, L., Jafarkhani, H.: Multi-user analog beamforming in millimeter wave mimo systems based on path angle information. IEEE Trans. Wireless. Commun. **18**(1), 608–619 (2019)
12. Zheng, L., Liu, D., Wen, Z., Zou, J.: Robust beamforming for multi-user miso full-duplex swipt system under non-linear energy harvesting model. IEEE Access **9**, 14387–14397 (2021)
13. Luo, Z., Zhao, L., Liu, H., Li, Y.: Robust hybrid beamforming in millimeter wave systems with closed-form least-square solutions. IEEE Wireless Commun. Lett. **10**(1), 156–160 (2021)
14. Zhang, R., Leung, S.H., Luo, Z., Wang, H.: Precoding design for correlated mimo-af relay networks with statistical channel state information. IEEE Trans. Signal Process. **66**(22), 5902–5916 (2018)

15. Xing, C., Ma, S., Fei, Z., Wu, Y.C., Poor, H.V.: A general robust linear transceiver design for multi-hop amplifyand-forward mimo relaying systems. IEEE Trans. Signal Process. **61**(5), 1196–1209 (2013)
16. Christensen, S.S., Agarwal, R., De Carvalho, E., Cioffi, J.M.: Weighted sum-rate maximization using weighted mmse for mimo-bc beamforming design. IEEE Trans. Wireless Commun. **7**(12), 4792–4799 (2008)

Based on Content Relevance Caching Strategy in Information-Centric Network

Xueqin Xiong[1]($\boxtimes$), Zhanjun Liu[1], Yuan Zhang[2], and Qianbin Chen[1]

[1] School of Communication and Information Engineering,
Chongqing University of Posts and Telecommunications, Chongqing, China
1710382196@qq.com
[2] School of Computer and Internet of Things,
Chongqing Institute of Engineering, Chongqing 400056, China

Abstract. Information-Centric Networking (ICN) replaces identifying endpoints with identifying content. One of the most common and important features of ICN architectures is in-network caching, which can significantly reduce content request latency and improve user quality of service(QoS) and network performance. Therefore, how to efficiently utilize cache resources and optimize cache performance has become one of the research hotspots in ICN. This paper proposes a local popularity caching strategy based on content relevance caching (CRC). In this strategy, the local popularity of the content is calculated based on the relevance of the content requested. Routing nodes make caching decisions based on local popularity. In the forwarding process of the interest packet, the cache node ID table in the interest packet is updated according to the local popularity, and the cache decision is made. In the backhaul process of the data packet, content caching and replacement strategy need to be performed according to the caching parameters and local popularity parameters. In cache replacement, if the remaining cache capacity of the current routing node cannot satisfy the required capacity of the cached content, the local popularity of the content needs to be used to replace the cached content. In this way, repeatedly requested content ends up being cached in routing nodes closer to the user. The simulation results show that CRC has better network performance than several other classical caching strategy.

Keywords: Information-Center Networking · Content Relevance · Local Popularity · Caching Strategy

1 Introduction

With the development of information technology, the traffic in the network continues to increase. The number of users who obtain information from the network

Q. Chen—This work was supported by the Chongqing Municipal Education Commission under Grant KJQN201900645.
Chongqing University of Posts and Telecommunications Doctoral Start-up Fund Project (A2019017).

F. Gao et al. (Eds.): ChinaCom 2022, LNICST 500, pp. 122–134, 2023.
https://doi.org/10.1007/978-3-031-34790-0_10

is gradually increasing, and users are more concerned about the content itself [1]. This has led to the Information-Centric Networking (ICN) [2] architecture as the research direction for future networks. ICN emerged as an architecture that includes caching at the edge of the network. Unlike traditional methods, users in ICN request content directly from the network only by their Named Data Object (NDO) names [3]. As shown in Fig. 1, ICN includes cache management modules in all routing nodes to realize the decoupling of content and address [4], and each routing node in the network can selectively store a copy of the content [5]. When the same content request occurs again, the corresponding content can be returned directly from the routing node without the need to obtain it from the source server. However, the cache capacity of each routing node is limited, and only reasonable cache deployment [6,7] can improve the cache utilization of nodes.

The current caching strategies in ICN include: Leave Copy Everywhere (LCE) [8], Leave Copy Down (LCD) [9], Probability [10], ProbCache [11] etc. LCE is the routing node caches every piece of content it passes through. It does not consider the influence of content popularity and network topology, which will lead to frequent replacement of cached content in routing nodes, resulting in low cache utilization of routing nodes. LCD is next-hop routing node that caches content at the hit routing node, which helps to gradually push popular content caches to edge routing nodes. It considers the network topology, however, popular content needs to move many times to reach the edge routing node, so the convergence speed is slow. Probability is that the routing node caches the arriving content with a fixed probability. It without considering the distance between the user and the routing node. Therefore, the QoS for users cannot be improved. ProbCache is the probability that content can be cached to a routing node inversely proportional to the distance between the routing node and the content requester. It enables content to be quickly cached to routing nodes closer to the user. The research found that in practical applications, there is a relevance between the content requested. However, some existing caching mechanisms [12] do not consider the relevance between the content requested.

Aiming at some existing caching mechanisms, this paper proposes a caching decision based on content relevance caching (CRC). Considering the relevance between the contents requested, the local popularity of the content is calculated according to the relevance between the contents [13]. Therefore, according to the local popularity of the content, the routing node decides whether to cache the content requested. During the forwarding of interest packet, make caching decisions based on local popularity and update the table of cache node IDs in interest packet. In the process of backhauling data packet, content caching and replacement strategy need to be performed according to cache parameters and local popularity parameters. In cache replacement, if the remaining cache capacity of the current routing node cannot satisfy the required capacity of the cached content, the local popularity of the content needs to be used to replace the cached content. This paper considers the user's QoS from the content request delay in the network [14,15], and the content copy is cached in the node closer

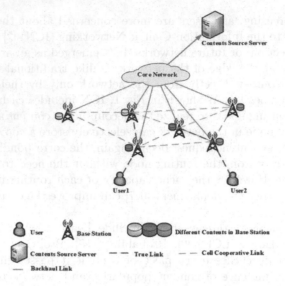

Fig. 1. Cache model in ICN.

to the user side, so as to realize the network performance and improve the user's QoS [16].

In this paper, it is assumed that all routers in the network have the same computing power and the same cache capacity. Furthermore, to simplify the model, this paper considers everything contents in the network to have the same capacity. Considering the content service model of the network, it is assumed that the requests sent by users satisfy the Poisson distribution, and the popularity of the content satisfies the Zipf-like distribution [17].

2   Cache Model and Modified Structure

2.1   Cache Model

In order to simultaneously satisfy the user's QoS and improve the cache utilization, the optimal cache location needs to be adopted when content caching. The optimization problem model is derived for the content cache location problem as follows.

$$\min \sum_{c \in C} \sum_{n \in N} d_n^c \left(1 - S_n^c\right)$$

$$\text{s.t} \begin{cases} \sum_{c \in C} S_n^c < C_n & \forall n \in N \\ S_n^c = \{0, 1\} & \forall n \in N, \forall c \in C \end{cases} \tag{1}$$

where d_n^c represents the distance from the content request initiated by node n to the routing node that provides content c. The S_n^c represents whether node n

caches content c, the value is 0 or 1. The content cached by each node cannot exceed the cache capacity of the routing node itself. The caching strategy proposed in this paper is a caching strategy based on content relevance, and the caching decision is made in the forwarding stage of the interest packet. In order to make the content relevance-based caching strategy proposed in this paper feasible, it is necessary to add the cache routing node ID table field to the interest packet and data packet, and add the cache parameter S_n^c and the popularity parameter pop to the routing node.

When the request interest packet sent by the user arrives at the routing node, the cache parameter S_n^c in the routing node needs to be queried first. If $S_n^c = 1$, it means that the content has been cached in the routing node, and the data packet is returned directly. If $S_n^c = 0$, it means that the routing node does not cache the content, and the local cache cannot satisfy the user's request. Continue to forward the interest packet upwards. In the forwarding process, a cache decision needs to be made in order to update the cache ID table in the interest packet. The caching decision proposed in this paper is a caching decision based on a greedy algorithm. If the remaining cache space of the current routing node is sufficient, the arriving content can be directly cached. At this time, the ID of the routing node needs to be added to the cache node ID table in the interest packet, the cache parameter S_n^c corresponding to the cache information table in the routing node is set to 1, and the interest packet continues to be forwarded upward. If the remaining space of the current routing node is insufficient, it is necessary to determine whether to add the ID of the current routing node to the interest packet after updating the local popularity. Assuming that $ID = n1, n2...$ represents the list of nodes on the forwarding path of the content request that have decided to cache the data packet, there are:

$$ID^c = \begin{cases} ID^c \cup \{n\} & pop_n^c > \min\left(\{ \ pop \ _n^i \mid i \in C_n\}\right) \\ ID^c & \text{otherwise} \end{cases} \tag{2}$$

where C_n represents the set of all content that have been cached in routing node n. The i represents the least popular content cached in the current routing node. The pop_n^i represents the content that has been cached in routing node the minimum popularity of the current routing node. If the local popularity c of the currently requested content is greater than the minimum local popularity among the cached content in the current routing node. Then the current routing ID of the node needs to be added to the node ID table of the cached interest packet. Set the cache parameter S_n^c corresponding to the cache information table in the routing node to 1, and the cache parameter of the modified content i to 0. Continue to forward interest packet up.

2.2 Modified Interest Packet, Data Packet and Routing Node Models

The modified the fromat of interest packet is shown in Fig. 2(a), the fromat of data packet is shown in Fig. 2(b), and the structure of the routing node is shown in Fig. 3.

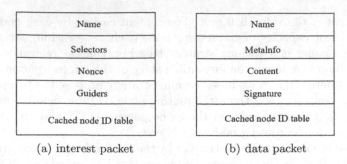

(a) interest packet   (b) data packet

Fig. 2. Modified packet of interest and data

Content Name	Cache parameter	Popularity
Name	S_n^c	Pop

Fig. 3. Structure of the modified routing node.

3 Local Popularity Caching Mechanism Based on Content Relevance

3.1 Calculation of Content Relevance

In practical applications, each user has its own access domain, which means that there is a high relevance between the content requested by the user, so the content with high relevance in the routing node is more likely to be accessed by the user in turn. In this paper, the proposed caching strategy exploits the semantic relevance of content as the relevance between content. The first step in semantic relevance analysis is to extract attributes that have an impact on relevance, and the more attributes with the same or similar semantics, the greater the relevance. When calculating the semantic relevance, this paper mainly considers the content name of the interest packet, and calculates the content relevance according to the content name attribute of the interest packet.

Relevance coefficient parameter: $\beta_{c'}^c$ represents the relevance between the content c and the content of the node cache c', $\beta_{c'}^c$ value of is 0, 1.

$$\beta_{c'}^c = \frac{|M \cap M'|}{|\max(M, M')|} \tag{3}$$

In this equation,M and M' represent the semantic vector spaces of content c and content c', respectively. Where $M = M_1, M_2 \ldots\ldots M_k$ denotes the set of name strings of content c and $M' = M_1', M_2' \ldots\ldots M_m'$ denotes the set of name strings of content c'. The number of elements in the intersection between the semantic vectors M and M' is used as the numerator. The maximum number of ideas of M and M' (i.e., the maximum number between k and m) is used as the denominator. According to the above formula, the relevance between the content c and the content c' is obtained.

3.2   Local Popularity Calculation

Since the content requested by the user is high relevance, data content with high relevance is more likely to be requested by the same user. Taking relevance into account when calculating local popularity can improve network performance. The local popularity of content c at routing node n is updated as follows.

$$pop_n^c = \frac{Ret_n^c}{\sum_{c_j \in C_n} Ret_n^{c_j}} + \sum_{c' \in C_n} \beta_{c'}^c \qquad (4)$$

where Ret_n^c indicates the number of requests for content c in routing node n, and C_n indicates all content cached by routing node n. The $\sum_{c_j \in C_n} Ret_n^{c_j}$ represents the total number of requests for all content at routing node n. The $\beta_{c'}^c$ indicates the relevance between content c and content c'. The $\sum_{c' \in C_n} \beta_{c'}^c$ indicates the sum of the relevances between the content c and all content already cached in the routing node.

3.3   Caching Decision Process

The caching decision proposed in this paper is made in each routing node along the forwarding path of interest packet sent by users. The decision-making process algorithm is as follows.

The algorithm proposed in this paper is based on the greedy algorithm. When the routing node receives the interest packet requested by the user, it firstly queries whether the remaining available cache capacity of the current routing node can satisfy the cache capacity for caching the content requested by the user. If possible, directly add the ID of the routing node to the cache node ID table of the interest packet, calculate the popularity of the interest packet in the current routing node, and update the cache node ID table interest packet and the cache information table in the routing node. If not, it is necessary to query the minimum popular content and its popularity in the cache information table of the routing node, and compare the popularity of the arriving content with the minimum popularity of the cached content in the node. If it is greater than, add the ID of the routing node to the cache node ID of the interest packet table, and update the cache node ID table interest packet and the cache information table in the routing node, and then forward the interest packet. The cache parameter of the replaced Interest in the routing node is set to 0. If the popularity of the content is less than the minimum popularity of the content in the routing node, the interest packet is forwarded directly.

Algorithm 1. Caching decisions based on content relevance

Input: interest packet for request content c received by node n

  $pop_n^c = 0$

Output: S_n^c

1. **if** $CacheAvailablecapacity > CacheContentCapacity$ **then**
2. $S_n^c = 1$
3.   Update the current local popularity of content c in the routing node pop_n^c
4. $ID^c \cup \{n\}$
5. $CacheAvailablecapacity = CacheAvailablecapacity - CacheContentCapacity$
6. **else**
7.   Calculate the current local popularity of content c in the routing node pop_n^c
8.   **if** $pop_n^c > pop_n^i$ **then**
9. $S_n^c = 1$
10. $ID^c \cup \{n\}$
11. $S_n^i = 0$
12.   **else**
13. $S_n^c = 0$
14. $ID^c = ID^c$
15.   **end if**
16. **end if**

---

4   Simulation and Performance Analysis

In order to verify the performance of the caching strategy proposed in this paper in the network. This paper uses the ndnSIM2.7 simulation tool to compare the caching strategy with several other existing caching strategies. And verify the effectiveness of the strategy through simulation processing. MATLAB is used for the result data.

4.1   Experimental Environment and Parameter Settings

Simulation is performed in Linux (ubuntu 18) environment using NS3-based ndnSIM2.7 [18] emulator. The main modified parts are:

(1) The format of interest packet is modified, and the cached message ID table is added to the interest packet.
(2) The format of data packet is modified and the cached message ID table is added to the data packet.
(3) Modify the structure of the routing node and add the cache message ID table in the routing node.

The cache strategy proposed in this paper is simulated and implemented, and compared with other cache strategies. The experimental simulation parameters are shown in Table 1.

The network structure used in this paper is a tree structure, divided into 7 layers, each internal node has 2 child nodes, and there are 127 nodes in total, including 64 leaf nodes, 62 intermediate nodes, and 1 root node. In the simulation process, the leaf node is set as the user request node, the intermediate node is

Table 1. Experimental parameter setting.

Experimental parameters	Experimental setup
Frequency of content requests per node	100
Cache capacity per node	50–150(100)
Content Capacity	1
Content Popularity Parameter (Zipf)	0.6–1.4(1)
Simulation time	10 s

set as the routing node that needs to make caching decisions, and the root node is set as the content source node. It is assumed that the content source node can provide all the content requested by users in the network, and the cache required to cache each content is 1 unit. The content popularity obeys Zipf distribution, the parameter of Zipf is set between 0.6 and 1.4, the default value of Zipf parameter is 1. The cache capacity of each node is set to 50–150 units, and the default value of node cache capacity is 100 units.

4.2 Experimental Performance Indicators

In order to be able to effectively compare the results of the caching decision proposed in this paper with several other caching decisions, several common network performance in the network are selected as evaluation metrics.

(1) Cache hit ratio: cache hit ratio is the ratio of the number of content requests satisfied by a routing node to the total number of content requests made by all content requesters over a period of time. cache hit ratio can be used to measure the cache performance metrics in the network, and the cache utilization of a routing node can be reflected by the cache hit ratio. The higher the value of cache hit ratio, the higher the cache utilization of the routing node. Suppose the number of cache hits of a routing node is R_{hit}, the total number of requests for all contents sent by a requester is R_{total}, and the cache hit ratio is $cache_{hit}$, then there is a cache hit ratio of:

$$Cache_{hit} = \frac{R_{hit}}{R_{total}} \tag{5}$$

Figure 4 reflects the variation of cache hit rate with Zipf parameter when the cache capacity is the default value, from the figure, It can be seen that in different cache decision strategies, with the increase of the Zipf parameter, the cache rate increases, but the cache hit rate in CRC is better than the cache hit rate in other caching strategies, which is because when the cache capacity of the routing node is certain, the cache hit rate in the same routing This is because when the cache capacity of a routing node is certain, users are more likely to request content with high relevance in the same routing node, and the relevance of users' requested content is taken into account when calculating the content popularity in CRC, which can improve the cache hit ratio. Moreover, the local popularity calculation method is introduced in the CRC strategy proposed in this paper, which can more accurately sense the dynamic changes of the popularity of interest packet in the routing nodes, so the cache hit rate changes more obviously. From the figure, It can be seen that when the Zipf parameter is equal to 1, the cache hit rate of the routing node increases significantly, and the cache hit rate at this time is better than several other cache strategies.

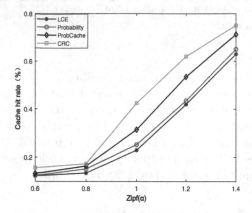

Fig. 4. Variation of cache hit rate with Zipf parameters.

Figure 5 shows the variation of the cache hit rate with the change in the cache capacity of the routing node when the Zipf parameter is set to its default value. From the figure, it can be seen that the cache hit rate of the routing node increases with the increase of the cache capacity of the routing node. The higher cache hit ratio of CRC compared to several other caching policies is due to the real-time update of the popularity of the cached content in the CRC strategy, which makes the content cached in the routing node reach the real-time update with the popularity of the content.

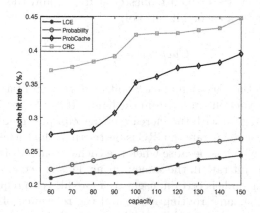

Fig. 5. Variation of cache hit rate with cache capacity.

(2) Average delay: The average delay is the average time for a user to send a content request and receive a content response. The average delay can reflect the retrieval efficiency of the content in the network and the QoS of the user. The lower the average delay, the higher the retrieval efficiency., the better the QoS of the user.

Figure 6 shows the average delay as a function of Zipf parameters. It can be seen that as the Zipf parameter increases, the average latency decreases across several caching decisions. When the Zipf parameter is 1, the caching decision proposed in this paper is quite different from other caching decisions. In this experiment, the delay of one-hop routing node is set to 10 ms. From the simulation results, it can be seen that the average delay is about 35 ms, indicating that most of the user's requests are responded between two hops, which improves the user's QoS.

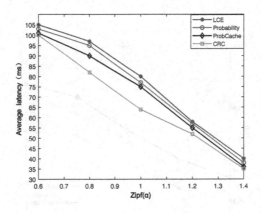

Fig. 6. Variation of average access latency with Zipf parameters.

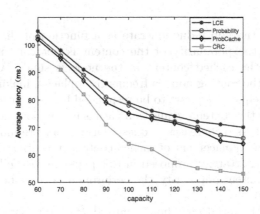

Fig. 7. Variation of average access latency with cache capacity.

Figure 7 shows the average delay with the cache capacity is recorded, indicating that the average delay decreases with the increase of the cache capacity. Compared with other caching strategies, the CRC average delay reduction is more obvious. Because the CRC considers the relevance between the content requested by the user, the content copy is cached in the routing node closer to the user, which can respond to the user's request faster.

(3) Hop reduction rate: Assuming that $hop_r(t)$ is the number of hops elapsed in a single request and $Hop_r(t)$ is the number of hops elapsed by the corresponding user of this request to obtain content from the content-providing source, the hop reduction rate is $H(t)$:

$$H(t) = \frac{\sum_{r=1} \text{Hop}_r(t) - \sum_{r=1} \text{hop}_r(t)}{\sum_{r=1} \text{Hop}_r(t)} \tag{6}$$

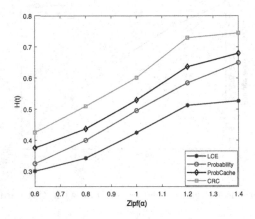

Fig. 8. Variation of hop count reduction rate with Zipf parameters.

Figure 8 shows the hop reduction rate as a function of the zipf parameter. When α is small, the popularity of the content is not concentrated, and the residence time of the cached content in the node is small. At this time, the cached content in the routing node is frequently replaced, making it difficult for the content of subsequent requests to be responded by the routing node, and the effect of shortening the content acquisition path is not obvious, and the reduction rate of hops is low. As α increases, requests for content are more concentrated, and at this time, the replacement of cached content in routing nodes is reduced. Because the caching strategy proposed in this paper makes full use of the local characteristics of content popularity, the performance can be better than several other caching strategies.

Figure 9 shows the variation of hop count reduction rate with the cache capacity of the routing node. When the cache capacity of the routing node is small, most of the content requests need to be forwarded to the content-providing source server to get a response, and the hop count reduction rate is lower at this time. The performance improvement of CRC is more stable compared to the other caching strategies.

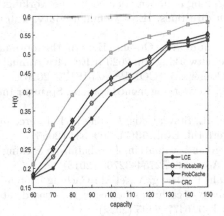

Fig. 9. Variation of hop count reduction rate with cache capacity.

5   Conclusion

In order to effectively utilize the cache space of routing nodes in ICN and improve the service quality of users, a cache strategy based on CRC is proposed. Based on the local popularity of the content, the ultimate goal is to minimize the forwarding distance of content sent by users. The simulation results show that CRC can cache content in routing nodes closer to the user, obtain a higher cache hit rate, reduce the user's request delay, and improve the user's QoS and network performance.The next step will be based on the research of this paper, combined with the diversity of user requests in the network, to analyze some key problems existing in the current caching strategy. Combined with the relationship between routing nodes, the cache strategy is studied to further optimize the cache performance of the network.

References

1. Li, J., Xue, K., Liu, J., Zhang, Y.: An ICN/SDN-based network architecture and efficient content retrieval for future satellite-terrestrial integrated networks. IEEE Netw. **34**(1), 188–195 (2019)
2. Ngaffo, A.N., El Ayeb, W.: Information-centric networking challenges and opportunities in service discovery: a survey. In: 2020 IEEE Eighth International Conference on Communications and Networking (ComNet), pp. 1–8. IEEE (2020)
3. Lederer, et al.: Adaptive multimedia streaming in information-centric networks. IEEE Netw. Mag. Comput. Commun. **28**(6), 91–96 (2014)

4. Nour, B., et al.: A unified hybrid information-centric naming scheme for IoT applications. Comput. Commun. **150**, 103–114 (2020)
5. Qian., H.U., et al.: Random cache placement strategy for content-centric networking. In: Journal of Xidian University (2014)
6. Din, I.U., et al.: Caching in information-centric networking: strategies, challenges, and future research directions. IEEE Commun. Surv. Tutorials **20**(2), 1443–1474 (2017)
7. Hagikura, J., Nakamura, R., Ohsaki, H.: On the optimal cache allocation in information-centric networking. In: 2020 IEEE 44th Annual Computers, Software, and Applications Conference (COMPSAC) IEEE (2020)
8. Jacobson, V., et al.: Networking named content. Springer International Publishing (2015)
9. Laoutaris, N., Che, H., Stavrakakis, I.: The LCD interconnection of LRU caches and its analysis. Perform. Eval. **63**(7), 609–634 (2006)
10. Wu, H., et al.: Design and evaluation of probabilistic caching in information-centric networking. IEEE Access **6**, 32754–32768 (2018)
11. Naeem., M.A., Ullah, R., Meng, Y., et al.: Caching content on the network layer: a performance analysis of caching schemes in ICN-based Internet of Things. IEEE Internet of Things J. **9**, 6477–6495 (2022)
12. Zhang, G., Yang, L., Tao, L.: Caching in information centric networking: a survey. Comput. Netw. **57**(10), 3128–3141 (2013)
13. Kang, M.W., et al.: A content caching optimization scheme based on content popularity in ICN. In: Proceedings of Symposium of the Korean Institute of communications and Information Sciences (2018)
14. Qian, H.U., et al.: Random cache placement strategy for content-centric networking. In: Journal of Xidian University (2014)
15. Jiang, Y., et al.: User preference learning-based edge caching for fog radio access network. IEEE Trans. Commun. **67**(2), 1268–1283 (2019)
16. Ibrahim, et al.: Survey on caching approaches in information centric networking. J. Netw. Comput. Appl. **56**, 48–59 (2015)
17. Yang, et al.: Optimal caching and scheduling for cache-enabled D2D communications. IEEE Commun. Lett. Publ. IEEE Commun. Soc. **21**, 1155–1158 (2017)
18. Afanasyev, A., Ilya, M., Zhang, L.: ndnSIM: NDN simulator for NS- 3. In: Tech. Rep. 4, (2012)

Network Communication Performance Enhancement

Performance Analysis and Optimization Strategy over Cell-Free Massive MIMO in the Finite Blocklength Regime

Qingqin Xu[1(✉)], Zhong Li[1], Teng Wu[1], and Jie Zeng[2]

[1] School of Communication and Information Engineering, Chongqing University of Posts and Telecommunications, Chongqing 400065, China
{s210131272,s190131188,s200131102}@stu.cqupt.edu.cn
[2] Department of Electronic Engineering, Tsinghua University, Beijing 100084, China
zengjie@tsinghua.edu.cn

Abstract. The sixth generation (6G) mobile networks need to meet various performance requirements such as the number of connections, latency, reliability, and energy efficiency. In particular, for the Internet of Things (IoT) scenarios with short packet transmission, it is necessary to analyze and optimize various performances while achieving massive connections. In addition, practical constraints (such as imperfect channel state information, limitations of classical Shannon's capacity, inter-cell interference, massive user interference, etc.) further aggravate the difficulties of theoretical analysis and performance improvement. We propose a performance analysis and optimization strategy for short packet transmission systems based on cell-free massive multiple-input multiple-output (CF mMIMO), which points out the idea of improving system performance with large-scale connections under practical constraints. Furthermore, with the combination of simultaneous wireless information and power transfer (SWIPT) technology and finite blocklength (FBL) information theory, we derive the closed-form expressions of downlink signal-to-interference-plus-noise ratio (SINR), achievable data rate, and energy collected based on CF mMIMO. Simulation results verify the effectiveness of the proposed strategy, which is also expected to support massive ultra-reliable and low latency communications (mURLLC) with ultra-high energy efficiency or spectral efficiency in the future.

Keywords: Cell-free massive multiple-input multiple-output (CF mMIMO) · Finite blocklength (FBL) · Massive ultra-reliable and low latency communications (mURLLC) · Performance analysis and optimization · Simultaneous wireless information and power transfer (SWIPT)

This work was supported by the National Natural Science Foundation of China (No. 62001264) and the Natural Science Foundation of Beijing (No. L192025).

F. Gao et al. (Eds.): ChinaCom 2022, LNICST 500, pp. 137–148, 2023.
https://doi.org/10.1007/978-3-031-34790-0_11

1   Introduction

From the fifth generation (5G) to the sixth generation (6G), in addition to the number of access users that need to be significantly improved, ultra-high spectral efficiency, ultra-low latency and ultra-high reliability have also become basic indicators that 6G needs to be guaranteed [7,10]. In response to these changes, new theories, methods and technologies are urgently needed for 6G.

Related research has been made by some scholars recently. Saad *et al.* [7] first proposed massive ultra-reliable and low latency communications (mURLLC) and pointed out that mURLLC covers four performance indicators: massive connections, ultra-high reliability, ultra-low latency, and scalability (e.g., ultra-high spectral efficiency, wide area coverage, etc.). Zhang *et al.* [11] analyzed the quality-of-service (QoS) for mURLLC with statistical delay. Liu *et al.* [2] optimized indicators such as the number of user accesses, latency, and reliability to achieve mURLLC. In addition, the cell-free massive multiple-input multiple-output (CF mMIMO) which has great potential to become one of the key technologies for 6G greatly reduces the user-to-base station distance in traditional cellular cells and has a strong anti-fading capability [1]. Ngo *et al.* [5] analyzed the user achievable data rate and system throughput for the first time for an uplink CF mMIMO system considering the effects of channel estimation error and power control. Nasir *et al.* [4] studied a CF mMIMO system implementing downlink ultra-reliable and low latency communications (URLLC) and optimized the system data rate and energy efficiency.

Although mURLLC, CF mMIMO and other new theories and technologies have been proposed, the related research is still in the exploration stage. There is still much room for exploration to achieve the requirements of 6G multiple performance indicators (reliability, latency, user capacity, etc.). Furthermore, for 6G key performance indicators differentiation and linkage characteristics, how to build an evaluation system to break through the bottleneck of system performance improvement and accelerate program design and simulation verification has not been solved.

The key contributions of this paper can be summarized as follows.

- A performance analysis and optimization strategy over CF mMIMO for short packet transmission is proposed for large-scale IoT scenarios, which is expected to support future mURLLC with ultra-high energy or spectral efficiency.
- Combining simultaneous wireless information and power transfer (SWIPT), we derive closed-form expressions for downlink signal-to-interference-plus-noise (SINR), achievable data rate, and energy collected with finite block-length (FBL) information theory over CF mMIMO.

The remainder of this paper is organized as follows. Section 2 describes the strategy of performance evaluation. In Sect. 3, we analyze a case of CF mMIMO. In Sect. 4, simulation results are shown and analyzed. Finally, conclusions are given in Sect. 5.

Notations: $\mathbb{C}^{K \times N}$ collects $K \times N$ complex-valued matrices. $\mathbb{E}(\bullet)$ denotes expectation. $(\bullet)^H$ denote transpose and conjugate. $\mathcal{CN}(0,1)$ denotes the zero-mean complex Gaussian distribution with variance 1.

2   System Model and Performance Evaluation

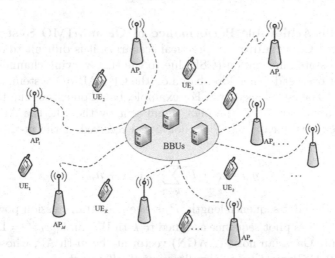

Fig. 1. Architecture diagram of the CF mMIMO system.

A CF mMIMO system contains M access points (APs) and K user equipments (UEs) as shown in Fig. 1. By deploying massive APs in a distributed manner, the spatial diversity gain is obtained, and the path loss is greatly reduced, thereby significantly improving the achievable data rate and reliability. In addition, high-performance base band units (BBUs) are used to collectively process the signals of multiple APs, which improve the number of access users and the performance of multi-user detection. Assuming that each AP or UE has a single antenna, the received signal can be modeled as

$$Y = GX + Z, \tag{1}$$

where $G \in \mathbb{C}^{M \times K}$ is the channel matrix. $X \in \mathbb{C}^{K \times N}$ is the transmitted signal and N is the number of channel uses (CUs). $Y \in \mathbb{C}^{M \times N}$ is the received signal. $Z \in \mathbb{C}^{M \times N}$ is the noise at the receiver and other co-channel interference. We assume that g_{mk} represents the channel coefficient between the m-th AP and the k-th UE, then the channel can be modeled as

$$g_{mk} = h_{mk} \sqrt{\beta_{mk}}, \tag{2}$$

where $h_{mk} \sim \mathcal{CN}(0,1)$ is the small-scale Rayleigh fading coefficient between the m-th AP and the k-th UE, and remains unchanged throughout the coherent interval [3]; β_{mk} is the large-scale fading between the m-th AP and the k-th UE and considers path loss $\beta_{mk}(d_{mk}) = \min(1, d_{mk}^{-\alpha_{\mathrm{PL}}})$ as a nonsingular bounded path loss model, which d_{mk} is the distance and $\alpha_{\mathrm{PL}} > 0$ is the path loss factor. It is usually assumed that β_{mk} is known in advance [3,5].

In light of various needs of 6G, the following describes the performance evaluation strategy based on CF mMIMO for short packet transmission, combined with FBL information theory, mainly including the following three contents.

Analyze the Achievable Performance of CF mMIMO System Based on Practical Constraints. In practical scenarios, it is difficult to obtain perfect channel state information (CSI) due to the time-varying channel state and limited pilot overhead. Therefore, based on the CF mMIMO system, a CSI error model need to be established first. For example, based on expressing the channel coefficients above, by using the pilot signal sent by the UE, the AP estimates the uplink channel locally [5]. The pilot signal received at the m-th AP can be expressed as [3,5]

$$\boldsymbol{y}_m = \sqrt{n_p P_p} \sum_{k=1}^{K} g_{mk} \boldsymbol{\varphi}_k + \boldsymbol{n}_m, \tag{3}$$

where n_p is the pilot sequence length, P_p is the pilot transmission power of each UE, $\boldsymbol{\varphi}_k \in \mathbb{C}^{1 \times n_p}$ is pilot sequence assigned to k-th UE, and $\|\boldsymbol{\varphi}_k\|^2 = 1$. $\boldsymbol{n}_m$ is the additive white Gaussian noise (AWGN) vector at the m-th AP, whose elements follow $\mathcal{CN}(0,1)$. Project $\boldsymbol{y}_m$ in the direction of $\boldsymbol{\varphi}_k^H$ to get

$$y_{mk} = \boldsymbol{y}_m \boldsymbol{\varphi}_k^H = \sqrt{n_p P_p} g_{mk} + \sqrt{n_p P_p} \sum_{\substack{k'=1 \\ k' \neq k}}^{K} \boldsymbol{\varphi}_{k'} \boldsymbol{\varphi}_k^H + n_m, \tag{4}$$

where $n_m = \boldsymbol{n}_m \boldsymbol{\varphi}_k^H \sim \mathcal{CN}(0,1)$. Using the minimum mean-squared error (MMSE) criterion, the estimation of channel coefficients g_{mk} can be expressed as [8]

$$\hat{g}_{mk} = \frac{\mathbb{E}\left[y_{mk}^* g_{mk}\right]}{\mathbb{E}\left[|y_{mk}|^2\right]} y_{mk} = c_{mk} y_{mk}, \tag{5}$$

where c_{mk} is expressed as

$$c_{mk} \triangleq \frac{\sqrt{n_p P_p} \beta_{mk}}{n_p P_p \sum_{k'=1}^{K} \beta_{mk} |\boldsymbol{\varphi}_k^H \boldsymbol{\varphi}_{k'}|^2 + 1}. \tag{6}$$

The actual channel can be expressed as $g_{mk} = \hat{g}_{mk} + \tilde{g}_{mk}$, where $\tilde{g}_{mk}$ is the estimation error, due to the orthogonality of MMSE criterion [8], $\tilde{g}_{mk}$ and $\hat{g}_{mk}$ is independent of each other. Then, through the massive user access and detection scheme, the post-processing signal-to-noise ratio, achievable data rate and other performance indicators can be derived under imperfect CSI.

Establish a Performance Evaluation System Around Indicators. The classical Shannon's capacity is based on the assumption of infinite coding block-length, which cannot accurately describe the achievable data rate of short packet communication. Therefore, we can use FBL information theory to model and analyze data rate and error probability. The achievable data rate R_k of the k-th UE is [6]

$$R_k \approx C\left(\gamma_k\right) - \sqrt{\frac{V\left(\gamma_k\right)}{n'}} Q^{-1}\left(\varepsilon_k\right), \tag{7}$$

where ε_k $(0 \leq \varepsilon_k < 1)$ is the decoding error probability at the k-th UE; n' is the length of coding block; $Q^{-1}\left(.\right)$ represents the inverse function of a function Q; γ_k is the SINR at the k-th UE, $C\left(\gamma_k\right) = \log_2\left(1 + \gamma_k\right)$ and $V\left(\gamma_k\right) = 1 - \frac{1}{(1+\gamma_k)^2}$. The decoding error probability $\varepsilon_k\left(n_d, \gamma_k\right)$ of the k-th UE is

$$\varepsilon_k\left(n_d, \gamma_k\right) \approx Q\left(\frac{C\left(\gamma_k\right) - R_k}{\sqrt{V\left(\gamma_k\right)/n'}}\right). \tag{8}$$

Furthermore, theoretical relationships between the achievable data rate and other performance indicators can be deduced.

Optimize the Transmission Scheme for Typical Scenarios. The performance evaluation and analysis system is beneficial for providing references for scheme design and simulation. For example, based on (7), the latency t_D and spectral efficiency η_{SE} can be expressed as

$$t_D = \max_k \frac{D_k}{R_k}, \quad \eta_{SE} = \frac{\sum\limits_{k=1}^{K} R_k}{B_{total}}, \tag{9}$$

where D_k is the packet size of k-th user, and B_{total} is the total bandwidth of the system. For specific scenarios, we can optimize the performance of one or several indicators. Then, we can analyze the relationship between the achievable data rate, reliability, latency and spectral efficiency with simulation. By adjusting the parameters, the transmission scheme is further adjusted to meet the performance requirements. Because of using the CF mMIMO system that supports massive connections and considering short packet transmission, the above strategy is expected to support mURLLC with ultra-high energy efficiency or spectral efficiency in the future.

3   Use Case and Performance Analysis

In this section, a use case of a CF mMIMO system in Fig. 1 is introduced. Combined with SWIPT technology, we assume that each UE is equipped with information and energy receivers, and the energy collection model of each UE is generalized by using time-switching (TS) and power-splitting (PS). Each coherent interval n_c $(n_c = B_c T_c$, where B_c refers to coherent bandwidth and T_c refers to coherent time) is divided into two orthogonal time slots, which are used for uplink pilot training and downlink SWIPT transmission respectively. The system model is shown in Fig. 2.

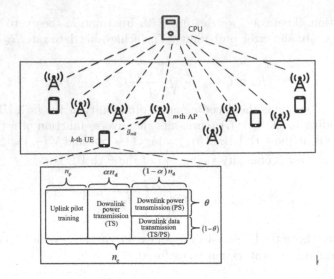

Fig. 2. System model of CF MIMO with SWIPT.

3.1 Downlink Data Transmission

Channel estimation in uplink has been done in Sect. 2. Using the joint TS-PS protocol, based on the TS factor α and PS factor θ, the downlink SWIPT transmission phase is divided into two sub-phases. In the first downlink power transmission sub-phase, UE uses αn_d CUs to collect energy from AP based on TS protocol, and n_d is the number of CUs used in downlink transmission phase. At this time, each UE is fully represented as an energy collection device and collects energy from the AP. In the second downlink information transmission sub-phase, the remaining $(1-\alpha)\,n_d$ CUs are used for downlink information transmission. If PS protocol is adopted, the received signal energy is divided into two streams, which are used for energy collection and information decoding respectively. $\tilde{n}_d \triangleq (1-\alpha)\,n_d$ indicates the blocklength of the downlink data, and the transmission signal vector $x_m^{\tilde{n}_d}$ at the m-th AP can be expressed as

$$x_m^{\tilde{n}_d} = \sqrt{(1-\theta)\,P_d} \sum_{k=1}^{K} \sqrt{\eta_{mk}}\hat{g}_{mk}^* s_k^{\tilde{n}_d}, \tag{10}$$

where $s_k^{\tilde{n}_d} = \left[s_k^{(1)}, ..., s_k^{(\tilde{n}_d)}\right]$ is the symbol vector sent to the k-th UE, $s_k^{(l)}, l \in \{1, ..., \tilde{n}_d\}$ is the l-th data symbol sent to the k-th UE, and $\mathbb{E}\left[\left|s_k^{(l)}\right|^2\right] = 1, l \in \{1, ..., \tilde{n}_d\}$. η_{mk} is the power allocation coefficient between the m-th AP and the k-th UE, and meets the following power constraints at each AP

$$\sum_{k=1}^{K} \eta_{mk}\mathbb{E}\left[\left|\hat{g}_{mk}^*\right|^2\right] \le 1 \;\Rightarrow\; \sum_{k=1}^{K} \eta_{mk}\rho_{mk} \le 1, \tag{11}$$

where the expression of ρ_{mk} is

$$\rho_{mk} \triangleq \mathbb{E}\left[|\hat{g}_{mk}^*|^2\right] = \sqrt{n_p P_p}\beta_{mk}c_{mk}. \tag{12}$$

Thus, the signal received by the k-th UE from the M APs can be expressed as

$$y_k^{\tilde{n}_d} = \sum_{m=1}^{M} g_{mk}x_m^{\tilde{n}_d} + n_k$$

$$= \sqrt{(1-\theta)P_d} \sum_{m=1}^{M} \sum_{k'=1}^{K} \sqrt{\eta_{mk'}}g_{mk}\hat{g}_{mk'}^* s_{k'}^{\tilde{n}_d} + n_k, \tag{13}$$

where $n_k \sim \mathcal{CN}(0,1)$ represents the AWGN at the k-th UE. Further, the received signal $y_k^{\tilde{n}_d}$ in (13) can be rewritten as

$$y_k^{\tilde{n}_d} = \sqrt{(1-\theta)P_d} \sum_{m=1}^{M} \sqrt{\eta_{mk}}g_{mk}\hat{g}_{mk}^* s_k^{\tilde{n}_d}$$

$$+ \sqrt{(1-\theta)P_d} \sum_{\substack{m=1 \\ }}^{M} \sum_{\substack{k'=1 \\ k'\neq k}}^{K} \sqrt{\eta_{mk'}}g_{mk'}\hat{g}_{mk'}^* s_{k'}^{\tilde{n}_d} + n_k, \tag{14}$$

Thus, the SINR at the k-th UE can be expressed as [12]

$$\gamma_k = (1-\theta)P_d \left(\sum_{m=1}^{M} \sqrt{\eta_{mk}}\rho_{mk}\right)^2$$

$$\times \left\{ (1-\theta)P_d \sum_{\substack{k'=1 \\ k'\neq k}}^{K} \left[\sum_{m=1}^{M} \sqrt{\eta_{mk'}}\rho_{mk'}\frac{\beta_{mk}}{\beta_{mk'}}\right]^2 |\varphi_k\varphi_{k'}^H|^2 \right.$$

$$\left. + (1-\theta)P_d \sum_{m=1}^{M} \sum_{k'=1}^{K} \eta_{mk'}\rho_{mk'}\beta_{mk} + 1 \right\}^{-1}. \tag{15}$$

Then, according to (7), (8) and (15), we can get the achievable data rate and the decoding error probability with $n' = (1-\alpha)n_d$.

3.2   Energy Collection

According to reference [9], the collected energy can be modeled as

$$EH(P_R) = \left[\frac{a}{1-b}\left(\frac{1}{1+\exp(-c(P_R-d))} - b\right)\right]^+$$

$$= \left[\frac{a(1-\exp(-cP_R))}{1+\exp(-c(P_R-d))}\right]^+, \tag{16}$$

where $EH(P_R)$ refers to the energy collected instantaneously, $b = 1/(1+\exp(cd))$, $[z]^+ = \max(0,z)$. According to the literature [8], $a = 20$ mW, $c = 6400/\mu$W, $d = 2.9$ μW.

Instantaneous Energy Collection. Based on TS and PS protocols, the total instantaneous energy E_k collected by the k-th UE can be expressed as

$$E_k = \alpha n_d EH\left(P_k\right) + \left(1 - \alpha\right) n_d EH\left(\theta P_k\right), \tag{17}$$

where $EH\left(P_R\right)$ represents the energy collected instantaneously [9] and P_k represents the received power of the k-th UE. Let $s_k \in \left\{s_k^{(1)}, ..., s_k^{(\tilde{n}_d)}\right\}$, then according to (13), the received power P_k of the k-th UE can be expressed as

$$P_k = P_d \left| \sum_{m=1}^{M} \sum_{k'=1}^{K} \sqrt{\eta_{mk'}} g_{mk} \hat{g}_{mk'}^* s_{k'} \right|^2. \tag{18}$$

Average Energy Collection. The total average energy $\bar{E}_k$ collected by the k-th UE can be expressed as

$$\bar{E}_k = \alpha n_d \mathbb{E}\left[EH\left(P_k\right)\right] + \left(1 - \alpha\right) n_d \mathbb{E}\left[EH\left(\theta P_k\right)\right]. \tag{19}$$

Since the closed-form expression of (17) is mathematically difficult to calculate, we use Jensen inequality to get an upper bound $\bar{E}_k^{\text{UB}}$ of $\bar{E}_k$, that is

$$\bar{E}_k \leq \bar{E}_k^{\text{UB}} = \alpha n_d EH\left(\mathbb{E}\left[P_k\right]\right) + \left(1 - \alpha\right) n_d EH\left(\theta \mathbb{E}\left[P_k\right]\right). \tag{20}$$

Combined with (5), (6), and (18), the derived expression of $\mathbb{E}\left[P_k\right]$ is

$$\mathbb{E}\left[P_k\right] = P_d \mathbb{E}\left[\left|\sum_{m=1}^{M} \sqrt{\eta_{mk}} g_{mk} \hat{g}_{mk}^*\right|^2\right] + P_d \mathbb{E}\left[\left|\sum_{m=1}^{M} \sum_{\substack{k'=1 \\ k' \neq k}}^{K} \sqrt{\eta_{mk'}} g_{mk} \hat{g}_{mk}^*\right|^2\right]$$

$$= P_d \sum_{m=1}^{M} \eta_{mk} c_{mk}^2 \beta_{mk} \left(2 n_p P_p \beta_{mk} + 1\right)$$

$$+ P_d \sum_{m=1}^{M} \sum_{\substack{k'=1 \\ k' \neq k}}^{K} \eta_{mk'} c_{mk'}^2 \beta_{mk} \left(n_p P_p \beta_{mk'} + 1\right)$$

$$= P_d \sum_{m=1}^{M} \eta_{mk} \rho_{mk}^2 + P_d \sum_{m=1}^{M} \sum_{\substack{k'=1 \\ k' \neq k}}^{K} \eta_{mk'} \rho_{mk'} \beta_{mk}. \tag{21}$$

4   Simulation Results and Analysis

In this section, we validate our analysis through simulations. The specific parameters are set as shown in Table 1.

Table 1. Simulation parameter settings

Parameters	Value
Number of AP M	[100, 200]
Number of UE K	[50, 100]
Coherence Bandwidth B_c	200 kHz
Coherence Time T_c	1 ms
Bandwidth B	20 MHz
Transmitting Power of Uplink Pilot P_p	100 mW
Average Transmitting Power of Downlink p_d	[100, 200] mW
Decoding Error Probability ε_k	10^{-6}
Path Loss Factor α_{PL}	3.4

Figure 3 shows the relationship between the decoding error probability $\varepsilon_k (n_d, \gamma_k)$ and the coding block length n_d for the k-th UE. The decoding error probability ε_k decreases continuously as the coding blocklength n_d keeps increasing in the finite blocklength regime. By comparing the blue ($K = 100$), orange ($K = 75$) and green ($K = 50$) curves, we see that the decoding error probability increases when the number of UE K rises. Therefore, to meet different service requirements, when the number of UE K increases, the coding blocklength n_d can be increased appropriately to keep the reliability within an acceptable range.

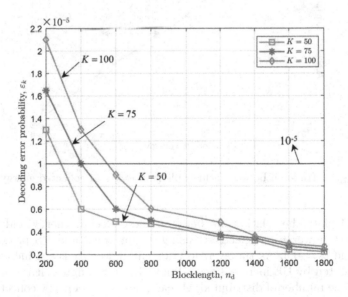

Fig. 3. Relationship between error probability ε_k and blocklength n_d.

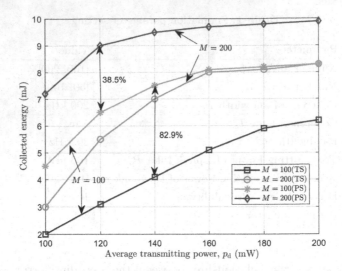

Fig. 4. Collected energy versus average transmitting power p_{d}.

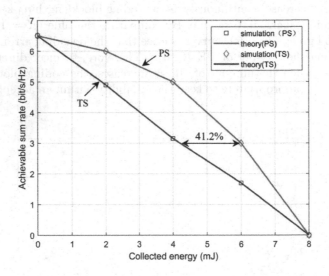

Fig. 5. Trade-off between achievable sum rate and collected energy.

Figure 4 plots the relationship between the collected energy and the average transmit power p_{d}, respectively using TS protocol and PS protocol, with $\alpha = 0.5$ and $\theta = 0.5$. As the average transmit power p_{d} keeps increasing, the energy collected by UE increases accordingly. From the figure, it is obvious that increasing the number of distributed AP can increase the energy collected by the UE regardless of whether TS or PS protocol is used. Specifically, increasing the number of AP from 100 to 200 increases the energy collected by the UE by 38.5

% when the PS protocol is used and the average transmitting power is $p_d = 120$ mW. In addition, the PS protocol is superior to the TS protocol.

Figure 5 depicts the trade-off between achievable rate and collected energy with $M = 100$, $K = 50$, $p_d = 200$ mW and $\alpha = 0$ corresponds to PS protocol and $\theta = 0$ corresponds to TS protocol. When α or θ tends to 0, the achievable rate will reach its maximum. Meanwhile, the CU allocated for downlink transmission will be used only for data transmission, while the energy collected by UE becomes infinitesimal. When α or θ converges to 1, the energy collected by UE reaches the maximum, CU allocated for downlink transmission is only used for energy transmission and the achievable rate of UE becomes infinitesimal. Therefore, by adjusting the value of TS factor α or PS factor θ, the compromise curve in Fig. 5 can be traversed to meet different rate-energy requirements.

5 Conclusion

In this paper, we have proposed a performance analysis and optimization strategy over CF mMIMO for short packet transmission. The main steps of the strategy are expected to support mURLLC with ultra-high energy or spectral efficiency in the future. Furthermore, we have combined CF mMIMO with SWIPT to derive the SINR and energy collected under imperfect CSI. At the same time, combined with FBL information theory, the downlink achievable data rate and error probability have been deduced. The simulation results have shown the correlation between performances and that CF mMIMO can improve the system performance, which has verified the effectiveness of the proposed strategy.

References

1. Elhoushy, S., Ibrahim, M., Hamouda, W.: Cell-free massive MIMO: a survey. IEEE Commun. Surveys Tutorials **24**(1), 492–523 (2021)
2. Liu, Y., Deng, Y., Elkashlan, M., Nallanathan, A., Karagiannidis, G.K.: Optimization of grant-free noma with multiple configured-grants for mURLLC. IEEE J. Sel. Areas Commun. **40**(4), 1222–1236 (2022)
3. Marzetta, T.L., Yang, H.: Fundamentals of massive MIMO. Cambridge University Press (2016)
4. Nasir, A.A., Tuan, H.D., Ngo, H.Q., Duong, T.Q., Poor, H.V.: Cell-free massive MIMO in the short blocklength regime for URLLC. IEEE Trans. Wireless Commun. **20**(9), 5861–5871 (2021)
5. Ngo, H.Q., Ashikhmin, A., Yang, H., Larsson, E.G., Marzetta, T.L.: Cell-free massive MIMO versus small cells. IEEE Trans. Wireless Commun. **16**(3), 1834–1850 (2017)
6. Polyanskiy, Y., Poor, H.V., Verdú, S.: Channel coding rate in the finite blocklength regime. IEEE Trans. Inf. Theor. **56**(5), 2307–2359 (2010)
7. Saad, W., Bennis, M., Chen, M.: A vision of 6G wireless systems: Applications, trends, technologies, and open research problems. IEEE Network **34**(3), 134–142 (2020). https://doi.org/10.1109/MNET.001.1900287
8. Steven, M.K.: Fundamentals of statistical signal processing. PTR Prentice-Hall, Englewood Cliffs, NJ **10**, 151045 (1993)

9. Wang, S., Xia, M., Huang, K., Wu, Y.C.: Wirelessly powered two-way communication with nonlinear energy harvesting model: Rate regions under fixed and mobile relay. IEEE Trans. Wireless Commun. **16**(12), 8190–8204 (2017)
10. You, X., et al.: Towards 6G wireless communication networks: Vision, enabling technologies, and new paradigm shifts. SCIENCE CHINA Inf. Sci. **64**(1), 1–74 (2021)
11. Zhang, X., Wang, J., Poor, H.V.: Statistical delay and error-rate bounded QoS provisioning for mURLLC over 6G CF M-MIMO mobile networks in the finite blocklength regime. IEEE J. Sel. Areas Commun. **39**(3), 652–667 (2020)
12. Zhang, X., Wang, J., Poor, H.V.: Statistical delay and error-rate bounded QoS provisioning for SWIPT over CF M-MIMO 6G mobile wireless networks using FBC. IEEE J. Selected Topics Signal Process. **15**(5), 1272–1287 (2021)

Admission Control Mechanism of Wireless Virtual Network Assisted by Vehicular Fog Computing

Zhanjun Liu, Ruifeng Hu$^{(\boxtimes)}$, Shuaishuai Xia, and Xia Peng

School of Communication and Information Engineering,
Chongqing University of Post and Telecommunications, Chongqing, China
939278797@qq.com

Abstract. In order to solve the problem of resources waste caused by insufficient computing resources and the lack of an effective admission mechanism in the service environment of wireless virtual network (WVN), this paper proposes an effective robust admission control mechanism. This mechanism mainly controls the access of user groups of WVN in a dynamic resource environment, which is in the assistance environment of vehicular fog computing (VFC). Firstly, considering the resource uncertainty caused by the characteristics of VFC, a robust optimization access model is established. It predicts the change of resources during the association of user time to determine whether to allow user groups access. Secondly, task offloading and the allocation of computing resources are processed. Since the coupling of task offloading and resource allocation leads to the non-convexity of the problem, we convert it into a convex optimization problem to resolve. Simulation results show that the admission control mechanism proposed in this paper can admit larger user groups in the assistance computing environment of VFC while ensuring the quality of user experience.

Keywords: Wireless virtual network · Vehicular fog computing · Admission control · Robust optimization

1 Introduction

With the development of 5th Generation Mobile Communication Technology, the network has increasingly shown heterogeneous characteristics [1], which brings challenges to the wireless network. To effectively overcome this situation, virtualizing the wireless network has been considered. The wireless virtual network (WVN) technology can improve resource utilization and integrates heterogeneous wireless networks efficiently. WVN also improves users' experience by

Supported by Chongqing University of Posts and Telecommunications Doctoral Initial Fund (A2019017) and the Chongqing Municipal Education Commission under Grant KJQN201900645.

F. Gao et al. (Eds.): ChinaCom 2022, LNICST 500, pp. 149–162, 2023.
https://doi.org/10.1007/978-3-031-34790-0_12

fragmenting and efficient processing of the network [2]. Moreover, it can not only provide wireless access services to individual users, but also can request wireless access service for user groups in the future virtual network. The user groups are assigned a network virtual slice called virtual network (VN), and they can be provided services through mobile virtual network operators (MVNOs) [3]. In summary, using WVN technology to build a future network architecture can better meet the requirements of emerging network status [4,5].

However, there is a problem with the existing technology in WVN. When a large number of VN customers with computation tasks arrive at the same time, only relying on the computing resources of the infrastructure service provider may easily reach the peak of the resource load due to the unbalance of resources, which affects the quality of experience (QoE) of users and leads some unnecessary waste of resources. Consequently, it is necessary to find assistance computing resources.

Vehicle Fog Computing (VFC), an excellent assistant computing resource for task offloading and resources utilization, has certain computing and communication capabilities by aggregating vehicles. By integrating and utilizing the computing resources, vehicles can be turned into small infrastructure [6] to alleviate the load pressure of base stations (BSs). VFC also significantly reduce deployment costs and latency given that it relies on the cooperation of nearby vehicles, rather than sending information to a remote server. Recently, the research on VFC has been gradually developed. The works [7,8] regarded the parked vehicles as infrastructure, and they proposed the concept of parking vehicle assistance so that parked vehicles can join the vehicle network as static nodes. In addision, the authors in [9] considered using the resources of the available vehicles in the parking lot to assist BS for computation and proposed an incentive measure to encourage vehicles to share their resources. The authors in [10] proposed a task offloading mechanism in the case of information asymmetry and uncertainty. And the authors studied the system of VFC and proposed an effective parallel offloading scheme to solve the problem of task decomposition and task offloading delay in [11].

In the research of WVN technology, random access to user groups will result in the waste of resources and low service provider revenue. Therefore, effective access control for WVN is very necessary. A robust optimization problem for admission control of VNs has been proposed in [12], but this method is only suitable for single-user admission, having low benefits for user groups admission. In [13,14], the authors considered a fixed snapshot of user equipment for admission control, but they did not incorporate statistical specifications for traffic demand. And in [15], the authors formulated an admission control mechanism of WVN with heterogeneous traffic profiles and various quality of experience requirements. Most studies have achieved certain results in admission control, but using the auxiliary computing resources to assist BS is considered by few people in the admission control of WVN.

Although we have been devoted to study VFC and the admission control of WVN to improve resource utilization and task computation efficiency, the admission control for user groups, which is in the assistance computing environment of VFC, has not been involved. According to the previous description, using VFC to provide services for WVN is a feasible solution to realize high resources utilization. Since the uncertainty of vehicles will result in the continued changes of resources in the assistance computing environment of VFC, the problem of the admission control for WVN is very difficult to solve. To solve the difficult problem, this paper further studies an admission control mechanism for user groups of WVN in the assistance computing environment of VFC, which is based on the traditional allocation problem of computing resources. The main contributions of this paper are as follows:

- This paper proposes a two-stage robust admission control mechanism. In the first stage, the user groups of WVN requesting service can be admitted in the assistance computing environment. And in the second stage, computing resource allocation and task offloading are performed for the admitted user groups.
- Since changes in the number of vehicles will cause fluctuations in computing resources, this paper models the WVN user group admission mechanism as a robust optimization problem in the first stage. Robust optimization can better solve some problems with uncertain data. At this stage, we need to predict the resource changes during the association time of users to determine whether to respond to the user's request.
- In the second stage, task offloading and resource allocation are performed for the user groups that have been admitted. Since the coupling of task offloading and resource allocation leads to the problem of non-convex, this paper decouples the problem of resource allocation and task offloading and transforms it into a convex optimization problem to solve. The task offloading position of users must be obtained firstly, and then computing resources will be allocated to users in this stage.
- Simulation results show that the admission control mechanism can effectively access the user groups of WVN while also ensuring the user's quality of experience (QoE).

The rest of this paper is organized as follows. In Sect. 2, we describe the system model under consideration and propose the problems that need to be solved. The admission control mechanism is elaborated and divided into two parts to solving them separately in Sect. 3. Section 4 presents and discusses the simulation results. Finally, this research is concluded in Sect. 5.

2 System Model and Problem Formulation

In this section, we firstly introduce the system model considered in this paper. And then, the wireless transmission model and delay model in the communication process are described, followed by the problem formulation is presented.

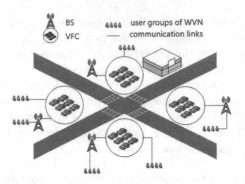

Fig. 1. System model

2.1 System Model

We assume that there are multiple BSs providing wireless access services in a two-dimensional region. According to the coverage of BS, we divide the area into multiple sub-areas. The computation capacity of vehicles with VFC in the sub-areas can be used by the BS to serve WVN. Among them, $b = \{1, 2, ..., B\}$ represents the set of BSs. Since the sub-area is defined as the coverage area of the BS, it also represents both the BS and the area. ϕ_b is used to indicate the number of vehicles with the function of VFC in area b, and its number obeys Poisson distribution. $w = \{1, 2, ..., W\}$ is represented as a set of WVN, and $m_{w,b} = \{1, 2, ..., M\}$ represents the user's set of the wth WVN in area b. Considering that users have two requirements: Firstly, each user carries a computing task, and $d_{m,w,b}^{comp}$ represents the amount of computing task of the wth WVN user which is represented by m in area b. The second, each user has a maximum tolerated delay, denoted by $T_{m,w,b}^{\max}$. The scene model in each area is shown in Fig. 1.

2.2 Wireless Transmission Model

In the Orthogonal Frequency Division Multiplexing (OFDM) communication environment, we assume that the position of users and vehicles will not change during the transmission process. The user tasks are processed in two cases, one is processed directly by the BS and the other is transmitted by the BS to vehicles for processing. The processed results are transmitted directly from the BS or vehicle to the user. Due to the orthogonality of OFDM resources, we assume that both vehicles and BSs have the same transmission mode, and there is no interference between them during communication. We suppose that the spectrum resource owned by vehicles is smaller than BSs and that the vehicle has the same bandwidth as the BS because of its own nature and limitations of the vehicle. Then the transmission rate between BS and users is $R = W \log(1 + S/N)$, where W is the fixed-size of sub-channel transmission bandwidth allocated to users by the BS or vehicles, S is the average transmission power of the channel, and N

is the additive white Gaussian noise with zero mean and its variance is σ^2. It is also applies between vehicles and users.

2.3   Delay Model

In this paper, the task processing time and the downlink transmission time are considered only in the whole process. For each user group of WVN, we use $\varepsilon \in \{0,1\}$ to indicate whether it is admitted or not. $\varepsilon = 0$ means that users are blocked, and when users are accessed, $\varepsilon = 1$. Assuming that BSs can offload the user's computing task to the BS or VFC, the binary variable $\alpha \in \{0,1\}$ is used to indicate the offloading position. When $\alpha = 1$, the task is handled by BSs, and the task is handled by the VFC as $\alpha = 0$.

Delay Model of BS. When BSs transfer the computing task of users to the local, the computation delay of task is

$$t_{m,w,b}^{comp} = \frac{d_{m,w,b}^{comp} Q_m}{q_{m,w,b}^B} \tag{1}$$

where $d_{m,w,b}^{comp}$ is the size of data of the computing task carried by the user, Q_m is the computation rate depending on the data type, and $q_{m,w,b}^B$ is the computation rate allocated by the BS to users of WVN. When the task is completed and transmitted to the user, downlink time data transmission of the user is

$$t_{m,w,b}^{tran} = \frac{d_{m,w,b}^{in}}{R_{m,w,b}^B} \tag{2}$$

where $d_{m,w,b}^{in}$ is the size of downlink data transmitted by the BS to users, and $R_{m,w,b}^B$ is the rate of data transmission, which depends on the sub-channel transmission bandwidth allocated by the BS. In summary, the total delay for users who offload tasks to the base station is

$$T_{m,w,b} = t_{m,w,b}^{comp} + t_{m,w,b}^{tran} \tag{3}$$

Delay Model of VFC. When tasks of users are offloaded to vehicles, the delay can be divided into three parts: (1) The transmission delay that BS transmits the data to target vehicles. (2) The computation delay of VFC. (3) The downlink transmission delay. The transmission delay of the first part is

$$t_{m,w,b}^{tran1} = \frac{d_{m,w,b}^{comp}}{R_{m,w,b}^{BV}} \tag{4}$$

where $R_{m,w,b}^{BV}$ is the transmission rate, and its value depends on the transmission bandwidth of the sub-channel when BS communicates with vehicles. The delay of the second part is

$$t_{m,w,b}^{comp} = \frac{d_{m,w,b}^{comp} Q_m}{q_{m,w,b}^V} \tag{5}$$

where $q_{m,w,b}^V$ is the computation rate of VFC to serve the users of WVN. The delay of the third part is

$$t_{m,w,b}^{\text{tran}\,2} = \frac{d_{m,w,b}^{in}}{R_{m,w,b}^V} \tag{6}$$

where $R_{m,w,b}^V$ is the data transmission rate when VFC communicates with users, depending on the transmission bandwidth of the sub-channel allocated by VFC. Therefore, the total delay of the user who offloads tasks to VFC is

$$T_{m,w,b} = t_{m,w,b}^{comp} + t_{m,w,b}^{tran1} + t_{m,w,b}^{tran2} \tag{7}$$

In summary, the user's delay mainly consists of two parts: the transmission delay and the computation delay. The required computing resources are only related to the amount of the calculation task, and the transmission delay is related to the position of the task offloading after admission. Since the unload location of tasks cannot be determined before the network access, the downlink transmission delay is only considered when admitting. The minimum amount of computation required at each time is

$$\bar{q} = \frac{d^{comp}}{T^{\max} - t^{tran}} \tag{8}$$

Since the resources of VFC are affected by vehicle density in time-varying, estimating the total utilization computing resources of vehicles is necessary. At the same time, when users are applying for access, the system can judge whether the network is admitted to accessing based on the existing available computing resources.

To ensure that enough computing resources can be obtained for the access of user groups, the computing resources in the system need to be considered. We use C_b to represent the total computing resources that can be used by BS in area b, and its total amount remains unchanged. $C_v(t)$ denotes the sum of available computing resources of VFC in area b at time t. Consequently, the available computing resources at each moment can be expressed as $C_b + C_v(t)$. Considering the continuous association of user tasks, we estimate the computing resources in subsequent moments and analyze the number of computing resources required by users in the network through multiple time scales. We use δ to represent a time interval. During the associated time, sufficient computing resources should be available for users at each $T^{\max}/\delta$ moment, which is represented by n.

2.4   Problem Formulation

To sum up, the problem of the admission control mechanism proposed in this paper is formulated as admission control for simultaneously incoming user groups of WVN. The strategy for the allocation of computing resources is executed for the user groups that are allowed, and the rejection strategy is executed for the blocked user groups. In order to ensure the quality of service for users after being admitted by WVN, we minimize the delay of users. Therefore, the problem can be expressed as

$$\min_{\{\varepsilon,\alpha,q\}} \sum_b^B \varepsilon \sum_w^W \sum_m^M T_{m,w,b}$$

$$s.t.\ C1 : \varepsilon, \alpha \in \{0,1\}$$

$$C2 : \varepsilon \sum_w^W \sum_m^M \alpha q_{m,w,b}^B \leq q_b^B, \forall m, w, b$$

$$C3 : \varepsilon \sum_w^W \sum_m^M (1-\alpha) q_{m,w,b}^V \leq q_b^V \phi_b, \forall m, w, b$$

$$C4 : T_{m,w,b} \leq T_{m,w,b}^{\max}, \forall m, w, b$$

$$C5 : \sum_0^n C_b + C_v(t) \geq n\varepsilon \sum_m^M \bar{q}_m, \forall m, w, b$$

Constraint C1 indicates the binary variable for admission and task offloading. The constraint C2 represents that the computing resources used by users whose tasks are offloaded to the BS cannot exceed the total computing resources owned by BS, and q_b^B represents the maximum computation rate of that the BS can provide for services. Constraint C3 means that the computing resources used by users whose tasks are offloaded to the VFC cannot exceed the total computing resources owned by VFC, where q_b^V is the maximum computation rate that the VFC can serve the users of WVN, and its value which is not fixed, determined by the total amount of computing resources owned by the vehicles forming the VFC. Constraint C4 expresses that the delay of users cannot exceed the maximum delay tolerated by users, which ensures the user quality of service. Constraint C5 denotes that the computing resources required for the admitted user groups cannot exceed the total computing resources possessed by the system. Since the total computing resources in this constraint include the computing resources of transient vehicles, it will change with the dynamics of the number of vehicles, and this change is not negligible, otherwise it will lead to access failure, which is very bad for the experience of users.

3   Admission Control Mechanism in WVN

In this section, we divide the admission control mechanism into two stages. Firstly, we implement robust admission control for user groups. Secondly, task offloading and resources allocation are processed for the admitted user groups.

3.1   Robust Admission Control

The problem mentioned in (9) cannot be solved directly since it contains two binary variables. In this paper, problem (9) is decomposed into two sub-problems to solve them separately. As the offloading position and the computation rate to be allocated are difficult to determine before the admission control for WVN, we model the two sub-problems as an admission problem and a resource allocation problem, which will be described in detail as follows.

The admission problem is a mixed-integer linear problem because ε is a binary variable in the problem (9), where $\varepsilon_{w,b}$ will be extended to a range of real numbers. Accordingly, the admission problem can be expressed as

$$\max_{\{\hat{\varepsilon}_{w,b}\}} Q(\{\hat{\varepsilon}_{w,b}\})$$

$$s.t. \; C6 : \hat{\varepsilon}_{w,b} \in [0,1] \tag{10}$$

$$C7 : n\hat{\varepsilon}_{w,b} \sum_m^M \bar{q}_m \leq \sum_0^n C_b + C_v(t), \forall m, w, b$$

The problem (10) is formulated as the maximum number of users allowed. We need to note that in constraint C7, the number of vehicles in each area mentioned earlier is variable. Changes in the number of vehicles can lead to changes in the resources that can be aggregated by VFC. This is an obvious uncertainty problem, and the quality of service for user groups of WVN is not guaranteed due to the uncertainty of resources. Therefore, it is necessary to optimize this problem using robust optimization.

Since ϕ_b is time-varying, the amount of VFC resources C_v is also time-varying. But in the long time run, the number of vehicles is averaged at a certain value, that is $\bar{\phi}_b$. To simulate the variability of density, we suppose that the relationship between the actual number of vehicles and the average number of vehicles is affected by two bounded but random parameters, which are γ and θ. At any time $\phi_b = (1+\gamma\theta)\bar{\phi}_b$, where $\gamma > 0$ is the parameter with the largest magnitude that affects the uncertainty of ϕ_b, and θ is the zero-mean random variable between $[-1,1]$, which defines the possible volatility of the number of vehicles. It means that the number of vehicles cannot deviate from the estimated number of vehicles by more than $\theta\bar{\phi}_b$, and the possible deviation level is controlled by the parameter γ.

The BS can change parameters for robustness adjustments based on robustness levels and historical statistics, which is the data on the number of vehicles. Problem (10) can be expressed as a robust problem based on the definition of the robust linear problem and similar expressions in [16–18]. When $\theta = 0$, it means that there is no uncertainty in the problem, otherwise, the problem (10) is represented by a robust correspondence problem. In the robust model proposed by the authors in [16], the corresponding robust feasible solution must satisfy the constraint of high probability if the uncertainty coefficient has bounded symmetry. Since $\bar{\phi}_b$ in $[\bar{\phi}_b - \gamma\bar{\phi}_b, \bar{\phi}_b + \gamma\bar{\phi}_b]$ has boundedness and symmetry, and the mean value is $\bar{\phi}_b$, the problem (10) follows the model proposed in [16]. The constraint C7 also can find a feasible solution $\hat{\varepsilon}_{w,b}$ when the condition is satisfied with a high probability.

Dealing with the problem (10) is very simple according to the conclusions in [17,18]. According to the method, if this paper defines the reliability level as ζ, which means that the maximum probability of dissatisfying the constraint C7 is ζ, then finding a feasible solution to problem (10) is equivalent to solving the following problem

$$\max_{\{\hat{\varepsilon}_{w,b}\}} Q(\{\hat{\varepsilon}_{w,h}\})$$

$$s.t.\ C6 : \hat{\varepsilon}_{w,b} \in [0,1]$$

$$C8 : n\hat{\varepsilon}_{w,b} \sum_{m}^{M} \bar{q}_m - nC_b - \sum_{0}^{n} C_v(t) \tag{11}$$

$$- \gamma\tau\sqrt{\sum_{0}^{n} C_v^2(t)}) \leq 0, \forall m, w, b$$

where $\zeta = \exp\{-\tau^2/2\}$. ζ can be interpreted as the overload probability of the embedded WVN. Allowing some users of WVN to exceed the system capacity with such a low probability is reasonable since the network capacity and vehicle traffic conditions change with time in practical applications. Therefore, this paper can also use the probability constraint (12) to express the constraint C8

$$\Pr\{n\hat{\varepsilon}_{w,b} \sum_{m}^{M} \bar{q}_m \leq \sum_{0}^{n} C_b + C_v(t)\} \leq \zeta, \forall m, w, b \tag{12}$$

Since ε is non-negative, the problem (11) is a convex problem based on robustness parameters (γ, ζ) and the constraint C8 is convex, whose objective functions are all linear functions. Solving the problem (11) has many ways when specific parameters (γ, ζ) are given, and in this paper, we use convex optimization to solve the problem. It is necessary to note that $\hat{\varepsilon}_{w,b} \in \{0,1\}$ is a real value bounded on [0,1], which can represent some users who are admitted to the network. However, marginal benefit [19] will be used to recover $\hat{\varepsilon}_{w,b}$ from $\varepsilon_{w,b}$ if partial admission is not allowed in the network.

3.2 Task Offloading and Resource Allacation

At this stage, we conduct traditional task offloading and resource allocation to users of WVN who have already been admitted. We do not consider the multiple associations for the time being between users and BSs or between users and VFC. For the users of WVN that have been admitted, the paper uses w_b^ε to indicate the set of them, which is denoted as

$$w \in \begin{cases} w_b^\varepsilon, & \varepsilon_{w,b} = 1 \\ w_b - w_b^\varepsilon, & others \end{cases} \tag{13}$$

As mentioned above, the unload position of users task is represented by a binary variable α, and the optimization goal of resources allocation and task offloading is the total delay of users. Thus, the problem of resource allocation and task offloading can be represented as

$$\min_{\{\alpha,q\}} \sum_b^B \sum_w^W \sum_m^M T_{m,w,b}$$

$$s.t. \; C1 : \alpha \in \{0,1\}$$

$$C2 : \sum_w^W \sum_m^M \alpha q_{m,w,b}^B \le q_b^B, \forall m, w, b \qquad (14)$$

$$C3 : \sum_w^W \sum_m^M (1-\alpha) q_{m,w,b}^V \le q_b^V \phi_b, \forall m, w, b$$

$$C4 : T_{m,w,b} \le T_{m,w,b}^{\max}, \forall m, w, b$$

The simultaneous presence of variables α and q makes constraints C2 and C3 non-convex, resulting in problem (14) not being solved directly by convex optimization. Therefore, it is necessary to make a decision on the user's offloading position firstly by fixing the average rate $\bar{q}_{m,w,b}^B$ and $\bar{q}_{m,w,b}^V$. The offloading problem can be expressed as follows

$$\min_{\{\alpha\}} \sum_b^B \sum_w^W \sum_m^M \alpha t_{m,w,b}^{tranb} + (1-\alpha) t_{m,w,b}^{tranv}$$

$$s.t. \; C1 : \alpha \in \{0,1\}$$

$$C2 : \sum_w^W \sum_m^M \alpha \bar{q}_{m,w,b}^B \le q_b^B, \forall m, w, b \qquad (15)$$

$$C3 : \sum_w^W \sum_m^M (1-\alpha) \bar{q}_{m,w,b}^V \le q_b^V \phi_b, \forall m, w, b$$

$$C4 : T_{m,w,b} \le T_{m,w,b}^{\max}, \forall m, w, b$$

Problem (15) is a mixed-integer linear programming problem, which can be solved by methods such as the branch-and-bound method to obtain the user offloading location. Once the user's offloading decision is obtained, it is substituted into the problem (14) so that it can be transformed into a convex optimization problem to be solved with the CVX tool.

4   Performance Simulation and Discussions

In this section, the proposed model is systematically verified and simulated in various aspects to demonstrate the effectiveness of the admission mechanism. We use the MATLAB platform to carry on the simulation, and the concrete parameters used in the simulation process are shown in Table 1. Considering that the focus of this paper is admission control, we carried out the admission

Table 1. The Simulation Parameters

parameters	Numerical value
System Bandwidth	10 MHz
Transmission Power	24 dbm
Noise Power Density	−174 dbm/H
Task Size	1–10 Mbits
Task Rate	500–1000 CPU Cycle/bit
Computing Rate of BS	15*10^11 CPU Cycle/s
Computing Rate of VFC	1*10^10 CPU Cycle/sehicles
Vehicles	Poisson distribution
User Groups of WVN	5–20/group /area
Users of WVN	5–9/person/WVN

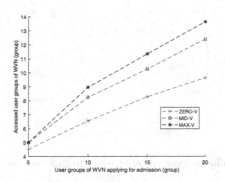

Fig. 2. Accessed number of WVNs in three cases

control simulation for user groups of WVN applying for admission. We also simulate the total delay of users after the resource allocation. The simulation results are as expected.

In order to verify the effectiveness of the admission mechanism proposed in this paper, we conduct simulation for the system performance of the different number of vehicles in the VFC assistance environment, as shown in Fig. 2. The simulation result of non-vehicular fog computing assistance is called ZERO-V. In addition, two cases with different numbers of vehicles are selected for simulation. One scenario has 30 vehicles in each area to form the VFC environment and the simulation result is called MID-V. And another has 50 vehicles, called MAX-V. It can be seen from Fig. 2 that with the assistance of VFC, more user groups of WVN can be admitted, and the more assistance vehicles, the more users will be admitted. On the other hand, the figure reflects that the system with VFC assistance can improve the admission rate effectively only when more user groups applying.

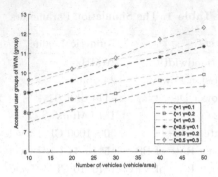

Fig. 3. Accessed number of WVNs in different environment

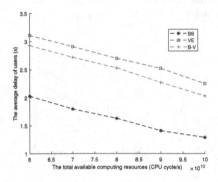

Fig. 4. The average delay of users in different environment

In Fig. 3, different robustness optimization parameters are set to evaluate its effect on the number of accessed user groups in the environment of VFC assistance in different vehicle densities. From Fig. 3, we can conclude that when ζ (user tolerance probability) is constant, the larger γ (resource fluctuation parameter) is, the more user groups can be admitted. When γ is constant, the lower ζ is, the existing system, with enough resources, can better meet the requirements of user groups so that the system can access more user groups of WVN. The number of admitted user groups will also increase as the density of vehicles increases. From the analysis of the results, it is noticeable that setting different robustness parameters plays an effective role in the admission mechanism proposed.

For verifying the total delay of the users with the assistance of VFC, we use the average delay to simulate it. The case without VFC assistance is called BS. As VFC assistance is provided, it is called B-V, and when only VFC is used for computation, we call it VE. Under three different environments, the relationship between the total available resources and the average user delay is shown in Fig. 4. When all tasks are offloaded to BSs, the users can obtain the minimum delay. However, the load of BS can easily reach the peak level, which also affect the system to access more user groups. When all tasks are offloaded to VFC

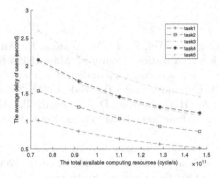

Fig. 5. The average delay of different types of users

to deal with, the delay will increase relatively. While in the case of B-V, the latency is not too high and the computational resources are guaranteed, which keeps the load of BS in a balanced state. Therefore, with the assistance of VFC, the system can increase the total number of available resources, greatly relieving the load pressure of BS, and ensuring the delay requirements of users effectively.

Finally, the task processing delay of users is evaluated. As the available computing resources will inevitably increase linearly when the number of vehicles increases, we use the total available computing resources for simulation. When the number of admitted networks is constant, we simulate the task processing delay, analyzing the relationship between the task type (mainly point to the size of the task) and the delay, as well as the task delay and the total available computing resources. The simulation result is shown in Fig. 5. It can be concluded that the average delay of users will decrease as the number of available resources increases when a certain number of WVN are admitted, which will inevitably decrease the total delay.

5   Conclusions

In this paper, we propose a robust admission mechanism for user groups of WVN in VFC assisted environment, mainly for the problems of the uncertainty of resources and low resource utilization caused by random access of user groups. This mechanism can provide effective access control for user groups of WVN with guaranteed user latency requirements and dynamic changes in resources. The mechanism has two stages. Firstly, the robust optimization model is performed to solve the admission problem of user groups in a resource-uncertain environment, and the best user groups are admitted to improve resource utilization. The second stage is traditional task offloading and resource allocation for admitted users to ensure users latency requirements. Simulation results show that the mechanism can solve the problems of user-resource mismatch and resource uncertainty in VFC. In addition, it can guarantee the QoE of users as well while accessing more user groups.

References

1. Feng, Z., Qiu, C., Feng, Z., Wei, Z., Li, W., Zhang, P.: An effective approach to 5G: wireless network virtualization. Commun. Mag. IEEE **53**(12), 53–59 (2015)
2. Liang, C., Yu, F.R.: Wireless network virtualization: a survey, some research issues and challenges. IEEE Commun. Surv. Tutorials **17**(1), 358–380 (2014)
3. Riggio, R., Bradai, A., Harutyunyan, D., Rasheed, T., Ahmed, T.: Scheduling wireless virtual networks functions. IEEE Trans. Netw. Serv. Manage. **13**(2), 240–252 (2016)
4. Anderson, T., Peterson, L., Shenker, S., Turner, J.: Overcoming the internet impasse through virtualization. Computer **38**(4), 34–41 (2005)
5. Turner, J.S., Taylor, D.E.: Diversifying the Internet. In: Global Telecommunications Conference, 2005. GLOBECOM 2005. IEEE (2005)
6. Hoang, D.T., Wang, P., Niyato, D., Hossain, E.: Charging and discharging of plug-in electric vehicles (PEVs) in vehicle-to-grid (V2G) systems: a cyber insurance-based model. IEEE Access **5**(99), 732–754 (2017)
7. Liu, N., Ming, L., Wei, L., Chen, G., Cao, J.: PVA in VANETs: Stopped cars are not silent. In: INFOCOM, 2011 Proceedings. IEEE (2011)
8. Malandrino, F., Casetti, C., Chiasserini, C.F., Sommer, C., Dressler, F.: The role of parked cars in content downloading for vehicular networks. Veh. Technol. IEEE Trans. **63**(9), 4606–4617 (2014)
9. Zhang, Y., Wang, C., Wei, H.Y.: Parking reservation auction for parked vehicle assistance in vehicular fog computing. IEEE Trans. Veh. Technol. **PP**(99), 1–1 (2019)
10. Zhou, Z., Liao, H., Zhao, X., Ai, B., Guizani, M.: Reliable task offloading for vehicular fog computing under information asymmetry and information uncertainty. IEEE Trans. Veh. Technol. **PP**(99), 1–1 (2019)
11. Xie, J., Jia, Y., Chen, Z., Nan, Z., Liang, L.: Efficient task completion for parallel offloading in vehicular fog computing. China Commun. **16**(11), 14 (2019)
12. Liang, C., Yu, F.R.: Mobile virtual network admission control and resource allocation for wireless network virtualization: a robust optimization approach. In: 2015 IEEE Global Communications Conference (GLOBECOM). IEEE (2015)
13. Park, K.M., Kim, C.K.: A framework for virtual network embedding in wireless networks. ACM(2009)
14. Yun, D., Yi, Y.: Virtual network embedding in wireless multihop networks. In: International Conference on Future Internet Technologies. ACM (2011)
15. Mirahsan, M., Senarath, G., Farmanbar, H., Dao, N.D., Yanikomeroglu, H.: Admission control of wireless virtual networks in HetHetN ets. IEEE Trans. Veh. Technol. **67**(5), 4565–4576 (2018)
16. Bertsimas, D., Brown, D.B., Caramanis, C.: Theory and applications of robust optimization. SIAM Review (2011)
17. Ben-Tal, A., Nemirovski, A.: Robust solutions of linear programming problems contaminated with uncertain data. Math. Program. **88**(3), 411–424 (2000)
18. Yun, S., Caramanis, C.: System-level optimization in wireless networks: managing interference and uncertainty via robust optimization. IEEE/ACM Trans. Netw. **20**(2), 339–352 (2012)
19. Liu, G., Yu, F.R., Ji, H., Leung, V.C.M.: Energy-efficient resource allocation in cellular networks with shared full-duplex relaying. IEEE Trans. Veh. Technol. **64**(8), 3711–3724 (2015)

Convolutional Recurrent Neural Network Based on Short-Time Discrete Cosine Transform for Monaural Speech Enhancement

Jinzuo Guo[1]($\boxtimes$), Yi Zhou[1], Hongqing Liu[1], and Yongbao Ma[2]

[1] School of Communication and Information Engineering,
Chongqing University of Posts and Telecommunications, Chongqing, China
s200131221@stu.cqupt.edu.cn
[2] Suresense Technology, Chongqing 400065, China

Abstract. Speech enhancement algorithms based on deep learning have greatly improved speech's perceptual quality and intelligibility. Complex-valued neural networks, such as deep complex convolution recurrent network (DCCRN), make full use of audio signal phase information and achieve superior performance, but complex-valued operations increase the computational complexity. Inspired by the deep cosine transform convolutional recurrent network (DCTCRN) model, in this paper real-valued discrete cosine transform is used instead of complex-valued Fourier transform. Besides, the ideal cosine mask is employed as the training target, and the real-valued convolutional recurrent network (CRNN) is used to enhance the speech while reducing algorithm complexity. Meanwhile, the frequency-time-LSTM (F-T-LSTM) module is used for better temporal modeling and the convolutional skip connections module is introduced between the encoders and the decoders to integrate the information between features. Moreover, the improved scale-invariant source-to-noise ratio (SI-SNR) is taken as the loss function which enables the model to focus more on the part of signal variation and thus obtain better noise suppression performance. With only 1.31M parameters, the proposed method can achieve noise suppression performance that exceeds DCCRN and DCTCRN.

Keywords: Speech enhancement · Deep learning · Convolutional recurrent neural network · Discrete cosine transform

1 Introduction

Speech enhancement refers to the extraction of the purest possible target speech from noisy speech. It belongs to an important branch of audio front-end processing. Traditional single-channel speech enhancement algorithms include spectral-subtractive algorithms [1], minimum mean square error estimation [2], and wiener filtering [3]. These algorithms have fast calculations and require low-performance

F. Gao et al. (Eds.): ChinaCom 2022, LNICST 500, pp. 163–173, 2023.
https://doi.org/10.1007/978-3-031-34790-0_13

hardware, but their robustness is poor, and they usually can not handle non-stationary noise well. Deep learning-based methods treat speech enhancement as a supervised learning problem and use neural networks' powerful nonlinear fitting ability to remove non-stationary noise in complex acoustic environments. These methods can be divided into two main categories: mapping and mask-based methods. The mapping methods learn the mapping relationship between the noisy speech and the clean speech by training a neural network model. The mask-based methods estimate a mask to classify noise and clean speech signals and then obtain the enhanced speech signal by weighting it with the noisy signal. Common masks include the ideal binary mask (IBM) [4], the ideal ratio mask (IRM) [5], the phase sensitive mask (PSM) [6] and the complex ratio mask (CRM) [7], which show better performance than direct spectral mapping.

The end-to-end model is a typical time-domain method by inputting the original speech signal and directly outputting the final enhanced speech signal, for example, Conv-tasnet [8], which belongs to the encoder-decoder framework. It extracts features from the speech waveform by a 1-D convolutional neural network (Conv1d) in the encoding stage and then passes them through the temporal convolutional network (TCN) as the enhancement module. Finally, the speech is reconstructed by a 1-D convolutional transpose neural network (ConvTranspose1d) in the decoding stage. Although the performance is excellent, a large number of Conv1d layers used to obtain a suitable receptive field lead to large latency and computational complexity, which limits its application in the low-latency domain.

Another popular method is to convert the speech signal to the time-frequency domain by short-time fast Fourier transform (STFT) and then estimate the amplitude spectrum of the original signal from the amplitude spectrum of the noisy signal, and finally combine it with the phase information of the noisy signal to obtain the enhanced speech signal [9]. It focuses on signal amplitude and neglects the phase information which greatly limits the performance of the model. The deep complex convolution recurrent network DCCRN [10] model combines the advantages of deep complex u-net (DCUNET) [11] and convolutional recurrent network (CRNN) [12] using the complex-valued network to estimate CRM and reconstruct the magnitude and phase of speech by simultaneously augmenting the real and imaginary components of the spectrogram of the speech signal. It has shown excellent performance in the 2020 Deep Noise Suppression (DNS) challenge. However, complex-valued networks increase computational complexity. To address this issue, the recently proposed deep cosine transform convolutional recurrent network DCTCRN [13] model, which uses discrete cosine variation as input, is trained using a real-valued network, which reduces the number of parameters and improves the performance compared with DCCRN.

In this paper, we make full use of the advantages of DCCRN and DCTCRN. Firstly, discrete cosine transforms are used in preparing input features. Secondly, the F-T-LSTM [14] is used for temporal modeling, and the convolutional module is employed to integrate inter-feature information in the skip connections part [15]. Lastly, we modify the scale-invariant source-to-noise ratio (SI-SNR) as a loss function. Experimental results show that the proposed model with fewer parameters outperforms those of both DCCRN and DCTCRN in terms of objective metrics.

2 Proposed Model

2.1 System Architecture

CRNN is a single-channel real-time speech enhancement model proposed by Ke Tan in 2018 [12], which is an encoder-decoder architecture with a two-layer LSTM as the processor. We have made several revisions to the CRNN model: 1. Introduce the F-T-LSTM module to temporal modeling [14]. 2. Add the convolutional module in the skip connections section between the encoders and the decoders [15]. 3. Optimize SI-SNR as loss function. The structural diagram of the proposed model is shown in Fig. 1.

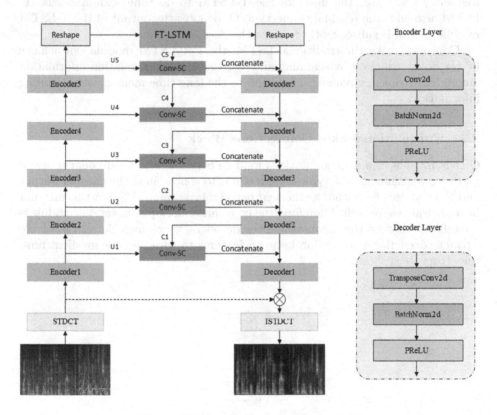

Fig. 1. The proposed network structure

2.2 F-T-LSTM Block

The frequency-time-LSTM (F-T-LSTM) module first scans the frequency bands to generate a summary of the spectral information, then uses the output layer activations as the input to a traditional time-LSTM (T-LSTM) for time scale summarization. It can be described as follows:

$$\text{F-LSTM:} \begin{cases} U_f = \text{BLSTM}(E[i, :, :]), i = 1 \cdots F \\ O_f = U_f + E \end{cases},$$
$$\text{T-LSTM:} \begin{cases} U_t = \text{LSTM}(O_f[:, i, :]), i = 1 \cdots T \\ O_t = U_t + O_f \end{cases} \tag{1}$$

where $E \in R^{F \times T \times C}$ denotes the output of the encoder. Send E to BLSTM to obtain U_f, then add a residual connection to obtain O_f (the output of the frequency-LSTM) as the input of the T-LSTM to do time scale analysis. T-LSTM also adds the residual connection, O_t denotes the output of the T-LSTM module, which is subsequently fed into the decoder.

Compared with the traditional LSTM, the F-T-LSTM module can achieve better noise reduction by scanning and aggregating the correlation information among the frequency points, in addition to the long time memory of the timing information.

2.3 Convolutional Skip Connections Block

CRNN introduces a skip connections module between encoder-decoder to avoid gradient vanishment. The typical approach is to concatenate the encoder output and the last decoder output as the next decoder layer input [12], but this may not be a favorable approach. Therefore, the convolutional skip connections module is introduced between the encoders and the decoders, which uses Conv2d blocks to extract correlation information between features to speed up the gradient flow, the structure is shown in Fig. 2.

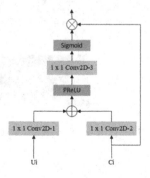

Fig. 2. Convolutional skip connections block

U_i is the output of the encoder layers and C_i is the output of F-T-LSTM or the decoder layers. There are two 1×1 Conv2D layers with output channels being twice that of the input channels, mapping U_i and C_i to a high-dimensional space for information integration, with corresponding weights W_C and W_U, respectively. The high-dimensional space feature layer output can be described as:

$$A_i = PReLU\left(W_U \otimes U_i + W_C \otimes C_i\right) \tag{2}$$

where U_i and C_i represent the ith layer of the encoder and the decoder, respectively. $PReLU$ is Parametric Rectified Linear Unit (PReLU, the range is -inf to inf). The output of the convolutional skip connections block is

$$B_i = \sigma\left(W_f \otimes A_i\right) \cdot C_i \tag{3}$$

where W_f represents a 1×1 Conv2D layer with output channels being half of the input channels. σ is the sigmoid function, and the range is 0 to 1.

2.4 Input Feature

DCT is a transform related to DFT but uses only real numbers [13]. In addition to the general orthogonal transform properties, the basis vectors of the transform array of DCT can well describe the correlation characteristics of speech and image signals. Therefore, DCT is considered as a quasi-optimal transform in transforming speech signals and image signals. DCT is defined as:

$$F(u) = c(u) \sum_{n=0}^{N-1} f(n) \cos\left[\frac{\pi u(2n+1)}{2N}\right], u = 0, 1, \ldots, N-1, \tag{4}$$

and the inverse DCT is defined as:

$$f(n) = \sum_{n=0}^{N-1} c(u) F(u) \cos\left[\frac{\pi u(2n+1)}{2N}\right], n = 0, 1, \ldots, N-1 \tag{5}$$

where $c(u)$ is a compensation factor that allows the DCT transformation matrix to be orthogonal.

$$c(u) = \begin{cases} \sqrt{\dfrac{1}{N}}, & u = 0, \\ \sqrt{\dfrac{2}{N}}, & u = 1, 2, \ldots, N-1. \end{cases} \tag{6}$$

where $f(n)$ is the original signal. $F(u)$ is the DCT-transformed coefficient, and N is the number of points of the original signal.

2.5 Training Target

The training target is an ideal cosine mask (ICM) optimized by signal approximation (SA). The ICM can be defined as:

$$ICM_{t,f} = \frac{S_{t,f}}{Y_{t,f}} \tag{7}$$

where $S_{t,f}$ and $Y_{t,f}$ denote the DCT coefficients of the clean speech and the noisy speech in a particular T-F unit respectively.

2.6 Loss Fuction

The loss function is based on SI-SNR, which is an important metric of speech quality and defined as:

$$\begin{cases} s_{\text{target}} = \frac{<\hat{s},s> \cdot s}{\|s\|_2^2}, \\ e_{\text{noise}} = \hat{s} - s, \\ SI - SNR = 10 * \log_{10}\left(\frac{\|s_{\text{target}}\|_2^2}{\|e_{\text{noise}}\|_2^2}\right). \end{cases} \tag{8}$$

where s and $\hat{s}$ are the clean and estimated time-domain speech data, respectively. $< .,. >$ denotes the dot product between two vectors, and $\|.\|_2$ is the Euclidean norm (L2 norm).

Improved SI-SNR uses the noisy signal and clean signal to calculate the value of SI-SNR and then uses the enhanced signal and clean signal to calculate the value of SI-SNR. The final result is the subtraction of the above two values. The advantage of the improved SI-SNR is it enables the model to focus more on the part of the signal variation, and our experiments prove that the improved SI-SNR works better than the SI-SNR in noise suppression tasks. The improved SI-SNR is defined as:

$$SI - SNR_i = SI - SNR_{(S,\hat{S})} - SI - SNR_{(S,Y)} \tag{9}$$

where $SI - SNR_{(S,\hat{S})}$ and $SI - SNR_{(S,Y)}$ represent the SI-SNR score of the enhanced and clean signal and the SI-SNR score of the noisy and clean signal, respectively.

3 Experiment

3.1 Datasets

In our experiments, we evaluate the proposed models on two datasets.

3.1.1   Dataset 1 (DNS 2020): The first dataset is generated based on the Interspeech 2020 DNS Challenge dataset [16], all the waveforms are sampled at 16kHz. The DNS Challenge clean speech dataset was derived from the public audiobook dataset Librivox1. It has a recording of volunteers reading over 10,000 public domain audiobooks in different languages, most of which are in English. It contains over 500 h of speech from 2150 speakers. And the noise dataset consists of a 180-hour noise set which includes 150 classes and 65,000 noise clips, which were selected from Audioset2 and Freesound3. We randomly select speech clips and noise clips to create a 500-hour noisy training set, with a signal-to-noise ratio being set at -10db to 20db. Each selected audio clip is set to 10 s. We estimated the proposed model with the DNS-2020 synthetic no reverb test set.

3.1.2   Dataset 2 (Noisy Speech Database): The clean data in the second dataset are from [17], which is widely used in speech enhancement research. This clean set is obtained from sentence recordings of various text passages and 30 English speakers were selected from the Voice Bank corpus [18], including males and females with various accents. 28 and 2 speakers were assigned to the training and test sets, respectively. The noise data are obtained from NoiseX-92 [19], which contains 15 types of noise such as White noise, Pink noise, HF channel noise, Speech babble, factory floor noise, etc. We use the above clean speech and noise to synthesize a 50 h training set with a signal-to-noise ratio (SNR) of 0 db-20 db, 40% of the data set without reverberation, and 60% of the data set with reverberation (T60 from 0.3 s to 1.3 s). Room impulse response (RIR) is randomly-selected from the DNS RIR dataset. To verify the noise suppression performance of the model under different SNR and reverberation or non-reverberation. We generate two test sets: reverberant and non-reverberant test sets, and the SNR are set to (0 db,5 db,10 db,15 db,20 db).

3.2   Training Setup and Baselines

The baseline structure is shown in Fig. 1, with the difference that instead of introducing the convolutional module in the skip connections section between the encoders and the decoders, simple stacking is used. The details of the setup are as follows: In the DCT transform, the window function is the periodic Hanning window, the window length and frameshift are 32 ms and 8 ms, and the DCT length is 512 points. The optimizer is Adam gradient, with an initialized learning rate of 1e–3, and it will decay 0.5 when the validation loss goes up. The model is selected by early stopping. The loss function is SI-SNR or Improved SI-SNR. We compare the proposed model with DTLN, DCCRN-E and DCTCRN, and their detail settings are as follows.

- DTLN: The window length and hop sizes are 32 ms and 8 ms, and the FFT length is 512. The number of each LSTM nodes is set to 128. During training, 25% of dropout is applied between the LSTM layers. The 1D-Conv Layer to create the learned feature representation has 256 fifilters.

- DCCRN-E: the window length and hop sizes are 25 ms and 6.25 ms, and the FFT length is 512. The number of channels for the DCCRN-E is {32, 64, 128, 128, 256, 256}. The kernel size and stride are set to (5,2) and (2,1). The number of two-layer LSTM nodes is set to 256. There is a 1024*256 fully connected layer after the LSTM. In the encoder module, pad one zero-frame in front of the time dimension at each convolutional encoder layer. In the decoder module, look ahead with one frame in each convolutional layer.
- DCTCRN: the window length and hop sizes are 32 ms and 8 ms, and the DCT length is 512. The number of channels for the DCTCRN is {8, 16, 32, 64, 128, 128, 256}. The kernel size and stride are set to (5,2) and (2,1). The number of two-layer LSTM nodes is set to 256. In the encoder module, pad one zero-frame in front of the time dimension at each Conv2ds. In the decoder module, remove the last time frame at each transpose convolutional decoder.
- Baseline: the window length and hop sizes are 32 ms and 8 ms, and the DCT length is 512. The number of channels for the baseline is {16, 32, 64, 128, 128}. The kernel size and stride are set to (5,2) and (2,1). The number of F-T-LSTM nodes is set to 128. As with DCCRN-E, pad one zero-frame in front of the time dimension at each encoder and look ahead a frame at each decoder, totally $5 \times 8 = 40$ ms, confined with the DNS challenge limit—40 ms.

3.3 Evaluation Results and Discussions

The perceptual evaluation of speech quality (PESQ) [20] is employed to verify the noise reduction performance of DTLN, DCTCRN, DCCRN-E, and our model on dataset 1. We conduct ablation experiments to verify the performance of each module. Our proposed model achieves the highest PESQ scores among all models, which are shown in Table 1. In addition, we use flops-counter. Pytorch to compute the MACs and parameters of the models. Our model only has 1/3 parameters and 60% GMACs when compared with DCCRN, but the PESQ score on the DNS-2020 synthetic no reverb test set is 0.18 higher. Compared with DCTCRN, although our model is more computationally intensive, it can achieve a better noise reduction effect with fewer parameters.

Table 1. Various models' PESQ on DNS-2020 synthetic no reverb test set

Modle	Para.(M)	GMacs	look ahead(ms)	PESQ
Noisy	–	0	0	2.45
DTLN	1.0	1.58	0	3.04
DCTCRN	2.86	2.69	0	3.24
DCCRN-E	3.98	10.1	37.5	3.26
Baseline	1.08	5.12	40	3.39
+Convolutional SC	1.31	6.06	40	3.43
+Improved SI-SNR	1.31	6.06	40	**3.44**

To verify the noise reduction performance of the models at each dB and with or without reverberation. The PESQ and STOI [21] scores of the models in the test set 2 are tested. Table 2 and Table 3 show the objective results on the test set without reverberation, and Table 4 and Table 5 show the results under reverberant conditions, respectively (In the table, PROPOSED stands for Baseline + Convolutional SC + Improved SI-SNR). In each case, the best result is highlighted by a boldface number.

Table 2. Various models' PESQ on the non-reverberation dataset 2

test SNR	0 dB	5 dB	10 dB	15 dB	20 dB	Avg.
Noisy	1.559	1.876	2.222	2.560	2.870	2.217
DCTCRN	2.443	2.482	3.148	3.403	3.617	3.018
DCCRN-E	2.542	2.907	3.207	3.460	**3.704**	3.164
PROPOSED	**2.622**	**2.954**	**3.236**	**3.476**	3.684	**3.194**

Table 3. Various models' STOI(IN%) on the non-reverberation dataset 2

test SNR	0 dB	5 dB	10 dB	15 dB	20 dB	Avg.
Noisy	73.58	82.01	88.68	93.24	96.06	86.71
DCTCRN	83.62	90.13	93.81	96.05	97.52	92.22
DCCRN-E	84.97	90.71	94.01	96.11	97.54	92.66
PROPOSED	**85.65**	**91.03**	**94.22**	**96.24**	**97.65**	**92.95**

From the results of the non-reverberant set, it can be found that the PESQ score of DCCRN-E is slightly higher than our model at 20 dB. In all other cases, our model outperforms DCCRN-E and DCTCRN in both PESQ and STOI. Our model achieves state-of-the-art performance, with DCCRN-E being the second and DCTCRN being the worst. As can be seen from Tables 2 and 3, our model outperforms DCCRN-E at low SNRs and is similar to that of DCCRN-E at high SNRs.

Table 4. Various models' PESQ on the reverberation dataset 2

test SNR	0 dB	5 dB	10 dB	15 dB	20 dB	Avg.
Noisy	1.687	1.980	2.299	2.628	2.911	2.301
DCTCRN	2.412	2.804	3.134	3.408	3.626	3.076
DCCRN-E	2.433	2.801	3.128	3.416	3.653	3.086
PROPOSED	**2.511**	**2.905**	**3.235**	**3.507**	**3.724**	**3.176**

Table 5. Various models' STOI(IN%) on the reverberation dataset 2

test SNR	0 dB	5 dB	10 dB	15 dB	20 dB	Avg.
Noisy	72.38	82.95	90.57	95.37	97.86	87.82
DCTCRN	82.78	90.68	95.11	97.52	98.73	92.96
DCCRN-E	83.35	90.96	95.22	97.57	98.80	93.18
PROPOSED	**84.14**	**91.38**	**95.43**	**97.69**	**98.84**	**93.49**

On the reverberation test set, our model gets the best results among all conditions. DCTCRN and DCCRN-E yield similar PESQ and STOI scores, while our model performs much better than DCTCRN and DCCRN-E. Unlike the non-reverberant case, our model is much better than DCCRN-E in all dB conditions, and the results indicate that it is more promising for denoising with reverberation.

3.4 Conclusions

In this work, we propose a DCT-based real-valued CRNN for single-channel speech enhancement. We introduce the F-T-LSTM module and the convolutional skip connections module on the original CRNN and improve the loss function SI-SNR. Experimental results show that our model has only 1/3 parameters and 60% computational effort of DCCRN-E, but it outperforms both DCCRN-E and DCTCRN. In addition, our model has excellent noise suppression performance in the reverberation case.

References

1. Boll, S.: Suppression of acoustic noise in speech using spectral subtraction. IEEE Trans. Acoust. Speech Sig. Process. **27**(2), 113–120 (1979)
2. Hendriks, R.C., Heusdens, R., Jensen, J.: MMSE based noise PSD tracking with low complexity. In: 2010 IEEE International Conference on Acoustics, Speech and Signal Processing, pp. 4266–4269. IEEE (2010)
3. Abd El-Fattah, M., Dessouky, M.I., Diab, S., Abd El-Samie, F.: Speech enhancement using an adaptive wiener filtering approach. Prog. Electromagnet. Res. M **4**, 167–184 (2008)
4. Hu, G., Wang, D.: Speech segregation based on pitch tracking and amplitude modulation. In: Proceedings of the 2001 IEEE Workshop on the Applications of Signal Processing to Audio and Acoustics (Cat. No. 01TH8575), pp. 79–82. IEEE (2001)
5. Srinivasan, S., Roman, N., Wang, D.: Binary and ratio time-frequency masks for robust speech recognition. Speech Commun. **48**(11), 1486–1501 (2006)
6. Wang, X., Bao, C.: Mask estimation incorporating phase-sensitive information for speech enhancement. Appl. Acoust. **156**, 101–112 (2019)
7. Williamson, D.S., Wang, Y., Wang, D.: Complex ratio masking for monaural speech separation. IEEE/ACM Trans. Audio Speech Lang. Process. **24**(3), 483–492 (2015)

8. Luo, Y., Mesgarani, N.: Conv-TasNet: surpassing ideal time-frequency magnitude masking for speech separation. IEEE/ACM Trans. Audio Speech Lang. Process. **27**(8), 1256–1266 (2019)
9. Xu, Y., Du, J., Dai, L.R., Lee, C.H.: An experimental study on speech enhancement based on deep neural networks. IEEE Sig. Process Lett. **21**(1), 65–68 (2013)
10. Hu, Y., et al.: DCCRN: deep complex convolution recurrent network for phase-aware speech enhancement. arXiv preprint arXiv:2008.00264 (2020)
11. Choi, H.S., Kim, J.H., Huh, J., Kim, A., Ha, J.W., Lee, K.: Phase-aware speech enhancement with deep complex U-Net. In: International Conference on Learning Representations (2018)
12. Tan, K., Wang, D.: A convolutional recurrent neural network for real-time speech enhancement. In: Interspeech. vol. 2018, pp. 3229–3233 (2018)
13. Li, Q., Gao, F., Guan, H., Ma, K.: Real-time monaural speech enhancement with short-time discrete cosine transform. arXiv preprint arXiv:2102.04629 (2021)
14. Li, J., Mohamed, A., Zweig, G., Gong, Y.: LSTM time and frequency recurrence for automatic speech recognition. In: 2015 IEEE Workshop on Automatic Speech Recognition and Understanding (ASRU), pp. 187–191. IEEE (2015)
15. Zhou, L., Gao, Y., Wang, Z., Li, J., Zhang, W.: Complex spectral mapping with attention based convolution recurrent neural network for speech enhancement. arXiv preprint arXiv:2104.05267 (2021)
16. Reddy, C.K., et al.: ICASSP 2021 deep noise suppression challenge. In: ICASSP 2021–2021 IEEE International Conference on Acoustics, Speech and Signal Processing (ICASSP), pp. 6623–6627. IEEE (2021)
17. Valentini-Botinhao, C., et al.: Noisy speech database for training speech enhancement algorithms and TTS models (2017)
18. Veaux, C., Yamagishi, J., King, S.: The voice bank corpus: Design, collection and data analysis of a large regional accent speech database. In: 2013 International Conference Oriental COCOSDA Held Jointly with 2013 Conference on Asian Spoken Language Research and Evaluation (O-COCOSDA/CASLRE), pp. 1–4. IEEE (2013)
19. Varga, A.: The NOISEX-92 study on the effect of additive noise on automatic speech recognition. ICAL Report, DRA Speech Research Unit (1992)
20. Rix, A.W., Beerends, J.G., Hollier, M.P., Hekstra, A.P.: Perceptual evaluation of speech quality (PESQ)-a new method for speech quality assessment of telephone networks and codecs. In: 2001 IEEE International Conference on Acoustics, Speech, and Signal Processing. Proceedings (Cat. No. 01CH37221). vol. 2, pp. 749–752. IEEE (2001)
21. Taal, C.H., Hendriks, R.C., Heusdens, R., Jensen, J.: A short-time objective intelligibility measure for time-frequency weighted noisy speech. In: 2010 IEEE International Conference on Acoustics, Speech and Signal Processing, pp. 4214–4217. IEEE (2010)

Data Balancing Technique Based on AE-Flow Model for Network Instrusion Detection

Xuanrui Xiong[1], Yufan Zhang[1(✉)], Huijun Zhang[2], Yi Chen[1], Hailing Fang[1], Wen Xu[1], Weiqing Lin[1], and Yuan Zhang[3]

[1] College of Communication and Information Engineering, Chongqing University of Posts and Telecommunications, Chongqing 400065, China
xiongxr@cqupt.edu.cn, zhanghj@ctbu.edu.cn, s200101041@stu.cqupt.edu.cn
[2] College of Environmental Resources, Chongqing Technology and Business University, Chongqing 400067, China
[3] School of Computing, Chongqing Institute of Engineering, Chongqing 400056, China
zhangyuan@cqie.edu.cn

Abstract. In network intrusion detection, the frequency of some rare network attacks is low, and such samples collected are relatively few. It results in an imbalanced proportion of each category in the dataset. Training the classifier with imbalanced datasets will bias the classifier to majority class samples and affect the classification performance on minority class samples. In response to this problem, researchers usually increase minority class samples and reduce majority class samples to get a balanced dataset. Therefore, we propose a data balancing technique based on AutoEncoder-Flow (AE-Flow) Model. Firstly, we use AutoEncoder (AE) to improve the deep generative model-Flow, obtaining AE-Flow. Then we use it to learn the distribution of minority class samples and generate new samples. Secondly, we use K-means and OneSidedSelection (OSS) algorithms to finish the undersampling of majority class samples. Finally we get a balanced dataset and use machine learning (ML) classifier to finish intrusion detection. We conducted comparative experiments on NSL-KDD dataset. The experimental results show that the balanced dataset obtained by our proposed method can effectively improve the Recall rate on minority class samples and the classification performance on overall samples.

Keywords: Imbalanced data · Deep generative model-Flow · AutoEncoder · Network Intrusion Detection

Supported by the National Natural Science Foundation of China (51808079), Chongqing Research Program of Basic Research and Frontier Technology (cstc2017jcyj AX0470, cstc2017jcyjAX0135), the Science and Technology Research Program of Chongqing Municipal Education Commission (No. KJQN201801908).

F. Gao et al. (Eds.): ChinaCom 2022, LNICST 500, pp. 174–190, 2023.
https://doi.org/10.1007/978-3-031-34790-0_14

1   Introduction

The task of network intrusion detection is to identify the abnormal traffic in network and judge which attack it belongs to. Therefore, network intrusion detection is essentially a multi-classification task. Now classical machine learning classifiers such as Decision Tree (DT), Random Forest (RF), Logistic Regression (LR) and eXtreme Gradient Boosting (XGBoost) are widely used in network intrusion detection [1]- [2]. However, the frequency of various types of intrusions is different in network, so the number of different categories samples in collected network intrusion records varies greatly, which makes the relative datasets have the problem of category imbalance. Because the quantity of some rare attacks is too small, it is difficult for classifier to learn its general characteristics during training. Therefor, it is easy to misjudge minority class samples into majority class during testing, which makes the recall rate of minority class samples especially low.

Training models with imbalanced datasets has always been a challenge for researchers. The traditional ways dealing with imbalanced datasets are oversampling of minority class and undersampling of majority class. The commonly used undersampling methods are generally Random Undersampling and its improvements based on various clustering algorithms. While the oversampling algorithms are generally various improvements based on Synthetic Minority Oversampling Technique (SMOTE) algorithm [3]. But SMOTE is easy to generate redundant samples and noise samples, which will affect the classification performance. With the development of deep learning, many researchers choose deep generative model to generate new samples.

In recent years, Generative Adversarial Network (GAN), Variational Auto-Encoders (VAE) and Flow-based generative model are widely used in the fields of image, speech and text generation. Now both VAE and GAN have been widely used in network intrusion detection domain. In literature [4], the authors used Conditional VAE model to learn the feature of real samples for generating more samples. In this way they rebalanced the data proportion of training datasets. In [5], the authors improved VAE by using overall covariance Gaussian distribution as posterior probability distribution, obtaining the Variational Laplace AutoEncoder (VLAE) model. It enhanced the expressiveness of posterior data and can generate high-quality minority samples. In [6], the authors used conditional generative adversarial network (CGAN) to input samples and their labels simultaneously into its generator network for training, which can specify the category of new samples generated.

The deep generative model uses its powerful learning ability to learn the distribution of samples through training, and generates new samples that conforms to this distribution [7]. The generated samples can effectively expand the quantity and the diversity of original data. Therefore, we select the Flow-based model to generate minority class samples. We propose an AE-Flow model combined with K-means and OSS algorithms to achieve the goal of data balancing, and test the balanced dataset by using ML classifier. The main contributions of this paper are as follows:

1. Aiming at the problem that Flow-based model has a long training time and a huge structure, we introduce AE to simplify it by sharing the tasks of it. In this way we get the AE-Flow model and train it to generate high-quality minority class samples.
2. We use K-means to cluster majority class samples and undersampling from them for removing redundant ones in them. And we use OSS to remove majority class noise samples located near the boundary of minority class samples.
3. A balanced dataset can be obtained by applying aboved methods. The effectiveness of our proposed method is proved by comparing the classification performance of the classifiers before and after the data balancing operation.
4. We compared our proposal with other data balancing methods: SMOTE, VAE, GAN. The experimental results demonstrate the superiority of our proposal.

The structure of this paper is organized as follows: Sect. 2 briefly introduces the theories related to our approach. Section 3 details the proposed method. Section 4 presents the experimental results and analysis, and we conclude in Sect. 5.

2   Backgroud

The method proposed in this paper has mainly used the deep generative model-Flow, the unsupervised model-AutoEncoder. Next, we will introduce their theories and usages in detail.

2.1   Flow-Based Model

The goal of generative model is to use a known probability density model to fit the distribution of real data samples. But the distribution of real sample is complex, so the flow-based model applies a series of invertible transformation to convert a simple distribution to a complex distribution. It means Flow performs multiple invertible transformations on the input samples, making it become a latent variable of a known distribution (generally Gaussian distribution), completing the mapping from real data space to latent variables space [8]. Since each step of transformation in flow model is invertible, when the model training is completed, it can sample a random vector from the latent variable space and transform it to a new data sample through multiple inverse transformations.

If we represent the real sample and its probability distribution as $x \sim p_\theta(x)$, the latent variable and its probability distributions as $z \sim p_\varphi(z)$, and the $p_\varphi(z)$ taking a Gaussian distribution, then the flow model is to require the reversible transformation to make

$$z = F(x)$$
$$x = F^{-1}(z) \tag{1}$$

where F represents the invertible transformation. Because the single-step reversible transformation cannot achieve a strong nonlinearity, but the entire model needs a strong nonlinear transformation to complete the mapping from x to z. So Flow requires many steps of invertible transformations to be coupled [9]. Hence, F is a combination of multi-step invertible transformations: $F = f_1 * f_2 \cdots * f_n$. Then the mapping from x to z is

$$x = h_0 \overset{f_1}{\leftrightarrow} h_1 \overset{f_2}{\leftrightarrow} h_2 \cdots \overset{f_i}{\leftrightarrow} h_i \cdots \overset{f_n}{\leftrightarrow} h_n = z \tag{2}$$

where h_i is the hidden variable of middle layer output after each step of invertible transformation f_i .

Because the density of z is known as $p_\varphi(z)$,and $z = F(x)$, according to the variation theorem, the probability density function of x can be expressed as

$$p_\theta(x) = p_\varphi(z)| \det \frac{\partial F(x)}{\partial x}| \tag{3}$$

where $\frac{\partial F(x)}{\partial x}$ is the Jacobian matrix of $F(x)$ at x .

The task of Flow is to maximize the log-likelihood probability density $p_\theta(x)$ by updating the parameters of invertible transformations through training, which means

$$\max \log p_\theta(x) = \max \log p_\varphi(z) + \log |\det \frac{\partial F(x)}{\partial x}| \tag{4}$$

So the loss function of Flow is to minimizing the negative log-likelihood as

$$\begin{aligned} L_{Flow} &= -\log p_\theta(x) \\ &= -(\log p_\varphi(z) + \log |\det \frac{\partial F(x)}{\partial x}|) \end{aligned} \tag{5}$$

Where $\log p_\theta(x)$ is maximized indirectly by reducing the loss function through model training. However, the computational cost of Jacobian matrix determinant in formula(5) can be very high. If the transformation can be designed to make the Jacobian be an upper or a lower triangular, the determinant can easily be computed as the product of its diagonal terms. In order to make this Jacobian easy to compute, researchers devised different methods to solve this problem. Bengio, the authors of NICE [10] has divided the input samples into two parts by designing an additive coupling layer, and performed the following transformations as

$$\begin{aligned} y_1 &= x_1 \\ y_2 &= x_1 + f(x_2) \end{aligned} \tag{6}$$

where f represents a one-step reversible transformation. This way makes the Jacobian matrix be a triangular matrix, and the diagonal elements are all 1. The whole transformation is also invertible [10]. Its inverse transformation is

$$\begin{aligned} x_1 &= y_1 \\ x_2 &= y_2 - f(y_1) \end{aligned} \tag{7}$$

So far, the two major requirements of flow that transformation is invertible and the corresponding Jacobian determinant is easy to calculate has been solved by this design. Later, Bengio proposed a more generalized affine coupling layer in model Real-NVP [11] to improve NICE.

2.2   AutoEncoder

AutoEncoder is a typical unsupervised neural network model that mainly includes two modules: Encoder and Decoder, which is often used for feature extraction and dimensionality reduction [12]. Its network structure is shown in Fig. 1.

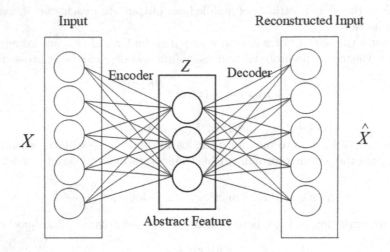

Fig. 1. AutoEncoder model

As shown in Fig. 1, the model maps the input data X to feature space through Encoder to obtain the feature vectors Z, and then maps the feature vectors Z back to original data space through Decoder to obtain the reconstructed samples $\hat{X}$. Its loss function is the reconstruction error between reconstructed data and the original data, which is the mean-square error (MSE) of $\hat{X}$ with X. During model training, the Encoder and Decoder are optimized simultaneously by minimizing the reconstruction error, so as to learn the feature vectors for the input data.

3   Proposed Method

We propose an AE-Flow model to learn the distribution of minority class samples and generate new samples, combined with K-means and OSS algorithms to obtain a balanced dataset. After that, we train the classifier with the balanced dataset, and perform classification detection on test set. The process of the entire network intrusion detection is shown in Fig. 2.

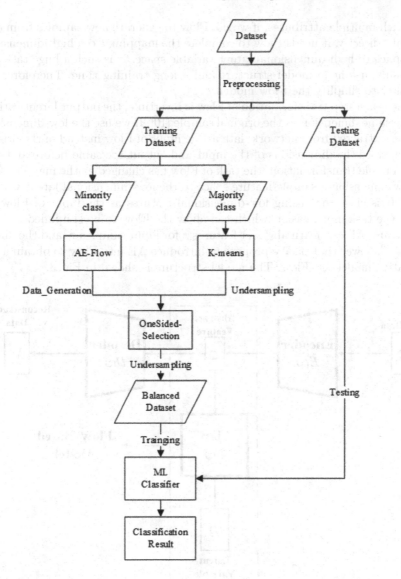

Fig. 2. Flowchart of the proposed network intrusion detection method.

3.1 AE-Flow Based Minority Class Generating

Flow needs multi-step invertible transformations coupled to achieve a strong non-linear transformation for completing the mapping from sample space to latent variable space. Therefor, its model usually has a large structure and the training time is especially long [13]. While network intrusion records are high-dimensional data with multiple attributes, if we use Flow to generate new samples from original data directly, it needs Flow to complete the mapping from high-dimensional data space to high-dimensional latent variable space. It is such a huge task that will result in a huge model structure and a long training time. Therefore, it is necessary to simplify the Flow model.

Since each step transformation of Flow is invertible, the output latent variable has the same dimension as the original sample [10]. If we use the low-dimensional features extracted from network data as the input of Flow instead of the original sample, since the dimensions of the input and output are same before and after the invertible transformation, the task of Flow has changed as the mapping from the low-dimensional sample feature space to the low-dimensional latent variable space. It is clear that using low-dimensional features as the input of Flow can makes the task much easier, which can allow the Flow to be simplified.

Because AE can learn abstract features z for input samples x, and the dimension of z is lower than x. We propose to introduce AE into Flow to obtain a new generative model AE-Flow. The model structure is shown in Fig. 3.

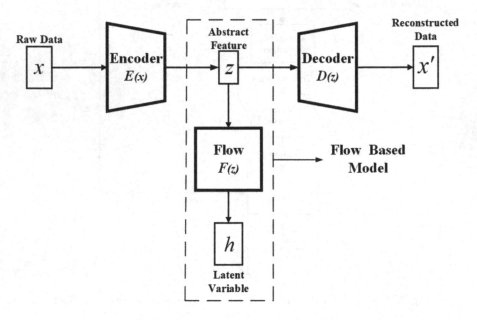

Fig. 3. The proposed AE-Flow model.

As shown in Fig. 3, the data input into AE-Flow firstly pass through the encoder network to become dimensionality-reduced feature vector z. Then on the one hand, through the Flow model, z becomes a latent variable h ,which is of the same dimension and has a known probability density. And on the other hand, z becomes a reconstructed sample x' through the decoder network.

So the loss function of AE from x to x' is:

$$
\begin{aligned}
L_{AE} &= ||x - x'||^2 \\
&= ||x - D(z)||^2 \\
&= ||x - D(E(x))||^2
\end{aligned}
\tag{8}
$$

Where z represents the encoded features of data sample, E represents the encoder network, and D represents the decoder network.

Well the loss function of the Flow model can be expressed as:

$$
\begin{aligned}
L_{Flow} &= -\log p_\theta(z) \\
&= -(\log p_\varphi(h) + \log|\det \tfrac{\partial F(z)}{\partial z}|)
\end{aligned}
\tag{9}
$$

Where h represents the latent variable that conforms to the Gaussian distribution, F represents the Flow network.

Finally the loss function of the entire AE-Flow model is the sum of L_{AE} and L_{Flow}, which can be expressed as:

$$
\begin{aligned}
L_{AE-Flow} &= L_{AE} + L_{Flow} \\
&= ||x - D(z)||^2 - (\log p_\varphi(h) + \log|\det \tfrac{\partial F(z)}{\partial z}|)
\end{aligned}
\tag{10}
$$

During model training, AE and Flow are simultaneously optimized by minimizing the loss function $L_{AE-Flow}$. When the training is completed, we can sample a random vector from the latent variable space. And after a series of inverse transformations of Flow, it becomes a low-dimensional feature, then the feature through reconstruction by decoder to becomes a new sample that conforms to the distribution of original data.

We use the proposed AE-Flow model to generate new samples for minority class: R2L and U2L in NSL-KDD dataset, and add them to original training set to complete data augmentation.

3.2   K-means Based Undersampling

Besides expanding the quantity of minority class samples, we also need to eliminate the redundant samples of majority class, to avoid the bias of classifier to this class. We use the K-means algorithm to cluster the majority class samples, and determine the sampling proportion from each cluster according to its density. If the density of a sample cluster is very high, samples in this cluster are with high similarity, and a large number of redundant samples need to be removed. On the contrary, if the density of a sample cluster is very low, it means there are few samples with high similarity in this cluster, so we need to keep them in the whole cluster.

3.3   OSS Based Undersampling

In addition to removing redundant majority class samples, we also need to pay attention to the majority class samples that are at the boundaries of minority class and majority class. Because they are relatively close to the minority class samples, it is easy to interfere with the judgment of minority class for classifier. They are noisy samples for minority class and we need to eliminate them. The OSS algorithm can find the nearest neighbor for each minority class sample located near the class boundary [14]. If its nearest neighbor belongs to majority class, the majority class sample is removed correspondingly. By applying OSS algorithm, we can obtain a dataset with a clear class boundary.

3.4   Classification

Combining the processing of above methods, we obtain a balanced dataset. We use the original training set and the balanced set to train the classifier, and compare the classification performance of classifier on the test set. If the balanced dataset obtained by our proposal can improve the performance of classifier, it proves that our proposal is effective.

4   Experiments and Analysis

4.1   Dataset

We conduct experiments with the NSL-KDD dataset, which is a publicly available dataset in the field of network intrusion detection. This dataset contains 5 categories: Normal, Dos, Probe, U2R and R2L. Each data record has 41-dimensional features and a label. The quantity of each category in the training set KDD Train+ and the test set KDD Test+ is shown in Table 1.

Table 1. The quantity of each category in KDD Train+ and KDD Test+.

Dataset	Normal	Dos	Probe	R2L	U2R	Total
KDD Train+	67343	45927	11656	995	52	125973
KDD Test+	9710	7457	2421	2754	200	22544

It can be seen that the quantity of R2L and U2L samples in training set is far less than that of Normal and Dos. Therefore, R2L and U2R are regarded as minority classes, and Normal and Dos are regarded as majority classes. Training a classifier model with such imbalanced data will bias the model towards majority class, thus requiring processing of imbalanced datasets.

4.2 Data Preprocessing

Numericalization Processing. Each sample in the dataset has 41-dimensional features, including 3 character-type features. Character-type features are inconvenient to input into model to participate in calculation, so they need to be encoded into numerical values. We use the LabelEncoder method to encode 3 character features ("protocol-type", "service", "flag") as numerical features. For example, the "protocol-type" has three attributes: "TCP", "UDP", "ICMP" and they are encoded as "0", "1", "2" respectively. In this way, different attributes can be distinguished by numerical value, and it is easy to input into models to participate in calculation.

Normalization Processing. The 41-dimensional features of original sample data have different value ranges, If these value ranges can be scaled down to around 0 and the variance is 1, the feature value of each data will be greatly reduced, and the operation speed of the entire model will be greatly improved. we choose Z-score standardization method to realize it, and the formula of Z-score is:

$$x^* = \frac{x - u}{\sigma} \tag{11}$$

where x^* is the transformed output value, x is the original data, u and σ is the mean and variance of each feature in original data record.

4.3 Balanced Dataset Processing

Use our proposed AE-Flow model to generate new samples for the two minority class in KDD Train+. We have generated 10,000 new samples for R2L and U2L respectively. Then we perform K-means clustering undersampling on the two majority class-Normal and Dos. The number of Normal has been reduced from 67342 to 16836, and the number of the Dos has dropped from 45972 to 16714. Finally we apply OSS algorithm to the obtained dataset and reduce the number of Normal and Dos data to 16353, 15445 respectively. The data balancing procedure is completed and a balanced dataset is obtained. The number of each category in the dataset before and after data balancing is shown in Table 2. And the proportion of each category in raw dataset and the balanced dataset are shown in Fig. 4.

Table 2. The number of each category in raw dataset and balanced dataset.

Class	Raw dataset	Balanced dataset
Dos	45927	16353
Normal	67343	15445
Probe	11656	11656
R2L	995	11995
U2L	52	11052

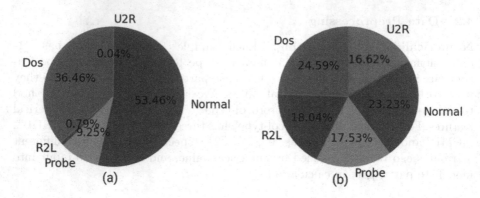

Fig. 4. The proportion of each category in: (a) raw dataset; (b) the balanced dataset.

As shown in Fig. 4, in raw dataset, the proportion of each category is extremely imbalanced. While after our data balancing processing, each category counts a balanced proportion in balanced dataset.

4.4   Evaluation Metric

Network intrusion detection is a multi-classification problem. When judging a category of samples, this category can be regarded as a positive example, and the other types of samples are negative examples, then the classified data can be divided into four types: True Positive (TP), True Negative (TN), False Positive (FP), False Negative (FN). Therefore, this paper uses Precision, Recall, and F1-score as evaluation metrics. The calculation formulas of them are as follows.

$$Precision = \frac{TP}{TP + FP} \tag{12}$$

$$Recall = \frac{TP}{TP + FN} \tag{13}$$

$$F1 - score = \frac{2 * Precision * Recall}{Precision + Recall} \tag{14}$$

As for the evaluation of overall Precision, Recall, and F1-score of all samples in test set, it is generally calculated by the average of the metric of each category. Now there are two main ways to calculate the average: *Macro* and *Weighted*. *Macro* is calculated by arithmetic mean. It means each category has the same weight. *Weighted* takes the proportion of each category in the entire data set as the weight of this class when calculating the overall mean. Because the quantity of each category in our test set KDD Test+ is still imbalanced (as shown in Table 1), to calculate the average of above metrics on all samples in entire dataset. The formulas are as follows.

$$Weighted\_P = \sum_{i=1}^{n} \frac{Support_i}{Total} * Precision_i \qquad (15)$$

$$Weighted\_R = \sum_{i=1}^{n} \frac{Support_i}{Total} * Recall_i \qquad (16)$$

$$Weighted\_F1 = \sum_{i=1}^{n} \frac{Support_i}{Total} * F1 - score_i \qquad (17)$$

$Support_i$ refers to the quantity of the ith class samples in test set, and $Total$ refers to the total number of all class samples in the test set. $Precision_i$, $Recall_i$, $F1 - score_i$ refer to the Precision, Recall, and F1-score value of the ith class samples. This calculation method can avoid the bad influence of imbalanced data in test set.

4.5   Experimental Results and Analysis

Classification Performance Comparison Before and After Data Balancing. We select the commonly used classifiers in machine learning: DT, RF, LR and XGBoost to verify the effectiveness of our proposed method. These classifiers are trained by original training set KDD Train+ (before data balancing) and the Balanced Dataset obtained in Sect. 4.5(after data balancing) respectively, then tested on KDD Test+. Comparing the $Weighted\_P$, $Weighted\_R$, $Weighted\_F1$ before and after data balancing, the result is shown in Fig. 5.

From Fig. 5, it can be seen that compared with original training set, training the classifier with balanced dataset makes each classifier have a greater improvement in each evaluation metric on the test set, and it has the most obvious improvement on the performance of LR and XGBoost. So we propose to use VotingClassifier [15] to combine the advantages of these two classifiers by making a decision fusion from their classification results. This means they are trained in parallel and the final result is voted upon their output classifications. We conduct comparative experiments on the VotingClassifier (XGBoost+LR). The experimental results are shown in Table 3.

As can be seen from Table 3, compared with the original training set, the Recall of the minority class samples has been greatly improved. The Recall of R2L has increased from 1.38% to 34.50%, and it has increased from 0.5% to 58.50% for U2R. And on the weighted average of overall classification metric, the Precision increased by 3.48%, the Recall increased by 7.37%, and the F1-score increased by 10.89%.

In addition, compared with the experimental results of using LR or XGBoost alone in Fig. 5, the classification performance of VotingClassifier combining them is better than both. This proves that VotingClassifier can combine the advantages of both XGBoost and LR to achieve high-performance network intrusion detection.

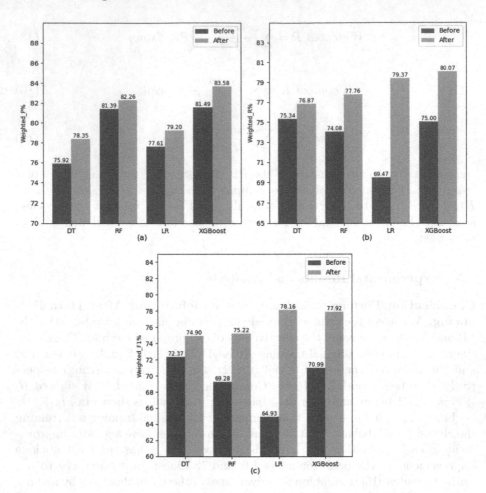

Fig. 5. Classification performance of each classifier on test set before and after data balancing: (a) *Weighted_P*; (b) *Weighted_R*; (c) *Weighted_F*1.

So far, we have obtained a high-performance network intrusion detection system combined AE-Flow data balancing strategy with VotingClassifier (XGBoost+LR).

Comparison with Other Data Balancing Method. We compared the popular data balancing methods in other papers. They are SMOTE [3], VAE [5] and GAN [6]. We choose Precision, Recall, and F1-score of each category as the evaluation metric for comparison. Then the classifier we used is the VotingClassifier (XGBoost+LR). The experimental results are shown in Table 4, Table 5, and Table 6.

From Table 5 we can find that the Recall of Normal data in Raw dataset is higher than the results of other balanced datasets, which is because it accounts

Table 3. The classification performance of VotingClassifier (XGBoost+LR) before and after data balancing.

Class	Precision(%)		Recall(%)		F1-score(%)	
	before	after	before	after	before	after
Dos	96.61	96.08	77.91	82.45	86.26	88.74
Normal	64.36	74.63	97.32	95.19	77.48	83.67
Probe	80.30	75.93	59.77	**80.50**	68.53	78.15
R2L	97.44	91.97	1.38	**34.50**	2.72	50.17
U2R	33.33	74.05	0.5	**58.5**	0.99	65.36
Weighted avg	80.50	**83.98**	74.29	**81.66**	69.61	**80.50**

Table 4. Comparison of *Precision* with different data balancing method.

Model	Dos(%)	Normal(%)	Probe(%)	R2L(%)	U2R(%)
Raw	95.80	66.92	**81.23**	39.34	10.74
SMOTE	**97.07**	68.41	76.12	39.64	66.67
VAE	94.95	71.71	75.83	51.11	50.0
GAN	91.71	**77.49**	62.61	62.97	49.02
Proposed	96.08	74.63	75.93	**91.97**	**74.05**

Table 5. Comparison of *Recall* with different data balancing method.

Model	Dos(%)	Normal(%)	Probe(%)	R2L(%)	U2R(%)
Raw	73.34	**97.09**	67.74	8.24	8.0
SMOTE	77.38	96.75	62.54	12.09	12.0
VAE	78.69	96.32	72.73	17.50	13.5
GAN	76.03	96.56	74.85	30.07	12.5
Proposed	**82.45**	95.19	**80.50**	**34.50**	**58.5**

Table 6. Comparison of *F*1 with different data balancing method.

Model	Dos(%)	Normal(%)	Probe(%)	R2L(%)	U2R(%)
Raw	83.08	79.24	73.87	13.63	9.17
SMOTE	86.12	80.15	68.66	18.53	20.33
VAE	86.05	82.21	74.25	26.07	21.25
GAN	83.13	85.98	68.18	40.70	19.92
Proposed	**88.74**	**83.67**	**78.15**	**50.17**	**65.36**

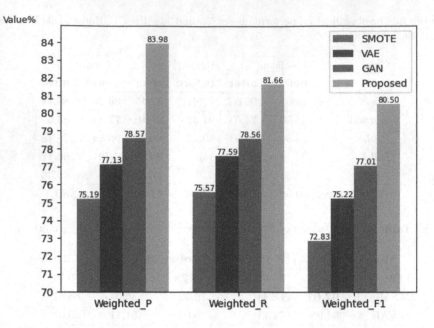

Fig. 6. Comparison of $Weighted\_P$, $Weighted\_R$, $Weighted\_F$ with different data balancing methods.

for the largest number in the original imbalanced data set. This result confirms the phenomenon that training a classifier with an imbalanced dataset biases the classifier towards the majority class. While after applying different data balancing methods, the Recall of the minority class samples R2L and U2R have a certain improvement compared to the raw dataset, moreover our method has the highest improvement.

Then we compared the $Weighted\_P$, $Weighted\_R$, $Weighted\_F$ of each data balancing method. The experimental results are shown in Fig. 6:

As can be seen from Fig. 6, the evaluation results of the data balancing method based on deep generative models (VAE, GAN and AE-Flow) are higher than SMOTE, then GAN outperforms VAE, and our proposal outperforms GAN. It is because SMOTE only synthesizes new samples by "interpolating" sampling between the minority class samples, while the deep generative model can learn the distribution of the original samples to generate new sample data that conforms to this distribution. The result of GAN is better than that of VAE. Because VAE directly assumes the probability distribution of features as a Gaussian distribution, while the distribution of real sample features may be much more complex than Gaussian distribution actually. If the two are far from each other, the VAE will poorly fit the real samples and generate new samples of low quality. GAN distinguishes the real samples with fake samples generated by the generator model through the discriminator model, and modeling data generation (an unsupervised learning problem) as a supervised problem bypasses the challenge of finding complex distributions of real samples. Our AE-Flow model establishes a probabilistic relationship between real samples and generated samples by training a reversible neural network, and this relationship is deterministic and one-to-one, which is where AE-Flow outperforms VAE and GAN. Therefore, our proposal achieves the best experimental results in the end.

5 Conclusion

Aiming at the problem with poor classification performance of minority class samples caused by the imbalance data in network intrusion detection, this paper proposes a data balancing method based on AE-Flow combined with K-means and OSS. Our method uses AE-Flow to learn the minority class samples for generating this kind of samples, then it uses the K-means algorithm to cluster the majority class samples and completes undersampling. Finally, the OSS algorithm is used to eliminate the majority class samples located near the boundary, and so far a new balanced data set is obtained. Using this dataset as a new training set, the experimental results of the classifier on the test set show that our method can effectively improve the classification performance on the minority class samples and the entire dataset. Comparing with the experimental results of data balancing methods in other papers, our method also outperforms them all.

References

1. Besharati, E., Naderan, M., Namjoo, E.: LR-HIDS: logistic regression host-based intrusion detection system for cloud environments. J. Ambient. Intell. Humaniz. Comput. **10**, 3669–3692 (2019)
2. Dong, R.H., Shui, Y.L., Zhang, Q.Y.: Intrusion detection model based on feature selection and random forest. Int. J. Netw. Security **23**(6), 985–996 (2021)
3. Chawla, N.V., Bowyer, K.W., Hall, L.O., Kegelmeyer, P.: SMOTE: Synthetic Minority oversampling Technique. Journal of Artificial Intelligence Research **16**, 321–357 (2002)
4. Yang, Y.Q., Zheng, K.F., Wu, C.H., Yang, Y.X.: Improving the classification effectiveness of intrusion detection by using improved conditional variational autoencoder and deep neural network. Sensors **19**(11), 1–20 (2019)
5. Azmin, S.H., Islam, A.B.: Network Intrusion Detection System based on Conditional Variational Laplace AutoEncoder. In: 7th International Conference on Networking, Systems and Security, pp. 82–87. ACM, Dhaka, Bangladesh (2020). https://doi.org/10.1145/3428363.3428371
6. Dlamini, G., Fahim, M.: DGM: a data generative model to improve minority class presence in anomaly detection domain. Neural Comput. Appl. **33**(20), 13635–13646 (2021). https://doi.org/10.1007/s00521-021-05993-w
7. Liu, X.D., et al.: A GAN and feature selection-based oversampling technique for intrusion detection. Security Commun. Netw. **2021**, 1–15 (2021)
8. Kingma, D.P., Dhariwal, P.: Glow: Generative Flow with Invertible 1x1 Convolutions. arXiv preprint arXiv:1807.03039 (2018)

9. Dinh, L., Krueger, D., Bengio, Y.: NICE: Non-linear Independent Components Estimation. arXiv preprint arXiv:1410.8516 (2014)
10. Rezende, D.J., Mohamed, S.: Variational Inference with Normalizing Flows. In: the 32nd International Conference on Machine Learning, pp. 1530–1538. ACM, Lille, France (2015)
11. Dinh, L., Sohl-Dickstein, J., Bengio, S.: Density estimation using Real NVP. arXiv preprint arXiv:1605.08803 (2017)
12. Andresini, G., Appice, A., Malerba, D.: Autoencoder-based deep metric learning for network intrusion detection. Inf. Sci. **569**, 706–727 (2021)
13. Grover, A., Dhar, M., Ermon, S.: Flow-GAN: Combining Maximum Likelihood and Adversarial Learning in Generative Models. In: the Thirty-Second AAAI Conference on Artificial Intelligence (AAAI-18), pp. 3069–3076. AAAI, New Orleans, USA (2018). https://doi.org/10.1609/aaai.v32i1.11829
14. Guo, T., Lu, X.P., Yu, K.P., Zhang, Y.X., Wei, W.: Integration of light curve brightness information and layered discriminative constrained energy minimization for automatic binary asteroid detection. IEEE Trans. Aerosp. Electron. Syst. **2022**, 1–20 (2022)
15. Khan, M.A., Khattk, M.A.K., Latif, S.: Voting Classifier-Based Intrusion Detection for IoT Networks. In: Advances on Smart and Soft Computing ICACIn 2021 (AAAI-18), pp. 313–328. Springer, Casablanca, Morocco (2021). https://doi.org/10.1007/978-981-16-5559-326

Robust Hybrid Beamforming
for Full-Duplex OFDM mmWave Systems
with Partially-Connected Structure

Zhen Luo[1,2], Yanzi Hu[1(✉)], Yangfan Xiang[1], and Hongqing Liu[1]

[1] The School of Communication and Information Engineering,
Chongqing University of Posts and Telecommunications, Chongqing 400065, China
yanzihu09@163.com

[2] College of Electronic and Information Engineering, Southwest University,
Chongqing 400715, China

Abstract. In this paper, a full-duplex orthogonal frequency division multiplexing (OFDM) millimeter wave systems with correlated estimation errors and partially-connected structures is investigated to improve the spectral efficiency and energy efficiency. To attenuate the self-interference caused by full-duplex mode, a zero-space projection based method is proposed. Then, a two-stage hybrid beamforming scheme is developed. In the fist stage, the correlated channel estimation errors are considered to design the robust fully digital beamformers. In the second stage, an alternating algorithm with closed-form solutions is proposed to solve the hybrid processors. The numerical results show that the proposed scheme has superior performance over existing designs.

Keywords: mmWave · hybrid beamforming · full-duplex ·
partially-connected · OFDM · correlated estimation errors

1 Introduction

The combination of characteristics of millimeter wave (mmWave) signals and massive multiple-input multiple-output (MIMO) architectures can obtain considerable system gains to combat the severe path loss. For conventional massive MIMO systems with fully digital beamformers, each transmitting or receiving antenna need to assign one radio frequency (RF) chain. Applying such structure to mmWave systems with large antenna arrays results in extremely high power consumption and hardware complexity. Thus, the hybrid analog and digital beamforming structure has been commonly adopted in mmWave systems due to its high system gains and low hardware complexity compared to fully digital beamforming techniques [1].

The full-duplex (FD) communication mode based mmWave systems has the potential to further improve the spectral efficiency by supporting simultaneous transmission and reception. It can nearly achieve twice the spectral efficiency

F. Gao et al. (Eds.): ChinaCom 2022, LNICST 500, pp. 191–203, 2023.
https://doi.org/10.1007/978-3-031-34790-0_15

of the half-duplex (HD) mode. Whereas, the severe self-interference (SI) caused by the co-frequency co-time transmission makes the spectral efficiency far less than expected [2]. SI cancellation (SIC) based on the hybrid beamforming has been studied in the literature. In [3,4], passive SIC schemes at the base station are adopted by utilize RF absorber material and cross-polarization. Hence, the SI channel is considered as a far-field transmission channel. The FD scheme at the base station is proposed for the cellular system in [3], by scheduling the uplink and downlink single-antenna HD users based on the beam-domain distributions of the associated channels to mitigate the SI. The beam-domain based SIC scheme is extended in [4] to design a hybrid time switching and power splitting simultaneous wireless information and power transfer protocol for the FD base station.

However, the line-of-sight (LoS) SI channel cannot be ignored in mmWave systems due to the antenna placement and device packaging [5]. Considering the LoS SI channel, a zero-space projection based SIC method is proposed in [6] to eliminate the SI by replacing the digital beamformer with the vectors in the zero-space of the analog equivalent channel. In [7], the widespread hybrid beamforming design procedure is adopted in point-to-point FD mmWave systems. The fully digital processors and the hybrid processors are solved sequentially. This design procedure would result in a sub-optimal solution, but it is attractive for its ease of use. It has been utilized to design hybrid beamforming schemes for multi-user FD orthogonal frequency division multiplexing (OFDM) mmWave systems in [8]. The aforementioned works all adopt fully-connected structures in which each RF chain is connected to all antennas. However, such a structure leads to severe insertion losses and degrades the energy efficiency [9]. Thus, the partially-connected structure, in which each RF chain is only connected with part of the antennas with fewer phase shifters, is more attractive in energy efficiency sensitive scenarios. In [10], an alternating minimization algorithm is proposed to decompose the fully digital processors into hybrid ones with partially-connected structures.

It is noted that the above designs are restricted to perfect channel state information (CSI) assumptions, which is impractical due to the imperfect channel estimations. The robust hybrid FD beamforming designs dealing with imperfect channel estimates are reported in [11]. However, the users therein are all equipped with single-antenna, and the estimation errors are assumed to be independent and identically distributed (i.i.d.). The general Kronecker model of the estimated channel is adopted in [12], and the robust beamformers are investigated for mmWave HD relay systems. To our best knowledge, energy efficient hybrid beamforming designs for FD broadband mmWave systems that are robust to correlated channel estimation errors have not been investigated yet.

In this paper, we develop a robust hybrid beamforming designs with partially-connected structure for point-to-point FD OFDM mmWave systems. First, a zero-space projection based method is proposed to mitigate the SI, and the fully digital robust beamformers are optimized based on the general estimated channel model. According to the relationship between the lower bound of averaged mutual information and the weighted minimum mean squared error (WMMSE), the original highly complicated optimization problem is transformed into a tractable one. To improve the energy efficiency, an alternating method is utilized to decompose the fully digital processors into hybrid ones with partially-connected structures. The performances of the proposed hybrid beamformers and SIC scheme are examined by numerical simulations.

2   System and Channel Model

2.1   System Model

Consider a point-to-point FD OFDM mmWave system, where one node with N_i, $i \in \{a, b\}$ antennas and $N_{i,rf}$ RF chains transmit $N_{i,s}$ data streams to another node that has M_i antennas and $M_{i,rf}$ RF chains. The above parameters are subject to constraints $N_{i,s} \leq N_{i,rf} \leq N_i$, $N_{i,s} \leq M_{i,rf} \leq M_i$. Node a and node b are all operating in FD mode, and both of them adopt hybrid analog-digital beamformers with partially-connected structure. We assume the data stream numbers of node a and node b are identical.

At the transmitter, the transmitted signal vector $\mathbf{s}_i[k] \in \mathbb{C}^{N_{i,s} \times 1}$ of node i at k^{th} subcarrier $k = 1, ..., K$, is first fed into the digital precoder, $\mathbf{F}_{i,bb}[k] \in \mathbb{C}^{N_{i,rf} \times N_{i,s}}$. Then the precoded signals are transformed into time-domain using inverse fast Fourier transformations (IFFTs). After adding proper cyclic prefix (CP), the processed signals are phase-shifted using the following analog beamformer matrix $\mathbf{F}_{i,t} \in \mathbb{C}^{N_i \times N_{i,rf}}$. At the receiver side, assuming perfect carrier and frequency offset synchronization, the received signals for each subcarrier are processed using the analog combiner $\mathbf{W}_{i,r} \in \mathbb{C}^{M_i \times M_{i,rf}}$. Then, the CP is removed and the signals in time-domain are transformed into frequency-domain through the fast Fourier transformation (FFT). Finally, the combiner $\mathbf{W}_{i,bb}[k] \in \mathbb{C}^{M_{i,rf} \times N_{i,s}}$ is employed to obtain the processed signal at the kth subcarrier. The received signal vector of node i at k^{th} sub-carrier is given by

$$\mathbf{y}_i[k] = \underbrace{\sqrt{P_j} \mathbf{W}_{i,bb}^H[k] \mathbf{W}_{i,r}^H \mathbf{H}_{ji}[k] \mathbf{F}_{j,t} \mathbf{F}_{j,bb}[k] \mathbf{s}_j[k]}_{\text{desired signal}}$$

$$+ \underbrace{\sqrt{P_{i,si}} \mathbf{W}_{i,bb}^H[k] \mathbf{W}_{i,r}^H \mathbf{H}_{i,si}[k] \mathbf{F}_{i,t} \mathbf{F}_{i,bb}[k] \mathbf{s}_i[k]}_{\text{SI}}$$

$$+ \underbrace{\mathbf{W}_{i,bb}^H[k] \mathbf{W}_{i,r}^H \mathbf{n}_i[k]}_{\text{noise}}, \tag{1}$$

where $i, j \in \{a, b\}, i \neq j$; P_j and $P_{i,si}$ denote the transmit power of node j and the SI power of node i, respectively. The transmitted signal vector $\mathbf{s}_j[k]$ is subject to $E\{\mathbf{s}_j[k]\mathbf{s}_j^H[k]\} = \mathbf{I}_{N_{j,s}}$. $\mathbf{H}_{ji}[k] \in \mathbb{C}^{M_i \times N_j}$ is the mmWave channel matrix from the transmitter of node j to the receiver of node i at the kth subcarrier; $\mathbf{H}_{i,si}[k] \in \mathbb{C}^{M_i \times N_i}$ is the SI channel matrix of node i at the kth sub-carrier; $\mathbf{n}_i[k]$ is the additive complex white Gaussian noise (AWGN) vector of node i at the kth subcarrier with zero mean and covariance matrix $\delta_i^2 \mathbf{I}$.

It is worth noting that the analog processor is a post-IFFT module, so it is identical for all subcarriers, which is the key challenge of hybrid beamformer designs in broadband mmWave systems. Furthermore, every element in the analog processing matrices has an equal modulus, i.e., $|\mathbf{F}_{i,t}^{(m,n)}|^2 = |\mathbf{W}_{i,r}^{(m,n)}|^2 = 1, \forall m, n$.

2.2   Channel Model

The geometric channel model that incorporating the wideband and limited scattering characteristics of mmWave channel is adopted in this paper. The delay-d channel matrix from the transmitter of node j to the receiver of node i with uniform linear arrays (ULAs) is given by [13]

$$\mathbf{H}_{ji}[d] = \sqrt{\frac{N_j M_i}{N_p}} \sum_{l=1}^{N_p} \alpha_{ji,l} p\left(dT_s - \tau_l\right) \mathbf{a}_r\left(\theta_{ji,l}^r\right) \mathbf{a}_t^H\left(\theta_{ji,l}^t\right) \tag{2}$$

where N_j and M_i are the numbers of transmit and receive antenna arrays, N_p is the number of propagation paths. $p(\tau)$ denotes the pulse shaping filter with T_s-spaced signalling evaluated at τ seconds. $\alpha_{ji,l} \sim \mathcal{CN}(0,1)$ denotes the complex gain of the lth path. $\mathbf{a}_r\left(\theta_{ji,l}^r\right)$ and $\mathbf{a}_t\left(\theta_{ji,l}^t\right)$ are the normalized receive and transmit array response vectors with the azimuth angle of arrival (AoA) and departure (AoD) $\theta_{ji,l}^r$ and $\theta_{ji,l}^t$, respectively. The vector $\mathbf{a}_r\left(\theta_{ji,l}^r\right)$ and $\mathbf{a}_t\left(\theta_{ji,l}^t\right)$ can be expressed as

$$\mathbf{a}_r\left(\theta_{ji,l}^r\right) = \frac{1}{\sqrt{N_r}} \begin{bmatrix} 1 & e^{j\pi \sin \theta_{ji,l}^r} & \cdots & e^{j\pi(N_r-1)\sin \theta_{ji,l}^r} \end{bmatrix}^T \tag{3}$$

$$\mathbf{a}_t\left(\theta_{ji,l}^t\right) = \frac{1}{\sqrt{N_t}} \begin{bmatrix} 1 & e^{j\pi \sin \theta_{ji,l}^t} & \cdots & e^{j\pi(N_t-1)\sin \theta_{ji,l}^t} \end{bmatrix}^T \tag{4}$$

Assuming perfect synchronization, the channel matrix at k^{th} sub-carrier can be expressed as [13]

$$\begin{aligned} \mathbf{H}_{ji}[k] &= \sum_{d=0}^{D-1} \mathbf{H}_{ji}[d] e^{-\frac{j2\pi kd}{K}} \\ &= \sqrt{\frac{N_j M_i}{N_p}} \sum_{l=1}^{N_p} \alpha_{ji,l} \mathbf{a}_r\left(\theta_{ji,l}^r\right) \mathbf{a}_t^H\left(\theta_{ji,l}^t\right) \times \sum_{d=0}^{D-1} p\left(dT_s - \tau_l\right) e^{-\frac{j2\pi kd}{K}} \end{aligned} \tag{5}$$

Considering the antenna placement and size of mmWave devices, the SI channel matrix of node i at the kth subcarrier $\mathbf{H}_{i,si}[k]$ is given by [5]

$$\mathbf{H}_{i,si}[k] = \sqrt{\frac{\kappa}{1+\kappa}} \mathbf{H}_{i,los} + \sqrt{\frac{1}{1+\kappa}} \mathbf{H}_{ii}[k], \tag{6}$$

where κ is the Rician factor; $\mathbf{H}_{ii}[k]$ is the reflected path component of the SI channel at k^{th} subcarrier, which can be modelled as Eq. (5) with corresponding

AoAs and AoDs; The LoS component of the SI channel, $\mathbf{H}_{i,los}$, is adopted to a frequency flat near-field model. For more details please refer to [5].

Due to the packaging of a FD mmWave device, the propagation circumstances of the LoS component are basically stable [5]. So we assume an accurate estimation of $\mathbf{H}_{i,los}$ in this paper. For other channels, i.e., $\mathbf{H}_{ji}[k]$ and $\mathbf{H}_{ii}[k]$, the general Kronecker model in [12] is adopted, and the estimated channel is given by

$$\mathbf{H}[k] \& = \bar{\mathbf{H}}[k] + \mathbf{T}\mathbf{\Delta}\mathbf{R}, \tag{7}$$

where $\mathbf{T}$ and $\mathbf{R}$ are the transmitting and receiving covariance matrices of the channel estimation errors; $\mathbf{\Delta} \sim \mathcal{CN}\left(\mathbf{0}, \sigma^2\mathbf{I}\right)$ is the unknown part of the channel mismatch, with σ^2 being the variance of estimation errors. Here we drop the subscripts for the ease of notation.

3   Robust Hybrid Beamforming Design

In this section, we first proposed a zero-space projection based SIC method. Under imperfect CSI, the singular value decomposition (SVD) of estimated channel matrix can no longer provide the optimal fully digital beamformers [14]. Then, we derived the optimal fully-digital precoder and combiner by utilizing the relationship between the lower bound of mutual information and the WMMSE. After obtaining the fully-digital beamformers, we decompose them into hybrid ones with partially-connected structures by an alternating decomposition method.

3.1   Self-interference Cancellation

Considering the SI term in Eq. (1), the SIC method should eliminate this term, i.e., $\mathbf{W}_{i,bb}^H[k]\mathbf{W}_{i,r}^H\mathbf{H}_{i,si}[k]\mathbf{F}_{i,t}\mathbf{F}_{i,bb}[k] = \mathbf{0}$. Given that the strength of the reflected path component is much weaker than that of the LoS component and the accurate assumption of $\mathbf{H}_{i,los}[k]$, we propose a zero-space projection based SIC method, which is an extension from narrowband systems in [15] to broadband systems. The main difference between these two SIC schemes is the design of analog beamformers, which is common to all sub-carriers. As there is no power constraint at the receiver side, we insert an SIC module, i.e., $\mathbf{W}_{i,sic}$, between the baseband combiner $\mathbf{W}_{i,bb}$ and analog combiner $\mathbf{W}_{i,r}$ to mitigate the interference. The SIC matrix can be designed by finding the zero-space of the equivalent channel.

As we only know the estimated SI channel $\bar{\mathbf{H}}_{i,si}[k]$, we construct the equivalent channel of the kth subcarrier as follows

$$\mathbf{H}_{i,eq}[k] = \mathbf{W}_{i,r}^H\bar{\mathbf{H}}_{i,si}[k]\mathbf{F}_{i,t}\mathbf{F}_{i,bb}[k], \tag{8}$$

By taking the SVD of the above equivalent channel, we have

$$\mathbf{H}_{i,eq}[k] = [\mathbf{U}_{i,eq1}[k] \quad \mathbf{U}_{i,eq0}[k]]\,\mathbf{\Lambda}_{i,eq}[k]\mathbf{V}_{i,eq}^H[k], \tag{9}$$

where $\mathbf{U}_{i,eq1} \in \mathbb{C}^{M_{i,rf} \times N_{i,s}}$ and $\mathbf{U}_{i,eq0} \in \mathbb{C}^{M_{i,rf} \times (M_{i,rf} - N_{i,s})}$ contain the left singular vectors corresponding to non-zero and zero singular values, respectively. $\mathbf{U}_{i,eq0}$ is the zero-space of $\mathbf{H}_{i,eq}$, which satisfies

$$\mathbf{U}_{i,eq0}^{H}[k]\mathbf{H}_{i,eq}[k] = \mathbf{0}, \tag{10}$$

By selecting the corresponding vectors in $\mathbf{U}_{i,eq0}^{H}[k]$, the SIC matrix $\mathbf{W}_{i,sic}$ can be obtained, and the combiner of node i at the kth subcarrier is finally constructed as

$$\mathbf{W}_{i}[k] = \mathbf{W}_{i,r}\mathbf{W}_{i,sic}[k]\mathbf{W}_{i,bb}[k], \tag{11}$$

The solutions of $\mathbf{W}_{i,r}$ and $\mathbf{W}_{i,bb}[k]$ will be given in Sect. 3.3.

Remark: The necessary condition to preserve the number of data streams after SIC is rank$(\mathbf{W}_{i,sic}) \geq N_{i,s}$, which is equivalent to $M_{i,rf} \geq 2N_{i,s}$. Otherwise, the number of data streams, i.e., the dimensions of received signal vectors, may be decreased after processing. Compared with the zero-space projection based SIC method in [6], in which the equivalent channel is constructed as $\mathbf{W}_{i,r}^{H}\bar{\mathbf{H}}_{i,si}\mathbf{F}_{i,t}$, the necessary condition to preserve the number of data streams should be $M_{i,rf} \geq N_{i,s} + N_{i,rf}$. Combined with the condition $N_{i,s} \leq \min\{N_{i,rf}, M_{i,rf}\}$, the proposed SIC method requires less RF chains to preserve the number of data streams.

3.2   Fully Digital Beamforming Design

The SI can be effectively attenuated by utilizing the proposed SIC scheme, which will be verified by numerical results in Sect. 4. In this subsection, we design the fully digital beamformers by ignoring the SI term temporarily. Then, the SIC modules is appended to finish the design. By removing the SI term, the combined signal of node i at the kth subcarrier can be written as

$$\mathbf{y}_{i}[k] = \sqrt{P_{j}}\mathbf{W}_{i}^{H}[k]\mathbf{H}_{ji}[k]\mathbf{F}_{j}[k]\mathbf{s}_{j}[k] + \mathbf{W}_{i}^{H}[k]\mathbf{n}_{i}[k], \tag{12}$$

where $\mathbf{W}_{i}^{H}[k] = \mathbf{W}_{bb,i}^{H}[k]\mathbf{W}_{i,r}^{H}$ and $\mathbf{F}_{j}[k] = \mathbf{F}_{j,r}\mathbf{F}_{j,bb}[k]$ represent the fully digital combiner and precoder, respectively.

At the receiver side, the MMSE receiver is adopted, which is given by

$$\begin{aligned}\mathbf{W}_{i,fd}[k] &= \left[E_{\mathbf{H}_{ji}}\left\{\tilde{\mathbf{y}}_{i}[k]\tilde{\mathbf{y}}_{i}^{H}[k]\right\}\right]^{-1}E_{\mathbf{H}_{ji}}\left\{\tilde{\mathbf{y}}_{i}[k]\mathbf{s}_{j}^{H}[k]\right\}\\ &= \left(P_{j}\bar{\mathbf{H}}_{ji}[k]\mathbf{F}_{j}[k]\mathbf{F}_{j}^{H}[k]\bar{\mathbf{H}}_{ji}^{H}[k] + \mathbf{Q}_{i}[k]\right)^{-1} \times \sqrt{P_{j}}\bar{\mathbf{H}}_{ji}[k]\mathbf{F}_{j}[k]\end{aligned} \tag{13}$$

where $\tilde{\mathbf{y}}_{i}[k] = \sqrt{P_{j}}\mathbf{H}_{ji}[k]\mathbf{F}_{j}[k]\mathbf{s}_{j}[k] + \mathbf{n}_{i}[k]$ is the received signal vector before combining of the node i and $\mathbf{Q}_{i}[k] = P_{j}\sigma_{ji}^{2}\text{tr}\left(\mathbf{T}_{j}\mathbf{F}_{j}[k]\mathbf{F}_{j}[k]^{H}\mathbf{T}_{j}^{H}\right)\mathbf{R}_{i}\mathbf{R}_{i}^{H} + \delta_{i}^{2}\mathbf{I}$.

Then, the MMSE matrix can be calculated as

$$
\begin{aligned}
\mathbf{M}_i[k] &= E_{\bar{\mathbf{H}}_{ji}}\left[\left(\mathbf{W}_{i,fd}^H[k]\tilde{\mathbf{y}}_i[k] - \mathbf{s}_j[k]\right)\left(\mathbf{W}_{i,fd}^H[k]\tilde{\mathbf{y}}_i[k] - \mathbf{s}_j[k]\right)^H\right] \\
&= \mathbf{I}_{N_{i,s}} - P_j\mathbf{F}_j^H[n]\bar{\mathbf{\Pi}}_{ji}^H[n]\left(P_j\bar{\mathbf{\Pi}}_{ji}[k]\mathbf{F}_j^H[k]\bar{\mathbf{H}}_{ji}^H[k] + \mathbf{Q}_i[k]\right)^{-1} \times \bar{\mathbf{H}}_{ji}[k]\mathbf{F}_j[k] \\
&= \left(\mathbf{I}_{N_{i,s}} + P_j\mathbf{F}_j^H[k]\bar{\mathbf{H}}_{ji}^H[k]\mathbf{Q}_i^{-1}[k]\bar{\mathbf{H}}_{ji}[k]\mathbf{F}_j[k]\right)^{-1}
\end{aligned}
\tag{14}
$$

Optimizing the sum rate directly is found to be intractable. In this paper, we adopt the lower bound of mutual information as the objective, which is given by [16]

$$
I_{lb}\left(\mathbf{s}_j[k], \tilde{\mathbf{y}}_i[k]\right) = -\log\det\mathbf{M}_i[k], \tag{15}
$$

The optimization problem of the fully digital beamformers can be constructed as

$$
\min_{\{\mathbf{F}_{j,fd}[k]\}} -\frac{1}{K}\sum_{k=1}^{K}\sum_{i,j} I_{lb}\left(\mathbf{s}_j[k], \tilde{\mathbf{y}}_i[k]\right) \tag{16}
$$
$$
\text{s.t.} \quad \text{tr}\left(\mathbf{F}_{j,fd}[k]\mathbf{F}_{j,fd}^H[k]\right) \leq 1, i,j \in \{a,b\}, i \neq j
$$

The above problem can be divided into two sub-problems as follows

$$
\min_{\{\mathbf{F}_{a,fd}[k]\}} -\frac{1}{K}\sum_{k=1}^{K} I_{lb}\left(\mathbf{s}_a[k], \tilde{\mathbf{y}}_b[k]\right) \tag{17}
$$
$$
\text{s.t.} \quad \text{tr}\left(\mathbf{F}_{a,fd}[k]\mathbf{F}_{a,fd}^H[k]\right) \leq 1
$$

$$
\min_{\{\mathbf{F}_{b,fd}[k]\}} -\frac{1}{K}\sum_{k=1}^{K} I_{lb}\left(\mathbf{s}_b[k], \tilde{\mathbf{y}}_a[k]\right) \tag{18}
$$
$$
\text{s.t.} \quad \text{tr}\left(\mathbf{F}_{b,fd}[k]\mathbf{F}_{b,fd}^H[k]\right) \leq 1
$$

Due to the equivalence of formulas (17) and (18), we just provide the solution for (17) in the next, and the solution for (18) can be obtained by corresponding substitutions. According to [17], the optimization problem (17) is identical to the following WMMSE problem.

$$
\min_{\{\mathbf{F}_{a,fd}[k],\mathbf{A}_b[k]\}} \frac{1}{K}\sum_{k=1}^{K} \text{tr}\left(\mathbf{A}_b[k]\mathbf{M}_b[k]\right), \tag{19}
$$
$$
\text{s.t.} \quad \text{tr}\left(\mathbf{F}_{a,fd}[k]\mathbf{F}_{a,fd}^H[k]\right) \leq 1.
$$

where $\mathbf{A}_b[k]$ is a weighting matrix. The points are that the KKT conditions of (17) and (19) can be satisfied simultaneously when $\mathbf{A}_b[k] = (\mathbf{M}_b[k])^{-1}$. In the next, we proposed an alternating algorithm to solve (19), and update the fully digital precoder $\mathbf{F}_{a,fd}[k]$, the fully digital combiner $\mathbf{W}_{b,fd}[k]$ and the weighted matrix $\mathbf{A}_b[k]$ iteratively.

Algorithm 1. Proposed design for $\mathbf{F}_{a,fd}[k]$ and $\mathbf{W}_{b,fd}[k]$

Require: Construct $\mathbf{F}_{a,fd}[k]$ randomly; set λ_{min}, λ_{max}, and the termination criteria ϵ_1 and ϵ_2;

1: **repeat**
2:     Calculate $\mathbf{W}_{b,fd}[k]$ according to Eq. (13);
3:     Calculate $\mathbf{M}_b[k]$ according to Eq. (14);
4:     Update $\mathbf{A}_b[k] = (\mathbf{M}_b[k])^{-1}$;
5:     **while** $\lambda_{max} - \lambda_{min} > \epsilon_1$ **do**
6:         setting $\lambda_m = \frac{\lambda_{max} + \lambda_{min}}{2}$;
7:         calculate $\mathbf{F}_{a,fd}[k]$ according to Eq. (21);
8:         **if** $\mathrm{tr}\left(\mathbf{F}_{a,fd}[k]\mathbf{F}_{a,fd}^H[k]\right) < 1$ **then**
9:             $\lambda_{min} = \lambda_m$;
10:        **else**
11:            $\lambda_{max} = \lambda_m$;
12:        **end if**
13:    **end while**
14: **until** The change of $\mathrm{tr}\left(\mathbf{A}_b[k]\mathbf{M}_b[k]\right)$ is below ϵ_2.

First, we calculate $\mathbf{W}_{b,fd}[k]$ according to Eq. (13) and $\mathbf{M}_b[k]$ according to Eq. (14) with fixed $\mathbf{F}_{a,fd}[k]$. Then, we set $\mathbf{A}_b[k] = (\mathbf{M}_b[k])^{-1}$, and update $\mathbf{F}_{a,fd}[k]$. The corresponding Lagrange function to solve $\mathbf{F}_{a,fd}[k]$ can be formulated as follows

$$L_{\mathbf{F}_{a,fd}[k]} = \&\frac{1}{K}\sum_{k=1}^{K}\mathrm{tr}\left(\mathbf{A}_b[k]\mathbf{M}_b[k]\right) + \lambda\left[\mathrm{tr}\left(\mathbf{F}_{a,fd}[k]\mathbf{F}_{a,fd}^H[k]\right) - 1\right], \quad (20)$$

where λ is the Lagrange multiplier. By setting the derivative of $L_{\mathbf{F}_{a,fd}[k]}$ w.r.t. $\mathbf{F}_{a,fd}[k]$ to zero, $\mathbf{F}_{a,fd}[k]$ can be solved as

$$\begin{aligned}
\mathbf{F}_{a,fd}[k] = &\left[P_a\bar{\mathbf{H}}_{ab}^H[k]\mathbf{W}_{b,fd}[k]\mathbf{A}_b[k]\mathbf{W}_{b,fd}^H[k]\bar{\mathbf{H}}_{ab}[k]\right.\\
&+ P_a\sigma_{ab}^2\mathrm{tr}\left(\mathbf{A}_b[k]\mathbf{W}_{b,fd}^H[k]\mathbf{R}_b\mathbf{R}_b^H\mathbf{W}_{b,fd}[k]\right)\mathbf{T}_a^H\mathbf{T}_a \quad (21)\\
&\left.+ \lambda\mathbf{I}\right]^{-1}\sqrt{P_a}\bar{\mathbf{H}}_{ab}^H[k]\mathbf{W}_{b,fd}[k]\mathbf{A}_b[k].
\end{aligned}$$

Based on Eq. (21), a bisection search method can be adopted to obtain λ. Notice that $\lambda \geq 0$, so we set the minimum Lagrange multiplier as $\lambda_{min} = 0$, and calculate $\mathbf{F}_{a,fd}[k]$. If the power constraint is satisfied, we set $\lambda = 0$. Otherwise, we set the maximum Lagrange multiplier λ_{max} to a pre-defined value and start the bisection search until the power constraint is satisfied. The proposed iterative algorithm is summarized in Algorithm 1.

Due to the alternating minimization process, the objective function in (19) decreases monotonically. Combined with the fact that the WMMSE is lower bounded, the convergence of Algorithm 1 can be guaranteed. A similar approach can be found in [17]. The fully digital beamformers $\mathbf{F}_{b,fd}[k]$ and $\mathbf{W}_{a,fd}[k]$ can be obtained by directly substituting the corresponding matrices into Algorithm 1. We omit further details here to avoid repetitions.

3.3   Hybrid Beamforming Design for Partially-Connected Structure

Different from fully-connected structure, the output signal of each RF chain in the partially-connected structure is connected to a sub-array to improve the energy efficiency and further reduce the hardware implementation complexity. Therefore, the analog beamforming matrix in the partially-connected structure can be formulated as a block diagonal format, and each block is an vector that satisfies the constant modulus constraint. Taking the precoder at node a as an example, each RF chain is connected to $\frac{N_a}{N_{a,rf}}$ antennas, and the analog precoder is given by

$$\mathbf{F}_{a,t} = \text{blkdiag}\left[\mathbf{f}_1, \mathbf{f}_2, \ldots, \mathbf{f}_{N_{rf}}\right] \tag{22}$$

where $\mathbf{f}_i = \left[\exp\left(j\theta_{\frac{(m-1)N_a}{N_{a,rf}}+1}\right), \ldots, \exp\left(j\theta_{\frac{mN_a}{N_{a,rf}}}\right)\right]^T$, $m = 1, \ldots, N_{a,rf}$, with θ_i being the phases of the corresponding phase shifter. So the total number of phase shifters in this structure is N_a, indicating that the hardware complexity of RF beamformers is one $N_{a,rf}$ fold lower than that of fully connected structures.

In this section, we aim for decomposing the fully digital beamformers into hybrid ones with partially connected structure. The hybrid beamformer optimization problem is constructed as an Euclidean distance minimization problem of all the subcarriers, which can be formulated as follows

$$\min_{\{\mathbf{F}_{a,t}, \mathbf{F}_{a,bb}[k]\}} \sum_{k=1}^{K} \|\mathbf{F}_{a,fd}[k] - \mathbf{F}_{a,t}\mathbf{F}_{a,bb}[k]\|^2$$
$$\text{s.t.} \quad \|\mathbf{F}_{a,t}\mathbf{F}_{a,bb}[k]\|_F^2 = 1, \tag{23}$$
$$\mathbf{F}_{a,t} \in \mathcal{F}$$

where $\mathcal{F}$ is the set of feasible analog beamformers induced by the equal-modulus constraint. In our previous work [18], we have proved that if the unconstrained solution for the problem (23) is sufficiently close to $\mathbf{F}_{a,fd}[k]$, the corresponding normalization that satisfies the power constraint can achieve the Euclidean distance in the same order. This conclusion can also be extended to broadband systems. The corresponding unconstrained optimization problem is formulated as

$$\min_{\{\mathbf{F}_{a,t}, \mathbf{F}_{a,bb}[k]\}} \sum_{k=1}^{K} \|\mathbf{F}_{a,fd}[k] - \mathbf{F}_{a,t}\mathbf{F}_{a,bb}[k]\|^2$$
$$\text{s.t.} \quad \mathbf{F}_{a,t} \in \mathcal{F} \tag{24}$$

We alternatively optimize $\mathbf{F}_{a,t}$ and $\mathbf{F}_{a,bb}[k]$ in the next. In nth iteration, by taking advantage of the special properties of block diagonal structure of $\mathbf{F}_{a,t}$ and with fixed $\mathbf{F}_{a,bb}[k]$, problem (24) can be rewritten as

$$\min_{\theta_i} \& \sum_{k=1}^{K} \|\left(\mathbf{F}_{a,fd}[k]\right)_{i,:} - \exp\left(j\theta_i^{(n)}\right)\left(\mathbf{F}_{a,bb}^{(n)}[k]\right)_{l,:}\|^2 \tag{25}$$

where $l = \lceil i\frac{N_{a,rf}}{N_a} \rceil$. This is a vector rotation problem, and the closed-form solution is given by

$$\&\theta_i^{(n)} = \arg\left\{ \sum_{k=0}^{K-1} (\mathbf{F}_{a,fd}[k])_{i,:} \left(\mathbf{F}_{a,bb}^{(n)}[k]\right)_{l,:}^H \right\}, i = 1, \ldots, N_a. \tag{26}$$

Then, we optimize $\mathbf{F}_{a,bb}[k]$ with the fixed $\mathbf{F}_{a,t}$. Since the digital precoder is optimized for each subcarrier, we can get rid of the summation notation in (24) when optimizing the baseband precoder $\mathbf{F}_{a,bb}[k]$. The closed-form solution is given by

$$\&\mathbf{F}_{a,bb}^{(n)}[k] = \left[\left(\mathbf{F}_{a,t}^{(n)}\right)^H \mathbf{F}_{a,t}^{(n)}\right]^{-1} \left(\mathbf{F}_{a,t}^{(n)}\right)^H \mathbf{F}_{a,fd}[k] \tag{27}$$

The iteration terminates when the change of the objective function is below a pre-defined threshold. At last, $\mathbf{F}_{a,bb}[k]$ is normalized to satisfy the power constraint, which is given by

$$\mathbf{F}_{a,bb}[k] = \frac{\mathbf{F}_{a,bb}[k]}{\|\mathbf{F}_{a,t}\mathbf{F}_{a,bb}[k]\|_F} \tag{28}$$

4   Simulation Results

In the following, we present numerical results of the proposed robust hybrid FD OFDM beamforming designs. The propagation paths for different channels are all set as $Np = 4$. The elements of mmWave channels, i.e., complex gains of propagation paths, and AWGN matrices obey complex Gaussian distribution. Furthermore, the azimuth AoAs and AoDs for each of the channel paths follow Laplacian distribution with uniformly distributed means over $[0, 2\pi)$, and angular spread of $5°$. The Rician factor κ in Eq. (6) is set to 20 dB and path gain α is complex Gaussian distributed with zero mean and unit variance. The transmitted powers and SI powers of different links are set to be equal, i.e., $P_a = P_b$, $P_{a,si} = P_{b,si}$. The transmitted signal-to-noise ratio (SNR) is defined as $\text{SNR} = 10\log_{10}\frac{P_i}{\delta_i^2}$, the interference-to-noise ratio (INR) is defined as $\text{INR} = 10\log_{10}\frac{P_{i,si}}{\delta_i^2}$. The termination criteria in Algorithm 1 are set as $\epsilon_1 = \epsilon_2 = 1 \times 10^{-4}$. The maximum number of iterations is set to 50 to control the convergence rate. All the simulations are averaged over 1000 channel realizations.

Figure 1 shows the spectral efficiency comparison between the proposed design for different INR settings with other existing designs. The fully-connected structure design is obtained by replacing sub-connected structures in the proposed design with fully-connected structures. The antenna configurations are set as $N_a = M_a = 64$, $N_b = M_b = 32$, $N_{a,rf} = N_{b,rf} = M_{a,rf} = M_{b,rf} = 4$, $N_{a,s} = N_{b,s} = 2$. The estimation error covariances are $\sigma_{e,aa}^2 = \sigma_{e,bb}^2 = 0.7$. As we can see, the proposed design is only inferior to the fully-connected design. The proposed design outperforms the design in [14] by 11.1% at SNR = 10 dB.

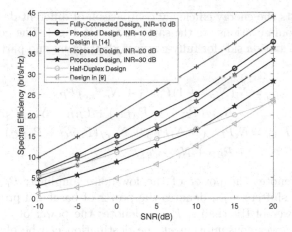

Fig. 1. Spectral efficiency at different SNR settings. $N_a = M_a = 64$, $N_b = M_b = 32$, $N_{a,rf} = N_{b,rf} = M_{a,rf} = M_{b,rf} = 4$, $N_{a,s} = N_{b,s} = 2$, $\sigma_{e,aa}^2 = \sigma_{e,bb}^2 = 0.7$.

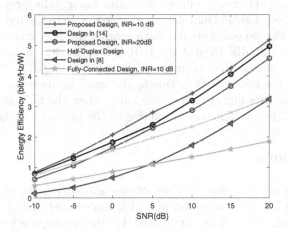

Fig. 2. Energy efficiency at different SNR settings. $N_a = M_a = 64$, $N_b = M_b = 32$, $N_{a,rf} = N_{b,rf} = M_{a,rf} = M_{b,rf} = 4$, $N_{a,s} = N_{b,s} = 2$, $\sigma_{e,aa}^2 = \sigma_{e,bb}^2 = 0.7$.

When INR goes higher, the performance curves of the proposed designs intersect with the HD mode due to the imperfect SIC effect caused by estimation errors, e.g., the HD mode outperforms the proposed designs when SNR ≤ -5 dB at INR = 20 dB and SNR ≤ 10 dB at INR = 30 dB. However, the proposed design still prevails the HD mode at high SNR regime, e.g., 20.81% gains can be seen at SNR = 20 dB when INR = 30 dB. Moreover, when the INR rises to 30 dB, the proposed design still outperforms the design in [8]. The design in [8] suppresses the power of SI plus noise covariance. However, the performance degrades severely under imperfect channel estimations.

Figure 2 plots the energy efficiency comparison of different designs appeared in Fig. 1. The configurations are the same as that in Fig. 1. The power consumption at the base station side for fully-connected structure and partially-structure can be expressed as

$$P_{fully} = N_i(N_{i,rf} + 1)P_{LNA} + N_i N_{i,rf} P_{PS}$$
$$+ N_{i,rf}(P_{RFC} + P_{ADC}) + P_{BB} + N_{i,rf} P_{SI},$$
$$P_{sub} = N_i P_{LNA} + N_i P_{PS} + N_{i,rf}(P_{RFC} + P_{ADC})$$
$$+ P_{BB} + N_{i,rf} P_{SI},$$

where P_{LAN} denotes the power of the low-noise amplifier; P_{PA} denotes the power of phase shifters. P_{BB} denotes the power of baseband processing; P_{RFC} denotes the power of RF chains; P_{DAC} denotes the power of digital-to-analog converts. The power consumption at the destination can be obtained by corresponding substitutions. The value of each component follows the setting in [6]. As shown in this figure, although the fully-connected design provides higher spectral efficiency, its energy efficiency is the worst. The proposed partially-connected designs provide higher energy efficiency due to the reduced number of phase shifters. The proposed design outperforms the fully-connected design by 174.7% at SNR = 20 dB. Even if the INR is increased to 20 dB, the proposed design still outperforms the design in [8] by 44.6% at SNR = 20 dB and performs closely to the design in [14]. Due to the lower hardware complexity of the HD mode, it provides higher energy efficiency when the SNR is low. With the increase of SNR, its performance is inferior to the proposed design.

5   Conclusions

In this paper, partially-connected structures and correlated estimation errors are considered to develop a robust hybrid beamforming design for FD OFDM mmWave systems. The SI is attenuated by the zero-space projection based method. Then, the fully digital beamformers and the corresponding hybrid ones are solved sequentially. Simulation results verify the superiority of the proposed robust design over other existing designs.

References

1. Heath, R.W., Jr., Gonzalez-Prelcic, N., Rangan, S., Roh, W., Sayeed, A.M.: An overview of signal processing techniques for millimeter wave MIMO systems. IEEE J. Sel. Topics Signal Process. **10**, 436–453 (2016)
2. Xia, X., Xu, K., Wang, Y., Xu, Y.: A 5G-enabling technology: benefits, feasibility, and limitations of in-band full-duplex mMIMO. IEEE Veh. Technol. Mag. **13**(3), 81–90 (2018)
3. Xia, X., Xu, K., Wang, Y., Xu, Y.: Beam-domain full-duplex massive MIMO: realizing co-time co-frequency uplink and downlink transmission in the cellular system. IEEE Trans. Veh. Technol. **66**(10), 8845–8862 (2017)

4. Xu, K., Shen, Z., Wang, Y., Xia, X., Zhang, D.: Hybrid time-switching and power splitting SWIPT for full-duplex massive MIMO systems: a beam-domain approach. IEEE Trans. Veh. Technol. **67**(8), 7257–7274 (2018)
5. Xiao, Z., Xia, P., Xia, X.-G.: Full-duplex millimeter-wave communication. IEEE Wirel. Commun. **24**(6), 136–143 (2017)
6. Zhang, Y., Xiao, M., Han, S., Skoglund, M., Meng, W.: On precoding and energy efficiency of full-duplex millimeter-wave relays. IEEE Trans. Wirel. Commun. **18**(3), 1943–1956 (2019)
7. Satyanarayana, K., El-Hajjar, M., Kuo, P.-H., Mourad, A., Hanzo, L.: Hybrid beamforming design for full-duplex millimeter wave communication. IEEE Trans. Veh. Technol. **68**(2), 1394–1404 (2019)
8. Satyanarayana, K., El-Hajjar, M., Mourad, A., Hanzo, L.: Multi-user full duplex transceiver design for mmWave systems using learning-aided channel prediction. IEEE Access **7**, 66068–66083 (2020)
9. Garcia-Rodriguez, A., Venkateswaran, V., Rulikowski, P., Masouros, C.: Hybrid analog-digital precoding revisited under realistic RF modeling. IEEE Wirel. Commun. Lett. **5**(5), 528–531 (2016)
10. El Ayach, O., Heath, R.W., Rajagopal, S., Pi, Z.: Multimode precoding in millimeter wave MIMO transmitters with multiple antenna sub-arrays. In: 2013 IEEE Global Communications Conference (GLOBECOM), pp. 3476–3480 (2013)
11. Cai, Y., Xu, Y., Shi, Q., Champagne, B., Hanzo, L.: Robust joint hybrid transceiver design for millimeter wave full-duplex MIMO relay systems. IEEE Trans. Wirel. Commun. **18**, 1199–1215 (2019)
12. Jiang, L., Jafarkhani, H.: mmWave amplify-and-forward MIMO relay networks with hybrid precoding/combining design. IEEE Trans. Wirel. Commun. **19**(2), 1333–1346 (2020)
13. Park, S., Alkhateeb, A., Heath, R.W.: Dynamic subarrays for hybrid precoding in wideband mmWave MIMO systems. IEEE Trans. Wirel. Commun. **16**(5), 2907–2920 (2017)
14. Yu, X., Shen, J.-C., Zhang, J., Letaief, K.B.: Alternating minimization algorithms for hybrid precoding in millimeter wave MIMO systems. IEEE J. Sel. Topics Signal Process. **10**(3), 485–500 (2016)
15. Luo, Z., Zhao, L., Tonghui, L., Liu, H., Zhang, R.: Robust hybrid precoding/combining designs for full-duplex millimeter wave relay systems. IEEE Trans. Veh. Technol. **70**(9), 9577–9582 (2021)
16. Xing, C., Ma, S., Fci, Z., Wu, Y.-C., Poor, II.V.: A general robust linear transceiver design for multi-hop amplify-and-forward MIMO relaying systems. IEEE Trans. Signal Process. **61**(5), 1196–1209 (2013)
17. Christensen, S.S., Agarwal, R., de Carvalho, E., Cioffi, J.M.: Weighted sum-rate maximization using weighted MMSE for MIMO-BC beamforming design. IEEE Trans. Wirel. Commun. **7**(12), 4792–4799 (2008)
18. Luo, Z., Zhao, L., Liu, H., Li, Y.: Robust hybrid beamforming in millimeter wave systems with closed-form least-square solutions. IEEE Wirel. Commun. Lett. **10**(1), 156–160 (2021)

Deep Learning Applications
and Optimization

Optimization of Tensor Operation in Compiler

Chenguang Qiu[1]([✉]), Jun Wu[2], Haoqi Ren[1], and Zhifeng Zhang[1]

[1] Department of Computer Science, Tongji University, Shanghai, China
chenguangqcg@163.com, {renhaoqi,zhangzf}@tongji.edu.cn
[2] School of Computer Science, Fudan University, Shanghai, China
wujun@fudan.edu.cn

Abstract. This paper proposes an AI compiler architecture, which can compile the trained model and deploy it on DSP chip. The biggest difficulty in deploying the reasoning model on DSP is the multiplication between tensors. Tensor multiplication is the main operation and the most time-consuming operation in the process of model reasoning. Therefore, the operation efficiency of tensor multiplication directly restricts the performance of reasoning. However, there is no matrix computing unit in DSP chip, instead of vector computing unit. We define a new dialect in MLIR(Multi-Level Intermediate Representation) to efficiently compile AI models, especially GEMM and conv operations. The dialect is based on the basic features of mhlo, so this new dialect can make full use of the existing optimized pass of mhlo. Moreover, we have added some functions to support architecture related optimization, mainly the lower algorithm of operation, such as GEMM and conv. we finally map dialect to LLVM dialect and convert it into LLVM IR(immediate representation). The advantage of converting to LLVM IR is that more detailed instruction scheduling can be carried out at the backend of the compiler. We compare the efficiency of a speech model in the code generated by the traditional compiler clang and the code generated by our compiler. The experimental results show that this conversion method has greatly improved the efficiency.

Keywords: MLIR · Deep learning · Compiler · Vector processor

1 Introduction

AI development tools were designed for the data center infrastructure behind applications like internet queries, voice search, and online facial recognition. But as AI technology advances, so does the desire to leverage it in all sorts of use cases – including those that run on small, resource-constrained, MCU-based platforms at the edge. So instead of focusing solely on high-end hardware accelerators running cloud-based recommendation systems, for example, tools like compilers must also be able to optimize AI data and algorithms for smaller footprint devices.

High performance digital signal processor (DSP) is a high-performance processor composed of VLSI chips for signal processing. It is mainly used to realize various

F. Gao et al. (Eds.): ChinaCom 2022, LNICST 500, pp. 207–219, 2023.
https://doi.org/10.1007/978-3-031-34790-0_16

digital signal processing algorithms in real time and quickly, especially various audio and video processing algorithms. DSP generally has a multi-bus structure, the data storage space is separated from the program space, and has an independent data bus and address bus. It can fetch instructions and read data at the same time. DSP has an efficient hardware multiplier, which can complete the multiplication instructions in a short period, and speed up the multiplication operations such as FFT, matrix operation, convolution, digital filtering and so on. Therefore, DSP chip is very suitable for the reasoning of audio processing model. DSP chips are widely used in all kinds of smart phones. In addition, the scene of smart home needs frequent voice interaction with users. With the help of the trained effective AI model and the powerful computing power of DSP, speech recognition can be carried out more accurately and timely.

Matrix multiplication calculation is the core of many architectures based on transformer (such as BERT). It is the key factor restricting the speed of model training and reasoning. The operation efficiency of matrix multiplication can be used as an important index to measure the compilation efficiency. However, compared with some hardware designed for AI operation, DSP lacks matrix operation unit. Compared with other embedded processors, DSP has vector operation unit, that is, SIMD instruction. The training of the algorithm and the implementation of the reasoning algorithm are the two most important parts, which also need the most computing resources. Compared with training, the hardware resources required for model reasoning are much smaller. In addition, the tensor dimension used by models such as speech recognition is small. These factors improve the feasibility of deploying the model reasoning process on DSP chip.

At present, various high-level IR optimizations focus on optimizing the combination form of the kernel, rather than the code generation of a single kernel. And most of the implementation of kernel is still based on handwritten assembly library. This method can make great use of the ability of hardware, but it also loses the opportunity to generate better code to a certain extent, because the compiler is difficult to optimize deeply from a global perspective.

MLIR is a general-purpose IR that also supports hardware specific operations. Many hardware targets can use this infrastructure and will benefit from it. MLIR is more suitable for high-level compilation optimization, but not for generating final machine code. Moreover, LLVM IR does not provide good support for matrix data types and GEMM, which is consistent with the SIMD operation characteristics of DSP [1–3].

Therefore, this paper proposes a method to convert the kernel in AI model into DSP supported operations through the MLIR framework. This process converts the matrix multiplication operation lower into the LLVM IR representation, and generates machine code with the help of the mature compiler back-end LLC. The front end is mainly responsible for converting the trained model into DSP dialect, and doing some operator level optimization on the intermediate code of DSP dialect, and generating LLVM IR code with the help of the infrastructure of MLIR. Finally, the LLVM IR is handed over to the LLVM backend for more architecture related instruction level optimization, and finally binary machine code is generated. Compared with traditional methods, the proposed method can convert operators into corresponding machine opcode at the IR level, and make use of various optimization passes provided by the LLVM backend.

2 Relate Work

MLIR is a basic compilation framework, which is mainly used in AI compilation. MLIR is committed to building reusable, scalable and powerful compilers, and can be combined with LLVM to take advantage of the existing back-end compilation framework [4, 5]. Thanks to its hybrid IR structure, MLIR can support a variety of different needs under the condition of providing a unified infrastructure. MLIR can represent data flow graph, including dynamic shape, user extensible OP ecosystem, tensorflow variable, etc. In addition, MLIR can optimize loops in high-performance computing across cores, such as fusion, loop switching, tiling and so on. MLIR can also convert the memory layout of data to suit different hardware architectures. MLIR can complete the "reduced" conversion of code generation, such as DMA insertion, explicit cache management, memory tiling, and vectorization of one-dimensional and two-dimensional register architecture. MLIR can decompose some patterns into more fine-grained combinations of small local patterns through pass, and supports rewriting specific patterns at the granularity of a single operation [17, 23].

TVM / NNVM mainly hopes to reduce the gap between the deep learning framework and the underlying hardware[6]. However, on different hardware, there are inevitable differences in various hardware resources, such as memory, L1 / L2 cache, bandwidth, etc. Therefore, TVM / NNVM adopts the philosophy of separating calculation from schedule. All hardware platforms share the compute attribute to ensure the consistency of the final results; Different hardware platforms enjoy the schedule attribute exclusively according to their own characteristics to ensure the efficiency of their execution [24–27]. TVM is mainly responsible for how to compile the operators in the calculation diagram into code that can be executed efficiently on different hardware. This can be abstracted into an optimization problem. Therefore, in this process, TVM will also use the method of deep learning to optimize different hardware platforms, which is called autotvm. Using automation methods such as deep learning to optimize different hardware platforms can be well applicable to the diversity of end-to-end devices in the future [10–12].

XLA (accelerated linear algebra) is a compiler for tensorflow launched by Google in 2017. XLA uses JIT compilation technology to analyze tensorflow diagrams created by users at runtime, converts tensorflow OP into HLO (high level optimizer) intermediate representation [7], and completes various graph optimization including OP fusion on the HLO layer. Finally, it completes the automatic generation of CPU / GPU and other machine codes based on LLVM. XLA adopts a relatively simple technical path [8, 9, 17]. For computationally intensive operators with high requirements for automatic CodeGen, such as matmul / convolution, like tensorflow, they will directly call libraries such as cuBLAS/cuDNN; For other memory access intensive operators, XLA will conduct fully automatic OP fusion and underlying code generation (CodeGen) [23–27]. In addition to the compilation body, XLA also includes a set of static execution engines. This statically is reflected in the static fixed shape compilation (that is, a complete compilation is carried out for each set of input shapes at run time and the compilation results are retained), the static operator scheduling sequence, and the static display memory / memory optimization. It is expected that better performance / storage optimization results can be obtained compared with tensorflow for the dynamic interpretation and execution of the calculation graph [13–15].

LLVM began a research project at the University of Illinois. Its goal is to provide a modern SSA based compilation strategy that can support static and dynamic compilation of any programming language [1–3]. LLVM has developed into a comprehensive project composed of many sub-projects, many of which are widely used in the production of various commercial and open source projects, as well as academic research. The LLVM core library provides a modern optimizer independent of source code and target, and provides code generation support for many popular CPUs (and some less common CPUs). These libraries are built around an intermediate code representation called LLVM IR. Clang is the compiler front end provided by LLVM, which can provide fast compilation and accurate error and warning information. LLC is responsible for IR parsing, instruction selection, optimization, register allocation, assembly code generation, machine code generation and other functions. LLVM intermediate code is an IR (immediate representation) in the form of SSA. The instruction set used is LLVM virtual instruction set. The instruction set is a three address instruction set similar to RISC (reduced instruction set computer). It contains simple control instructions and memory access instructions with type pointers. It has syntax independent of high-level language and target processor, and is easy to conduct code analysis and optimization. LLVM intermediate code instruction set has rich types of instructions, including scalar instructions such as bit and bit by bit instructions and vector instructions such as extraction element, insertion element and shift [28–31].

3 Implement

3.1 Compiler Structure

As shown in Fig. 1 Compiler framework, the compiler is mainly divided into two parts. The front end supports the input of various models, such as tensorflow and pytorch. MLIR provides a basic framework for converting these models into corresponding dialects. XLA can convert tensorflow graphs into HLO dialects, which is a dialect supported by MLIR. Then, using the basic framework of MLIR, the compiler can convert HLO dialect to dialect designed for DSP architecture [18–20], and finally convert it to LLVM IR. The compiler will perform some high-level operator optimization in the MLIR phase, including data format conversion, dead code elimination, Op fusion and other operations. We call the infrastructure provided by MLIR to complete these optimization. In addition, we can also do some architecture related optimization at the front end, which is also the focus of this article, the lower optimization of tensor multiplication.

LLC is a reusable compiler back-end, which does not distinguish the front-end language framework, so we can use LLC to complete the process from LLVM to machine code. LLC takes LLVM IR as input, and finally generates machine code through instruction selection, register allocation and other processes.

The SIMD instruction of DSP provides powerful vector operation capability [16].First, we define the corresponding instruction at the backend and provide the form of intrinsics function to call the intrinsics function in LLVM IR. Assume that the vector width supported by DSP is 2048bit (Fig. 2).

In order to realize architecture related optimization in the MLIR phase, it is necessary to call DSP supported instructions in the MLIR. Therefore, we need to expose some

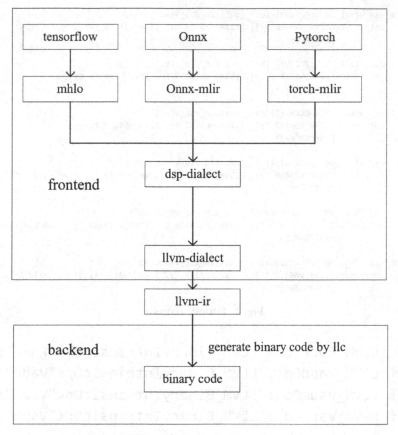

Fig. 1. Compiler framework.

instructions in the DSP to the front end of the MLIR in the form of intrinsic instructions. And rewrite the conversion pattern in the process of dialect conversion to complete the conversion from matrix multiplication to vector multiplication. For other operations, we convert them to affine and other dialects, which are the infrastructure provided by MLIR, and for which MLIR defines the relevant patterns converted to LLVM. Through the delivery optimized infrastructure provided by MLIR, all the code is finally lowered to the LLVM IR phase (Fig. 3).

```
def int_dsp_vfmul_10  :GCCBuiltin<"__builtin_dsp_vfmul_10">,
        Intrinsic<[llvm_v256i8_ty], [llvm_v256i8_ty, llvm_v256i8_ty],
                  [IntrNoMem]>;

def int_dsp_vfmul_20  :GCCBuiltin<"__builtin_dsp_vfmul_20">,
        Intrinsic<[llvm_v128i16_ty], [llvm_v128i16_ty, llvm_v128i16_ty],
                  [IntrNoMem]>;

def int_dsp_vfmul_40  :GCCBuiltin<"__builtin_dsp_vfmul_40">,
        Intrinsic<[llvm_v64i32_ty], [llvm_v64i32_ty, llvm_v64i32_ty],
                  [IntrNoMem]>;

def int_dsp_vfmac_10  :GCCBuiltin<"__builtin_dsp_vfmac_10">,
        Intrinsic<[llvm_v256i8_ty], [llvm_v256i8_ty, llvm_v256i8_ty, llvm_v256i8_ty],
                  [IntrNoMem]>;

def int_dsp_vfmac_20  :GCCBuiltin<"__builtin_dsp_vfmac_20">,
        Intrinsic<[llvm_v128i16_ty], [llvm_v128i16_ty, llvm_v128i16_ty, llvm_v128i16_ty],
                  [IntrNoMem]>;

def int_dsp_vfmac_40  :GCCBuiltin<"__builtin_dsp_vfmac_40">,
        Intrinsic<[llvm_v64i32_ty], [llvm_v64i32_ty, llvm_v64i32_ty,llvm_v64i32_ty],
                  [IntrNoMem]>;
```

Fig. 2. Intrinsic function.

```
def LLVM_FmacOp : LLVM_BinaryIntrinsicOp<"Fmac">;
def LLVM_VaddOp : LLVM_BinaryIntrinsicOp<"Vadd">;
def LLVM_VsumOp : LLVM_BinaryIntrinsicOp<"Vsum">;
def LLVM_VsubOp : LLVM_BinaryIntrinsicOp<"Vsub">;
```

Fig. 3. Mlir intrinsic op.

3.2 Tensor Multiply

Tensor multiplication in AI model is mainly divided into two types: the first is full connection and dot. The two inputs of this tensor multiplication are feature and weight. Feature is the feature extracted from the input data, which can only be determined at runtime. Weight is the value that is continuously updated by iteration through the back-propagation algorithm during the model training process. Therefore, the weight data is represented as static data in the model reasoning process, that is, the data that can be determined in the model compilation process, which is similar to the literal constant in the C language program. Therefore, we can optimize the layout of weight data during compilation, and convert it to a data format more suitable for SIMD instructions, so as to speed up the operation.

The arrangement of data has a great impact on matrix multiplication. At present, in order to adapt to the tensor core or matrix operation unit, most feature matrices are arranged in rows, while weight is transposed, which is arranged in columns. This format is very suitable for chips with matrix computing units, and has the advantage of sequential access to memory. However, for deploying voice model on DSP, storing weight matrix by line can generate better code. Therefore, in order to make full use of the operation characteristics of DSP, we can transpose the weight matrix arranged in columns. We can insert a transfer node into DSP dialect to represent the transpose of weight matrix. However, the DSP chip does not provide matrix transpose instructions, or load and store instructions accessed according to stripe. One method is to insert transpose instructions during compilation, but the load and store instructions are expensive, and additional memory is required to implement matrix transpose, which puts great pressure on the memory of DSP chip. However, the weight data is obtained in the training process and remains unchanged in the reasoning process, so we can transpose it in the compilation stage.

The second is that the two tensors that perform operations are dynamic, and the data is determined at runtime. This kind of tensor is obtained through pre-node operation. Because the pre-running and post-running environment cannot be determined for this kind of data, its data format cannot be changed in the compiler. Fortunately, current compiler frameworks are arranged in rows for dynamic tensors. Therefore, we propose an algorithm to realize matrix multiplication by exchanging matrix operation sequence. This algorithm does not need additional memory overhead, and is better than transpose algorithm in time complexity.

In the traditional algorithm, one value of an objective matrix is obtained each time. For example, for the evaluation of multiplication, $C = AB$, we can get the value of c_{11} by $c_{11} = a_{11}b_{11} + a_{12}b_{21} + \cdots + a_{1m}b_{m1}$. the basic idea of our algorithm is to obtain only one item of all elements in all rows of the objective matrix each time, and continue to multiply and accumulate. Finally, after m cycles, the elements in one row of the objective matrix are obtained.

The description of the algorithm is as follows:
Input: matrix A(m*n) and matrix B(n*k), both of which are closely arranged in rows.
Output: product of matrix A and matrix B.

Because the pipeline of DSP chip has been carefully designed and optimized, it is considered that after the pipeline is started, the average execution cycle of each instruction is 1 cycle, that is, the next instruction can directly use the calculation result of the previous instruction without waiting.

> For i = 0 to n:
> For j = 0 to m:
>
> 1. vloadr a_{ij} : there are 64 a_{ij} duplicate in a vector register VR1
>
> 2. load $b_1, b_2, \cdots, b_{jg}$ to vector register
>
> 3. vfmac VR0, VR1, VR2: multiply VR1 and VR2, add their results to VR0, and store the results in VR0
>
> store VR0: 64 target values can be calculated per cycle

So the final time complexity is: $3mnk/64$.
Inner circulation diagram:

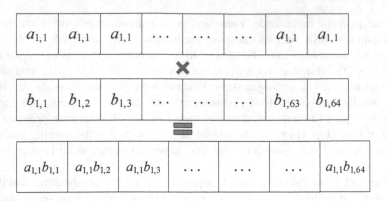

outer circulation diagram:

$a_{1,1}b_{1,1}$ $+$ $a_{1,2}b_{2,1}$ $+$ ... ... $+$ $a_{1,m}b_{m,1}$	$a_{1,1}b_{1,1}$ $+$ $a_{1,2}b_{2,2}$ $+$ ... ... $+$ $a_{1,m}b_{m,2}$	$a_{1,1}b_{1,1}$ $+$ $a_{1,2}b_{2,3}$ $+$ ... ... $+$ $a_{1,m}b_{m,3}$	...	...	...	$a_{1,1}b_{1,64}$ $+$ $a_{1,2}b_{2,64}$ $+$ ... ... $+$ $a_{1,m}b_{m,64}$

The image below is part of the LLVM IR generated by the compiler front end, corresponding to the innermost loop in the algorithm:

```
1   for.body:
2     %j.019 = phi i32 [ 0, %for.cond1.preheader ], [ %inc, %for.body4 ]
3     %0 = call <64 x i32> @LLVM.dsp.vloadr.32(i32 x, i32 x) #1, !dbg !49
4     %1 = call <64 x i32> @LLVM.dsp.vload.32(i32 x, i32 x)
5     %2 = call <64 x i32> @LLVM.dsp.vfmac.40(<64 x i32> %3, <64 x i32> %4, <64 x i32> %5) #3, !dbg !43
```

3.3 Kernel Fusion

The basic form of full connection formula in deep learning is that $Y = WX + b$, we can see that there is an offset b in the formula. The general operator method is to multiply first and then add once. In the stage of model reasoning, we can fuse the two operations through reasonable optimization. Therefore, based on the matrix multiplication proposed above, the offset calculation algorithm is integrated as follows.

The description of the algorithm is as follows:
Input: matrix A(m*n) and matrix B(n*k), both of which are closely arranged in rows.
Output: product of matrix A and matrix B.

Because the pipeline of DSP chip has been carefully designed and optimized, it is considered that after the pipeline is started, the average execution cycle of each instruction is 1 cycle, that is, the next instruction can directly use the calculation result of the previous instruction without waiting.

For i = 0 to n:
  For j = 0 to m:

    1. vloadr a_{ij} : there are 64 a_{ij} duplicate in a vector register VR1

    2. load $b_{j1}, b_{j2}, \cdots, b_{jg}$ to vector register

    3. vfmac VR0, VR1, VR2: multiply VR1 and VR2, add their results to VR0, and store the results in VR0
  vadd VR0, VR0, VR3: add VR0 with VR3, and store result to VR0

  store VR0: 64 target values can be calculated per cycle

By operator coincidence, we can optimize the space-time cost of repeated load of the target matrix, so as to improve the performance.

3.4 Loop Tiling

Tensor multiplication is a typical computation intensive operator, but it still needs to access a large amount of memory space. In order to speed up matrix operation, we should reduce the overhead caused by memory access as much as possible. When the input matrix used for tensor multiplication cannot be placed in the SRAM, and in order to adapt to the computational bit width of the vector instruction, the data needs to be divided into tiles so that each tile can be placed in the SRAM.

3.5 Quantization

The training of neural network is a process of continuously fine adjustment of weights, which usually requires floating-point precision representation and operation, and cannot be directly replaced by fixed-point numbers. However, in the model prediction stage, due to the strong robustness of the deep neural network model, it can well deal with a certain intensity of input noise and eliminate the interference of irrelevant information in the data. Therefore, if the low-precision operation is regarded as a noise source, the neural network model should be able to give relatively accurate results. Therefore, we reduce the precision of the tensor multiplication of fp32 to fp16 for operation, which greatly improves the operation efficiency while retaining the expected results [32].

4 Evaluation

Based on the manually written assembler library, we compare the performance of a single operator with that of the whole model by taking the cycles required for the end of the running of the machine code generated by the compiler as the performance index.

216   C. Qiu et al.

Take the 1024*1024 tensor multiplication operator as an example. At the single operator scale, because we have optimized the operator implementation at the operator level, the code generated by the AI compiler and the handwritten assembly library have similar performance.

However, in AI model reasoning with more operators, the AI compiler shows better performance because the AI compiler supports both operator level and instruction level optimization, and can schedule instructions across operators. Instructions between operators without dependency can be executed in parallel, further improving performance. As shown in Fig. 4. Performance comparison between mlir compiler and tradition compiler which uses assembler library, in the test of a part of the recommendation model, the AI compiler achieved 21.27% performance optimization compared with the manually optimized operator library. The Fig. 5 explains why code generation through IR is more advantageous in the model formed by the combination of multiple operators. Store operations of different operators and computations of subsequent operators, such as vfmac, can be executed in parallel.

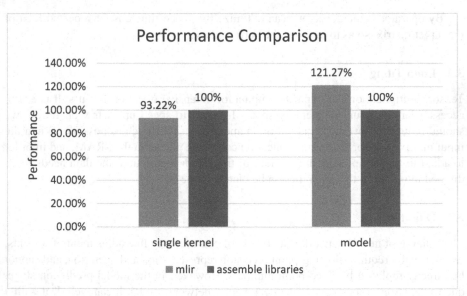

Fig. 4. Performance comparison between mlir compiler and tradition compiler which uses assembler library.

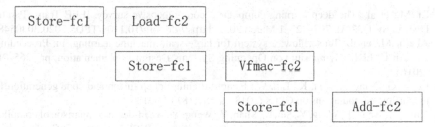

Fig. 5. Instructions in parallel

5 Conclusion

This paper presents an AI compiler, which can deploy the trained AI model to the embedded processor DSP. This compiler architecture can optimize the operator level and instruction level, and further reduce the model reasoning overhead. This AI compiler can well lower the important tensor multiplication operation in AI reasoning to the SIMD processor supported by DSP, so as to support AI reasoning on the embedded processor, and its performance can be comparable to that of the handwritten assembly operator library. This work can reduce the overhead of manually designing algorithm libraries for various AI chips.

Acknowledgement. The authors would like to thank the editors and the reviewers for providing comments and suggestions for this paper. This work was supported by National Key R&D Program of China under Grant 2020YFA0711400, National Natural Science Foundation of China under Grants 61831018 and U21A20452, the Jiangxi Double Thousand Plan under Grant jxsq2019201125, and the S&T plan projects of Jiangxi Province Education Department GJJ201003.

References

1. Lattner, C., Adve, V.: LLVM: a compilation framework for lifelong program analysis and transformation. In: Proceedings of the International Symposium on Code Generation and Optimization: Feedback-directed and Runtime Optimization, ser. CGO 2004. IEEE Computer Society, Washington, DC, p. 75 (2004). http://dl.acm.org/citation.cfm?id=977395.977673
2. Cytron, R., Ferrante, J., Rosen, B.K., Wegman, M.N., Zadeck, F.K.: Efficiently computing static single assignment form and the control dependence graph. ACM Trans. Program. Lang. Syst., **13**(4), 451–490 (1991). https://doi.org/10.1145/115372.115320
3. Vasilache, N., et al.: The next 700 accelerated layers: from mathematical expressions of network computation graphs to accelerated GPU kernels, automatically. ACM Trans. Archit. Code Optim. **16**(4), pp. 38:1–38:26 (2019). https://doi.org/10.1145/3355606
4. Lattner, C., et al.: MLIR: scaling compiler infrastructure for domain specific computation. In: 2021 IEEE/ACM International Symposium on Code Generation and Optimization (CGO), pp. 2–14 (2021). https://doi.org/10.1109/CGO51591.2021.9370308
5. Schweitz, E.: An MLIR dialect for high-level optimization of fortran. In: LLVM Developer Meeting, October 2019

6. Li, M., et al.: The deep learning compiler: a comprehensive survey. IEEE Trans. Parallel Distrib. Syst. **32**(3), 708–727, 1 March 2021. https://doi.org/10.1109/TPDS.2020.3030548
7. Abadi, M., et al.: TensorFlow: a system for large-scale machine learning. In: Proceedings of 12th USENIX Symposium on Operating Systems Design Implementation, pp. 265–283 (2016)
8. Long, G., Yang, J., Zhu, K., Lin, W.: FusionStitching: deep fusion and code generation for tensorflow computations on GPUs (2018). arXiv:1811.05213
9. Xing, Y., Weng, J., Wang, Y., Sui, L., Shan, Y., Wang, Y.: An in-depth comparison of compilers for deep neural networks on hardware. In: Proceedings of IEEE International Conference on Embedded Software Systems, pp. 1–8 (2019)
10. Chen, T., Moreau, T., Jiang, Z., et al.: TVM: an automated end-to-end optimizing compiler for deep learning. In: 13th USENIX Symposium on Operating Systems Design and Implementation (OSDI 2018), pp. 578–594 (2018)
11. Adachi, Y., Kumano, T., Ogino, K.: Intermediate representation for stiff virtual objects. In: Proceedings Virtual Reality Annual International Symposium 1995, pp. 203–210. IEEE (1995)
12. Yao, L., Mimno, D., McCallum, A.: Efficient methods for topic model inference on streaming document collections. In: Proceedings of the 15th ACM SIGKDD International Conference on Knowledge Discovery and Data Mining, pp. 937–946 (2009)
13. Gopinath, K., Hennessy, J.L.: Copy elimination in functional languages. In: Proceedings of the 16th ACM SIGPLAN-SIGACT Symposium on Principles of Programming Languages, pp. 303–314 (1989)
14. Wei, R., Schwartz, L., Adve, V.: DLVM: a modern compiler infrastructure for deep learning systems. arXiv preprint arXiv:1711.03016 (2017)
15. Griewank, A., Walther, A.: Evaluating derivatives: principles and techniques of algorithmic differentiation. SIAM (2008)
16. Ren, H., Zhang, Z., Jun, W.: SWIFT: A Computationally-intensive DSP architecture for communication applications. Mob. Netw. Appl. **21**(6), 974–982 (2016)
17. Mullapudi, R.T., Vasista, V., Bondhugula, U.: PolyMage: automatic optimization for image processing pipelines. In: International Conference on Architectural Support for Programming Languages and Operating Systems (ASPLOS), pp. 429–443 (2015)
18. Zerrell, T., Bruestle, J.: Stripe: tensor compilation via the nested polyhedral model. CoRR, vol. abs/1903.06498 (2019). http://arxiv.org/abs/1903.06498
19. Zhou, Y., Qin, J., Chen, H., Nunamaker, J.F.: Multilingual web retrieval: an experiment on a multilingual business intelligence portal. In: Proceedings of the 38th Annual Hawaii International Conference on System Sciences, Big Island, HI, USA, p. 43a (2005)
20. Korra, R., Sujatha, P., Chetana, S., Naresh Kumar, M.: Performance evaluation of Multilingual Information Retrieval (MLIR) system over Information Retrieval (IR) system. In: 2011 International Conference on Recent Trends in Information Technology (ICRTIT), Chennai, India, pp. 722–727 (2011)
21. Yang, H., Lee, C.: Multilingual Information Retrieval Using GHSOM. In: 2008 Eighth International Conference on Intelligent Systems Design and Applications, Kaohsuing, Taiwan, pp. 225–228 (2008)
22. Curzel, S., et al.: Automated generation of integrated digital and spiking neuromorphic machine learning accelerators. In: 2021 IEEE/ACM International Conference on Computer Aided Design (ICCAD), Munich, Germany, pp. 1–7 (2021)
23. Tian, R., Guo, L., Li, J., Ren, B., Kestor, G.: A high performance sparse tensor algebra compiler in MLIR. In: 2021 IEEE/ACM 7th Workshop on the LLVM Compiler Infrastructure in HPC (LLVM-HPC), St. Louis, MO, USA, pp. 27–38 (2021)
24. Wei, W., Zeng, Q., Ye, T., Lomone, D.: Adaptive differentiated integrated routing scheme for GMPLS-based optical Internet. J. Commun. Netw. **6**(3), 269–279 (Sept. 2004)

25. Li, H., Peng, Y.: Effective multi-level image representation for image categorization. In: 2010 20th International Conference on Pattern Recognition, Istanbul, Turkey, pp. 1048–1051 (2010)
26. Zhuhadar, L., Nasraoui, O., Wyatt, R., Romero, E.: Multi-language ontology-based search engine. In: 2010 Third International Conference on Advances in Computer-Human Interactions, Saint Maarten, Netherlands Antilles, pp. 13–18 (2010)
27. Siemieniuk, A., et al.: OCC: an automated end-to-end machine learning optimizing compiler for computing-in-memory. IEEE Trans. Comput. Aided Des. Integr. Circuits Syst. **41**(6), 1674–1686 (June2022)
28. Komisarczyk, K., Chelini, L., Vadivel, K., Jordans, R., Corporaal, H.: PET-to-MLIR: a polyhedral front-end for MLIR. In: 2020 23rd Euromicro Conference on Digital System Design (DSD), Kranj, Slovenia, pp. 551–556 (2020)
29. Junod, P., Rinaldini, J., Wehrli, J., Michielin, J.: Obfuscator-LLVM - software protection for the masses. In: 2015 IEEE/ACM 1st International Workshop on Software Protection, Florence, Italy, pp. 3–9 (2015)
30. Wei, J., Thomas, A., Li, G., Pattabiraman, K.: Quantifying the accuracy of high-level fault injection techniques for hardware faults. In: 2014 44th Annual IEEE/IFIP International Conference on Dependable Systems and Networks, Atlanta, GA, USA, pp. 375–382 (2014)
31. Sharma, V.C., Haran, A., Rakamaric, Z., Gopalakrishnan, G.: Towards formal approaches to system resilience. In: 2013 IEEE 19th Pacific Rim International Symposium on Dependable Computing, Vancouver, BC, Canada, pp. 41–50 (2013)
32. Alvarez, R., Prabhavalkar, R., Bakhtin, A.: On the efficient representation and execution of deep acoustic models. CoRR, abs/1607.04683 (2016)

Self-supervised Anomalous Sound Detection for Machine Condition Monitoring

Ying Zeng$^{(\boxtimes)}$, Hongqing Liu, Yu Zhao, and Yi Zhou

School of Communication and Information Engineering,
Chongqing University of Posts and Telecommunications, Chongqing, China
s200101158@stu.cqupt.edu.cn

Abstract. Automatic detection of anomalous sounds is very important for industrial equipment maintenances. However, anomalous sounds are difficult to collect in practice, and self-supervised methods have received extensive attentions. It is well-known that the self-supervised methods show poor performances on certain machine types. To improve the detection performance, in this work, we introduce other types of data as targets to train a general classifier. After that, the model has certain prior knowledge, and then we fine tune the parameters of the model for a specific machine type. We also studied the impact of input features on performance, and it is shown that for machine types, filtering out low-frequency noise interference can significantly improve model performance. Experiments conducted using the DCASE 2021 Challenge Task2 dataset showed that the proposed method improves the detection performance on each machine type and outperforms the DCASE 2021 Challenge first-placed ensemble model by 8.73% on average according to the official scoring method.

Keywords: Machine condition monitoring · Anomalous sound detection · Self-supervised learning

1 Introduction

Anomalous sound detection (ASD) is receiving increasing attentions, especially in the industrial fields, where mechanical failures cause companies a great financial risk. Due to the shortage of maintenance workers in companies around the world, there is a growing need for automatic diagnostic technology using machine sounds [1,2].

The purpose of ASD is to identify whether the sound emitted from a machine is normal or abnormal in determining the machine operation status. If the anomaly score of the data exceeds a threshold, the said sound is identified as

This work is supported by the Natural Science Foundation of Chongqing, China (No. cstc2021jcyj-bshX0206).

F. Gao et al. (Eds.): ChinaCom 2022, LNICST 500, pp. 220–230, 2023.
https://doi.org/10.1007/978-3-031-34790-0_17

the outlier. Because of the variability of the anomaly data and the high cost of damaging machines, it is difficult to collect them, and the unsupervised anomaly detection methods are usually preferred.

The Challenge on Detection and Classification of Acoustic Scenes and Events (DCASE) has played a great role in advancing this technology. In DCASE 2020 Challenge Task 2, teams from all over the world participated and a good detection performance was achieved [3], but this was under ideal conditions. In order to simulate more realistic scenarios, the DCASE 2021 Challenge added a domain shift condition [4]. The task is performed under the condition that the acoustic properties of training data and testing data are different, i.e., domain shift, and the differences include speed, machine load, ambient noise, etc. Compared to 2020, this task only provides very little normal audio data for the target domain, and this extra setting simulates a more realistic situation.

The traditional approaches are to train an autoencoder that maps normal data to a low-dimensional space through the encoder, and then reconstruct the data with the decoder, and the reconstruction error is used as the loss function [5]. The parameters in the network are continuously updated to reduce the reconstruction error. Since the network is trained with normal data, the basic assumption is that normal data can be well reconstructed after training, but the abnormal data cannot. During the test, the reconstruction error is used as the anomaly score. However, under the influence of complex environments, the model trained by this method often cannot distinguish the normal and abnormal sounds.

The normalized flow (NF) is another commonly used method [6], which is a series of reversible transformations between the input data distribution $p(x)$ and the known distribution $p(z)$ to perform accurate likelihood estimation. The negative log-likelihood function is used as optimization objective and anomaly score. It can fit the distribution of normal samples well, but for other normal samples whose domain is shifted, it is easy to be judged as abnormal.

The latest research is often based on self-supervised learning [7–9], and the assumption is that there are sound data from multiple machines of the same machine type. This is a realistic assumption since multiple machines of the same type are often installed in factories. For a specific machine type, by training a dedicated classifier to distinguish between different machine ID, the model can learn the inherent attributes of the machine ID and anomalies are determined based on the output probability of the corresponding IDs. In this case, the normal sound often outputs a higher probability, while the output probability of abnormal data corresponding to ID is often lower than normal output.

The key to self-supervised anomalous sound detection is to use normal sound samples to learn the inherent properties of normal sound samples, so as to distinguish abnormalities. However, due to the powerful fitting ability of the neural network, it is very easy to distinguish different machine IDs of the same machine type, which means that it is very easy to overfit. Although these methods improved detection performance on average, research showed that the significant low scores were obtained on some machine types, see DCASE 2021. To overcome the above problems, we propose a more robust self-supervised anomaly detection model. First, we use all machine types to train a classifier that can simultaneously distinguish different machine types with different IDs. Second, we fine-tune the model parameters to train a dedicated classifier for each machine type. Since the features of some machine types are mainly concentrated in high frequencies, we design a high-pass filter to filter out low-frequency noise signal to improve the detection performance.

In addition to classifier confidence, Mahalanobis distance is served as an additional option for computing the anomaly scores. The experimental results show that the proposed method is superior to the first-place model of DCASE 2021 challenge task2, especially on the target domain.

The main contributions of this paper can be summarized as follows.

- We found that by selecting an appropriate anomaly score, the detection performance of the same model will be greatly improved.
- We preprocess the input features to reduce the interference caused by noise. Specifically, we adopt a high pass filter for some machine types to filter out the low frequency interference before Mel filtering.
- We train a general anomalous sound detection model, and finally fine tune the parameters of the model to obtain a special anomalous sound detection model for a specific machine type. After this, the model can learn more discriminative and robust latent acoustic representations.

The rest of the paper is organized as follows. Section 2 gives an overview of the proposed method in details. Section 3 describes the experiment settings and the experimental results. Finally, Sect. 4 concludes the paper.

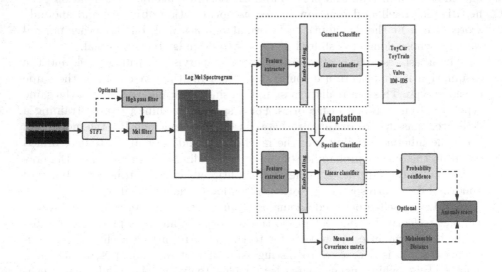

Fig. 1. A overview of our anomalous sound detection model.

2   Proposed Method

The overall structure of our model is shown in Fig. 1. First, we use all machine types to train a classifier that can simultaneously distinguish different machine types with different IDs. Finally, we fine tune the model parameters to train a dedicated classifier for each machine type. In the fine-tuning phase, we use the enhanced input features, the time spectrum after short-time Fourier transform is passed through a high-pass filter with a selectable cut-off frequency. The model will continuously optimize the parameters according to the loss function. We use the training dataset to calculate the average vector and covariance matrix of each class separately to measure the anomaly score.

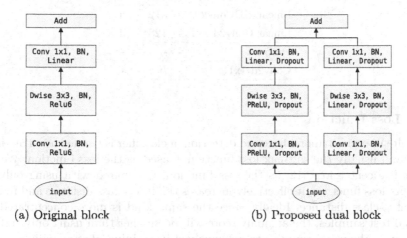

(a) Original block   (b) Proposed dual block

Fig. 2. Comparison of Inverted residuals block when stride = 2.

2.1   Model

We use the inverted residuals proposed by Mobilenet v2 [10] to build our model. Similar to mobilefacenet [11], PRelu is selected as the activation function, and a linear branch without using any activation function is added to reduce the loss of information caused by PRelu. Figure 2 shows the case of stride = 2. When stride = 1, the input is added to the output through skip connection. By utilizing this structure, our final model is depicted in Table 1, where the global depthwise convolution (GDConv) [11] means that the kernel size is equal to the input dimension size, and the bottleneck consists of n numbers of the proposed inverted residuals. This model first uses two layers of 2D Convs to extract features and three layers of the proposed bottleneck, and followed by convolutional layers and finally outputs the probability of section IDs.

Table 1. Model architecture, where k is the number of section IDs, t indicates the expansion factor, c is the output channels, and s is the stride. The first layer of each sequence has a stride s and others use stride 1, and linear means that the activation function is not employed.

Operator	t	c	n	s
Conv2d 3x3	-	64	-	2
Conv2d 3x3	-	64	-	1
Dual block	2	128	2	2
Dual block	4	128	2	2
Dual block	4	128	2	2
Conv2d 1x1	-	512	-	1
Linear GDConv2d	-	512	-	1
Linear Conv2d 1x1	-	128	-	1
Dropout	-	-	-	-
Conv2d 1x1	-	k	-	-

2.2 Loss Function

For self-supervised anomaly sound detection, a classifier is trained as an auxiliary task, and usually the softmax loss function is used as the loss function. We also select the center loss [12] as the loss function. Compared with using only the softmax loss function, it effectively increases the inter-class distance and reduces the intra-class distance. Ideally, since the same kind is more concentrated, for normal test samples, the anomaly score will be smaller than using only softmax loss. Since abnormal sounds are not involved in training, its anomaly score has little change compared with only softmax loss, and then AUC and pAUC can be improved. The joint loss function now is

$$\mathcal{L}_S = -\sum_{i=1}^{m}\sum_{j=1}^{k} y_{ij} \log \hat{y}_{ij}, \tag{1}$$

$$\mathcal{L}_C = \frac{1}{2}\sum_{i=1}^{m} \|x_i - c_{y_i}\|_2^2, \tag{2}$$

$$\mathcal{L} = \lambda \mathcal{L}_S + \mathcal{L}_C, \tag{3}$$

where (1) and (2) respectively represent the softmax loss and center loss, λ is a tunable parameter, and m is the size of mini-batch. In (1), $\hat{y}_i \in \mathbb{R}^k$ denotes that the i-th sample passes through the output of the network and then passes through the output value of the softmax function, y_i is the one-hot encoding of the label, $\hat{y}_{ij}$ and y_{ij} are the j-th values of $\hat{y}_i$ and y_i, respectively. In (2), $c_{y_i} \in \mathbb{R}^{128}$ denotes the real class center of i-th sample and x_i is the output of Linear Conv2d 1x1 layer. In actual training, we first initialize a class center for each class, and then continuously update the class center.

2.3 Calculation of Anomaly Score

The calculation of anomaly scores is very important. We found that the results obtained by using different calculation anomaly scores for the same model are often very different. This indicates that the model might be good enough, but we only need to select appropriate anomaly scores for different machine types.

Classifier Confidence. The models is trained to identify from which section the observed signal was generated and outputs softmax value for each machine section ID. After feature extraction, the features of an audio segment are segmented into B segments. The anomaly score is calculated as

$$Score = \frac{1}{B} \sum_{i=1}^{B} \log \frac{1 - P_i}{P_i}, \tag{4}$$

where P_i is the prediction probability of machine ID corresponding to the i-th feature segment.

Mahalanobis Distance. Mahalanobis distance [13,14] is commonly used as an indicator of similarity measure. During the experiments, it is found that using Mahalanobis distance as anomaly score effectively classify anomalies, and it also shows a high performance under the condition that the target domain has very few normal data. The formula for calculating Mahalanobis distance is

$$Score_{ma} = \sqrt{(\mathbf{x} - \boldsymbol{\mu})^T \Sigma^{-1} (\mathbf{x} - \boldsymbol{\mu})}, \tag{5}$$

where $\mathbf{x}$ is the mean vector, $\boldsymbol{\mu}$ is the mean vector representation corresponding to the ID and Σ is the covariance matrix corresponding to the ID. For the source domain and the target domain, we use the data of different domains to calculate the average vector, and use all the training data of the machine ID to calculate the covariance matrix. Because the amount of data corresponding to the target domain is too small, the covariance matrix will be inaccurate if calculation only uses the data from the target domain.

2.4 Data Augmentation

Data augmentation is an effective way to improve neural network generalization and prevents overfitting. In our system, we use the Mixup method [15] in the training phase to randomly introduce other samples as noise to the original data. The mixing operation on the training samples is

$$\tilde{x} = \eta x_i + (1 - \eta) x_j, \tag{6}$$

where x_i is considered as the original sample and x_j is considered as the random sample of this mini-batch.

Since the sound characteristics of some machine types are mainly concentrated in high frequencies, we pass a high-pass filter with a manually tuneable cutoff frequency to produce better embedding.

3   Experiments

3.1   Datasets

We conduct experiments using the DCASE 2021 Challenge Task2 dataset, which includes recordings of 10 s in length and a sampling rate of 16 kHz, and in this dataset, ToyCar and ToyTrain belong to ToyADMOS2 [16], and Fan, Gearbox, Pump, Slider, Valve belong to MIMIIDUE [17]. The dataset for each machine type has 6 different machine numbers, and for each number, about 1000 normal samples belong to the source domain and 3 normal samples are in the target domain. We use sections 3, 4, and 5 for each machine type as the test set. For both domains, the same number of test samples is provided, with approximately 100 normal samples and 100 abnormal samples.

3.2   Experimental Setup

We load the audio data using the default sample rate and apply a short time Fourier transform (STFT) with a window size of 1024 and a hop length of 512 samples. We pass the data through a high pass filter, and then convert the STFT spectrogram into a Mel spectrogram with a 128-band Mel filter. After this, we generate a 128×313 logarithmic Mel spectrogram. We used Adam as the optimizer and the learning rate of the model was set to 0.001. Training runs with a batch size of 64 for 50 epochs.

Table 2. The effect of anomaly scores on results, where m represents Mahalanobis distance and p represents probability confidence.

	m		p	
	AUC	pAUC	AUC	pAUC
ToyCar	**62.92%**	**54.42%**	54.58%	54.17%
ToyTrain	**68.21%**	**56.04%**	49.04%	49.50%
fan	72.64%	54.59%	**86.15%**	**71.45%**
gearbox	**66.18%**	**57.68%**	52.02%	51.95%
pump	63.31%	54.94%	**78.81%**	**67.57%**
slider	74.17%	61.30%	**89.15%**	**73.82%**
valve	57.51%	52.46%	**59.23%**	**59.67%**

3.3   Results and Discussions

To show the performance, we evaluate the detection performance of the area under the receiver operating characteristic curve (AUC) and the partial AUC (pAUC) with $p = 0.1$.

Table 3. Anomaly detection results for different machine types, where General represents pre-training with all data, and Specific represents the final result after fine-tuning.

	Machine Type	Baseline	Top1	general	specfic
AUC	ToyCar	65.93%	75.27%	65.09%	**78.40%**
	ToyTrain	68.51%	69.15%	71.24%	**73.43%**
	fan	60.68%	61.01%	86.15%	**91.44%**
	gearbox	65.49%	63.07%	71.09%	**73.40%**
	pump	58.30%	86.76%	78.81%	**89.06%**
	slider	57.22%	83.18%	**89.15%**	89.11%
	valve	51.87%	65.36%	74.78%	**80.03%**
pAUC	ToyCar	52.32%	59.71%	58.24%	**68.73%**
	ToyTrain	57.56%	59.91%	59.33%	**62.19%**
	fan	50.50%	60.79%	71.45%	**82.78%**
	gearbox	56.86%	61.56%	60.48%	**64.06%**
	pump	50.98%	**81.55%**	67.57%	77.32%
	slider	51.41%	63.60%	73.82%	**75.03%**
	valve	50.07%	60.15%	61.03%	**67.18%**
	harmonic mean	56.38%	66.80%	69.43%	**75.53%**

Table 4. Results for different machine types in Source Domain and Target Domain. h-mean means harmonic mean.

	Source domain				Target domain			
	Top1		ours		Top1		ours	
	AUC	pAUC	AUC	pAUC	AUC	pAUC	AUC	pAUC
ToyCar	**81.44%**	59.05%	78.63%	**68.94%**	69.97%	60.39%	78.18%	68.53%
ToyTrain	**77.56%**	62.21%	75.89%	**62.83%**	62.38%	57.78%	71.12%	61.56%
fan	51.45%	61.70%	**94.63%**	**85.43%**	74.93%	59.91%	88.45%	80.29%
gearbox	63.52%	61.38%	**76.13%**	**64.02%**	62.62%	61.75%	70.87%	64.10%
pump	**88.72%**	**82.19%**	86.39%	73.11%	84.88%	80.91%	91.90%	82.05%
slider	85.56%	66.10%	**91.10%**	**75.85%**	80.92%	61.28%	87.20%	74.24%
valve	69.56%	64.03%	**79.35%**	**68.06%**	61.64%	56.71%	80.72%	66.33%
h-mean	71.66%	64.56%	**82.59%**	**70.49%**	70.00%	61.91%	80.45%	70.26%

Table 2 shows the performance of the general anomalous sound detection model without using a high-pass filter. It is obvious that choosing different anomaly scores for the same model has a great impact on the results, which means that the model is often good enough, and the only thing to do is to choose an appropriate anomaly score. In order to better compare the performance of the model, we choose the anomaly scores that are more suitable for this machine type from the Mahalanobis distance and probability confidence in the following results.

In Table 3, baseline is built by Autoencoder, a classic method of anomalous sound detection. Top1 is the first-placed model in the DCASE 2021 challenge [7], which is an ensemble of three different models including two self-supervised classifier models and a probabilistic model. The harmonic mean obtained in the table is the average of AUC and pAUC. The harmonic mean of our general model reach 69.43%, which is a great improvement over previous methods. After fine-tuning the model parameters to fit the specific machine type, our method finally reached 75.53%. It can be clearly seen that our method outperforms the previous results.

In Table 4, the detection results in the source domain and the target domain are shown. The average performance of our model outperforms state-of-the-art models in both source and target domains. In particular, the performance of the target domain is only slightly degraded compared to the source domain, which means that our method is very robust.

Table 5. The impact of high-pass filtering on detection performance, we do not show the results of fan and pump after high-pass filtering because the model cannot converge.

	w/o hpss		hpss	
	AUC	pAUC	AUC	pAUC
ToyCar	62.92%	54.42%	**65.09%**	**58.24%**
ToyTrain	68.21%	56.04%	**71.24%**	**59.33%**
fan	**86.15%**	**71.45%**	-	-
gearbox	66.18%	57.68%	**71.09%**	**60.48%**
pump	**78.81%**	**67.57%**	-	-
slider	**89.15%**	**73.82%**	86.41%	69.16%
valve	59.23%	59.67%	**74.78%**	**61.03%**

To verify the effectiveness of the high-pass filter, we conducted ablation experiments to compare the performance without and with high-pass filtering. In Table 5, we found that the performance after the high-pass filter has been improved, which shows that filtering out a low-frequency noise is beneficial for detections. Specifically, for fan, pumps and slider, the detection performance will decrease, and we conjecture that it may be because the low-frequency signals of these machine types contain a lot of feature information. Table 6 shows the performance of our specfic model when using the centerloss. For fan, gearbox, pump and valve, centerloss can improve the performance. But the performance of other machine type has been decrease, we speculate that it may be because the centerloss destroys the details of features, so that the abnormal sound is mapped to the normal feature space. In Table 7, we summarize the best experimental setups in the fine-tuning stage.

Table 6. The impact of centerloss on detection performance.

	w/o centerloss		centerloss	
	AUC	pAUC	AUC	pAUC
ToyCar	**78.40%**	**68.73%**	65.12%	61.10%
ToyTrain	**73.43%**	**62.19%**	67.11%	56.97%
fan	89.70%	78.66%	**91.44%**	**82.78%**
gearbox	71.56%	62.59%	**73.40%**	**64.06%**
pump	80.35%	69.37%	**89.06%**	**77.32%**
slider	**89.11%**	**75.03%**	81.21%	66.48%
valve	76.20%	61.50%	**80.03%**	**75.53%**

Table 7. Experiment configurations, f_{min} represents the cut-off frequency of high pass filter.

	ToyCar	ToyTrain	Fan	Gearbox	pump	Slider	Valve
Centerloss	False	False	True	True	True	False	True
Highpass filter	True	True	False	True	False	False	True
f_{min}	1000	2000	0	2000	0	0	2000

4   Conclusion

We propose a self-supervised anomaly detection model that outperforms the DCASE 2021 first-placed Ensemble model. To achieve that, We first use all the training data to train a general anomalous sound detection model, and then fine tune the model parameters to better adapt to specific machine types. The findings are that for some machine types, the model will perform better by simply filtering out low frequency noise interference. Experiments show that the anomaly detection ability can be effectively improved by using our method. With less target domain data, our method achieves a superior performance in the target domain.

References

1. Koizumi, Y., Saito, S., Uematsu, H., Harada, N.: Optimizing acoustic feature extractor for anomalous sound detection based on Neyman-Pearson lemma. In: 25th European Signal Processing Conference (EUSIPCO), pp. 698–702. IEEE (2017)
2. Koizumi, Y., Saito, S., Uematsu, H., Kawachi, Y., Harada, N.: Unsupervised detection of anomalous sound based on deep learning and the Neyman-Pearson lemma. IEEE/ACM Trans. Audio Speech Lang. Process. **27**(1), 212–224 (2018)
3. Koizumi, Y., et al.: Description and discussion on DCASE 2020 challenge task2: unsupervised anomalous sound detection for machine condition monitoring. arXiv preprint arXiv:2006.05822 (2020)

4. Kawaguchi, Y., et al.: Description and discussion on DCASE 2021 challenge task 2: unsupervised anomalous sound detection for machine condition monitoring under domain shifted conditions. arXiv preprint arXiv:2106.04492 (2021)
5. Chandola, V., Banerjee, A., Kumar, V.: Anomaly detection: a survey. ACM Comput. Surv. (CSUR) **41**(3), 1–58 (2009)
6. Dohi, K., Endo, T., Purohit, H., Tanabe, R., Kawaguchi, Y.: Flow-based self-supervised density estimation for anomalous sound detection. In: 2021 IEEE International Conference on Acoustics, Speech and Signal Processing (ICASSP), ICASSP 2021, pp. 336–340. IEEE (2021)
7. Lopez, J., Stemmer, G., Lopez-Meyer, P., Singh, P.S., del Hoyo Ontiveros, J.A., Courdourier, H.A.: Ensemble of complementary anomaly detectors under domain shifted conditions. DCASE2021 Challenge, Technical report (2021)
8. Morita, K., Yano, T., Tran, K.: Anomalous sound detection using CNN-based features by self supervised learning. DCASE2021 Challenge, Technical report (2021)
9. Wilkinghoff, K.: Utilizing sub-cluster adacos for anomalous sound detection under domain shifted conditions. DCASE2021 Challenge, Technical report (2021)
10. Sandler, M., Howard, A., Zhu, M., Zhmoginov, A., Chen, L.-C.: MobileNetv2: inverted residuals and linear bottlenecks. In: Proceedings of the IEEE Conference on Computer Vision and Pattern Recognition, pp. 4510–4520 (2018)
11. Chen, S., Liu, Y., Gao, X., Han, Z.: MobileFaceNets: efficient CNNs for accurate real-time face verification on mobile devices. In: Zhou, J., et al. (eds.) CCBR 2018. LNCS, vol. 10996, pp. 428–438. Springer, Cham (2018). https://doi.org/10.1007/978-3-319-97909-0_46
12. Wen, Y., Zhang, K., Li, Z., Qiao, Y.: A comprehensive study on center loss for deep face recognition. Int. J. Comput. Vis. **127**(6), 668–683 (2019)
13. De Maesschalck, R., Jouan-Rimbaud, D., Massart, D.L.: The mahalanobis distance. Chemom. Intell. Lab. Syst. **50**(1), 1–18 (2000)
14. Xiang, S., Nie, F., Zhang, C.: Learning a mahalanobis distance metric for data clustering and classification. Pattern Recogn. **41**(12), 3600–3612 (2008)
15. Thulasidasan, S., Chennupati, G., Bilmes, J., Bhattacharya, T., Michalak, S.: On mixup training: improved calibration and predictive uncertainty for deep neural networks. arXiv preprint arXiv:1905.11001 (2019)
16. Harada, N., Niizumi, D., Takeuchi, D., Ohishi, Y., Yasuda, M., Saito, S.: Toy-ADMOS2: another dataset of miniature-machine operating sounds for anomalous sound detection under domain shift conditions. arXiv preprint arXiv:2106.02369 (2021)
17. Tanabe, R.: MIMII due: sound dataset for malfunctioning industrial machine investigation and inspection with domain shifts due to changes in operational and environmental conditions. arXiv preprint arXiv:2105.02702 (2021)

Safety Modeling and Performance Analysis of Urban Scenarios Based on Poisson Line Process

Kong Shi[1]([✉])[iD] and Xinyu Gu[2][iD]

[1] Beijing University of Posts and Telecommunications, Beijing, China
18801372153@163.com
[2] Purple Mountain Laboratories, Beijing University of Posts and Telecommunications, Nanjing 211111, China
guxinyu@bupt.edu.cn

Abstract. Secrecy Performance is one of the focus of research on physical layer security in vehicle-to-everything (V2X). Poisson line process (PLP) is regarded as a more suitable model to study the vehicle communication performance of urban scenarios. However, due to the high theoretical difficulty in the analysis of PLP, research in this area has not been widely conducted yet. In this paper, we take a secure transmission scheme that can improve physical layer security as an example, use PLP model to model urban scenarios. We analyze the performance of coverage probability, secrecy probability and secrecy throughput and draw some effective conclusions to improve secrecy performance. We import a typical urban scenario - part of the map data of Xi'an urban area in China, compare the performance derived by PLP and two-dimensional Poisson point process (2D PPP) model with those modeled on the real urban map respectively, it is demonstrated that PLP is more suitable as the model for urban scenarios.

Keywords: Poisson line process · urban scenario · safety performance analysis · stochastic geometry

1 Introduction

As the number of vehicles increases worldwide, traffic problems can no longer be ignored. We need intelligent transportation systems to update and disseminate information related to road safety and traffic congestion through communication transmission between vehicles or between vehicles and other devices, to improve people's travel efficiency and driving experience. Under this trend, vehicle-to-everything (V2X) technology has become an important technical means to improve the existing transportation system.

Security problems in the process of vehicle communication cannot be ignored. Vehicle communication involves the exchange of information about the user's identity, location and trajectory, and securing vehicle communication is crucial to ensure the user's personal safety. There are two popular strategies for

© ICST Institute for Computer Sciences, Social Informatics and Telecommunications Engineering 2023
Published by Springer Nature Switzerland AG 2023. All Rights Reserved
F. Gao et al. (Eds.): ChinaCom 2022, LNICST 500, pp. 231–246, 2023.
https://doi.org/10.1007/978-3-031-34790-0_18

vehicular security: password-based solutions and physical layer security (PLS)-based solutions [1]. Among them, password-based solutions may face challenges due to the strict latency requirements in vehicle communication, especially for large-scale access scenarios. However, physical layer security-based solutions can complement the former very well [2]. In [3], the authors provide a comprehensive overview of the PLS strategy adopted for V2X, presenting the security threats and the basic principles of PLS techniques. The authors in [4] investigated the PLS performance of mobile vehicle networks, derived exact closed-form expressions for secrecy performance and verified the secrecy performance under different conditions.

Based on the well-known PLS theory analysis, artificial noise (AN) and cooperative jamming (CJ) strategies have been proposed to improve the secrecy performance [5]. In [6], AN schemes for secrecy enhancement are investigated and the balance between communication reliability and security is analyzed. The authors in [7] proposed a practical uncoordinated cooperative jamming scheme to enhance the physical layer security of single-input-single-output eavesdropping channels. In [8], in addition to applying AN and CJ approaches, a full-duplex legal receiver is applied to further enhance the physical layer security. The authors in [9] investigates the confidential transmission of cooperative interference and artificial noise schemes by considering two types of eavesdroppers.

The stochastic geometry not only has high analytical and computational efficiency, but also provides assistance in assessing the influence of system parameters on network performance. There have been many studies applying stochastic geometry to analyze the performance of vehicular communication. It has also been widely used to study the physical layer security. In urban scenarios, the location of nodes on each road is usually irregular and can be considered as a one-dimensional Poisson point process, and the number of roads is usually irregular and can be modeled as Poisson line process (PLP). The authors in [10] presents the evolution history of PLP theory, discusses in detail the basic features and application of PLP, PLCP and other models in wireless domain. The authors in [11] propose a transmitter selection criterion to enhance the reliability performance of downlink transmission in a wireless vehicular network using Manhattan Poisson line process model.

In this paper, the secrecy performance analysis is performed using the current emerging PLP model for urban scenarios.

2   System Model

In the actual urban scenarios, vehicles travel along the road. In order to reflect the random distribution of roads, we use PLP to model the urban roads, and since in most urban areas, the roads are mostly distributed perpendicular or parallel to each other, we model the urban roads as some straight lines that are randomly distributed and parallel or perpendicular to each other - Manhattan Poisson line process (MPLP), with road distribution density λ_l. MPLP belongs to a special case of PLP. Since vehicles are randomly distributed on each road,

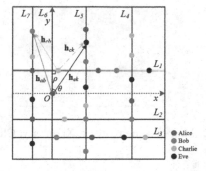

Fig. 1. MPLP model.

we model the vehicles on each road as a one-dimensional Poisson point process (1D PPP) with a vehicle density of λ_v.

The scenario is equipped with four vehicles, as shown in Fig. 1, which are the transmitting vehicle (Alice), the legitimate receiving vehicle (Bob), the eavesdropping vehicle (Eves) and the jamming vehicle (Charlies). We assume that each Alice and Charlie is equipped with N_a and N_c antennas respectively. Each Eve and Bob is equipped with only one antenna [12]. The fast fading channels from Alice to Bob and Eve are denoted by $h_{ab} \in C^{N_a}$ and $h_{ek} \in C^{N_a}$ respectively, and the fast fading channels from Charlie to Bob and Eve are denoted by $h_{cb} \in C^{N_c}$ and $h_{ck} \in C^{N_c}$ respectively. We call the channel h_{ab} the legitimate channel and h_{ek} the eavesdropping channel, where $h_{ab} \sim CN(0, I_{N_a})$, $h_{ek} \sim CN(0, I_{N_a})$ and $h_{ck} \sim CN(0, I_{N_c})$. According to the knowledge of stochastic geometry, we can get the following channel distribution, that is, $\|h_{ab}\|^2 \sim \Gamma(N_a, 1)$, $\|h_{ek}^T w_a\|^2 \sim exp(1)$, $\|h_{ek}^T W_a\|^2 \sim \Gamma(N_a - 1, 1)$ and $\|h_{ck}^T T_c\|^2 \sim \Gamma(N_c - 1, 1)$ [13]. Where $CN(p, q)$ denotes a circularly symmetric complex Gaussian distribution with mean p and covariance q. $\Gamma(k, \mu)$ denotes a gamma distribution with shape parameter k and scale parameter μ. $exp(a)$ denotes an exponential distribution with mean a. $|\cdot|$ and $\|\cdot\|$ denote the absolute value and the two-parameter number, respectively.

In order to make the theoretical results more convincing, we selected a typical urban scenario, a part of roads in the urban area of Xi'an, China, to verify the applicability of PLP on real urban roads. This part of the map was downloaded with openstreetmap, as shown in Fig. 2, and all the road data of this part of the map was saved as osm files, and the osm files were converted into readable xml files, which store all the road information, and then vehicle modeling was performed on these real roads. The schematic diagram of the real roads displayed with sumo-gui software is shown in Fig. 3.

3   Secure Transmission Scheme

We use the PLP to analyze the performance of the secure transmission scheme proposed in [14] with the addition of interfering vehicles and artificial noise (AN). The idea of this secure transmission scheme is as follows.

Fig. 2. Map of some roads in Xi'an city, China.

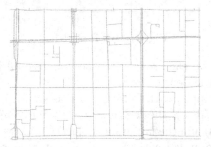

Fig. 3. Modeling diagram of some roads in Xi'an, China.

In order to ensure that the confidential information is transmitted to the legitimate receiving vehicle Bob while causing a certain degree of interference to Eves, Alice transmits confidential messages with AN to Bob, where the predefined channel distribution prevents Bob from receiving interference from AN. Eves tries to capture the confidential information and also receives interference from AN. Charlies transmits jamming signals to interfere with Eves, and due to the preset channel distribution, Bob does not receive the jamming information from Charlies.

The total transmission signal vector s_a formed by the superposition of the confidential information and AN can be expressed as $s_a = \sqrt{P_a\theta}w_a x + \sqrt{\frac{P_a(1-\theta)}{N_a-1}}W_a z_a$, $\sqrt{P_a\theta}w_a x$ denotes the portion of confidential information to be transmitted and $\sqrt{P_a(1-\theta)/(N_a-1)}W_a z_a$ denotes the portion of increased AN interference. where $\theta \in [0,1]$, denotes the ratio of the confidential information power to the total transmit power P_a. $\theta = 1$ means that the message sends only confidential information without AN, and $\theta = 0$ means that the message sends no confidential information to be transmitted. $x \sim CN(0,1)$ denotes the vector of confidential information to be sent to Bob, and $z_a \in C^{N_a-1}$ is an AN vector whose distribution satisfies $CN(0, I_{N_a-1})$. $[w_a, W_a]$ constitutes an orthogonal vector, $w_a = h_{ab}/\|h_{ab}\|$, which is a beamforming precoding vector of h_{ab}, and $W_a \in C^{N_a \times N_a-1}$ denotes the beamforming matrix of AN, which forms a null vector with h_{ab}, that is, $h_{ab}^H W_a = 0$. This setting determines that the AN information will not bring interference to the legitimate receiver Bob.

Meanwhile, the interference signal generated by Charlies will further enhance the security performance. The interference signal of Charlies s_c is designed to interfere Eves without generating interference to Bob. s_c can be expressed as $s_c = \sqrt{\frac{P_c}{N_c-1}} T_c z_c$, where P_c denotes the transmitting power of each Charlie. $T_c \in C^{N_c \times N_c-1}$ and h_{cb} form the null vector, that is, $T_c{}^H h_{cb} = 0$. This setting determines that Charlies do not interfere Bob. $z_c \sim CN(0, I_{N_c-1})$ is a Gaussian interference signal vector. The received signals from Bob and Eve are denoted as

$$
\begin{aligned}
y_b &= h_{ab}{}^H s_a d_{ab}{}^{-\frac{\alpha}{2}} + h_{cb}{}^H s_c d_{cb}{}^{-\frac{\alpha}{2}} + n_b \\
&= \sqrt{P_a \theta} \|h_{ab}\| d_{ab}{}^{-\frac{\alpha}{2}} w_a x + n_b,
\end{aligned}
\tag{1}
$$

$$
\begin{aligned}
y_k &= \sqrt{P_a \theta} h_{ek}{}^T d_{ek}{}^{-\frac{\alpha}{2}} W_a x + \sqrt{\frac{P_a(1-\theta)}{N_a-1}} h_{ek}{}^T W_a d_{ek}{}^{-\frac{\alpha}{2}} z_a \\
&\quad + \sum_{c \in \varphi_c} \sqrt{\frac{P_c}{N_c-1}} h_{ck}{}^T T_c d_{ck}{}^{-\frac{\alpha}{2}} z_c + n_e, \ k \in \varphi_E,
\end{aligned}
\tag{2}
$$

where d_{ab}, d_{ek} and d_{ck} denote the propagation distances from Alice to Bob, Alice to Eve and Charlie to Eve respectively. $n_b \sim CN(0, \sigma_b{}^2)$ and $n_e \sim CN(0, \sigma_e{}^2)$ denote the independent Gaussian noise variables received by Bob and Eve respectively. α denotes the path loss factor.

According to (1) (2), the SINR (Signal to Interference plus Noise Ratio) received by Bob and Eves respectively is as follows.

$$
SINR_b = \frac{P_a \theta \|h_{ab}\|^2 d_{ab}{}^{-\alpha}}{\sigma_b{}^2},
\tag{3}
$$

$$
SINR_{ek} = \frac{P_a \theta \left| h_{ek}{}^T w_a \right|^2 d_{ek}{}^{-\alpha}}{\frac{P_a(1-\theta)}{N_a-1} \|h_{ek}{}^T W_a\|^2 d_{ek}{}^{-\alpha} + I + \sigma_e{}^2}, \ k \in \varphi_E,
\tag{4}
$$

where $\frac{P_a(1-\theta)}{N_a-1} \|h_{ek}{}^T W_a\|^2 d_{ek}{}^{-\alpha}$ is the interference to Eves caused by AN. The channel capacity of the legitimate channel and the eavesdropper channel can be expressed as $C_B = log_2(1 + SINR_b)$ and $C_{ek} = log_2(1 + SINR_{ek})$ respectively. They will be used to derive the following performance indicators.

4   Secrecy Performance Analysis

The eavesdropping code can be designed by choosing these two code rates, namely the coding rate R_b and the confidential information rate R_s [15]. R_b and R_s are fixed before data transmission, and the redundancy rate $R_e = R_b - R_s$ is artificially added to interfere Eves. We use the secrecy throughput proposed in [11] to quantify the secrecy performance, which contains coverage probability and secrecy probability.

4.1 Coverage Probability

The coverage probability represents the probability that a legitimate receiver will successfully receive the message sent by the transmitting vehicle and is defined as the probability that C_B can support R_b. The expression of the coverage probability is

$$P_c = P[C_B = log_2(1 + SINR_b) > R_b]$$
$$= P(SINR_b > \beta = 2^{R_b} - 1),$$ (5)

where $SINR_b$ is the SINR received at Bob, $R_b = log_2(1 + \beta)$, β is a threshold and $\beta = 2^{R_b} - 1$.

First we derive expressions for the coverage probability under PLP model. We choose an Alice and a Bob as typical vehicles respectively. We assume that Alice is at the round point $(0,0)$, the distance between Alice and Bob is s_n, y_n is the projected distance of s_n on the y-axis, and x_n is the projected distance of s_n on the x-axis. When discussing the coverage probability for Bob, Eves are not considered, and the preset channel makes Bob receive no interference information from Charlies, so Eves and Charlies do not appear in the model. The expression of P_c is derived as follows.

$$P_c = P(SINR_b > \beta)$$
$$= \int_{s_n} P(SINR_b > \beta \mid s_n) f_{S_n}(s_n) ds_n$$
$$= \int_{y_n} \int_{s_n} P(SINR_b > \beta \mid Y_n) f_{Y_n}(y_n) \cdot f_{S_n}(s_n \mid y_n) ds_n dy_n$$ (6)
$$\overset{(a)}{=} \int_0^\infty \int_{y_n}^\infty P(SINR_b > \beta \mid Y_n) f_{Y_n}(y_n) \cdot f_{S_n}(s_n \mid y_n) ds_n dy_n,$$

where step (a) follows $s_n \geq y_n$. Next we derive $f_{Y_n}(y_n)$, $f_{S_n}(s_n \mid y_n)$, and $P(SINR_b > \beta \mid Y_n)$ respectively, where y_n is the real numerical representation of Y_n and s_n is the real numerical representation of S_n.

Assume that the road where Bob is located is parallel to the y-axis, the vehicles obey the 1D PPP distribution on this road with density λ_v. y_n is the vertical distance from Bob to the x-axis, according to the Probability Distribution Function (PDF) of 1D PPP [16],

$$f_{Y_n}(y_n) = 2\lambda_v exp(-2\lambda_v y_n).$$ (7)

The conditional CDF for s_n is as follows.

$$F_{S_n}(s_n \mid y_n)$$
$$= P\left(\sqrt{X_n^2 + y_n^2} < s_n \mid Y_n\right)$$
$$= F_{X_n}\left(\sqrt{s_n^2 - y_n^2} \mid y_n\right)$$ (8)
$$\overset{(b)}{=} 1 - exp\left(-2\lambda_s \sqrt{s_n^2 - y_n^2}\right),$$

where step (b) because the vertical distance of the road where Bob is located from the y-axis is x_n, and x_n obeys the 1D PPP distribution with density λ_s. $f_{S_n}(s_n \mid y_n)$ can be derived from $F_{S_n}(s_n \mid y_n)$ as follows.

$$f_{S_n}(s_n \mid y_n) = \frac{2\lambda_s s_n}{\sqrt{s_n^2 - y_n^2}} \, exp\left(-2\lambda_s \sqrt{s_n^2 - y_n^2}\right). \tag{9}$$

The expression of $P(SINR_b > \beta \mid Y_n)$ is derived as follows.

$$
\begin{aligned}
&P\left(SINR_b > \beta \mid Y_n\right) \\
&= P\left(\frac{P_a \theta \, \|h_{ab}\|^2 \, s_n^{-\alpha}}{\sigma_b^2} > \beta \mid Y_n\right) \\
&= P\left(\|h_{ab}\|^2 > \frac{\beta s_n^\alpha \sigma_b^2}{P_a \theta} \mid Y_n\right) \\
&\overset{(c)}{=} \sum_{k=0}^{N_a-1} \left(\frac{\beta s_n^\alpha \sigma_b^2}{P_a \theta}\right)^k \cdot \frac{1}{k!} \cdot exp\left(-\frac{\beta s_n^2 \sigma_b^2}{P_a \theta}\right).
\end{aligned}
\tag{10}
$$

Step (c) because $\|h_{ab}\|^2 \sim \Gamma(N_a, 1)$, according to the CDF of gamma distribution, $P(\|h_{ab}\|^2 \le x) = 1 - \sum_{k=0}^{N_a-1} \frac{x^k}{k!} \cdot exp(-x)$. According to (6) (7) (9) (10), we can derive P_c under the PLP model.

To verify that PLP model is more applicable to urban scenarios, we compare P_c under PLP modeling with that under 2D PPP modeling. We derived the expressions for the coverage probability P_c under 2D PPP modeling as follows.

Due to space limitation, some of the derivation procedures similar to MPLP are not repeated in the 2D PPP derivation. Only the simple derivation results of 2D PPP are given here. Under the 2D PPP model, assuming Alice is at the circle point $(0,0)$ and the distance from Bob to Alice is r.

$$P_c = P\left(SINR_b > \beta\right) = \int_0^\infty P\left(SINR_b > \beta \mid r\right) f_r(r) dr. \tag{11}$$

$$f_r(r) = 2\pi \lambda r \, exp\left(-\lambda \pi r^2\right). \tag{12}$$

$$P\left(SINR_b > \beta \mid r\right) = \sum_{k=0}^{N_a-1} \left(\frac{\beta r^\alpha \sigma_b^2}{P_a \theta}\right)^k \frac{1}{k!} \cdot exp\left(-\frac{\beta r^\alpha \sigma_b^2}{P_a \theta}\right). \tag{13}$$

P_c under the 2D PPP model are derived from (11) (12) (13).

4.2 Secrecy Probability

Secrecy probability is defined as the probability that the capacity of the eavesdropping channel is lower than the rate redundancy R_e. The expression of secrecy probability is

$$
\begin{aligned}
P_{sec} &= P\left[C_E = log_2\left(1 + SINR_e\right) < R_e\right] \\
&= P\left(SINR_e < \gamma = 2^{R_e} - 1\right),
\end{aligned}
\tag{14}
$$

where $SINR_e$ is the SINR received at Eves, $R_e = log_2(1+\gamma)$, γ is a threshold and $\gamma = 2^{R_e} - 1$.

First we derive P_{sec} under Poisson line process modeling model. We choose an Alice and an Eve as typical vehicles respectively. Suppose Eve is at the round point $(0,0)$, s_n is the distance between Alice and Eve, y_n is the projected distance of s_n on the y-axis and x_n is the projected distance of s_n on the x-axis. When discussing P_{sec} for Eves, we do not consider Bob. The expression of P_{sec} is derived as follows.

$$
\begin{aligned}
P_{sec} &= P\left(SINR_e < \gamma\right) \\
&= \int_0^\infty \int_{y_n}^\infty P\left(SINR_e < \gamma \mid Y_n\right) f_{Y_n}\left(y_n\right) f_{S_n}\left(s_n \mid y_n\right) ds_n dy_n.
\end{aligned}
\tag{15}
$$

The derivation of (15) is similar as (6), we do not repeat the detailed derivation process here. Next we will derive $f_{Y_n}(y_n)$, $f_{S_n}(s_n \mid y_n)$ and $P(SINR_e < \gamma \mid Y_n)$ respectively. $f_{Y_n}(y_n)$ is derived in (7) and $f_{S_n}(s_n \mid y_n)$ is derived in (9) without repeating the derivation. $P(SINR_e > \gamma \mid Y_n)$ is derived as follows.

$$
\begin{aligned}
&P\left(SINR_e > \gamma \mid Y_n\right) \\
&\stackrel{(b)}{=} P\left(\frac{P_a \theta \left|h_{ek}{}^T w_a\right|^2 s_n{}^{-\alpha}}{\frac{P_a(1-\theta)}{N_a-1}\left\|h_{ek}{}^T W_a\right\|^2 s_n{}^{-\alpha} + I + \sigma_e{}^2} > \gamma \mid Y_n\right) \\
&\stackrel{(c)}{=} E_I\left[P\left(\left|h_{ek}{}^T w_a\right|^2 > \gamma \frac{(1-\theta)}{\theta} + \frac{\gamma\left(I + \sigma_e{}^2\right) s_n{}^\alpha}{P_a \theta} \mid Y_n, I\right)\right] \\
&\stackrel{(d)}{=} exp\left(-\frac{\gamma(1-\theta)}{\theta}\right) exp\left(-\frac{\gamma \sigma_e{}^2 s_n{}^\alpha}{P_a \theta}\right) L_I\left(s \mid Y_n\right)\Bigg|_{s=\frac{\gamma s_n{}^\alpha}{P_a \theta}}.
\end{aligned}
\tag{16}
$$

The interference $I = \sum_{c \in \varphi_c} \frac{P_c}{N_c-1}\left\|h_{ck}^T T_c\right\|^2 d_{ck}^{-\alpha}$ in step (b). Step (c) is derived since $\left\|h_{ek}^T W_a\right\|^2 \sim \Gamma\left(N_a - 1, 1\right)$ and the mean value of $\left\|h_{ek}^T W_a\right\|^2$ is $N_a - 1$. Step (d) is derived due to $\left|h_{ek}^T w_a\right|^2 \sim \exp(1)$ and the mean value of $\left|h_{ek}^T w_a\right|^2$ is 1 and $E_I\left(e^{-AI}\right) = L_I(s)|_{s=A} = \int_I e^{-AI} f_I(I) dI$, where $A = \frac{\gamma s_n{}^\alpha}{P_a \theta}$. $f(I)$ is PDF of I, and $L_I(s)$ is the Laplace transform of I. I is divided into two parts, which are the interfering vehicles I_0 on the same road as the typical vehicle Eve (referred to as typical road in the following paper) and the interfering vehicles I_n on the other roads, the expression of $L_I(s)$ is as follows.

$$
L_I\left(s \mid Y_n\right) = L_{I_0}\left(s \mid Y_n\right) \cdot L_{I_n}\left(s \mid Y_n\right).
\tag{17}
$$

The expression of $L_{I_0}(s \mid Y_n)$ is derived as follows.

$$L_{I_0}(s \mid Y_n) = E\left[e^{-sI_0}\right]$$

$$= E\left[E_{G_{0I_0}}\left[\prod_{I_0} exp\left(-s\frac{P_c}{N_c-1}G_{0I_0}x^{-\alpha}\right)\right]\right]$$

$$\overset{(a)}{=} E\left[\prod_{I_0}\left(1+\frac{sP_cx^{-\alpha}}{N_c-1}\right)^{-(N_c-1)}\right] \tag{18}$$

$$\overset{(b)}{=} exp\left[-2\lambda_v\int_{s_n}^{\infty}\left(1-\left(1+\frac{sP_cx^{-\alpha}}{N_c-1}\right)^{-(N_c-1)}\right)dx\right].$$

G_{0I_0} represents the channel between Charlies and Eves. Step (a) is derived due to $\|h_{ck}^T T_c\|^2 \sim \Gamma(N_c-1,1)$ and the Moment Generating Function (MGF) of gamma distribution, step (b) is derived from the Probability Generating Function (PGF) of the 1D PPP [17], and assume that the distance $x > s_n$ from the interfering vehicle to the round point.

Then the expression of $L_{I_n}(s \mid Y_n)$ is derived as follows.

$$L_{I_n}(s \mid Y_n) = E\left[\prod_y L_{I_0}(s \mid Y_n)\right]$$

$$= exp\left[-2\lambda_s\int_0^{s_n}1-exp\left(-2\lambda_v\int^{\infty}\sqrt{s_n^2-y^2}\right.\right. \tag{19}$$

$$\left.\left.1-\left(1+\frac{sP_c\left(x^2+y^2\right)^{-\frac{\alpha}{2}}}{N_c-1}\right)^{-(N_c-1)}dx\right)dy\right].$$

where assuming that the coordinates of the interfering vehicle position (x,y) satisfies $x^2 + y^2 > s_n{}^2$. $L_I(s \mid Y_n)$ is derived from (17)–(19). $P(SINR_e > \gamma \mid Y_n)$ is derived from (16)–(19), and then

$$P_r(SINR < \gamma \mid Y_n) = 1 - P(SINR_e > \gamma \mid Y_n). \tag{20}$$

P_{sec} for the Poisson line process modeling can be derived from (7) (9) and (15)–(20).

In order to verify that PLP model is more applicable to urban scenarios, we compare P_{sec} under PLP model with those under the 2D PPP model. P_{sec} under 2D PPP model is shown as follows.

Assume that the typical vehicle Eve is at the circle point $(0,0)$ and the distance from Alice to Eve is r.

$$P_{sec} = P(SINR_e < \gamma) = \int_0^{\infty} P(SINR_e < \gamma \mid r) f_r(r)dr. \tag{21}$$

$$P(SINR_e > \gamma \mid r)$$

$$= exp\left(-\frac{\gamma(1-\theta)}{\theta}\right)exp\left(-\frac{\gamma\sigma_e^2r^{\alpha}}{P_a\theta}\right)L_I(s \mid r)\Big|_{s=\frac{\gamma r^{\alpha}}{P_a\theta}}. \tag{22}$$

$$L_I(s \mid r)$$

$$= exp\left[-2\pi\lambda\int_r^\infty x\left(1 - \left(1 + \frac{sP_cx^{-\alpha}}{N_c - 1}\right)^{-(N_c-1)}\right)dx\right]. \qquad (23)$$

$$P\left(SINR_e < \gamma \mid r\right) = 1 - P\left(SINR_e > \gamma \mid r\right). \qquad (24)$$

P_{sec} under the 2D PPP model are derived from (12) and (21)–(24).

4.3   Secrecy Throughput

We use the secrecy throughput proposed in the literature [11] to quantify the confidentiality performance, which contains both P_c and P_{sec}. The secrecy throughput η is defined as the rate of information, in bps, transmitted from the legitimate source node to the destination node in complete secrecy, and the expression for secrecy throughput η is

$$\eta = P_c \cdot P_{sec} \cdot R_s \qquad (25)$$

The relationship between the η and each influencing factor is studied in order to analyze how to choose the appropriate parameters to ensure that the information is reliably transmitted to the receiver while not leaking to the eavesdropper. That is, the confidential information sent by Alice is received by the legitimate receiver Bob, to ensure the transmission quality. Meanwhile, the confidential information sent by Alice is not eavesdropped by Eves as much as possible, so that the confidential information is not leaked, that is, secure transmission is guaranteed.

However, the above two situations cannot be satisfied at the same time, but are mutually restrictive. For example, the more confidential information Alice sends, the more confidential information Bob receives and the greater P_c. But at the same time, the more confidential information Eves receives, the less P_{sec}. The next section analyzes how to select the appropriate parameters to achieve a balance between P_c and P_{sec} by studying the relationship between η and related parameters.

5   Simulation Results and Analysis

In this section, we plot the graphs of coverage probability, secrecy probability and secrecy throughput versus each important parameter under PLP and 2D PPP model respectively. In order to make the theoretical results more convincing, we chose a typical urban scenario - part of the roads in the urban area of Xi'an, China, modeled the vehicles on real roads and simulated the communication performance of the vehicles, compared the performance curves under two models with those under real urban road. The simulation modeling parameters are shown in Table 1.

Table 1. Parameters of Simulation

Parameter	Value
λ_s	0.001
λ_v	0.05
α	7
$noise$	10^{-20}
$P_a(dBm)$	30
$P_c(dBm)$	30

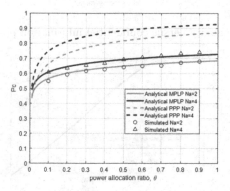

Fig. 4. Coverage probability versus confidential information power ratio θ, $R_b = 3$. (Color figure online)

5.1 Coverage Probability Simulation Results and Analysis

As shown in Fig. 4, the larger θ is, the more confidential information Alice transmits to Bob and the larger P_c is. The curves of different colors in the figure represent different antenna numbers of Alice, the more antennas Alice has, the larger P_c. We can improve the P_c by appropriately increasing θ or N_a.

The solid and dashed lines represent P_c under PLP and 2D PPP model respectively, the black triangles and black circles indicate P_c derived from vehicle modeling on some roads in Xi'an urban area with different N_a. We can find that the curves of the real urban scenario match better with those under PLP model, which indicates that the PLP model is more applicable to the modeling of urban scenarios than 2D PPP. This conclusion can be drawn from all the graphs below, so it is not repeated in the following. And the phenomenon that the theoretical curves fit the curves of the real scenarios proves the correctness of the theoretical formulation derived above. According to $\beta = 2^{R_b} - 1$, different R_b represents different threshold β. We can find in Fig. 5 that the lower β, the larger P_c. We conclude that P_c can be improved by appropriately decreasing the preset R_b value from the figure.

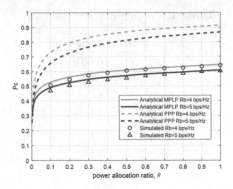

Fig. 5. Coverage probability versus confidential information power ratio θ, $N_a = 2$.

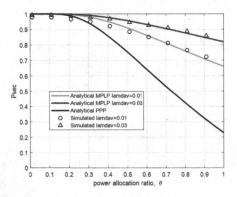

Fig. 6. Secrecy probability versus confidential information power ratio θ, $R_e = 1$, $N_c = 4$. (Color figure online)

5.2   Secrecy Probability Simulation Results and Analysis

As shown in Fig. 6, the larger θ, the more effective information sent to the eavesdropping vehicle Eves, the smaller the interference caused by AN to Eves, the smaller P_{sec}, and the worse the security performance. We can learn that decreasing θ can improve P_{sec} and thus improve security performance.

The blue and green curves in Fig. 6 represent different densities of interfering vehicles, we can find that the higher the density of interfering vehicles, the higher P_{sec}. This is because the greater the density of interfering vehicles, the greater the interference of Charlies to Eves, the greater the P_{sec}, and the better the secrecy performance. Therefore, we can increase P_{sec} by appropriately increasing the density of interfering vehicles, thus improving the secrecy performance. According to $\gamma = 2^{R_e} - 1$, different R_e represents different threshold γ. We can find that in Fig. 7, the larger γ, the higher P_{sec}. We can increase the size of R_e appropriately by changing the preset R_b and R_s to improve P_{sec}. We can find in Fig. 8 that the more N_c, the higher P_{sec}. This is because N_c, the more the interference to Eves, so the higher P_{sec} and the better secrecy performance.

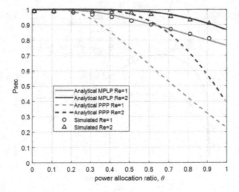

Fig. 7. Secrecy probability versus confidential information power ratio θ, $\lambda_v = 0.02$, $N_c = 4$.

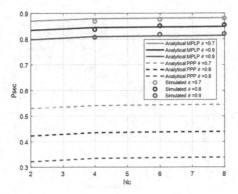

Fig. 8. Secrecy probability versus confidential information power ratio θ, $R_e = 1$, $\lambda_v = 0.02$.

Therefore, we can increase N_c to improve the P_{sec} and thus improve the secrecy performance. Different color curves represent different θ. We can see that the larger θ, the lower the P_{sec}, the reason is that the higher θ, the more secrecy information transmit to Eves, the lower P_{sec}.

5.3 Secrecy Throughput Simulation Results and Analysis

From Fig. 9, it can be seen that η increases and then decreases with the increase of θ. The reason is that as θ increases, the confidential information received by the receiving vehicle Bob increases, and P_c improves. At the same time, the secrecy information received by Eves also increases and the P_{sec} decreases. We can try to choose the parameter θ near the peak point so that Bob receives as much confidential information as possible, and Eves eavesdrops on as little confidential information as possible. The parameters can also be selected appropriately according to the specific needs in different situation. For example, for high security performance requirements, the parameter θ with the peak point a

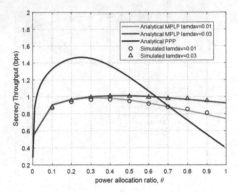

Fig. 9. Secrecy throughput versus confidential information power ratio θ with different interfering vehicle densities, $N_a = 2$. (Color figure online)

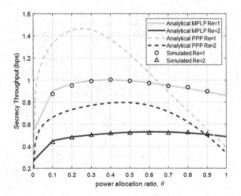

Fig. 10. Secrecy throughput versus confidential information power ratio θ with different R_e, $N_a = 2$.

little to the left can be chosen to achieve a higher P_{sec} at the expense of the P_c appropriately.

The blue and green curves in Fig. 9 indicate different interfering vehicle densities. We can find that the higher the density of interfering vehicles, the higher η, so increasing the density of interfering vehicles can increase η. The different color curves in Fig. 10 indicate different R_e. We can find that the larger R_e, the smaller η. That is because $\eta = P_c \cdot P_{sec} \cdot R_s$, and $R_s = R_b - R_e$. With P_c, P_{sec} and R_b determined, the larger R_e and the smaller R_s, the smaller η.

6   Conclusion

In this paper, we use Poisson line process model to model urban scenarios of V2X, and derive coverage probability, secrecy probability and secrecy throughput based on a secure transmission scheme with the addition of interfering vehicles and artificial noise using stochastic geometry. Some effective conclusions are drawn to improve secrecy performance by controlling the parameters. At the same time, we verify that the Poisson line process model is more suitable for modeling urban scenarios by modeling vehicles on the real urban map.

Acknowledgement. This work was supported in part by the State Major Science and Technology Special Projects (Grant No. 2018ZX03001024) and in part by the National Key Research and Development Program (Grant No. 2022YFF0610303).

References

1. Chen, X., Ng, D., Gerstacker, W.H., et al.: A survey on multiple-antenna techniques for physical layer security. IEEE Commun. Surv. Tutor. **19**, 1027–1053 (2017)
2. Furqan, H.M., Solaija, M.S.J., Arslan, H.: Intelligent physical layer security approach for V2X communication. arXiv preprint (2019). https://arxiv.org/pdf/1905.05075.pdf
3. ElHalawany, B.M., El-Banna, A.A.A., Wu, K.: Physical-layer security and privacy for vehicle-to-everything. IEEE Commun. Mag. **57**(10), 84–90 (2019). https://doi.org/10.1109/MCOM.001.1900141
4. Xu, L., Yu, X., Wang, H., et al.: Physical layer security performance of mobile vehicular networks. Mob. Netw. Appl. **25**(4) (2019)
5. Wu, Y., Qian, L.P., Mao, H.W., et al.: Secrecy-driven resource management for vehicular computation offloading networks. IEEE Netw. **32**(3), 84–91 (2018)
6. Tolossa, Y.J., Vuppala, S., Kaddoum, G., Abreu, G.: On the uplink secrecy capacity analysis in D2D-enabled cellular network. IEEE Syst. J. **12**(3), 2297–2307 (2018)
7. Hu, X., Mu, P., Wang, B., Li, Z.: On the secrecy rate maximization with uncoordinated cooperative jamming by single-antenna helpers. IEEE Trans. Veh. Technol. **26**(5), 4457–4462 (2019)
8. Ma, R., Yang, S., Du, M., Ou, J.: Improving physical layer security jointly using full-duplex jamming receiver and multi-antenna jammer in wireless networks. IET Commun. **13**(10), 1530–1536 (2019)
9. Si, J., Cheng, Z., Li, Z., Cheng, J., Wang, H.-M., Al-Dhahir, N.: Cooperative jamming for secure transmission with both active and passive eavesdroppers. IEEE Trans. Commun. **68**(9), 5764–5777 (2020). https://doi.org/10.1109/TCOMM.2020.3003946
10. Dhillon, H.S., Chetlur, V.V.: Poisson line cox process: foundations and applications to vehicular networks (2020)
11. Tang, Z., Sun, Z., Li, C., et al.: Reliability performance of transmitter selection in wireless vehicular networks. In: 2020 IEEE/CIC International Conference on Communications in China (ICCC). IEEE (2020)
12. Hu, L., Wen, H., Wu, B., Tang, J., Pan, F., Liao, R.-F.: Cooperative jamming aided secrecy enhancement in wireless networks with passive eavesdroppers. IEEE Trans. Veh. Technol. **67**(3), 2108–2117 (2018)
13. Yang, Y., Wang, W., Zhao, H., Zhao, L.: Transmitter beamforming and artificial noise with delayed feedback: secrecy rate and power allocation. J. Commun. Netw. **14**(4), 374–384 (2012)
14. Qiu, B., Jing, C.: Performance analysis for cooperative jamming and artificial noise aided secure transmission scheme in vehicular communication network (2020)
15. Klinc, D., Ha, J., McLaughlin, S.W., Barros, J., Kwak, B.-J.: LDPC codes for the Gaussian wiretap channel. IEEE Trans. Inf. Forensics Secur. **6**(3), 532–540 (2011)

16. Krishnan, S., Dhillon, H.S.: Spatio-temporal interference correlation and joint coverage in cellular networks. IEEE Trans. Wirel. Commun. **16**(9), 5659–5672 (2017)
17. Sial, M.N., Deng, Y., Ahmed, J., Nallanathan, A., Dohler, M.: Stochastic geometry modeling of cellular V2X communication on shared uplink channels (2018)

An Efficient Memory Management Method for Embedded Vector Processors

Shengxuan Li[1], Haoqi Ren[1], Zhifeng Zhang[1], Bin Tan[2], and Jun Wu[3]([✉])

[1] Department of Computer Science, Tongji University, Shanghai, China
{lsx1998,renhaoqi,zhangzf}@tongji.edu.cn
[2] School of Electronic and Information Engineering, Jinggangshan University, Ji'an, China
tanbin@jgsu.edu.cn
[3] School of Computer Science, Fudan University, Shanghai, China
wujun@fudan.edu.cn

Abstract. For processors with vectorial computing units like DSP, it is very important to ensure vector load/store operations alignment of memory blocks, and minimize space wastage when making memory allocations. In this paper, we design and implement a memory management method, vector memory pool, suitable for embedded vector processors. By partitioning an entire block of memory space into many aligned vector objects and making efficiently use of vector processing units, the processing of memory manipulation library functions such as memset/memcpy is accelerated. The implementation and comparative verification of vector memory pool on RT-Thread Nano based on SWIFT DSP was completed, and the running efficiency reached a tens of times improvement compared to the original method.

Keywords: DSP · RT-Thread Nano · vector memory pool

1 Introduction

DSP is an embedded processor that is very good at realizing various digital signal processing operations (such as digital filtering, spectrum analysis, etc.) at high speed. The strengths of high-performance DSP are their ability to perform vector operations, pointer linear addressing, and other data processing with large amounts of operations. Generally, DSP chips are mostly used in embedded scenarios, but they also have the need to support multitasking. In order to realize multitasking scheduling and memory management functions on embedded devices while ensuring the real-time performance of embedded DSP chips, the porting and targeted optimization of real-time operating systems on embedded devices are especially important [1].

A real-time operating system is an operating system that can support the operation of real-time control systems. Compared to improving the efficiency of using computer systems, the primary task of real-time operating systems is to schedule all available resources to accomplish real-time control tasks as much as possible. Real-time operating

F. Gao et al. (Eds.): ChinaCom 2022, LNICST 500, pp. 247–258, 2023.
https://doi.org/10.1007/978-3-031-34790-0_19

system programs are small, task switching is fast, and interrupts are blocked for a very short time [2].

The resource environment of embedded systems is also various. Some systems are resource constrained with only tens of KB of memory available for allocation, while others have several MB of memory, and it becomes complicated to choose an efficient memory allocation algorithm for these different systems that is suitable for them.

In this paper, we design a new static memory management method, vector memory pool, for a real-time operating system, RT-Thread Nano, running on SWIFT DSP developed by the CIC lab of Tongji University, and verify its correctness and performance.

2 Relate Work

2.1 RT-Thread Nano

RT-Thread is a free open source embedded real-time operating system platform created by a group of open-source enthusiasts in China, mainly for small and medium-sized microcontrollers, using the GPLv2 license, which can be applied to commercial projects for free and does not require the project to be open source [3–5]. RT-Thread Nano is a minimalist version of the hard real-time kernel, developed in C language, using object-oriented programming The RT-Thread Nano is a cuttable, preemptive real-time multitasking RTOS developed in C with an object-oriented programming mindset.

The RT-Thread operating system provides different memory allocation management algorithms in a targeted manner, depending on the upper layer applications and system resources. In general, they can be divided into two categories: memory heap management and memory pool management. And memory heap management is further divided into three cases according to specific memory devices: the first is for allocation management of small memory blocks (small memory management algorithm); the second is for allocation management of large memory blocks (slab management algorithm); and the third is for allocation cases of multiple memory heaps (memheap management algorithm).

The memory heap manager can allocate memory blocks of arbitrary size, which is very flexible and convenient. However, it also has obvious drawbacks: first, it is not efficient in allocation, and free memory blocks have to be looked up at each allocation; second, it is easy to generate memory fragmentation. To improve the efficiency of memory allocation and avoid memory fragmentation, RT-Thread provides an alternative memory management method: Memory Pool [6–9].

Memory pool is a memory allocation method used to allocate a large number of small memory blocks of the same size, which can greatly speed up memory allocation and release and avoid memory fragmentation as much as possible. In addition, RT-Thread's memory pool supports thread hang function, when there is no free memory block in the memory pool, the application thread would be hung until there is a new available memory block in the memory pool, and then the hung application thread would be woken up.

The memory pool's thread pending feature is ideal for scenarios that require synchronization via memory resources, such as when playing music, the player thread decodes the music file and sends it to the sound card driver, which drives the hardware to play the music.

The following is a description of the static memory pool implementation.

A memory pool is created by first requesting a large block of memory from the system, and then dividing it into multiple smaller blocks of the same size, which are directly connected by a link list (this link list is also called free block link list). At each allocation, the first memory block at the head of the chain is taken from the free link list and provided to the requestor. As you can see in the Fig. 1, there are multiple memory pools of different sizes allowed in physical memory, each of which in turn consists of multiple free memory blocks, which the kernel uses for memory management. When a memory pool object is created, the memory pool object is assigned to a memory pool control block whose parameters include the pool name, memory buffer, memory block size, number of blocks, and a queue of waiting threads [10–12].

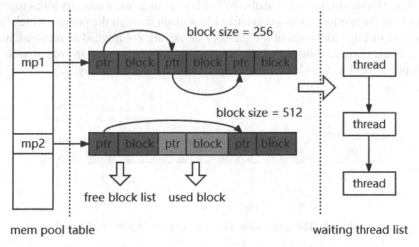

Fig. 1. The design of a typical memory pool in RT-Thread.

2.2 SWIFT DSP

Swift is a SIMD VLIW DSP chip, from hardware architecture to assembly instruction set are developed by CIC lab of Tongji University, is an 8-launch, 13-stage pipeline very long instruction word DSP processor, while the on-chip by a set of bit width of 2560bit vector registers, and for the vector registers designed a variety of memory load/store and calculation instructions. It also provides a complete tool chain, including LLVM-based compiler, assembler, linker, and functional/structural simulator, and supports GDB debugging and FPGA test verification [13–15].

The CIC lab of Tongji University has previously implemented RT-Thread support for SWIFT DSP and completed the porting and correctness testing of RT-Thread Nano on DSP. Now, we are considering the optimization of its memory management performance, mainly considering the efficient use of memory and vector optimization of some system library functions like memset by using the existing vector register resources on chip.

3   Design and Implementation

3.1   Vector Memory Pool

For embedded processors like DSPs, there is no memory mapping and all applications access the real physical address. Memory pools are suitable for this class of systems without MMU. 0 address corresponds to the real memory starting address (so it must also be accessible).

For processors with vector registers, the load/store instruction is usually designed separately for vector processors, and the access address alignment of such instructions is strongly related to the width of the vector, while the general-purpose memory pool design usually does not give special consideration to vector load/store, and the adoption of the previously described memory pool design leads to the following phenomenon.

Although many memory pool designs are designed with multiple block size structures of different bit widths, they are handled by linking a pointer and a memory block together and linking the memory blocks into a free block chain through the pointer, which leads to the fact that the addresses of the memory blocks are not aligned as required, and a large amount of space is often wasted for vector structure alignment in order to meet the needs of vector object read and write usage. As we can see in the Fig. 2.

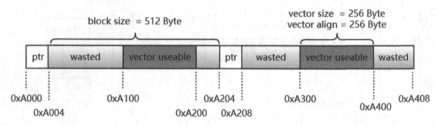

Fig. 2. The space wasted in memory pool for vector align.

For the special case of vector registers mentioned above, this paper designs a new vector memory pool that splits the memory block from the original chain structure so that each memory block is guaranteed to be address aligned, adds a pointer to the memory block in the original chain architecture, and records the pointer from the memory block to the original structure through an external hash table. The specific logic structure is as follows Fig. 3.

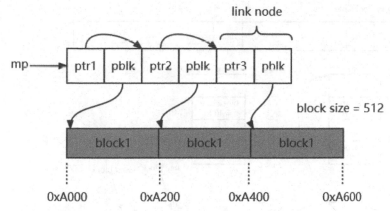

Fig. 3. The logic design of vector memory pool.

3.2 Design Details

Top-Level Design

At the top level, a mptable is created to record the mp structures according to different vector sizes, each mp structure points to the whole memory segment allocated to it, and the memory blocks are aligned according to the vector width, and each memory segment is divided into blocks according to its block size, and a free block linklist is created. The specific structure is shown in the Fig. 4.

The mp structure records the memory space and size allocated to this thread pool, as well as the size of the memory blocks divided, the total number of free blocks and the chain of free blocks, and the chain of threads currently requesting memory from this mp and the number.

Initialization

Get a whole block of memory and complete vectorization alignment, divide it into multiple block blocks according to the desired size, generally, the size of the block could be much larger than the number of blocks divided, so it is only necessary to simply put the first $\lceil 8*n/block\_size + 1 \rceil$ blocks used to save the linklist structure of the head area, give each block used for memory allocation number 0-n, create an array of linked node structures of size n in the head area, each pointer structure and memory block one by one, ptr points to the next node structure, pblk points to the memory block corresponding to the current structure, and also create a hash table for block addressing.

Finally, the free block linklist is saved in the vector memory pool structure to complete the initialization.

Allocation and Free

The process of allocating a vector memory pool is relatively simple. After finding a free block, it is plucked from the chain table and the pointer is pointed to the original mp structure, which is not much different from the general memory pool allocation.

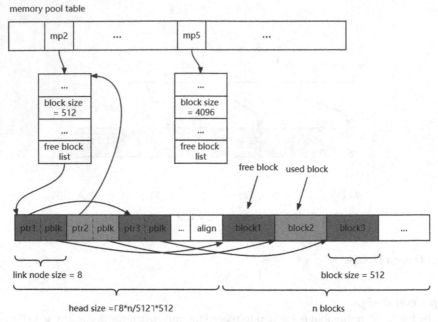

Fig. 4. The top-level design of vector memory pool.

The memory free process, because of the separation of memory blocks and pointers, cannot directly find the mp structure to which the current memory block belongs as in a regular memory pool implementation, so extra space and time are needed to complete the process by finding the corresponding structure of the memory block through an external hash table mapping and inserting the memory block back into the free list, using the header insertion method.

Figure 5 shows an example of a vector memory pool usage, where memory block 1 is first requested and then block 4 is freed.

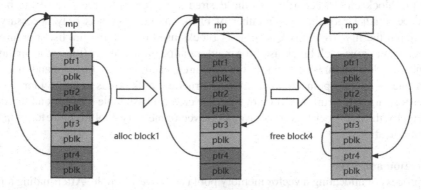

Fig. 5. An example of vector memory pool.

Memory Library Vectorization

Since the space arrangement of the vector memory pool is aligned according to the vector load/store format, we can use vector registers to accelerate some memory operations, typically such as memset/memcpy and other operations.

For the space allocated using vector memory pool, if we want to do batch memory read/write, by using vector registers, we can get a theoretical 64 times efficiency improvement, as the vector size is 2560 bits which can be considered as 64 cells of 40 bits. Here is a detailed example comparison of memcpy in Fig. 6, for larger memory copy, if we don't use vector registers, we need to loop n times, if we use vector registers + normal memory pool, we need to use additional scalar copy to handle memory space close to a vector size, if we use vector registers + vector memory pool method, we can maximize the efficiency of batch copy.

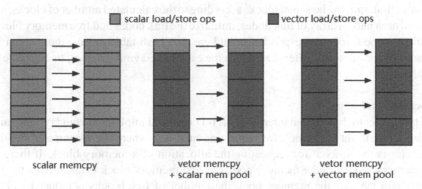

Fig. 6. An example comparison of memcpy.

Since vector registers also support the special instruction called vmovg2v, it is possible to rewrite individual scalar values to each group of the vector, allowing efficient optimization for operations such as memset. By reusing hardware loop and step read/write instructions, the efficiency of mem operations can be further improved.

3.3 Implementation

RT-thread internally encapsulates the memory pool call interface, so we can keep the interface consistent by adding our designed vector memory pool to the original base memory allocation method of RT-Thread, which could simplify our work on other unrelated aspects, allowing us to focus on the vector memory pool implementation, and enabling us to compare the vector memory pool with the existing methods, which is beneficial for performance analysis.

The SWIFT DSP is a high-performance vector processor with a 256 bytes wide data bus and up to 2560 bits vector arithmetic units. CIC lab has equipped it with a complete and efficient tool chain and completed the port of RT-Thread Nano, so the implementation and verification of our designed vector memory pool can be done using RT-Thread Nano running on the SWIFT DSP.

Initialization

To create a vector memory pool, refer to the standard memory pool interface provided by RT-Thread, we design the following static vector memory pool initialization interface. rt_err_t rt_vmp_init(rt_mp_t mp, void *start, rt_size_t size, rt_size_t block_size);

Initialize the vector memory pool, first pass in the relevant data via parameters, including the target address used to allocate space, the address needs to be externally aligned to the actual vector situation before passing in, the size of the space, and the size of the memory block, after which the actual number of available memory blocks is calculated based on the two sizes, while the relevant counters are configured to set all blocks to idle and the number of waiting threads to 0.

After that, split the head and blocks according to the calculated number of blocks, map the head area into an array of link nodes, initialize the link nodes and free memory blocks, establish a one-to-one correspondence, and create a hash table to save the mapping of memory blocks to nodes, after that, return the established vmp structure to complete the initialization.

Allocation and Free

Similarly, refer to the original interface of RT-Thread and implement void *rt_vmp_alloc (rt_mp_t mp, rt_int32_t time); for requesting memory, where the meaning of the time parameter is the timeout for requesting the allocation of a memory block. If there are free memory blocks in the memory pool, the first memory block is taken from the free block chain table of the memory pool, the number of free blocks is reduced and this memory block is returned; if there are no more free memory blocks in the memory pool, the timeout time setting is judged: if the timeout time is set to zero, the empty memory block is returned immediately; if the waiting time is greater than zero, the current thread is hung on this memory pool object until there are free memory block available in the memory pool, or until the wait time is reached.

For memory freeing, implement void rt_vmp_free (void *block); interface. When using this function interface, first find out the connection node corresponding to the memory block that needs to be freed through the hash table, calculate the memory pool object that the memory block is in (or belongs to), then increase the number of available memory blocks in the memory pool object, and add the freed memory block to the free memory block chain table. Then determine if there is a pending thread on that memory pool object, and if so, wake up the first thread on the pending thread chain table.

Memory Library Vectorization

For mem-related operations, according to the original interface, implement void *rt_vmemset(void *src, int c, rt_ubase_t n); and void *rt_vmemcpy(void *dest, const void *src, rt_ubase_t n); this two mem library functions, mixed in c and assembly language, call special vector operation instructions to complete the vector mem operation. The core operators of these two memory operations are vmovrg2v10 and vstore10.

4 Evaluation

By comparing with RT-Thread Nano's existing memory pool and mem operation library, we can analyze the operational efficiency of the static vector memory pool we designed.

We use the RT-Thread Nano running on the SWIFT DSP structure simulator to perform the test. This structure simulator is able to get the exact running time of the program on the DSP, which can be used for our experimental results verification and comparative analysis. And the simulator could record and output the number of cycles the program runs when it stops at a breakpoint, so that we can calculate the running time of each library function by adding breakpoints before and after the target code segment to be tested. The test case is a simple multi-threaded code, configuring the vector bit width used by the DSP to 2048 bits, designing two threads with the same priority, and the entire execution of each thread is much smaller than the size of a time slice allocated by the operating system, so there is no problem with the impact of task scheduling on the clock cycle. One thread use the Rt-Thread memory pool and mem library functions, and the other use vector memory pool and vector mem library, and each operation is looped 10 times to calculate the average number of running cycles.

We analyze the operational efficiency by comparing the number of the program running clock cycles, including the initialization /allocation and free of the memory pool, and focusing on the efficiency of mem-related operations. As can be seen in Figs. 7 and 8, the vector memory pool does not have a particularly large additional overhead in establishing allocation and recovery compared to the standard implementation, except for the free operation, which requires an additional time overhead of reverse lookup.

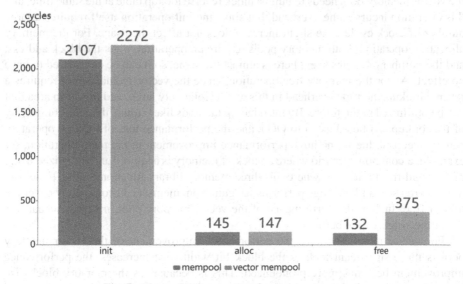

Fig. 7. The evaluation results of vector memory pool

We can see that by using vector arithmetic units, both memset and memcpy operations have a large performance improvement, and the magnitude of the improvement varies

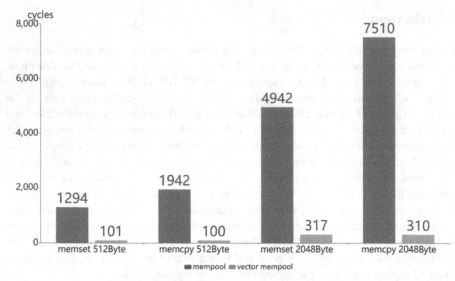

Fig. 8. The evaluation results of vector memory library

according to the bit width size. The performance improvement is 12.8 times, and at 2048 bits, the performance improvement is 15.6 times, the efficiency improvement of memcpy also reaches 19.42 times and 24.22 times.

Analyzing the above results, first, during the initialization phase of the memory pool, the vector memory pool needs to build a block reverse lookup table at the same time, and this operation incurs some overhead, but since the init operation itself requires a large number of clock cycles, the slight increase does not affect the usage. For the memory allocation operation, both memory pools require an operation to get the block address, and the number of cycles spent here is almost the same, so it can be considered to have no effect. As for the memory free operation, since the vector memory pool requires a reverse lookup, the time overhead in this area is relatively large, and this is an area that can be optimized in the future. By introducing methods like bitmap, the time complexity of the lookup can be adjusted to O(1), and the performance loss of the free operation can be accepted due to the huge performance improvement in the mem operation, for example, a common scenario where a block of memory is acquired and initialized using malloc and freed after use, where this three memory library functions, alloc + memset + free, are used, and the huge performance gain from memset can completely cover the loss of free. In fact, the performance of the vector memory pool in such a scenario is 6.22 times higher than before.

For vector mem functions, the performance improvement of the vector memory pool is more significant and, as the block bit width size increases, the performance improvement becomes more pronounced. This is because, as the memory block size increases, the percentage of call overhead generated by the system gradually decreases and the efficiency of vector utilization becomes more obvious.

5 Conclusion

In this paper, we design and implement a memory management method, vector memory pool, suitable for use in embedded vector processors. By dividing the contiguous address space according to the vector bit-width alignment, it solves the space wastage problem in memory allocation for processors like DSP that need to use a lot of vector load/store, and by using vector units, the processing of memory manipulation library functions such as memset/memcpy is accelerated. The implementation of vector memory pooling and comparison verification was done on rt-thread nano running on SWIFT DSP. Compared with the original method, there is only a slight loss of efficiency in the creation of memory pools for allocation and free, but it is able to ensure that the allocated space has been aligned according to the vector load/store requirements, and to achieve a tens of times improvement in the operational efficiency of mem operations.

Acknowledgement. The authors thank the editors and the anonymous reviewers for their invaluable comments to help to improve the quality of this paper. This work was supported by National Key R&D Program of China under Grant 2020YFA0711400, National Natural Science Foundation of China under Grants 61831018 and U21A20452, the Outstanding youth project of Natural Science Foundation of Jiangxi Province 20212ACB212001, and the Jiangxi Double Thousand Plan under Grant jxsq2019201125.

References

1. Shang, Q., Liu, W.: Multi-function DSP experimental system based on TMS320VC5509. In: Proceedings of 2016 2nd International Conference on Social, Education and Management Engineering (SEME 2016), pp. 107–111. DEStech Publications (2016)
2. Tarasiuk, T., Szweda, M.: DSP instrument for transient monitoring. Comput. Stand. Interfaces **33**(2) (2010)
3. Shen, J.Q., Wu, J., Zhang, Z.F., et al.: Design and implementation of binaryutilities generator. Appl. Mech. Mater. **644**, 3260–3265 (2014). Trans Tech Publications Ltd.
4. Fridman, J., Greenfield, Z.: The TigerSHARC DSP architecture. IEEE Micro **20**, 66–76 (January 2000)
5. Zhou, Y., He, F., Hou, N., Qiu, Y.: Parallel ant colony optimization on multi-core SIMD CPUs. Future Gener. Comput. Syst. **79** (2018)
6. Maiyuran, S., Garg, V., Abdallah, M.A., et al.: Memory access latency hiding with hint buffer: U.S. Patent 6,718,440, 6 April 2004
7. Adachi, Y., Kumano, T., Ogino, K.: Intermediate representation for stiff virtual objects. In: Proceedings Virtual Reality Annual International Symposium 1995, pp. 203–210. IEEE (1995)
8. Vanholder, H.: Efficient Inference with TensorRT (2016)
9. Chadha, P., Siddagangaiah, T.: Performance analysis of accelerated linear algebra compiler for TensorFlow
10. Sivalingam, K., Mujkanovic, N.: Graph compilers for AI training and inference
11. Griewank, A., Walther, A.: Evaluating derivatives: principles and techniques of algorithmic differentiation. SIAM (2008)
12. Paszke, A., Gross, S., Massa, F., et al.: PyTorch: an imperative style, high-performance deep learning library. In: Advances in Neural Information Processing Systems, pp. 8024–8035 (2019)

13. Moore, R.C., Lewis, W.: Intelligent selection of language model training data. In: Proceedings of the ACL 2010 Conference Short Papers, pp. 220–224. Association for Computational Linguistics (2010)
14. Abadi, M., Barham, P., Chen, J., et al.: TensorFlow: a system for large-scale machine learning. In: 12th USENIX Symposium on Operating Systems Design and Implementation (OSDI 2016), pp. 265–283 (2016)
15. Yang, Y., Wu, R., Zhang, L., Zhou, D.: An asynchronous adaptive priority round-robin arbiter based on four-phase dual-rail protocol. Chin. J. Elec. **24**(01), 1–7 (2015)

A Reconfigurable Convolutional Neural Networks Accelerator Based on FPGA

Yalin Tang[1]([✉]), Haoqi Ren[2], and Zhifeng Zhang[2]

[1] Tongji University, Shanghai, China
2030815@tongji.edu.cn
[2] School of Electronics and Information Engineering, Tongji University, Shanghai, China

Abstract. With the development of lightweight convolutional neural networks (CNNs), these newly proposed networks are more powerful than previous conventional models [4, 5] and can be well applied in Internet-of-Things (IoT) and edge computing. However, they perform inefficiently on conventional hardware accelerators because of the irregular connectivity in the structure. Though there are some accelerators based on unified engine (UE) architecture or separated engine (SE) architecture which can perform well for both standard convolution and depthwise convolution, these versatile structures are still not efficient for lightweight CNNs such as EfficientNet-lite. In this paper, we propose a reconfigurable engine (RE) architecture to improve the efficiency, which is used in communications such as IoT and edge computing. In addition, we adopt integer quantization method to reduce computational complexity and memory access. Also, the block-based calculation scheme is used to further reduce the off-chip memory access and the unique computational mode is used to improve the utilization of the processing elements. The proposed architecture can be implemented on Xilinx ZC706 with a 100 MHz system clock for EfficientNet-lite0. Our accelerator achieved 196 FPS and 72.9% top-1 accuracy on ImageNet classification, which is 27% and 18% speedup compared to CPU and GPU of Pixel 4 respectively.

Keywords: convolutional neural network · depthwise convolution · quantization · hardware accelerator · EfficientNet

1 Introduction

In recent years, convolutional neural networks (CNNs) play significant roles in researches on some hot issues like Artificial Intelligence (AI) and Deep Learning (DL), especially their applications in image processing [1, 2, 3]. Since AlexNet won the Image-Net Large Scale Vision Recognition Challenge competition in 2012 [4], more and more deeper CNNs for image classification with high predictive accuracy have been proposed. This comes with some challenges such as increasing computations, parameters and memory accesses. In order to solve these problems, lightweight CNNs such as ShuffleNet [6], MobileNet [7] and EfficientNet [8] were proposed, which adopt depthwise separable convolution to reduce the size of parameters and enhance the speed of inference with limited loss in accuracy.

© ICST Institute for Computer Sciences, Social Informatics and Telecommunications Engineering 2023
Published by Springer Nature Switzerland AG 2023. All Rights Reserved
F. Gao et al. (Eds.): ChinaCom 2022, LNICST 500, pp. 259–269, 2023.
https://doi.org/10.1007/978-3-031-34790-0_20

Even though these lightweight CNN models are more powerful than previous conventional models, they are still costly to be implemented on hardware. Thus, the call for efficient hardware implementations which are able to tackle the above problems arises. At the very beginning, Central processing units (CPUs) are used for the infrastructure of the CNN models [9]. But they are very inefficient in dealing with a large number of complicated convolutional calculations. Graphics processing units (GPUs) are more widely used with remarkable performance in handling large amounts of parallel computations because of its plentiful computing resources and high memory bandwidth [10]. However, it is not suitable for edge computing or Internet of Things (IoT) due to the disadvantage of its high energy consumption. Application-specific integrated circuit (ASIC) is much better in terms of power, performance and area [11]. Nevertheless, it is a fully custom designed chip for certain functionality and the hardware structure remains fixed once it is produced. With the rapid development of CNN models, it is lack of flexibility to be adapted to the advances. In this scenario, FPGAs have the advantages of flexible reconstruction and customizability with its programmable architecture to implement any target applications on hardware while maintain the benefits of low power and high performance of ASICs.

Despite the use of FPGAs to accelerate CNN models has become an academic hotspot, some FPGA accelerators [12, 13, 14], which aimed at large and conventional models such as AlexNet, VGG16 and ResNet, are not well applied in lightweight CNN models with irregular connectivity mentioned above. On account of the depthwise separable convolution adopted in these lightweight CNNs, those FPGA accelerators mentioned above are inefficient and underutilized. Therefore, it is necessary to design customized architectures to deploy the lightweight CNNs.

Shivapakash proposed a Multi-bit accelerator to enhance the power efficiency, which achieves $4.5 \times$ lower power consumption than 32-bit architectures by truncating the bits of parameters and activations sequentially [15]. But it still needs too much off-chip memory access. [16] proposed a SE architecture optimized for MobileNet to schedule the different data-path for standard convolution and depthwise convolution. It is underutilized due to the workload imbalance in EfficientNet. LETA, proposed in [17], adopted UE architecture to improve the efficiency and resource utilization. Its main problem is the high off-chip memory traffic.

This paper presents a customized hardware accelerator with a reconfigurable calculation core based on FPGA which targets quantized lightweight CNNs: both activations and weights are 8 bits. This accelerator is used in communications (IoT or edge computing). The main contributions of this work are as follows:

- A reconfigurable engine architecture with a reconfigurable computational core for both standard convolution and depthwise convolution.
- A block-based convolutional calculation scheme (pointwise-depthwise-pointwise) is designed to reduce off-chip memory access.
- Efficiently scheduling the calculation mode and blocking the image to maximize the utilization of both processing elements and on-chip memory.

The rest of the paper is organized as follows. Section 2 introduces the inverted residual with linear bottleneck module which contains depthwise separable convolution, the EfficientNet-lite model and quantization. In Sect. 3, we present the proposed customized architecture of the accelerator and some details. The results are shown in Sect. 4, and Sect. 5 gives the conclusions.

2 Backgroud

2.1 Inverted Residual with Linear Bottleneck Module

Recent state-of-the-art CNNs such as MobileNet, EfficientNet are based on an inverted residual structure with linear bottleneck. It consists of a pointwise convolution (*Pwcv*) layer, a depthwise convolution (*Dwcv*) layer and a pointwise convolution layer again sequentially which is similar to the basic structure of ResNet [5]. If skipping connections is applied, the input feature maps will add to the results after convolution. The main difference is that the standard convolution (*Scv*) in the middle layer is replaced by the *Dwcv* which greatly reduces the size of parameters. Figure 1 shows the difference. Both of the *Pwcv* is actually *Scv* with a 1×1 filter while the former one is used to expand the dimensionality, the other is the opposite. The *Dwcv* in the middle layer, the channels of which are computed independently, is spilt from the *Scv*. The separable channels make the *Dwcv* faster and smaller than the *Scv*.

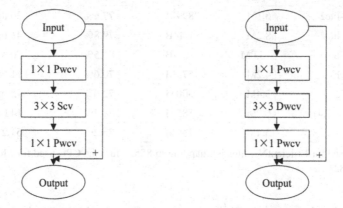

Fig. 1. The basic residual block in ResNet (left) and EfficientNet (right).

Assume that the height and width of the input feature map are H_i and W_i respectively, and the number of input channels is C_i. *Scv* and *Dwcv* apply the same convolutional kernel $K \times K$ with the stride length of 1 to generate the output feature map of which size is $H_o \times W_o \times C_o$. But the amount of operations is different as follows (In the case of *Dwcv*, $C_i = C_o$):

$$O_{Scv} = C_i \cdot H_o \cdot W_o \cdot C_o \cdot K^2 \qquad (1)$$

$$O_{Dwcv} = H_o \cdot W_o \cdot C_o \cdot K^2 \qquad (2)$$

Thus, we can see that *Scv* requires C_i times as much operations as *Dwcv*.

2.2 EfficientNet-Lite

EfficientNets are generated by using neural architecture search (NAS) and compound scaling method, which is based on a mobile-size baseline network manually designed. The main structure of EfficientNets is the *mobile inverted bottleneck block* like MobileNets, but with an additional *squeeze-and-excitation* optimization.

EfficientNet-lite makes some changes. All nonlinear activations called *swish* in EfficientNets [8] are replaced with *RELU6* activations for easier post-quantization and all *squeeze-and-excitation modules* are removed which makes the model to be easily implemented on hardware. All these changes is to make the model mobile and IoT friendlier. As shown in Table 1, EfficientNet-lite is more powerful than MobileNets with similar parameters and higher accuracy. The most accurate model, EfficientNet-lite4, is about 6% more accurate than MobileNetV3.

Table 1. EfficientNet-lite and MobileNet Performance Results on ImageNet.

Model	Params	MAdds	Top-1 Acc	CPU
EfficientNet-lite0	4.7M	407M	75.1%	12 ms
EfficientNet-lite1	5.4M	631M	76.7%	18 ms
EfficientNet-lite2	6.1M	899M	77.6%	26 ms
EfficientNet-lite3	8.2M	1.44B	79.8%	41 ms
EfficientNet-lite4	13.0M	2.64B	81.5%	76 ms
MobileNetV1	4.2M	575M	70.6%	113 ms
MobileNetV2	3.4M	300M	72.0%	75 ms
MobileNetV2(1.4)	6.9M	585M	74.7%	143 ms
MobileNetV3	5.4M	219M	75.2%	51.2 ms

[*] The CPU used for EfficientNet-lites is Snapdragon 855, while the CPU used for MoblieNets is Snapdragon 821.

Considering the area and real time, we target EfficientNet-lite0 to be implemented on hardware accelerator. Other EfficientNet-lite models can be well extended.

2.3 Integer Quantization

Model integer quantization has been widely applied in academia and industry as an optimization technology that can effectively reduce the size of the model and speed up the inference of CNNs with limited loss in accuracy. The width of quantized data can be 8-, 4-, 2- or 1-bit. Since 8-bit low-precision inference is commonly used, we target 8-bit integer quantization in the following discussion.

The aim of the quantization algorithm is to map 32-bit floating-point values to 8-bit integers. This can be written as:

$$q = round\left(\frac{r}{s} + Z\right) \tag{3}$$

$$S = \frac{r_{max} - r_{min}}{q_{max} - q_{min}} \quad (4)$$

$$Z = round\left(q_{max} - \frac{r_{max}}{S}\right) \quad (5)$$

where q, r is quantized integer and floating-point real number respectively. S denotes the scaling factor that represents the map ratio between q and r, and Z denotes the zero-point that represents the quantized integer of zero in real number. Function $round()$ means the value is rounded to the nearest integer. R_{min} and r_{max} are the maximum and minimum values of r respectively, and q is the same. For 8-bit integer quantization, q_{min} is -128 and q_{max} is 127 for symmetric scheme while q_{min} is 0 and q_{max} is 255 for asymmetric scheme.

In order to reduce the accuracy loss caused by quantization, we adopt different schemes for weight and activation. For the weight quantization, the per-channel symmetric scheme is used, which means each channel of the feature map has independent scaling factor S_W and zero-point Z_W. To simplify the calculation, we just apply S_W and Z_W to the bias quantization. And we just use a constant scaling factor S_A and zero-point Z_A within a layer for activation quantization with asymmetric scheme. Particularly, we need to collect the range of activations during the inference and choose the appropriate r_{min} and r_{max} to minimize the KL-Divergence between the quantized activations distribution and the original since the range of activations is not fixed for different inputs.

Assume that the weight of convolution is W, the bias is B, the input is X, and the output is A. Since convolution is essentially a matrix operation, the computation can be written as:

$$A = \sum_{i}^{N} W_i X_i + B \quad (6)$$

After quantization and adjustment, it becomes:

$$q_A = \frac{S_W S_X}{S_A}\left(\sum_{i}^{N}(q_W - Z_W)(q_X - Z_X) + q_B\right) + Z_A \quad (7)$$

where q_X, q_A, q_W, q_B are quantized input, output, weight and bias respectively. And S_X, S_A, S_W denote the scaling factors of input, output and weight respectively, which is same to Z. In order to compute with 8-bit integer during the quantitative inference, the results need to be multiplied by a scaling factor in the above equation for each channel after convolution.

Table 2 shows the performance of the quantized EfficientNet-lite0 based on Pytorch compared with the floating-point model and the official implementation based on Tensorflow [8]. Note that the batch normalization layers and activation layers have been merged into the convolutional layers during the quantization to enhance the accuracy.

Table 2. Performance Results of Different Framework After Quantization or Not.

Model	Framework	Precision	Top-1 Acc	CPU
EfficientNet-lite0	Pytorch	FP32	73.6%	57.3 ms
EfficientNet-lite0	Pytorch	INT8	72.9%	13.6 ms
EfficientNet-lite0	Tensorflow	FP32	75.1%	12 ms
EfficientNet-lite0	Tensorflow	INT8	74.4%	6.5 ms

* The CPU we used (Intel Core i5-6300HQ) is different from the official one (Snapdragon 855).

3 Proposed Architecture

3.1 Overall Architecture

Figure 2 Presents the block diagram of the proposed architecture. The accelerator is a reconfigurable engine architecture and is driven by pre-compiled instructions. In the whole system, the Processing System (PS) tiles the input image into blocks and schedules the computations sequentially. The data blocks and instructions are put into the off-chip memory from PS before run time.

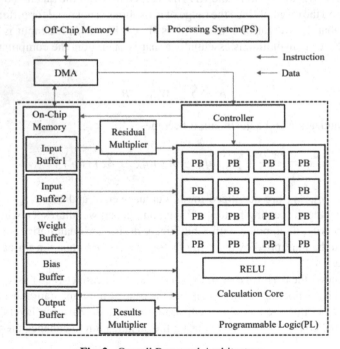

Fig. 2. Overall Proposed Architecture.

When the accelerator is started, the controller fetched instructions from off-chip memory. These instructions will be parsed and dispatched to the computational core.

The input feature maps, weights and biases will be filled into on-chip memory from the off-chip memory. Both standard convolution and depthwise convolution are computed in the core as well as the *RELU* function. The residual multiplier is used to scale the input feature maps for skipping connection, and the result multiplier is to quantize the results with the factor as in *Eq. (7)*. After convolution computations, the results are written back into off-chip memory. The final results of all these convolution layers are sent back to PS. Since we target EfficientNet-lite model, the pooling and full connection operation are computed in PS.

3.2 Reconfigurable Calculation Core

There are 16 processing blocks (PBs) inside the core, where each consists of 8 processing elements (PEs) and adder tree. The details are shown in Fig. 3. The calculation core can compute up to 1024 multiply-accumulate operations per cycle.

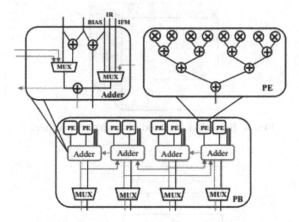

Fig. 3. The details of processing block.

In the inverted residual with linear bottleneck module, the number of the channels first increases then decreases. In order to improve the resource utilization of the processing elements, we enhance the structure and dataflow in [17]. For standard convolution, we only perform parallel computing along the channel dimension. And the parallelism of I/O channels can be configured as 16–64, 32–32 and 64–16. For depthwise convolution, we perform both the channel parallelism and the pixel parsallelism. The pixel parallelism can be configured as 2 or 4 (the corresponding channel parallelism is 64 or 32) according to the computation mode of the preceding pointwise convolution layer, and the total output is 128. The different parallelism can be performed by changing the output connections of the Adders. The red line input of the mux in Fig. 3 is the yellow line output from other adder within the PB and the black line output of the Adder in Fig. 3 is only used in depthwise convolution.

3.3 Image Blocking and Block-Based Data-Path

Due to the limited on-chip memory, we partition the input image and design a unique computation scheme as shown in Fig. 4. The inter-channel computation is scheduled with weight reuse and input feature map fully reuse within a convolution layer. The inverted residual block is regarded as a basic computing block. The input feature maps are fetched into the first input buffer as shown in Fig. 2. After the pointwise convolution layer, the results are sent to the second input buffer to prepared for depthwise convolution. Then, the results are sent to the first input buffer again to be used in the next pointwise convolution layer. The output buffer is used to store the intermediate results and the final results of the above convolution. After the basic block complete all the computations, the final results are written back to the off-chip memory. The data path of activations is shown in Fig. 5 briefly.

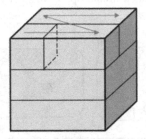

Fig. 4. Image blocking and computation schedule.

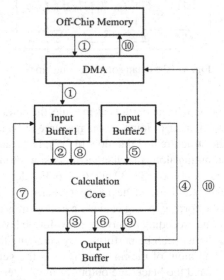

Fig. 5. The brief data path of activations.

4 Experiments

We evaluate the performance of the proposed architecture and compare it with previous works in this section. The whole system is implemented by Verilog HDL and runs at 100 MHz frequency on Xilinx ZC706 board. This platform is based on Zynq-7000 SoC with a dual-core ARM Cortex-A9 core processor. Vivado (v17.4) is used to synthesize and place-and-route the hardware design. The data set used for inference in this experiment is from ImageNet ILSVRC2012. The size of the images is $224 \times 224 \times 3$ and the batch size is 20. We implement EfficientNet-lite0 on this hardware accelerator and it takes about 384M multiply-accumulate operations to compute the inference of one single image.

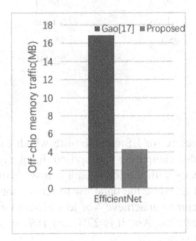 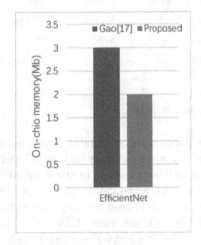

Fig. 6. Comparisons of off-chip memory traffic and on-chip memory.

Table 3 shows the results of the proposed architecture and comparisons with other works. The CPU of Pixel 4 is Snapdragon 855 and the GPU is Adreno 640. The proposed architecture is faster than CPU and GPU of Pixel 4 with limited accuracy loss (1–2% lower). Our reconfigurable engine (RE) architecture uses large on-chip memory size while reducing off-chip memory traffic. And compared with the unified engine (UE) architecture in [17], our architecture has about 4 × less off-chip traffic and still less on-chip memory, achieve a performance of 196 FPS in EfficientNet-lite0 as shown in Fig. 6. Though there is a small gap in latency because of lower frequency, our architecture still performs well.

Table 3. Performance Comparisons.

	CPU[8]	GPU[8]	Gao[17]	Proposed
Platform	Pixel4	Pixel4	Xilinx XCVU37P	Xilinx ZC706
Model	lite0	Lite0	B0	Lite0
Precision	INT8	FP32	INT8	INT8
Frequency	2.84 GHz	2.84 Hz	300 MHz	100 MHz
Off-chip Traffic	N/A	N/A	16.9 MB	4.3 MB
On-chip Memory	N/A	N/A	3 Mb	2 Mb
MAC Operation	407 M	407 M	390 M	384 M
Latency	6.5 ms	6.0 ms	4.1 ms	5.1 ms
GOPS	N/A	N/A	95.1	75.3
Accuracy	74.4%	75.1%	73.9%	72.9%

5 Conclusion

In this paper, a reconfigurable engine architecture for EfficientNet-lite which can be applied in communications such as IoT and edge computing is proposed. Integer quantization method is used to improve the efficiency with limited accuracy loss. Also, we design a block-based calculation scheme and schedule the dataflow to reduce the off-chip traffic and on-chip memory. Our architecture can achieve $4 \times$ less off-chip traffic than the latest FPGA-based EfficientNet accelerator. And it is 27% and 18% speedup compared to CPU and GPU of Pixel 4 respectively.

References

1. Can, F., Eyüpoğlu, C.: Convolutional neural network architectures used in computer vision. In: 5th International Symposium on Multidisciplinary Studies and Innovative Technologies, pp. 305–311. IEEE Press, New York (2021)
2. Dong, Y., Liu, Q., Du, B., Zhang, L.: Weighted feature fusion of convolutional neural network and graph attention network for hyperspectral image classification. IEEE Trans. Image Process. **31**, 1559–1572 (2022)
3. Pinckaers, H., Ginneken, B.V., Litjens, G.: Streaming convolutional neural networks for end-to-end learning with multi-megapixel images. IEEE Trans. Pattern Anal. Mach. Intell. **44**, 1581–1590 (2022)
4. Russakovsky, O., et al.: ImageNet large scale visual recognition challenge. Int. J. Comput. Vision **115**(3), 211–252 (2015). https://doi.org/10.1007/s11263-015-0816-y
5. He, K., Zhang X., Ren, S., Sun, J.: Deep residual learning for image recognition. In: CVPR, pp. 770–778. IEEE Press, New York (2016)
6. Ma, N., Zhang, X., Zheng, H.-T., Sun, J.: ShuffleNet V2: Practical guidelines for efficient CNN architecture design. In: Ferrari, V., Hebert, M., Sminchisescu, C., Weiss, Y. (eds.) Computer Vision – ECCV 2018. LNCS, vol. 11218, pp. 122–138. Springer, Cham (2018). https://doi. org/10.1007/978-3-030-01264-9_8

7. Howard, A., et al.: Searching for mobileNetV3. In: ICCV, pp. 1314–1324. IEEE Press, New York (2019)
8. Tan, M., Le, Q.V.: EfficientNet: rethinking model scaling for convolutional neural networks. In: ICML, pp. 6105–6114. PMLR, California (2019)
9. Abadi, M.: TensorFlow: a system for large-scale machine learning. In: 12th USENIX Symposium on Operating Systems Design and Implementation, pp. 265–283. USENIX Association, Savannah, GA (2016)
10. Hazelwood, K., et al.: Applied machine learning at Facebook: a datacenter infrastructure perspective. In: IEEE International Symposium on High Performance Computer Architecture, pp. 620–629. IEEE Press, New York (2018)
11. Jouppi, N.P., et al.: A domain-specific supercomputer for training deep neural networks. Commun. ACM **63**, 67–78 (2020)
12. Yin, S., et al.: A high energy efficient reconfigurable hybrid neural network processor for deep learning applications. IEEE J. Solid-State Circuits **53**, 968–982 (2018)
13. Nguyen, D.T., Nguyen, T.N., Kim, H., Lee, H.: A high-throughput and power-efficient FPGA implementation of YOLO CNN for object detection. In: IEEE Transactions on Very Large Scale Integration (VLSI) Systems, vol. 27, pp. 1861–1873 (2019)
14. Venieris, S.I., Bouganis, C.: fpgaConvNet: mapping regular and irregular convolutional neural networks on FPGAs. IEEE Trans. Neural Netw. Learn. Syst. **30**, 326–342 (2019)
15. Shivapakash, S., Jain, H., Hellwich, O., Gerfers, F.: A power efficiency enhancements of a multi-bit accelerator for memory prohibitive deep neural networks. IEEE Open J. Circ. Syst. **2**, 156–169 (2021)
16. Wu, D., et al.: A high-performance CNN processor based on FPGA for MobileNets. In: 29th International Conference on Field Programmable Logic and Applications, pp. 136–143. IEEE Press, New York (2019)
17. Gao, J., et al.: LETA: a lightweight exchangeable-track accelerator for efficientnet based on FPGA. In: 2021 International Conference on Field-Programmable Technology, pp. 1–9. IEEE Press, New York (2021)

Deep Learning and Network Performance Optimization

CARN-Conformer: Conformer in Attention Spectral Mapping Based Convolutional Recurrent Networks for Speech Enhancement

Bo Fang[1(✉)], Hongqing Liu[1], Yi Zhou[1], Yizhuo Jiang[2], and Lu Gan[2]

[1] School of Communication and Information Engineering,
Chongqing University of Posts and Telecommunications, Chongqing, China
s200131155@stu.cqupt.edu.cn
[2] College of Engineering, Design and Physical Science, Brunel University,
London UB8 3PH, UK

Abstract. In recent years, the attention transformer model has been widely used in the field of speech enhancement. With the introduction of a convolutionally enhanced transformer (Conformer), it models both the local and the global information of the speech sequence to achieve a better performance. In this paper, we propose a speech enhancement structure using conformer with time-frequency (TF) domain in DCCRN. To that aim, the second layer LSTM in DCCRN is replaced with TF-Conformer. By doing this, information between and within frames can be better utilized. An attention convolution path between the convolutional encoder and decoder is also developed to better convey nonlinear information. The results show that the model's PESQ surpasses DCCRN and DCCRN+ on the testset of Interspeech 2020 Deep Noise Suppression (DNS) Challenge, with the best model size of 2.3 M. At the same time, the excellent results have been obtained on the blind test set of ICASSP 2021 DNS Challenge, and the overall MOS score exceeds the winner team by 0.06.

Keywords: Speech enhancement · Attention · Time-frequency domain

1 Introduction

Noise is widespread in the natural environments and interferes with our language communications. Speech enhancement aims at suppressing noise components from noisy speech, and to improve the quality and intelligibility of audio. An excellent speech enhancement system can help people or machines better understand the meaning of speech such as speech recognition, hearing aids, and sentiment analysis [6]. Traditional speech enhancement algorithms usually estimate the noise spectrum theoretically based on statistical signals, and use filters to suppress the noise. The rise of deep learning has turned the speech enhancement into a

© ICST Institute for Computer Sciences, Social Informatics and Telecommunications Engineering 2023
Published by Springer Nature Switzerland AG 2023. All Rights Reserved
F. Gao et al. (Eds.): ChinaCom 2022, LNICST 500, pp. 273–282, 2023.
https://doi.org/10.1007/978-3-031-34790-0_21

data-driven supervised learning task. In recent years, DNN-based speech enhancement [18] methods have achieved great results in noise suppression. However, in practical applications, it is still difficult to suppress the noise in the case of low signal-to-noise ratios (SNR). The ICASSP 2021 deep noise suppression (DNS) challenge [12] is dedicated to speech enhancement task in harsh environments, and the corresponding dataset and evaluation metric (DNSMOS) [10] are provided for participants. For single-channel speech enhancement, the algorithms can be mainly divided into time domain [7,8] and time-frequency domain [21] structures. The time-domain algorithms mainly use convolutional encoder and transposed convolutional decoder to simulate the Fourier and inverse transforms, and directly estimate the clean target speech sequence through an end-to-end data-driven concept. Although it is not necessary to estimate the phase in the time domain, it is difficult to model the long speech sequences. The time-frequency domain algorithms extract the complex spectrum or power spectrum of the target speech from the noisy speech. After the short-time Fourier transform (STFT), the spectrums are processed to remove the noise in frequency domain.

In terms of the training goal, there are two common methods in deep learning: direct mapping and mask estimation. Due to the limited dynamic ranges of mask as a training target, the convergence speed is very fast, which is usually desired. The common masks mainly include ideal ratio mask (IRM) [11], ideal binary mask (IBM) [17], and target magnitude spectrum (TMS) [18]. However, many of these methods ignore the phase information of speech, and ambiguous phase information can make the modeling of recovered speech difficult [19]. The recent studies have shown that phase ratio mask (PSM) [2] and complex ratio mask (CRM) [20] achieved a good performance in phase estimation. The CRM respectively acts on the real and imaginary parts of the spectrogram, which estimates the phase information more accurately and improves the speech quality. With this concept and using complex operations, DCCRN [4] combines the advantages of two networks of DCUNET [1] and CRN [13], and develops a new complex speech enhancement network [14], where LSTM layers between convolutional encoder and decoder model the temporal context to reconstruct speech by simultaneously enhancing the real and imaginary parts of the speech in frequency domain.

In this paper, we propose a complex convolutional network [4], which uses DCCRN as a backbone structure. The difference is the conformer [3] attention mechanism, we use Multihead-Attention in frequency domain to process the relevant information between frequencies in the frame. In addition to that, we use the skip connection attention mechanism of attention convolution to improve the information aggregation between the encoder and decoder, which is also different from DCCRN+ [9]. To train the network, the weighted loss of mean square error (MSE) and scale-invariant signal-to-noise ratio (SI-SNR) [8] is developed to better balance the speech distortion and noise suppression. Under the framework of the proposed model, we perform comparisons on the DNS test sets, and it is found that the proposed model outperforms DCCRN in all scenarios, with a significantly less computation. Under the P808 subjective evaluation system, the proposed model outperforms DCCRN and TSCN-PP [5].

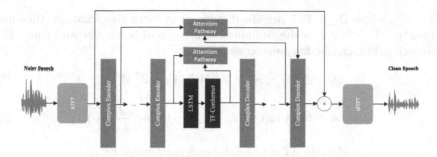

Fig. 1. CARN-Conformer Network

2 The CARN-Conformer Network

As shown in Fig. 1, our time-frequency domain network adopts a multi-layer convolution structure, where the complex convolution structure is utilized. The attention pathway is added between the encoder and decoder. LSTM and one layer TF-Conformer Module is used as the middle layer. The detailed information for each layer is provided below.

2.1 Time-Frequency Conformer

The conformer is widely used in the field of speech recognition(ASR), which adds a convolution module to the original transformer. We use Conformer to extract information and intra-frame frequency correlations between temporal contexts. The TF-Conformer Module is mainly composed of a stack of five blocks, namely two feed forward modules (FFM), the multi-head self attention (MHSA) module, the convolution module, and the LayerNormlization, depicted in Fig. 2. We use $X(t, f)$ to represent the first input of TF domain features, and suppose the input of the ith block is z and the output of the ith block is

$$\hat{z} = z + \frac{1}{2}\text{FFM}(z), \tag{1}$$

$$z' = \text{MHSA}(\hat{z}) + \hat{z}, \tag{2}$$

$$z'' = conv(z') + z', \tag{3}$$

$$output = layernorm(z'' + \frac{1}{2}\text{FFM}(z)). \tag{4}$$

The FFM follows a pre-normalized residual unit and applies layer normalization on the input within the residual unit. It is similar to a macaron-structured network and consists of a linear layer that includes a swish activation function and dropout. We improve MHSA to explore contextual information in the frequency dimension. Therefore, the frequency dimension is used as the sequence dimension, the time dimension is combined into batch size, and the channel dimension is used as the feature dimension. The reshape operators are applied before and after MHSA layer between the features of $Z \in R^{B \times C \times T \times F}$ and $Z \in$

$R^{BT \times F \times C}$, where B, C, T, F are the dimension of batch size, channel, time and frequency, $BT = B \times T$ is the combined dimension of batch size and time. The improved MHSA can be formulated as follows:

$$Q_i = Z^Q W_i^Q, K_i = Z^K W_i^K, V_i = Z^V W_i^V, \tag{5}$$

$$head_i = Attention(Q_i, K_i, V_i) = softmax(\frac{Q_i K_i^T}{\sqrt{d}})V_i, \tag{6}$$

$$MultiHead = Concat(head_1, ..., head_h)W^O, \tag{7}$$

In the formula, i $\in$ [1, h] is the head index. Z^Q, Z^K, $Z^V \in R^{F \times C}$ are the input features with length F and dimension C, Q_i, K_i, $V_i \in R^{F \times C/h}$ are queries, keys and values. W^Q, W^K, $W^V \in R^{C \times C/h}$ and $W^O \in R^{C \times C}$ are parameter matrices.

The convolution module helps extract the information that the model extracts the temporal context, starting with point convolution and gated linear units, Then a 1D depthwise convolution where normalization helps the model better deep training.

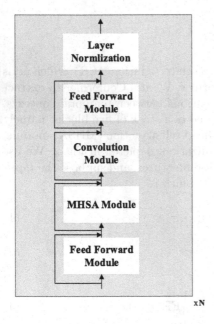

Fig. 2. TF-Conformer Module.

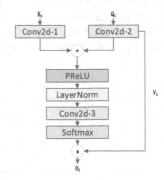

Fig. 3. Attention pathway.

2.2 Attention Pathway (AP)

In past DCCRN networks, skip connections were used to map encoder features directly to decoders. This paper proposes a new skip connection method based on the attention mechanism, which uses the output of the encoder and decoder (conformer) of the ith layer as the input of the attention path, and obtains the input of the $(i-1)th$ layer. In the Fig. 3, K_i is the output of the $Conv2d$ encoder and Q_i is the output of the decoder. There are two causal 2D convolutions with kernel $(3, 2)$ and stride $(1, 1)$ to process K_i and Q_i. The first layer $Conv2d$ doubles the output channels to extract high-dimensional spatial features, referring as W_1 and W_2, and then sums the outputs. The output A_i of high-dimensional spatial features can be described as:

$$A_i = LayerNorm(PReLU(W_1 \cdot K_i + W_2 \cdot Q_i)) \qquad (8)$$

After that, utilize the PReLU activation function and normalization layer, then recover the number of channels and generate the attention mask using causal $Conv2d$ with the same kernel and stride, refering as W_3. Finally, the feature V_i of the original input to the decoder is multiplied by the attention mask element, and the resulting mask feature is concatenated with the output Q_i to get the final output to the next decoder. The output B_i of AP can be described as:

$$B_i = Softmax(PReLU(W_3 \cdot A_i) \cdot V_i \qquad (9)$$

2.3   Learning Target and Loss Function

In our model, we use CRM [20] as our training target. During training, CARN-Conformer estimates CRM. Given the complex-valued STFT spectrogram of clean speech S and noisy speech Y, CRM is defined as

$$CRM = \frac{Y_r S_r + Y_i S_i}{Y_r^2 + Y_i^2} + j\frac{Y_r S_i + Y_i S_r}{Y_r^2 + Y_i^2}, \qquad (10)$$

where Y_r and Y_i refer to the real and imaginary parts of the noisy spectrum, respectively, and S_r and S_i represent the real and imaginary parts of the clean complex spectrum, and M_r and M_i denote the real and imaginary parts of the CRM, respectively.

We multiply the input noisy speech $X = X_r + jX_i$ and the CRM mask to generate the enhanced spectrogram

$$\hat{S} = X_r M_r - X_i M_i + i(X_r M_i + X_i M_r). \qquad (11)$$

Applying inverse Fourier transform (iSTFT) to $\hat{S}$ yields a time-domain waveform $\hat{s}$

$$\hat{s} = iSTFT(\hat{S}). \qquad (12)$$

To train the network, the weighted loss functions is developed by considering both SI-SNR and MSE. The SI-SNR is defined

$$\begin{cases} s_{target} := \frac{<\hat{s},s>\cdot s}{||s||_2^2} \\ e_{noise} := \hat{s} - s_{target} \\ L_{SI-SNR} := -10log_{10}(\frac{||s_{target}||_2^2}{||e_{noise}||_2^2}) \end{cases} \qquad (13)$$

Therefore, the final weighted loss is

$$Loss = L_{SI-SNR} + log(MSE(S_r, \hat{S}_r) + MSE(S_i, \hat{S}_i) \\ + MSE(|S|, |\hat{S}|)). \tag{14}$$

where $<\cdot, \cdot>$ denotes the dot product between two vectors and $||\cdot||_2$ is Euclidean norm (L2 norm). The added MSE part measures the real, imaginary, and magnitude differences between the estimated spectrum and the true spectrum. We take the logarithm of the MSE loss to ensure it is of the same order of magnitude as the negative SNR.

3 Experiments

We first evaluate the performance of our model on both Interspeech 2020 and ICASSP 20201 DNS challenge datasets [12]. For the Interspeech 2020 dataset, it contains 180 h of noise sets, which includes 150 lessons and 65,000 noise clips, and more than 500 h of clean speech, which includes 2,150 speaker audio clips, and has 80,000 RIR clips. We generated 500 h each for the unreverb and reverberated datasets with a sampling rate of 16 kHz and 10 s segments, and the SNR was set in the range of −5 to 20 dB. The ratio of training set and test set is 9:1. The generation method for the ICASSP dataset is consistent with the method for the Interspeech dataset. Additionally, we also Voice Bank+DEMAND [15] dataset to test the our model, where a total of 824 samples from 8 speakers are used.

3.1 Training Setup and Parameters

For our model, the window length and frame shift used are 32 ms and 16 ms, respectively, corresponding to an STFT length of 512, and we stack the real and imaginary parts together as the input to the network. The model is trained using the Adam optimizer with a bach size of 6. The initial learning rate is 1e−3, the learning rate is halved if the validation loss does not drop within 3 epochs, and training is stopped if the validation loss does not drop within 10 epochs. We compare several models on dataset, described as follows.

DCCRN [4]: The number of channels of the encoder and decoder is {32, 64, 128, 128, 256,256}. The kernel size and stride of each layer are (5, 2) and (2, 1), respectively. The middle layer uses a two-layer LSTM with 256 nodes. There is a 1024 * 256 fully connected layer after the LSTM. Each encoder processes the previous frame and the current frame. An additional future frame is processed by a later layer of the decoder, and each layer only uses the previous and current frame.

CARN-Conformer: Three models consist of ours-1, ours-2 and ours-3. The number of channels of the encoding layer is [32, 32, 64, 64, 64, 64, 64, 64]. The kernel size and stride are (5, 2) and (2, 1) respectively, and all the convolutional encoders and decoders are causal. In the middle layer of ours-1, we set up a conformer block instead of LSTM, with 16 attention heads, 64 attention dimensions,

256 FFM dimensions, using relative position coding, dropout settings in FFM is 0.15. Based on ours-1, we set AP between the encoder and decoder to get ours-2. In ours-3, we replace the SI-SNR in ours-2 with our proposed constraint function.

Table 1. PESQ on DNS2020 synthetic test set.

Model	Para.(M)	no reverb	reverb	Ave.
Noisy	-	2.45	2.75	2.60
NSNet(Baseline)	1.3	3.07	2.81	2.94
DCUNET [1]	3.6	3.22	2.79	3.01
DCCRN [4]	3.7	3.26	3.20	3.23
DCCRN+ [9]	3.3	3.33	3.30	3.32
DCCRN +TF-conformer (ours-1)	2.1	3.28	3.26	3.27
+attention pathway(ours-2)	2.3	3.40	3.35	3.37
+new loss(ours-3)	2.3	**3.42**	**3.36**	**3.39**

3.2 Experimental Results and Discussions

We evaluate model performance in terms of perceptual evaluation of speech quality (PESQ) and DNSMOS [15], which is provided by the Challenge organizer. In Table 1, we perform ablation experiments on the models using the DNS-2020 synthetic test set, in terms of PESQ. It is seen that all proposed models outperform DCCRN [4] with the smaller parameters. After adding the conformer, it can be found that the parameters of the model are significantly reduced, and the noise reduction ability is improved to a certain extent. The model after adding the attention path only adds a small amount of parameters and the performance is significantly improved. It is seen that our best model outperforms DCCRN [4] by 0.16 and DCCRN+ [9] 0.07 on the test set.

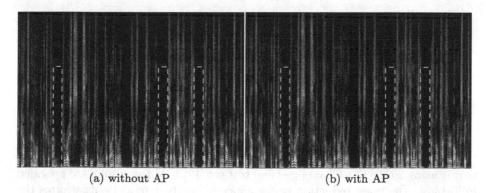

(a) without AP   (b) with AP

Fig. 4. The denoising result on a testing noisy clip for the cases with/without AP: (a) without AP, (b) with AP.

In Fig. 4, to visually see the performance of AP, we compare the spectrograms of a test segment without AP and with AP. We can find that the spectrogram with AP is clearer and the residual noise is better suppressed.

Table 2. DNSMOS on DNS2020 blind test set.

Model	Para.(M)	no reverb	reverb	realrec	Ave.
Noisy	-	3.13	2.64	2.83	2.85
NSNet(Baseline)	1.3	3.49	2.64	3.00	3.03
DCCRN[T1]	3.7	4.00	2.94	3.37	3.42
ours-1[T1]	2.1	4.00	3.16	3.28	3.49
ours-2[T1]	2.3	4.04	3.34	3.35	3.56
ours-3[T1]	2.3	**4.04**	**3.36**	**3.37**	**3.59**
DCCRN[T2]	3.7	3.90	2.96	3.34	3.38
ours-1[T2]	2.1	3.92	3.02	3.38	3.43
ours-2[T2]	2.3	3.97	3.14	3.40	3.50
ours-3[T2]	2.3	**3.98**	**3.16**	**3.42**	**3.52**

In Table 2, the blind test set is used to evaluate the performance in terms of DNSMOS [6], where [T1] and [T2] respectively represent the real-time track and non-real-time track. It is noted that the proposed models outperform the baselines. With attention path and new loss function, the performance of the proposed model is superior to that of DCCRN [4] in both tracks.

In Table 3, the experiments with the Voice Bank + DEMAND dataset [15] are provided. It is seen that our model has a significantly lower parameter quantity, and outperforms DCCRN [4] and DCCRN+ [9].

Table 3. PESQ on Voice Bank + DEMAND.

Model	Para.(M)	External Data	PESQ-WB
Noisy	-	-	1.97
RNNoise [16]	0.06	√	2.29
DCCRN [4]	3.7	√	2.68
DCCRN+ [4]	3.3	√	2.84
ours-3	2.3	√	**2.90**

Finally, we further compare the performances in more complex acoustic scenarios using 2021 DNS Challenge blind test set [12], and the results are provided in Table 4. The noise reduction performance of our best model outperforms the winning model of TSCN-PP [5] in all scenarios, which indicates our model generalizes better.

Table 4. DNSMOS on the DNS2021 blind test set.

Model	singing	Tinal	Non-English	English	Emotional	Overall
Noisy	2.96	3.00	2.96	2.80	2.67	2.86
NSnet2(Baseline)	3.10	3.25	3.28	3.30	2.88	3.21
TSCN-PP [5]	3.14	3.44	3.50	3.49	2.92	3.38
ours-3	**3.18**	**3.46**	**3.54**	**3.52**	**2.96**	**3.44**

4 Conclusion

In this paper, we propose a model CARN-Conformer that uses conformer and adopts attention pathway skip connections to perform speech enhancement. Conformer is used to combine local and global information for modeling and the new loss function constrains both the time and frequency domains. Especially, the attention pathway is utilized to map between the encoder and the decoder, and as a result, the ability of the model to suppress noise is improved. The proposed model achieves excellent MOS scores on the ICASSP 2021 DNS Challenge blind test set, proving the effectiveness of the model structure.

References

1. Choi, H.S., Kim, J.H., Huh, J., Kim, A., Ha, J.W., Lee, K.: Phase-aware speech enhancement with deep complex u-net. In: International Conference on Learning Representations (2018)
2. Erdogan, H., Hershey, J.R., Watanabe, S., Le Roux, J.: Phase-sensitive and recognition-boosted speech separation using deep recurrent neural networks. In: 2015 IEEE International Conference on Acoustics, Speech and Signal Processing (ICASSP), pp. 708–712. IEEE (2015)
3. Gulati, A., et al.: Conformer: convolution-augmented transformer for speech recognition. arXiv preprint arXiv:2005.08100 (2020)
4. Hu, Y., et al.: DCCRN: deep complex convolution recurrent network for phase-aware speech enhancement. arXiv preprint arXiv:2008.00264 (2020)
5. Li, A., Liu, W., Luo, X., Zheng, C., Li, X.: ICASSP 2021 deep noise suppression challenge: Decoupling magnitude and phase optimization with a two-stage deep network. In: 2021 IEEE International Conference on Acoustics, Speech and Signal Processing (ICASSP), ICASSP 2021, pp. 6628–6632. IEEE (2021)
6. Li, J., et al.: Developing far-field speaker system via teacher-student learning. In: 2018 IEEE International Conference on Acoustics, Speech and Signal Processing (ICASSP), pp. 5699–5703. IEEE (2018)
7. Luo, Y., Chen, Z., Yoshioka, T.: Dual-path RNN: efficient long sequence modeling for time-domain single-channel speech separation. In: 2020 IEEE International Conference on Acoustics, Speech and Signal Processing (ICASSP), ICASSP 2020, pp. 46–50. IEEE (2020)
8. Luo, Y., Mesgarani, N.: Conv-TasNet: surpassing ideal time-frequency magnitude masking for speech separation. IEEE/ACM Trans. Audio Speech Lang. Process. **27**(8), 1256–1266 (2019)

9. Lv, S., Hu, Y., Zhang, S., Xie, L.: DCCRN+: channel-wise subband DCCRN with SNR estimation for speech enhancement. arXiv preprint arXiv:2106.08672 (2021)
10. Naderi, B., Cutler, R.: An open source implementation of ITU-T recommendation p. 808 with validation. arXiv preprint arXiv:2005.08138 (2020)
11. Narayanan, A., Wang, D.: Ideal ratio mask estimation using deep neural networks for robust speech recognition. In: 2013 IEEE International Conference on Acoustics, Speech and Signal Processing, pp. 7092–7096. IEEE (2013)
12. Reddy, C.K., et al.: ICASSP 2021 deep noise suppression challenge. In: 2021 IEEE International Conference on Acoustics, Speech and Signal Processing (ICASSP), ICASSP 2021, pp. 6623–6627. IEEE (2021)
13. Tan, K., Wang, D.: A convolutional recurrent neural network for real-time speech enhancement. In: Interspeech, vol. 2018, pp. 3229–3233 (2018)
14. Trabelsi, C., et al.: Deep complex networks (2017). arXiv preprint arXiv:1705.09792
15. Valentini-Botinhao, C., Wang, X., Takaki, S., Yamagishi, J.: Investigating RNN-based speech enhancement methods for noise-robust text-to-speech. In: SSW, pp. 146–152 (2016)
16. Valin, J.M.: A hybrid DSP/deep learning approach to real-time full-band speech enhancement. In: 2018 IEEE 20th International Workshop on Multimedia Signal Processing (MMSP), pp. 1–5. IEEE (2018)
17. Wang, D.: On ideal binary mask as the computational goal of auditory scene analysis. In: Divenyi, P. (ed.) Speech Separation by Humans and Machines, pp. 181–197. Springer, Boston (2005). https://doi.org/10.1007/0-387-22794-6_12
18. Wang, D., Chen, J.: Supervised speech separation based on deep learning: an overview. IEEE/ACM Trans. Audio Speech Lang. Process. **26**(10), 1702–1726 (2018)
19. Wang, D., Lim, J.: The unimportance of phase in speech enhancement. IEEE Trans. Acoust. Speech Signal Process. **30**(4), 679–681 (1982)
20. Williamson, D.S., Wang, Y., Wang, D.: Complex ratio masking for monaural speech separation. IEEE/ACM Trans. Audio Speech Lang. Process. **24**(3), 483–492 (2015)
21. Zhao, Y., Wang, D., Merks, I., Zhang, T.: DNN-based enhancement of noisy and reverberant speech. In: 2016 IEEE International Conference on Acoustics, Speech and Signal Processing (ICASSP), pp. 6525–6529. IEEE (2016)

An Elite Genetic Algorithm for Power Allocation in Cell-Free Massive MIMO Systems

Yehao Li[1], Chaowei Wang[1]([✉]), Danhao Deng[1], Mingliang Pang[1], Weidong Wang[1], and Lexi Xu[2]

[1] Beijing University of Posts and Telecommunications,
Beijing, People's Republic of China
{liyehao,wangchaowei,dengdanhao,pangmingliang,wangweidong}@bupt.edu.cn
[2] China United Network Communications Corporation,
Beijing, People's Republic of China
xulx29@chinaunicom.cn

Abstract. Network-assisted full-duplex (NAFD) cell-free massive MIMO can greatly improve the spectral efficiency and reduce the unmet system capacity ratio (USCR) by simultaneous downlink and uplink transmission with massive access points (APs). As most existing works focus on the system throughput maximization while ignoring the user requirements. In this paper, we jointly study the dynamic power allocation under the constraint of USCR. An elite genetic algorithm for power allocation is proposed to solve the above problems. Simulation results show that the proposed algorithm significantly reduces the USCR of the cell-free massive MIMO while sufficiently meeting the user requirements.

Keywords: Massive MIMO · Cell-free · User-centered · Power allocation

1 Introduction

Beyond 5G networks are expected to own the ability to handle more access users with great energy efficiency and ultra-low latencies as well as providing exceptionally high transmission rates while supporting more equitable quality of service (QoS) over the coverage area, which can tackle the problems left by 5G [1]. Therefore, cell-free massive MIMO has a strong appeal to the researchers nowadays due to its ability to overcome the inherent intercell-interference in cellular networks through coherent cooperation between APs [2–4]. Specifically, cell-free massive MIMO uses numerous distributed access points (APs) with simple linear processing capability, which can serve many users coherently with the same time and frequency resources [5–7]. The benefits of massive MIMO and full duplex are

This work is supported by the National Key R&D Program of China under Grant 2020YFB1807204.

F. Gao et al. (Eds.): ChinaCom 2022, LNICST 500, pp. 283–293, 2023.
https://doi.org/10.1007/978-3-031-34790-0_22

combined. Moreover, cell-free massive MIMO are much more robust to shadow fading correlation than traditional cellular networks [8]. Therefore, it can provide greatly improved services for all users, regardless of their location. However, the cell-free massive MIMO also brings in several challenges including the severe multi-user interference [9]. Therefore, the concept of network-assisted full-duplex (NAFD) system is proposed [10], which aims to reduce the system performance degradation due to self-interference between uplink and downlink. In a NAFD cell-free massive MIMO system, APs with multiple antennas are distributed in an area and connected to a central processor unit (CPU), which can estimate the channel state information (CSI) among APs with pilot arrangement, via fronthaul to serve users with different communication requirements [11]. Since considering only maximizing the total system spectral efficiency (SE) may lead to poor QoS of users, different from the previous works, we investigate the power allocation in NAFD cell-free massive MIMO to find the optimal power allocation to achieve flexible allocation of system resources and improved system performance. Accordingly, we propose a power allocation algorithm based on elite genetic algorithm. Simulation results show that the proposed power allocation scheme has better QoS under various types of user requirements conditions.

2   System Model and Problem Formulation

2.1   System Model

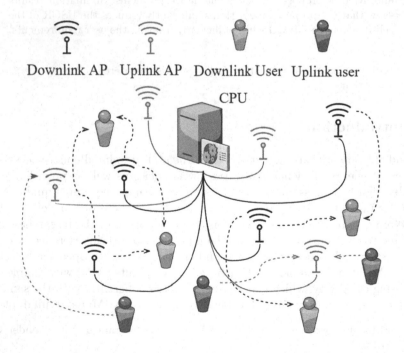

Fig. 1. NAFD cell-free massive MIMO systems.

As depicted in Fig. 1, we consider a NADF cell-free massive MIMO system containing K users. Based on the user-centric concept, each user considers itself as the center and selects APs whose distances to the user are smaller than the selection radius R_s. Then, the system will also contain M APs, which are connected to a CPU by downlink or uplink fronthaul. Moreover, each AP is equipped with L antennas, and each user is equipped with single antenna, each DL-AP or uplink user is considered as a transmitter, who allocates its power according to the power allocation method to the corresponding downlink users or UL-APs, which are considered as receivers. Theoretically, each full-duplex AP is considered either a downlink transmitting AP (DL-AP) or an uplink receiving AP (UL-AP), and each user is considered either a downlink user or an uplink user as well [3]. Accordingly, we divide the APs into M_d DL-APs indexed by $\mathbf{M}_d = \{1, 2, \cdots, m_d\}$, and M_u UL-APs indexed by $\mathbf{M}_u = \{1, 2, \cdots, m_u\}$. Meanwhile, we divide the users into K_d downlink users indexed by $\mathbf{K}_d = \{1, 2, \cdots, k_d\}$ and K_u uplink users indexed by $\mathbf{K}_u = \{1, 2, \cdots, k_u\}$.

2.2 Downlink Transmission Model

For downlink transmission, in each scheduled time slot, the CPU computes, compresses and transmits the beamforming signals to each DL-AP. Specifically, the received signal at DL-AP m_d is given as:

$$\mathbf{x}_{d,m_d} = \sum_{k_d=1}^{K_d} \mathbf{p}_{d,m_d,k_d} s_{d,k_d} + \mathbf{q}_{d,m_d}, \tag{1}$$

where $\mathbf{p}_{d,m_d,k_d} \in \mathbb{C}^{L \times 1}$ represents the linear transmit beamforming and power allocation vector between DL-AP m_d and downlink user k_d, and user k_d, s_{d,k_d} is the download transmitted signal for downlink user k_d with $\mathbb{E}[s_{d,k_d} s_{d,k_d}^H] = 1$. $\mathbf{q}_{d,m_d} \sim \mathcal{CN}(0, \sigma_{q,d,m_d}^2 \mathbf{I}_L) \in \mathbb{C}^{L \times 1}$ denotes the downlink quantization noise at DL-AP m_d, where σ_{q,d,m_d}^2 is the corresponding compression noise power.

Then, the DL-APs transmit their received signals to the downlink users. The signal received at downlink user k_d can be expressed as:

$$y_{d,k_d} = \sum_{m_d=1}^{M_d} \mathbf{h}_{d,m_d,k_d}^H \mathbf{x}_{d,m_d} + \sum_{k_u=1}^{K_u} h_{k_u,k_d} \sqrt{p_{u,k_u}} s_{u,k_u} + \mathbf{n}_{d,k_d}, \tag{2}$$

where $\mathbf{h}_{d,m_d,k_d} \in \mathbb{C}^{L \times 1}$ represents the CSI vector between DL-AP m_d and downlink user k_d, h_{k_u,k_d} denotes the CSI between uplink user k_u and downlink user k_d. p_{u,k_u} is the uplink transmission power of the uplink user k_u, and s_{u,k_u} is the corresponding uplink transmitted signal with $\mathbb{E}[s_{u,k_u} s_{u,k_u}^H] = 1$. $\mathbf{n}_{d,k_d} \sim \mathcal{CN}(0, \sigma_{d,k_d}^2)$ is the additive white gaussian noise (AWGN) at downlink user k_d. Overall, the downlink SE of downlink user k_d can be expressed as:

$$R_{k_d} = \log_2(1 + \frac{\mid \mathbf{h}_{d,k_d}^H \mathbf{p}_{d,k_d} \mid^2}{\eta_{d,k_d}}) \tag{3}$$

where η_{d,k_d} is the covariance interference at downlink user k_d and can be expressed as:

$$\eta_{d,k_d} = \sum_{k'_d=1,k'_d \neq k_d}^{K_d} | \mathbf{h}_{d,k_d}^H \mathbf{p}_{d,k'_d} |^2 + \sum_{k_u=1}^{K_u} p_{u,k_u} | h_{k_u,k_d} |^2$$
$$+ \sigma_{q,d,m_d}^2 \| \mathbf{h}_{d,m_d,k_d} \|^2 + \sigma_{d,k_d}^2, \tag{4}$$

where $\mathbf{h}_{d,k_d} = [\mathbf{h}_{d,1,k_d}^T, \cdots, \mathbf{h}_{d,M_d,k_d}^T]^T \in \mathbb{C}^{LM_d \times 1}$ denotes the CSI matrix between all DL-APs and downlink user k_d, $\mathbf{p}_{d,k_d} = [\mathbf{p}_{d,1,k_d}^T, \cdots, \mathbf{p}_{d,M_d,k_d}^T]^T \in \mathbb{C}^{LM_d \times 1}$ denotes the transmit beamforming and power allocation vector between DL-APs and downlink user k_d.

2.3 Uplink Transmission Model

For uplink transmission, in each scheduled time slot, M_u UL-APs jointly receive signals from uplink users. The received signal by UL-AP m_u can be expressed as:

$$y_{u,m_u} = \sum_{k_u=1}^{K_u} \mathbf{h}_{u,k_u,m_u} \sqrt{p_{u,k_u}} s_{u,k_u} + \sum_{k_d=1}^{K_d} \mathbf{H}_{m_u} \mathbf{p}_{d,k_d} s_{d,k_d} + \mathbf{n}_{u,m_u}, \tag{5}$$

where $\mathbf{h}_{u,k_u,m_u} \in \mathbb{C}^{L \times 1}$ represents the CSI vector between UL-AP m_u and downlink user k_u, and $\mathbf{n}_{u,m_u}$ denotes the AWGN at UL-AP m_u. $\mathbf{H}_{m_u} \in \mathbb{C}^{L \times LM_d}$ denotes the CSI between UL-AP m_u and all DL-APs. Then, the UL-APs compress the received signals and transmit them to the CPU. The received signal at the CPU can be expressed as:

$$y_u = \sum_{k_u=1}^{K_u} \mathbf{h}_{u,k_u} \sqrt{p_{u,k_u}} s_{u,k_u} + \mathbf{H}\mathbf{x_d} + \mathbf{n}_u + \mathbf{q_u}, \tag{6}$$

where $\mathbf{h}_{u,k_u} = [\mathbf{h}_{u,k_u,1}^T, \cdots, \mathbf{h}_{u,k_u,M_u}^T]^T \in \mathbb{C}^{LM_u \times 1}$ denotes the CSI between the uplink user k_u and all UL-APs. $\mathbf{H} = [\mathbf{H}_1^T, \cdots, \mathbf{H}_{M_u}^T]^T \in \mathbb{C}^{LM_u \times LM_d}$ denotes the CSI between all UL-APs and DL-APs, $\mathbf{x}_d = [\mathbf{x}_{d,1}^T, \cdots, \mathbf{x}_{d,M_d}^T]^T \in \mathbb{C}^{LM_d \times 1}$ represents the received signal at all DL-APs, $\mathbf{n}_u = [\mathbf{n}_{u,1}^T, \cdots, \mathbf{n}_{u,M_u}^T]^T \in \mathbb{C}^{LM_u \times 1}$ is the AWGN at all UL-APs, $\mathbf{q}_u = [\mathbf{q}_{u,1}^T, \cdots, \mathbf{q}_{u,M_u}^T]^T \in \mathbb{C}^{LM_u \times 1}$ is the uplink compression noise at all UL-APs, $\mathbf{q}_{u,m_u} \sim \mathcal{CN}(0, \sigma_{q,u,m_u}^2 \mathbf{I}_L) \in \mathbb{C}^{L \times 1}$ denotes the quantization noise at UL-AP m_u, where σ_{c,u,m_u}^2 is the corresponding compression noise power. In order to detect the transmitted signal s_{u,k_u}, the CPU employs a receive beamforming and power allocation vector $\mathbf{p}_{u,k_u} = [\mathbf{p}_{u,k_u,1}^T, \cdots, \mathbf{p}_{u,k_u,M_u}^T]^T \in \mathbb{C}^{LM_u \times 1}$.

In addition, since the CPU has the full information of the downlink signal s_{d,k_d}, the inter-AP interference (IAI) can be modeled as $\mathbf{H} = \hat{\mathbf{H}} + \tilde{\mathbf{H}}$, where $\hat{\mathbf{H}} \in \mathbb{C}^{LM_u \times LM_d}$ denotes the imperfect channel and $\tilde{\mathbf{H}} \in \mathbb{C}^{LM_u \times LM_d}$ denotes the channel estimation error, and since the IAI power can be much stronger than the others, we assume that only the IAI channel is imperfect, and other channel estimates are perfect.

Overall, the uplink SE of uplink user k_u can be expressed as:

$$R_{k_u} = \log_2(1 + \frac{p_{u,k_u} |\, \mathbf{p}_{u,k_u}^{\mathbf{H}} \mathbf{h}_{u,k_u} \,|^2}{\eta_{u,k_u}}), \tag{7}$$

where η_{u,k_u} is the interference-plus-noise at uplink user k_u and can be expressed as:

$$\eta_{u,k_u} = \sum_{k_u'=1, k_u' \neq k_u}^{K_u} p_{u,k_u'} |\, \mathbf{p}_{u,k_u}^{\mathbf{H}} \mathbf{h}_{u,k_u'} \,|^2 + \mathbf{p}_{u,k_u}^{\mathbf{H}} \sum_{m_d=1}^{M_d} p_{d,m_d} \widetilde{\mathbf{H}}_{m_d} \mathbf{p}_{u,k_u} \tag{8}$$
$$+ \mathbf{p}_{u,k_u}^{\mathbf{H}} (\mathbf{N}_u + \mathbf{Q}_u) \mathbf{p}_{u,k_u},$$

where $p_{d,m_d} = \sum_{k_d'=1}^{K_d} \|\, \mathbf{h}_{d,m_d,k_d} \,\|^2 + L\sigma_{q,d,m_d}^2$, $\widetilde{\mathbf{H}}_{m_d} = diag(\sigma_{1,m_d}^2 \mathbf{I}_L, \cdots, \sigma_{M_u,m_d}^2 \mathbf{I}_L)$, $\mathbf{N}_u = \mathbf{n}_u \mathbf{n}_u^H = diag(\sigma_{u,1}^2 \mathbf{I}_L, \cdots, \sigma_{u,m_u}^2 \mathbf{I}_L)$ and $\mathbf{Q}_u = \mathbf{q}_u \mathbf{q}_u^H = diag(\sigma_{q,u,1}^2 \mathbf{I}_L, \cdots, \sigma_{q,u,m_u}^2 \mathbf{I}_L)$.

2.4 Problem Formulation

Most existing works focused on maximizing the sum SE of users in the system, i.e. $\sum_1^K R_k$, which ignores user requirements, leads to poor insufficient user satisfaction and waste of resources. To solve this problem, we define the unmet system capacity ratio (USCR) in Eq. 9 (note that there is no extra benefit in providing data rate that exceeds the requirements) [12]:

$$USCR = \sum_1^K \max(R_{r,k} - R_k, 0) / \sum_1^K R_{r,k}, \tag{9}$$

where $R_{r,k}$ indicates the SE requirement of k-th user at the current time slot. In terms of constraints, we assume that both the uplink and downlink transmissions are limited by the maximum transmit power. To maximize QoS, our object is to minimizes USCR by allocating power subject to the constraints, as mentioned before, this can be formulated as the following mathematical program:

$$\begin{aligned} \min \quad & USCR \\ s.t. \quad & 0 \leq p_{d,m_d} \leq P_d, \\ & 0 \leq p_{u,k} \leq P_u, \end{aligned} \tag{10}$$

where Ineq. 10 indicates the lower and upper limits of transmission power of each DL-AP and user respectively.

3 The Power Allocation Based on Elite Genetic Algorithm

Due to the high computational cost of finding the optimal solution to solve the resource allocation problem, we turn to the metaheuristic optimization method. Genetic algorithm is one of the effective ways to address these problems, and in this section, we will briefly introduce the genetic algorithm. Genetic algorithm searches for optimal solutions by simulating natural evolutionary processes. The process of solving the problem is transformed into a process similar to the intersection and mutation of chromosomal genes in biological evolution. The basic framework of genetic algorithm includes encoding, initial population selection, genetic operations, and fitness function evaluation. The initial individuals are changed by genetic operators such as selection, crossover and variation. Finally, the individual with the greatest fitness will be selected as the optimal solution through the evaluation and the judgment of termination criterion.

Algorithm 1. Elite Genetic Algorithm-based Power Allocation

1: $pop \leftarrow$ INITPOPULATION(N_{ind})
2: **for** $gen = 1$ to N_{gen} **do**
3:      **for** ind in pop **do**
4:          $ind.fitness \leftarrow$ EVALUATESOLUTIONFITNESS(ind, env)
5:      **end for**
6:
7:      $elites, pop' \leftarrow$ SORTBYFITNESS(pop)
8:      $pop'' \leftarrow$ MAINTAINPOPULATION(pop')
9:
10:      $stop \leftarrow$ TERMINATIONCRITERION$()$
11:      **if** stop **then**
12:          **break**
13:      **end if**
14:
15:      $offspring \leftarrow$ TOURNAMENTSELECTION(pop'')
16:      $offspring' \leftarrow$ CROSSOVERANDMUTATION$(offspring)$
17:      $pop \leftarrow offspring' + elites$
18:
19: **end for**
20: **return** $pop.top$
21:
22: **function** EVALUATESOLUTIONFITNESS(ind, env)
23:      $ind \leftarrow$ CONSTRAINTHANDLING(ind)
24:      $scheme \leftarrow$ DEPLOYMENT(ind, env)
25:      $USCR \leftarrow$ CALCULATEUSCR$(scheme)$
26:      **return** $-USCR$
27: **end function**

Algorithm 1 presents details of our proposed algorithm. Initially, a population of individuals is created by assigning random values of power allocation vectors, and in practice, in order to avoid invalid search and speed up convergence, we take some proven excellent power allocation vectors as part of the initial individuals. Then, for each generation, all individuals will be evaluated and ranked. Next, to protect individuals with better fitness, the top ranked individuals will be set as elites according to the elite rate. In addition, to maintain the stability of the size of population, the last few individuals will be eliminated, while the others, a subset of individuals from the population will be selected and applied through the crossover and mutation operators. To be specific, crossover operations randomly combine the characteristics (some elements in the power distribution vector) of two individuals (parents) to produce a pair of new individuals (offspring), and mutation operations assign new values randomly to the power allocation vector, making it possible for the algorithm to derive different solutions. Finally, the offspring are born, and they will form a new population with the elites in the next generation. In order to ensure that the solution can be obtained in time, we set the maximum number of iterations of the algorithm, which means the process will continue until generation N_{gen} is reached. Furthermore, to avoid the algorithm falling into invalid iterations, we set termination criterion as well which will terminate the iterations when the convergence criterion in Ineq. 11 is met.

$$\frac{\max(USCR_{i-1}, \cdots, USCR_{i-20}) - USCR_i}{USCR_i} \leq threshold, \qquad (11)$$

where $USCR_i$ indicates the i-th generation lowest USCR and the convergence criterion ensures that the algorithm will stop when the optimization beyond the threshold cannot be achieved in all last 20 generations. In this paper, we generate new power allocation vectors through initialization, crossover and mutation. Then, the negative value of USCR is set as the fitness function to iteratively select the optimal power allocation vector that can minimize USCR. In addition, due to the limitation of uplink and downlink transmission power, when the total power allocated by the new power allocation vector is greater than the corresponding upper power limit, the allocated power needs to be reduced proportionally to ensure that the total power is no more than the corresponding upper power limit. Similarly, the allocated power will not be less than the lower power limit to ensure that it will not allocation negative power.

4   Numerical Results and Discussion

In this section, some numerical results are provided to validate the performance of our proposed scheme under different system parameters. We consider a cell-free system in a circular area, and in order to simplify the system, the density of uplink and downlink APs is equal to ρ_{AP}. Besides, we model the variance and mean value of user requirements as $\sigma^2(R_r)$ and R_r respectively. Moreover, the detailed system configurations are listed in Table 1 [13].

Table 1. Simulation parameters

Parameter	Value
Radius	120 m
Density of downlink/uplink users	0.001
Number of antennas	4
The maximum power of the DL-APs	30 dBm
The maximum power of the users	20 dBm
Path loss	128.1+27.6lg(d)
Lognormal shadowing	8 dB
Rayleigh fading	0 dB
Size of population	2000
Threshold	0.1%

Three commonly used algorithms are compared with ours: In Uniform Allocation, each transmitter allocates power uniformly to all receivers. While in Random Allocation, the transmitter randomly allocates power to the receivers. In Exclusive Allocation, the transmitter allocates all its power to a particular receiver which has the best channel state.

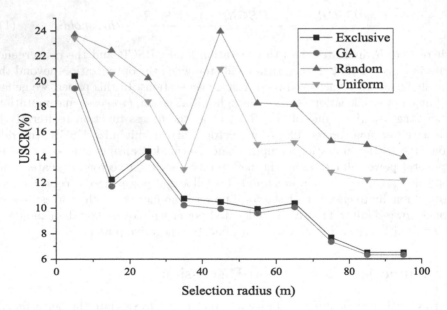

Fig. 2. USCR versus user selection radius with $\sigma^2(R_r) = 10, \overline{R_r} = 7bps/Hz$ and $\rho_{AP} = 0.01$

Figure 2 and Fig. 3 depict the user selection radius and density of AP versus USCR respectively. As we can see, the proposed scheme is superior to other

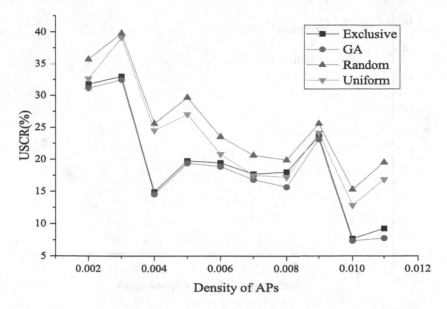

Fig. 3. USCR versus density of AP with $\sigma^2(R_r) = 10, \overline{R_r} = 7bps/Hz$ and $R_s = 75m$

schemes under various conditions. Specifically, as the user selection radius and density of AP increase, which means the number of APs increase, USCRs have the overall declining trend for all four schemes, which indicates that the increase in the number of APs can enhance the data rates and thus decrease the USCRs. However, all curves in the two figures do not monotonically decrease similarly also suggests that simply increasing the number of APs is not a panacea for our problems, it is because that as the number of APs increases, the complexity of the system increases as well, which leads to more interference that offsets the data rates it provides.

Figure 4 and Fig. 5 illustrate the mean value and variance of user requirements verse USCR respectively. As expected, the proposed scheme outperforms the traditional schemes under each user requirements case. In addition, the USCR of all four schemes increases with the mean value and variance of user requirements, but the proposed scheme increases more slowly and has a more significant advantage over the traditional allocation scheme especially when the mean value and variance of user requirements are large due to the ability to dynamically select a better power allocation method to meet the current user requirements and to achieve lower USCR.

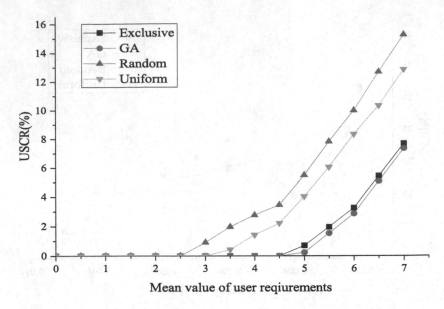

Fig. 4. USCR verses mean value of user requirements with $\sigma^2(R_r) = 10$, $R_s = 75m$ and $\rho_{AP} = 0.01$

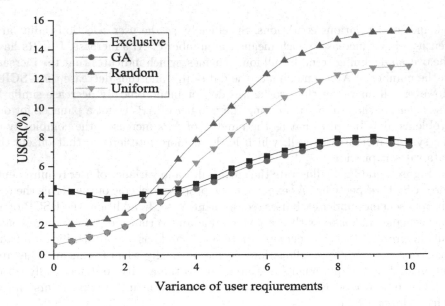

Fig. 5. USCR versus variance of user requirements with $\overline{R_r} = 7bps/Hz$, $R_s = 75m$ and $\rho_{AP} = 0.01$

5   Conclusion

In this paper, the power allocation problem in NAFD cell-free massive MIMO systems is investigated. The USCR is minimized by adjusting the power distribution method according to the dynamic user requirements. An elite genetic algorithm-based power allocation algorithm is proposed to solve this problem. Simulation results show that the proposed scheme achieves higher improvements than the uniform, exclusive and random allocations under various user requirements. In future work, we will study the power allocation method with user fairness in continuous communication scenarios.

References

1. Zhang, J., Bjornson, E., Matthaiou, M., Ng, D.W.K., Yang, H., Love, D.J.: Prospective multiple antenna technologies for beyond 5G. IEEE J. Sel. Areas Commun. **38**(8), 1637–1660 (2020)
2. Chen, S., Zhang, J., Bjornson, E., Zhang, J., Ai, B.: Structured massive access for scalable cell-free massive MIMO systems. IEEE J. Sel. Areas Commun. **39**(4), 1086–100 (2021)
3. Xia, X., et al.: Joint user selection and transceiver design for cell-free with network-assisted full duplexing. IEEE Trans. Wirel. Commun. **20**(12), 7856–7870 (2021)
4. Bjornson, E., Sanguinetti, L.: Making cell-free massive MIMO competitive with MMSE processing and centralized implementation. IEEE Trans. Wirel. Commun. **19**(1), 77–90 (2020)
5. Mai, T.C., Ngo, H.Q., Tran, L.-N.: Energy efficiency maximization in large-scale cell-free massive MIMO: a projected gradient approach. arXiv preprint arXiv:2201.08136 (2022)
6. Qiu, J., et al.: Secure transmission scheme based on fingerprint positioning in cell-free massive MIMO systems. IEEE Trans. Signal Inf. Process. Netw. **8**(8), 92–105 (2022)
7. Papazafeiropoulos, A., Kourtessis, P., Renzo, M.D., Chatzinotas, S., Senior, J.M.: Performance analysis of cell-free massive MIMO systems: a stochastic geometry approach. IEEE Trans. Veh. Technol. **69**(4), 3523–3537 (2020)
8. Ngo, H.Q., Ashikhmin, A., Yang, H., Larsson, E.G., Marzetta, T.L.: Cell-free massive MIMO versus small cells. IEEE Trans. Wirel. Commun. **16**(3), 1834–1850 (2017)
9. Shakya, I.L., Ali, F.H.: Joint access point selection and interference cancellation for cell-free massive MIMO. IEEE Commun. Lett. **25**(4), 1313–1317 (2021)
10. Wang, D., Wang, M., Zhu, P., Li, J., Wang, J., You, X.: Performance of network-assisted full-duplex for cell-free massive MIMO. IEEE Trans. Commun. **68**(3), 1464–1478 (2020)
11. Guo, M., Gursoy, M.C.: Joint activity detection and channel estimation in cell-free massive MIMO networks with massive connectivity. IEEE Trans. Commun. **70**(1), 317–331 (2022)
12. Paris, A., Del Portillo, I., Cameron, B., Crawley, E.: A genetic algorithm for joint power and bandwidth allocation in multibeam satellite systems. In: 2019 IEEE Aerospace Conference, Big Sky, MT, USA, pp. 1–15. IEEE (2019)
13. Xia, X., Zhu, P., Li, J., Wang, D., Xin, Y., You, X.: Joint sparse beamforming and power control for a large-scale DAS with network-assisted full duplex. IEEE Trans. Veh. Technol. **69**(7), 7569–7582 (2020)

DPNet: Depth and Pose Net for Novel View Synthesis via Depth Map Estimation

Ge Zhu, Yu Liu[✉], and Yumei Wang

Institute of Artificial Intelligence, Beijing University of Posts
and Telecommunications, Beijing, China
{zhuge2020110241,liuy,ymwang}@bupt.edu.cn

Abstract. Novel view synthesis is regarded as one of the efficient ways to realize stereoscopic vision, which paves the way to virtual reality. Image-based rendering (IBR) is one of the view synthesis strategies, which warps pixels from source views to target views in order to protect low-level details. However, IBR methods predict the pixels correspondence in an unsupervised way and have limits in getting accurate pixels. In this paper, we propose Depth and Pose Net (DPNet) for novel view synthesis via depth map estimation. We introduce two nearby views as implicit supervision to improve the pixels correspondence accuracy. Besides, the depth net firstly predicts the source depth map and then the pose net transforms the source depth map to the target depth map which is used to calculate pixels correspondence. Experimental results show that DPNet generates accurate depth maps and thus synthesizes novel views with higher quality than state-of-the-art methods on the synthetic object and real scene datasets.

Keywords: view synthesis · IBR · depth map · pixels correspondence · DPNet

1 Introduction

Novel view synthesis (NVS) solves the problem of generating new view images of a scene or an object in the condition that one or more input views are given, which can be used to generate all possible viewpoints of real-world scenes in virtual reality (VR). As shown in Fig. 1, given one image of the chair, we generate a new image of the same chair from a novel viewpoint (GT represents the real target view image). However, traditional NVS methods often rely on parallax plots or depth maps, which have the limitations of high computational costs. With the development of neural networks, supervision-based learning methods can synthesize high-quality novel views. NVS can be used in different application areas, including image editing, and animating still photographs.

© ICST Institute for Computer Sciences, Social Informatics and Telecommunications Engineering 2023
Published by Springer Nature Switzerland AG 2023. All Rights Reserved
F. Gao et al. (Eds.): ChinaCom 2022, LNICST 500, pp. 294–308, 2023.
https://doi.org/10.1007/978-3-031-34790-0_23

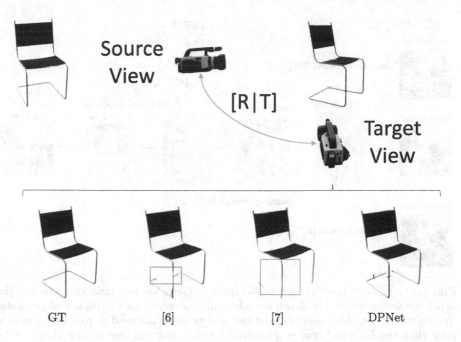

Fig. 1. With an input image, a novel view of the same object or scene is synthesized. It shows the results of DPNet compared to other two methods and all of them synthesis the target view by predicting target depth map. □ and □ prove that DPNet produces more clear result than other two depth guided view synthesis methods (Color figure online)

The NVS methods that have been approached in the last few years fall into two main types: 3D geometry-based methods and IBR methods. For 3D geometry-based methods, comprehensive 3D understanding is important so that the first step is to get the approximate underlying 3D structure. Some methods estimate the underlying 3D geometry in form of voxels [1] and mesh [2], and then put the corresponding camera transformations to the pixels of the 3D structure to produce the final output [3]. However, they not only require a commitment of time and resources, but also produce holes where lack of a prior information. In such conditions, hole-filling algorithms are needed but sometimes these algorithms are not effective [4].

Unlike 3D geometry-based methods, IBR methods generate novel images based on input images. The pixels from source views can be reprojected to the target view, low-level details such as colors and textures are well-protected. Zhou et al. [5] directly estimates the appearance flow and get final pixels value of target views from input views, and Chen et al. [6] predicts the target depth map to obtain the pixel-to-pixel correspondences with 3D warping. Hou et al. [7] also predicts the depth map of target view, but warps feature maps to generate the final target view image rather than directly warping pixels from source view. These IBR methods all achieve great view synthesis quality.

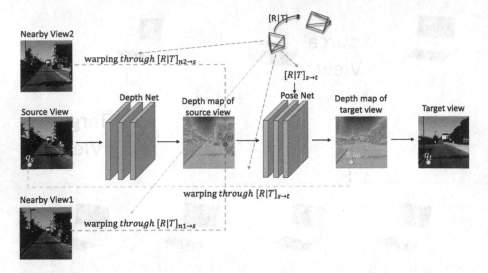

Fig. 2. Overview of the view synthesis pipeline. There are two main components: the depth net and pose net. The depth net takes only the source view as input and generates the depth map $\hat{D}_s$. Moreover, $\hat{D}_s$ and two nearby views are used to reconstruct source view that the L1 loss between generated source view and real source view can be alleviated to train the depth net. Then the pose net extracts the feature points of $\hat{D}_s$ to produce the depth map of target view $\hat{D}_t$ Finally, the $\hat{D}_t$ is used to warp pixels of source to the target view with bilinear interpolation.

In this paper, we design a reasonable frameworks to improve the view synthesis quality. Motivated by the advantage of IBR method, we take the method that it warps pixels from source view to target view with the help of target depth map. More specifically, we propose the DPNet consisting of a depth net and a pose net as shown in Fig. 2. DPNet firstly predicts the source depth map and subsequently deduces the target depth map rather than directly producing target depth map. In such way, the short-connection structure can be introduced into pose net. So multi-level feature maps extracted from source depth map can be transferred to target depth map to improve the depth map accuracy. To further improve the accuracy of predicted depth map of source view, two nearby view images are reprojected to source view through predicted depth map of source view. Then the camera transformation and the predicted source depth map are put into pose net to generate the target depth map. Subsequently, the generated target depth map is used to calculate the dense correspondences between the source view and the target view via perspective projection. Finally, the final output image is synthesized via pixel warping.

To get clear and continuous synthesis results, four specially designed loss functions are used to train the DPNet. The supervision loss is used to improve the depth map estimation accuracy. And the L1 reconstruction loss and VGG perceptual loss are used to generate realistic images. Moreover, the edge smoothness loss can make the final target depth map more continuous in edge. Detailed experiments are conducted on real scene [8] and synthetic object [9] datasets, the depth estimation accuracy and image quality are evaluated qualitatively and quantitatively. The experiment results demonstrate that DPNet actually improves the depth estimation accuracy and image quality.

2 Related Work

Study of novel view synthesis has a long history in computer vision and graphics. These researches differ based on whether they use pure images or 3D geometry structure and on whether a single view image or multiple view images are put into neural network. Recently, neural radiance fields and generative models are the new directions.

2.1 Geometric View Synthesis

If multiple images of a scene are provided, with the help of COLMAP [10,11], a 3D geometry scaffold can be constructed. Riegler et al. [3] firstly ran structure-from-motion [10] to get camera intrinsic and camera poses, then ran multi-view stereo [11] on the posed images to obtain per-image depth maps, and finally fused these maps into a point cloud. Similarly, Penner et al. [12] warped the extracted source feature maps into the target view using the depth map which was derived from the 3D geometry scaffold. A confidence image and a color image for each input image are obtained through these warped feature maps. Then these confidence images and color images were aggregated to get a final output. More recently, deep learning techniques created a new level of possibility and flexibility. Lombardi et al. [13] learned an implicit voxel representation of an object given many training views and generated a new view of that object when tested.

2.2 3D from Single Image

Inference about 3D shapes can serve as an implicit step in view synthesis. Given the serious inadequacy of recovering 3D shapes from a single image, recent work deployed neural networks for this task. They could be categorized by their output representation into mesh, point cloud, and voxel. With a single image as input, Tatarchenko et al. [14] predicted many unseen views and their depth maps from input, and these views were fused into a 3D point cloud which was later optimized to obtain a mesh. In [4], the features extracted from single input and the depth map estimated from the same input were used to create a point cloud carrying features. Many works explore using a DNN to predict 3D object shapes [15] or the depth map of a scene given an image [16]. These works focus on the quality of the 3D predictions as opposed to the view-synthesis task.

2.3 Image-Based Rendering Methods

Recently, many deep neural networks are developed to learn the image-to-image mapping between source view and target view [5–7,17,18]. Zhou *et al.* [5] directly estimated the appearance flow map in order to warp pixels of source view to their position of target view, Sun *et al.* [17] further refined the output by fusing multiple views with confidence map. With the help of predicted target depth map, Chen *et al.* [6] directly warped pixels of source view to target view and Hou *et al.* [7] warped the multi-level feature map extracted from source view to synthesize the final output. To improve the quality of synthesized image, Park *et al.* [18] used two consecutive encoder-decoder networks, firstly predicting a disocclusion aware flow and then refining the transformed image with a completion network. And in this paper, the target depth map couldn't be predicted from inputs directly, instead, the source depth map is firstly estimated by depth net and then the source depth net is transformed to target depth map through pose net.

2.4 Generative Models and Neural Radiance Fields

View synthesis can also be thought as an image generation task, and it has a lot to do with the field of generative modeling of images [19,20]. In [21], explicit pose control was allowed, they also used voxel. Although these methods can be used for view synthesis, the resulting view lacks consistency and has no control over the objects to be synthesized. The neural radiation field [22] produced impressive results by training an multi-layer perception (MLP) to map 3D rays to occupancy and color. Images are synthesized from this representation by volume rendering. This approach has been extended to an unlimited collection of outdoor scenes and crowdsourced images.

3 The Proposed Method for Novel View Synthesis

Figure 2 shows an overview of DPNet, it consists of two subnets: the depth net Ψ_D and the pose net Ψ_P. The depth net estimates the depth map of source view firstly. For the depth net, we use the skip-connection structure with four downsampling and upsampling layers to give a final prediction of the same spatial resolution with the input. This is followed by a sigmoid layer and a renormalization step, so the depth of prediction falls within the minimum and maximum values for each dataset. The predicted depth map is used to warp two nearby view images to source view, and L1 distance between generated source view and real source view is used to train the depth net. As for pose net, the given transformation matrix is applied on the 3D feature points extracted from the

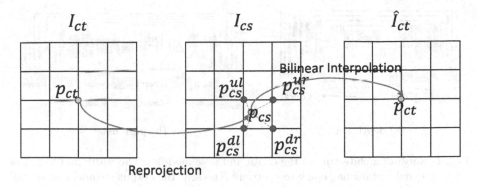

Fig. 3. Illustration of the pixels warping process from source view to target view. For each pixel point p_{ct} in the target view, it is firstly reprojected onto the source view based on the predicted depth map and camera pose transformation, and then the pixels value in target view are obtained by bilinear interpolation.

predicted source depth map to obtain the 3D feature points of the target depth map. Later, when the transformed 3D feature points are given, the depth map of the target view is predicted. Then the estimated depth map is used to find dense correspondences between target and source views. Finally, the source image is warped into the target image via bilinear interpolation.

3.1 Pixels Warping

The reprojection process and the bilinear interpolation process are shown in Fig. 3. For the reprojection process, the per-pixel correspondence C is obtained from the target depth map D_{ct} by converting from a depth map to 3D coordinates [X, Y, Z] and perspective projections:

$$[X, Y, Z]^T = D_{ct}(x_{ct}, y_{ct}) K^{-1} [x_{ct}, y_{ct}, 1]^T, \tag{1a}$$

$$[x_{cs}, y_{cs}, 1]^T \sim T_{ct \to cs} [X, Y, Z, 1]^T, \tag{1b}$$

where each pixel (x_{ct}, y_{ct}) in the target view corresponds to the pixel position (x_{cs}, y_{cs}) in the source view. Moreover, K is the camera intrinsic matrix and $T_{ct \to cs}$ represents the transformation matrix from target view to source view. For the bilinear interpolation process, with the obtained per-pixel correspondences $C_{ct \to cs}$, the pixels in the correspondences source view can be warped to the correspondences target view:

$$I_{ct}(x_{ct}, y_{ct}) = \sum_{x_{cs}} \sum_{y_{cs}} max(0, 1 - |x_{cs} - C_{ct \to cs}(x_{ct}, y_{ct})|)$$
$$max(0, 1 - |y_{cs} - C_{ct \to cs}(x_{ct}, y_{ct})|) I_{cs}(x_{cs}, y_{cs}). \tag{2}$$

Introducing the intermediate step of predicting depth map enforces the network to adhere to geometric constraints, resolving ambiguous correspondences. This process is substituted by $I_{ct} = PW(I_{cs}, D_{ct}, T_{ct \to cs})$.

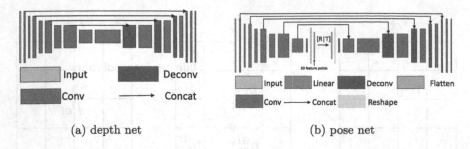

(a) depth net   (b) pose net

Fig. 4. Network architecture of the depth and pose modules. The width and height of each blue/red rectangular block respectively represent the output channel and spatial dimension of the feature map at the corresponding layer, and each decrease/increase in width and height size represents a change by the factor of 2 (the last conv layer is the output, it does not obey the rules). For depth net, it consists of 4 downsampling lawyers and 4 upsampling lawyers with the skip-connection structure. For pose net, inspired by [6], we also extract the latent code (3D feature points) to inject the camera transformation and predict the target depth map. (Color figure online)

3.2 Depth Map Estimation

The depth net takes a single input image to get the source depth map $D_s = \Psi_D(I_s)$. Moreover, two additional nearby view images I_{n1} and I_{n2} plus their camera transformation $T_{s\to n1}$ and $T_{s\to n2}$ are introduced to warp their pixels to source view to improve the depth estimation accuracy. $\hat{I}_{s1} = PW(I_{n1}, D_s, T_{s\to n1})$ and

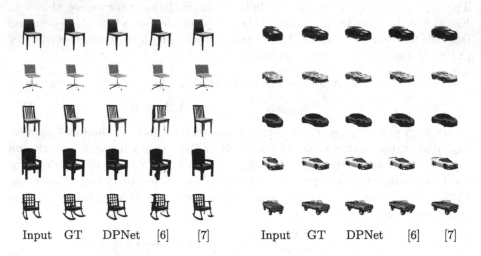

Input   GT   DPNet   [6]   [7]   Input   GT   DPNet   [6]   [7]

Fig. 5. Results on ShapeNet chair and car datasets. DPNet generates more structure-consistent predictions than [6] (for example, it can't generate a distorted leg in line 5); on the other hand, the generated images of the DPNet are more clear than [7] that it can rebuild rich low-level details (for example, it generates more clear chair surface in line 2).

$\hat{I}_{s2} = PW(I_{n2}, D_s, T_{s \to n2})$. And the two L1 distance between I_s and $\hat{I}_{s1}$ and between I_s and $\hat{I}_{s2}$ are the important part of final training loss function. The specific structure is described in Fig. 4(a), it consists of four downsampling layers and four upsampling layers, and the skip-connection structure transfers multi-level feature maps to create more stable predictions.

3.3 Depth Map Transformation and Target View Generation

In pose net, transformation matrix are applied to latent code to predict depth map of the target view, and the pose network is used to learn compact latent representations that are transformation equivariant. Given the source depth map, the 3D feature points z_s extracted from predicted source depth map can be regarded as a set of points $z_s \in R^{n \times 3}$. Then the 3D feature points are multiplied with the given transformation $T_{s \to t} = [R|t]_{s \to t}$ to get the transformed 3D feature points for the target view:

$$\widetilde{z}_s = T_{s \to t} \cdot \dot{z}_s \tag{3}$$

where $\dot{z}_s$ is the homogeneous representation of z_s. Then the target depth map D_t is created through $\widetilde{z}_s$. With the generated target depth map D_t and corresponding camera transformation $T_{s \to t}$, the target view image is synthesized $\hat{I}_t = PW(I_s, D_t, T_{t \to s})$. Because the input to pose net is a source depth map and not a source view image, the skip-connection structure can be introduced to transfer multi-level feature maps to make the pose net more effective (as shown in Fig. 4(b)).

3.4 Training Loss Functions

The framework can be trained in an end-to-end manner. For each input sample, a single source image, two nearby view images, one target view image and their relative transformation are provided. The depth net and the pose net are optimized jointly. To train the depth net in an implicit supervised manner, the supervision loss is used to improve the depth map estimation accuracy. For pixels regression, the L1 reconstruction loss and VGG perceptual loss are used to

Table 1. Results on ShapeNet objects. DPNet performs better than [6,7] for both chair and car objects, showing that it can deal with complex shape of chairs and rich colors and textures of cars ($\downarrow$ suggests the smaller the better, $\uparrow$ suggests the larger the better).

METHODS	CHAIR		CAR	
	L1$\downarrow$	SSIM$\uparrow$	L1$\downarrow$	SSIM$\uparrow$
Chen *et al.* [6]	0.0559	0.9224	0.0338	0.9424
Hou *et al.* [7]	0.0583	0.9237	0.0346	0.9392
DPNet	**0.0413**	**0.9381**	**0.0295**	**0.9491**

generate realistic images. Moreover, the edge smoothness loss can make the final target depth map more continuous in edge.

L1 Reconstruction Loss. The L1 reconstruction loss is the L1 loss between the predicted target view $\hat{I}_t$ and the ground truth I_t. Described as:

$$L_{recon} = \|\hat{I}_t - I_t\| \tag{4}$$

To minimize this reconstruction loss, the network learns to produce realistic new views by predicting the necessary depth maps.

Supervision Loss. The supervision loss consists of two parts, both of them are the L1 distance between the ground truth source view I_s and the generated source view $\hat{I}_s$:

$$L_{sup} = \|\hat{I}_{s1} - I_s\| + \|\hat{I}_{s2} - I_s\| \tag{5}$$

To minimize this supervision loss, the depth net learns to produce more accurate source depth map.

VGG Perceptual Loss. In addition to the L1 reconstruction loss, we also employ VGG perceptual loss to obtain realistic synthesis results. The pre-trained VGG16 network is used to extract features from the generated fake results and ground-truth images, and the perceptual loss is the sum of feature distances (L1 distance) calculated from multiple layers.

Edge Smoothness Loss. The edge smoothness loss encourages local smoothing of the predicted depth map. The loss is weighted because depth discontinuities usually occur at the edges of the image:

$$L_{edge} = \frac{1}{N} \sum_{i,j} |\partial x \widetilde{D}_t^{ij}| e^{-\|\partial x I_t^{ij}\|} + |\partial y \widetilde{D}_t^{ij}| e^{-\|\partial y I_t^{ij}\|} \tag{6}$$

where $\widetilde{D}_t$ is the predicted depth map of the target view and I_t is the ground-truth target view.

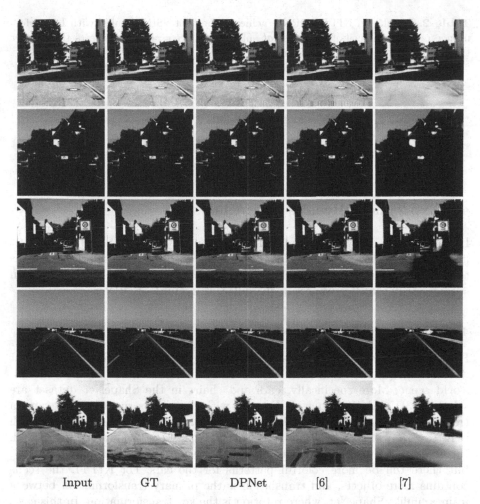

| Input | GT | DPNet | [6] | [7] |

Fig. 6. Qualitative results of KITTI. DPNet produces clear and structurally consistent predictions, while the depth guided pixels warping [6] method produces distortion and the depth guided multi-level feature map warping method [7] produces blurry .

In summary, the final loss function of the joint training framework will be:

$$L = \lambda_r L_{recon} + \lambda_s L_{sup} + \lambda_v L_{vgg} + \lambda_e L_{edge} \tag{7}$$

where the λ_r, λ_s, λ_v, and λ_e are weights for different loss functions.

Table 2. Results on KITTI. DPNet achieves the best SSIM results, with L1 performance outperforming both Chen *et al.* [6] and Hou *et al.* [7]. (↓ suggests the smaller the better, ↑ suggests the larger the better).

METHODS	KITTI	
	L1↓	SSIM↑
Chen *et al.* [6]	0.1803	0.6751
Hou *et al.* [7]	0.1635	0.7253
DPNet	**0.1634**	**0.7273**

4 Experiment Results and Analysis

In this section, experiments are conduct on public datasets, ShapeNet dataset [8] and KITTI dataset [9]. DPNet is compared with state-of-the-art algorithms to evaluate the performance qualitatively and quantitatively. Further ablation studies verify the effectiveness of the different modules of DPNet.

4.1 Dataset and Experiment Setup

For datasets, two different types of datasets are used for experiment: ShapeNet dataset [8] is used for synthetic objects and KITTI dataset [9] is used for real-world scene. More specifically, cars and chairs in the ShapeNet dataset are selected. 3D understanding of datasets with complex structures and camera transformations are a great challenge (*e.g.* depth estimation) and datasets with rich textures will show whether these methods preserve fine-grained detail well. In these selected datasets, the chairs have more complex shapes and structures, but there will be more colorful patterns for the cars. For KITTI, the scene contains more objects, and translation is the primary transformation between frames, unlike ShapeNet, where rotation is the key transformation. In this case, there is less need for accurate depth estimation, and the ability to recover low-level detail is more important for performance.

ShapeNet.   Rendered images are used with the dimension of 256×256 from 54 viewpoints (the azimuth from $0°$ to $360°$ with $20°$ increments, and the elevation of $0°$, $10°$, and $20°$) for each object. The training and test pairs are two views with the azimuth difference within the range $[-40°, 40°]$. For ShapeNet chairs, there are 558 chair objects in the training set and 140 chair objects in the test set; For ShapeNet cars, there are 5,997 car objects in the training set and 1,500 car objects in the test set.

KITTI.   There are 11 sequences and each sequence contains around 2,000 frames on average. The training pairs are restricted to be separated by at most 7 frames.

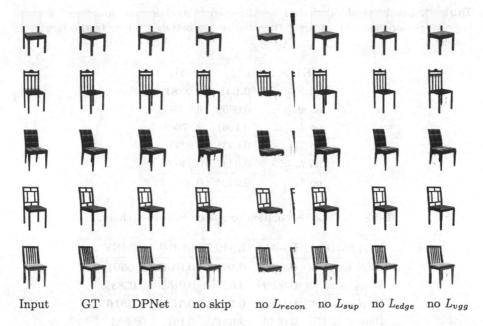

Input   GT   DPNet   no skip   no L_{recon} no L_{sup} no L_{edge} no L_{vgg}

Fig. 7. Ablation studies results. We compare the performance of the full model with its variants. The results show that the lack of L_{recon} leads to incomplete objects (like the chair in the 5th column). The lack of skip-connection structure in depth net and pose net results in the chair leg shortage (like the chair in the 5th column). The L_{vgg} makes the results sharper. And the L_{sup} and the L_{edge} leads to more accurate depth map estimation that it makes the results more stable.

For experiment setup, the depth net and the pose net are jointly trained using the Adam solver same with [7] that $\beta_1 = 0.9$ and $\beta_2 = 0.99$, and learning rate of 6×10^{-5}.

4.2 Evaluation Metrics and Evaluation Results

For evaluation metrics, Mean Absolute Error (L_1 error) and Structural SIMilarity (SSIM) Index are used as metrics to evaluate the synthetic results. For L1 metric, smaller is better; for the SSIM metric, larger is better. For image synthesis quality, DPNet is compared with two state-of-the-art depth map guided methods: one pixels warping method proposed by [6] and one multi-level feature map warping method proposed by [7]. For depth map estimation, DPNet is compared with one source depth map estimation method [4] and one target depth map estimation method [6]. Table 1 shows the results on test set of ShapeNet objects. DPNet performs best for both the chair and the car objects, showing that it can handle both the complex 3D structure of the chair and the rich texture of the car. Fig. 5 shows the qualitative results for all methods. The depth map guided pixels warping method [6] suffers from distortion and the depth map guided multi-level feature maps warping method [7] leads to blurry results. Two

Table 3. Results of ablation studies. All designed modules and loss functions help improve performance. (↓ suggests the smaller the better, ↑ suggests the larger the better).

METHODS	L1↓	SSIM↑
DPNet	**0.0414**	**0.9381**
no skip	0.0609	0.9199
no L_{recon}	0.1261	0.8786
no L_{sup}	0.0538	0.9295
no L_{edge}	0.0437	0.9360
no L_{vgg}	0.0423	0.9361

Table 4. Depth estimation results on ShapeNet chairs.

METHODS	L1-ALL	L1-REL	L1-INV	SC-INV
DPNet-source	**0.0576**	**0.0286**	**0.0145**	**0.0501**
Wiles *et al.* [4]	0.0699	0.0354	0.0184	0.0583
DPNet-target	**0.0598**	**0.0294**	**0.155**	**0.0516**
Hou *et al.* [7]	0.0610	0.0305	0.161	0.0523

nearby views are introduced to improve the accuracy of depth map estimation so that more impressive results are generated (*e.g.*, more complete chair leg and more detailed car roof are generated in line 5). All the methods are also evaluated on KITTI. Table 2 shows the quantitative results. DPNet performs better than [6] and obtains comparable results to [7]. Figure 6 shows the qualitative results, it can be seen that DPNet produces more clear predictions and better preserves the structure (check the bottom part of row 1, manhole cover in row 5). In a conclusion, DPNet can achieve high image synthesis quality.

4.3   Ablation Studies and Depth Estimation Results

To understand how the different modules of the framework work, we conduct an ablation study on ShapeNet chair as it is the most challenging dataset for 3D structures. Figure 7 and Table 3 show the performance of the different variants. No skip stands for removing the skip-connection structure in depth net and pose net. No L_{recon}, no L_{sup}, no L_{edge}, no L_{vgg} separately represents removing corresponding loss function from total loss function. The results show that the lack of L_{recon} leads to incomplete objects (like the chair in the 5th column). The lack of skip-connection structure in depth net and pose net leads to the chair leg shortage (like the chair in the 5th column). The L_{vgg} makes the results sharper. And the L_{sup} and the L_{edge} leads to more accurate depth map estimation that it makes the results more stable.

Moreover, to prove that more accurate depth maps are predicted, four metrics are used to evaluate depth map quality [7]. L1-all compute the mean absolute difference. L1-rel compute the mean absolute relative difference L1-rel $= \frac{1}{n}\sum_i |gt_i - pred_i|/gt_i$, and L1-inv metric is mean absolute difference in inverse depth L1-inv $= \frac{1}{n}\sum_i |gt_i^{-1} - pred_i^{-1}|$. Except L1 metrics, we also utilize sc-inv $= \left(\frac{1}{n}\sum z_i^2 - \frac{1}{n^2}\left(\sum z_i\right)^2\right)^{\frac{1}{2}}$, where $z_i = \lg(pred_i) - \lg(gt_i)$. The source depth map estimation is compared with [4] and the target depth map estimation is compared with [6]. Table 4 shows that our predicted depth is more accurate, which can explain why the DPNet can achieve better results than other methods.

5   Conclusion and Discussion

In this paper, DPNet is put forth to solve the novel view synthesis task. And it consists of two subnets: depth net and pose net. The depth net predicts the depth map of the source view from a single input view and two nearby view images are introduced to improve the accuracy of predicted depth map. Then the pose net is used for transformation between source depth map and target depth map. Moreover, the warping from source view pixels to target view pixels enables the preservation of low-level details, so more clear predictions are produced. Experimental results show that compared with above depth map guided warping methods, the performance of DPNet is better.

References

1. Choy, C.B., Xu, D., Gwak, J., Chen, K., Savarese, S.: A unified approach for single and multi-view 3d object reconstruction. In: European Conference on Computer Vision, pp. 628–644(2016)
2. Kato, H., Ushiku, Y., Harada, T.: Neural 3d mesh renderer. In: Proceedings of the IEEE Conference on Computer Vision and Pattern Recognition, pp. 3907–3916(2018)
3. Riegler, G., Koltun, V.: Stable view synthesis. In: Proceedings of the IEEE/CVF Conference on Computer Vision and Pattern Recognition, pp. 12216–12225 (2021)
4. Wiles, O., Gkioxari, G., Szeliski, R., Johnson, J.: Synsin: End-to-end view synthesis from a single image. In: Proceedings of the IEEE/CVF Conference on Computer Vision and Pattern Recognition, pp. 7467–7477 (2020)
5. Zhou, T., Tulsiani, S., Sun, W., et al.: View synthesis by appearance flow. In: European Conference on Computer Vision, pp. 286–301 (2016)
6. Chen, X., Song, J., Hilliges, O.: Monocular neural image based rendering with continuous view control. In: Proceedings of the IEEE/CVF International Conference on Computer Vision, pp. 4090–4100 (2019)
7. Hou, Y., Solin, A., Kannala, J.: Novel view synthesis via depth-guided skip connections. In: Proceedings of the IEEE/CVF Winter Conference on Applications of Computer Vision, pp. 3119–3128 (2021)
8. Chang, A., X., Funkhouser, T., Guibas, L., et al. Shapenet: An information-rich 3d model repository. In: IEEE Conference on Computer Vision and Pattern Recognition, pp. 1512–3012 (2015)

9. Geiger, A., Lenz, P., Urtasun, R.: Are we ready for autonomous driving? The KITTI vision benchmark suite. In: IEEE Conference on Computer Vision and Pattern Recognition, pp. 3354–3361 (2012)

10. Schonberger, J.L., Frahm, M.: Structure-from-motion revisited. In: Proceedings of the IEEE Conference on Computer Vision and Pattern Recognition, pp. 4104–4113 (2016)

11. Schönberger, J.L., Zheng, E., Frahm, J.M., et al.: Pixelwise view selection for unstructured multi-view stereo. In: European Conference on Computer Vision, pp. 501–518 (2016)

12. Penner, E., Zhang, L.: Soft 3D reconstruction for view synthesis. In: ACM Transactions on Graphics, pp. 1–11 (2017)

13. Lombardi, S., Simon, T., Saragih, J., et al.: Neural volumes: Learning dynamic renderable volumes from images. arXiv preprint 2019)

14. Tatarchenko, M., Dosovitskiy, A., Brox, T.: Multi-view 3d models from single images with a convolutional network. In: European Conference on Computer Vision, pp. 322–337 (2016)

15. Insafutdinov, E., Dosovitskiy, A.: Unsupervised learning of shape and pose with differentiable point clouds. In: Proceedings of the 32nd International Conference on Neural Information Processing Systems, pp. 2807–2817 (2018)

16. Li, Z., Snavely, N.: Megadepth: Learning single-view depth prediction from internet photos. In: Proceedings of the IEEE Conference on Computer Vision and Pattern Recognition, pp. 2041–2050 (2018)

17. Sun, S.H., Huh, M., Liao, Y.H., et al.:Multi-view to novel view: Synthesizing novel views with self-learned confidence. In: Proceedings of the European Conference on Computer Vision, pp. 155–171(2018)

18. Park, E., Yang, J., Yumer, E., et al.:Transformation-grounded image generation network for novel 3d view synthesis. In: Proceedings of the IEEE Conference on Computer Vision and Pattern Recognition, pp. 3500–3509 (2017)

19. Goodfellow, I., Pouget-Abadie, J., Mirza, M., et al.: Generative adversarial nets. Commun. ACM **63**(11), 139–144 (2020)

20. Brock, A., Donahue, J., Simonyan, K.: Large scale GAN training for high fidelity natural image synthesis. arXiv preprint (2018)

21. Nguyen-Phuoc, T., Li, C., Theis, L., et al.:Hologan: Unsupervised learning of 3d representations from natural images. In: Proceedings of the IEEE/CVF International Conference on Computer Vision, pp. 7588–7597 (2019)

22. Niemeyer, M., Mescheder, L., Oechsle, M., et al.: Differentiable volumetric rendering: Learning implicit 3d representations without 3d supervision. In: Proceedings of the IEEE/CVF Conference on Computer Vision and Pattern Recognition, pp. 3504–3515 (2020)

Vehicle Trajectory Prediction Model Based on Fusion Neural Network

Xuemei Mou[✉], Xiang Yu, Binbin Wang, Ziyi Wang, and Fugui Deng

School of Communication and Information Engineering, Chongqing University of Posts and Telecommunications, Chongqing, China
mouxuemei175101@163.com

Abstract. To address the problem of the lack of interpretability of vehicle trajectory prediction models based on deep learning, this paper proposes a Fusion Neural network with the Spatio-Temporal Attention (STA-FNet) model. The model outputs a predictive distribution of future vehicle trajectories based on different vehicle trajectories and traffic environment factors, with an in-depth analysis of the Spatio-temporal attention weights learned from various urban road traffic scenarios. In this paper, the proposed model is evaluated using the publicly available NGSIM dataset, and the experimental results show that the model not only explains the influence of historical trajectories and road traffic environment on the target vehicle trajectories but also obtains better prediction results in complex traffic environments.

Keywords: Intelligent traffic · Trajectory prediction · Deep learning · Spatial-temporal relationships

1 Introduction

Urban traffic congestion is becoming increasingly serious, and accurate prediction of vehicle trajectories is crucial for urban intelligent transportation. Currently, most trajectory predictions rely mainly on historical traffic data to predict and find rules from temporal features [1–3]. In recent years, with the development of neural network models, more and more scholars use neural networks as trajectory prediction models. Yang et al. [4] used Long Short Term Memory (LSTM) to predict the trajectory of the preceding vehicle with good results by joint time series modeling of vehicles with different driving styles around the target vehicle. Kaushik et al. [5] used Recurrent Neural Network (RNN) model to analyze the real-time series data acquired by in-vehicle sensors and the model showed good performance in predicting the future trajectory of an obstacle vehicle.

In complex data prediction, it is often difficult for a single model to capture the complexity and variability of trajectory data at the same time, failing to maintain good prediction performance, while combined models have good results. Ip et al. [6] utilize a combined model of LSTM and RNN to predict vehicle trajectories in the case the current

F. Gao et al. (Eds.): ChinaCom 2022, LNICST 500, pp. 309–320, 2023.
https://doi.org/10.1007/978-3-031-34790-0_24

and previous positions of the vehicle are known. Rossi et al. [7] used a combined model of LSTM and Generative Adversarial Network (GAN) to predict vehicle trajectories and performed well in scenes with high multimodal effects. Based on the data collected by the sensor, Wang et al. [8] used the combined model of Convolutional Neural Network (CNN) and RNN to conduct an in-depth analysis of the vehicle motion data collected by the sensor, to achieve the purpose of protecting the scene texture information of the environment and the interaction between the surrounding vehicles.

The attention mechanism proposed by Bahdanau et al. [9] can be naturally integrated with RNN to improve model interpretability. Cai et al. [10] used Graph Convolution Network (GCN) to pay attention to the interaction between the vehicle and the non-Euclidean-related structures existing in the environment and used the attention mechanism to enhance the extraction of image features by GCN. Yu et al. [11] managed the importance of the driving flow of the target and neighboring vehicles and the dynamics of the target vehicle in each driving situation by using an attention mechanism and utilizing LSTM to predict future trajectories.

To sum up, most of the related research focuses on the prediction of the vehicle's motion state and historical trajectory, while the interaction between the target vehicle and the road traffic environment, the spatial position of the surrounding vehicles, and the interaction with the target vehicle still need further research. Taking this as a motivation, this paper proposes a Fusion Neural Network with Spatio-Temporal Attention (STA-FNet) model through the analysis of the real urban vehicle running state data set. To predict the trajectory, it is proposed to extract the Spatio-temporal relationship between the target vehicle, surrounding vehicles, and road environment information through a model combined with a Convolutional Social pooling (CS) and a Bidirectional Recurrent Gating Unit (BiGRU). The main contributions of this paper are as follows:

1. Combination of BiGRU and CS, a novel and robust vehicle trajectory prediction structure are proposed. The model can not only explain the Spatio-temporal features between vehicle trajectory data but also quantify these factors for trajectory prediction.
2. The convolutional social pooling layer captures the target vehicle trajectory data and the spatial relationship between the target vehicle and surrounding vehicle trajectory data, and introduces a spatial attention mechanism to increase the extraction of key influencing factors.
3. BiGRU instead of traditional RNN can not only fully consider the Spatio-temporal relationship between data, but also make up for the defect that CS cannot effectively extract long-term sequence features. And through the attention module for mapping weighting and learning parameter matrix to give different weights to the hidden state of BiGRU to further improve the prediction accuracy of the model.

The organization of this paper is as follows: Sect. 2 related definitions and questions; Sect. 3 discusses the work related to the research in this paper; Sect. 4 describes the proposed method and models it; Sect. 5 experimental results; Sect. 6 summarizes the related work done in this paper.

2 Problem Analysis

First, in a static traffic scene at a certain moment, the eigenvalues (parking space, vehicle speed, acceleration, etc.) of the historical trajectory of the target vehicle at the current moment in various states will affect the future trajectory of the vehicle. Second, the historical spatial positions of the surrounding vehicles and the interaction with the target vehicle also affect the future trajectory of the vehicle. Therefore, this paper establishes a local reference frame for the predicted scene, making the model independent of the curvature of the road. The origin of the prediction at time t is on the target vehicle, as shown in Fig. 1, the y-axis points to the direction of movement of the road, and the x-axis points to the direction perpendicular to the road. T is the observation period.

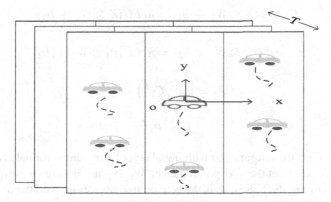

Fig. 1. Reference coordinate system.

Combined with the above content, this paper will initialize the state features contained in the historical trajectories of all vehicles in the traffic scene at the current moment. The historical trajectory state feature of the k-th vehicle is expressed as:

$$\tilde{x}_k = \{x, y, v, a, d, c\} \tag{1}$$

$$\tilde{x}_k^{(t-t_i)} = x_k^{(t-t_i)} - x_k^{(t)} \tag{2}$$

Among them, $t_i \in T$, $k \in n$, and n is the number of all vehicles in the current traffic scene, and T is the time length of the historical trajectory. (x, y) is the position coordinates of the above-relativized vehicles, respectively. v, a, and d are the vehicle speed, acceleration, and the relative distance between the surrounding vehicles and the target vehicle respectively. c is the road congestion coefficient index at the current moment. X_k is the historical trajectory feature sequence of the vehicle, which is expressed as:

$$X_k = \left\{ \tilde{x}_k^{(t-T)}, \cdots, \tilde{x}_k^{(t-1)}, \tilde{x}_k^{(t)} \right\} \tag{3}$$

3 Related Theory

3.1 Convolutional Social Pooling

CNN adopts the method of weight sharing, which has advantages in mining local relevant information in space. While convolving the trajectory vectors of the surrounding vehicles, to improve the accuracy of the local position of the vehicle, the influence of the existence of the target vehicle on the decision-making of the surrounding vehicles is also considered. In this paper, CS is used to learn the interdependence in the process of vehicle motion more robustly, to analyze the upstream and downstream spatial relationship between the vehicle trajectory data, extract multiple key features, and select the ReLU for activation.

$$C_1 = f(X \otimes W_1 + b_1) = ReLU(X \otimes W_1 + b_1) \tag{4}$$

$$C_2 = f(P_1 \otimes W_2 + b_2) = ReLU(P_1 \otimes W_2 + b_2) \tag{5}$$

$$P_1 = \max\left(C_2{}^{\mathrm{T}}\right) + b_3 \tag{6}$$

$$h_c = P_1{}^{\mathrm{T}} \tag{7}$$

where C_1 and C_2 is the output of convolutional layer 1 and convolutional layer 2 respectively, P_1 is the output of the max pooling layer, W_1, W_2 and W_3 are the weight matrices, b_1, b_2, b_3 and b_4 are the biases, $\otimes$ is the convolution operation. And the local positions between the target vehicle and neighboring vehicles, the interaction between the target vehicle and the environment and the spatial relationships between the trajectory data are captured by the CS network in $(t - T), \cdots, (t - 1), t$ period. The output feature vector H_C can be expressed as:

$$H_c = \left[h_{c_1}, h_{c_2}, \cdots, h_{c_i}\right]^T \tag{8}$$

3.2 Prediction Model

After multi-feature extraction is performed on the observation data of the vehicle running state, the observation data sequence is represented as a vector matrix. When the traditional RNN network processes time series information, the problem of gradient explosion or gradient disappearance occurs, as the length of the time series increases. Considering the advantage that Bidirectional GRU can process both forward and backward information of long-term series at the same time, this paper chooses BiGRU as the prediction model. It is a double-layer structure composed of two GRU in different directions. Trajectory sequences can provide not only forward information but also backward derivation references if known below. At time t, the specific calculation formula of BiGRU is as follows:

$$\overleftarrow{h}_t = GRU\left(W_t, \overleftarrow{h}_{t-1}\right), t \in [1, m] \tag{9}$$

$$\overleftarrow{h}_t = GRU\left(W_t, \overleftarrow{h}_{t-1}\right), t \in [1, m] \tag{10}$$

$$h_t = [\overrightarrow{h}_t, \overleftarrow{h}_t] \tag{11}$$

The final output of BiGRU is denoted as:

$$H_B = [h_1, h_2, \cdots, h_t] \tag{12}$$

3.3 Attention Mechanism

To improve the efficiency of trajectory prediction, this paper uses the Soft Attention model proposed by Bahdanau et al. [9], in which the degree of attention of each information area is represented by a weighted score in the range of [0,1]. The calculation formula of the weight coefficient of the Attention mechanism layer can be expressed as:

$$e_t = \mu tanh(wh_t + b) \tag{13}$$

$$\alpha_t = \frac{\exp(e_t)}{\sum_{j-1}^{t} e_j} \tag{14}$$

$$s_t = \sum_{t=1}^{i} \alpha_t h_t \tag{15}$$

Among them, e_t represents the attention vector at time t, u and w are the weight coefficients, b is the bias coefficient; α_t is the attention weight; the context vector s_t of each data will be calculated, that is, the output of this layer.

4 Model Building

4.1 Model Frame

According to the definition and description in Sect. 2 of this paper, the input of the STA-FNet model is the historical trajectories of all vehicles in the $(t - T), \cdots, (t - 1), t$ period, the motion state information, and road congestion status information. The input matrix is represented as:

$$X_T = \{X_1, \cdots X_k, \cdots X_n\} \tag{16}$$

To formally express the problem to be solved in this paper, let $P_{X_T}(X)$ denote the probability that the trajectory X appears in the trajectory X_T. Based on the definition above, the method proposed in this paper can obtain the trajectory set that maximizes $P_{X_T}(X)$. A more explicit definition is as follows:

$$maxP_{X_T}(X_1, \cdots X_k, \cdots X_n) \to Y = \{X_1^{(t+t_m)}, \cdots, X_k^{(t+t_m)}, \cdots X_n^{(t+t_m)}\} \tag{17}$$

4.2 Model Implementation

To comprehensively consider the influence of surrounding vehicles and road traffic environment on driving trajectories, a fusion neural network model with Spatio-temporal attention is built in this paper. Firstly, the road network is modeled, and the road congestion condition at the current moment is one-hot encoded so that the encoded vector can better reflect the dynamic change of road congestion conditions over time. And the local positions between the target vehicle and neighboring vehicles, the interaction between the target vehicle and the environment, and the spatial relationships between the trajectory data are captured by the convolutional social pooling (CS) network in $(t - T), \cdots, (t - 1), t$ period. Meanwhile, spatial attention acts to increase the extraction of key features. Secondly, after training through the CS network the above key features are represented as vector matrices, and the Spatio-temporal relationships between the trajectory data are continued to be extracted and fused by the two-layer BiGRU network to make reasonable predictions of future trajectories and filter out the vehicle trajectory sequences with the highest probability. Meanwhile, temporal attention acts to adjust the weight coefficients to extract the key features affecting the vehicle trajectory. The system framework is shown in Fig. 2:

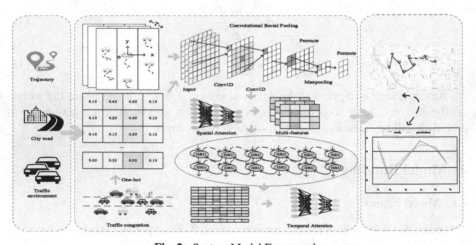

Fig. 2. System Model Framework.

4.3 Algorithm Complexity Analysis

In the stage of feature extraction using CS, the time complexity is $O(n^3)$; in the stage of prediction using vector matrix, the time complexity of the BiGRU model is $O(n^2)$, and the Spatio-temporal attention acts on the above models. The time complexity of the two stages of data processing is $O(n)$. Through the above analysis, the time complexity of the entire algorithm is $O(n^3) + O(n^2) + O(n) \sim O(n^3)$.

5 Experimental Results and Analysis

5.1 Dataset

This paper adopts the Lankershim Boulevard Urban Roads dataset from the NGSIM dataset, which exhibits real urban road traffic trajectories captured over a time of 30 min. The running status information of the vehicle in 5 different road sections is recorded, including information such as vehicle position, GPS coordinates, speed, acceleration, and vehicle type, as shown in Fig. 3. This paper selects the trajectory data of 800 consecutive frames as samples, and divides them according to the proportion of 62.5%, of which the first 500 sets of data are used as the training set, and the last 300 sets of data are used as the test set. The continuous variables are normalized to normalize the mean and variance of the data. The algorithm is optimized using the ADAM function with a learning rate of 0.01, and the number of samples per batch is 16.

Fig. 3. Distribution map of 5 road sections.

Due to the complex and changeable traffic operating environment in the urban road environment, the classification of traffic operating conditions is often inaccurate and there is a certain degree of ambiguity. Therefore, this paper uses the fuzzy comprehensive evaluation method of traffic flow to calculate the congestion coefficient of this road section. Referring to the "American Traffic Congestion Evaluation Index System", the Congestion Coefficient is defined as the ratio (V/C) of the actual volume of road traffic to the road capacity. When the Congestion Coefficient is in [0, 0.77], [0.78, 0.85], [0.86, 0.99], [1.0, 1.2], it is defined as "unblocked", "slightly congested", "moderately congested" and "severe congestion", associated with variables 1, 2, 3, and 4. One-hot coding is performed on discrete variables in this paper to unify the types of discrete variables and continuous variables. Therefore, after adopting the fuzzy evaluation method, the congestion coefficients of the five road sections can reflect the dynamic changes in road congestion to a certain extent, as shown in Fig. 4. By calculating the Congestion Coefficient, the current running state of the road section can be well understood, which is helpful for the subsequent prediction of the vehicle trajectory.

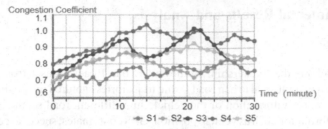

Fig. 4. Congestion Coefficient of 5 road sections.

5.2 Baseline Models

To explore the predictive performance of the proposed STA-FNet model, several baseline models are also trained and used to predict vehicle trajectories at the same time.

4. CS-LSTM [12]: Introduce a convolutional social pooling layer and LSTM to predict vehicle trajectories.
5. DCS-LSTM [13]: A dilated convolutional social pooling layer and LSTM are introduced to predict vehicle trajectories.
6. BiLSTM [14]: Predicting vehicle trajectories using Bidirectional LSTM.
7. STA-FNet: The fusion neural network prediction model based on the spatiotemporal attention mechanism proposed in this paper uses the convolutional social pooling layer to extract the spatiotemporal relationship between the historical social vectors of the target vehicle and completes the prediction through BiGRU.

5.3 Evaluation Indicators

This paper uses Root Mean Squared Error (RMSE), Mean Absolute Error (MAE), and Mean Absolute Percent Error (MAPE) for evaluation. The loss function quantifies how close the neural network model is to the ideal situation it was trained on. To facilitate the calculation, using the root mean square error as the loss function of the model.

$$\text{RMSE} = \sqrt{\frac{1}{N} \sum_{i=1}^{N} (y_i - \widehat{y}_i)^2} \tag{18}$$

$$\text{MAE} = \frac{1}{N} \sum_{i=1}^{N} |\widehat{y}_i - y_i| \tag{19}$$

$$\text{MAPE} = \frac{100\%}{N} \sum_{i=1}^{N} \left| \frac{\widehat{y}_i - y_i}{y_i} \right| \tag{20}$$

Among them, $\widehat{y}_i$ represents the predicted value, y_i represents the true value, and N is the number of samples.

5.4 Performance Analysis

Determination of Basic Parameters. To select the optimal number of hidden layer units, this paper compares the MAPE values under different hidden units. First, select the number of hidden layer units in [5, 10, 15, 30, 50] for testing, and their MAPE values are 0.8300%, 0.3818%, 0.5834%, 0.4834% and 0.3850%, respectively. Therefore, the number of hidden layer units (10) with the smallest MAPE value (0.3818%) is selected as the number of hidden layer units in this experiment. For different time steps, the STA-FNet model proposed in this paper has different evaluation performances. To select the best time step for the next experiment, this model tests the RMSE, MAE, and MAPE under the time step [5, 10, 15, 20, 25, 30], and the corresponding evaluation distribution is shown in Fig. 5. It can be seen that the RMSE, MAE and MAPE values of the model are relatively minimal when the time step is 20. Therefore, the time step selected for this experiment is 20.

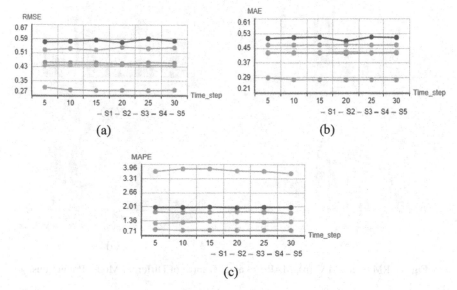

Fig. 5. Evaluation values at different time steps.

Performance Analysis. After determining the parameters of the model, use the designed training set and test set to verify the prediction performance of the model. The loss function curve generated by the model in 5 different road segments during the training process is shown in Fig. 6. It is not difficult to find that with the increase in the number of iterations, the loss function curves of the training set and the test set decrease rapidly and gradually converge, which indicates that the design of the model is reasonable.

Comparison of Baseline Methods. To further compare the prediction performance of different algorithms, CS-LSTM, DCS-LSTM, and BiLSTM are selected for comparison with the STA-FNet model. It can be seen from Fig. 7 and Table 1 that the proposed model outperforms the baseline models after 200 iterations. The average MAPE of the 5 road segments is 2.7320%, and the prediction accuracy is 97.2620%

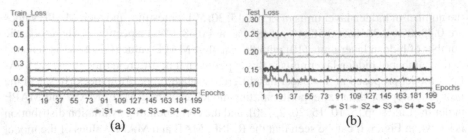

Fig. 6. Training set loss and Test set loss for 5 road segments with Epochs of 200.

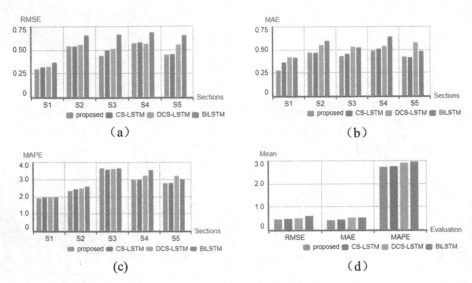

Fig. 7. RMSE(a), MAE(b), MAPE(c) and Mean(d) of Different Model Predictions.

The average MAPE values of STA-FNet, DCS-LSTM, and CS-LSTM are 0.2235%, 0.2065%, and 0.0563% higher than those of BiLSTM, respectively. The experimental results show that modeling the position interaction of surrounding vehicles and exploring the interaction between surrounding vehicles and target vehicles have a positive effect on improving the accuracy of vehicle trajectory prediction. In addition, DCS-LSTM, which introduces a convolutional social pooling layer, achieves the same prediction effect as CS-LSTM, while maintaining more accurate vehicle local position information, and its prediction performance is further improved.

The average MAPE value of the algorithm proposed in this paper is 0.0170% higher than that of DCS-LSTM. Because the algorithm in this paper takes into account the historical trajectory of the target vehicle itself and the historical location interaction between the target vehicle and the surrounding vehicles, while further considering the current traffic congestion of the road. At the same time, the accuracy of the prediction is further improved by using the Spatio-temporal attention mechanism acting on the whole process of extracting temporal and spatial features of the data. The comprehensive

Table 1. RMSE, MAE, and MAPE of Different Model Predictions.

Models	Evaluation	S1	S2	S3	S4	S5	Mean
STA-FNet (proposed)	RMSE	0.2968	0.5420	0.4425	0.5705	0.4487	**0.4601**
	MAE	0.2781	0.4694	0.4305	0.4901	0.4217	**0.4180**
	MAPE	1.9198	2.3349	3.6612	2.9660	2.7783	**2.7320**
DCS-LSTM	RMSE	0.3185	0.5405	0.501	0.5792	0.4535	0.4785
	MAE	0.3628	0.4679	0.4547	0.5092	0.4153	0.4420
	MAPE	1.9628	2.4374	3.5738	2.985	2.7858	2.7490
CS-LSTM	RMSE	0.3234	0.5565	0.5157	0.564	0.555	0.5029
	MAE	0.4201	0.551	0.5323	0.5393	0.5768	0.5240
	MAPE	1.9667	2.4839	3.6167	3.2207	3.2081	2.8992
BiLSTM	RMSE	0.3708	0.657	0.6651	0.6854	0.6536	0.6064
	MAE	0.4153	0.5967	0.5243	0.6395	0.4839	0.5319
	MAPE	1.9764	2.5963	3.6505	3.5435	3.0106	2.9555

consideration and analysis of the influencing factors around the target vehicle further enhance the interpretability of vehicle trajectory prediction.

In summary, the STA-FNet model proposed in this paper outperforms other models in predicting vehicle trajectories. The model starts from the historical trajectory of the target vehicle retrospectively and also explores the influence of the spatial distribution of neighboring vehicles on the future decision of the target vehicle. In addition, the impact of the road congestion state on the trajectory of the target vehicle at the current moment is quantified. The above influencing factors are combined to study the future trajectory of the target vehicle, which makes the model more comprehensive and interpretable in terms of trajectory prediction.

6 Conclusion

To effectively predict the motion trajectories of target vehicles in complex traffic scenes, this paper proposes a Fusion Neural network with the Spatio-Temporal Attention (STA-FNet) model. The novelty of this model is that it comprehensively considers the effects of attention factors, Spatio-temporal feature relationships among data, and the decision-making effects of the interaction between the target vehicle and surrounding vehicles on vehicle trajectory prediction. The comparative experimental results show that the prediction accuracy of the STA-FNet model constructed in this paper is 97.2620%, which is 0.0170%, 0.1672%, and 0.2235% higher than the DCS-LSTM model, CS-LSTM model, and BiLSTM model respectively. The effect is significantly better than other models, and the model has a stronger interpretability interpretation. In addition, objectively speaking, this paper sacrifices the complexity of the model to improve prediction accuracy.

The next step will consider reducing the complexity of the model based on improving or maintaining the existing prediction accuracy, which will be considered in the next research. Long-term prediction of vehicle trajectories enables a more accurate prediction of vehicle trajectories.

References

1. Liang, Y., Zhao, Z.: Vehicle trajectory prediction in city-scale road networks using a direction-based sequence-to-sequence model with spatiotemporal attention mechanisms. arXiv e-prints, arXiv: 2106.11175 (2021)
2. Leon, F., Gavrilescu, M.: A review of tracking and trajectory prediction methods for autonomous driving. Mathematics **9**(6), 660 (2021)
3. Huang, Z., Wang, J., Pi, L., et al.: LSTM based trajectory prediction model for cyclist utilizing multiple interactions with environment. Patt. Recogn. **112**, 107800 (2021)
4. Wang, J., Wang, P., Zhang, C., Su, K., Li, J.: F-Net: fusion neural network for vehicle trajectory prediction in autonomous driving. In: 2021 IEEE International Conference on Acoustics Speech and Signal Processing (ICASSP), pp. 4095–4099 (2021)
5. Bahdanau, D., Cho, K., Bengio, Y.: Neural machine translation by jointly learning to align and translate. In: 2015 Proceedings of 3rd *International Conference* on *Learning* Representations (ICLR), pp. 1049–0473 (2015)
6. Cai, Y., Wang, Z., Wang, H., et al.: Environment-attention network for vehicle trajectory prediction. IEEE Trans. Veh. Technol. **70**(11), 11216–11227 (2021)
7. Yu, D., Lee, H., Kim, T., et al.: Vehicle trajectory prediction with lane stream attention-based LSTMs and road geometry linearization. Sensors **21**(23), 8152 (2021)
8. Wang, S., Shao, C., Zhai, Y., et al.: A Multifeatures Spatial-Temporal-Based Neural Network Model for Truck Flow Prediction. J. Adv. Transp. **2021** (2021)
9. Lin, L., Li, W., Bi, H., et al.: Vehicle trajectory prediction using LSTMs with spatial-temporal attention mechanisms. IEEE Intell. Transp. Syst. Mag. **14**(2), 197–208 (2021)
10. Xi, P., Gu, Y.: Research on expressway travel time prediction based on deep learning. In: 2021 Fifth International Conference on Traffic Engineering and Transportation System (ICTETS), SPIE, 12058, pp. 399–403 (2021)
11. Jin, J., Guo, H., Xu, J., et al.: An end-to-end recommendation system for urban traffic controls and management under a parallel learning framework. IEEE Trans. Intell. Transp. Syst. **22**(3), 1616–1626 (2020)
12. Deo, N., Trivedi, M.M.: Convolutional social pooling for vehicle trajectory prediction. In: 2018 IEEE Conference on Computer Vision and Pattern Recognition Workshops (ICCVPR), pp. 1468–1476 (2018)
13. Zhang, H., Wang, Y., Liu, J., et al.: A multi-modal states based vehicle descriptor and dilated convolutional social pooling for vehicle trajectory prediction. arXiv preprint arXiv:2003.03480 (2020)
14. Li, T., Ni, A., Zhang, C., et al.: Short-term traffic congestion prediction with Conv–BiLSTM considering spatio-temporal features. IET Intel. Transport Syst. **14**(14), 1978–1986 (2020)

A Low-Overhead Routing Protocol for FANET Based on Ant Colony Algorithm

Ziyi Wang[⊠], Xiang Yu, Binbin Wang, and Shilong Cheng

School of Communication and Information Engineering, Chongqing University of Posts and Telecommunications, Chongqing, China
1286227136@qq.com

Abstract. To address the problems of low network throughput and delivery rate and high communication overhead between nodes due to frequent topology changes of flight self-assembled networks, this paper proposes a SE-AODV routing protocol optimized based on the traditional on-demand distance vector routing protocol. The new protocol takes into account the actual influencing factors such as energy and received signal strength, and combines the pheromone calculation rules of the ant colony algorithm to update the routing table, while optimizing the optimal path selection basis. Simulation results show that compared with traditional on-demand distance vector routing and EE-AODV, the new routing protocol not only shows more obvious advantages in throughput and packet delivery rate, but also reduces routing overhead, and is more suitable for scenarios where nodes are in high-speed motion.

Keywords: UAV · Flying Ad Hoc Network · AODV Routing Protocol · ACO

1 Introduction

With the development of technology, multiple miniature unmanned aerial vehicles (UAVs) coordinating and cooperating with each other can form a multi-UAV system. Compared with a single large UAV, a multi-UAV system composed of multiple small UAVs has the characteristics of low cost, high flexibility, and high reliability [1, 2]. However, there are still many problems that need to be solved in multi-UAV systems, among which, it is very meaningful work to design efficient routing protocols for multi-UAV systems to ensure efficient systems of multi-UAV systems.

Flying Ad hoc network (FANET) is a special kind of Ad hoc networks with UAVs as nodes and are considered by many as a special example of Mobile Ad hoc network (MANET) [1]. Communication between FANET nodes is a challenging task that requires routing protocols that support the effectiveness of such transmissions. Since FANET are special in nature and operate in a specific environment, routing techniques need to be tailored for it.

The routing technology of FANET needs to be adapted to its unique mobility model and operating environment in order to guarantee correct data forwarding. Therefore, its

F. Gao et al. (Eds.): ChinaCom 2022, LNICST 500, pp. 321–333, 2023.
https://doi.org/10.1007/978-3-031-34790-0_25

requirements are completely different from those of mobile and vehicular self-assembly networks. Establishing communication links with low latency, high throughput, and low routing overhead can greatly improve the communication benefits of flight self-assembled networks [2], so the development of routing for FANET is of great interest. The scheme proposed in this paper is based on the Ad hoc on-demand distance vector (AODV) routing protocol for mobile self-organizing networks, based on the special characteristics of FANET [3, 4], considering the energy factor and the received signal strength factor in practical applications, and referring to the pheromone calculation rules of the ant colony algorithm to select the optimal path, and proposes a new On-demand routing protocol SE-AODV. This scheme aims to improve packet throughput and packet delivery rate in the network and reduce the routing overhead of the whole network during packet transmission.

This article focuses on the classical on-demand vector routing protocol (AODV) for mobile self-organizing networks, and proposes an optimized routing protocol SE-AODV (Signal and Energy-AODV) for in-flight self-organizing networks considering the received signal strength and energy as well as the number of hops.

2   Related Work

In recent years, many routing protocols for FANET have been proposed by domestic and foreign experts and scholars [5–7], aiming at improving packet delivery rates and reducing overhead and packet loss rates. Existing routing protocols can generally be classified into two broad categories [8]: single-hop routing and multi-hop routing. Single-hop routing is mainly used in situations where the topology is fixed, which results in very poor fault tolerance and is unsuitable for dynamic environments. Multi-hop routing can be divided into two categories: topology-based routing and location-based routing. The details are shown in Fig. 1 below.

Single-hop routing uses a fixed static routing table to transmit messages. This routing protocol is lightweight, not suitable for dynamic environments, and is commonly used in situations where the topology is fixed. In multi-hop routing, message information is transmitted between multiple nodes and is not directly transmitted to the destination node. Therefore, how to choose the appropriate data forwarding path is the core of route discovery.

Topology-based routing protocols can be further divided into two categories: active routing and passive routing. In active routing, routing information is pre-recorded and stored in each drone, so that packets can be transmitted in real time without waiting. However, the disadvantage of this routing protocol is that it incurs a high communication overhead because each node needs packets to establish a route. Passive routing, also known as on-demand routing, looks up routing paths on demand only when packets need to be sent. Unlike active routing, passive routes are constructed only when the source node needs to send information and are not pre-built, creating routing tables as needed. The advantage of this is that it is not necessary to collect topological information about the entire network, but it is sufficient to obtain only a portion of it.

Therefore, passive routing is more energy efficient than active routing, can effectively reduce the control message overhead, and is more adaptable to the high dynamics of UAV nodes.

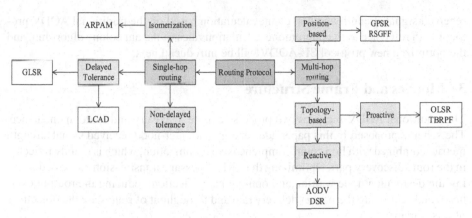

Fig. 1. Classification of Existing Routing Protocol.

In the literature [9], Rao et al. proposed a backup routing protocol AODV nth BR, which provides multiple alternate routes to the source node in case of link failures in the network. It is based on the classical AODV routing protocol and achieves efficient transmission of packets by establishing multiple routes.

In the literature [10], scholar Shubhajeet Chatterjee and his team proposed a new routing protocol E-Ant-DSR based on the existing dynamic source routing protocol (DSR), considering the combination with Ant colony optimization (ACO). The new protocol improves the optimal path selection by considering The new protocol improves the optimal path selection by considering multiple measures of link quality, congestion and hop count, calculates the pheromone of the path, and selects the optimal path for packet transmission based on the pheromone count of multiple paths.

An energy efficient AODV routing protocol EE-AODV is proposed in the literature [11]. The original RREQ packet field of AODV is modified using node residual energy and hop count as cost metric to find the optimal energy efficient routing. The protocol is then simulated using NS-2 to compare the performance output benefits of EE-AODV routing protocol with classical routing protocols in terms of network lifecycle, delivery ratio, routing overhead and energy consumption.

AODV, as a traditional passive routing protocol, was often used in mobile self-assembly networks in the past. Compared with other traditional routing protocols, such as OLSR, it has more advantages in terms of packet delivery rate and throughput. However, if it is used directly in FANET, it still leads to problems such as excessive routing overhead, low throughput and packet delivery rate.

In FANET, the rapid movement of nodes makes the topology of the network prone to great dynamic changes, which leads to easy breakage of links between nodes. This characteristic poses an unprecedented challenge to design a routing protocol with good scalability, robustness and high performance. The ant colony algorithm has strong robustness and is easy to combine with other algorithms. It has good distributed computing capability and all these advantages are compatible with the requirements of Ad hoc networks. Therefore, this article considers a new scheme SE-AODV that integrates energy, received signal strength and hop count calculation based on the traditional AODV protocol with reference to the pheromone calculation rules of the ant colony algorithm, and the optimized new protocol SE-AODV will be introduced next.

3   Metrics and Frame Structure

The traditional AODV includes two processes, route discovery and route maintenance. The scheme proposed in this paper adds energy and inter-node received signal strength metric, combined with hop count comprehensive optimization, which is mainly reflected in the route discovery part. Optimizing the RREQ message transmission process, designing the destination node waiting and optimal path selection, reducing the routing overhead, and improving the packet delivery rate and throughput of routes are the objectives of this scheme.

At the intermediate node, the energy threshold is first set for the node, and if a route request SE_REQ message is received from the source node, the energy of the node itself and the received signal strength between that node and the previous node need to be calculated. If the remaining energy of this node cannot satisfy the threshold, this intermediate node is dropped; if the threshold value is met, the received signal strength between the current node and the previous node is calculated.

For the received signal strength between nodes, if the distance between two nodes is too large, although there will be high broadcasting efficiency, but the link state is unstable; if the distance between two nodes is too small, although the link state is more stable, but the broadcasting efficiency is not high. Considering the above factors, for the received signal strength coefficient between nodes, the following definition is made.

$$S_{ij} = \begin{cases} 3, 0 < D_{ij} \leq 0.3R \\ 7, 0.3 < D_{ij} \leq 0.7R \\ 2, 0.7 < D_{ij} \leq R \end{cases} \tag{1}$$

where D_{ij} denotes the distance between node i and node j; R denotes the communication range of the node, S_{ij}, the link stability coefficient of the node, and D_{ij} is calculated as in Eq. 2.

$$D_{ij} = \sqrt{(x_i - x_j)^2 + (y_i - y_j)^2} \tag{2}$$

where x_i and y_i are the obtained coordinate values of the current node i, and x_j and y_j are the coordinates of the previous hop node j.

After calculating the received signal strength of a node, its energy parameters need to be processed for subsequent pheromone counting operations, and drawing on the energy calculation in the literature [12], this paper proposes the energy parameters calculation method in the following way.

Each node has an energy value which is set in its initial state. During the route discovery process, the energy of each node decreases after a period of time as the nodes consume a certain amount of energy for both receiving and forwarding packets. Here we define the energy of the node is calculated as Eq. 3.

$$E_i^{res} = E_i^0 - E_{cost} \tag{3}$$

where E_i^{res} denotes the remaining energy of node i at time t, E_i^0 denotes the initial energy of node i, and E_{cost} denotes the total energy consumed by node i from time 0 to t.

$$E_{\cos t} = E_f(i) + E_r(i) \qquad (4)$$

$E_f(i)$ denotes the energy consumed by node i for forwarding packets in time t, and $E_r(i)$ denotes the energy consumed by node i for receiving packets in time t.

The ACO algorithm is derived from real ants' foraging behavior. When ants search for food, they start from the nest and move around randomly to find food; in this process, ants secrete a substance called "pheromone" to mark. When ants choose the next path, they compare the concentration of pheromones left by the previous paths and release more pheromones to intensify the marking of the path after they have chosen a suitable path. This foraging process is characterized by a positive feedback.

In this paper, we define pheromones as follows.

After the intermediate node receiving the route request message meets its energy threshold and has calculated the received signal strength, it needs to update its pheromone count value using the above parameters and the information in the SE_REQ message, which is calculated as in Eq. 5.

$$P_{ij} = \frac{S_{ij} \times E_j}{H_{ij}} \qquad (5)$$

In the above Eq. 5, H_{ij} denotes the number of hops that a routing request passes through node i from the source node to node j.

Until the route request message is forwarded to the destination node. At the destination node, it first determines whether the current time has exceeded the waiting time, if not, it compares the current pheromone count with the highest recorded historical pheromone value and selects the higher message to update the routing table. Otherwise, when the destination node receives a new SE_REQ message and the current time has exceeded the route waiting time, it sends a SE_REP, i.e., a route reply message, to the source node according to the established reverse routing table until the SE_REP message is forwarded to the source node.

When RREQ is propagated in the network, intermediate nodes update their respective routes to the source node, called reverse routes. The route is considered to be valid.

The original frame structure of AODV contains several modules, such as RREQ ID, destination node address, etc. In this paper, we propose the SE-AODV protocol to add the pheromone count value to the original frame structure, as shown in Fig. 2. The modified frame structure is more convenient for route optimization, as the route request message is transmitted in the path, the pheromone count value is accumulated and recorded until it reaches the destination node.

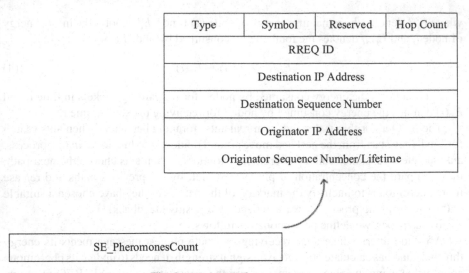

Type	Symbol	Reserved	Hop Count
RREQ ID			
Destination IP Address			
Destination Sequence Number			
Originator IP Address			
Originator Sequence Number/Lifetime			

SE_PheromonesCount

Fig. 2. SE-AODV frame structure.

4 SE-AODV

The whole SE-AODV route discovery process can be summarized as follows.

If a node wishes to deliver some packets to a destination, the packets are sent through the route if it exists; if no available route exists, the route request sending process is initiated.

The source node broadcasts the route request message SE_REQ, and the neighboring nodes receive it and first perform the pre-processing to receive SE_REQ, a process shown in Algorithm 1. After that they perform route request forwarding process and they will create a backlink to the SE_REQ originator. Then they calculate the value of the pheromone and update the routing table of the current node. After that they rebroadcast SE_REQ and add 1 to the hop count metric value.

Algorithm1. Intermediate node preprocessing that receives SE_REQ

1: **while** received SE_REQ
2:   **if** (index == source node of REQ)
3:     packed free
4:   **end if**
5:   **if** (index! == destination node of REQ && source node of REQ!= Broadcast id)
6:     packed free
7:   **end if**
8:   Calculate the energy value
9:   **if** (this energy < REM)
10:     packed free
11:   **else**
12:     Calculate the signal strength
13:     Calculate the RSSM
14:   **end if**
15:   hopcount++
16:   Create reverse routing table rt0 and update routing table rt
17:   Calculate the pheromone count pherCount
18:   update pheromone in REQ
19: **end while**

All intermediate nodes follow this process until SE_REQ reaches the destination. When the destination node receives SE_REQ, like the process in Algorithm 2, it starts the wait time function and after waiting for some time, it selects the path with the highest pheromone as the best selected path.

Afterwards, it updates the directional routing table of the destination node using the information in SE_REQ, and then sends a routing answer message (SE_REP) in the direction of the source node until it reaches the SE_REQ initiator.

Algorithm2. The destination node receives SE_REQ processing

1: **while** received SE_REQ
2:    Calculate the signal strength
3:    Calculate the RSSM
4:    P_{ij} = pheromone in REQ+pherCount
5:    Create or update reverse routing table rt0
6:    **if** (sequence number in REQ== sequence number in routing table rt)
7:      **if** (CURRENT-TIME <= DE-TIME)
8:        Pheromone in rt = Pheromone in REQ/Hop in REQ
9:        **if** (Pheromone in rt > calculated current pheromone value)
10:         update reverse routing table rt0
11:         update the pheromone in reverse routing table rt0
12:       **end if**
13:     **else**
14:       update sequence number
15:       send SE_REP
16:     **end if**
17:   **end if**
18: **end while**

When the intermediate node receives the SE_REP message, it will choose whether to update the routing table based on the sequence number and hop count information it carries; after that, it will continue to forward the SE_REP message until it reaches the destination node, which is the source node of SE_REQ. When it reaches the destination node, it will update the source node routing table of SE_REQ based on its information. At this point, the whole route discovery process is completed and a path from the source node to the destination node has been built, and the source node will send packets through this path.

5   Simulation and Analysis

Due to the specificity of FANET, we need to set the scenarios according to their characteristics when selecting them. In this paper, we use the ns-2.35 simulation platform [13, 14] to verify the above proposed innovative method, and we also choose the EE-AODV routing algorithm proposed in the literature [11] and the classical AODV routing algorithm as a comparison.

The selected simulation scenario is in a 1000 m × 1000 m area composed of 50 nodes, the nodes' movement model is RWP movement model, the running speed of each node varies from 20 to 100 m/s, and the node pause time is set to 0 s. The specific parameters are shown in the following Table 1.

Table 1. Simulation parameter.

Parameter	Value/Type
Channel type	Channel/Wireless channel
Simulation area	1000 × 1000 m
Simulation time	100 s
Mobility model	Random WayPoint
Agent type	UDP
Application type	CBR
MAC protocol	IEEE802.11
Initial energy	100 J

Routing overhead is one of the performance metrics that measure the effectiveness of the network and is calculated as follows.

$$\text{Routing overhead} = \frac{P_C}{P_D} \tag{6}$$

In the above equation, P_C is the total number of packets sent in the network and P_D is the total number of packets received.

The routing overhead at different node speeds is shown in Fig. 3. As can be seen from the figure, when the movement rate of the nodes increases, the routing overhead of the network also increases. The reason for this is that as the node speed increases, the energy required by the UAV increases and the network topology also changes more rapidly, resulting in an increase in overhead.

Compared to the classic AODV routing protocol, the routing overhead of EE-AODV has been reduced, but SE-AODV reduces the routing overhead even more significantly. And the increase in routing overhead is smaller when the node speed is higher.

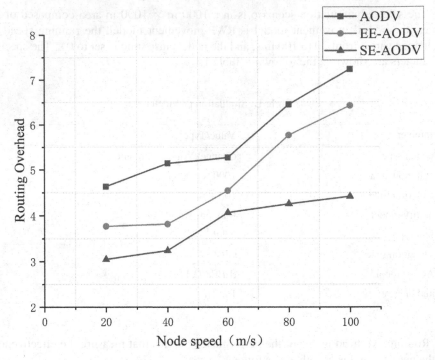

Fig. 3. Routing overhead as a function of node speed.

Throughput, which is the actual amount of data transmitted per unit of time, is an important indicator of routing performance. It is calculated as shown in Eq. 7.

$$\text{Throughput} = \frac{recevied \times 8}{Simulation\ time \times 1024} \tag{7}$$

Figure 4 shows the variation of network throughput with the change in node movement speed. Since the maximum number of connections in the simulation parameter is set to 15, the throughput is high because the nodes are well connected and the received signal strength is relatively stable when the node speed is maintained at about 20 m/s. When the node speed increases to 40, the topology in the network starts to change frequently because the maximum number of connections does not change, and it causes a sudden drop in throughput. SE-AODV has a certain improvement in throughput compared to EE-AODV and the classical AODV routing protocol.

This is due to the fact that the optimized SE-AODV routing takes more cases into account, ensuring node energy, received signal strength and hop count. As a result, the number of path breaks is significantly reduced and the packets sent per second are increased. As the node speed increases, the network energy is consumed, the received signal strength decreases, and the throughput of all scenarios decreases accordingly. But overall, the network throughput of SE-AODV is significantly more advantageous.

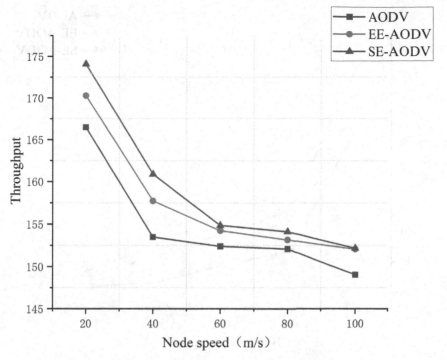

Fig. 4. Thoughtput as a function of node speed.

The grouped delivery rate is calculated as in Eq. 8.

$$\text{Packed Delivery Ratio} = \frac{P_R}{P_S} \times 100\% \qquad (8)$$

where P_R is the number of packets arriving at the target node; and P_S is the number of packets that the source node has sent.

Figure 5 shows that SE-AODV exhibits a better performance in terms of packet delivery rate compared to the classic AODV and EE-AODV. At lower node speeds, again due to the maximum number of connections and network topology, it exhibits a sudden drop in the variation from 20 to 40.

After that, as the network node speed increases and the network topology changes faster, the packet transmission rate in the path inevitably decreases. Packets will be cached in the queues of the nodes and when the queues are filled, packets will be dropped, so the packet delivery rate will drop accordingly. With the optimized SE-AODV, the link considers the received signal strength to select the next hop node, so the stability factor of the path is higher and the packet loss is greatly reduced.

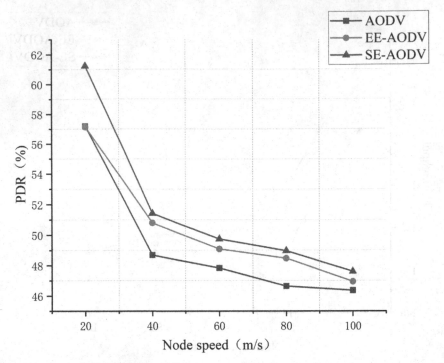

Fig. 5. Packet delivery rate as a function of node speed.

6 Conclusions

In this paper, we propose an optimized AODV routing protocol SE-AODV considering energy and received signal strength to address the problems of high routing overhead, low throughput and packet delivery rate of FANETs routing protocols. The new protocol provides multi-path selection and network energy balancing in terms of energy, received signal strength and hop count. By comparing with the classical AODV and EE-AODV protocols in real simulations, the results show that the SE-AODV protocol has lower routing overhead and has a significant improvement in throughput and packet delivery rate. The effectiveness and superiority of the proposed protocol in this paper are proved.

References

1. Wu, Q., Zeng, Y., Zhang, R.: Joint trajectory and communication design for multi-UAV enabled wireless networks. IEEE Trans. Wireless Commun. **17**(3), 2109–2121 (2018)
2. Wei, H., Jun-liang, C., You-hai, L.: Review and development prospect of UAV ad hoc network technology. Telecommun. Eng. **62**(01), 138–146 (2022)
3. Cameron, S., Hailes, S., Julier, S., et al.: SUAAVE: combining aerial robots and wireless networking (2010)
4. Yanmaz, E., Kuschnig, R., Bettstetter, C.: Channel measurements over 802.11 a-based UAV-to-ground links. IEEE GLOBECOM Workshops (GC Wkshps), pp. 1280–1284 (2011)

5. da Costa, L.A.L.F., Kunst, R., de Freitas, E.P.: Q-FANET: Improved Q-learning based routing protocol for FANETs. Comput. Netw. **198**, 108379 (2021)
6. Kakamoukas, G.A., Sarigiannidis, P.G., Economides, A.A.: FANETs in agriculture-A routing protocol survey. Int. Things **18**, 100183 (2022)
7. Liu, C., Zhang, Z.: Towards a robust FANET: Distributed node importance estimation-based connectivity maintenance for UAV swarms. Ad Hoc Netw. **125**, 102734 (2022)
8. Jiang, J., Han, G.: Routing protocols for unmanned aerial vehicles. IEEE Commun. Mag. **56**(1), 58–63 (2018)
9. Rao, M., Singh, N.: An improved routing protocol (AODV nthBR) for efficient routing in MANETs. In: Kumar Kundu, M., Mohapatra, D., Konar, A., Chakraborty, A. (eds.) Advanced Computing, Networking and Informatics - Volume 2. Smart Innovation, Systems and Technologies, vol. 28. Springer, Cham (2014). https://doi.org/10.1007/978-3-319-07350-7_24
10. Chatterjee, S., Das, S.: Ant colony optimization based enhanced dynamic source routing algorithm for mobile Ad-hoc network. Inf. Sci. **295**, 67–90 (2015)
11. Er-rouidi, M., Moudni, H., Mouncif, H., et al.: A balanced energy consumption in mobile ad hoc network. Proc. Comput. Sci. 1182–1187 (2019)
12. Sarkar, D., Choudhury, S., Majumder, A.: Enhanced-Ant-AODV for optimal route selection in mobile ad-hoc network. J. King Saud Univ.-Comput. Inf. Sci. **33**(10), 1186–1201 (2021)
13. Qiong-pei, W.: Research on wireless Ad-Hoc network routing protocol based on NS2. J. Pu'er Univ. **33**(3), 37–39 (2017)
14. Chao, L.: Research and improvement of AODV based on NS2. Wuhan University of Technology (2010)

Edge Computing and Artificial Intelligence Applications

Traffic-Tran: A Parallel Multi-encoder Structure for Cellular Traffic Prediction

Shilong Fan[1], Boyuan Zhang[1], and Xinyu Gu[1,2(✉)]

[1] Beijing University of Posts and Telecommunications, Beijing, China
guxinyu@bupt.edu.cn
[2] Purple Mountain Laboratories, Nanjing 211111, China

Abstract. Wireless cellular traffic prediction is a critical research topic for the realization of intelligent communications. The high nonlinearities and mutability of wireless cellular network traffic bring great challenges to accurate prediction. Due to the lack of dynamic spatio-temporal correlation modeling ability and complex network structure, the existing prediction methods cannot meet the requirements of accuracy and complexity in real scenes. By generating time series data for network traffic of a single grid, and spatial series data for network traffic of all grids with the same timestamp, this paper proposes a multi-encoder structure named "Traffic-Tran", which learns sequence correlation independently and in parallel by multiple network units. Meanwhile, in order to improve the recognition ability of multi-encoder feature information, an information supplement method is proposed. In addition, the design of sampling output module realizes the parallel multi-step flow prediction, which enlarges the application range of the model. Experimental results on a large real dataset verify the effectiveness of Traffic-Tran. The model complexity of Traffic-Tran is greatly reduced, with less memory usage and shorter runtime than other models. Under the premise of the same predictive performance, the number of training parameters of Traffic-Tran is reduced by 44.9%.

Keywords: Cellular traffic prediction · Spatio-temporal correlation · Transformer · Multi-step prediction

1 Introduction

In recent years, with the comprehensive coverage and popularization of new information infrastructure such as the Fifth Generation (5G) mobile network, people's demand for wireless cellular network is growing rapidly. According to the "Cisco Annual Internet Report" [1], the total number of global Internet users will reach 5.3 billion (66% of the global population) by 2023, up from 3.9 billion in 2018. How to configure cellular network resources, optimize network management strategy, improve network service quality and reduce energy consumption needs to be further thought and solved in the next generation of mobile communication.

© ICST Institute for Computer Sciences, Social Informatics and Telecommunications Engineering 2023
Published by Springer Nature Switzerland AG 2023. All Rights Reserved
F. Gao et al. (Eds.): ChinaCom 2022, LNICST 500, pp. 337–346, 2023.
https://doi.org/10.1007/978-3-031-34790-0_26

Accurate wireless traffic prediction helps optimize network management strategies to improve service quality and prevent network congestion, while reducing base station power consumption and operating costs. However, accurately predicting wireless cellular network traffic is a very challenging problem for the following two reasons. First, due to the emergence of new types of transportation, people can get from one end of the city to the other in a short time. The mobility of wireless users makes the cellular traffic between regions spatially dependent. Secondly, due to the regularity of the daily life and work of wireless users, the wireless cellular traffic also shows the pattern of regular changes in time. The traffic value at a certain moment is highly correlated with the traffic value at a similar moment (short-term dependence) and a relative moment of a certain day (periodicity). The modeling ability of time dependence and space dependence determines the performance of the final prediction results.

Data-driven artificial intelligent algorithms play an important role in improving network service quality. Among deep learning methods, convolutional neural networks (CNN) [2] and recurrent neural networks (RNN) [3] are the basic structures for modeling spatio-temporal dependence. Among them, spatial features are modeled mainly by convolutional neural networks [4] and graph neural networks (GCN) [5]. Some researchers also use transfer learning [6] and meta-learning [7] to improve the modeling ability. In addition, some researchers tried to enhance the representation of feature information through cross-domain data, so as to obtain more accurate prediction results [8].

Transformer [9] is a parallel encoder-decoder structure with many successful applications, and the ability of its internal attention layer to model sequence data has been proven in many practical scenarios. In terms of wireless cellular network traffic prediction, Transformer is also trying to be used to model the spatial-temporal correlations, and ST-Tran [10] is the first to apply the transformer architecture to predict cellular traffic. However, the combination of four transformer blocks in ST-Tran increases the parameter size, resulting in more memory usage and longer runtime. Therefore, this paper aims to build a simpler and more efficient model based on Transformer.

The sequence modeling ability of Transformer is utilized in this paper to model the space-time sequence of wireless cellular network traffic. We design a multi encoder-single decoder structure named Traffic-Tran to model sequence data by using the attention mechanism in each encoder. Multiple encoders in Traffic-Tran capture the spatio-temporal characteristic in parallel. After decoding this information, the output module will be used for multi-step prediction. Traffic-Tran can achieve effective cellular network traffic prediction with fewer training parameters.

2   System Model

2.1   Milan Data Description

The wireless cellular traffic data used in this paper comes from the Milan Telecom Data set [11], which is jointly initiated by Telecom Italia and European Institute of Innovation and Technology (EIT), and records the real wireless traffic data of Milan, Italy. Milan has a total population of about 1.3 million and covers an area of about 522 square kilometers. To collect wireless traffic data, Milan is evenly divided into $H \times W$ grids, each with a size of about (235 m $\times$ 235 m), where H and W are both 100. This data set records the traffic data of wireless mobile users in Milan, including five traffic services: receiving and dialing call services(Call-in, Call-out), receiving and sending short message services(SMS-in, SMS-out) and mobile internet services(Internet).

In the data set, wireless service traffic was recorded for 62 days from November 1, 2013 to January 1, 2014. Five kinds of wireless traffic of each grid are recorded and stored every ten minutes, that is, every ten minutes is a time granularity. The data at each time granularity is called a timestamp. Since there are many blank values in the data set collected by the 10-minute time granularity, which will lead to experimental errors. Therefore, the 10-minute time granularity is further aggregated into the one-hour time granularity before the experiment. Therefore, we finally got a time series data set of hourly time granularity in 62 days with a sequence length of 1488.

2.2   Problem Statement

The prediction of cellular traffic is further introduced as follows. This paper will finally realize the multi-step prediction of cellular flow, and the time step of the prediction result is expressed by T_{target}. As mentioned in the previous chapter, the predicted traffic value is highly correlated with similar times on the same day and relative times in the preceding days. In this paper, as shown in Fig. 1, the similar times on the same day is called close data $X_{close} \in \mathbb{R}^{N \times T_{close}}$, and its time step is T_{close}. In the same way, the relative times in the preceding days is called period data $X_{period} \in \mathbb{R}^{N \times T_{period} \times p}$, its time step is T_{period} for each of the previous p days, where N is the number of grids.

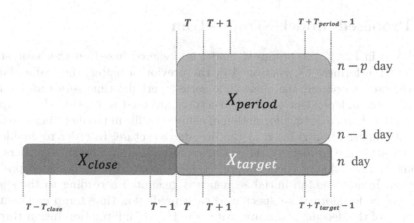

Fig. 1. Construction of X_{close}, X_{period} and X_{target}.

In order to capture the correlation between different grids, we use each grid data under the same timestamp to generate spatial sequence data. However, due to the large number of grids N, the correlation between all grids cannot be constructed. Therefore, we use (1) to quantify the correlation between grids and select K grids most related to grids as sequence data $X_{spatial}$.

$$R_{X,Y} = \frac{cov(X,Y)}{\sigma_x \cdot \sigma_y}, \tag{1}$$

where X and Y represent two grids.

The system model of wireless cellular network traffic prediction is roughly expressed as:

$$X_{target} = f(X_{close}, X_{period}, X_{spatial}), \tag{2}$$

where X_{close} and X_{period} are time sequence data, $X_{spatial}$ is spatial sequence data, and $f(*)$ is a nonlinear function constructed by deep learning algorithm.

The objective of the entire network is to reduce the error between the predicted value and the real value. We quantify the final performance using the following three evaluation indexes:

$$MAE = \frac{1}{n} \sum_1^n |\hat{y}_i - y_i|, \tag{3}$$

$$RMSE = \sqrt{\frac{1}{n} \sum_1^n (\hat{y}_i - y_i)^2}, \tag{4}$$

$$R^2 = 1 - \frac{\sum_1^n (\hat{y}_i - y_i)^2}{\sum_1^n (y_i - \bar{y})^2}, \tag{5}$$

where n is the number of the sample, $\hat{y}_i$ is the predicted value of the sample, y_i is the label of the sample and $\bar{y}$ is the mean of the sample.

3   Proposed Model—Traffic-Tran

As shown in Fig. 2, the proposed model is designed based on the basic structure of Transformer. As mentioned in the previous chapter, the traffic data is preprocessed to obtain the close time series, periodic time series and spatial series. Three independent encoder structures are used to capture the temporal and spatial characteristic information of cellular traffic in parallel, then the characteristic information is fused in the decoder structure. In order to enable the decoder structure to identify the feature information of different encoders, the outputs of the different encoders are further encoded by the designed position function. In addition, an initial sequence is generated according to the spatio-temporal node information specific to each prediction timestamp as the input sequence of the decoder structure. After the feature information fusion through the decoder, the final cellular traffic prediction is carried out through the output module.

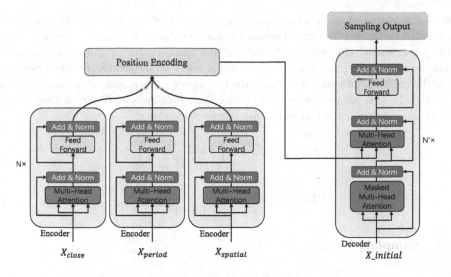

Fig. 2. Overview of Traffic-Tran.

3.1   Multi Encoder-Single Decoder Structure

The close data, periodic data and spatial data have different correlations, so it is necessary to construct different nonlinear functions to represent the correlations between the data and predict values. In this paper, multiple independent encoders structures are proposed to capture the feature information carried by different data in parallel. In addition, a single decoder is used to fuse the information captured by different encoders in order to balance the dependence between predicted values and different feature information. The core operation in encoders and decoders is the multi-head attention layer. The multi-head attention layer can effectively process sequence data. Note that the decoder needs to input an initial sequence to process the information from the encoder. In order to better realize the multi-step prediction of cellular flow, the predicted value of each step will generate a unique initial sequence called $X_{initial}$ according to its spatio-temporal position. Specifically, the initial sequence of the predicted values of each step carries the close information of T_{close} step and the periodic information of p step.

3.2   Position Encoding

Since recurrence and convolution are not included in our model, in order to recognize order of the sequences based on our model, we must inject some information about the relative or absolute positions of sequences. Among Traffic-Tran, two modules use position encoding to inject order information. One is to inject internal relative position information into the input sequence of each encoder structure, the other is to inject external relative position information into the output sequence of all encoders. Among them, the effectiveness of infusing information into the encoder input sequence has been proved in many scenarios, and this paper creatively proposes to infuse information into the output sequence of encoder. Different from the previous single-encoder structure, Traffic-Tran uses the design of multi-encoder structure to capture more feature information in parallel. In this paper, we use sine and cosine functions of different frequencies [9] as supplementary information for relative positions:

$$PE_{(pos,2i)} = \sin\left(\frac{pos}{10000^{\frac{2i}{d_{model}}}}\right), \tag{6}$$

$$PE_{(pos,2i+1)} = \cos\left(\frac{pos}{10000^{\frac{2i}{d_{model}}}}\right). \tag{7}$$

3.3 Sampling Output

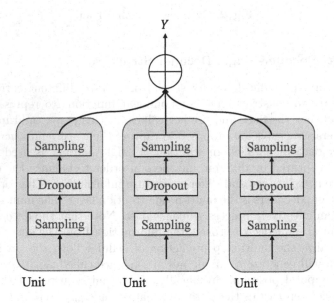

Fig. 3. Sampling output structure.

The prediction of each time step corresponds to the initial sequence of the decoder input one by one, and the prediction of each time step does not share parameters in the output module. This paper presents a multi-step prediction of cellular traffic, so this output module contains multiple independent network units. This section takes the prediction of three time steps as an example to illustrate the output module. The prediction of three timestamps is shown in Fig. 3, thus containing three network units. Each network unit is composed of the dropout layer, which is to prevent overfitting, and two sampling layers, where the sampling layer downsample the feature information. After the initial sequence of each prediction time step is fused with feature information in the decoder, the network unit in the output module is used to predict the output of this time step. Multiple network units in the output module are parallel to achieve multi-step prediction.

Most of the research works is to predict the output directly through fully connected layer after the feature information fusion. The output module uses a more advanced network structure to get more accurate prediction results than the output directly through the fully connected layer. In addition, because the output module can independently use the sequence vector output by the decoder structure, the design of output module realizes multi-step prediction of traffic data using different learnable parameters in parallel.

4   Experimental Results and Analysis

4.1   Experiment Setup

Experiments were conducted on Call-in data from Telecommunication activities mentioned in Sect. 2.1. We chose 400 from all 10000 grids. The time dimension T_{close}, T_{period} and T_{target} of the sequence data are all 3, and the period days $p = 3$. In other words, each sample contains a total of 15 timestamps, and each timestamp contains 400 grid Call-in data, among which the sequence data of twelve timestamps will be used as the input of the model, and the remaining three timestamps will be used as labels. In the data set containing 1488 time stamps, a total of 1413 samples are generated, among which 168 samples are used as test dataset D_{test} and the remaining 1245 samples are used as training dataset D_{train}.

In the same experimental environment (GeForce RTX 2080Ti), the comparison experiments of Traffic-Tran and other strategy are conducted. The network models are trained with the widely used optimization technique, Adam [12] with 500 epochs. The size of mini-batch is determined according to the complexity of the model. The initial learning rate is set to 0.001, and the effective learning rate follows a polynomial decay.

4.2   The Depth of Decoder

The decoder of Transformer is composed of a stack of $N = 6$ identical layers. In order to improve the ability of Traffic-Tran to fuse feature information, we conducted an experiment on the structural depth of the decoder. The effect of decoder depth is shown in Table 1. MAE and $RMSE$ are the lower the better, and R^2 is the closer to 1 the better. When N is 8, the values of MAE and $RMSE$ are the smallest, and R^2 is the closest to 1, achieving the best prediction performance. So the decoder of our model is composed of a stack of $N = 8$ identical layers.

Table 1. Effect of decoder depth.

N	MAE	RMSE	R^2	Params
6	10.29568	0.56877	0.80760	3593219
7	10.08085	0.56832	0.80790	3791235
8	10.04836	0.55609	0.81608	3989251
9	10.13335	0.56944	0.80714	4187267
10	10.16580	0.56759	0.80840	4385283

4.3 Performance Evaluation

We compared the results of Traffic-Tran with two widely used methods:

- STDenseNet: STDenseNet [4] learns spatial-temporal features using densely connected CNNs and fuse feature information by fully connected layer.
- ST-Tran: ST-Tran [10] is the first to apply the transformer architecture to predict cellular traffic. The combination of four transformer blocks is used to model temporal and spatial correlations.

Table 2. Comparison on Traffic-Tran and two widely used methods.

Model	MAE	RMSE	R^2	Params
STDenseNet	12.74558	0.62273	0.76935	249816
ST-Tran	10.00348	0.53643	0.82885	7239844
Traffic-Tran	10.04836	0.55609	0.81608	3989251

The effectiveness of Traffic-Tran compared to other methods is shown in Table 2. Compared with STDenseNet, Traffic-Tran has a significant advantage in predicting performance, but it also uses more trainable parameters. Compared with ST-Tran, Traffic-Tran's prediction performance is similar to that of ST-Tran, but the training parameters are greatly reduced, which achieves significant advantage in model complexity. Figure 4 shows the results of Traffic prediction using Traffic-Tran for one of the grids.

In general, Traffic-Tran can complete multi-step Traffic prediction, and its prediction performance is almost the same as that of the best prediction scheme. Moreover, the model complexity of Traffic-Tran is greatly reduced, with less memory usage and shorter runtime than other models.

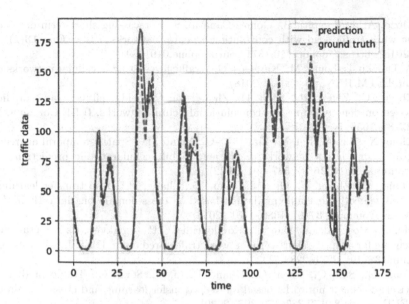

Fig. 4. Results of traffic prediction using Traffic-Tran.

5   Conclusion

Traffic-Tran can complete multi-step Traffic prediction, and the model complexity of Traffic-Tran is greatly reduced, with less memory usage and shorter runtime than other models. Traffic-Tran can construct complex nonlinear data caused by user movement, service randomness and regional limitations in wireless services, and obtain a prediction model with strong generalization performance. Experimental results on a large real dataset verify the effectiveness of Traffic Tran. Compared with existing prediction schemes, Traffic-Tran can realize parallel multi-step prediction, and its model architecture is simpler and more efficient. The number of parameters to be trained in the model decreases by 44.9%. However, its prediction accuracy has not improved, and more advanced architectures will be developed to further improve performance in the future. When the data set is limited, the combination of Traffic-Tran and transfer learning can be considered, so that only parameters in the output module can be trained in the target domain to improve the prediction performance.

Acknowledgment. This work was supported in part by the State Major Science and Technology Special Projects (Grant No. 2018ZX03001024) and in part by the National Key Research and Development Program (Grant No. 2022YFF0610303).

References

1. Cisco annual internet report (2018–2023) white paper. https://www.cisco.com/c/en/us/solutions/collateral/executive-perspectives/annual-Internet-report/white-paper-c11-741490.html. Accessed 9 Mar 2020

2. Mozo, A., Ordozgoiti, B., Gómez-Canaval, S.: Forecasting short-term data center network traffic load with convolutional neural networks. PLOS One **13**(2), 1–31 (2018). https://doi.org/10.1371/journal.pone.0191939
3. A. Dalgkitsis, Louta, M., Karetsos, G.: Traffic forecasting in cellular networks using the LSTM RNN, pp. 28–33 (2018)
4. Zhang, C., Zhang, H., Yuan, D., Zhang, M.: Citywide cellular traffic prediction based on densely connected convolutional neural networks. IEEE Commun. Lett. **22**(8), 1656–1659 (2018)
5. Zhao, N., Wu, A., Pei, Y., Liang, Y.-C., Niyato, D.: Spatial-temporal aggregation graph convolution network for efficient mobile cellular traffic prediction. IEEE Commun. Lett. **26**(3), 587–591 (2022)
6. Zhang, C., Zhang, H., Qiao, J., Yuan, D., Zhang, M.: Deep transfer learning for intelligent cellular traffic prediction based on cross-domain big data. IEEE J. Sel. Areas Commun. **37**(6), 1389–1401 (2019)
7. He, Q., Moayyedi, A., Dán, G., Koudouridis, G.P., Tengkvist, P.: A meta-learning scheme for adaptive short-term network traffic prediction. IEEE J. Sel. Areas Commun. **38**(10), 2271–2283 (2020)
8. Zeng, Q., Sun, Q., Chen, G., Duan, H., Li, C., Song, G.: Traffic prediction of wireless cellular networks based on deep transfer learning and cross-domain data. IEEE Access **8**, 172 387–172 397 (2020)
9. Vaswani, A., et al.: Attention is all you need. In: Guyon, I., et al. (eds.) Advances in Neural Information Processing Systems, vol. 30. Curran Associates Inc. (2017)
10. Liu, Q., Li, J., Lu, Z.: ST-Tran: Spatial-temporal transformer for cellular traffic prediction. IEEE Commun. Lett. **25**(10), 3325–3329 (2021)
11. Barlacchi, G., et al.: A multi-source dataset of urban life in the city of Milan and the Province of Trentino. Sci. Data **2**, 150055 (2015)
12. Kingma, D.P., Ba, J.: Adam: a method for stochastic optimization. CoRR, vol. abs/1412.6980 (2015)

Beam Illumination and Resource Allocation for Multi-beam Satellite Systems

Xiaorui Tang$^{(\boxtimes)}$, Rong Chai, and Kang'an Gui

School of Communications and Information Engineering, Chongqing University of Posts and Telecommunications, Chongqing 400065, People's Republic of China
2958788464@qq.com

Abstract. Multi-beam satellite communication systems have received considerable attentions in recent years. By generating multiple beams at the transmitting satellites, the coverage areas can be enlarged and the transmission capacity can be improved. In this paper, we study beam illumination and resource allocation problem in multi-beam satellite communication systems. Jointly considering the revenue received from successful packet transmission and the energy consumption required for packet transmission, we define a system utility function and formulate joint user grouping, beam illumination, and time-frequency resource allocation problem as a constrained utility function maximization problem. Since beam illumination and time-frequency resource allocation problems are of different time and regional scales, this paper proposes a two-stage resource allocation algorithm. On relatively large temporal scale, we propose an offline user grouping algorithm and a group-oriented beam illumination scheme. Then based on the obtained user grouping and beam assignment strategy, an online resource scheduling algorithm is proposed, which schedules time and frequency resources for individual users. Numerical results verify the effectiveness of the proposed algorithm.

Keywords: Multi-beam satellite systems · Resource allocation · Two-stage resource allocation algorithm

1 Introduction

With the rapid development of mobile Internet applications, the exponential growth of data traffic brings huge challenges to terrestrial cellular networks. Benefited from their wide coverage, high throughput and low cost, satellite communication systems are expected to act as an efficient complementary to the terrestrial systems and offer high-performance data transmission services to the terrestrial users [1]. To further enhance the transmission performance of satellite communications, multiple beams (multi-beam) satellite systems can be exploited. Specifically, by generating multiple satellite beams and allowing individual beams to provide services for different areas, the coverage area of

© ICST Institute for Computer Sciences, Social Informatics and Telecommunications Engineering 2023
Published by Springer Nature Switzerland AG 2023. All Rights Reserved
F. Gao et al. (Eds.): ChinaCom 2022, LNICST 500, pp. 347–361, 2023.
https://doi.org/10.1007/978-3-031-34790-0_27

the satellites can be enlarged and system throughput is expected to increase significantly [2].

In multi-beam satellite communication systems, the diverse user service requirements and time-varying channel characteristics pose challenges to the resource management schemes. In [3], the problem of user grouping was investigated for a multiuser multi-beam satellite system where each user group is illuminated by one individual satellite beam, and a sum-rate maximization-based user grouping algorithm was proposed. The beam scheduling and time-frequency resource allocation issue was considered for multi-beam satellite systems in [4–6]. Reference [4] proposed a sub-channel allocation scheme which maximizes the throughput of the satellite communication system. Reference [5] studied the wavelength and time slot allocation issue in satellite optical networks, and proposed an elastic resource allocation algorithm to reduce the communication blocking rate. An optimal power control and subchannel allocation scheme was proposed to maximize the total data rate and the number of accessing users [6].

Aiming to reduce inter-beam interference in multi-beam satellite systems, [7] proposed a heuristic beam shut off algorithm to minimize the number of active beams. Joint beam illumination and resource allocation problem was investigated for low-orbit satellites in [8]. The authors proposed a hybrid multi-beamforming-based low-power channel allocation method so as to minimize the number of handovers. Reference [9] studied the joint resource allocation problem and formulated the problem of frequency selection, beam allocation and power allocation as a sum-rate maximization model.

In this paper, we investigate the problem of user grouping and resource allocation for multi-beam satellite communication systems. Considering different time scales of user grouping and time-frequency resource scheduling, we first propose an offline user grouping algorithm. Given user grouping strategy, a beam illumination strategy is designed for user groups, then an intra-group time-frequency resource allocation strategy is proposed for ground users (GUs) inside individual user groups.

2   System Model

In this paper, we consider a satellite communication system consisting of a multi-beam low orbit satellite (LEO) satellite and multiple GUs, where the LEO satellite is equipped with an onboard transceiver thus is capable of transmitting data packets to GUs via service links. In order to improve data transmission capacity, the satellite supports a number of spot beams with each beam covering certain GUs. Let K denote the number of spot beams, and r denote the coverage radius of each beam. The total bandwidth of the satellite is divided into F sub-channels, and the sub-channels are full-frequency multiplexed among beams. Let B represent the bandwidth of each sub-channel. Denote user n as GU_n and (x_n, y_n) as the coordinate of GU_n, $1 \leq n \leq N$.

For convenience, system time T is divided into consecutive equal-length time slots, and the time slot length is τ. Without loss of generality, we assume that the channel characteristics of the links from the satellite to the GUs may change over time, however, they remain unchanged in each time slot. The system model considered in this paper is shown in Fig. 1.

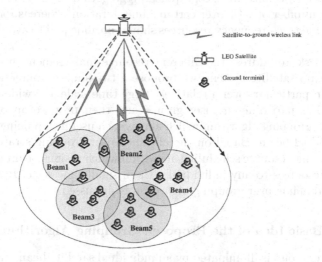

Fig. 1. System Model

2.1   Mission Executing Scenario

Let q_n denote the service characteristics of GU_n, which can be described as: $q_n = <s_n, w_n, T_n^{\max}>$, where s_n represents the size of the data packets of GU_n, and w_n denotes the service weight of the data packets of GU_n. Note that w_n indicates the relative importance and urgency of the service of GU_n. $T_n^{\max}$ denotes the transmission deadline of the packets of GU_n. Specifically, the data packets of GU_n should be transmitted before $T_n^{\max}$, otherwise, the packets will be dropped.

Let $h_{t,n,f}$ represent the channel gain of the service link from the satellite to GU_n in time slot t on sub-channel f, which can be modelled as $h_{t,n,f} = g^t g_n^r L_{t,n,f}$, where $g^t = \frac{2\pi - (2\pi - \theta)\delta}{\theta}$, is the transmit antenna gain of satellite beams, θ is the antenna beam width, $\delta \ll 1$ is a constant, g_n^r is the receive antenna gain of GU_n and $L_{t,n,f}$ represents the free space loss of the link from the satellite to GU_n in time slot t on sub-channel f, which can be expressed as $L_{t,n,f} = \left(\frac{c}{4\pi d_{t,n}\xi_f}\right)^2$, where c represents the speed of light, $d_{t,n}$ is the distance between the satellite and GU_n in time slot t, and ξ_f is the carrier frequency of sub-channel f.

3   Proposed Offline User Grouping Algorithm

To enable efficient data transmission from the satellite to the GUs in the considered satellite system, each GU should be illuminated by one satellite beam and specific time-frequency resources should be assigned to the GU. However, it should be noted that beam illumination and time-frequency resource allocation are of different time and region scales. Specifically, on account of the given beam width of satellite beams and geographical aggregation of GUs, one beam may illuminate a number of GUs over certain time duration, whereas for an individual GU, unique time-frequency resources should be allocated to avoid intra-beam interference.

In this work, to address the different resource management granularities in the multi-beam satellite system, we propose a two-stage resource management algorithm. In particular, over a relatively large time scale and wide region scale, we divide GUs into different user groups and then propose an offline beam-oriented user grouping algorithm which allows each user group being illuminated by an individual beam. Based on the obtained user grouping strategy, we then present an online resource scheduling algorithm which assigns beam and time slot scheduling resources to any individual GUs in small time scale. In this section, the proposed offline user grouping algorithm is discussed.

3.1   The Basic Idea of the Proposed Grouping Algorithm

Since one user group is illuminated by an individual satellite beam, in an attempt to utilize the beam resources in an efficient manner, the number of user groups should be highly limited under the constraint of beam coverage area. Aiming to achieve a tradeoff between the number of groups and the characteristics of user aggregation, we assign high priority to boundary users and propose a heuristic priority-based grouping algorithm.

Given the geographical distribution of the GUs, we form a minimum convex hull containing all the GUs. For convenience, we refer the GUs located at the boundary of the convex hull as boundary users and the remaining users as the internal users. The basic idea of the proposed algorithm is that starting from one boundary user, the neighboring boundary users are grouped, then by moving the circle covering all the grouped users using minimum enclosing circle method, as many internal users are grouped as possible. The procedure repeats until all the users are grouped.

3.2   Algorithm Description

The steps of the proposed user grouping algorithm are summarized as follows.

a) Initialization: Let Φ_m be the set of GUs in the m-th user group, and Φ_m^c be the m-th candidate user group. Set $m = 1$, $\Phi_m = \Phi_m^c = \emptyset$, where $\emptyset$ denotes the empty set.
b) Determine boundary users and internal users: Create a convex hull containing all the users, determine the boundary users and internal users of the hull. Let the sets of boundary users and internal users be N_b and N_{in}, respectively.

c) Evaluate the distance degree of GUs: Let $d_{n,n'}$ represent the distance between GU_n and $GU_{n'}$, $1 \leq n \neq n' \leq N$. Let ρ_n denote the distance degree of GU_n, which is defined as the sum of the distances between GU_n and all other GUs, i.e., $\rho_n = \sum_{n'=1,n' \neq n}^{N} d_{n,n'}$.

d) Select the ungrouped boundary user with the highest distance degree: Among all the ungrouped boundary users, i.e., $GU_n \in \mathbb{N}_b$, select the one with the highest distance degree, i.e., if $\rho_{n_0} = \max\{\rho_1, \ldots, \rho_N\}$, then GU_{n_0} is selected to initiate user grouping, update the set of the m-th group and the boundary set as $\Phi_m = \Phi_m \cup \{GU_{n_0}\}$ and $\mathbb{N}_b = \mathbb{N}_b/\{GU_{n_0}\}$.

e) Determine the GUs of the m-th user group: Collect the boundary users whose distance with GU_{n_0} is less than or equal to r into the m-th user group, i.e., $\forall GU_n \in \mathbb{N}_b$, check if $d_{n_0,n} \leq r$, if yes, then put GU_n into the m-th user group. Update the set of Φ_m as $\Phi_m = \Phi_m \cup \{GU_n\}$. Remove GU_n from the set of boundary users, i.e., $\mathbb{N}_b = \mathbb{N}_b/\{GU_n\}$. Denote C_m as the circle with the center being GU_{n_0} and the radius being r.

f) Determine the m-th candidate user set: If there exist boundary users whose distance with GU_{n_0} is greater than r and less than or equal to $2r$, then put these users into the m-th candidate user set. That is, if $\forall GU_n \in \mathbb{N}_b$ and $r < d_{n_0,n} \leq 2r$, then put GU_n into the m-th candidate user set. Update the candidate user set as $\Phi_m^c = \Phi_m^c \cup \{GU_n\}$.

g) Move C_m to cover as many candidate users as possible: Under the condition that all the GUs in Φ_m are covered by C_m, move the center of C_m to cover as many candidate users as possible by applying the minimum enclosing circle algorithm (discussed in next subsection). Update the corresponding sets. In particular, if $GU_{n_1} \in \mathbb{N}_b \cap \Phi_m^c$ and GU_{n_1} is covered by C_m, then put GU_{n_1} into the m-th user group, i.e., $\Phi_m = \Phi_m \cup \{GU_{n_1}\}$, remove GU_{n_1} from the sets of boundary users and candidate users, i.e., $\mathbb{N}_b = \mathbb{N}_b/\{GU_{n_1}\}$, $\Phi_m^c = \Phi_m^c/\{GU_{n_1}\}$. Let $\overline{GU}_m$ denote the virtual center user of the m-th user group, and $(\bar{x}_m, \bar{y}_m)$ denote the location of $\overline{GU}_m$.

h) Put the internal users covered by C_m into the m-th user group: Calculate the distance between internal user $GU_{n_1} \in \mathbb{N}_{in}$ and $\overline{GU}_m$, denoted by $\bar{d}_{n_1,m}$. If $\bar{d}_{n_1,m} \leq r$, then put GU_{n_1} into the m-th user group, update the m-th user set, i.e., $\Phi_m = \Phi_m \cup \{GU_{n_1}\}$, remove GU_{n_1} from the set of internal users, i.e., $\mathbb{N}_{in} = \mathbb{N}_{in}/\{GU_{n_1}\}$.

i) Evaluate the termination of the algorithm: If all the users are grouped, that is, $\mathbb{N}_b = \mathbb{N}_{in} = \emptyset$, the algorithm terminates, otherwise, let $m = m + 1$, return to Step d).

3.3   The Minimum Enclosing Circle Method-Based Group Position Update Algorithm

In this work, the minimum enclosing circle algorithm is applied to determine the optimal positions of individual groups.

The main idea of the minimum enclosing circle method is that given existing users, a circle with a minimum radius is determined which covers all the existing users. The procedure of the minimum enclosing circle method-based group position update algorithm is summarized as below.

a) Select two users in Φ_m: Give the set Φ_m, which consists of the boundary users with the distance from GU_{n_0} being less than or equal to r, two users of the farthest distance are selected and denoted as GU_{n_1} and GU_{n_2}, respectively.
b) Form an initial circle: Draw a circle with the diameter being the line connecting the two points GU_{n_1} and GU_{n_2}. If the circle covers all the GUs, put all the ungrouped GUs in Φ_m, update user sets and the algorithm completes, otherwise, move to Step c).
c) Select an ungrouped GU: From the candidate user set Φ_m^c, select one GU which is located outside the circle. That is, if $GU_{n_3} \in \Phi_m^c$ and $\bar{d}_{m_0,n_3} > r$, then GU_{n_3} is selected. Remove GU_{n_3} from Φ_m^c, i.e., $\Phi_m^c = \Phi_m^c / GU_{n_3}$.
d) Determine the minimum circle covering three GUs: Based on the three GUs, form the minimum circle. If the radius of the circle is less than or equal to r, and the circle covers all the GUs in Φ_m, then put GU_{n_3} in Φ_m, set $\Phi_m = \Phi_m \cup GU_{n_3}$, otherwise, check if $\Phi_m^c = \emptyset$, if yes, the algorithm terminates, else, move to Step c).

4   Resource Allocation Problem Formulation

In this section, given the obtained user grouping strategy, system utility function is defined which jointly considers the reward received for transmitting data packets and the consumed energy of the satellite. Then, a constrained resource allocation optimization problem is formulated to maximize system utility.

4.1   System Utility Function Formulation

Considering the overall utility of all the GUs in the system, we define system utility function U as

$$U = \sum_{n=1}^{N} U_n \tag{1}$$

where U_n represents the utility function of GU_n, which can be modeled as the difference between reward and cost for transmitting data packets from the satellite to GU_n, i.e.,

$$U_n = \lambda_1 \eta_n - \lambda_2 \tilde{E}_n \tag{2}$$

where λ_1 and λ_2 are weighting factors, η_n represents the reward that the satellite earns from transmitting the data packets of GU_n. Without loss of generality, it is assume that only if the data packets are received before the predefined deadline, the satellite is rewarded certain payment, hence, the reward function η_n can be modeled as $\eta_n = w_n \alpha_n$, where α_n represents the packet drop identifier, which is given by

$$\alpha_n = 1_{\{T_n \leq \lceil \frac{T_n^{\max}}{\tau} \rceil\}} \tag{3}$$

where $1_{\{\cdot\}}$ is an indicator function. If a logical variable x is true, $1_{\{x\}} = 1$; otherwise, $1_{\{x\}} = 0$, T_n is the time slot that the data transmission of GU_n is completed. It can be shown that in order to transit all the data packets of GU_n, T_n should meet the following constraints.

$$\text{C1}: \sum_{t=1}^{T_n-1} \sum_{m=1}^{M} \sum_{k=1}^{K} \sum_{f=1}^{F} z_{t,m,k} x_{t,n,m,f} R_{t,n,m,f} \tau < s_n \tag{4}$$

$$\text{C2}: \sum_{t=1}^{T_n} \sum_{m=1}^{M} \sum_{k=1}^{K} \sum_{f=1}^{F} z_{t,m,k} x_{t,n,m,f} R_{t,n,m,f} \tau \geq s_n \tag{5}$$

where $z_{t,k,m} \in \{0,1\}$ is the beam illumination variable of user groups, i.e., $z_{t,k,m} = 1$, if user group m is illuminated by satellite beam k at time slot t, otherwise, $z_{t,k,m} = 0$, $x_{t,n,m,f}$ denotes the time-frequency allocation variable of GUs, $x_{t,n,m,f} = 1$, if sub-channel f is assigned to GU_n in user group m at time slot t, otherwise, $x_{t,n,m,f} = 0$, $1 \leq t \leq T$, $1 \leq n \leq N$, $1 \leq m \leq M$, $1 \leq f \leq F$, $R_{t,n,m,f}$ denotes the achievable data rate of GU_n in user group m when receiving data from the satellite on sub-channel f in time slot t. $R_{t,n,m,f}$ can be expressed as

$$R_{t,n,m,f} = B \log(1 + \frac{x_{t,n,m,f} p g^t g_n^r L_{t,n,f}}{N_0 B}) \tag{6}$$

where p represents the transmit power of satellite beams and N_0 is the power spectral density of additive white Gaussian noise (AWGN).

$\tilde{E}_n$ in (3) is the normalized energy consumption of the satellite when transmitting the data packets of GU_n, which is defined as

$$\tilde{E}_n = \frac{E^{\max} - E_n}{E^{\max} - E^{\min}} \tag{7}$$

where $E^{\max} = \max_n \{E_n\}$, $E^{\min} = \min_n \{E_n\}$, and E_n represents the energy consumption of the satellite when transmitting data packets to GU_n, which can be computed as

$$E_n = \sum_{t=1}^{T_n} \sum_{m=1}^{M} \sum_{k=1}^{K} \sum_{f=1}^{F} z_{t,m,k} x_{t,n,m,f} p \tau \tag{8}$$

4.2   Optimization Problem Formulation

Aiming to maximize the system utility function under the constraints, we formulate the beam illumination and resource allocation problem of the considered multibeam satellite system as follows

$$
\max_{x_{t,n,m,f},z_{t,m,k}} U
$$

$$
\text{s.t.} \quad C1, C2
$$

$$
C3 : \sum_{m=1}^{M} y_{n,m} \leq 1
$$

$$
C4 : \sum_{k=1}^{K} z_{t,m,k} \leq 1
$$

$$
C5 : \sum_{m=1}^{M} \sum_{f=1}^{F} x_{t,n,m,f} \leq 1 \tag{9}
$$

$$
C6 : \sum_{m=1}^{M} \sum_{GU_n \in \Phi_m} \sum_{f=1}^{F} x_{t,n,m,f} \leq \min\{F, \left\lfloor \tfrac{p_b}{p} \right\rfloor\}
$$

$$
C7 : x_{t,n,m,f} 1_{\{z_{t,m,k}=0\}} = 0
$$

$$
C8 : R_{t,n,m,f} \geq x_{t,n,m,f} R_n^{\min}
$$

where C1 and C2 are the data packet transmission time constraints, C3 indicates that a user can only be associated with one user group, C4 represents that a user group can only be associated with one beam, C5 is the sub-channel association constraint. C6 is the maximum transmit power constraint of the satellite, where p_b is the maximum transmit power of a single satellite beam. C7 describes the coupling constraint between beam illumination and sub-channel allocation. C8 is the minimum transmission rate constraint, where $R_n^{\min}$ is the minumum data rate requirement of GU_n.

The formulated problem involves joint optimization of beam illumination and time-frequency resource allocation, which is difficult to solve conveniently due to the tight coupling of these problems. Considering the different granularities of beam illumination and resource allocation, we split the original optimization problem into two sub-problems, i.e., beam illumination sub-problem and time-frequency resource scheduling sub-problem, and design user group-oriented beam illumination algorithm and GU-oriented time-frequency resource scheduling algorithm, respectively.

5   User Group-Oriented Beam Illumination

Considering the fact that the distance between the satellite and the GUs is much longer than that between two GUs inside one user group, we ignore the variation of the link transmission performance of the GUs in one user group, employ virtual users to represent individual user groups and design a proportional fairness-based beam illumination strategy.

5.1   Service Model of Virtual Users

According to the user grouping algorithm discussed in Sect. 4, the virtual user of user group m is denoted by $\overline{GU}_m$, which is located in the center of the group. Given user grouping strategy $y_{n,m}^*$, the weighted aggregation traffic of $\overline{GU}_m$, denoted by $\bar{S}_m$, can be computed as

$$\bar{S}_m = \sum_{n=1}^{N} y_{n,m}^* w_n s_n \tag{10}$$

To characterize the diverse transmission deadline requirements of the GUs in user groups, we denote $\bar{T}_m$ as the maximum deadline of the GUs in user group m, which is computed as $\bar{T}_m = \max\{T_n^{\max}\}, \forall GU_n \in \Phi_m$.

6   Number of Beam-Slot Elements Allocated for User Groups

It can be understood in a straightforward manner that if one user group is of higher aggregate traffic requirement, a larger amount of beam and time slot resources should be assigned. To describe the beam illumination status of user groups, we introduce the concept of beam-slot element for convenience. Specifically, in the case that in one time slot, a satellite beam is assigned to illuminate one user group, we refer that one beam-slot element is allocated to the user group.

Let $N_0 = KT$ denote the total number of beam-slot elements and ϵ_m denote the number of beam-slot elements allocated to user group m. Applying proportional fairness scheme, we obtain

$$\frac{\epsilon_1}{\bar{S}_1} \approx \frac{\epsilon_2}{\bar{S}_2} \approx \cdots \approx \frac{\epsilon_m}{\bar{S}_M} \tag{11}$$

Under the constraint $\sum_{m=1}^{M} \epsilon_m = N_0$, we may solve the above equation and obtain ϵ_m, $1 \leq m \leq M$. ϵ_m represents the number of beam-slot elements which should be assigned to user group m, however, the specific beam-slot scheduling strategy still should be determined. To this end, we examine the transmission performance of user groups in different time slots. According to the definitions of utility function specified in (5) and (6), under the circumstance that the transmission deadline constraint is satisfied, maximizing the utility function is equivalent to minimizing the energy consumption of the satellite beams. Furthermore, as the transmit power is a given constant, when multiple transmission slots are required, minimizing the energy consumption is equivalent to assigning GUs to the time slots with the highest data rate, so as to reduce the overall time slots. As a consequence, we may assign satellite beams to user groups in the time slots when higher data rate is achieved.

6.1   Beam Illumination Sub-problem Formulation

Let $\bar{U}_m$ denote the aggregate utility function of user group m, suppose $\overline{\mathrm{GU}}_m$ is assigned satellite beam k at time slot t. For simplicity, it is assumed that the transmission performance of $\overline{\mathrm{GU}}_m$ on different sub-channels is similar, and the difference is negligible. Denote $\bar{R}_m$ as the transmission data rate of $\overline{\mathrm{GU}}_m$ in time slot t when a satellite beam is assigned, we obtain

$$\bar{R}_{t,m,f} = B\log(1 + \frac{pg^t g_n^r \bar{L}_{t,m,f}}{N_0 B}) \tag{12}$$

where $\bar{L}_{t,m,f}$ is the path loss from the satellite to $\overline{\mathrm{GU}}_m$.

To characterize the beam-slot scheduling strategy, we further apply resource virtualization scheme, and virtualize user group m into ϵ_m virtual groups with each virtual group being assigned one beam-slot element. Accordingly, the beam illumination sub-problem can be formulated as

$$\begin{aligned}
\max_{\bar{z}_{t,m,a_m,k}} \quad & \sum_{t=1}^{T}\sum_{m=1}^{M}\sum_{k=1}^{K} R_{t,m,k} \\
\text{s.t.} \quad & \sum_{t=1}^{T}\sum_{k=1}^{K} \bar{z}_{t,m,a_m,k} \le 1 \\
& \sum_{m=1}^{M}\sum_{a_m=1}^{\epsilon_m} \bar{z}_{t,m,a_m,k} \le 1 \\
& \bar{z}_{t,m,a_m,k} 1_{\{t>\bar{T}_m\}} = 0
\end{aligned} \tag{13}$$

The above formulated optimization problem can be regarded as a one-to-one matching problem which maps beam-slot element (t,k) to virtual user group (m, a_m). To solve the problem, we first map the optimization problem into a weighted complete bipartite graph with bipartite division $G^0 = (V_1, V_2, E, W)$, where V_1 and V_2 are the set of vertices, $V_1 = \{(m, a_m)\}$ denotes the set of virtual groups, where (m, a_m) represents the virtual group a_m in user group m, $V_2 = \{(t,k)\}$ represents the set of beam-slot elements, $E = \{e(v_1, v_2)\}$ denotes the set of edges which connect vertex $v_1 \in V_1$ to another vertex $v_1 \in V_2$, $W = \{w(v_1, v_2)\}$ is the set of edge weights, $\{w(v_1, v_2)\}$ denotes the weight of the edge $e(v_1, v_2) \in E$. If $v_1 = \{(m, a_m)\}$, $v_2 = \{(t,k)\}$, then $w(v_1, v_2) = R_{t,m,k}$. Applying Kuhn-Munkres algorithm, we are able to solve the optimization problem and obtain the beam illumination strategy for the virtual groups, denoted by $\bar{z}^*_{t,m,a_m,k}$. Denote $z^*_{t,m,k}$ as the beam illumination strategy of user groups, we obtain that if $\bar{z}^*_{t,m,a_m,k} = 1$, then $z^*_{t,m,k} = 1$.

7   Intra-group Time-Frequency Resource Assignment Algorithm

Based on the obtained user grouping and beam illumination strategy $y^*_{n,m}$ and $z^*_{t,m,k}$, we now assign time-frequency resources to the individual GUs.

7.1 Sub-problem Formulation

Suppose $z^*_{t_0,m_0,k} = 1$, i.e., at time slot t_0, user group m_0 is assigned a satellite beam. As there are F sub-channels offered by each satellite beam, the sub-channel resources should be allocated to GUs in group m_0. Let $\bar{U}_{m_0}$ denote the utility of the GUs in user group m_0, we obtain

$$\bar{U}_{m_0} = \sum_{GU_n \in \Phi_{m_0}} \lambda_1 \eta_n - \sum_{t=1}^{T} \sum_{k=1}^{K} \sum_{f=1}^{F} \lambda_2 z^*_{t,m_0,k} x_{t,n,m_0,f} p\tau \tag{14}$$

For user group m_0, the time-frequency resource assignment sub-problem can be formulated as follows

$$\min_{x_{t,n,m_0,f}} \quad \bar{U}_m \\ \text{s.t.} \quad C1, C2, C6 - C8 \tag{15}$$

Solving the above problem involves the time-frequency resource allocation over multiple slots. Obviously, the preceding resource allocation strategy will affect the successive solution as well as the total number of resource elements. Therefore, it is difficult to solve by using optimization tools. To tackle this problem, we present a priority-based resource allocation strategy. Specifically, stressing the importance of service weight and transmission deadline of GUs, we assign priority to GUs in user group m_0, then rank the GUs in descending order. Starting from the GU with the highest priority, the optimal time-frequency resource allocation strategy is designed. Updating the available resources, and assigning resources to the GU with the second highest priority. The procedure continues until all the GUs in the group are assigned resources or no available resources left.

7.2 Assigning Priority for GUs

To jointly consider user service weight and transmission deadline, we propose a two-level prioritizing scheme. Firstly, examining the service weight of GUs in Φ_{m_0} and assigning higher priority to the GUs with higher service weight. Let ξ_n denote the priority of GU_n. For $GU_{n_1} \in \Phi_{m_0}$ and $GU_{n_2} \in \Phi_{m_0}$, if $w_{n_1} > w_{n_2}$, we assign $\xi_{n_1} > \xi_{n_2}$, otherwise, set $\xi_{n_1} < \xi_{n_2}$. In the case that $w_{n_1} = w_{n_2}$, we then evaluate the transmission deadline of the two GUs, if $T^{max}_{n_1} < T^{max}_{n_2}$, we set $\xi_{n_1} > \xi_{n_2}$.

In this section, we compare the priorities of GUs in Φ_{m_0}, assign resources to the GU with the highest priority. Suppose GU_{n_0} is of the highest priority, we then design time-frequency resource allocation strategy for GU_{n_0}. To this end, we first evaluate the transmission performance of GU_{n_0} in various time-frequency elements and successively assign GU_{n_0} the resource elements which offer the highest performance, until all the data packets of GU_{n_0} can be transmitted. In order to complete the data transmission of GU_{n_0} before the given deadline $T^{max}_{n_0}$, only the time slots earlier than $\lceil T^{max}_{n_0}/\tau \rceil$ can be allocated.

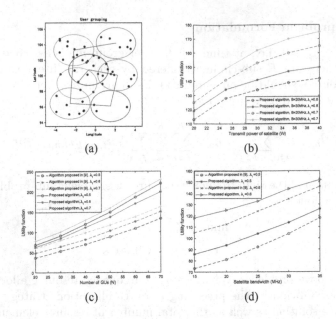

Fig. 2. (a) An example of user grouping results. (b) Utility function versus the transmit power of satellite. (c) Utility function versus the number of GUs. (d) Utility function versus satellite bandwidth.

The detail steps of the proposed time-frequency allocation algorithm can be summarized as follows:

a) Initialization: Given the set of GUs in user group m_0, Φ_{m_0}, user priority ξ_n, set $l = 1$.

b) Select the GU with the highest priority in Φ_{m_0}: Suppose $n_l = \arg\max \xi_n$, $\forall \mathrm{GU}_n \in \Phi_{m_0}$, assign time-frequency resource to GU_{n_l}.

c) Evaluate the transmission performance of GU_{n_l} on various sub-channels: Under the assumption $z^*_{t_i,m_0,k} = 1$, $1 \leq i \leq i'$, where $i' = \lceil \epsilon_{m_0}/K \rceil$, we evaluate the transmission performance of GU_{n_l} on various sub-channels in time slot t_i. Assume that $R_{t_i,n_l,m_0,f_i^*} \geq \cdots \geq R_{t_i,n_l,m_0,f_F^*}$, i.e., in time slot t_i, among all the sub-channels, sub-channel f_i^* yields the locally optimal performance.

d) Examine the transmission performance of GU_{n_l} over different time slots: Compare the locally optimal performance of GU_{n_l} over time slot t_i, suppose $R_{t_1,n_l,m_0,f_1^*} \geq R_{t_2,n_l,m_0,f_i^*} \geq \cdots \geq R_{t_{i'},n_l,m_0,f_{i'}^*}$.

e) Assign the locally optimal time-frequency resource element to GU_{n_l}: We assign time-frequency resource element (t_1, f_1^*) to GU_{n_l}, set $x^*_{t_1,n_l,m_0,f_1^*} = 1$, update the available resources by removing the element (t_1, f_1^*), then check whether there are still data packets of GU_{n_l} which need to be transmitted, i.e., whether $R_{t_1,n_l,m_0,f_1^*}\tau < s_{n_l}$, if yes, assign the remaining optimal resource element to GU_{n_l}, repeat the process, until all the data packets of GU_{n_l} are transmitted, update the set of Φ_{m_0}, i.e., $\Phi_{m_0} = \Phi_{m_0}/\mathrm{GU}_{n_l}$, otherwise, check whether there are still GUs in Φ_{m_l}.

f) Check algorithm terminates: If $\Phi_{m_0} = \emptyset$, then the algorithm terminates, otherwise, $l = l + 1$, return to Step b).

It should be noted that for certain GUs, the data packets may not be transmitted completely before the transmission deadline. In this case, we do not assign any resources to the GUs and assign the corresponding packet drop identifiers as 0. For instance, if for GU_n, the available resources are insufficient for transmitting s_n, i.e., $\sum_{i=1}^{i'} R_{t_i,n,m_0,f_i^*}\tau < s_n$, where the resource elements (t_i, f_i^*) are the remaining available resources for offering data transmission service of GU_n, then we set $\alpha_n = 0$ and $x_{t,n,m_0,f} = 0$, $\forall t, f$.

7.3 Mission Scheduling Strategy

It should be mentioned that the proposed mission assignment algorithm is capable of allocating various missions to individual UAVs, however, the exact mission execution time is still unknown. This can be tackled in a simple way by integrating the obtained trajectory planing strategy with mission assignment strategy. In particular, we may start from one specific MA, for instance, the MA located in the boundary region of the overall MAs, examine all the UAVs arrival at the MA, compute the UAV arrival time, and determine the time slots for executing missions. The procedure repeats until the scheduling strategy is determined for all the missions in MAs. Accordingly, the association strategy between MAs nd UAVs, denoted by $\alpha_{n,m,t}^*$, the mission schedule strategy, denoted by $\beta_{n,m,k,t}^*$ and mission partition strategy, i.e., $\eta_{n,m,k,t}^*$ can be obtained.

8 Simulation Results

In this section, we examine the performance of the proposed algorithm. In the simulation, set the system bandwidth B as 20MHz, the carrier frequency ξ_f as 20 GHz, and noise spectral density N_0 as 3×10^8 m/s. The number of beams K is set to 4, the user receive antenna gain g_n^r is 15 dB and the maximum transmit power p_b is 43 dB.

Figure 2(a) plots an example of user grouping results which is obtained from our proposed heuristic user grouping algorithm. In Fig. 2, the circles represent different user groups and the red polyline connects the center of groups. As can be seen from Fig. 2(a), all the GUs are clustered into groups with equal coverage ranges determine by the width of satellite beams.

In Fig. 2(b), we show the utility function versus the transmit power of the satellite. It can be seen from the figure, as the transmit power increases, the utility function also increases. This is because the increase in transmit power results in the increase of the data transmission rate and the possibility of successful transmissions as well. Comparing the effects of transmission bandwidth and the weighting factor λ_1 on utility function, we can observe that as the transmission bandwidth becomes larger, higher utility function can be obtained which is benefited from higher data rate. In addition, when the weighting factor λ_1 increases, the utility function also increases. The reason is that higher reward function is obtained from larger λ_1.

Figure 2(c) depicts the utility function versus the number of GUs. In the figure, we compare the performance of the algorithm proposed in this paper with the one proposed in [9]. In [9], a time-frequency resource allocation algorithm was proposed to maximize user transmission rate. It can be seen from the figure that as the number of GUs increases, the utility functions obtained from both algorithms increase accordingly. Comparing the performance obtained from our proposed algorithm and the one proposed in [9], we can observe that our proposed algorithm offers higher utility function. The reason is that while data transmission rate was considered in [9], the authors failed to examine the successful transmission of data packets, thus may result in relatively high packet loss rate, and low utility function in turn.

Figure 2(d) depicts utility function versus satellite bandwidth. In the figure, we also compare the performance of the algorithm proposed in this paper with the one proposed in [9]. As can be seen from the figure, the utility function increases as the bandwidth increases. This is because the increase in bandwidth leads to higher data transmission rate, resulting in less packet loss and higher utility. It can also be seen that the utility function of the algorithm proposed in [9] is lower than that of the algorithm proposed in this paper. Comparing the utility functions corresponding to different values of λ_1, we can observe that the increase of the weighting factor λ_1 offers higher utility function.

9   Conclusions

In this paper, we have studied the problem of beam illumination and resource allocation for multibeam satellite communication systems. An large scale offline user grouping algorithm and a group-oriented beam illumination scheme have been proposed. Then, an online time-frequency resource allocation algorithm has been designed. Numerical results demonstrate the our proposed algorithms offered better performance than existing algorithm.

References

1. Di, B., Song, L., Li, Y., et al.: Ultra-dense LEO: integration of satellite access networks into 5G and beyond. IEEE Wirel. Commun. **26**(5), 62–69 (2019)
2. You, L., Liu, A., Wang, W., et al.: Outage constrained robust multigroup multicast beamforming for multi-beam satellite communication systems. IEEE Wireless Commun. Lett. **8**(2), 352–355 (2018)
3. Chen, H., Qi, C.: User grouping for sum-rate maximization in multiuser multibeam satellite communications. In: IEEE International Conference on Communications (ICC). IEEE (2019)

4. Kawamoto, Y., Kamei, T., Takahashi, M., et al.: Flexible resource allocation with inter-beam interference in satellite communication systems with a digital channelizer. IEEE Trans. Wireless Commun. **19**(5), 2934–2945 (2020)
5. Li, Y., Zhang, Q., Gao, R., et al.: An elastic resource allocation algorithm based on dispersion degree for hybrid requests in satellite optical networks. IEEE Internet Things J. **9**(9), 6536–6549 (2021)
6. Di, B., Zhang, H., Song, L., et al.: Ultra-dense LEO: integrating terrestrial-satellite networks into 5G and beyond for data offloading. IEEE Trans. Wireless Commun. **18**(1), 47–62 (2018)
7. Liu, S., Lin, J., Xu, L., et al.: A dynamic beam shut off algorithm for LEO multibeam satellite constellation network. IEEE Wireless Commun. Lett. **9**(10), 1730–1733 (2020)
8. Ivanov, A., Bychkov, R., Tcatcorin, E.: Spatial resource management in LEO satellite. IEEE Trans. Veh. Technol. **69**(12), 15623–15632 (2020)
9. Zuo, P., Peng, T., Linghu, W., et al.: Resource allocation for cognitive satellite communications downlink. IEEE Access **6**, 75192–75205 (2018)

MAML-Based D2D Power Control Scheme in User-Variable Scenario

Zhenyu Fan[1(✉)] and Xinyu Gu[1,2]

[1] School of Artificial Intelligence, Beijing University of Posts and Telecommunications, Beijing 100876, China
{salam,guxinyu}@bupt.edu.cn
[2] Purple Mountain Laboratories, Nanjing 211111, China

Abstract. Meta-Learning has been extensively studied since it has the ability of quickly learning new skills by leveraging prior few-shot tasks, which is capable of relieving the problem of relying on large amount of data sample existed in deep learning. In this paper, we apply an algorithm of model-agnostic meta-learning (MAML) to cope with Device-to-Device (D2D) transmit power control issue in user-variable scenario. Specifically, MAML first learns good weight initializations of D2D power control neural network in initial D2D scenario, contributing to a meta-learner. When the number of D2D user changes, the network loads the meta learner and quickly adapts to a new scenario on a few shots of samples. Simulation results demonstrate that MAML shows good performance in generalization and MAML better conducts D2D user-variety power control issues than regular deep neural network power control methods.

Keywords: Model-agnostic meta-learning · deep neural network · user-variable · weight initialization · optimization

1 Introduction

Device-to-Device (D2D) communication has been considered as a promising technology, which enables nearby D2D user equipment (DUE) to communicate directly without the transition of the base station (BS) and undertakes an ability of communicating in the same channel to increase spectrum utilization efficiency. Nevertheless, channel reuse may prompt severe mutual interference among DUEs and it impairs D2D system throughput. Transmit power control becomes a critical technique to alleviate DUE mutual interference. For the purpose of adjusting transmit power of different DUEs in the same channel to maximize total throughput, most researches formulate it as non-convex problems, which entail large quantities of iterations and has high computational complexity. Machine learning (ML), e.g., deep learning has been exploited in D2D power control since ML based methods can approximate traditional optimization algorithms with much lower computational complexity. However, most neural networks in ML possess fixed-dimensional input and output which is only applied to D2D scenarios with specific number of D2D users [1], when facing a scenario where the number of D2D

F. Gao et al. (Eds.): ChinaCom 2022, LNICST 500, pp. 362–374, 2023.
https://doi.org/10.1007/978-3-031-34790-0_28

users is changing, the behavior of former network may be degraded, a new power control network has to be established and the training process would be conducted again.

Due to the correlation between the network structure and the number of D2D pairs in the scene, applying deep neural network (DNN) power control network to user-variable scenarios may lead to a result that the size of power control DNN for previous moment is not available for this moment, which is inappropriate for real-time operation and leads to the redundancy of rebuilding and retraining new power control network. Meta-learning is a category of machine learning that learns the representation on various learning tasks, forming prior experience and yielding a meta-learner, such that meta-learner teaches to initialize a base-learner and base-learner adapts new tasks quickly using only a small number of training samples. Moreover, model-agnostic meta-learning (MAML) proposed in [2] is a popular meta-learning approach which can be directly applied to any learning problem and model trained with a gradient descent procedure without the constraints on the number of learning parameters or model architecture. Compared with other machine learning methods, MAML can bring better generalization performance to the network and has attracted wide attention of many researchers. The author in [3] applied a modified model-agnostic algorithm capable of performing tasks just trained on a few shots of samples. In [4], the author involved L_1 regularization in standard MAML and proposed a sparse model-agnostic meta-learning (SMAML) to further enhance the efficiency in MAML. [5] applied a practical implementation of MAML to conduct image classification tasks and the result showed that MAML can transfer the prior experience extracted from pre-training on to new tasks and led to good generalization performance. Considering the transfer characteristic of MAML, in this paper, we exploit MAML method to D2D power control in user-variable scenario, i.e., first, we build a DNN power control network and acquire initial parameters in an initial scenario, second, when D2D user number changes, the network reloads initial parameters such that get trained for power control in a new scenario quickly, thereby enhancing network adaptability and real-time operation.

The rest of this paper is organized as follows. Section 2 describes the considered D2D communication scenario and formulates the D2D power control problem. In Sect. 3, we introduce MAML algorithm and propose MAML-based power control policy. Numerical results are shown and discussed in Sect. 4 and we finally conclude the paper in Sect. 5.

2 System Model and Problem Formulation

2.1 System Model

As can be seen in Fig. 1, we consider a Device-to-Device communication scenario with the size of $D \times D$, where a BS is located in the center to manage the power control information and channel state information (CSI) for D2D. Meanwhile, there are N pairs of D2D users, whose maximum distance between transmitter and receiver is 25 m [6], randomly distributed in the area and they simultaneously reuse the same frequency for transmissions. Let $\mathbb{I} = \{1, 2, 3, ..., N\}$ and $\mathbb{J} = \{1, 2, 3, ..., N\}$ respectively represents the set of D2D transmitters and receivers, accordingly, a D2D receiver $k \in \mathbb{J}$ may receive interference from other D2D transmitter $i \in \mathbb{I} \backslash \{k\}$. To address the cochannel interference, transmit power control is necessary such that cochannel interference can be relieved and D2D system throughput is maximized.

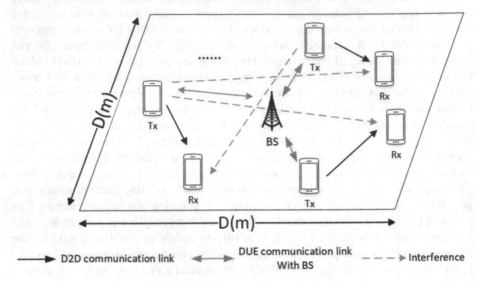

Fig. 1. D2D communication scenario network topology.

2.2 Problem Formulation

In the present work, we evaluate the D2D system weighted sum-rate (WSR) and the mean squared error (MSE) between predicted power and theoretical optimal power to characterize the merit of ML-based power control scheme, while comparing the adaptability of regular neural network and MAML to user-variable areas. Denote the distance from the i-th D2D transmitter to the j-th receiver as $d_{i,j}$ and the multipath fading between the i-th D2D transmitter and the j-th receiver as $G_{i,j}$, specifically, each multipath fading $G_{i,j}$ satisfies $G_{i,j} \sim N(0, 1)$. Thus, the channel gain from the i-th D2D transmitter to the j-th receiver can be written as $h_{i,j} = \beta(d_{i,j})^{-\alpha} |G_{i,j}|$ [7], where β and α represent the path loss coefficient and path loss exponent, and **H** is the matrix of $h_{i,j}$.

We analyze the overall system throughput and formulate the transmit power control problem in the work based on the Signal to Interference plus Noise Ratio (SINR) of D2D receivers. Let P_i denote the predicted transmit power of the i-th transmitter, where $0 \leq P_i \leq P_{max}$, and **P** is the matrix of P_i. Furthermore, we assume that N_0 is noise spectral density and W is the carrier bandwidth that D2D users access [8], and the WSR model can be expressed as follows:

$$\text{maximize} \sum_{k=1}^{N} W log_2 (1 + \frac{h_{i,j} P_i}{N_0 W + \sum_{k \in \mathbb{I} \setminus \{i\}} h_{k,i} P_k}) \tag{1}$$

The objective of power control scheme is to maximize the D2D WSR model such that an ideal power control policy for CSI in a certain scenario can be achieved.

Given that weighted minimum mean square error (WMMSE) is capable of reaching a stationary solution of non-convex problem, e.g., problem (1) [9], we regard WMMSE as the upper limit of D2D network communication performance and denote P_{WMMSE} as the theoretical optimal power generated by WMMSE. Since P_{WMMSE} generated according to certain CSI channel gain utilizing WMMSE scheme represents an optimal power allocated policy in a specific scenario, the MSE between P_{WMMSE} and P is capable of indicating the adaptability of ML power control method. The adaptability of ML power control method to user-variable areas can be written as:

$$\text{minimize} \, L = \sqrt{(P_{WMMSE} - P)^2} \tag{2}$$

The smaller the value of L, the greater approximating performance of ML power control and the better adaptability to certain D2D scenario can be achieved. Thus, the objective of power control scheme includes minimizing the MSE between theoretical optimal power and predicted power.

3 Model-Agnostic Meta-learning Based D2D Power Control Scheme

In this section, the detailed MAML algorithm is presented first. Then, we construct the neural network used for determining D2D transmit power and apply the MAML to ML-based power control procedure for D2D power control in user-variable scenarios.

3.1 Model-Agnostic Meta-learning Algorithm

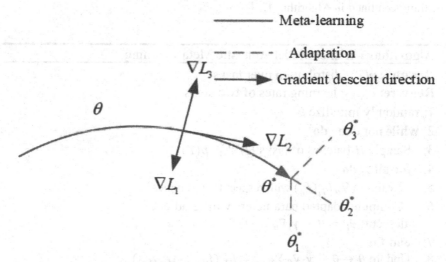

Fig. 2. Diagram of model-agnostic meta-learning algorithm (MAML).

As depicted in Fig. 2, meta-learning possesses an ability of training good model's initial parameters θ, contributing to a generic meta-learner on various similar tasks, such that the learner can quickly create adapted parameters $\theta_1^*, \theta_2^*, \theta_3^*$, thereby achieving rapid adaptation and providing an ideal feature representation towards most deep learning models trained for new tasks [2], and that is defined as model-agnostic. In K-shot MAML scenario, we consider a distribution over tasks $T \sim p(T)$ where H batches of task, $\{T_i\}_{i=1}^H$, are collected from this distribution and K samples are drawn in each task T_i. Accordingly, a generic model f_θ with parameters θ is trained on K samples in each task from $p(T)$, i.e., when training on T_i, the model will adapt to new parameters θ_i', which is calculated via gradient descent update, as is given as follows:

$$\theta_i' = \theta - \gamma_1 \nabla_\theta L_{T_i}(f_\theta) \tag{3}$$

where $L_{T_i}(f_\theta)$ is the loss computed using K samples for task T_i, γ_1 is the learning rate in the first step of gradient updating. To achieve good adaptability for f_θ, the model parameters are trained by minimizing total loss from tasks in $p(T)$, and the meta-objective can be expressed as follows:

$$\min_\theta \sum_{T_i \sim p(T)} L_{T_i}(f_{\theta_i'}) = \sum_{T_i \sim p(T)} L_{T_i}(f_{\theta - \gamma_1 \nabla_\theta L_{T_i}(f_\theta)}) \tag{4}$$

with the total loss computed across tasks from $p(T)$ minimized, the optimal initialization parameters for meta-learner can be acquired as follows:

$$\theta \leftarrow \theta - \gamma_2 \nabla_\theta \sum_{T_i \sim p(T)} L_{T_i}(f_{\theta - \gamma_1 \nabla_\theta L_{T_i}(f_\theta)}) \tag{5}$$

where γ_2 is the learning rate in the second step of gradient update, and the K-shot MAML algorithm is outlined in Algorithm 1.

Algorithm 1 K-shot Model-Agnostic Meta-Learning

Require: $p(T)$: distribution over tasks

Require: γ_1, γ_2: learning rates of two steps

1: randomly initialize θ

2: **while** not done **do**

3:   Sample H batches of tasks $\{T_i\}_{i=1}^H \sim p(T)$

4:   **for all** T_i **do**

5:     Evaluate $\nabla_\theta L_{T_i}(f_\theta)$ with respect to K samples

6:     Compute adapted parameters with gradient
      descent: $\theta_i' = \theta - \gamma_1 \nabla_\theta L_{T_i}(f_\theta)$

7:   **end for**

8:   Update $\theta \leftarrow \theta - \gamma_2 \nabla_\theta \sum_{T_i \sim p(T)} L_{T_i}(f_{\theta - \gamma_1 \nabla_\theta L_{T_i}(f_\theta)})$

9: **end while**

3.2 MAML-Based Power Control Scheme

In ML D2D transmit power allocation problem, a DNN is constructed to optimize problems in (1) and (2), thereby determining an optimal transmit power allocation policy of all D2D transmitters according to channel state information $\mathbf{H}$, whose size is $N \times N$ and is related to the number of D2D transceiver pairs N in the scenario. As shown in Fig. 3, a four-layer fully connected neural network is employed for feature extraction, and the channel state information $\mathbf{H}$ is flattened into one-dimensional vector, whose length is N^2, contributing to the input of DNN. In each hidden layer, 40 hidden neurons are included and the Rectified Linear Unit (ReLU) is used as the activation function to relieve gradient vanishing and overfitting.

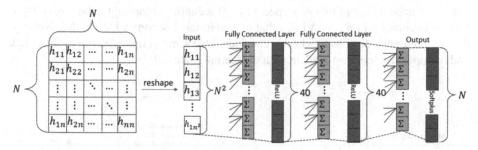

Fig. 3. Deep neural network architecture for power control.

The output of the network keeps the length of N and is fed into the Softplus part, i.e., when the input of Softplus part is x_S, the i-th output of Softplus part comes to $\log(e^{[x_S]_i} + 1)$, which restricts the output range and prevents negative values such that it can be treated as the predicted power allocation result.

In terms of DNN power control in D2D user-variable scenarios, the number of D2D transceiver pairs N is always changing, since the length of input layer and output layer are related to N, a phenomenon may happen that a well-trained DNN used for power control for previous second may not be applicable for this second and we have to establish a new DNN, initializing the whole model parameters again, which leads to unnecessary repetition of steps. Meta-learning has an ability of leveraging previous experience to train a model that can quickly adapt to new tasks using only a few samples and training iterations, furthermore, MAML is a well-studied meta-learning algorithm that has shown impressive results over many problems, e.g., supervised regression, classification, and reinforcement learning, and its feature has potential to handle the phenomenon. Therefore, in this paper, we propose a MAML-based power control scheme to address the changing of D2D transceiver pairs in the scenario.

As can be seen in Fig. 4, the scheme is divided into two phases, meta-training phase and meta-test phase [10], specifically, data samples used for both meta-training phase and meta-test phase are generated through system-level simulation of respective D2D scenarios. In meta-training phase, the number of D2D transceiver pairs in scenario is N_0, where a DNN is initialized and a K-shot MAML is conducted. The data sample used for meta-training phase includes M_0 batches and the value of M_0 includes 10000 and 20000.

Each batch contains K sample shots, consequently, the size of input feature fed into DNN becomes $[M_0, K, N_0, N_0]$ and the size of output label becomes $[M_0, K, N_0]$. After meta-training phase, a well-trained DNN emerges and we save the model parameters, which is defined as meta-learner. In meta-test phase, we aim to apply the meta-learner to the power control network in scenarios with different number of D2D pairs. Considering the number of D2D pairs is variable in meta-test phase and the corresponding power control network has different size of input and output layer, we denote the number of D2D transceiver pairs in user-variable scenario as the variable parameter N and reinitialize the input and output weight parameters of power control network with N dimensions while in hidden layers the network directly loads weight parameters of the meta-learner, and then the network transferred with meta-learner contributes to a base-learner. After loading meta-learner, the base-learner will be finetuned under only a few data samples with M batches to adapt to a new specific D2D scenario, accordingly, the size of input feature becomes $[M, K, N, N]$ and that of output label becomes $[M, K, N]$. Notably, during finetuning, the loss function is considered the same as optimization problem (2), and the optimizer comes to Adam with the learning rate of 0.001.

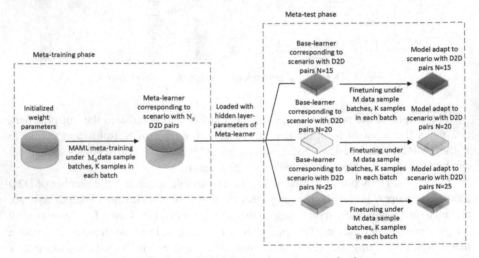

Fig. 4. Schematic of MAML-based power control scheme.

Through MAML, the base-learner can adapt to user-variable scenarios quickly and behave better generalization performance under only a few training samples without rebuilding a new power control network or conducting large number of training iterations.

4   Simulation Results and Analysis

In this section, we conduct extensive numerical experiments to verify the functionality and performance of the proposed MAML-based power control scheme and compare the performance of the proposed scheme with that of the following schemes: 1) WMMSE-based power control policy [9]; 2) regular DNN power control policy mentioned in [6].

Specially, for comparing the adaptability of DNN policy and MAML-based policy, we train the raw DNN network with M batches of data samples, the same as the finetuning process of base-learner in meta-test phase, and we subsequently compare the trained DNN with the finetuned base-learner in MAML-based power control. Moreover, the structure of raw DNN is the same as that of the base-learner such that other irrelevant variables can be controlled. The simulation program is operated in Python 3.6.2 with Tensorflow 2.6.2 on the computer equipped with 16GB of RAM and one 8-core Intel CPU, besides, Keras library is used for the construction and training of a neural network. The specific parameter settings are given in Table 1.

Table 1. System Parameters.

Parameter	Value
Number of D2D pairs in meta-training phase N_0	10
Number of D2D pairs in meta-training phase N	{15, 20, 25}
Number of samples in each batch K	10
Number of batches in meta-training phase M_0	{10000, 20000}
Number of batches in meta-test phase M	{100, 200, 300, 400}
D2D Max/Min transmit power P_{max}/P_{min}	24/0 dBm
Size of D2D area D	700 m
Channel Bandwidth W	20 MHz
Noise spectral density N_0	−174 dBm/Hz
Learning rate in the first step γ_1	0.01
Learning rate in the second step γ_2	0.001
Path loss coefficient β	$10^{-3.453}$
Path loss exponent α	3.8

Firstly, the simulation evaluates the WSR performance of D2D scenarios with different number of D2D pairs when exploiting WMMSE, MAML-based and regular DNN power control policy. In Fig. 5(a), 5(b) and 5(c), we show the average WSR result finetuned by different number of training batches in scenarios with different number of D2D pairs. It can be observed that for arbitrary sample shot, no matter how many batches conducted in the finetuning process, the WSR of MAML-based power control policy always performs better than regular DNN power control policy, and both of them performs slightly inferior to WMMSE-based scheme. Besides, as the number of batches M increases in finetuning process, both the WSR of MAML-based power control and that of DNN power control achieve closer to optimal WSR value while the gap between them decreases or even decreases to 0 under certain conditions. This is because with the increase of batches, both raw DNN and base-learner have been finetuned more thoroughly such that both of them have reached saturation and their performance gap may not be obvious, meanwhile, we may infer from the result that the superiority of MAML-based policy is more obviously highlighted with the descent of training batches or with the growth of D2D pairs.

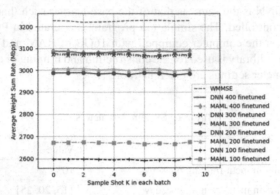

(a) WSR performance in scenario where N=15.

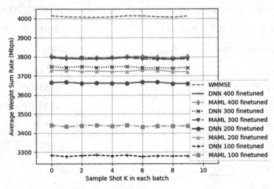

(b) WSR performance in scenario where N=20.

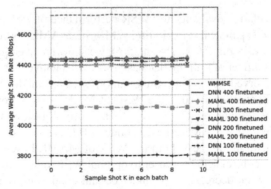

(c) WSR performance in scenario where N=25.

Fig. 5. The WSR performance of D2D scenarios with different number of D2D pairs.

Secondly, the simulation evaluates the MAML model transfer ability and adaptability towards D2D user-variable scenarios under 400 sample batches of finetuning process, mainly by comparing the MSE value respectively derived from raw DNN, base-learner loaded with half-trained meta-learner and base-learner loaded with totally trained meta-learner. Particularly, half-trained meta-learner is trained under 10000 batches in meta-training phase where M_0 is 10000, while meta-learner is trained under 20000 batches in meta-training phase where M_0 is 20000. As can be seen from results in Fig. 6(a), 6(b) and 6(c), regardless of the number of D2D pairs in the scenario, base-learner always experiences lower MSE than DNN with direct weight initializations when trained with any number of batches, moreover, the base-learner equipped with totally trained meta-learner experiences lower MSE value than base-learner equipped with half-trained meta-learner. Simulation results demonstrate that when the number of D2D pairs changes, the base-learner can better approximate the WMMSE policy than raw network with direct weight initializations. Besides, the more batches applied to the training of meta-learner, the more prior knowledge base-learner would accumulate, thereby accomplish better generalization performance. MAML-based power control behaves better adaptability in D2D user-variable scenario.

Thirdly, to analyze the real-time operation of MAML-based power control scheme, the simulation evaluates the MAML model time complexity towards D2D user-variable scenario under 400 sample batches of finetuning process, mainly by comparing the probability histogram of time consumption derived from raw DNN, base-learner loaded with half-trained meta-learner and base-learner loaded with totally trained meta-learner. We can infer from results in Fig. 7(a), 7(b) and 7(c) that regardless of the number of D2D pairs in scenario, the time consumption distribution of MAML-based power control is more concentrated than that of raw DNN, i.e., MAML-based power control time consumption distribution is mainly concentrated in the low time consumption interval while the time consumption of raw DNN still exist individual distributions in the range of high time consumption interval. Simulation results indicate that with respect of D2D user-variable scenario, power control network loaded with prior knowledge could adapt to changes of the number of D2D pairs quickly, MAML-based power control achieves better real-time operation.

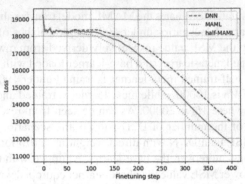

(a) MSE value in scenario where N=15.

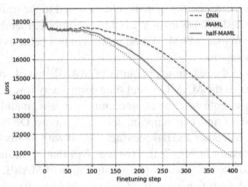

(b) MSE value in scenario where N=20.

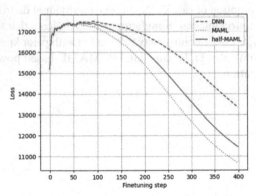

(c) MSE value in scenario where N=25.

Fig. 6. The MSE value between optimal power and predicted power in D2D scenarios with different number of D2D pairs.

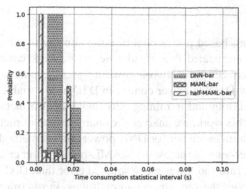

(a) CDF curve in scenario where N=15.

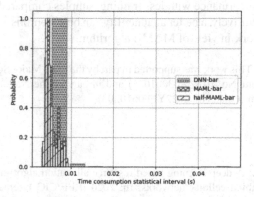

(b) CDF curve in scenario where N=20.

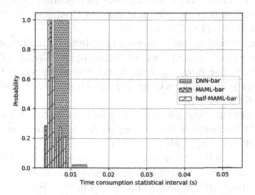

(c) CDF curve in scenario where N=25.

Fig. 7. Time consumption in D2D scenarios with different number of D2D pairs.

5 Conclusion

The Machine learning based power control issue considering dynamic user changing scenarios is more complicated than regular neural network-based power control due to the correlation between the network structure and the number of D2D pairs, and directly applying raw DNN to power control in D2D user-variable scenarios may leads to repetition of rebuilding and retraining new power control network, which increase time complexity. In this work, we analyze the characteristic of meta-learning and apply MAML to pre-train a meta-learner for DNN power control methods. Simulation results show that in D2D user-variable areas, the MAML-based power control method achieves better weighted sum rate and lower mean squared error than DNN power control without meta-learners under the same training conditions. Furthermore, the power control network loaded with meta-learner parameters can converge to optimal results faster and regress to similar performance with less training samples compared with regular power control network. Intuitively, a better adaptability can be accomplished for a user-variable power control network in view of MAML algorithm.

Acknowledgement. This work was supported in part by the State Major Science and Technology Special Projects (Grant No.2018ZX03001024) and in part by the National Key Research and Development Program (Grant No. 2022YFF0610303).

References

1. Pei, E., Yang, G.: A deep learning based resource allocation algorithm for variable dimensions in d2d-enabled cellular networks. In: 2020 IEEE/CIC International Conference on Communications in China (ICCC), pp. 277–281. IEEE (2020)
2. Finn, C., Abbeel, P., Levine, S.: Model-agnostic meta-learning for fast adaptation of deep networks. In: Proceedings of the 34th International Conference on Machine Learning, in PMLR, vol. 70, pp. 1126–1135 (2017)
3. Pawar, A.: Modified model-agnostic meta-learning. In: 2020 IEEE International Conference on Machine Learning and Applied Network Technologies (ICMLANT). IEEE (2020)
4. Gai, S., Wang, D.: Sparse model-agnostic meta-learning algorithm for few-shot learning. In: 2019 2nd China Symposium on Cognitive Computing and Hybrid Intelligence (CCHI), pp. 127–130. IEEE (2019)
5. So, C.: Exploring meta learning: parameterizing the learning-to-learn process for image classification. In: 2021 International Conference on Artificial Intelligence in Information and Communication (ICAIIC), pp. 199–202 (2021)
6. Lee, W., Kim, M., Cho, D.H.: Transmit power control using deep neural network for underlay device-to-device communication. IEEE Wirel. Commun. Lett. **8**(1), 141–144 (2019)
7. IEEE 802.20 WG: IEEE 802.20 channel models document. IEEE 802.20 PD-08rl (2007)
8. 3GPP TR 38.889: 3rd Generation Partnership Project; Technical Specification Group Radio Access Network; Study on NR-based access to unlicensed spectrum. Rel-16 V16.0.0, pp. 64–65 (2018)
9. Shi, Q., Razaviyayn, M., Luo, Z.Q., He, C.: An iteratively weighted MMSE approach to distributed sum-utility maximization for a MIMO interfering broadcast channel. IEEE Trans. Signal Process. **59**(9), 4331–4340 (2011)
10. Sun, Q., Liu, Y., Chua, T.S., et al.: Meta-transfer learning for few-shot learning. In: 2019 IEEE/CVF Conference on Computer Vision and Pattern Recognition (CVPR). IEEE (2019)

Interference-aware Spectrum and Power Coordination in Satellite-aided Cell-free Massive MIMO System

Mingliang Pang[1], Chaowei Wang[1(✉)], Danhao Deng[1], Yehao Li[1], Weidong Wang[1], and Lexi Xu[2]

[1] Beijing University of Posts and Telecommunications,
Beijing, People's Republic of China
{pangmingliang,wangchaowei,dengdanhao,liyehao,wangweidong}@bupt.edu.cn
[2] China United Network Communications Corporation,
Beijing, People's Republic of China
xulx29@chinaunicom.cn

Abstract. In this paper we construct a hybrid architecture that combines terrestrial cell-free massive MIMO system and multi-beam satellite communication system to maximize the throughput within the coverage. We propose an interference-level based user selection algorithm to divert terrestrial users with stronger interference to satellite service, thereby reducing the total system interference. For satellite users, to further increase the system throughput, we use the co-frequency across beams, which include two steps, inter-beam and intra-beam resource allocation. The former uses soft frequency reuse and the latter is allocated based on water-filling algorithm. The simulation results show that the proposed satellite-aided cell-free system has a significant improvement in throughput compared with the traditional system. At the same time, the throughput of satellite users is also improved compared with the traditional frequency reuse scheme.

Keywords: Cell-free massive MIMO · Multi-beam satellite · Frequency reuse · Resource management

1 Introduction

As one of the core technologies of the 5th generation mobile communication, the massive multiple-input multiple-output (MIMO) technology deploys dozens to hundreds of antennas in the base station (BS) [1]. The antenna can obtain strong array gain, diversity gain and spatial multiplexing gain, which can provide services for multiple mobile terminals (MT) on the same time-frequency resource block and greatly improve the system spectrum efficiency. However, with the

Supported by National Key R&D Program of China (2020YFB1807204).

F. Gao et al. (Eds.): ChinaCom 2022, LNICST 500, pp. 375–389, 2023.
https://doi.org/10.1007/978-3-031-34790-0_29

further densification of cells, inter-cell interference has become a major bottleneck limiting the performance of massive MIMO systems, which seriously affects the performance of cell-edge MT [2]. In order to suppress the above-mentioned interference and provide homogeneous service for all MTs, the cell-free massive MIMO system emerges as the times require. In this system, the traditional BS is replaced by numerous distributed access points (AP), and the same MT can be served by multiple APs on the same time-frequency resources [3]. This technology makes the MT break through the constraints of the cell boundary, and the MT is located in the center of the cell [4]. Compared with traditional cellular massive MIMO networks, cell-free massive MIMO has obvious advantages. It has large energy efficiency, which is brought about by the high array gain. Due to the strong macro diversity gain, cell-free massive MIMO can considerably improve the achievable sum-rate [5]. Furthermore, it can provide high throughput, reliability, and energy efficiency with simple signal processing [6]. In addition, the average distance between the closest antennas and an arbitrary MT is substantially reduced by invoking a large number of distributed antennas, which makes the deployment of cell-free massive MIMO more flexible and cost-effective [7].

In addition to cell-free massive MIMO, satellite networks are also an important part of 5G and even 6G. The satellite system has developed from the initial global beam and regional beam to the current multi-spot beam. The emergence of spot beam technology is one of the important advancements in the improvement of modern satellite communication capabilities. The spread of multi-beam antennas increase drastically the number of users that can potentially be served by single satellite [8]. Multi-beam satellites (MBS) have been widely used not only because the resource utilization rate of satellite systems can be effectively improved through the inter-beam frequency reuse technology [9], but also because it raises possibility for the sharing the satellite frequency with other radio network including terrestrial radio system [10]. Additionally, the introduction of phased array antenna technology can allow for reconfigurable beam numbers, aiming points, and beamforming to further enhance spot beam capabilities [11]. As multi-beam satellite communication system has the advantages of extensive coverage, high beam gain, small user terminals and high frequency utilization, it plays an irreplaceable and important role in mobile and emergency communication scenarios over a large area in complex environments such as floods, earthquakes and so on [12].

In this paper, we combine terrestrial cell-free massive MIMO system with satellite network. The terrestrial users and satellite users are distinguished by an interference-based user selection algorithm, and the satellite is used to reduce the interference of the system and enhance the throughput performance of the system. The main contributions of this paper can be summarized as follows:

1. Combining the advantages of cell-free massive MIMO and multi-beam satellite systems, we have established a hybrid communication architecture for satellite-terrestrial integration. The satellite network complements terrestrial communications to enhance the performance of the hybrid system.

2. Based on the interference level between users, a user selection algorithm was designed to classify users into terrestrial and satellite users. Users with higher interference are selected to provide services via satellite, thus significantly reducing the interference in the system.

3. For the resource allocation of satellite users, we split it into two steps, inter-beam resource allocation and intra-beam resource allocation. The former uses soft frequency reuse, and the latter uses water-filling algorithm to allocate power and bandwidth resources. Experimental results show that the proposed resource allocation algorithm can improve the throughput performance of the system.

The rest of this paper is organized as follows. Section 2 describes the work related to satellite-aided cell-free massive MIMO system and the multi-beam satellite resource management. Section 4 provides the user selection algorithm and resource allocation algorithm. Section 5 analyzes the simulation results. Finally, the conclusions are given.

2   Related Work

However, the inter-beam interference problem of multi-beam satellites cannot be ignored. For the problem of inter-beam interference, [8] lists three system characteristics that affect the co-channel interference (CCI) between satellite beams: beam layout, multiplexing scheme and scheduling. Among them, the beam layout depends on the design of the antenna, and the traditional hexagonal grid is being replaced by a more efficient beam layout, such as a square grid [13], which can greatly reduce the CCI by increasing the distance from the center of the same polarized beam. In the multiplexing scheme, the four-color multiplexing mostly adopts the form of 2 sub-bands and 2 polarizations, which has good interference isolation characteristics. If a smaller frequency reuse factor is adopted, the relationship between the increase of the beam bandwidth and the actual achievable system capacity needs to be weighed to ensure that it is beneficial to the satellite system. The third goal of scheduling is efficiency and fairness. Scheduling is usually performed by the beam's gateway, which generally only has local beam information, and the interference generated by other beams is unknown. The current trend is to centrally control the gateway through SatCloudRAN [14] to coordinate processing of all beams, which can better control interference.

In terms of satellite resource management, [15] established a model of maximizing the number of serviceable users under power constraints in a multi-beam satellite network, and proposed an intelligent search algorithm by applying the greedy idea. Compared to an exhaustive search, the algorithm limits the search to the case where the beam exhausts all available energy, thus reducing the computational complexity. Aiming at the optimal power allocation problem based on service matching service in MBS communication system, [16] adopts a two-stage power allocation method based on genetic algorithm and simulated annealing (GA-SA) algorithm to minimize the unsatisfied system capacity (USC). The proposed two-stage approach improves USC while reducing overall power consumption compared to uniform power distribution. In [17], the power allocation problem is formulated as a convex optimization problem, and the inter-beam interference problem is solved by Lagrangian theory and subgradient iteration. The evaluation results show that the algorithm has good performance in terms of delay, bandwidth utilization, capacity and fairness, and has strong robustness in practical applications. In [18], the power allocation problem in the flow matching of multi-beam satellite systems is reduced to an optimization problem, and the convex optimization framework is decomposed into different sub-problems, each sub-problem is executed by a given agent. The conjecture-based multi-agent Q-learning algorithm proposed in the literature is used to search for the optimal power allocation scheme, which improves the communication satisfaction and fairness of the system under the premise of low complexity.

In addition, there is few research on satellite-aided cell-free massive MIMO system. [19] proposes an algorithm for LEO satellite-aided cell-free massive MIMO network that forms an integrated space-terrestrial framework that combines the benefits offered by ultra-dense terrestrial deployment (cell-free massive MIMO) with the large coverage of the LEO satellite segment. The algorithm controls the transfer of users from the ground to the satellite segment, shifting those users who somehow limit the performance of the terrestrial network to the satellite segment, ultimately improving the worst user rate. In [20], the authors propose an optimization framework and a greedy solution for hybrid network architectures that combine a cell-free massive MIMO terrestrial layout with a low Earth orbit satellite segment to maximize the minimum per-user rate in the coverage area. When a single-antenna access point is operated on a surface section or when deployed sparsely, the hybrid network architectures have significant results.

3   System Model

We consider a scenario shown in Fig. 1, in which there is a multi-beam GEO satellite with a cell-free system in each beam, and the satellite and terrestrial access points assist in serving users. Specifically, satellite users and terrestrial users are selected through a suitable user selection algorithm. The terrestrial users are served by access points, and the satellite users are served by the satellite through the gateway station. Since the communication frequency bands used by the ground and satellite are different, the interference between the ground communication system and the satellite communication system can be ignored.

3.1   Terrestrial Communication Model

Duplexing Mode. To exploit the reciprocity of the uplink (UL) and downlink (DL) channels, TDD is the duplex mode adopted in the cell-free massive MIMO system [21]. For channel estimation, both UL and DL pilots can be used.

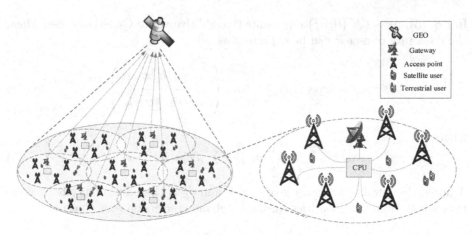

Fig. 1. Satellite-aided Cell-free Massive MIMO System.

Therefore, in the ground satellite fusion network architecture designed in this paper, the duplex mode of the ground cell-free system is TDD. Then, we mainly consider the user's downlink later in this paper.

Signal Model for Downlink Transmission. We consider a cell-free scenario with L APs and K users in this paper. Then, we adopt the compressed-based strategy downlink signal model shown in [22]. The CPU compresses the baseband signal by quantizing the fronthaul links and forwarding them to each AP; hence, the received signal at the ith AP is given as

$$x_l = \sum_k^K w_{l \cdot k} s_k + q_l, \tag{1}$$

where $w_k = \left[w_{1,k}^{\mathrm{T}}, \ldots, w_{L,k}^{T} \right]^{\mathrm{T}}$ represents the beamforming vector of downlink user k sent by all APs, and $s_k \sim \mathcal{CN}(0,1)$ is the signal for downlink user k. q_l represents the quantization noise which related to the compression noise power of AP.

The channel matrix of user k can be expressed as

$$\mathbf{h}_k = \left[\mathbf{h}_{1,k}^{\mathrm{T}}, \mathbf{h}_{2,k}^{\mathrm{T}} \cdots \mathbf{h}_{L,k}^{\mathrm{T}} \right]^{\mathrm{T}}, \tag{2}$$

where $h_{l,k}^{\mathrm{T}}$ denotes the channel state information matrix from lth AP to kth user. Then, the received signal of downlink user k can be expressed as

$$y_k = \sum_l^L \mathbf{h}_{l,k}^{\mathrm{H}} x_l + n_k. \tag{3}$$

In Eq. (3), $n_k \sim \mathcal{CN}\left(0, \sigma_k^2\right)$ represents the additive white Gaussian noise. Then, the data rate of user k can be expressed as

$$R_k = \log_2\left(1 + r_k\right) = \log_2\left(1 + \frac{\rho_k \left|\boldsymbol{h}_k^{\mathrm{H}} \boldsymbol{w}_k\right|^2}{\rho_k \gamma_k + \delta_k^2}\right), \tag{4}$$

where

$$\gamma_k = \sum_{k',k' \neq k} \left|\boldsymbol{h}_k^{\mathrm{H}} \boldsymbol{w}_{k'}\right|^2 + \sum_l \mu_l \left\|\boldsymbol{h}_{l,k}\right\|^2 + \sigma_k^2, \tag{5}$$

denotes the interference matrix of user k and δ_k^2 is the additional circuit noise that stems from nonlinearities during baseband conversion and phase offset.

3.2 Multi-beam Satellite System Model

Considering a single multi-beam GEO satellite, the satellite has M beams, there are N users under each beam, the mth user under the nth beam is denoted by (m, n), located at the position of $\Omega_{m,n}$. The total bandwidth of the satellite system is B_{total}, which is evenly divided into N_B sub-channels and the maximum transmit power of the satellite is P_{total}.

Channel Mode. The tth time slot satellite transmits data to the user (m, n) with power $P_{m,n,t}$, denoting the communication link with $[m, n, t]$, the link bandwidth is $B_{m,n,t}$, and $h_{m,n}$ is the gain of the satellite-ground link. Assume that the multi-beam satellite channel matrix is H_{matrix}:

$$H_{matrix} = [h_{1,1}, h_{1,2}, ..., h_{m,n}, ..., h_{M,N}], \tag{6}$$

in which $h_{m,n}$ can be expressed as

$$h_{m,n} = G_t\left(\theta\right) + PL + G_r\left(\varphi\right). \tag{7}$$

In Eq. (7), $G_t\left(\theta\right)$ is the transmit antenna gain of the link, θ is the angle that the user deviates from the beam antenna axis. PL denotes the loss and fading of the signal power due to the channel environment. $G_r\left(\varphi\right)$ is the receive antenna gain of the link and the angle at which the direction of the received signal deviates from the axis of the receiving antenna is denoted by φ.

Problem Formulation. Considering the problem of co-channel interference, the frequency of the user (m, n) at this moment is f, and the co-channel interference $I_{m,n,t}$ can be expressed as

$$I_{m,n,t} = \sum_{\varphi \in \Xi_f \, and \neq [m,n,t]} P_\varphi h_\varphi, \tag{8}$$

where Ξ_f denotes the set of all co-channel channels with frequency f. $\varphi \in \Xi_f$ and $\neq [m, n, t]$ indicates the channel $[m, n, t]$ causing co-channel interference. P_φ is the data transmission power of the link, and h_φ is the channel gain of the link. The signal-to-interference-noise ratio $SINR_{m,n,t}$ of the link is

$$SINR_{m,n,t} = \frac{P_{m,n,t} h_{m,n}}{I_{m,n,t} + N_0 B_{m,n,t}}, \tag{9}$$

where N_0 is the power spectral density of white Gaussian noise. The data rate $C_{m,n}^t$ of the communication link between the user (m, n) and the satellite in the tth slot can be expressed as

$$C_{m,n}^t = B_{m,n,t} \log_2(1 + SINR_{m,n,t}). \tag{10}$$

Based on Eq. (10), the sum of the system throughput over the time period T is

$$C_{total} = \sum_{m=1}^{M} \sum_{n=1}^{N} \sum_{t=1}^{T} C_{m,n}^t. \tag{11}$$

Then the complete optimization problem can be formulated as

$$\begin{aligned} &P: \max C_{total} \\ s.t. \ &C1: \sum_{m=1}^{M} \sum_{n=1}^{N} P_{m,n} \leq P_{total} \\ &C2: \sum_{n=1}^{N} B_{m,n} \leq B_{total} \forall m \end{aligned} \tag{12}$$

The optimization objective means maximizing the aggregate throughput of the system. Constraint 1 indicates that the total power of all users is not greater than the maximum transmit power of the satellite; Constraint 2 indicates that the total bandwidth of all users in the same beam is not greater than the total system bandwidth.

4   User Selection and Resource Allocation Algorithms

4.1   User Selection Algorithm

User selection algorithm has been designed in the satellite-ground fusion network in [23]. But the algorithm is more complex. On the basis of [23], this paper proposes a user selection algorithm based on interference. Specifically, it can be known from Eq. (5) that the closer the distance between users is, the greater the interference received by the users. Therefore, we use the distance between users to characterize the interference size of users, and select users based on this. The specific algorithm is shown in Algorithm 1.

First, we calculate the distance d_{ij} between user i and user j and sort it in ascending order. Then we take the first element in d_{1j} as the threshold value, and if the distance between the two users is less than this threshold, one of the users is determined as a satellite user. If the number of satellite users obtained by this threshold is exactly the preset number N_S, the algorithm ends. Otherwise, the threshold will be updated and the above operation will be repeated.

Algorithm 1. Interference-level Based User Selection Algorithm

---

Initial Set the total number of users in each beam N;
    Set the number of satellite users in each beam N_S;
    Set the distance threshold to $d_G = 0$.
Output The coordinates of ground users and satellite users.
 1: Randomly generate user coordinates based on the number of users;
 2: Calculate the distance d_{ij} between user i and user j based on user coordinates;
 3: Set $k = 1$;
 4: Set the number of satellite users $M = 0$;
 5: **for** $i = 1 : N$ **do**
 6:    Sort d_{ij} from smallest to largest as D_i;
 7:    $d_G = D_i(k)$;
 8:    **for** $j = 1 : N$ **do**
 9:      **if** $d_{ij} < d_G$ **then**
10:         Determine user j as a satellite user, $M = M + 1$;
11:      **end if**
12:    **end for**
13:    **if** $M = N_S$ **then**
14:      break;
15:    **else if** $M < N_S$ **then**
16:      Set $M = 0$, $k = k + 1$, jump to 8;
17:    **else**
18:      Set $M = 0$;
19:      continue;
20:    **end if**
21: **end for**

4.2 Resource Allocation Algorithm

The inter-beam resource allocation algorithm in this paper is a soft frequency reuse (SFR) based on fractional frequency reuse (FFR). According to [24] the schematic diagram of frequency reuse is shown in Fig. 2.

The left of Fig. 2 illustrates a strict FFR deployment with a beam edge reuse factor of 3. Users inside each beam are assigned a common frequency subband, while the bandwidth of beam edge users is divided across beams according to a reuse factor of N. In general, strict FFR requires a total of $N+1$ subbands. Center users do not share any spectrum with edge users, which reduces interference to center users and edge users.

Although strict FFR reduces the interference between systems, the frequency band utilization rate is relatively low. Based on strict FFR, the right of Fig. 2 illustrates a SFR deployment with a reuse factor of 3 on the beam-edge. SFR allows center users to share sub-bands of edge users in other beams. Because intra-beam users share bandwidth with neighboring beams, they typically transmit at lower power levels than beam-edge users. While SFR is more spectral efficient than Strict FFR, it causes more disturbance to users inside and at the edge of the beam. But we can reduce the interference in the system by controlling the power ratio of center and edge users.

Algorithm 2. Soft Frequency Reuse Based on Water-filling Algorithm (WSFR)

Initial Generate beams and user coordinates;
   Based on SFR set the value of R_{center}, N_{block}, N_{sfr} and β ;
   Set the water level $h_w = 0$.
Output The number of resource blocks allocated by the satellite user.
  1: Calculate H_{center}, H_{edge} and d according to the user coordinates;
  2: Calculate P_{center} and P_{edge} based on β;
  3: **if** $d < R_{center}$ **then**
  4:     $i = 1$;
  5:     Sort all central users by H_{center} and the corresponding channel matrix is $\widetilde{H}_{center}$,
       in which $\widetilde{H}_{center}(1)$ is worst;
  6:     **while** true **do**
  7:        Let $h_w = k / \widetilde{H}_{center}(i)$;
  8:        Allocate resource blocks with h_w and calculate the number of allocated
           resource blocks N_{ac};
  9:        **if** $N_{ac} < N_{sfr}$ **then**
 10:           The remaining resource blocks are divided equally between the central
              users;
 11:           break;
 12:        **else**
 13:           Remove the worst channel without allocating resource blocks, $i = i + 1$.
 14:        **end if**
 15:     **end while**
 16: **else**
 17:     $i = 1$;
 18:     Sort all edge users by H_{edge} and the corresponding channel matrix is $\widetilde{H}_{edge}$, in
       which $\widetilde{H}_{edge}(1)$ is worst;
 19:     **while** true **do**
 20:        Let $h_w = k / \widetilde{H}_{edge}(i)$;
 21:        Allocate resource blocks with h_w and calculate the number of allocated
           resource blocks N_{ae};
 22:        **if** $N_{ae} < N_{block} - N_{sfr}$ **then**
 23:           The remaining resource blocks are divided equally between the edge users;

 24:           break;
 25:        **else**
 26:           Remove the worst channel without allocating resource blocks, $i = i + 1$.
 27:        **end if**
 28:     **end while**
 29: **end if**

The intra-beam resource allocation is based on the water-filling algorithm, and the system resource blocks are adaptively allocated mainly according to the user channel state information. Users with good channel status are allocated more resource blocks, and users with poor channel status are allocated fewer resource blocks, thereby maximizing the total throughput. The complete resource allocation algorithm for satellite users is shown as Algorithm 2.

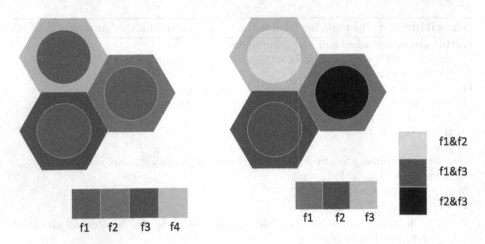

Fig. 2. Strict FFR (left) and SFR (right) resource allocation.

In Algorithm 2, R_{center} is the center radius. N_{block}, N_{sfr} denote the total number of resource blocks and number of central user resource blocks respectively. β indicates the ratio of central user power to total power and h_w is the water level of the water-filling algorithm. k is a constant that controls the water level. The channel state information of central users and edge users are indicated by H_{center} and H_{edge} respectively. d presents the distance between users and beam center. P_{center} and P_{edge} refer to the power of resource blocks occupied by central users and edge users.

5   Simulation Results and Analysis

In this section, simulation experiments are carried out for the algorithm proposed in the Sect. 4 . The main simulation parameters are shown in Table 1.

Table 1. Simulation Parameters.

Parameter	Value
Terrestrial users per beam N_T	500
Satellite users per beam N_S	50
Terrestrial channel bandwidth B_T	10 MHz
Satellite channel bandwidth B_S	30 MHz
Power of AP P_T	10 W
Power of Satellite P_S	200 W
Number of beams N	7
Beam radius R	125.26 KM

We compare the throughput performance using three-color, four-color, same frequency, FFR, USFR and WSFR. Three-color multiplexing refers to dividing the entire frequency band of the system into 3 orthogonal sub-bands, each beam sharing one of the 3 sub-bands, and different frequency bands are specified between adjacent beams, and uniform allocation is used for resource allocation within beams. Four-color divides the entire frequency band of the system into 4 orthogonal subbands on the basis of three colors. Same frequency means that each beam uses the same frequency band and the resource allocation within the beam is also uniformly allocated. FFR means inter-beam using FFR intra-beam using water-filling algorithm to allocate resources. USFR indicates that SFR is used for resource allocation between beams, and uniform allocation is used for resource allocation within beams. WSFR represents the resource allocation algorithm for satellite users proposed in this paper, that is, SFR is used for resource allocation between beams, and water-filling algorithm is used for resource allocation within beams.

The throughput comparison under different central area radii R_{center} is shown in Fig. 3. The throughput of our proposed WSFR algorithm first increases and then decreases as R_{center} increases. This is because when R_{center} is small, there are few central users in the beam, which affects the performance of the system. When R_{center} is large, there will be few users at the edge of the system, which will waste resources and degrade the performance. At the same time, no matter how R_{center} changes, WSFR always outperforms FFR and USFR. This is because WSFR improves the efficiency of frequency utilisation between beams compared to FFR and optimises the scheduling of resources for users within the

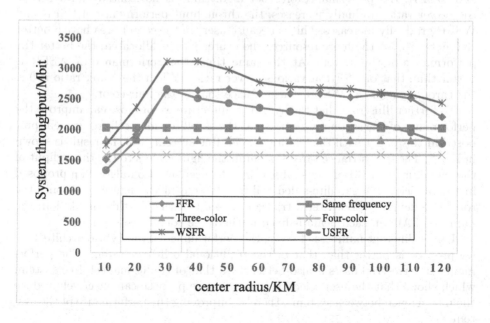

Fig. 3. Comparison of system throughput under different center radii.

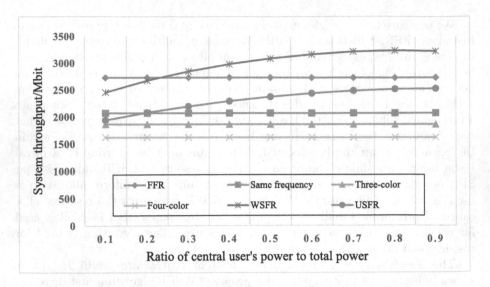

Fig. 4. Comparison of system throughput under different power ratios.

beam compared to USFR. When R_{center} is 30KM, the throughput performance of WSFR reaches 1.9 times that of four-color.

The system throughput under different power ratios is shown in Fig. 4. Power ratios refer to the ratio of power in the center area of the beam to the total power of the system. Since the power ratio only affects the performance of USFR and WSFR, the performance of other algorithms is horizontally straight. As the power ratio gradually increases, the throughput performance of USFR and WSFR gradually increases. This is because users in the center area have a better channel state, so the more resources the center user is allocated, the better the performance of the system. At the same time, the performance of WSFR is better than that of USFR at various power ratios. When the power ratio is 0.8, the throughput of the WSFR reaches twice that of the four-color.

To further illustrate that the hybrid architecture we propose can improve the performance of the system, we compared the satellite-aided cell-free system proposed in this paper with the traditional cell-free system, and the result is shown in Fig. 5. The terrestrial cell-free system in the figure refers to the throughput of the remaining terrestrial users after using the user selection algorithm proposed in this article. The satellite-aided cell-free system in the figure represents the total throughput of both terrestrial and satellite users. In this simulation, the number of APs in each beam is fixed in the three contrast scenarios.

Under different numbers of users, the performance of the hybrid architecture we propose is better than that of the traditional cell-free system. The performance of terrestrial users is also better than that of traditional cell-free system, which shows that the user selection algorithm we propose can effectively reduce the interference between systems, thereby improving the performance of the system.

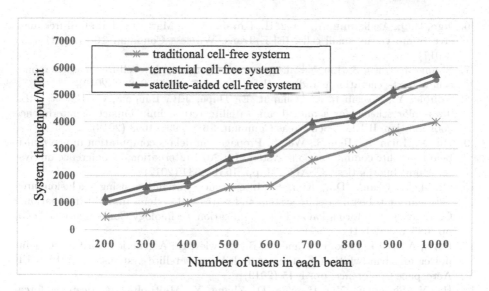

Fig. 5. Performance comparison of satellite-aided cell-free system and traditional cell-free system.

6   Conclusion

This paper proposes a hybrid communication framework that combines the benefits provided by cell-free massive MIMO with the large coverage of satellites. System models for the terrestrial and satellite segments are given separately. The simulation results show that the proposed user selection algorithm and resource allocation algorithm can reduce interference within the system and improve the throughput performance of the system.

References

1. Andrews, J.G., et al.: What will 5g be? IEEE J. Sel. Areas Commun. **32**(6), 1065–1082 (2014)
2. Pereira de Figueiredo, F.A.: An overview of massive mimo for 5g and 6g. IEEE Latin America Trans. **20**(6), 931–940 (2022)
3. Nayebi, E., Ashikhmin, A., Marzetta, T.L., Yang, H., Rao, B.D.: Precoding and power optimization in cell-free massive mimo systems. IEEE Trans. Wireless Commun. **16**(7), 4445–4459 (2017)
4. Buzzi, S., D'Andrea, C.: Cell-free massive mimo: User-centric approach. IEEE Wireless Commun. Lett. **6**(6), 706–709 (2017)
5. Zhang, J., Zhang, J., Ng, D.W.K., Jin, S., Ai, B.: Improving sum-rate of cell-free massive mimo with expanded compute-and-forward. IEEE Trans. Signal Process. **70**, 202–215 (2022)

6. Ngo, H.Q., Ashikhmin, A., Yang, H., Larsson, E.G., Marzetta, T.L.: Cell-free massive mimo versus small cells. IEEE Trans. Wireless Commun. **16**(3), 1834–1850 (2017)
7. Zhang, J., Chen, S., Lin, Y., Zheng, J., Ai, B., Hanzo, L.: Cell-free massive mimo: a new next-generation paradigm. IEEE Access **7**, 99878–99888 (2019)
8. Couble, Y., Rosenberg, C., Chaput, E., Dupé, J.B., Baudoin, C., Beylot, A.L.: Two-color scheme for a multi-beam satellite return link: impact of interference coordination. IEEE J. Sel. Areas Commun. **36**(5), 993–1003 (2018)
9. Hu, X., Luan, X., Ren, S., Wu, J.: Propagation delays computation in geo multibeam satellite communications system. In: 2012 International Conference on Systems and Informatics (ICSAI2012), pp. 1631–1634 (2012)
10. Oh, D.S., Chang, D.I., Kim, S.: Interference mitigation using exclusion area between multi-beam satellite system and terrestrial system. In: 2014 International Conference on Information and Communication Technology Convergence (ICTC), pp. 685–689 (2014)
11. Paris, A., Del Portillo, I., Cameron, B., Crawley, E.: A genetic algorithm for joint power and bandwidth allocation in multibeam satellite systems. In: 2019 IEEE Aerospace Conference, pp. 1–15 (2019)
12. He, Y., Sheng, B., Yin, H., Yan, D., Zhang, Y.: Multi-objective deep reinforcement learning based time-frequency resource allocation for multi-beam satellite communications. China Commun. **19**(1), 77–91 (2022)
13. Hirsch, A., Bosshard, P., Le Boulc'H, D., Pressence, J.: Broadband multibeam satellite radio communication system with improved reuse of frequencies on the forward channel, and associated method for reuse (Jun 20 2017), uS Patent 9,686,009
14. Ahmed, T., Dubois, E., Dupé, J.B., Ferrús, R., Gélard, P., Kuhn, N.: Software-defined satellite cloud ran. Int. J. Satell. Commun. Network. **36**(1), 108–133 (2018)
15. Srivastava, N.K., Chaturvedi, A.: Flexible and dynamic power allocation in broadband multi-beam satellites. IEEE Commun. Lett. **17**(9), 1722–1725 (2013)
16. Aravanis, A.I., MR, B.S., Arapoglou, P.D., Danoy, G., Cottis, P.G., Ottersten, B.: Power allocation in multibeam satellite systems: A two-stage multi-objective optimization. IEEE Trans. Wireless Commun. **14**(6), 3171–3182 (2015)
17. Jia, M., Zhang, X., Gu, X., Guo, Q., Li, Y., Lin, P.: Interbeam interference constrained resource allocation for shared spectrum multibeam satellite communication systems. IEEE Internet Things J. **6**(4), 6052–6059 (2018)
18. Chen, R., Hu, X., Li, X., Wang, W.: Optimum power allocation based on traffic matching service for multi-beam satellite system. In: 2020 5th International Conference on Computer and Communication Systems (ICCCS), pp. 655–659. IEEE (2020)
19. Riera-Palou, F., Femenias, G., Caus, M., Shaat, M., Pérez-Neira, A.I.: Scalable cell-free massive mimo networks with leo satellite support. IEEE Access **10**, 37557–37571 (2022)
20. Riera-Palou, F., Femenias, G., Caus, M., Shaat, M., García-Morales, J., Pérez-Neira, A.I.: Enhancing cell-free massive mimo networks through leo satellite integration. In: 2021 IEEE Wireless Communications and Networking Conference Workshops (WCNCW), pp. 1–7 (2021)
21. Ngo, H.Q., Ashikhmin, A., Yang, H., Larsson, E.G., Marzetta, T.L.: Cell-free massive mimo versus small cells. IEEE Trans. Wireless Commun. **16**(3), 1834–1850 (2017)
22. Xia, X., et al.: Joint user selection and transceiver design for cell-free with network-assisted full duplexing. IEEE Trans. Wireless Commun. **20**(12), 7856–7870 (2021)

23. Riera-Palou, F., Femenias, G., Caus, M., Shaat, M., Garcia-Morales, J., Pérez-Neira, A.I.: Enhancing cell-free massive mimo networks through leo satellite integration. In: 2021 IEEE Wireless Communications and Networking Conference Workshops (WCNCW), pp. 1 7. IEEE (2021)

24. Novlan, T., Andrews, J.G., Sohn, I., Ganti, R.K., Ghosh, A.: Comparison of fractional frequency reuse approaches in the ofdma cellular downlink. In: 2010 IEEE Global Telecommunications Conference GLOBECOM 2010, pp. 1–5 (2010)

Research on Crowd Movement Trajectory Prediction Method Based on Deep Learning

Ruikun Wang[1], Xinyu Gu[1,2(✉)], and Dongliang Li[1]

[1] Beijing University of Post and Telecommunication,
10 Xitucheng Road, Beijing 100876, China
guxinyu@bupt.edu.cn
[2] Purple Mountain Laboratories, Nanjing 211111, China

Abstract. Since the 21st century, the vigorous development of the Internet has brought about the rapid rise of social platforms. People's desire to share has been satisfied, and the information such as time and location shared by users has become the trajectory data of users. The analysis of these trajectory data is helpful to the study of crowd behavior, among which the prediction of crowd movement trajectory is an important content of trajectory data analysis.

This paper investigates the Transformer model which has an excellent performance in the field of Natural Language Processing (NLP). According to the characteristics of the data adopted in this paper, a prediction method of crowd movement trajectory based on the Transformer model is proposed and the future trajectory prediction is realized. Markov model, Long Short Term Memory Network (LSTM), and Gated recurrent unit network (GRU) are selected as baseline methods to compare with the model in this paper. The final results show that the prediction method proposed in this paper performs well in the dataset of this paper. The result also shows that the prediction methods based on deep learning have higher accuracy in predicting the future movement trajectory of the crowd compared with the prediction scheme based on the traditional model, even other parameters.

Keywords: Trajectory prediction · Deep learning · Transformer · Neural networks

1 Introduction

In human daily life, social platforms play a rather important role, and users use them to post information and communicate with other users. Some users often choose to upload their location when posting messages on social platforms, and this information shared by users is aggregated into a huge collection of user location data. For example, white-collar workers in cities usually go to

F. Gao et al. (Eds.): ChinaCom 2022, LNICST 500, pp. 390–402, 2023.
https://doi.org/10.1007/978-3-031-34790-0_30

work during the day and go home at night to rest. Students' locations usually change back and forth between school and home. Cab drivers' locations change irregularly throughout the city. By studying the movement patterns of humans in the real world, some reasonable inferences can be made about the content of human activities, which in turn can rationally explain various patterns of human behavior.

At present, the analysis of crowd movement patterns mainly faces demand from both academic and application aspects. From the academic aspect, the development of human society cannot be separated from the various activities carried out by human beings. Moving between various locations is an important part of human activities. An in-depth understanding of crowd movement patterns can only play a role in promoting the understanding of human activities. From the application aspect, with the deepening of city intelligence, personalized tertiary industries are also gradually appearing on the historical stage. Such as user location-based network service platforms, which have also developed rapidly in recent years and generated great market benefits. Their development path is to provide increasingly differentiated services for different groups of users and to provide customized service content according to each user. It is necessary to study the movement patterns of their service targets.

2   Previous Work

The research on the crowd movement trajectory prediction method is an important branch of crowd movement patterns research. By processing historical trajectory data and building a data model composed of various parameters, it can achieve the purpose of predicting the user's future arrival location. In this process, people's ideas about this direction are changing. For example, Gambs [1] built a Mobile Markov chain (MMC) model for the crowd's movement trajectory. Then, many prediction models based on the Markov model have emerged, such as the Hidden Markov model (HMM) proposed by Mathew [2]. In addition, many other traditional prediction methods based on parametric models have emerged one after another, such as the History average model (HA) [3], the Autoregressive integrated moving average model(ARIMA) [4], the Spatial-temporal autoregressive integrated moving average model (STARIMA) [5], and Vector autoregressive model (VAR) [6], the Decision tree model (DT) [7,8], and the Gaussian process model (GP) [9,10], etc., have all played their roles in the study of crowd movement trajectories.

With the continuous updating and iteration of the crowd movement trajectory prediction methods, the defects of various methods are gradually discovered. Methods based on traditional models perform poorly in solving nonlinear and non-smooth Spatio-temporal sequence prediction problems because traditional parametric models rely on fixed patterns for prediction, which are difficult to capture dynamic trajectory data features. Traditional models easily lose the ability to fit the data when dealing with massive trajectory data and fail to achieve the desired prediction accuracy [11]. In recent years, the research on crowd-moving trajectories based on deep learning has made remarkable progress. A series of research results show that methods based on deep learning have obvious advantages in solving the problems of dynamic trajectory updates and long-term moving trajectory prediction. For example, recurrent neural network (RNN) [12], long short-term memory network (LSTM) [13], gated recurrent unit network (GRU) [14] and Time-convolutional network (TCN) [15], the encoder-decoder-based crowd movement trajectory prediction model proposed by Jianwei Chen [16], and the attention mechanism-based recurrent neural network [17] proposed by Jie Feng et al. have shown far better performance than traditional prediction models. RNN can extract time-series features from trajectory data. LSTM solves the gradient explosion problem of RNN. GRU simplifies the structure of the LSTM and reduces training costs. These three methods ignore spatial correlations between time sequences when applied to Spatio-temporal sequences predicting. TCN uses the Convolutional Neural Network (CNN) structure to capture spatial relationships while using RNN structure to capture temporal relationships. Chen's model uses the Graph Convolutional Neural Network (GCN) structure to capture spatial relationships and uses Bi-LSTM to solve the problem of RNN structure. In recent years, the attention mechanism was beginning to be applied to the trajectory prediction areas. In this paper, we adopt a crowd movement trajectory prediction method based on deep learning and attention mechanism to solve the previous problem.

3 Method

The Transformer model was originally proposed by the Google team in 2017 and was first applied to machine translation [18], which abandoned the traditional RNN model to extract sequence information and pioneered the attention mechanism to achieve fast parallel computation, improving the defect of slow training speed of RNN model. The standard Transformer model consists of four modules: Input, Output, Encoder, and Decoder. In this paper, a position encoding mechanism is used to enable the neural network to obtain the order of the vectors, and a mask padding mechanism is used to improve the sparsity of the input data. The Encoder module is split from the standard Transformer model as the core part of the model, and the Dropout mechanism is added to prevent the model from overfitting. The final model outputs the prediction through a fully connected layer. Our model is shown in Fig. 1.

3.1 Position Encoding

After the vectors are input into the model, considering that the Transformer model does not have a sequential unit structure like RNN, positional encoding (PE) is performed on the input vectors for the neural network to obtain the position information of the vectors, i.e., the internal ordering of the sequence. There are two ways to obtain the positional encoding, one is to learn through data training, and the other is to generate the positional encoding directly using

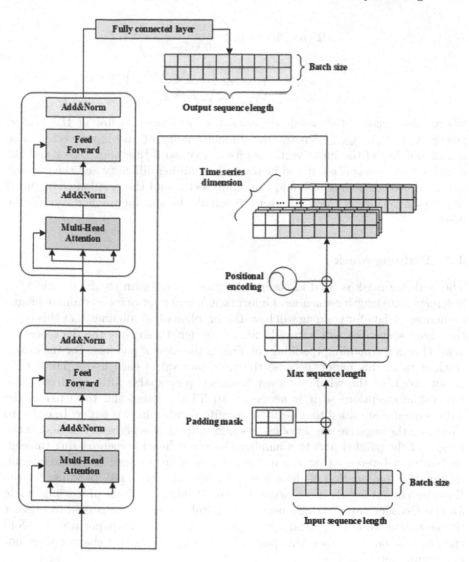

Fig. 1. Crowd movement trajectory prediction model

the formula. In this chapter, we use the positional encoding based on the sine and cosine function, which generates the corresponding encoding for each position by using the sine and cosine functions of different frequencies and adding it to the input vector of the corresponding position. The dimensionality of the position encoding vector must be the same as the dimensionality of the input vector during this calculation. The equation for calculating the position encoding based on the sine and cosine functions is shown in Eq. 1.

$$PE(pos, 2i) = \sin\left(\frac{pos}{10000^{\frac{2i}{d_{\text{model}}}}}\right)$$

$$PE(pos, 2i + 1) = \cos\left(\frac{pos}{10000^{\frac{2i}{d_{\text{model}}}}}\right)$$

(1)

where pos denotes the absolute position of a single feature in the vector, $pos = 0, 1, 2\ldots$, d_{model} denotes the dimensionality of the input vector, The dimensionality of the input vector is often large, so if the input vector and the position code are spliced, it will increase the training difficulty and the training time, so it is often chosen to add the input vector and the position code, but if the dimensionality of the input vector is small, the splicing method can also be used.

3.2   Padding Mask

The padding mask is used in Natural language procession (NLP) to deal with indeterminate length sequences of information, and a set of indeterminate length sequences of data for training will have the problem of misalignment, at this time, the short sequences will naturally fill in the length so that the data become neat, this is the padding (padding) of This is the idea of padding. For the crowd track data in this paper, because the time interval of each user's punch card is not fixed, so the whole data set becomes very sparse after the fixed time interval interception, so it is necessary to fill the gaps, and the gaps in the data sequence are filled to a negative infinite number in this paper. In order to eliminate the negative impact of useless information, it is necessary to change the weight of the padded part to a number close to 0 (mask) when passing through the softmax layer, so that the useless elements are masked to the maximum extent, the combination of these two mechanisms is the mask padding, for the Encoder part, it is only necessary to use the Padding mask for processing, while for the Decoder part, it is also necessary to Subsequent mask is used to prevent the test data from being read by the neural network, this paper uses five-fold cross-validation to replace this part of the function, so this chapter does not make more introduction.

3.3   Encoder Part

The Encoder module in the Transformer model structure consists of Multi-head attention and Feedforward neural network (FNN), which is used as the core part of the model in this chapter, shown in Fig. 2.

Attention, Self-attention and Multi-head Attention. The predecessors of Multi-head attention are attention and Self-attention. Attention is a mechanism designed to mimic human attention, shown in Fig. 3: The core attention mechanism is a weighted sum of the Value values of the elements in the Source, and the

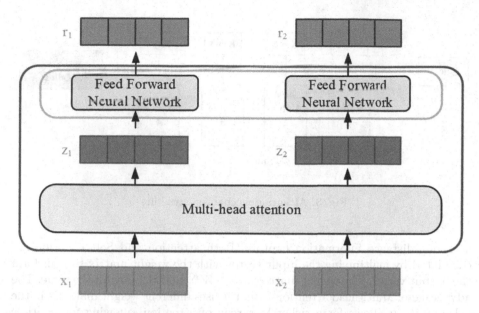

Fig. 2. Encoder part structure

Query and Key are used to calculate the weight coefficients of the corresponding Value, shown in Eq. 2:

$$Attention(Query, Source) = \sum_{i=1}^{L_x} Similarity(Query, Key_i) * Value_i \quad (2)$$

The calculation of Similarity in Eq. is to directly calculate the dot product of Query and Key, take this result as the similarity result of Query and Key, and later introduce the calculation method similar to SoftMax to numerically convert the similarity calculation result. The purpose of such calculation is twofold: on the one hand, the result can be normalized, and the original result can be organized into a probability distribution with the sum of all On the other hand, it is also possible to make the weights of relatively important elements larger through the inherent mechanism of SoftMax function, which makes them more prominent and helps to focus the attention of the network. After the similarity calculation, the weight coefficients are weighted and summed to obtain the attention coefficient.

The advantage of the attention mechanism is that it is fast because it no longer relies on RNN-based sequential decoders, solves the problem that RNNs cannot be computed in parallel, and can capture key information with excellent local performance. The disadvantage is that information is not available between medium and long distances. To improve this disadvantage, the Self-attention mechanism has emerged. In the attention mechanism, all computations occur between Source and Target, and the Self-attention mechanism makes a change by limiting the computation to the Source or Target, solving the problem of medium

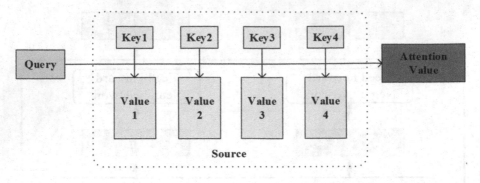

Fig. 3. Attention mechanism structure

and long-distance information capture. Both attention and Self-attention are calculated by multiplying the input vector with the weight matrix to transform the output vector. The weight matrixes W^Q, W^K, and W^V are all the same. The advantage of Multi-head attention is that it uses different weight matrixes in the calculation. It allows for a richer hierarchy of attention, allowing for multiple perspectives on the data being trained.

Feedforward Neural Network. Multi-head attention takes the position encoded data through different weight matrices, calculates multiple sets of output results, uses splicing processing to obtain a larger Z matrix as the output, and then inputs Z into the feedforward neural network, shown in Eq. 3

$$FFN(x) = \max(0, xW_1 + b_1)W_2 + b_2 \tag{3}$$

where x denotes the output Z of Multi-Head attention. The fully connected layer here uses a two-layer neural network, which first undergoes a linear transformation. Then a nonlinear transformation through the ReLU function, and finally another linear transformation. The purpose of the feedforward layer is to map the input Z to a higher dimensional space and then filter it by the nonlinear function ReLU. Finally, change Z back to the original dimension after the filtering.

Add&Normalize Part and Dropout. The final layer of the Encoder part is the Add&Normalize layer. Add means let the output vector be put into a Residual Neural Network (Res-net). In deep learning, we often encounter the problem of network degradation, which refers to the phenomenon that the network's Loss tends to stabilize at the beginning of training as the number of layers deepens, and then increases at the end of training when the number of layers continues to deepen, and the existence of residual blocks is to solve this problem. We choose Layer normalization in our model. Layer normalization is to calculate the mean and variance of all vectors in each layer and then normalize them to 0–1. The advantage of Layer normalization is that it is not affected by different Batch-size. The output of this layer will be input to the next Encoder layer.

The dropout mechanism is to turn off some neurons to make some limitations on the fitting ability of the neural network. Let the neurons in the hidden layer stop working with a certain probability p during the forward propagation, which will lead to the simplification of the network as well as random changes. The network will not be dependent on the local features, which can make the model more generalizable, as shown in Fig. 4. In the process of Dropout, each time the hidden neurons that are turned off are different, so it is equivalent to training different neural networks. So the training results are different. The result is more like training different neural networks and averaging them, which can offset some of the "opposite" fitting results, thus preventing overfitting overall. Moreover, Dropout forces the neural network to discard fixed implicit relations and learn more robust features instead, reducing the possibility that the neural network is sensitive to specific data, which is why the Dropout mechanism can prevent overfitting. Finally, just as the emergence of gender in biology allows species to reproduce offspring that are adapted to their environment, Dropout effectively prevents the effects of overfitting on the model through a similar mechanism.

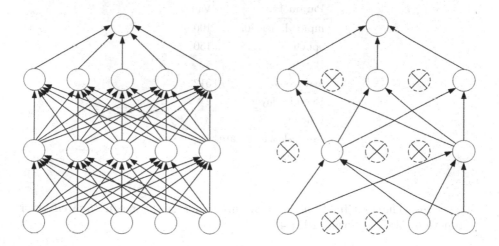

Fig. 4. The principle of the Dropout mechanism

4 Experiments

1) *Dataset*: The dataset [19] used in this paper is derived from user check-in data from the Foursquare website in Tokyo, Japan over a considerable period of time, including location information shared by users who visited various event venues to clock in over a ten-month period. As is shown in Table 1:

Table 1. Dataset

Dataset	Number of users	Check-in times	City	Duration	Number of venues
TSMC-Tky	2293	573703	Tokyo	10 months	61858

2) *Parameters*: Due to the sparsity of the trajectory sequence data, in this paper, the sequence is first complemented by the Padding Mask. Then enter Multi-head attention layer, where the number of attention heads is set to 8. The feature dimension is set to 512. The number of Encoder Layers is set to 2. The end part of the Encoder layer is Layer normalization, which is used to speed up training and improve training stability. Finally, a fully-connected layer is added to project the tensor into the form $[Batch - size, output - len]$. In this paper, we choose StepLR for the dynamic update of the learning rate. The initial learning rate is set to 0.00001, γ is set to 0.96, and step-size is set to 3, i.e., the learning rate is updated every 3 epochs. All parameters are shown in Table 2:

Table 2. Parameters of our model

Parameters	Values
input dimension	100
epoch	150
Batch-size	50
feature-size	512
Encoder-layer	2
n-head	8
Initial-learning rate	1e−5
Dropout	0.5

3) *Metrics*: The loss function used in this paper is the mean squared error function (MSE), shown in Eq. 4.

$$MSE = \frac{1}{n} \sum_{i=1}^{m} w_i \left(y_i - \hat{y}_i\right)^2 \qquad (4)$$

Since the trajectory data used in this paper are continuous rather than discrete, the problem under study is a regression problem. In order to compare with the Markov model, the problem is converted to a classification problem. We choose *top@k*, *Recall* and *F1 − score* as model performance metrics. The calculation formula of them are shown in Eq. 5, Eq. 6 and Eq. 7,

$$top @k = \frac{1}{|u|} \sum_{|u|} \sum_{j}^{|l_u^*|} \frac{\left|l_{u,j}^* \cap S_{u,j}^k\right|}{|l_u^*|} \qquad (5)$$

$$\text{Recall}@k = \frac{1}{|u|} \sum_{|u|} \sum_{j}^{|l_u^*|} \frac{|S_{u,j}^k \cap S_{u,j}^{visited}|}{|S_{u,j}^{visited}|}$$

$$\text{Precision}@k = \frac{1}{|u|} \sum_{|u|} \sum_{j}^{|l_u^*|} \frac{|S_{u,j}^k \cap S_{u,j}^{visited}|}{k} \tag{6}$$

$$F_1 - score = 2 \cdot \frac{\text{Precision} \cdot \text{Recall}}{\text{Precision} + \text{Recall}} \tag{7}$$

where $l^*(u, j)$ denotes the actual venue, and $S_k(u, j)$ denotes the set of the top k candidate predictions with the highest probability. In our Experiment, we choose $k = 1, 5$. $S_{u,j}^{visited}$.

4) *Baselines*: We compare our work with following several works based on generative models, including Markov, LSTM and GRU.

5   Disscusion

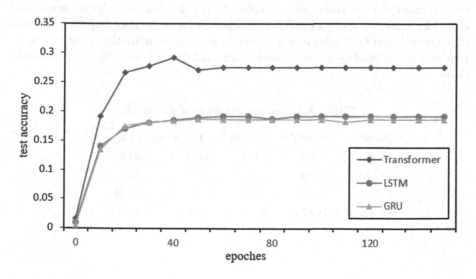

Fig. 5. Curves of test accuracy

It can be seen in Fig. 5 that the accuracy of our model performs best among all works. And as is shown in Fig. 6, the prediction accuracy of our model on the experimental dataset is 8.4% better than LSTM and 8.9% better than GRU. The Markov model cannot capture the non-Markovian properties in long-term trajectory data, such as periodicity, etc. The performance difference between the LSTM model and the GRU model is small, and both of them are greatly improved compared to the Markov model because they solve the information

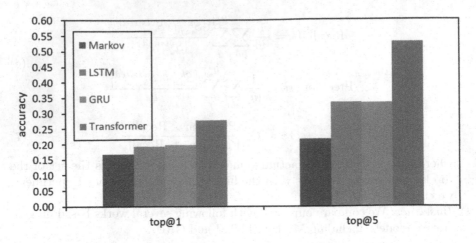

Fig. 6. Performance in TSMC_Tky

acquisition problem for long trajectories. In addition, Recall and F1-score of several models were compared in Table 3. We demonstrate the superiority of crowd movement trajectory prediction schemes based on deep learning methods over those based on traditional parametric models from another perspective, as well as the superiority of the Transformer model when dealing with sequential data.

Table 3. Recall and F1-score of all models

Model	Recall@1	Recall@5	F1-score@1	F1-score@5
Markov	0.091	0.132	0.091	0.147
LSTM	0.191	0.285	0.191	0.255
GRU	0.186	0.273	0.186	0.283
Our model	**0.275**	**0.401**	**0.275**	**0.434**

6   Conclusion

In this paper, the latest Transformer model is introduced to implement crowd movement trajectory prediction. The position encoding enables the model to obtain the position relationship of vectors. The sparsity of data is improved by the mask-filling mechanism. Attention and its variants Self-attention and Multi-head attention are introduced respectively, and the Encoder layer based on Multi-head attention and FNN is taken as the core of the model in this chapter, followed by adding residual blocks for preventing neural network degradation. We use a normalization mechanism to improve training stability as well as speed up training. We add a Dropout mechanism to prevent overfitting of the model. Several experiments on real datasets have demonstrated the effectiveness of the model. The model used in this paper has a relatively small number of network layers due to the small amount of data. For massive amounts of data, a deeper network structure can help capture more accurate crowd movement patterns.

Acknowledgment. This work was supported in part by the State Major Science and Technology Special Projects (Grant No. 2018ZX03001024)and in part by the National Key Research and Development Program (Grant No. 2022YFF0610303).

References

1. Gambs, S., Killijian, M.-O., del Prado Cortez, M.N.: Next place prediction using mobility Markov chains (2012)
2. Mathew, W., Raposo, R., Martins, B.: Predicting future locations with hidden Markov models. In: Proceedings of the 2012 ACM Conference on Ubiquitous Computing, UbiComp 2012, pp. 911–918. Association for Computing Machinery, New York (2012). https://doi.org/10.1145/2370216.2370421
3. Tikunov, D., Nishimura, T.: Traffic prediction for mobile network using holt-winter's exponential smoothing. In: 2007 15th International Conference on Software, Telecommunications and Computer Networks, pp. 1–5. IEEE (2007)
4. Xu, C., Xiang, W., Ji, M., et al.: Hybird forecasting model based on ARIMA and self-adaptive filtering. Comput. Appl. Softw. **35**(11), 302–306 (2018). (in Chinese)
5. Duan, P., Mao, G., Yue, W., Wang, S.: A unified STARIMA based model for short-term traffic flow prediction. In: 2018 21st International Conference on Intelligent Transportation Systems (ITSC), pp. 1652–1657. IEEE (2018)
6. Wu, L., Zeng, X., Zhou, W.: A prediction method of interval series based on vector autoregression a multiple linear regression. Guilin University of Electronic Technology (2021). (in Chinese)
7. Song, Y.-Y., Ying, L.: Decision tree methods: applications for classification and prediction. Shanghai Arch. Psychiatry **27**(2), 130 (2015)
8. Ma, K.: Spatiotemporal sequences prediction methods based on decision tree method. Inf. Technol. Inform. **10**, 35–37 (2017). (in Chinese)
9. Ye, W., Cai, C., Ping, Y., et al.: UKF estimation method incorporating gaussian process regression (2019)
10. Li, S., Zhou, Y., Yue, C., et al.: Application of gaussian process mixture model on network traffic prediction. Comput. Eng. Appl. **56**(5), 186–193 (2020). (in Chinese)
11. Yang, H., Pan, Z., Bai, W.: Review of time series prediction methods. Comput. Sci. **46**(1), 21–28 (2019). (in Chinese)
12. Yu, J., de Antonio, A., Villalba-Mora, E.: Deep learning (CNN, RNN) applications for smart homes: a systematic review. Computers **11**(2), 26 (2022)
13. Chandra, R., Jain, A., Singh Chauhan, D.: Deep learning via LSTM models for COVID-19 infection forecasting in India. PloS One **17**(1), e0262708 (2022)
14. Zhang, N., Zhang, N., Zheng, Q., Xu, Y.-S.: Real-time prediction of shield moving trajectory during tunnelling using GRU deep neural network. Acta Geotech. **17**(4), 1167–1182 (2022)
15. Sang, H., Chen, W., Wang, H., Wang, J.: Pedestrian trajectory prediction model based on multi-model space-time interaction. Acta Electon. Sinica 1 (2022)

16. Chen, J.: Research on crowd trajectory prediction based on deep learning (2020). (in Chinese)
17. Feng, J., et al.: DeepMove: predicting human mobility with attentional recurrent networks. In: Proceedings of the 2018 World Wide Web Conference, pp. 1459–1468 (2018)
18. Smith, L.N.: Cyclical learning rates for training neural networks. In: 2017 IEEE Winter Conference on Applications of Computer Vision (WACV), pp. 464–472 (2017)
19. Yang, D., Zhang, D., Zheng, V.W., Yu, Z.: Modeling user activity preference by leveraging user spatial temporal characteristics in LBSNS. IEEE Trans. Syst. Man Cybern.: Syst. 45(1), 129–142 (2015)

An Improved Hidden Markov Model for Indoor Positioning

Xingyu Ren[1], Di He[1(✉)], Xuyu Gao[1], Zhicheng Zhou[2], and Chih-Chun Ho[3]

[1] Shanghai Key Laboratory of Navigation and Location-Based Services,
Shanghai Jiao Tong University, Shanghai, China
{dihe,gao_xuyu}@sjtu.edu.cn
[2] Shenzhen Dashi Intelligent Co., Ltd., Shenzhen, China
zhouzhicheng@chn-das.com
[3] Beijing Jizhi Digital Techonology Co., Ltd., Beijing Longfor Blue Engine Industrial Park, Building 6, No.8 Beiyuan Street, Chaoyang District, Beijing, China

Abstract. This paper proposes an indoor positioning method combines machine learning, IMU (Inertial Measurement Unit) and an improved HMM (Hidden Markov Model). HMM is the base framework, the latent states correspond to the location grid, which uses two methods to divide the area into grids with different granularity. The fine-grained grids are used to compute transition probability, and the coarse-grained ones for emission probability. IMU data can help to adjust transition probability between fine-grained grids, and some machine learning methods to estimate the emission probability in each coarse-grained grid. And for the particularity of the model, there's an improved Viterbi algorithm proposed to calculate the most likely path, which is a more robust version compared with the original one.

Keywords: Indoor Positioning · Hidden Markov Model · IMU · Machine Learning

1 Introduction

The main contribution of this paper is the proposed improved HMM and the modeling method for indoor positioning that combines classical fingerprinting method and inertial navigation method.

1.1 Indoor Positioning

Indoor positioning is a hot topic recently, and there are many methods to achieve it. Not like the outdoor positioning, the precise indoor positioning is more difficult to be realized due to the complex environmental problems.

In outdoor environment, one can use GPS and the geometric relationship to locate the position. But this method is not suitable for indoor environment.

© ICST Institute for Computer Sciences, Social Informatics and Telecommunications Engineering 2023
Published by Springer Nature Switzerland AG 2023. All Rights Reserved
F. Gao et al. (Eds.): ChinaCom 2022, LNICST 500, pp. 403–420, 2023.
https://doi.org/10.1007/978-3-031-34790-0_31

Usually, GPS signal is not available in indoor environment, or the signal is weak and not accurate because of fading and multipath. So, the indoor positioning methods are mainly based on the signal features (like strength) of the wireless signals, such as WiFi, Bluetooth, Zigbee, etc. Nowadays, 5G technology is applying and deploying steps by steps. Because of the properties of 5G, there're many indoor stations, which can also provide many signal features.

The most popular method is fingerprinting. It's like machine learning method, requires a pre-collected database of signal features on each pre-demarcated location. And use some model to train the data, this is called offline stage. When the user is in the indoor environment, the signal features can be collected and input to the trained model to get the prediction. This is called online stage. This method bypass the geometric method.

Another main method is use Inertial Navigation System (INS) to locate a path of positions. This method use the IMU to measure the acceleration and angular velocity of the user. And then use calculus to calculate the speed and position [2]. The shortage of INS is drift error will accumulate over time span, so usually people only use INS as assistance for other system. But in a short period of time it is reliable.

In this paper, those methods are combined with Hidden Markov Model (HMM) to achieve more accurate positioning. This method can utilize the history of user's movement to predict the current position. The IMU data can help to adjust the transition probability between grids, and original fingerprinting method or machine learning method can provide emission probability.

1.2 Hidden Markov Model

HMM is a statistical Markov model in which the problem being modeled is assumed to be a Markov process with unobservable ("hidden") states. As part of the definition, HMM requires that there is observable process whose outcomes are "influenced" by the outcomes of hidden states in a known way. Since hidden states cannot be observed directly, the goal is to learn about hidden state sequence by observing the observable sequence. HMM has an additional requirement that the outcome of observable process at time $t = t_0$ must be "influenced" exclusively by the outcome of the corresponding hidden state, and that the outcomes of previous hidden states (and the observations) at $t < t_0$ must not affect the outcome of t_0's state and observation [12,18].

HMM are known for their applications to statistical mechanics, physics, chemistry, economics, finance, signal processing, information theory, pattern recognition – such as speech, handwriting, gesture recognition, part-of-speech tagging, musical score following, partial discharges and bio-informatics [5,10,11, 13,15].

HMM have five main factors:

- State space: The latent states
- Observation space: The observable outcomes

- Transition probability between states: 2-D matrix-like table $A[i][j]$ is the probability of transitioning from state i to state j
- Emission probability of each state: 2-D matrix-like table $B[o][j]$ is the probability of observing o in state i
- Initial probability of each state

Viterbi algorithm [16] is used to solve the HMM's latent state sequence from observation sequence. This article will propose a new HMM that can utilize the IMU data to dynamically update the transition probability, in order to do that, the gridding method should be refined, whose "side effect" is making the position estimation more accurate in some way. The corresponding Viterbi algorithm is also proposed to improve the robustness of the algorithm.

2 Mathematical Modeling

As the description in Sect. 1.2, the property of HMM is perfectly suited for indoor positioning. However, it's necessary to model the indoor environment to fit those five properties in the HMM.

Let's make the HMM-based indoor positioning idea clear first. In the indoor positioning problem, the state of HMM is the location, the observation is the signal features, the transition probability is the probability of moving from one location to another, the emission probability is the probability of observing the signal features in each location.

Some symbols are defined as follows:

- State space which is location (grid) set: $\mathcal{L}$
- Observation space which is signal features set: $\mathcal{O}$
- Transition Probability is still using the original notation: $A[i][j]$, where i and j are the locations
- Emission probability is still using the original notation: $B[i][o]$, where i is the location, o is the signal features
- Initial probability is noted as Π, where $\Pi[i]$ is the initial probability of in location i

And the input observation sequence to compute the best latent state sequence is noted as Y, where Y_i is the observation of the time i.

A location here is an abstract concept. In general, a location is a grid. So it relates to a coordinate in the real world.

Five main factors in HMM will be detailed in the following sections respectively.

2.1 Observation and Signal Features

The observation is one of the main concepts of HMM. As the name suggests, the observation is some observable that can be influenced by the hidden states. Here just use the signal features to describe the observation. In fingerprinting method, the popular signal feature is the strength of the signal, or RSS (Received Signal Strength). RSS data collection is carried out at each grid in pre-demarcated areas.

There should be several base stations or APs in the indoor environment, so that it's possible to synthesize RSS information from multiple APs. If there's only one or two APs, the same RSS values may appear in many different places, resulting in ambiguity for computation of emission probability.

The RSS data of those concerned APs should be arranged carefully. There's a simple method to organize the RSS information. Suppose there're a group of APs and each of them has an unique ID. At first, determine a specific order of those APs (using the ID), and then when collecting the RSS data in each grid, always use the same order to organize the RSS data. For example, suppose there're 4 APs, whose ID are listed as $122, 124, 133, 135$. For one collection of a single acquisition, there are usually 4 RSS values, like -101 for AP 122, -112 for AP 124, -88 for AP 133, and -94 for AP 135. Then the representation of the RSS data is $[-101, -112, -88, -94]$. It's important to sort the RSS data of the corresponding AP in the same and determined order as the APs.

But there're some corner cases. First is that the RSS data of some APs may be missing. In the example above, if the No.124 AP is missing, fill it with a reasonable default value. In general it should use the minimum RSS value. For 5G signal collected by Android phone, the minimum RSS value that phone can collect is -140 [8], so the missing AP's data should use -140 or value that is less than -140. Second situation is there're more APs than needed. In this case, just simply ignore the data from extra APs.

In conclusion, the observation is a vector of RSS values that sorted in a pre-defined AP's order.

2.2   Emission Probability

The emission probability is the probability of observing the signal features in each grid. Formally, use B to represent it, which is a function that takes the location and signal features as input and returns the probability of observing the signal features in that location.

In the original HMM, the signal features (Observation space) is generally a finite discrete set. But as it shows in Sect. 2.1, the observation is a vector of RSS values that, in most cases, belongs to an infinite set. So the emission probability needs to be calculated in other way.

Like traditional fingerprinting method, classification methods like KNN (K-Nearest Neighbors) [1] or DNN (Deep Neural Networks) [14] are usually used to classify the RSS vector into different classes, which here is the location grids. In the final step of classification, most of machine learning methods can produce a probability vector that represents the probability of each class/location. Declare the location (noted as l)'s probability given the signal features (noted as o) as $P(L = l | O = o)$, where L is a random variable of the grid and O is the observation.

So $P(O = o | L = l)$ can be deduced by $P(L = l | O = o)$:

$$P(O = o | L = l) = \frac{P(L = l | O = o)\, P(O = o)}{P(L = l)}$$

$$\sim P(L = l | O = o) \tag{1}$$

Considering required value for Viterbi algorithm is the maximum/minimum, not the accurate value, so as long as all the emission probability are proportional to the true value at the same scale, $P(O = o | L = l)$ can be replaced by $P(L = l | O = o)$ directly.

More formally,

$$B[l][o] = P(L = l | O = o) \tag{2}$$

In practice, to get the emission probability, use the similar approach as fingerprinting method. First collect the RSS data. For each grid, measure RSS many times to build the fingerprinting database. For each measurement, it is an observation as described in Sect. 2.1. This means for each grid, for each measurement, there's an RSS vector as an observation. And then those data will be used to train the KNN or some other machine learning models. Finally use the model to provide the emission probability.

In HMM, the input is an observation sequence, so each observation in that sequence will be passed to a machine learning method (like KNN) to compute $P(L = l | O = o)$, then there is a B for each Y_i. Y_i is input to a machine learning model and get a probability distribution of each grid l. That's the emission probability at time i. So there will be a sequence of emission probability, which has the same length as Y. Formally, the notation (and the definition) of emission probability becomes: B from now on is a sequence of emission probability, where B_i is the emission probability related to i-th observation Y_i.

2.3   State of HMM

To determine the state space, the model uses grid map to partition the indoor environment. In Fig. 1, the indoor area is divided into the meshed grids. In original HMM, a grid is associated with a state, and the transition probability between two grids is related to the distance between those two grids. The observation of each grid is some signal feature (e.g. the strength of the signal or some aggregated information, will discuss later) there. The emission probability can be estimated by some machine learning method, which basically is a function that maps the signal feature to the probability that the signal feature occurs at each location, e.g. SVM, KNN, DNN, etc. These methods are called "fingerprinting" methods, the fingerprinting means the signal features. As we know, those machine learning methods require pre-collected data to train the model. Basically, the state space of HMM is the grid of the indoor positioning area. But the original grids with coarse granularity is not usable for HMM, especially for the transition probability part.

But this leads to a problem: the grid can't be too small, otherwise there's too much work to collect each grid's signal feature. Meanwhile the grid can't be too large, otherwise the transition from one grid to its neighbor is kind of impossible, let alone the transition from one grid to further grids. So the transition probability doesn't make sense any more.

For example, consider the grid size (the length of side of each grid) d is as large as about 5 meters, while a man's walking speed is about $1\,\mathrm{m/s}$. And the measurement is at a frequency of about once per second. In this scenario, it's kind of impossible to transition from one grid to it's adjacent grid. So the transition probability between two grids is zero. Even we can set the transition probability from one grid to its neighbor grid to be some appropriate value, like 0.15 for four adjacent grid and 0.4 for current grid. But this would lead to another problem: when using Viterbi algorithm to solve HMM, every step will position at a grid's center point, and then the next step is still current grid if there's no large change of observation, or the next step will suddenly "jump" to the neighbor girds. And this is based on the assumption that the emission probability is accurate. This will reduce the HMM and Viterbi algorithm to original emission probability calculation, which is same as using the machine learning method directly: It can not utilize the historical information to predict the current location any more.

But the grid size can not be too small to just fit the measuring frequency. It is also difficult to measure and collect the RSS data and create fingerprints for each small grid. And further more, as described in the Sect. 2.1, for normal RSS measurement device, the resolution is not very high, so if the grid size is too small, there will be no difference of RSS between two adjacent grids. In the test environment later, we use an Android phone to measure the RSS. Because the accuracy of the phone is not very high, the size of the grid cannot be too small. Generally in the real indoor environment, when the size of the grid is less than 3m, the RSS of the adjacent grid is difficult to distinguish.

In order to utilize HMM, it's necessary to find a way to balance the two problems described above, or even solve both. That is to collect useful and distinguishable data easily and model the transition probability accurately.

In this study, we propose a solution to model the locations. Use two grid map with different granularity: a coarse grid map (which the grid size is large) for measuring RSS (observation) and computing emission probability, and a dense grid map (which the grid size is small) for transition probability computing. And then the states in HMM is now the small grids.

So now the location/state set $\mathcal{L}$ contains the fine-grained small grids. And l will represent the small grid in general context.

But there's another problem: how to determine the small grid's emission probability? To combine the information of both maps together, we set the emission probability of each small grid is equal to the big one which contains the small one. More formally, assume the big grid is l' and the small grid it contains is l. According to Eq. (2), the emission probability of the small grid is updated as follows:

$$B_i[l] = B[l][Y_i] = \mathrm{P}(L = l'|O = Y_i), \forall l \text{ belongs to } l' \tag{3}$$

Further more, this model will benefit the transition probability computation considering IMU data. This will be discussed in the Sect. 2.4.

This model has many advantages. It not only fixes the two problems about transition and observation, but also provides a simple way to describe the obstacles in the indoor environment. If the resolution of the small grid map is high enough, an obstacle, like a wall or a desk, can be modeled by simply removing a clique of some small grids.

2.4   Transition Probability and IMU

Another important part of HMM is the transition probability A, where $A[p][l]$ is the probability of transition from previous state (location/small grid) p to current state l.

The plain idea to describe transition probability is that the closer the distance between two location, the greater the probability of moving to each other. So firstly it is suggested to compute the distance between two small grids.

Consider the grid map as an undirected (a two-way directed) graph. Each small grid is a vertex in the graph. Each small grid is only connected to its four directly adjacent grid (north, south, east, west), or maybe counts the four diagonal grid in and there will be 8 adjacent grid. The edge weight is simply the distance between those directly or diagonally adjacent grids. For example, in the squared grid map, the distance between two directly adjacent grids is the grid length, and between two diagonally adjacent grids is $\sqrt{2}$ times the grid length.

In the undirected graph, there're several all-pair shortest path algorithms. And there exists two famous ones: Floyd-Warshall algorithm [6] and Johnson's algorithm [9]. Suppose there are V grids (vertices). Floyd's approach has the complexity of $O(V^3)$, and Johnson's approach usually has the complexity of $O(V^2 \log V)$.

But for simplicity, assume every grid is only connected to its four/eight neighbor grids. It's accurate enough for basic scenarios. Given this assumption, it's better to use BFS (Breadth-First Search) to compute the shortest path for each vertex. And the complexity is $O(V^2)$ [4].

It is worth noting that it's unnecessary to compute all vertices for each vertex, since normally when computing the transition probability, what matters is the grids around current one. But for simplicity and clear statements, we compute all vertices here, and will discuss this in Sect. 4.1 later.

Another thing worth mentioning is the obstacles in the environment will be modeled conveniently. As described in last section, the obstacles in the fine-grained grid map will simply be removed. So the distance between two grids that are across the obstacles will be large, resulting the transition probability is small, which makes sense.

For convenience, the distance map is noted as D, where $D[p][l]$ is the shortest path's length from p to l.

Another problem for transition probability is how to utilize the IMU data, because IMU is generally available in most of mobile devices. It's proper to use a vector $\mathbf{v}$ to model the IMU data. Although the IMU's output is acceleration, but one can use integral to get the speed, and this is reliable in a short period of time. The $|\mathbf{v}|$ is speed, the $\angle\mathbf{v}$ is the direction. Assuming IMU can provide data at given sampling rate r, the speed and direction, formally represented by vector $\mathbf{v}$, can be calculated. Base on the speed vector and the sample rate, HMM can predicate the possible movement between two sampling time. Assume current location of current grid p is $\mathbf{x}$, the speed is $\mathbf{v}$ and sampling period is $\Delta t = 1/r$. For convenience, let $\boldsymbol{\delta} = \mathbf{v}\Delta t$. To compute the next position $\mathbf{y}$:

$$\mathbf{y} = \mathbf{x} + \boldsymbol{\delta} \tag{4}$$

Then we can determine which grid position $\mathbf{y}$ belongs to, and suppose that grid is p'.

One more thing worth consideration is the connectivity of those two grids. Since if there're some obstacles between p and p', the transition is impossible. There's a simple way to determine the connectivity of two grids, as the shortest distance between two grids is already computed and the obstacle information is stored in the distance map. If the distance $D[p][p']$ is much larger than the supposed distance, then there must be some obstacles.

Consider a probability distribution with the density function Φ, this function should satisfy some conditions. The longer the distance between two grids, the smaller the probability will be. In general, normal distribution will satisfy. And then the transition probability between previous grid p and current grid l, considering the speed $\mathbf{v}$, can be computed as follows:

1. Use $\mathbf{v}$ and Eq. (4) to get the real grid for previous grid, and denote it as p'.
2. If p and p' is not connected, the transition probability from p to each other grid is 0. Because it is impossible to move from p to p', leaving alone the probability moving from p' to p.
3. If not, the current transition probability $A'[p][l]$ is $\Phi(D[p'][l])$. (Attention: here it is $D[p'][l]$ not $D[p][l]$, cause the IMU data is taken into account).

The pseudo-code is shown in Algorithm 1: A' is the transition function (which is a 2-D matrix) for a certain time.

For each observation in Y, the IMU data is usually different, so the transition probability for each observation is also different. So we use the original symbol A as a sequence of matrices, where $A_i[p][l]$ is the transition probability from previous state p to current state l, corresponding to the observation Y_i. And A_i is A' in Algorithm 1.

It is worth noting that the length of sequence A is equal to the length of Y minus 1. Because the IMU data and transition probability describes the movement from Y_{i-1} to Y_i. For example, if there're 3 observations in Y, then the length of sequence A is 2, where $A_2[i][j]$ uses the speed $\mathbf{v}$ at moment 1 to predict the movement from time 1 to 2, and A_3 use the speed at moment 2 to predict the movement from time 2 to 3 (note that there is no A_1).

As the algorithm delivered above, for some p and l, the value $A_i[p][l]$ is missing, resulting the sum of those probability is less than 1. But same as in Sect. 2.2, there's no need to compute the exact value for Viterbi algorithm, reasonable values are enough.

Algorithm 1: Build Transition Probability at time t

Data: $\mathcal{L}, \delta, D, \Phi$
Result: A' as the transition probability function
function $(\mathcal{L}, \delta, D, \Phi)$
begin
    for $p \in \mathcal{L}$ **do**
        let $\mathbf{x}$ be the coordination of p
        let p' be the new location that point $\mathbf{y}$ belongs to, such that $\mathbf{y} \leftarrow \mathbf{x} + \delta$
        if $p' \in \mathcal{L}$ and **not** $(D[p][p'] \gg |\delta|)$ **then**
            for $l \in \mathcal{L}$ **do**
                $A'[p][l] \leftarrow \Phi(D[p'][l])$

2.5 Initial Probability

Initial probability is the probability of user at grid p at time 1. Empirically the initial probability is set to be $1/|\mathcal{L}|$. Another option is to set the probability in proportion to the amount of data in each grid. Formally, the initial probability Π is defined as: $\Pi[l] = 1$ or $\Pi[l] =$ the number of the fingerprints in l (l is the small fine-grained grid here, but as revealed in Eq. (3) in Sect. 2.3, here it's fine using the information of the coarse grid that contains current small grid) in the database. And here it's unnecessary to use exact value (which is the proportion of the number in each coarse grids), the reason is same as in Sect. 2.2.

3 Improved Viterbi Algorithm

Viterbi algorithm is a dynamic programming algorithm that compute the latent state sequence that is most likely to produce the observation sequence. In order to introduce the improved version of this algorithm, we first investigate the basic idea of Viterbi algorithm [16].

Viterbi Algorithm is a dynamic programming algorithm that an compute the latent state sequence from the observation sequence. Dynamic programming is a method to solve optimization problems, such as finding the minimum/maximum value. Those problems can be divided into sub-problems, and solutions of sub-problems can be reused to solve the original problem. It's a kind of induction in mathematics. For HMM, the problem is to find the most likely (maximum probability) latent sequence given the observation sequence. The sub-problem can be defined as: find the probability of most likely latent for the first i moments (each observation is related to a moment), given the first i observations of Y, the last latent state (i-th state) is l. Suppose the solution of this sub-problem is $V[i][l]$, then the relation of bigger sub-problem and smaller sub-problem is:

$$V(i, l) = \max_{p}\{V[i-1][p] \times A_i[p][l] : p \in \mathcal{L}\} \times B_i[l] \tag{5}$$

And the base case is: at moment 1, for each l,

$$V[1][l] = \Pi[l] \times B_1[l] \tag{6}$$

While computing the solution of each sub-problem, it's necessary to record the previous state that leads to the maximum probability of current state. Formally, psi is a table, where

$$psi[i][l] = \arg\max_p \{V[i-1][p] \times A_i[p][l] : p \in \mathcal{L}\} \tag{7}$$

For the original problem, the maximum probability of the latent state sequence (the path) is:

$$\max_l V[|Y|][l] \tag{8}$$

To recover the total path, we start from the last state, which is

$$\hat{l}_{|Y|} = \arg\max_l V[|Y|][l] \tag{9}$$

Then the previous state can be calculated by looking up the table psi:

$$\hat{l}_{t-1} = psi[t][\hat{l}_t] , t = |Y|, |Y|-1, |Y|-2, \cdots, 2 \tag{10}$$

For the convenience, Viterbi Algorithm can be divided into the following 3 parts:

1. Initialization: use the Eq. (6) to initialize $V[1][l]$ for each l.
2. Forward Computation: use the Eq. (5) to compute $V[i][l]$ for each i and l, from 2 to $|Y|$. At same time record psi.
3. Backward Recovering: find the last state using Eq. (9), then use psi to recover the whole path (Eq. (10)).

The original Viterbi Algorithm has a problem. In the original model, both the transition probability A and the emission probability B contain a lot of zeros. In A, usually only the nearby grids have positive number. When computing B, depending on the machine learning method selected, usually it has $P(L = l|O = o) = 0$ for many l. Sometimes there's only one l that has non-zero probability (which is 1).

Combining the above two facts, and considering the Eq. (5), it's clear that as computing $V[i][*]$ from $t = 1$ to $|Y|$, there're more 0s in $V[i][*]$. Normally it it not a problem, since $V[i][l] = 0$ means that it's impossible to land on grid l at time i. And in fact, that's a good thing because it's more accurate. But sometimes in the real application it appears that

$$V[i][l] = 0 , \forall l \in \mathcal{L}$$

And then it can't use Eq. (5) to compute the next state. This will lead the algorithm to fail.

Although this situation is rare, it will still reduce the robustness of the proposed algorithm. So we propose an improved version of Viterbi Algorithm. The basic idea is re-initialize the algorithm on failure. There are some improvements in the corresponding 3 parts of the algorithm.

3.1   Initialization

For the initialization subroutine, enable it to re-initialize for each moment t. Then Eq. (6) becomes:

$$V[t][l] = \Pi[l] \times B_t[l] \tag{11}$$

The pseudo code for this simple subroutine is described in Algorithm 2. The input is the state space $\mathcal{L}$, the initial probability Π, the emission probability B (a sequence), and time t. The table V is going to be initialized, it's a kind of output, but here the reference of V is passed as a parameter so that it can be modified.

Algorithm 2: Initialize Subroutine

Data: $\mathcal{L}, V, \Pi, B$, and t
function init($\mathcal{L}, V, \Pi, B, t$)
begin
   for $l \in \mathcal{L}$ **do**
      $V[t][l] = \Pi[l] \times B_t[l]$
   if $V[t][l] = 0, \forall l \in \mathcal{L}$ **then**
      error

3.2   Backward Recovery

For the backward recovering subroutine, enable it to recover the path for any range $[s, t]$. Further more, it's possible that at time t, there's no valid previous state to reach current state. This will be explained in the next section. So the basic routine is still find the maximum state for t, such as Eq. (9), here it becomes:

$$\hat{l}_t = \arg\max_l V[t][l] \tag{12}$$

And then use psi to compute previous state from $t - 1$ to s, like Eq. (10). But if there's no valid previous state ($psi[i][seq]$ is null), then use (12) to calculate maximum state for i. It's worth mentioning that if the previous states are null for all i, then this will reduce to single point positioning (like using machine learning method to predict the location directly), which makes sense.

The pseudo code is described in Algorithm 3. The input is the state space $\mathcal{L}$, the subproblem's table V, recovering table psi, and the range $[s, t]$ for which the recovering subroutine runs. The output is the path seq for that range, but here it's passed as a reference. seq is a sequence of length $|Y|$ but not equal to $t - s + 1$, and the subroutine will fill the recovered path in seq from s to t. This will be more clear in the next Sect. 3.3.

Algorithm 3: Recover Subroutine

Data: $\mathcal{L}, V, psi, seq$, and $[s, t]$
function recover $(\mathcal{L}, V, psi, [s, t])$
begin

$\quad$ $seq[t] \leftarrow \arg\max_l \{V[t][l] : l \in \mathcal{L}\}$

$\quad$ **for** $i \leftarrow t - 1$ **downto** s **do**
$\quad\quad$ $seq[i] \leftarrow psi[i][seq[i+1]]$
$\quad\quad$ **if** $seq[i]$ is null **then**
$\quad\quad\quad$ $seq[i] \leftarrow \arg\max_l \{V[i][l] : l \in \mathcal{L}\}$

3.3 Forward Computation

The forward computation is the main part of Viterbi Algorithm. Same as the original Viterbi algorithm, first initialize the basic case at time 1, by calling Algorithm 2. And then start the forward computation from $t = 2$ to $|Y|$.

As mentioned before, the original Viterbi Algorithm will fail when $V[i][l] = 0$ for all l. So when it happens, just reset the algorithm.

There's a variable s to record the starting time of the current computation procedure. Initially, $s = 1$. While computing from $i = 2$, or if at some time i, $V[i][l] = 0$ for all l, then start the reset procedure: First, recover the path seq from last start point s to current break point $i - 1$, by calling Algorithm 3. After this, the path in range $[s, i - 1]$ is recovered. Then set $s = i$, to use for next recovering subroutine. Then time i becomes the initial time and re-initialize $V[i][*]$ by calling Algorithm 2.

The pseudo code is described in Algorithm 4. The input is the state space $\mathcal{L}$, the initial probability Π, the transition probability (sequence with length of $|Y| - 1$) A, the emission probability (sequence with length of $|Y|$) B. The output is the best path seq for the observation sequence Y.

Note that we use $|B|$ as the length of observation sequence Y because B is the sequence derived from Y (as described in Sect. 2.2), and they have the same length.

At line 11, it's possible that $V[i-1][p] \times A_i[p][l] = 0, \forall p \in \mathcal{L}$, then $psi[t-1][l]$ is null. That's why we need to consider this situation in Algorithm 3.

Actually, some small operations can also be realized through the proposed approach. For example, a threshold can be defined to indicate whether there is a failure in the process: if there are more than 95% of $V[i][*]$ is 0, it fails. Or if $\max_l V[i][l] < 0.001$, it fails. And then call the re-initialization procedure.

There's a degeneration case: if $V[i][*] \equiv 0 \forall i$, the reset procedure will be called each time. This will lead to a situation that the positioning algorithm is just using the initial probability Π and the emission probability of time i: B_i. As mentioned in Sect. 2.5, if $\Pi[l] \equiv 1$, the degeneration situation is just using the machine learning method for single prediction. If $\Pi[l] = $ the number of the

---

Algorithm 4: Improved Viterbi Algorithm

Data: $\mathcal{L}, A, B, \Pi$
Result: *seq*: best path
function viterbi($\mathcal{L}, A, B, \Pi$)
begin
    $s \leftarrow 1$
    allocate V as an array of size $|B|$
    allocate *psi* as an array of size $|B| - 1$
    allocate *seq* as an array of size $|B|$
    init($\mathcal{L}, V, \Pi, B, s$)
    for $i \leftarrow 2$ **to** $|B|$ **do**
        for $l \in \mathcal{L}$ **do**
            $V[i][l] \leftarrow \max_{p}\{V[i-1][p] \times A_i[p][l] : p \in \mathcal{L}\} \times B_i[l]$
            $psi[i-1][l] \leftarrow \arg\max_{p}\{V[i-1][p] \times A_i[p][l] : p \in \mathcal{L}\}$
        if $V[i][l] = 0, \forall l \in \mathcal{L}$ **then**
            recover($\mathcal{L}, V, psi, seq, [s, i-1]$)
            $s \leftarrow i$
            init($\mathcal{L}, V, \Pi, B, s$)
    recover($\mathcal{L}, V, psi, seq, [s, |B|]$)
    return *seq*

---

fingerprints in l in the pre-collected database, this will be a kind of naive Bayes method, or maximum a posteriori method [7].

3.4 Re-clarification of the Symbols

Since there are many changes of the symbols in HMM through the narration, those symbols are listed again:

- emission probability sequence B. $|B| = |Y|$. B_t is the emission probability at time t, which compute from the observation at time t.
- markov transition probability sequence A. $|A| = |Y| - 1$. A_t is the transition probability from $t - 1$ to t.
- state space is the small grid set $\mathcal{L}$ and the observation space is basically an infinite set.
- The large (coarse) grid is used to collect the fingerprints and the symbol is NOT $\mathcal{L}$.

4   Implementation Notes

4.1   Transition Probability

In Sect. 2.4, the transition probability is based on the IMU data (as speed). So for each moment, IMU data should be taken into consideration for the transition probability. This is a time consuming process.

Here we can define a threshold of distance d_t. If the distance between previous state (grid) is less than d_t, compute the transition probability. Otherwise, the transition is impossible. This will reduce the scale of computation. When compute V in Viterbi Algorithm, it can just ignore the impossible transition.

Another improvement is using cache. First, partition the IMU data (speed) into discrete values. It can partition on both direction and magnitude of speed. Then for each discrete value, compute the transition probability and store them to cache. When the new IMU data is updated, find which discrete value it belongs to, and then get the transition probability from cache.

Another thing is locality [3]. Define the transition probability as $A[l][p]$ where p is still previous state and l is current state. This will accelerate the computation of finding maximum previous state part in Viterbi Algorithm.

4.2 Probability Representation

Generally probability is a floating number, if we use the floating number directly, as we computing the chain of probability in Viterbi Algorithm, it will cause numerical error (called "underflow") [17].

It's better to use logarithm probability. And the change the multiplying operation to summarization operation. And this will avoid the numerical error.

5 Real Application

The real application ground is shown in Fig. 1. The size of the real application ground area is 20 m × 32 m. The size of coarse grid is 4 m × 4 m. This is used for fingerprints collection. The size of fine grid is 0.5 m × 0.5 m (not shown in Fig. 1). Because human step size is usually larger than 0.5m, so the transition between nearby grids makes sense. There are some places containing obstacles, which are marked as red X-shape. For those obstacles that are not large enough to fill the whole grid, it is counted as the whole grid.

First, we collect the RSS fingerprints for each coarse grid in the ground and train the KNN model.

Second, which is the real positioning process, we walk along the pre-defined test route (blue arrows in Fig. 1), and collect the RSS data, the direction and speed information. Meanwhile, we also record the real position for each collection as truth value.

Finally, we use the collected RSS data, the direction and speed information to predict the position using KNN model and HMM model. There're some preprocessing steps for the collected data. For the RSS data, we remove the outliers and normalize the data. For the direction and speed information, because the real output fluctuates a lot, we use the moving average method to smooth the data. And we round the direction to four directions: north, south, east and west.

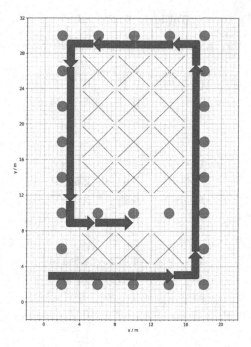

Fig. 1. Test Ground

Since we need to calculate the emission probability from each observation using KNN, in the Table 1, the results by using KNN method are also given. The first column is the No. of observation sequence, and there're 93 observations in Y. The second and third column is the error distance, which is, for each observation, the distance between truth value and prediction of KNN and HMM. Due to the limitation of page size, the table only shows some representative results and the full picture of 93 observations is shown in Fig. 2.

From Table 1 and Fig. 2, it can be found that the effect of HMM method is better than that of KNN. And HMM is smoother, there're no large jumps. Especially, at time 48, the error of KNN reaches 28 m. It is found in the test log that the real position is (13 m, 29 m), but KNN predicts it's at (11 m, 1 m). The reason is KNN's prediction depends on single observation, while HMM can utilize the observation sequence (and speed information) to predict the position.

The RMSE (Root Mean Square Error) of KNN is 3.83532 m, and the RMSE of HMM is 1.04212 m.

Table 1. Test Results

No. of Obs	Error Distance	
	KNN	*HMM*
1	2	0
2	0	1.58114
3	2	0
⋮	⋮	⋮
16	2	2.54951
17	5.65685	2.54951
18	6	3.53553
19	4	3
⋮	⋮	⋮
46	4.4724	1.58114
46	4.4724	1.58114
47	2	0
48	28.0713	0
⋮	⋮	⋮
RMSE	3.83532	1.04212

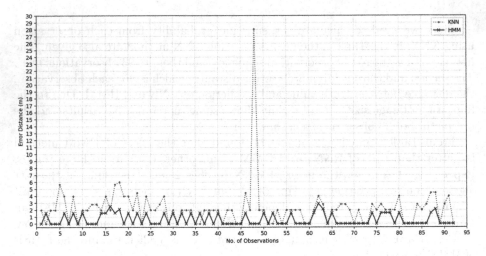

Fig. 2. Error Distance of KNN and HMM

6 Conclusion

The improved HMM is based on the emission probability sequence B and the markov transition probability sequence A. The emission probability is computed from the observation using machine learning method like KNN. This is based on fingerprinting method, requires onerous labor to collect fingerprints for each grid, and then build the database. The markov transition probability is computed from the IMU data (speed) and the distance between each location, so it contains the movement information of the user at that moment. The data collecting part requires the grid not too small, or it's too difficult to collect data and the data between small grids are not distinguishable because of the low resolution of normal sensors. But to compute transition probability, the grids can not be too large, or it will be impossible to move from one grid to another in one sampling period. To solve the contradiction of emission probability modeling and transition probability modeling, two kinds of girdding methods are used. The small one is used to calculate the transition probability and the large one is used to calculate the emission probability. And the small grids can also be used to model the obstacles in the environment.

After modeling, in real practice, sometimes the original Viterbi Algorithm can not work well due to the condition when all $V[i][l]$ become 0. So an improved algorithm which adds reset mechanism is proposed. Each time when the algorithm fails, it will reset the variables and output the best path of the last correct range. It will increase the robustness of the algorithm.

Finally, the real application results show that the proposed method is more accurate, smoother, and there're no large jumps between adjacent predications.

Acknowledgment. This research work is supported by the National Natural Science Foundation of China under Grant No. 61971278 and 62231010, the Longfor Group and Shanghai Jiao Tong University Joint Research Project under Grant No. XM22018 "Customer Flow Positioning and Analysis in Commercial Scenarios", and the Shenzhen Science and Technology Innovation Commission Undertaking Major National Science and Technology Project under Grant No. CJGJZD20210408092601004.

References

1. Altman, N.S.: An introduction to kernel and nearest-neighbor nonparametric regression. Am. Stat. **46**(3), 175–185 (1992)
2. Bejuri, W.M.Y.W., Mohamad, M.M., Omar, H., Omar, F.S., Limin, N.A.: Robust special strategies re sampling for mobile inertial navigation systems (2019)
3. Bryant, R., O'Hallaron, D.R.: Locality, pp. 604–608. Pearson (2016)
4. Cormen, T.H., Leiserson, C.E., Rivest, R.L., Stein, C.: Introduction to Algorithms. MIT press, Cambridge (2009)
5. Ernst, J., Kellis, M.: ChromHMM: automating chromatin-state discovery and characterization. Nature Methods **9**, 215–6 (2012)
6. Floyd, R.W.: Algorithm 97: shortest path. Commun. ACM **5**(6), 345 (1962)
7. Goodfellow, I., Bengio, Y., Courville, A.: Deep Learning. MIT Press (2016). http://www.deeplearningbook.org

8. Google Inc.: Cellsignalstrengthnr.getcsirsrp (2022). https://developer. android.com/reference/kotlin/android/telephony/CellSignalStrengthNr?hl=en# getCsiRsrp(). Online version of the Android API documentation

9. Johnson, D.B.: Efficient algorithms for shortest paths in sparse networks. J. ACM **24**(1), 1–13 (1977)

10. Li, N., Stephens, M.: Modeling linkage disequilibrium and identifying recombination hotspots using single-nucleotide polymorphism data. Genetics **165**, 2213–33 (2004)

11. Pardo, B., Birmingham, W.: Modeling form for on-line following of musical performances, vol. 2, pp. 1018–1023 (2005)

12. Ross, S.M.: 4 - Markov chains. In: Ross, S.M. (ed.) Introduction to Probability Models, 12th edn., pp. 193–291. Academic Press (2019)

13. Satish, L., Gururaj, B.I.: Use of hidden Markov models for partial discharge pattern classification. IEEE Trans. Electr. Insul. **28**(2), 172–182 (1993)

14. Schmidhuber, J.: Deep learning in neural networks: an overview. Neural Netw. **61**, 85–117 (2015)

15. Starner, T., Pentland, A.: Real-time American sign language recognition from video using hidden Markov models. In: Proceedings of International Symposium on Computer Vision - ISCV, pp. 265–270 (1995)

16. Viterbi, A.: Error bounds for convolutional codes and an asymptotically optimum decoding algorithm. IEEE Trans. Inf. Theory **13**(2), 260–269 (1967)

17. Wikipedia contributors. Arithmetic underflow – Wikipedia, the free encyclopedia (2021). https://en.wikipedia.org/w/index.php?title=Arithmetic_underflow& oldid=1043452199. Accessed 7 Aug 2022

18. Wikipedia contributors. Hidden Markov model—Wikipedia, the free encyclopedia (2022). Accessed 28 Sept 2022

Author Index

Printed in the United States
by Baker & Taylor Publisher Services